Implementing Systems for Supporting Management Decisions

IFIP – The International Federation for Information Processing

IFIP was founded in 1960 under the auspices of UNESCO, following the First World Computer Congress held in Paris the previous year. An umbrella organization for societies working in information processing, IFIP's aim is two-fold: to support information processing within its member countries and to encourage technology transfer to developing nations. As its mission statement clearly states,

> IFIP's mission is to be the leading, truly international, apolitical organization which encourages and assists in the development, exploitation and application of information technology for the benefit of all people.

IFIP is a non-profitmaking organization, run almost solely by 2500 volunteers. It operates through a number of technical committees, which organize events and publications. IFIP's events range from an international congress to local seminars, but the most important are:

- the IFIP World Computer Congress, held every second year;
- open conferences;
- working conferences.

The flagship event is the IFIP World Computer Congress, at which both invited and contributed papers are presented. Contributed papers are rigorously refereed and the rejection rate is high.

As with the Congress, participation in the open conferences is open to all and papers may be invited or submitted. Again, submitted papers are stringently refereed.

The working conferences are structured differently. They are usually run by a working group and attendance is small and by invitation only. Their purpose is to create an atmosphere conducive to innovation and development. Refereeing is less rigorous and papers are subjected to extensive group discussion.

Publications arising from IFIP events vary. The papers presented at the IFIP World Computer Congress and at open conferences are published as conference proceedings, while the results of the working conferences are often published as collections of selected and edited papers.

Any national society whose primary activity is in information may apply to become a full member of IFIP, although full membership is restricted to one society per country. Full members are entitled to vote at the annual General Assembly, National societies preferring a less committed involvement may apply for associate or corresponding membership. Associate members enjoy the same benefits as full members, but without voting rights. Corresponding members are not represented in IFIP bodies. Affiliated membership is open to non-national societies, and individual and honorary membership schemes are also offered.

Implementing Systems for Supporting Management Decisions

Concepts, methods and experiences

Edited by

Patrick Humphreys
London School of Economics and Political Science
UK

Liam Bannon
University of Limerick
Ireland

Andrew McCosh
University of Edinburgh
Scotland

Piero Migliarese
Politecnico di Milano
Italy

Jean-Charles Pomerol
LAFORIA, Université Paris VI
France

SPRINGER-SCIENCE+BUSINESS MEDIA, B.V.

First edition 1996

Originally published by Chapman & Hall in 1996
MyCopy version of the original edition 1996

DOI 10.1007/978-0-387-34967-1

A catalogue record for this book is available from the British Library

Printed on permanent acid-free text paper, manufactured in accordance with ANSI/NISO Z39.48-1992 and ANSI/NISO Z39.48-1984 (Permanence of Paper).
www.springer.com/mycopy

CONTENTS

Introduction

Patrick Humphreys
Department of Social Psychology
London School of Economics and Political Science, Houghton Street, London WC2A 2AE. Email: P.Humphreys@lse.ac.uk

This book presents a selection of contributions to the conference on *Implementing Systems for Supporting Management Decisions: Concepts, Methods, and Experiences* held in London in July, 1996. The conference was organized by the International Federation of Information Processing's Working Group 8.3 on Decision Support Systems and the London School of Economics and Political Science. (LSE). The Programme Committee for the Conference comprised Liam Bannon, University of Limerick; Patrick Humphreys, LSE, co-chairperson; Andrew McCosh, University of Edinburgh; Piero Migliarese, Politecnico di Milano, co-chairperson; Jean-Charles Pomerol, LAFORIA, Universite Paris VI. The chairperson of the organizing committee was Dina Berkeley, LSE. The programme committee members served also as the editors of this book. Each contribution was selected by the editors after peer review and was developed by its authors specifically for inclusion in this volume.

Working group 8.3 was formally established in 1981 on the recommendation of IFIP's Technical Committee on Information Systems (TC8). The scope of the working group covers:

> "Development of approaches for applying information systems technology to increase the effectiveness of decision makers in situations where the computer system can support and enhance human judgment in the performance of tasks that have elements that cannot be specified in advance."

The principal aim of the working group is:

> "To improve ways of synthesising and applying relevant work from reference disciplines to practical implementations of systems that enhance decision support capability."

The idea of "Decision support systems", initially conceived two decades ago as a rallying cry ("DSS") for a variety of system developers, academic theorists and intrigued potential end users (Keen and Scott Morton, 1978), has had a chequered history. Much vaunted systems development methodologies, together with a plethora of academic and commercial hyperbole in this area, have often led to products and implementations which sought to replace rather than support the end user, or to frustrate the actual decision making processes in practice. Conversely, real decision support has often been found through the innovative use of systems in ways their designers and builders never imagined (Humphreys, 1989; Garcia and Orellana, 1994).

It has not been easy to learn constructively from these experiences as they tend to be reported from within the particular perspective of the designer, the implementer or the end user, starting from quite different assumptions, using quite different languages, and writing for quite different audiences. The severity of this problem, threatening the development and commercial success of the whole field began to be appreciated at the end of the first decade of DSS (and was key topic of the IFIP Working Group 8.3 1986 working conference "Decision Support Systems: A decade in perspective", see Mclean and Sol, 1986). Since then the problem has been widely recognised, as evidenced by the fundamental emphasis now placed within the relevant areas of the work plan for the Commission of the European Communities' fourth framework programme (1995-1999) on the necessity to start from properly understood user requirements, involve end users at all stages of the system design and development process, and provide "best practice demonstrators" of all kinds of implementations of technology for business processes.

However, there is still a dearth of published material which provides any kind of exploration and integration of the range of experience amassed through implementations over the past decade in a way which could properly inform the work of users, researchers, developers, professionals and implementers seeking to avoid repeating the problems and pitfalls of the past and to find better ways of working together to make more useful and satisfying products and implementations. The motivation for this book is to provide, in a concise format, accounts of exploration and integration of this material in a way which is accessible and didactic for all the full range of participants in this process.

The range of experience integrated in this book is expressed in contributions which deal with all aspects of implementation, considered either from a theoretical or a practical standpoint. The perspectives taken include those of the corporate designer, of the end users, of the implementer, or any combination of these. All the following categories are spanned:

- The implementation of major corporate decision support systems which are at the stage of "rolling out" to the organisation at large;

- The implementation of business process alterations, including those in which DSS methods have been employed at the initiation or analysis stages, and including those in which the revised business process is itself a corporate decision aid;

- The use of implementation support systems, to help put a decision into effect, or to help put a business process alteration into effect;

- The special implementation issues which arise in connection with Executive Information Systems;

- Implementation issues which affect Management Information Systems and Project Management Systems;

1

Experimentation with Organisation Analyser, a tool for the study of decision making networks in organisations

Frédéric Adam
College Lecturer, Dept. of Accounting, Finance and Information Systems, University College Cork, Western Road, Cork, Ireland
Tel: 353 21 90 40 38
Fax: 353 21 27 15 66
Email: ster8004@iruccvax.ucc.ie

Abstract

This paper reports on experimentation with Organisation Analyser (OA), a prototype software aimed at supporting the identification and analysis of decision making networks in organisations. Previous research has identified that there was great benefit in adopting a network approach to the study of organisations. This research has viewed organisations as being composed of a variety of different types of networks: emergent networks, established networks, communication networks, grape vine etc. However, it is often difficult to operationalise such an approach when studying such complex phenomena as organisational decision making and implementation.

To facilitate the application of network analysis to entire organisations, we have developed Organisation Analyser (OA), a Windows-based tool for the representation and analysis of all the relevant kinds of networks which we tested in one Irish organisation. Central focus on a sample of decisions currently being made and implemented in that organisation brought to light the very political and unstable nature of the objectives and the unfolding of the decision-making processes in organisations. With the help of a novel framework for the analysis of organisational decision making, this paper describes the organisation where the research is taking place and the decisions selected for the purpose of the study. It shows the support which OA provided the researcher in the analysis of the information collected and presents preliminary conclusions regarding the nature of the decision making effected by groups of top managers in organisations and the way in which these decisions are implemented. In particular, it provides new insights into the concepts of structural hole, centrality and decision ownership. It reveals how decision implementation can be just as difficult as choice. OA appears to have potential as a DSS tool to assist managers in structuring their organisational networks better.

Keywords

AC402 Group decision making, AC403 organisational decision making, AD 102 information in organisations, AD04 information channels

1 CASE STUDY OF A DECISION PROCESS

In March 1995, Fun Ireland Ltd, a toy company based in Ireland and the subsidiary of a large American corporation, were trying to purchase an integrated software package which would cover the financial, distribution and manufacturing aspects of their business. The business was growing rapidly on all their European markets and they were also looking into expanding into a number of South American countries. They had been a mainly manufacturing organisation, but now 75% of their turnover was coming from trading goods produced by their suppliers in the Far East.

They had been telling their parent company about the failure of their current, largely manual systems for a long time, but everytime they had asked for clearance to purchase any system, it had been refused by the HQ in New York. At that time, Fun only had a few PCs on which a large number of spreadsheet reports were being produced covering most aspects of the business. They also had a payroll and an inventory control system that was provided to them by a supplier of computer bureau services. However, that software and the PDP 11 computer running it were now completely obsolete and Fun were the last customer using a service which was becoming more and more expensive and unreliable.

Dave, the finance director of Fun had been wrestling with the problem ever since he had joined the company 18 months earlier and had identified the potential failures threatening to occur in many areas. Sales order processing was his main concern as he was convinced that Fun was losing a significant portion of the ever growing business due to orders not being met on time or being forgotten about. But invoicing was crucial too and he wondered how long it would take before customers realised that Fun sometimes had no clear idea how much had been shipped to a particular customer.

After one year of work and a number of rejections from the US on technical grounds, Dave decided to hire a consultant in this area to help him produce the reports that would convince people at the HQ to give the go ahead. He got in contact with a research centre in the local university and started working with Brian, one of their researcher / lecturers.

Brian took four weeks to carry out an extensive analysis of requirements in Fun and to draw the outline of the systems required. In the report he wrote, he also pointed out the numerous weaknesses in the current systems. This report was presented to the top managers in Fun and the recommendations were approved. It was also forwarded to the HQ in the US who merely acknowledged reception. Brian then put together an Invitation to Tender which was sent to six potential suppliers of systems, of which four responded within the time allocated. Based on these proposals, Brian and Dave selected two organisations with which they pursued contacts including a formal presentation of their proposed solution and a visit of their premises. Both turned out to be local suppliers and that was largely due to Brian's perception that local support would be a very important asset during the implementation phase as people in Fun has little experience with large computer systems (there were no IT personnel in Fun at that time). They eventually selected one supplier who made a final presentation to the top management of Fun and received the approval of the Managing Director. The next step was to commit the money to this investment of roughly £150,000 and the signs were good when the IT Director at the HQ (the one who had stopped the investment until then) responded favourably to the request and agreed with the conclusions of the final report he had been sent. All that was now needed after 20 months of the decision making process was a signature of the finance Director at the HQ.

In the meantime, Fun's parent company had purchased Kiddies Clothing Ltd; a UK-based company similar in size to Fun but operating in a complementary market. Because of the numerous uncertainties regarding the sharing of business between Fun and Kiddies and the relations to be developed between the two companies, the HQ blocked the investment in Fun.

The bad news infuriated Dave who had put so many efforts into the whole project over a two year period. Brian helped him find his second wind and initiate a number of meetings with equivalent personnel in Kiddies and a new strand of reports were sent to the HQ to indicate how the systems in Fun and Kiddies would operate and the processes that would be shared between the two companies. A joint report signed by Fun and Kiddies was even sent to the US which emphasised the support that Kiddies were ready to give Fun in their implementation of the system that Brian and Dave had selected.

Still, after two more months of negotiating with people at the HQ, the request to commit the money was rejected and the whole project put on hold while a global IT strategy for Fun was put together by the IT director at the HQ. More than two years after the first alarming reports had been written and sent to the US about the weaknesses of the current systems in Fun, nothing had been done and the manual systems were still holding on. A computerised system for Fun Ireland had never seemed so far away.

This ultimate reversal of fortune discouraged Dave who was beginning to think that history was just going to repeat itself over and over again. But Brian found it difficult to accept that all the efforts of the last few months had been in vain. In an attempt to demonstrate that there were no managerial grounds for postponing any longer the commitment of Fun to the purchase of a platform and a software that had already been carefully selected, he convinced Dave and Mark to send a final report to the HQ. In this report, they particularly emphasised that a global IT strategy for the company made little sense as no truly shared processes requiring integration of computer systems had been identified either between Ireland and the US or between Fun and Kiddies. In addition, the implementation of such global strategy meant that Fun would have to sacrifice the possibility of using local support for the software, an added difficulty for a company without full-time resident IT expertise.

Much to their surprise, this report was to win them the battle. Mid-way through December 1995, Dave got the news that he could start implementing the decision to purchase an integrated computer system covering the financial and distribution activities of Fun. Before the end of January, the cabling had been put in place and discussions were on-going regarding the choice of a file server.

However, the implementation of the decision proved as difficult as the previous stages and Dave has to clear each purchase with the HQ. At times, it seems that the reluctance to implement the choices that have been made is as great as the reluctance to commit to these choices in the first instance. For Brian, who is now watching from the outside, there seems to be a risk that the whole process is further delayed at every stage of the implementation just as it has been in the earlier stages of the decision process. Implementing the project - actually spending the money - is even more difficult than planning - merely thinking about spending the money. Moreover, it appears that committing to a solution is not the most important aspects of decision making; implementing it, enacting the choices made, raises new issues and fresh interrogations which were overlooked or ignored throughout the previous stages.

The short scenario presented in the previous paragraphs is in no way an invention, it is the true story of a still unfinished decision process in which the author of this paper played the role of the consultant[1]. This story illustrates that the decision making processes used in organisations are on average very remote from the normative models prescribed by such areas of research as economics where actors seek to maximise their utility or their profit (Simon, 1955). People in organisations might attempt to behave in a way that optimises the outcomes of their decisions, ie 'rationally', (even though this has been questioned as well, eg: Feldman and March, 1981), but at the overall level of an organisation, the processes used and outcomes reached can appear very difficult to understand and follow for an outside observer. This has already been reported in the literature. March (1987) has described how the available empirical studies of decision making processes in organisations indicate that our current theories of choice overestimate the coherence of decision processes. In the case of Fun, both Dave and the people he was negotiating with in the HQ are following their own agendas and use everything in their power to convince the other managers that they are correct. But, seen from the outside, the two and a half year decision making process appears to be totally illogical and wasteful of people's time and energy, as a decision was reached several times during the period covered by the study, but kept being rejected until finally, it began being implemented as in slow motion. The fact that this case deals with the subsidiary of a multi-national company with limited autonomy for investment matters does not provide sufficient explanation for these decisional uncertainties as all managers involved agree on the nature of the problems and the goals of the project. It confirms that decision processes can sometimes appear to be without any order (March and Olsen 1986) and that the preferences of managers are often vague and contradictory, even when there is agreement on the overall objectives (March, 1987). Indeed, Keen (1977) has explained how decisions must often satisfy contradictory objectives whose relative priorities evolve over time. In addition, fresh questions seem to arise at the implementation stage of the decision making process which makes little managerial sense in the light of the traditional literature on normative decision making.

This paper reports on an experiment with a new way of studying the complex processes leading to the making and implementation of decisions in organisations and attempts to bring together results and observations of the behaviour of individuals, groups and sub-units within organisations to compare them with the resulting organisational processes. We use the data collected in a case study of multiple decision processes in an Irish organisation to test the validity of the network approach - a technique borrowed from the field of Sociology - to the study of decision-related tasks in real organisational settings.

2 ANALYTICAL LEVELS IN THE STUDY OF DECISION MAKING

As is demonstrated in the case study presented in this paper, it is difficult to establish a clear link between individual behaviour and the resulting organisational processes. This was observed by many previous researchers and research on the behaviour of people when they are associated with others has started as early as the 19th century. Gustave Le Bon (1896) has investigated the psychology of the 'Crowd', which he described as behaving like a single being

[1] The names of the organisations and the people studied in this case study have been changed to enable a more complete reporting of the behaviour of the actors and the context of the decisions.

subjected to 'the law of mental unity of crowds'. Individuals in crowd, says Le Bon, lose their conscious personality and adopt and follow a sort of collective mind. McGrath (1984), whose work on groups is often used as a reference, indicated how important groups are for organisations. He said that "groups are the instruments through which much work gets done" (McGrath, 1984: p 5) and Pennings concluded that:

> People (...) do not exist in a social vacuum; they are surrounded by fellow members and are embedded in a network of social relationships. They are also often associated with decision making groups such as work teams, budget committees, board of Directors (...). Groups are an important medium through which decisions are made and can greatly affect the way individuals arrive at decisions [Pennings, 1983 : vii].

Many empirical findings have emerged in this respect from the extensive study of a large variety of actual groups in society and in organisations. However, many researchers have argued that focusing on groups is not sufficient in the context of the study of managers' work. It seems that much of the interactions between managers may escape the notion of group. For example, previous studies of information exchange amongst managers involved many types of interaction between the managers of an organisation (Adam and Murphy, 1995 a; Daft *et al.*, 1988; Jones *et al.*, 1988), whereas much of the group research has focused on what happens within formalised groups where members know they are part of a group. As a result, the focus of the group research field has now shifted significantly as researchers turned to other analytical levels and other unit of analysis, namely the individual and the organisation.

In sociology, the need for additional analytical levels besides the individual and the group levels were also identified (Monge and Eisenberg, 1987). For example, Burt (1980) has described the personal level, the 'clique' level and the overall organisational network level, while Tichy (1981) has added a fourth level: the environmental or inter-organisational level. In support of such attempts to experiment with more realistic (but more complex) analytical levels, Hedberg pointed out that

> Although organisational learning occurs through individuals, it would be a mistake to conclude that organisational learning is nothing but the cumulative result of their members' learning. Organisations (...) have cognitive systems and memories. As individuals develop their personalities, personal habits and beliefs over time, organisations develop world views and ideologies. Members come and go, and leadership changes, but organisations' memories preserve certain behaviours, mental maps, norms and values over time. [Hedberg, 1981 : 6].

Thus, for this study, it is proposed to differentiate between the different levels at which interaction takes place among managers in organisations as a vehicle to support our study of organisational decision making. The contention is that any study of managerial activities must articulate what processes are used (1) by individuals, (2) by spontaneous groups of the kind that exist when managers form informal associations to tackle specific problems, (3) by identified groups, such as Steering Committees or Boards of Directors and (4) by the organisation as a whole (Adam and Murphy, 1995b). In the context of this study, the aim was to trace the decision-related activities accomplished at each of the four levels identified as relevant analytically and the decision-related activities which span several or all of these levels.

The network approach to organisations already used in sociology (Roethlisberger, 1977) seems to offer a mode of organisational inquiry which can accommodate the different analytical levels required for the study of organisational phenomena such as decision making and implementation (Nohria, 1992).

3 THE NETWORK APPROACH TO ORGANISATIONS - A NEW MODE OF INQUIRY FOR IS

Roethlisberger expressed the view that organisations and behaviour within them were such 'elusive phenomena' that no research should aim at providing a definitive theory for the study of organisations. He proposed that a framework that could be used as a 'walking stick' to investigate the field of organisational research would be more useful (Roethlisberger, 1977). Nohria has suggested that Network Analysis, a body of research which concentrates on networks defined as 'the observed pattern of organisation' can be such a walking stick 'likely to hold well in our intellectual inquiry of organisations' (Nohria, 1992).

Since the 50's the concept of networks has been used in a number of fields as diverse as psychology, sociology and molecular biology. Roethlisberger and Dickson (1939) used it in the 30's to emphasise the importance of people's webs of informal relations in organisations. Thus, the network perspective is born out of a careful observation of the life of actual organisations. Balbridge has observed that New York University makes decisions through 'a network that allows a cumulative build-up of expertise and advice' (Balbridge, 1971) while Kadushin observed that 'a core of 47 people (...) runs Detroit' (Kadushin, 1978). The work accomplished has enabled the capture of a number of significant organisational processes at different levels of analysis, i.e.: individual, groups, cliques, sub-units and organisation as a whole (Tichy, 1992).

This more realistic approach to organisations has been formally described by Nohria. He suggested a dynamic approach to the analysis of organisations whereby actors (or managers)

> are not seen as atoms locked in a crystalline grid, their every action determined by their structural location, (...)[but as] active, purposeful agents' [Nohria, 1992].

White indicated that individual ties are continuously added to and subtracted from formal networks as managers get involved in different projects or face different problems and he described management as an on-going process involving

> throwing up fresh network and changing existing networks (...) whole chunks of networks are added or rearranged in concert. Reorganisation never ends because struggles for control never end [White, 1992: 94].

Thus, the analysis of organisational networks examines the structure and patterning of relationship that establish amongst individuals and groups in organisations and attempts to draw conclusions for the study of individual behaviour in organisations. We intend to apply it to the study of decision making and decision implementation with the support of a computer-based tool developed especially for this research project.

4 OPERATING PRINCIPLES OF ORGANISATION ANALYSER

Because the principles of network analysis are not self evident when it comes to their operational application to studying decision making processes, the first step in this research project was to develop a computer-based tool called Organisation Analyser which would support the analysis of the different networks existing in the organisations studied at the different levels of analysis identified in section 2 of this paper.

Organisation Analyser (OA) uses the principles of message flow analysis (Stohl and Redding, 1987; O'Reilly, Chatman and Anderson, 1987). This research has demonstrated that the communication which is so crucial for organisations cannot exist without messages, these stimuli that 'trigger a meaning in someone's head' (Stohl and Redding, 1987). OA is focused on the study of the interaction between individuals and it uses messages as an indicator of such interaction. It helps researchers identify the mechanisms used for the transmission of typical messages between individuals (communication channels, frequency of interaction, nature of relationships) and concentrate on what it all means for organisational decision making.

OA also uses the principles of network analysis regarding the relative positions of individuals in organisational networks. Researchers who analysed organisational networks identified a number of standard individual roles that individuals can have: the stars, the linkers (or bridges) and the isolates (Monge and Eisenberg, 1987). They have also showed that individuals can be more or less central in a communication network: (1) central because they are involved in many relations, (2) central by betweenness because they are in the middle of paths that connect others or (3) central by closeness because they have immediate access to others who are connected (Brass and Burkart, 1992). According to Brass and Burkart, all these aspects of centrality are important to identify because they can confer a different basis of power. Granovetter (1973) and Burt (1992) have also argued that people who surround themselves with 'structural holes' (areas of an organisation where contacts between people or groups are disorganised) gain additional power and autonomy.

It can prove difficult to identify managers' degree of centrality and their position relative to structural holes in organisational networks because the complexity of these networks often makes it difficult to examine the whole network or to envisage all its characteristics at the same time. OA enables researchers to collect from managers large amounts of data regarding managers and their linkages to each others but also regarding the usage of the information exchanged and the managerial activities served by these transfers of information. It then provides a means to store all these data into a stable, but meaningful model of the organisation. It is therefore possible to visualise the networks and the relative strength of the linkages between managers in the stable environment provided by the software and to investigate what happens within the network as the organisation tackles a decision situation.

To support these goal, OA enables the creation of a number of objects: (1) managers, (2) groups, (3) internal links, (4) external links, (5) interdependencies and (6) decisions. The researcher can store the personal data required to identify each actor including their perception of their role, their goal within the organisation and their perceived environment uncertainty (Daft, Sormunen and Parks; 1988). Managers are visually represented by special icons as in Figure 1. Links between managers and their information content can be described as being emergent or formal (Monge and Eisenberg, 1987; Euske and Roberts, 1987), as communication or information oriented (Adam and Murphy, 1995a), as carrying primarily hard or soft information (Mintzberg, 1973); task related or non task related information (Bales, 1953, 1950); routine or unexpected information (Huber, 1982; Huber and McDaniel, 1986) and internal or external information (Blandin and Brown, 1977; Kefalas, 1973; Keegan, 1974). OA also uses Daft and Lengel's framework of communication channels to classify the media used in relationships (Daft and Lengel, 1986).

A special type of link with the environment can be attached to managers. It allows the same level of coding as with a normal link, but managers in contact with their environment are flagged by OA with a special icon as seen on Figure 1 (manager 1 and 2).

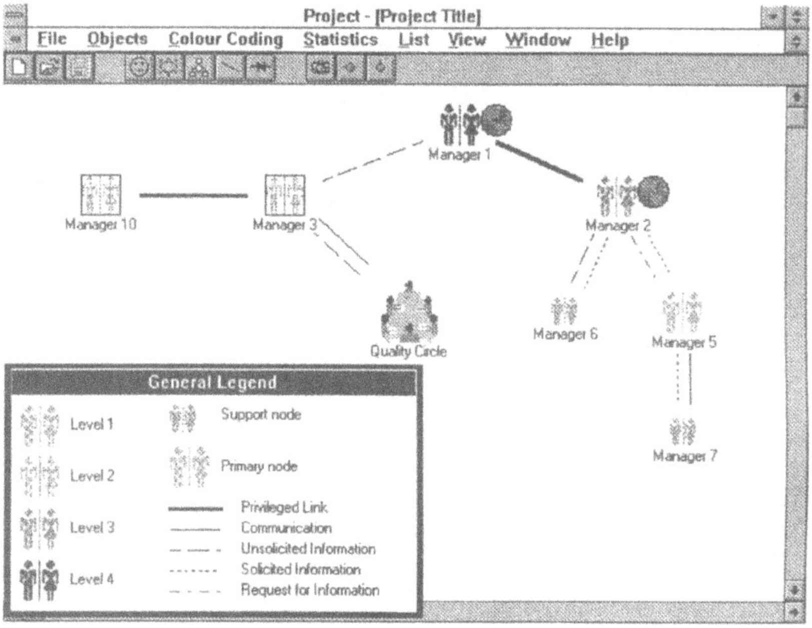

Figure 1 The main screen of OA with a sample of six managers
Note: The explanation of the legend in Figure 1 is given in section 5 of this paper

Groups can also be coded in OA by selecting the managers involved and assigning them the status of group. These groups can then be visualised by changing the view mode of OA to 'groups'. Groups are coded with a specific icon and an attached label (Figure 1 - quality circle).

Once the data collection steps have been accomplished, researchers can use the multiple analytical features of OA to obtain quickly a very high level of aggregation in the presentation of the data thanks to a number of built-in filters. For example, the user can get a visual breakdown of all the links used by the managers which differentiates between communication links, request for information, unsolicited information etc. Figure 1 shows the different types of links used by a sample of six managers. Other analytical filters that can be applied to the organisation analysed include a breakdown of the communication media used by the managers; a breakdown of the frequency of the interaction between the managers; channels used for the different types of information; new versus established channels of interaction and a hierarchical filter which maps the distribution of managers within the organisation by hierarchical level and by functional area.

Finally, OA enables the researchers to analyse the way in which managers use their information. The current prototype focuses on decisions made by individual managers and by groups as a way to discover how executives work out common visions of their world. Any number of actors can be attached to each decision, and actors may be assigned to a particular phase of the decision process (Mintzberg *et al.*, 1976; Simon, 1977).

5 THE STUDY AT FUN

The study of the decision making processes used in an organisation requires some form of classification of the different types of decisions with which managers can be faced. This must enable the selection of a meaningful sample of decisions representative of the decision making of that organisation (Keen and Scott Morton, 1978). A number of parameters can be put forward to differentiate amongst decision types such as: (1) the type, frequency, structure and complexity of the decision; (2) the characteristics, capabilities and needs of the decision maker; and (3) the organisational context (Keen and Scott Morton, 1978). A number of frameworks have been put forward to deal with this complexity (Gorry and Scott Morton, 1971, Moore and Chang, 1983, Adam *et al.*, 1995).

Adam, Fahy and Murphy (1995) have summarised much of the work carried out thus far in this area. Based on this review of existing research, they have identified that the *novelty* of the problem and its *specificity* appear to influence the processes used by managers when making a decision. Novelty in this instance refers to the prior experience which management have with a certain type of problem in a given organisation. March and Olsen have suggested that novelty is not a property of a situation so much as it is people's reaction to it; and the most common organisational response to novelty is to find a set of existing practices that can be used (March and Olsen, 1989). Thus, organisations, while relying on a limited set of 'stable, routine processes', are able to tackle a wide variety of new situations and give the impression that they changed themselves drastically to adapt to modifications in their environment (March, 1981).

The second factor, the specificity of the problem, is partially related to the first. It relates to the ability of management to set out the appropriate specifications for the problem they face and the information that they need to address the problem raised by a particular decision. This factor is problematic because the definition of problems is as much a human construct as the solutions of these solutions (Lévine and Pomerol, 1995; Pomerol, 1994).

Adam *et al.* (1995) formalised these comments in a framework of decision types which allows for an organisation's specific experience of dealing with the different types of problems and takes into account that the level of expertise of management in organisations may evolve over time. When decision situations are faced a certain number of times, managers' ability to tackle them may increase and, in any case, their ability to describe the cause and effects relationships between the parameters of the decision increases (and so does the level of specificity of these problems). Thus, the decision making processes used by managers will become more and more refined as their experience with the decision situation they address develops and the implementation of these decisions becomes more and more routine and automatic.

For the purpose of this study, Adam *et al.*'s framework was simplified to support the selection of a sample of decisions representative of the decision making of managers in Fun Ireland Ltd (see Table 1).

Table 1 Decision situations studied in Fun Ireland Ltd.

	Complete model available	Partial model available	No model available
Has happened before	Ordering goods from far east suppliers	Introduction of an existing product on a new market	Development of a new entertainment product
Has never happened before	Selection of an automatic telephone system	Selection and implementation of an integrated CBIS	Acquisition of another company in Europe

At the time this study began, the researcher already possessed a significant knowledge of the organisation studied thanks to the consultancy exercise described in section 1. This enabled the selection of the decisions in table 1. The next step consisted in interviewing all the actors involved in these decisions and the coding of the resulting data in OA for analysis. The results of this analysis are presented in the section below.

The Decision Groups at Fun

Organisation Analyser was used to study the managerial groups and the external agents involved in the decision making processes selected in Fun. First, the overall network was roughly coded starting from the Managing Director down through four layers of personnel, then the sub-sets of this network involved with each of the decisions were isolated and refined in light of the specific decision process they supported. Figure 2 shows the people involved in the integrated Computer-Based Information System (CBIS) selection decision described in the introduction of this paper in the different organisations to which they belong: Fun' people in Ireland (A) and in the Headquarters in the US (B), Kiddies' people (C), the consultant (D) and the vendor of systems (E). The clear focus on this particular decision is justified by the greater knowledge and the longitudinal exposure of the researcher to this decision situation.

Figure 2 shows in details the relationships existing between the people involved in the context of this decision. The thicker lines represent privileged links between nodes in the network whereby the people connected have full access to each other, share information on a equal basis and exchange opinions freely. This was the case, for instance, between Brian (the consultant), Dave (the project leader for Fun) and Mark (the accountant of Fun) who were at the core of the project and were the most active in designing potential solutions and producing reports for the others. The thin lines represent the communication links whereby people are in contact with each other in the context of the decision and exchange information and opinions at regular intervals or on an ad-hoc basis. This was the most common type of link identified between the people involved.

Finally, the dotted lines indicate a different kind of relationships where one manager is clearly subordinated to the other. The most fundamental characteristic of these relationships is that they are asymmetrical as opposed to the symmetrical (like the previous two kinds: privileged links and communication links). More specifically, relationships coded by double dashed lines indicate requests for information from the superior toward his/her subordinates and the resulting flow of requested information. In the case of Dave (the project leader for Fun in Ireland) and John (the Chairman of the Board of the parent company), a flow of unsolicited information (long dashes line) what also coded to account for the many reports Dave sent John to try and influence his decision making regarding the system. Very often, these relationships go by two as one manager report to the other. The only exceptions concerned Peter (the project leader for the software vendor) who kept sending unsolicited information to Brian to provide him with stronger arguments in favour of the system and Dave who was trying to persuade Veronica to clear the investment. Such flows of unsolicited information were often the mark of intense lobbying of top managers by lower levels.

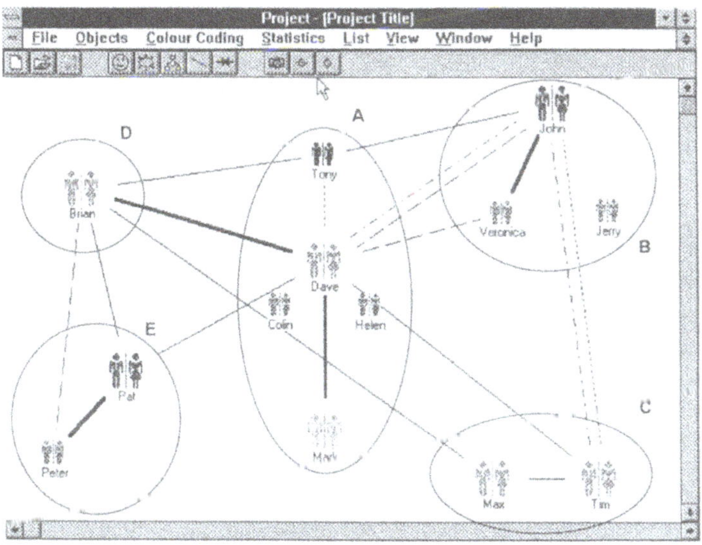

Figure 2 People involved in the system selection decision

Going to the other decisions of Table 1, the purchasing of goods from suppliers in the Far East is a good example of completely routinised decision, recurring every month and regularly involving large volumes of goods. This involved Dave and Colin getting together and making predictions for the volumes required in the coming months. Once they had reached a decision as to how much to order of each product, they clear their decision with Tony. The task of implementing the decision - including the monitoring of the movement of the goods through the Suez canal and into Rotterdam harbour - was left to Dave. The most striking characteristic of this decision was that it was made under considerable uncertainty and was often modified at the last minute based on little more than personnel hunches from either Dave, Colin or Tony.

This decision group was very complex as it included the apparently best connected managers in the organisation (according to the current organisational network developed in OA) and they all contributed their personal sources of information to the predictions of required volumes of product. But Tony (the Managing Director) often had the final say in this matter.

The purchase of the telephone system was completed by Mark from the analysis of the requirements to the purchase of the complete solution. The only support he got in this decision process was the go-ahead to spend £20,000 which was given by Tony (the MD for Fun Ireland) and Veronica (the vice-president for Finance in the US). Throughout the decision process, Mark was in contact with a number of potential suppliers, but he focused on one particular supplier very early on in the decision process. This decision was less interesting from the point of view of this study insofar as it only involved two individuals, the decision owner (Mark) and the decision taker (Tony).

The decisions regarding new products and new markets rarely involved many people. The exploration of new horizons was handled mostly by Tony, Colin (the Marketing director for Fun in Ireland) and his assistant. They initiated the contacts with new distributors and advertising agencies abroad. These complex decisions were made on the basis of very specific and accurate simulations of the potential contribution of each product on each market which enabled Fun to make an educated guess concerning the financial potential of new targets. These simulations were prepared by Dave and Mark who are often seen as the Lotus 123 wizards in Fun and then refined by Colin who had a better knowledge of the markets. An example of how short the decision loop could become if an opportunity arose was given recently when the launch of an existing product in Spain was initiated by Colin who sought and obtained the approval of Tony in one meeting and committed large amounts of product to this new market. This quick decision turned out to be very successful and enabled the company to perform well above its targets for the year.

Finally, the decision to acquire another company in Europe could not be included in Organisation Analyser for reasons of secrecy. Indeed, it proved difficult to identify how the decision had unfolded (it was only made public once the contracts had been signed so the data collection could only be historical and superficial). It was nevertheless possible to identify that mainly five people (John, the Chairman of the board for the parent company, three vice-presidents from the HQ in the US and Tony, the MD for Fun Ireland) were involved with the merger on Fun's side. According to the Irish Managing Director, the decision was extremely difficult and took a lot of time. The same care and slow approach was adopted for other decisions that had to be made as a result of the merger - eg: the people to let go, the people to keep and the autonomy to be given the newly acquired organisation. Tony said that this care was a result of the decision makers feeling that they were on 'new ground' where they had never been before and were 'experimenting' with the decision making process as it went along.

Findings of the Case Study at Fun

The decision groups studied in Fun turned out to be of variable size from nearly 20 people disseminated in four organisations for the selection of the CBIS to just 2 in the case of the purchase of the telephone system. This reflects the small size of the managerial group and the high degree of specialisation of the managers in Fun. This was a general characteristic in Fun where all the staff, managers and employees, have developed extremely personal and effective work practices in their positions and would be difficult to replace. Thus, the decision groups studied often involved the same people, but in radically different positions and roles.

This preliminary finding highlights the major difficulty in applying the principles of network analysis to the study of organisational decision making. Many attributes of the actors involved in the management of an organisation (eg: classification as support node or primary node, degree of centrality) are not stable and change drastically depending upon the focus of research. As coded in OA, a manager can be quite central and important in the context of a decisional network (the sub-network dealing with that decision), while being a mere support node or not being involved at all in other sub-networks. This was the case for Mark who was decision owner in one case and not connected in other cases, but also for Dave and Colin who were decision centres for a number of decision processes and were nevertheless excluded from the merger decision. This indicates the very relative nature of the concept of centrality in organisations as it can be visualised in OA. Being well connected to a lot of people is certainly a desirable attribute, but it does not confer decisional power. It gives a manager the potential to play an important role in the management of an organisation, but this potential can only be enabled by a prominent position in the formal structure of the organisation and by a positive reputation in the organisation for being a 'problem-solver' or having the proper skills. OA's main strength is that it allows the coding of the 'version' of the network which is activated by each specific decision within the overall organisational network.

When coding the global network of an organisation in OA, the researcher must interpret his or her overall knowledge of the organisation's activities to evaluate the role of a given manager. At the level of specific decisional networks, the role and centrality of each manager is entirely dictated by the actual processes observed. Organisation Analyser enables the researcher to break down the overall network to begin the investigation at a finer level of analysis, that of the decisional group. Thus, OA supports the coding of a sample of decisional groups and the aggregation of all this (sometimes contradictory) information into the organisational network. This confirms the validity of the methodology developed for this research project:

1) selection of a sample of decisions representative of current organisational processes
2) use of OA to switch from one analytical level to the next in an effort to get a complete picture of decision making in the organisation studied.

OA proved particularly useful in the analysis of structural holes. By their very nature, structural holes are very unlikely to appear at the level of decisional groups. In most cases, the formal structure of organisations ensures that decisions are dealt with by well-connected groups of people. Structural holes appear mainly when the organisational network is considered in its entirety and areas of decision making appear to be isolated. This causes the coordination of these different groups to be loose and can results in wrong decisions being made that clash with each other at implementation stage. In Fun, the communication between the headquarters (in the US) and the Irish subsidiary seemed very weak. This was not due to a lack of communication channels, but more to a reluctance from the part of the managers in the US to exchange their views with their Irish counterparts. It is the author's perception that this lack of clarity in the exchanges of information, which is obvious in OA (see Figure 2 where only Tony has real communication links with US managers), amounts to a 'purposeful' structural hole created and maintained by some of the top managers at the interface between the two entities. It would seem that Tony (who was also a member of the Board for Fun International) did not always disseminate all the information in his possession to his subordinates.

This structural hole identified at the overall level was found to cause a break-down of communication within the decisional group involved with the purchase of the CBIS. This can explain to a large degree why this decision process appears so difficult. Overall, this decision will have taken two and a half years to select a system which is now only implemented in slow motion. According to Eisenhardt (1990) and Carlsson (1993), this is the sign of a very uncertain company where decision making suffers from the lack of clarity of the goals or the lack of decisiveness of managers. Such companies, they say, are generally unable to make fast and accurate decisions and often fail to adapt to their environment. Carlsson gives the three characteristics of good decision making: a quick yet rational decision process, a decisive powerful CEO yet an equally empowered top management team and a bold yet safe incremental execution. These three characteristics appeared to be missing at Fun which was confirmed by the very long time it had taken to purchase Kiddies, the complementary company in the UK. That seemed to indicate that decision making was a slow process in Fun.

In fact, it can be argued that these two decision processes are not characteristic of the decision making in Fun for two different reasons. The purchase of the CBIS is the consequence of the structural hole mentioned above and the purchase of Kiddies constituted too radically new an adventure for Fun's managers. Indeed, a look at the other decisions in the sample, especially the decisions on the upper level of the framework which by their nature are recurrent decisions (even though they might occur only once a year) revealed that Fun was primarily a very fast and decisive organisation, quite in line with Carlsson's (1993) recommendations. In the areas where they felt confident that they understood the issues at hand, managers at Fun were very sharp. They never spent undue time debating whether to re-order from their Far East suppliers even though these purchasing decisions were of the order of a hundred thousand pounds. They would purchase several containers of goods in preparation for the launch of a new advertising campaign in any of the European markets and the goods could end up anywhere in Europe, pushed by the very strong marketing policies of the companies. The procurement policy was so aggressive that sales representatives were never short of stocks, but lasting situations of over-stock never seemed to occur in Fun.

Similarly, the decisions to expand to new markets were always taken very fast. Quantities were ordered, or sometimes they were available due to the relative failure of an advertising campaign in another market, and they were committed in one meeting and shipped to the distributors. When a market was completely new, the Managing Director and the Marketing Director would travel there and spend several weeks negotiating with potential distributors and creating reliable contacts and sources of feed-back for the monitoring of the launch on the new market. Procedures for such important moves were well-established and efficient and involved a small number of people used to working together. At times, it seemed like this group of executives displayed signs of Groupthink or feelings of invulnerability as described by Janis (1972), but the obvious, consistent success of the current strategy leaves no doubt as to how well managers at Fun understand their markets and their products.

Discussion of the Findings

These observations indicate that the presence of structural holes in organisations can cause decision making processes to break down or, at least, to slow down to a great extent. Furthermore, they suggest that structural holes have more to do with top managers' personal styles than with organisational structure. Analysis of the data coded in OA showed that it was up to a number of key individuals to remove the distortion in the network, but the sensitive nature of this issue did not allow the researcher to even attempt to clarify whether the individuals in question were aware of this distortion.

The findings also confirm that the degree of familiarity of managers with the problems they address is paramount in explaining the speed and the directness of the approaches used by organisations to adapt to their environment and make good decisions. In Fun, the recurring decisions regarding the products and markets were made with great certainty and great speed because the decision groups concerned by these decisions had developed a set of common behaviours and managerial tools that all managers understood and trusted to be appropriate. Two conditions seemed to be required for an organisation to benefit from the degree of familiarity of the team with a decision situation: (1) tools and procedures had to be developed that would become the accepted way to approach a problem and (2) once these techniques were developed, they had to be used consistently, not only to analyse future decisions, but also to analyse past decisions and review their outcomes. This was a readily identifiable form of organisational learning at Fun and one that gave great confidence to the managers when making their decisions. Such systematic review of the outcome of previous decisions proved crucial at Fun in enabling managers to keep up with their markets and products.

However, there was another reason why the decision making at Fun was so fast and aggressive for these recurrent decisions. The common point between all the decisions in the upper area of Table 1 (the recurrent decisions) is not only that they had occurred before, but that their outcome is reversible. In other words, the consequences of making a wrong decision are not perceived as being fatal for the company. In this instance, reversibility does not mean that managers feel confident that they can reverse the decision made and return to the previous state (this is almost never possible), but that they know that they will find alternative solutions if the future they had planned does not materialise. For example, the ease with which managers at Fun ordered big consignments of goods was justified by the existence of alternative markets where products can be shipped if the targeted market fails. Similarly, the decision to create a new product is not as important and difficult when toys are involved as when a new model of motorcar is concerned. A bad toy can be discarded, whereas a new car must be a success. The importance of the outcome of a decision was confirmed by the difficulties met by Fun's managers in relation to the probably irreversible merger decision.

Finally, the analysis of the decision groups at Fun based on the sub-networks coded in OA also indicated that all managerial groups seem to be organised around a central individual who becomes the owner of that decision (this phrase is actually used in Fun to describe the manager in charge of leading and implementing a project). This was the case with Dave for two of the decisions (the purchases from the Far East and the system selection), Mark for the purchase of the telephone system, Tony or Colin for the new markets and John for the merger. We have already described above the boundaries of the concept of centrality. Centrality is an essential characteristic of leadership, but it is not a stable characteristic in organisational networks. In fact, the centre of the decision groups was found to vary with the different decision situations as most decisions had a different leader. However, this were only true for the decision owners - i.e.: the people who lead the decision from start to finish either that they had volunteered to be project leaders or that they had been assigned the supervision of the decision. It did not hold for the overall control of the decision making process as all decisions were ultimately confirmed or approved by the same one or two people at Fun: John, the Chairman of Board in the US or Tony, the Managing Director for Ireland. In that sense, if decision *leadership* was variable and project based, decision *taking* was always centralised around the same people even though many other decision makers were heavily involved in managing and leading projects in the organisation. In particular, Dave and Colin were frequent decision owners because they were very active managers, but they often had to seek approval from Tony or to the vice-presidents in the US for important matters. In that sense, the analysis enabled by OA reveals that the concept of centrality as it has been described in the network literature ignores the reality of power in organisations. This highlights that the role of a top manager may often be that of a referee who accepts or rejects decisions that have already been designed by others rather than the more active role of shaping the decisions made by an organisation.

6 CONCLUSIONS

A lot of the research in management and in IS has focused on one specific aspect of organisational life such as decision making, communication, information processing or information interpretation. Very often this research has been aimed at developing normative processes and few studies have provided complete pictures of the activities involved in management. One of the reasons for this was highlighted by Nutt (1984) who stated that organisational processes are made up of so many activities that researchers are faced with a dilemma. Either they use a strict framework which they use to collect data on a large number of cases (ability to generalise the findings) or they use an emergent approach to examine the raw data of a small number of cases and use their intuition to find patterns, phases and sequences (richness and completeness). Both approaches have weak points as an artificial order may be imposed on what is essentially a chaotic process (framework based approach) or as the generalisability of the conclusions is somewhat sacrificed because the analysis of large data banks cannot be tackled (emergent approach).

The aim of this research project was to study the decision making processes used by managers in one organisation with the support of Organisation Analyser, a computerised tool based on a network approach to organisations which enables the collection and analysis of large volumes of data arising from an in-depth case study. The benefits of using such tools as OA are that they allow the consistent and rigorous comparison of data within cases - ie: across decisional groups, and across case studies of different organisations (which is the next step in this research project). Furthermore, OA enables researchers to begin their inquiry at a realistic analytical level, that of the decisional groups with the view to building up their knowledge of the overall network of an organisation incrementally and meaningfully. This seems to be a feasible way to reach reliable and generalisable conclusions regarding an organisation's decision making processes.

The preliminary findings reported in this paper confirm the benefits of using an approach based on the analysis of the decisional networks in organisations. In particular, the analysis of the concepts of centrality, decision ownership and decision authority in organisational decision making processes reveals a complex picture likely to confuse research results obtained if the decisional networks in existence were ignored. In Fun, the decision leadership was delegated to a large extent and the decisional groups evolved dynamically as the decisions unfolded, but overall control remained in the same hands whatever the decision.

Structural holes were found to have a great importance for the efficiency of organisational processes. OA turned out to greatly facilitate the identification of these accidental or purposeful discontinuities in the network of organisations. In supporting the identification of distortions and discontinuities in the networks of organisations, OA proved its potential as a DSS type tool to assist managers in identifying and removing the weaknesses in the formal and informal networks of their organisations. Thus, OA becomes a simulation tool, a kind of decision support system to study the shaping and reshaping of the organisation as it faces a variety of situations likely to heighten tensions, to create uncertainty or to require commitment to radically new policies. Such a tool seems particularly useful to researchers of organisation phenomena, but with some further developments of the interface and of the accuracy of the diagnostic it can formulate on an organisation's processes, OA could become a valuable managerial tool to evaluate the suitability of the current structure of an organisation and explain the difficulties encountered by some managers. Already, OA has demonstrated its potential in enriching the communication between the researchers and the people they interview as it enables interviewees to visualise how "their" data was interpreted by the researchers.

Another important finding for the continuation of this research was that the novelty of the problem, its specificity and the reversibility of the outcome are three fundamental dimensions for the study of decisions. Thus, Adam *et al.*'s framework (1995), which was used in this study for the selection of a sample of decisions, must be augmented so as to take into account the reversibility of the outcome of a decision in addition to the novelty of the problem and its specificity.

This project must now continue and investigate more companies and more decision processes until data covering a large sample of both decisions and organisations are available to the researcher and reliable and generalisable conclusions can be drawn on the issues identified in this paper.

7 REFERENCES

Adam F. and Murphy C. (1995 a) Information flows amongst executives: their implications for systems development, *Journal of Strategic Information Systems*, **4**(4).

Adam, F. and Murphy, C. (1995 b) Organisation Analyser - A Computer-Based Tool to Support The Analysis of Organisations from an Information Perspective, *Proceedings of the third SISnet Conference*, Bern, September 1995, 1-19.

Adam, F., Fahy, M. and Murphy, C. (1995) Cumulative research in decision support systems - a practical example, *Proceedings of the Third Conference on Information Systems (ECIS)*, Athens, June 1995, 1221-1233.

Balbridge J. V. (1971), *Power and Conflict in the University*, Wiley, New-York.

Bales, R. F. (1950) *Interaction Process Analysis: A Method for the Study of Small Groups*, Cambridge, MA: Addison-Wesley, 1950.

Bales, R. F. (1953) The equilibrium problem in small groups. In T. Parsons, R.F. Bales and E.A. Shils (Eds), Working Papers in the Theory of Action. Glencoe, IL: Free Press, 1953.

Blandin, J.S. and Brown, W.B. (1977) Uncertainty and management's search for information, *IEEE Transactions on Engineering Management*, **EM24**, 114-119.

Brass Daniel J. and Burkart Marlene E. (1992) Centrality and power in organisations, in Nitin Nohria and Robert Eccles (Eds.) *Networks and Organisations: Structure Form and Action*, Harvard Business School Press, Boston Mass, Chapter 7.

Burt, R. S. (1980) Models of Network Structure, *Annual Review of Sociology*, **6**, 79-141.

Burt, R. S. (1992) The social structure of competition, Nitin Nohria and Robert Eccles (Eds.) *Networks and Organisations: Structure Form and Action*, Harvard Business School Press, Boston Mass.

Carlsson S. A. (1993) Executive support systems for executive teams in organisations in high-velocity environments, Proceedings of the Twenty-six Annual Hawaii International Conference, III, 1-20.

Daft, R. L. and Lengel R. H. (1986) Organisational information requirements, media richness and structural design, *Management Science*, **32**(5), 554-571.

Daft, R.L., Sormunen, J. and Parks, D. (1988) Chief executive scanning, environmental characteristics and company performance: an empirical study, *Strategic Management Journal*, **9**, 123-139.

Eisenhardt Kathleen M. (1990) Speed and strategic choice: how managers accelerate decision making, *California Management Review*, **31**, 39-54.

Euske, N. and Roberts, K. (1987) Evolving perspectives in organisation theory: communication implications, in Jablin, F., Putnam, L., Roberts, K. and Porter, L. (eds.) (1987) *Handbook Of Organisational Communication: An Interdisciplinary Perspective*, pp. 41-69.

Feldman M. and March J. (1981) Information in organisations as signal and symbol, *Administrative Science Quarterly*, **26**, 171-186.

Gorry A. and Scott Morton. M. (1971) A Framework for Management Information Systems, *Sloan Management Review*, **Fall**, 55-70.

Granovetter, MS(1973) The strength of weak ties, *American Journal of Sociology*, **78**, 1360-1380.

Hedberg, Bo (1981) How organisations learn and unlearn, Nystrom, P.C. and Starbuck, W.H. (Eds.) *Handbook of Organisational Design*, 2, Oxford University Press, England, 3-27.

Huber G. (1982) Organisational information systems: determinants of their performance and behaviour, *Management Science*, **28**(2), 135-155.

Huber, G. and McDaniel, R. (1986) The decision-making paradigm of organisational design, *Management Science*, **32**, Number 5, pp. 572-589.

Janis, I. L (1972), *Victims of Groupthink*, Houghton Mifflin Comp, USA.

Jones J Saunders C and McLeod R (1988) Information media and source patterns across management levels: A pilot study, *Journal of Management Information Systems*, **5**(3), 71-84.

Kadushin C. (1978) Small world - How many steps to the top?, *Detroit News*, 106(26).

Keegan, W. (1974) Multinational scanning: a study of the information sources utilised by headquarters executives in multinational companies, *Administrative Science Quarterly*, 411-421.

Keen, P.G. (1977) The evolving concept of optimality, in Starr and Zeleny (Eds.), *TIMS studies in Management Science*, **6**, North Holland, 31-57.

Keen, P.G. and Scott Morton, M.S. (1978), *Decision Support Systems: An Organisational Perspective*, Addison-Wesley, Reading, Mass.

Kefalas, A. (1973) Scanning the business environment - some empirical results, *Decision Science*, **4**, 63-74

Le Bon, G. (1896), *The Crowd - A Study of the Popular Mind*, Fisher Unwin, London.

Lévine, P. and Pomerol, J.C. (1995) The role of the decision maker in DSSs and representation levels, in Nunamaker and Sprague (Eds.) *Proceedings of the 28th Annual Hawaii Conference on System Sciences*, 1995, 42-51.

March, J.P. (1981) Footnotes to organisational change, *Administrative Science Quarterly*, **26**, 563-577.

March, J.P. (1987) Ambiguity and Accounting: the elusive link between information and decision making, *Accounting, Organisations and Society*, **12**(2), 153-168.

March, J.P. and Olsen, J.P. (1989), *Rediscovering Institutions - The Organisational Basis of Politics*, The Free Press, New York.

March, J.P. and Olsen, J.P. (1986), Garbage can models of decision making in organisations, in J. March and R. Weissinger-Baylon (eds.) *Ambiguity and Command: Organisational Perspectives on Military Decision Making*, 11-35.

March, J. and Simon, H. (1993), *Organisations*, (2nd edition), Blackwell Publishers, Cambridge, Mass..

McGraph, Joseph E (1984), *Groups - Interaction and Performance*, (1st Edition), Prentice-Hall, Englewood Cliffs, N.J. 07632.

Mintzberg, H. (1973) *The Nature Of Managerial Work*, Prentice Hall.

Mintzberg, H., Raisinghani, D. And Théorêt, A. (1976) The Structure of "Unstructured" Decision Processes, *Administrative Science Quarterly*, **21**, 246-275.

Monge P. and Eisenberg E. (1987) Emergent communication networks, in Jablin F. Putnam L. Roberts K. and Porter L. (eds.) *Handbook Of Organisational Communication: An Interdisciplinary Perspective*, Sage Publication, London, 41-69.

Moore, J.H. and Chang, M. (1983) Meta-Design considerations, in J.L. Bennett (Ed.), *Building Decision Support Systems*, Addison-Wesley, 173-204.

Nohria N. (1992) Introduction: Is a network perspective a useful way to studying organisations, in Nitin Nohria and Robert Eccles (Eds.) *Networks and Organisations: Structure Form and Action*, Harvard Business Scholl Press, Boston Mass.

Nutt, Paul C. (1984) Types of organisational decision processes, *Administrative Science Quarterly*, **29**, 414-450.

O'Reilly, C., Chatman, J. and Anderson, J. (1987) Message flow and decision making, in Jablin, F., Putnam, L., Roberts, K. and Porter, L. (eds.) (1987) *Handbook Of Organisational Communication: An Interdisciplinary Perspective*, 600-623.

Pennings, J. M. (Ed.) (1983), *Decision Making: An Organisational Behaviour Approach*, Weiner, New York.

Pomerol, J.C. (1994) Des preferences au choix, des mathematiques a l'intelligence artificielle: le monde de l'aide a la decision, LAFORIA report 94 / 20, University Pierre et Marie Curie, Paris.

Roetlisberger F. J. (1977), *The Elusive Phenomena*, Harvard Business School Press., Boston.

Roetlisberger F. J. and Dickson W.J. (1939), *Management and the Worker*, Harvard University Press., Cambridge.

Simon, H. (1955), A behavioural model of rational choice, *Quarterly Journal of Economics*, **69**, 99-118.

Simon, H. (1977) *The New Science of Management Decisions*, Prentice Hall.

Stohl, C. and Redding, W. (1987) Messages and message exchange processes, in Jablin, F., Putnam, L., Roberts, K. and Porter, L. (eds.) (1987) *Handbook Of Organisational Communication: An Interdisciplinary Perspective*, 451-502.

Tichy N. M. (1992) Networks in organisations, in Nitin Nohria and Robert Eccles (Eds.) *Networks and Organisations: Structure Form and Action*, Harvard Business Scholl Press, Boston Mass, Chapter 10.

Tichy, N. M. (1981) Networks in organisations, Nystrom, P. and Starbuck, W. (Eds.) *Handbook of Organisational Design*, 2, Oxford University Press, New York, 225-249.

White H. C. (1992) Agency as control in organisational networks, in Nitin Nohria and Robert Eccles (Eds.) *Networks and Organisations: Structure Form and Action*, Harvard Business Scholl Press, Boston Mass, Chapter 3.

8 BIOGRAPHY

Frédéric Adam is college lecturer in the Department of Accounting, Finance and Information Systems at University College Cork in Ireland. He is also a senior researcher with the Executive Systems Research Centre. His main research interests include the usage of information in organisations and the study of research methodologies in the IS field. His research has been published in a number of journals including the *Journal of Strategic Information Systems* and he has presented his work in several recent IS conferences in Greece, Holland, Ireland and Switzerland. He is also involved in a number of consultancy projects in the area of information systems implementation and information systems for top managers.

The author would like to acknowledge the contribution of Brian Fitzgerald, Ciaran Murphy and Jean-Charles Pomerol.

2

A software process for management software systems

Alfs T. Berztiss
Department of Computer Science, University of Pittsburgh
Pittsburgh, PA 15260, USA
(e-mail: alpha@cs.pitt.edu; fax: +412-624-8854)

and

SYSLAB, University of Stockholm, Sweden

Abstract

The business world of today is characterized by very rapidly changing business conditions that require rapid responses. The responses are to be results of decision making, supported by carefully designed management software systems. This paper is a position statement that discusses various factors to be considered in the definition of a software process for developing such systems. Since the rapid change will extend to management software, the software process is to allow rapid configuration of new systems from existing components, and rapid reconfiguration of existing systems. Because the boundary between decision support systems and other classes of business-oriented software is becoming increasingly blurred, we use the term management software systems in preference to decision support systems.

Keywords

Decision support, domain model, management software system, pattern, reuse, software process

1 INTRODUCTION

Kroenke (1992) classifies business software systems into systems for transaction processing, management information, decision support, office automation, and executive support. In full agreement with Alter (1993), who observes that the separation between the DSS, EIS (Executive Information System), and ES (Expert System) worlds is largely artificial, we contend that the distinction between the different types of systems listed by Kroenke has become very blurred, and is in fact disappearing. For example, an order fulfillment system could, in addition to the processing of regular orders, generate periodic summaries for management, use the summaries to assist in decisions of when to increase inventory by initiating manufacturing runs, replace explicit orders as the basis for initiating shipments by automatic monitoring of client inventories, and produce surveys of long-term trends for top management.

Another trend that has to be considered is the very rapid change that characterizes the business environment of today. Daniel Bell's *The Coming of the Post-Industrial Society* (Bell, 1973) was published as early as 1973. Ten years later George Huber described what a postindustrial organization would look like (Huber, 1984). His basic premise is that postindustrial society will be characterized by accelerating increase in knowledge, complexity, and turbulence, and that postindustrial organizations will therefore have to be qualitatively different from the organizations of the industrial age. The qualitative differences are to be most noticeable in decision making, innovation, and the acquisition and distribution of information. Huber and McDaniel (1986) describe several organizational paradigms, and find that a decision-making paradigm is the most effective for the operation of organizations in the world of today. The main characteristic of this paradigm is the explicit provision of structures and processes that facilitate the making of decisions in the operation of an organization.

The rapid change phenomenon has given rise to the business reengineering (BRE) movement (Davenport, 1993; Hammer and Champy, 1993; Johansson *et al*, 1993). One aspect of BRE is the recognition of business processes as the defining features of an enterprise. We have discussed this in detail elsewhere (Berztiss, 1995). Another is the need for cooperation within an enterprise and between enterprises at the level of processes. Our order fulfillment system is an example of internal cooperation; a well-known example of inter-company cooperation is the automatic updating by Procter and Gamble of the inventory of its products in Wal-Mart stores (Hammer and Champy, 1993, pp. 60-62).

To summarize, businesses have to cope with rapidly changing business environments. This requires that they assume a decision-making structure, and that decision-making be built into the software systems of an enterprise. These software systems are to support business processes, and a major aspect of their design is to be cooperation, both intra- and inter-enterprise cooperation. These characteristics have to be taken into account in the design of the development process for decision support software, or, what is a more appropriate term, management software systems. In Section 2 we explore two classes of software development models. Section 3 deals in greater detail with the demands on management software systems, and in Section 4 we consider the software process from the BRE viewpoint. In Section 5 we introduce our software process model. Finally, Section 6 contains some conclusions and recommendations, which have been influenced by our practical experience with patterns.

2 MODELS OF THE SOFTWARE DEVELOPMENT PROCESS

Software process models fall into two major classes. One relates to the capabilities of the organization that develops the software. The other defines the steps that are to be followed in software development, and considers the representations that are to express such a definition of the software process. Let us call the models feature-oriented or managerial, and structure-oriented or technical, respectively.

The most comprehensive managerial model is the Capability Maturity Model (CMM), developed at the Software Engineering Institute (SEI) of Carnegie-Mellon University (Humphrey, 1989; Paulk *et al*, 1993). The CMM puts software developing organizations at five levels, and an organization moves to higher levels by showing that it has mastered all the "key process areas" that define the higher level. Another example is ISO 9001, which is a general quality standard (Paulk, 1995). It identifies minimal requirements for quality control in an organization in the form of 20 clauses. It is related specifically to software by ISO 9000-3. The Bootstrap model (Kuvaja *et al*, 1994) attempts to combine the SEI and ISO approaches. The CMM is very detailed on how an organization can improve its software development practices, but it is rather rigid, and its use is mainly confined to North America; ISO 9001 is not concerned with detailed steps to improvement. Bootstrap introduces CMM to Europe, but in a flexible form.

A technical model defines steps in the software development process, and recommends an ordering of the steps. Popular technical models have been the waterfall (Royce, 1970) and the spiral (Boehm, 1988) models. The waterfall model assumes a strict ordering of a sequence of steps. The steps could be requirements elicitation, specification, system design, detailed design, coding, testing, and maintenance. However, it has been shown that that these steps must inevitably be intertwined (Swartout and Balzer, 1982). The spiral model allows developers to define their own process steps, and the steps can be revisited over and over again. It can therefore serve as a very general framework for the software process. A generic model, such as the spiral model, has to be transformed into an application-specific software process. Thirteen notations in which the process can be described have been surveyed by Armenise *et al* (1993). For a detailed description of one of these notations, FUNSOFT, see Deiters and Gruhn (1994).

We have investigated concurrency in a software process model (Berztiss, 1993), and have developed a software process model (Berztiss and Bubenko, 1995) based on the enterprise model introduced by Bubenko *et al* (1994). The model to be discussed in Section 5 represents an extension of this work. Our model is somewhere between a pure managerial and a pure technical model.

3 MANAGEMENT SOFTWARE SYSTEMS FOR TODAY AND TOMORROW

In (Berztiss, 1995) we adapted some guidelines of Huber and McDaniel (1986) that are to facilitate the introduction of a decision-making paradigm into organizations. Here we shall extend and broaden the guidelines, and discuss the significance of the guidelines for the software process, and for the software systems developed by the process.

Decision-making authority is assigned to appropriate levels in an organizational hierarchy. A three-way partition identifies decisions relating to strategy, operational tactics needed to implement a strategy, and day-to-day operation of an organization. Strategic decisions cannot be generated automatically, but the decision-making process is to be supported by software, which we interpret to cover both programs and information bases. Tactical decision making can be partially automated, and the decisions that arise in day-to-day operation can be automated for the most part.

Decision makers must have the specialized knowledge appropriate to their level of decision making. This requires not only specialized skills to interpret information, but user-friendly access to all required information, and to software tools that are to support interpretation of the information and the actual decision making.

Situations are identified as standard and nonstandard. This refers to situations that arise in day-to-day operation of an organization. Decision making with respect to standard situations can be standardized and automated. Nonstandard situations require initiative and flexibility. This implies that management software systems must be constantly monitored by people, and that a switch to manual control of a situation can be effected seemlessly. In particular, messages flowing through an organization relate to standard and nonstandard situations. Response to "standard" messages is to be automated; "nonstandard" messages are to be rapidly chanelled to appropriate decision making personnel. A nonstandard message may affect strategy.

Decision making is managed. Under the decision-making paradigm the making of decisions is the central activity in an organization, and it cannot be left to chance. What this means is that all business processes are to be explicitly defined, and all routine decision making is to be supported by appropriate management software systems. Moreover, an organization should be able to switch into an exceptional mode of operation when truly exceptional situations arise, and this without throwing anybody into panic.

Processes are "owned". Business reengineering puts much emphasis on business processes, and it has been recommended that a process and the data that give primary support to the process should both be "owned" by the same manager — see, e.g., (Davenport, 1993, p.88). This implies that our current views on data bases, and a preference for their centralized management have to be reconsidered. Moreover, a process can then be regarded as being supported by an autonomous management software system that cooperates with software systems that support other business processes, all having the common aim of advancing the objectives of an enterprise.

Cooperation is emphasized, both within an organization and between organizations. This was briefly touched upon in Section 1. Cooperation within an organization relates to all three kinds of decision making, and is to be supported by appropriate tools that facilitate group decision making. Cooperation between organizations has related for the most part to day-to-day operation, but we can expect that in the future more attention will be given to software-supported strategy formulation in the setting up of alliances of companies and their suppliers — for a general discussion see (Lewis, 1995). Cooperation by means of software systems requires that they be properly coordinated — Malone and Crowston (1994) survey various aspects of coordination.

Intelligent agents are in use. When decision making by software reaches an advanced level, e.g., when a software system controls the investment portfolio of an enterprise, it becomes appropriate to talk of intelligent agents. However, there is wide disagreement on when exactly a piece of software becomes an agent — apart from the inclusion of a learning component in an agent, there is little to distinguish agents from expert systems. Although practical successes have been few as yet (Greif, 1994), learning components in management software systems are to be given greater attention. Agents can assume particular significance in the context of cooperative management software systems, where they are to cooperate, and are to facilitate cooperation.

Domain knowledge becomes part of software. We consider the incorporation of domain knowledge into management software systems as perhaps the most important of the trends considered in this section. Our interest is in domain knowledge, domain models, and domain analysis. Domain knowledge is the entire corpus of data, rules, and processes that characterizes a discipline. Some of it is codified in standards and handbooks, but most of it is distributed in the collective memory of practitioners of the discipline. A domain model is an abstraction that consists of only those parts of the domain knowledge that are relevant to a particular application. The purpose of domain analysis is to develop domain models. We classify domain models into occupation models, enterprise models, process models, and situation models. An occupation model captures the knowledge that relates to the practices followed by members of an occupation as an explicit structure. For the most part this is expressed in the form of business rules. An enterprise model provides insight into the objectives of an enterprise, i.e., the goals that a management software system is to assist in achieving. It also shows the management structure of the enterprise. The ownership of processes and their data ultimately depends on this structure. Process models are easiest to define: they capture the essence of business processes. A situation model relates to a specific context. An interesting aspect of situation analysis relates to exceptions. For example, overbooking can be incorporated into some reservation systems, with the degree of overbooking for a given setting determined from domain knowledge, which is to include a consideration of enterprise objectives. An exception arises when, due to overbooking, actual demand exceeds availability by an unexpectedly large margin.

4 REENGINEERING AND THE SOFTWARE PROCESS

In (Berztiss, 1995) we define BRE in terms of sixteen steps. We shall now use these reengineering steps as a framework for the definition of software development processes, and relate the reengineering steps to a process defined within the framework, and to the software systems to be developed under this process.

1. Management commitment. There has to be full management support for the introduction of a process-oriented approach to software development. In addition, management has to insist that each software project is well planned, subjected to a thorough cost-benefit study, and is smoothly integrated into the organizational structure. This necessitates some understanding of the software process by top management.

2. Manager selection. Most organizations now have a CIO (Chief Information Officer), and this executive officer must see to it that top management understands the ultimate benefits to be derived from an improved software process, i.e., a decision-making process that requires project planning and cost-benefit analysis. An operational manager is to supervise an initial overhaul of the operation of the IS (Information Systems) department, to bring it in line with modern practices as defined by the managerial process models of Section 2, and the introduction of incremental improvements after the initial overhaul.

3. Reengineering teams. The overhaul of information systems development is a typical BRE task, to be tackled exactly like any other BRE task. In particular, basing the software development process on the use of self-managing development teams is to be encouraged.

4. Initial education. The IS personnel must have full understanding of the software process, both under the feature- and the structure-oriented forms. This is essential for obtaining personnel support for the process. One task of education is to make clear that no spectacular improvement can be expected in the short term, but that long-term improvement will be achieved if software development follows a well-defined process.

5. Process identification. We have to distinguish between the software development process, and software systems that this process is to produce. In this step a generic software process is to be defined under consideration of both features and structure.

6. Process specification. This step relates to software systems, but an essential property of a software system is that it defines a process. There has to exist a precise requirements document for each software system. Preferably this should be a formal specification document.

7. Development of alternative implementation plans for each process. Although under Steps 5 and 6 we referred to software systems, our real concern is with total systems in which tasks are allocated to hardware, software, and people. At this stage different allocation schemes can be proposed, and an implementation plan developed for each scheme. Note that the software process itself can be implemented in various ways, and the various alternatives should be defined as part of this step.

8. Cost-benefit study for each plan and selection of an appropriate plan. Each of the schemes of Step 7 is now subjected to cost-benefit analysis. Moreover, the software components of these plans do not have to be implemented under the same software process, i.e., different specific processes can be derived from the generic process of Step 5, as noted under Step 7. Each relevant combination of software system and software process is to be considered in the cost-benefit analysis.

9. Infrastructure definition based on the selected plan. This relates primarily to the software process, and the infrastructure consists of CASE (Computer Assisted Software Engineering) tools, and groupware that is to allow IS personnel to work in collaboration. This in turn requires that there be adequate network facilities to support the groupware. The infrastructure requirements do not depend on individual software projects — they will be determined by the mix of the software systems that an organization develops.

10. Setting of priorities for implementation of processes and infrastructure. Here we have to consider two aspects. As explained above, software process and infrastructure are related, and the priorities in infrastructure upgrading will be determined by a cost-benefit analysis that will again depend on the product mix. Further, no organization possesses the resources to implement all the software systems it can use, so a cost-benefit analysis is to define a priority schedule. However, it has to be realized that cost-benefit analysis in this context is still very subjective, and will remain so until we have improved our understanding of the benefits that are to be derived from specific software systems.

11. Second education phase. This is an on-going effort, relating both to the software process and to the software systems. As our understanding of the effectiveness of different aspects of the software process grows, this understanding has to be conveyed to IS personnel. As regards software systems, one of the major problems is inadequate understanding of application domains (Curtis *et al*, 1988). There have to be institutionalized procedures for making the relevant IS personnel familiar with the domains for which they are developing software systems.

12. Pilot implementation. Just as there has to be a priority list for the implementation of software systems (Step 10), so there has to be a priority list for the components of a software process model. The taking of measurements that relate to the software process and to the software systems produced by the process is to begin at once, but the effective utilization of the measurements can only begin when there are enough of them, and this takes time. The first priority, then, is emphasis on measurements. At the same time, all other features that define a mature software process in accordance with a managerial process model are to be examined, and the sequence for their introduction is to be determined by the "organizational culture" of the IS department, i.e., by how ready IS is to accept responsibility for each feature.

13. Reexamination of the BRE effort. The activities of Steps 10 through 12 should not be considered in isolation. They depend on each other and reinforce each other, and an early demonstration of the effectiveness of this consolidated approach to the reengineering of IS will determine the willingness of top management to allocate additional resources to a continuation of the reengineering of IS.

14. Completion of implementation. The ultimate aim of any IS department should be to have an excellent software process in place, but, for example, to reach the higher levels on the SEI process maturity scale takes time, resources, and unreserved management support. In Step 13 it was essential to show that resources will be well spent; in Step 14 it is essential to spend the resources well.

15. Continuing automation of processes. Again we have to differentiate between the software process and software systems. At Level 5 on the SEI scale, the software process is to optimize itself. This will remain a manual activity, carried out by people supervising the process. However, reengineering of IS improves productivity and the skills of IS personnel. This allows software systems to become more sophisticated.

16. Automatic linkages to the environment. The environment of the IS department is the entire organization of which it is a part, and the software systems developed by IS should assist in a coordinated operation of the organization. One aim of BRE should be the integration of all activities of an organization — this depends greatly on how well the software systems that support these activities are integrated. A broader environment includes entities with which an organization cooperates, such as suppliers, government agencies, and trade groups.

5 A SOFTWARE PROCESS MODEL

Rapid construction of management software systems requires a well-defined process. In the preceding three sections we examined requirements for this software process from three viewpoints. In Section 2 a distinction was made between managerial and technical models. In Section 3 we examined some current trends relating to the operation of organizations. A most important trend is BRE, and we took a BRE approach to the software process in Section 3. All these trends and factors are to have an effect on the process for developing management software systems. However, to give full justice to this effect is beyond the scope of a conference paper, and here we merely state that the process model introduced below was developed under consideration of the material of Sections 2-4. Moreover, the process model can be presented in only a very sketchy form.

In (Berztiss and Bubenko, 1995) we introduced a software system development model, which, modified and extended, is shown here as Figure 1. In this model, system development begins with objectives and ends with a management software system. The objectives determine a domain model that consists of three basic components: a structured information base, procedures for changing the information base (events), and processes. This somewhat informal model is converted into a formal functional specification. There are also nonfunctional aspects of a software system, such as usability, which can rarely be stated in formal terms – they are represented by the "Nonfunctional requirements" box. This development process is defined in terms of various concepts, and different roles in the process are allocated to actors, which can be people or software tools. Several versions of the system can be generated, and, during the lifetime of a particular version, it is represented in different forms, such as requirements diagrams, specification, and code. There must always be a clear understanding of which version a particular representation belongs to (version control), and that all representations of a version are consistent (configuration control).

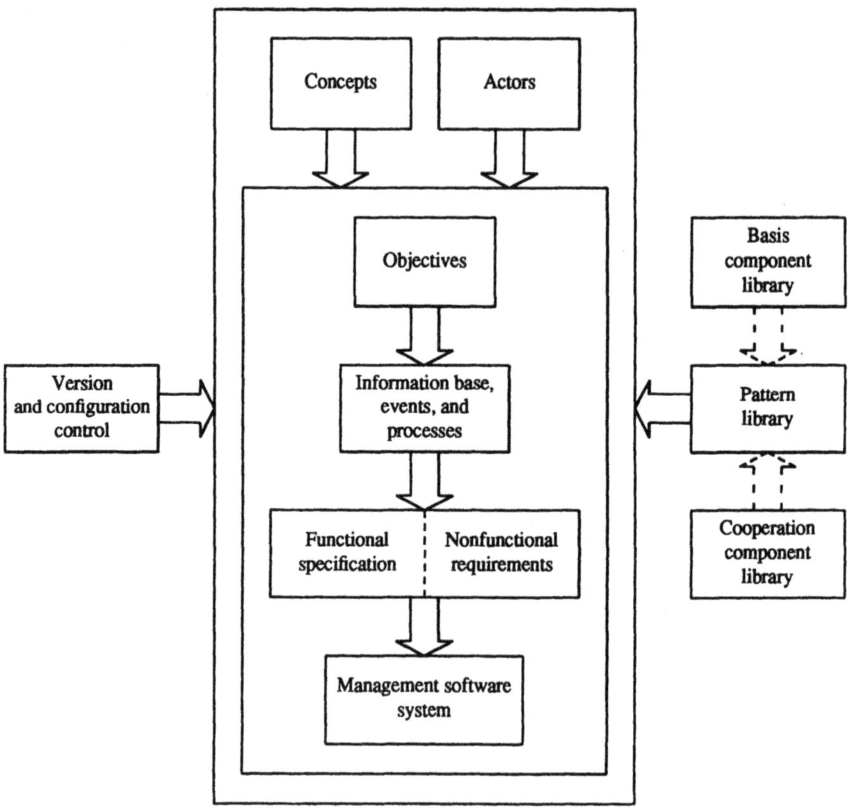

Figure 1 A software process model for management systems

The more enclosed a box, the more specific is its role in the process. The box for version and configuration control, and the three boxes for the libraries are not enclosed, which means that they are not influenced by what particular software product is being developed, i.e., they are fully application independent.

The main change in this model from the Berztiss and Bubenko (1995) model is the addition of the libraries. Lately some domain knowledge has been expressed as patterns — see, e.g., (Coplien and Schmidt, 1995). We interpret a pattern to be a generic template that defines the structure of a problem and its solution, but that has to be refined to become applicable in a specific situation. We can relate the four domain models of Section 3 to patterns. The occupation and enterprise models suggest what management software systems are needed and what patterns are relevant in the setting up of the systems. A process model imposes structure on a pattern, and a situation model relates a process to the setting in which it is to operate — in particular, exceptional conditions in the operation of a process are covered by the situation model. In Figure 1 we have a basis component library and a cooperation component library. These components are gathered up into a pattern.

Let us take a concrete example, a rental car company. A look at its operation allows us to identify a set of very general patterns that are constructed almost exclusively from "basis components". These patterns relate to reservations, actual rentals, acquisition and disposal of inventory, tracking of transaction trends, management of distributed sites, etc. The reservations and rental patterns arise in the hotel, airline, car rental, and formal wear rental businesses. This is by no means an exhaustive list — Maiden and Sutcliffe (1992) point out the similarity between a theatre reservation system and a university course registration system; we note that both are instances of the reservation pattern. Tracking of transaction trends should be practiced by every enterprise — a downward trend is a danger signal; an upward trend of car rentals should trigger inventory build-up; an upward trend in hotel occupancy rates can justify an increase in room charges. Management of distributed sites is particular to car rental: a car may be picked up and dropped off at different sites, and transaction trends at different sites may suggest a redistribution of cars.

An example of pattern constructed primarily from "cooperation components" is the scheduling of a meeting, which can involve personnel from several enterprises. This can be handled by an intelligent agent. The pattern requires the agent to consult intended participants regarding their availability, and negotiate a mutually acceptable time slot, which can be complicated if the participants' calendars show no common available time slot. Depending on the width of the negotiated time window, the agent has to decide whether to hold a face-to-face or an electronic meeting. In the worst case, there can be a switch to a group decision mode in which participants cooperate asynchronously via a blackboard structure. The selection of the blackboard structure is a decision relating to software architectures — see, e.g., (Shaw, 1995).

The actors box has a twofold significance. First, it has to be decided which parts of the software process are to be carried out by people and which by tools. Maiden and Sutcliffe (1993) advance strong arguments that reuse is to be very much people-oriented. In terms of Figure 1, the four boxes relating to objectives, the three-component requirements, patterns, and functional specifications define a difficult system construction task, and only people are capable of effectively carrying out this task.

Second, in the system that is being developed, various tasks are to be allocated to people, software, and hardware. Considering people and software alone, the allocation relates to routine tasks, routine exceptions, and unexpected exceptions. With regard to order fulfillment, this is a routine process when there are no shortages. Routine exceptions arise when there are inventory shortages, and an unexpected exception arises when the warehouse staff go out on strike. The first two cases can be handled by software, the last, because it is unexpected, has to be handled by people, but in cooperation with the software system.

6 CONCLUSIONS AND RECOMMENDATIONS

The two most important tasks for the future are the setting up of a pattern library, and the development of a "pattern selection apprentice". We have started work on the former, and in two directions – to prove that the approach is quite general. One direction is in computer science, and is concerned with patterns relating to safety-critical situations (Berztiss, 1996); the other relates to management software, and consists of patterns suggested by the analysis of the operation of a rental car business, which we referred to earlier. Some of the rental business patterns deal with the gathering of information that is to support decision making, and the actual making of decisions. For example, an analysis of rental data can suggest a redistribution of rental objects over the locations at which the enterprise operates, and an analysis of repair and resale data will suggest when a rental object is to be taken out of service. These generic patterns are as easily adaptable to rental videos as to rental cars. The rental data pattern can also indicate shortages, which in the case of rental cars may lead to purchase of additional cars, but in the case of a hotel to raised room rates.

The base of our pattern library consists of the generic patterns, which are merely capsule outlines in natural language. A pattern for a specific application has also a natural language version that consists of five entries. They are (1) *Triggered by*, which establishes what it is that initiates the activities grouped under the pattern; (2) *Activities*, which gives an outline of all activities that are part of the pattern, an indication of the conditions under which each activity takes place, and an indication of how the activities are related to each other; (3) *Information base changes*, which indicates those parts of the information base supporting the car-rental process that are to be affected by the activities of the pattern; (4) *Affects*, which identifies all patterns that can be affected by this pattern, and states the conditions under which this pattern would interact with other patterns; (5) *Notes*, which can contain any information deemed relevant by the author of the pattern, e.g., an explicit indication of what is *not* considered in the pattern. These patterns are next defined in the specification language SF – (Berztiss, 1990) is currently the best introduction to SF.

With the capsule summaries to refer to, the setting up of patterns for a reservation and the cancellation of a reservation in the rental-car context took about 25 minutes for initial design and about 10 minutes for review on the following day. These patterns were adapted for the reservation and cancellation of a restaurant table in approximately six minutes. Being given just the capsule summaries, teams of rather inexperienced undergraduate students in one of the author's courses have implemented and fairly thoroughly tested an information system for a rental-car operation in around 360 person-hours (a team consisted of six students, and each student contributed approximately 60 hours to the project).

The pattern selection apprentice is to be a specialization of the software apprentices described by Rich and Waters (1990). By consulting the requirements for a management software system and a pattern library, the apprentice is to decide which patterns are applicable in a given situation. Initially the apprentice is merely to help software developers navigate through a library of patterns.

The ultimate purpose of a management software system is to exercise control. We distinguish between three kinds of software: a conventional program that is fully deterministic and can exercise control over a process or part of a process entirely on its own; an ES that also exercises total control, but that may be under continuous modification as the understanding of the process continues to improve over time; a DSS that assists a human decision maker, but does not make control decisions entirely on its own. Thus, a fully understood process is controlled by a conventional program, a process that is reasonably well understood and about which our understanding continues to improve is under control of an ES, and a process that is not so well understood is under partial control of a DSS. If our understanding is so poor that we cannot express our knowledge about the process as software, then we have to depend entirely on human versatility in dealing with it. How far a management system can be advanced along this progression from full human control to a decision support system to an expert system to a conventional program depends on how well a control situation is understood, and how well it can be explicitly described. This applies both to the software process, and to the systems with which the software process is to deal.

7 REFERENCES

Alter, S. (1993) Why persist with DSS when the real issue is improving decision making? In *Decision Support Systems: Experiences and Expectations* (eds. T. Jelassi, M.R. Klein, and W.M. Mayon-White), 1-11, North-Holland.

Armenise, P., Bandinelli, S., Ghezzi, C., and Morzenti, A. (1993) A survey and assessment of software process representation formalisms. *Int. J. Software Eng. Knowledge Eng.* **3**, 401-426.

Bell, D. (1973) *The Coming of the Post-Industrial Society*. Basic Books.

Berztiss, A. (1990) Formal specification methods and visualization. In *Principles of Visual Programming Systems* (ed. S.-K. Chang), 231-290, Prentice Hall.

Berztiss, A. (1993) Concurrent engineering of information systems. In *Proc. IFIP WG8.1 Working Conf. on Information System Development Processes* (eds. N. Prakash, C. Rolland, B. Pernici), 311-324, North-Holland.

Berztiss, A.T. (1995) *Software Methods for Business Reengineering*. Springer-Verlag.

Berztiss, A.T. (1996) Unforeseen hazard conditions and software cliches. To appear in *High Integrity Systems* **1**.

Berztiss, A.T., and Bubenko, J.A. (1995) A software process model for business reengineering. In *Information Systems Development for Decentralized Organizations*, 184-200, Chapman & Hall.

Boehm, B.W. (1988) A spiral model of software development and enhancement. *Computer* **21**, (5), 61-72.

Bubenko, J.A., Rolland, C., Loucopoulos, P., and DeAntonellis, V. (1994) Facilitating "fuzzy to formal" requirements modelling. In *Proc. IEEE Internat. Conf. on Requirements Eng.*

Coplien, J.O., and Schmidt, D.C, eds. (1995) *Pattern Languages of Program Design*. Addison Wesley.

Curtis, B., Krasner, H., and Iscoe, N. (1988) A field study of the software design process for large systems. *Communications of the ACM*, **31**, 1268-1287.

Davenport, T. H. (1993) *Process Innovation: Reengineering Work through Information Technology*. Harvard Business School Press.

Deiters, W., and Gruhn, V. (1994) The FUNSOFT net approach to software process management. *Int. J. Software Eng. Knowledge Eng.* **4**, 229-256.

Greif, I. (1994) Desktop agents in group-enabled products. *Comm. ACM* **37**, (7), 100-105.

Hammer, M., and Champy, J. (1993) *Reengineering the Corporation: A Manifesto for Business Revolution*. Harper Business.

Huber, G.P. (1984) The nature and design of post-industrial organizations. *Management Science* **30**, 928-951.

Huber, G.P., and McDaniel, R.R. (1986) The decision-making paradigm of organizational design. *Management Science* **32**, 572-589.

Humphrey, W.S. (1989) *Managing the Software Process*. Addison-Wesley.

Johansson, H. J., McHugh, P., Pendlebury, A. J., and Wheeler, W. A. (1993) *Business Process Reengineering: BreakPoint Strategies for Reengineering*. Wiley.

Kroenke, D. (1992) *Management Information Systems*. McGraw-Hill.

Kuvaja, P., Simila, J., Krzanik, L., Bicego, A., Saukkonen, S., and Koch, G. (1994) *Software Process Assessment and Improvement — The BOOTSTRAP Approach*. Blackwell Business.

Lewis, J.D. (1995) *The Connected Corporation*. Free Press.

Maiden, N.A., and Sutcliffe, A.G. (1992) Exploiting reusable specifications through analogy. *Comm. ACM* **35**, (4), 55-64.

Maiden, N.A.M., and Sutcliffe, A.G. (1993) People-oriented software reuse: the very thought. In *Advances in Software Reuse* (eds. R. Prieto-Diaz and W.B. Frakes), 176-185, IEEE Computer Society Press.

Malone, T.W., and Crowston, K. (1994) The interdisciplinary study of coordination. *ACM Computing Surv.* **26**, 87-119.

Paulk, M.C. (1995) How ISO 9001 compares with the CMM. *IEEE Software* **10**, (4), 74-83.

Paulk, M.C., Weber, C., Garcia, S., Chrissis, M.B., and Bush, M. (1993) Key practices of the Capability Maturity Model Version 1.1. SEI Report CMU/SEI-93-TR-25, Software Engineering Institute of Carnegie-Mellon University.

Rich, C., and Waters, R.C. (1990) *The Programmer's Apprentice*. ACM Press, 1990.

Royce, W.W. (1970) Managing the development of large software systems. In *Proc. IEEE WESCON*, 1-9.

Shaw, M. (1995) Architectural issues in software reuse: it's not just functionality, it's the packaging. In *Proc. ACM SIGSOFT Symp. Software Reusability* (special issue of *ACM SIGSOFT Software Engineering Notes*), 3-6.

Swartout, W., and Balzer, R. (1982) On the inevitable intertwining of specification and implementation. *Comm. ACM* **25**, 438-440.

8 BIOGRAPHY

Prof. Berztiss received the PhD in Theoretical Physics from the University of Melbourne in Australia. Since 1970 he has been with the Computer Science Department of the University of Pittsburgh. Since 1984 he has also been a research associate of SYSLAB of the University of Stockholm. Dr. Berztiss is a Fellow of the Australian Computer Society, and belongs to ACM, IEEE, European Association for Theoretical Computer Science, and IFIP Working Groups 8.1 (Design and Evaluation of Information Systems) and 8.3 (Decision Support Systems). He has published three books and numerous technical papers. He has been a consultant with UNIDO, SEI, IBM, etc. His research interests include conceptual modeling in the reengineering of organizations, specification and prototyping of software, reliability engineering of software, treatment of uncertain data, and curriculum development for software engineering education.

3

A management decision support system for allocating housing loans

Marko Bohanec [(1)] *Bojan Cestnik* [(3,1)] *Vladislav Rajkovič* [(2,1)]
[(1)] *"Jožef Stefan" Institute, Jamova 39, SI-1000 Ljubljana, Slovenia*
[(2)] *University of Maribor, Faculty of Organizational Sciences, Kranj*
[(3)] *Temida, d.o.o., Ljubljana*
e-mail: (marko.bohanec bojan.cestnik vladislav.rajkovic)@ijs.si

Abstract

A system for supporting management decisions in the allocation of housing loans is presented. The system has been used in the Housing Fund of the Republic of Slovenia since 1991 for granting loans to citizens. Various activities are supported, such as priority ranking of applications, financial evaluation and analyses. The system is based on a knowledge base that contains several qualitative and quantitative decision models, and is combined with a database. In the paper, we present the design of the system, the principal stages of its development and utilization, and practical experience obtained in 11 completed floats of loans.

Keywords

Management decision support systems, knowledge-based systems, decision models, loan allocation, housing

1 INTRODUCTION

The Housing Fund of the Republic of Slovenia was founded in 1991 under provisions of the Housing Law for the purpose of financing the national housing programme and encouraging the construction, renovation and maintenance of housing. The Fund obtains financial resources for its operations from: an allocation from the Republic's budget, part of the proceeds of the sales of flats, subsidies from local and foreign organizations, the proceeds of the sale of the Fund's securities, and income earned by the Fund's business operations. The resources are earmarked primarily for loans with favorable terms (low interest rates and long repayment time) to citizens and non-profit housing organizations.

So far the Fund has granted more than 11 thousand loans in 11 floats with a total value of about 12 billion Slovenian tolars (approximately 74 million ECU). The floats differed from each other in the amount of available funds and the purpose of loan consumption (e.g., construction, renovation, maintenance). These differences reflected in different criteria that determine the priority of applicants, such as the present state of housing, family status, and the age of family members.

The amount requested by applicants usually exceeds the available financial resources. In such cases, applicants must be ranked in a loan priority order. A system that supports the loan allocation activities must, among other things, facilitate an efficient determination of priority order, considering both, the housing law and prescribed conditions within the float. Fast, reliable and transparent determining of priorities, which is fair for all applicants, is required. Transparency requires effective explanation of loan priority order, which is an important demand because of the sensitivity of housing affairs and interconnection of different factors. The problem increases due to the high number of applicants.

In this paper, we describe a management decision support system for supporting the activities related to loan allocation in the Housing Fund of Slovenia. The system is based on a combination of a knowledge-based system (Klein, Methlie 1995; Mallach 1994) and a database that contains numerous data items about applications, loans and priorities for all floats of loans. The central component of the knowledge base is a qualitative multi-criteria decision model (Rajkovič, Bohanec 1991; Gumesson 1991; Angehm 1992) for the evaluation of loan priority.

In the following section, the problem of loan allocation is presented. Section 3 describes our approach to the development of the system. Its utilization is illustrated in section 4 by focusing on some of its important phases. The paper is concluded by presenting some critical success factors.

2 PROBLEM DESCRIPTION AND REQUIREMENTS

The Housing Fund distributes financial resources in floats of loans. The Fund invites applicants to apply for the loans by filling in an application form. The financial resources are limited, and are usually exceeded by applicants' requests. Therefore, all applicants must be ranked in a priority order for the distribution of financial resources in accordance with criteria, prescribed in the corresponding tender. Those criteria may vary from tender to tender. In addition to priority, the amount that is granted to an applicant depends also on some other factors, such as the amount already granted to the applicant in previous floats.

Due to a high number of applicants, which varies from several hundreds to several thousands per float, a fast and efficient supporting system is required. Other important demands are transparency, comprehensibility, and flexibility. The transparency is needed to report reasons for the calculated results and explain the loan priority order to both the Fund's management and applicants. The comprehensibility of the system means that its procedures should be well understood and trusted. All the system activities and obtained results should be presented to the management and applicants in a form that facilitates an overview of the underlying activities and procedures, and justification of the results. For instance, the system must enable tracing the path from application form data to the final determination of the loan to be granted to the applicant. Flexibility of the system is required due to substantial differences between the tenders, which affect its components. The usual rate of the Fund's floats is two to three per year, so there is a permanent need for the adaptation of the system.

3 DESIGN OF THE SYSTEM

In order to facilitate flexibility and transparency, we centered the design of our loan allocation system around a *knowledge base* (Vadera, Nechab 1991; Klein, Methlie 1995). The knowledge base contains various evaluation and computational models related to priority ranking of applications and determining financial aspects of each application. The knowledge base was the first component of the system we developed and is still the starting point whenever the system is adapted for the specifics of a new tender (Figure 1). The structure of the knowledge base largely determines the requested data from each applicant, so it serves as a basis for the design of an application form, entities in a database, and specific procedures and activities to be performed on these data.

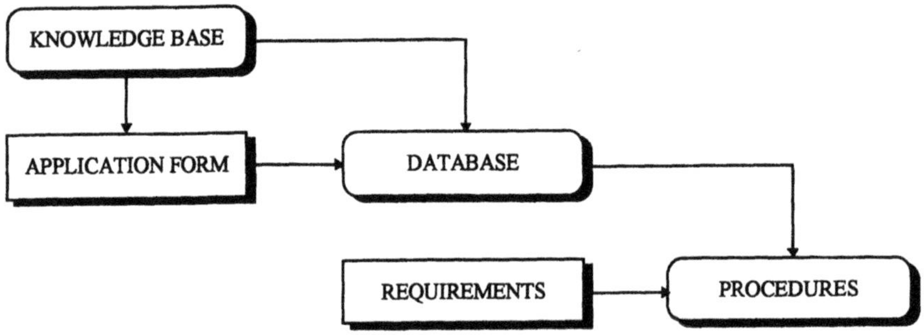

Figure 1 Development of the loan allocation system.

3.1 A model for the evaluation of application priority

The most important single model in the knowledge base is a hierarchical qualitative evaluation model for determining the priority of applications. Each application is ranked into one of five priority classes based on the hierarchy of criteria shown in Figure 2. The priority thus depends on three main groups of assessments:

1. applicant's *housing* conditions in terms of the ownership and suitability of *present* housing, the way of *solving* his or her housing problem, and the *stage* of solving;
2. applicant's *status* in terms of earnings, employment, and the number of children;
3. *social* and *health* conditions.

All the criteria in this model are qualitative: their values are words that typically express a level of priority. For example, there are three priority levels for the SOCIAL criterion: (1) *normal,* (2) *priority,* and (3) *high_priority*. The specific value for each applicant is determined from his or her FAMILY status and AGE, where the highest priority is typically granted for young families. Once the priority with respect to SOCIAL is known, it is combined further with the HEALTH criterion, which can be (1) *normal* or (2) *priority* (typically for disabled persons). The aggregation that yields the value of the criterion SOCIAL-HEALTH is defined by decision rules shown in Table 1, where the asterisk stands for any value of the corresponding criterion. Similar decision rules are defined for the remaining aggregate criteria in the model.

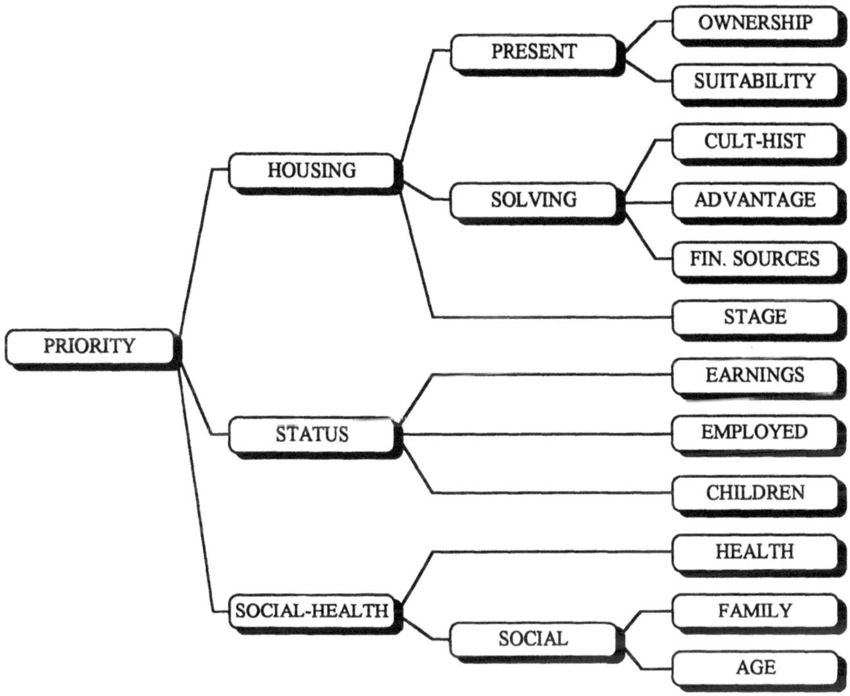

Figure 2 Criteria structure for determining loan priority

Table 1 Decision rules for the criterion SOCIAL-HEALTH

HEALTH	SOCIAL	SOCIAL-HEALTH
(1) normal	(1) normal	(1) normal
(1) normal	(2) priority	(2) high_priority
*	(3) high_priority	(3) high_priority
(2) priority	*	(3) high_priority

In such an evaluation model, the Fund's policy is explicitly articulated in terms of criteria structure and decision rules. However, the Fund's floats differ substantially in their purposes and the earmarked amount of money. This requires different policies and, consequently, different evaluation models. Therefore, before each float is announced, the evaluation model is carefully investigated by the Fund's managers and redesigned if necessary. Typically, the first two levels of criteria in the model remain stable, while some leaves and decision rules are modified, added or deleted.

For a technical support of this process, we use DEX, an expert system shell for multi-attribute decision making (Bohanec, Rajkovič 1990). In addition to the creation and adaptation of the model itself, DEX provides a number of useful tools for the verification and explanation of decision rules and analysis of the evaluation process (Bohanec, Rajkovič 1993; Bohanec *et al* 1995).

3.2 Computational models

The application priority is just one of the factors that affect the amount of the loan granted to an applicant. Some other factors are also important, such as the amount the applicant has actually asked for, the size of the owned flat (if applicable), and the amounts already granted to the applicant in previous tenders. The involved calculations tend to be rather complex and difficult to comprehend, especially if they change from tender to tender. For this reason, we included in the knowledge base a number of *computational models* with which we tried to *visualize* these calculations.

An example of such a visualization is shown in Figure 3. It is based on a computational model for determining the final approved amount of a loan. This amount is a minimum of (1) requested amount, (2) difference between the normalized price of the credited flat and an already owned one, (3) the maximal amount that can be granted in this float with respect to priority ranking and the size of the applicant's family, and (4) the maximal amount that remained available for the applicant from previous floats. Note that the calculation of the third value depends on the evaluation of application priority, which is obtained from the qualitative model in Figure 2. Therefore, the two models are actually connected.

In addition to computational models that are related to finance, the knowledge base contains some other models for verifying the completeness and consistency of applications.

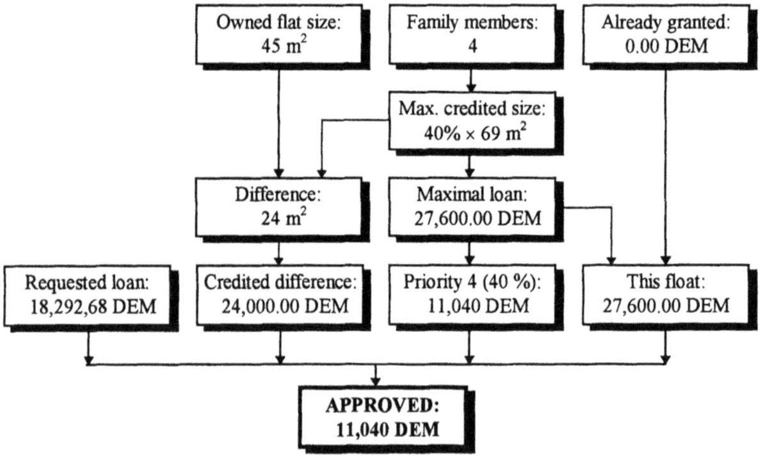

Figure 3 A calculation of approved loan amount.

3.3 Database design

Once the various models in the knowledge base have been built, they provide a valuable source of information for the initial design and subsequent adaptation of the remaining components of the system, particularly the database (see Figure 1). In order to perform their functions, all the models need some inputs; these are, for example, represented by leaves in the priority evaluation model (the rightmost criteria in Figure 2) and the topmost cells of the computational model in Figure 3. A collection of these inputs almost completely defines the data that has to be requested from applicants and stored in the database. In our case, we only extended this collection by applicants' personal data, which do not enter any of the models.

4 IMPLEMENTATION AND EXPERIENCE

In this section we illustrate the system's implementation by focusing on some of its important phases. For each phase, we present its essential features and highlight our experience obtained from the completed floats. The phases, which are captured from the time perspective, are the following: application gathering, data entry, loan approval, applicant notification, complaint handling, contract input, global database maintenance, and loan consumption verification.

The system supports three arrangements for gathering applications for a float: by a personal visit, by mail and by a personal visit at local municipalities. In the first issued tender, we decided to collect applications by mail. It was observed that due to the relatively high number of incomplete applications a substantial amount of time was spent just to contact the applicants and to inform them how to complete the applications. As a consequence, in the next float we had arranged that every citizen had to apply in person. We expected to achieve a higher standard of completed forms by having the applicants complete the forms on the spot. This eventually turned out to be correct. Besides, since a few thousands of citizens were expected to respond to the tender, we felt that we had to schedule their arrivals. To resolve that, every application form was labeled with a date and time of the suggested arrival. A special subsystem was developed for the task. Much to our surprise, the majority of applicants stuck to the suggested times; in this way, the waiting lines were drastically reduced. However, a considerable shortcoming was that citizens from distant regions of Slovenia had to come to the capital city. Therefore, in the next float we allowed application gathering and data entry in local municipalities. However, such arrangement turned out to be hard to control. So, in the next tenders we decided to use a combination of mail and personal visits with scheduled arrivals, which turned out to be the most effective.

Relevant data from each application are stored in the system's database in a local area network environment. For a typical float, up to 20 workstations are used for data entry. A printed application form, which contains data from an application, includes also a list of possible imperfections. Namely, the entered data are checked for completeness and consistency by computational models that contain specific restrictions of the tender. Every applicant can, therefore, determine the status of his or her application just by reading the printout. Moreover, since all applications are checked by the same computational model, the objectivity of evaluations increases.

Table 2 What-if analysis of an evaluation

Criterion	Value−1	Value	Value+1
PRIORITY		**4**	
HOUSING		2	
PRESENT		2	
ownership		1	2: **PRIORITY=5**
suitability	2: no change	3	
SOLVING		2	
cult-hist		1	2: no change
advantage	1: no change	2	
fin. sources		1	2: no change
stage		1	2: **PRIORITY=5**
STATUS		2	
earnings		1	2: no change
employed	1: no change	2	3: no change
children	1: no change	2	3: no change
SOCIAL-HEALTH		4	
health		1	2: no change
SOCIAL		4	
family	2: no change	3	4: no change
age	1: **PRIORITY=2**	2	

Soon after the applications are gathered and the data are stored in the database, a loan approving decision has to take place. The process of approving the loans consists of two phases: ranking the applications into five classes, and determining the percentage of approved amount for each class. Each complete application, which fulfills the tender requirements, is classified by the evaluation model according to their priority to be granted a loan.

At this stage, the what-if analysis turned out to be particularly valuable. The analysis points out the criteria that could, by changing the value for just one step, influence the final class. An example is shown in Table 2. The leftmost column displays the criteria structure, where the lower and upper-case entries represent basic and aggregate criteria, respectively. The column labeled 'Value' gives the evaluation results of an application at hand. This application has been classified into the fourth priority class. In the remaining two columns, the value of each basic criterion is independently varied for one step (if possible) and the influence of this change to the final priority is displayed. For example, if *ownership* changed from 1 to 2 (with all the remaining basic criteria unchanged), the application would be classified into the fifth priority class. On the other hand, the change of *suitability* from 3 to 2 does not affect the priority.

The utility of the analysis is not only in explaining why an applicant falls into a particular class, but also in understanding the model as a whole. To determine the percentage of approved amount for each rank, one has to first take into account the planned amount of funds for a specific tender. Usually, the approved sum should roughly equal to the earmarked amount. On the other hand, the decision is typically based on the known approximate description of classes. For example, since class four includes also young applicants with no children and an average family income for whom this was their first loan application, the percentage for the class was around 80 % in all issued tenders. This factor prevailed also in the tenders where the approved amount was eventually more than three times greater than the earmarked amount.

An important role in the process of approving loans is played by statistical analyses. In fact, the analyses are useful in many phases, so the system includes a wide variety of them. For example, a distribution of applicants and requested amounts over priority ranks is a prerequisite for the decision. Some other distributions, like for instance over the criteria used in the priority evaluation model, are useful to obtain an overall impression of the database.

After the loans are approved, the applicants have to be informed about the outcome. Mailmerge technology is used for the task. Every applicant receives the final printout of his or her application data together with the notification of the approved amount. At the same time, the list of approved applicants is sent to a subcontracted bank that is responsible for completing loan contracts.

After the notification some of the applicants complain. Some of them argue that the data in the final printout are incorrect, while the others just disagree with the rejection explanation. Handling the complaints adds a time dimension to the database. Namely, it is desirable to know both the data before the complaint and after the correction. After collecting all complaints, the process of assessing the loans is carried out again for the complainants.

The bank that completes the loan contracts sends them to the Fund. The data from the contracts are added to the database. This phase is important since two events can happen. First, an applicant may for various reasons withdraw from the contract. Second, the granted amount in the contract can slightly deviate from the approved amount.

Another important phase is maintaining the global database of all applicants that responded to the tenders. First, it can serve as an archive of all applicants. More importantly, it is used to verify the upper limit of approved amount for every citizen that applies to more than one tender. Namely, the highest amount available to an individual borrower is 40 % of the value of the appropriate housing floor space determined according to the size of the family. This limit is regarded as a cumulative limit for all tenders. However, note that the limit for an individual citizen may change by, for example, increasing the size of the family.

Last but not least, there is a phase of verifying the purpose of the loan consumption. It typically takes place a year after a completed tender For this phase, a small number of randomly selected approved applicants are selected according to their municipality and purpose of the loan consumption. Then, they are notified about the selection and are asked to contact the responsible person at the Fund in order to settle the date for the verification. We believe that the existence of such a procedure substantially decreases the number of approved applicants who spend the granted loan non-intentionally.

5 CONCLUSION

The system described in this paper is regularly used in the Housing Fund of the Republic of Slovenia and supports the Fund's principal activity: allocation of housing loans to citizens. In addition to a robust implementation of commonly used information system techniques (Rupnik-Miklič, Zupančič 1995), it incorporates some recently developed research methods from the area of qualitative decision support. The central component of the system is a knowledge base that consists of several qualitative and quantitative models.

This approach offers some important features regarding system design, utilization and maintenance. First, the system is flexible. A majority of adaptations to frequently changing requirements can be achieved by local modifications of the underlying models. The structure of the models themselves largely determines the remaining components of the system, i.e., the database and procedures. The second characteristic is transparency that is required for the users to comprehend and verify the information flow. This is particularly important in the design stage, which involves an intensive communication between the designer and managers. Here, the models provide an effective framework for the articulation of management's requirements. In the loan approval stage, the transparency facilitates explanation of the procedure and its results to the applicants.

According to the experience gained so far, it appears that problems of this type require permanent development and adaptation of the supporting system. Not only do the floats substantially differ from each other, but also unpredictable events occur that may alter the decision making policy within one float. For this reason, permanent participation of knowledge owners in the process is vital. Moreover, their participation is essential to provide the comprehensibility of the process in spite of its high complexity.

6 ACKNOWLEDGMENT

The system presented in this paper could not have been developed without substantial support and collaboration from the Fund's side. The authors wish to thank Mira Becele, Nevenka Fajdiga and Breda Kutin for their contribution in all phases of the system development and exploatation. We are also grateful for the support of Edvard Oven, the General Manager of the Fund. Special thanks to Janet Efstathiou for suggestions and corrections of an earlier draft.

7 REFERENCES

Angehm, A.A. (1992) Supporting multi-criteria decision making. In: Holtham, C. (ed.): *Executive information systems and decision support*. Chapman & Hall. London.

Bohanec, M., Rajkovič, V. (1990) DEX: An expert system shell for decision support. *Sistemica* **1**(1).

Bohanec, M., Rajkovič, V. (1993) Knowledge-based explanation in multiattribute decision making. In: Nagel, S. (ed.): *Computer aided decision analysis: Theory and applications*. Quorum Books. London.

Bohanec, M., Rajkovič, V., Semolič, B., Pogačnik, A. (1995) Knowledge-based portfolio analysis for project evaluation. *Information & Management* **28**.

Gumesson, E. (1991) *Qualitative methods in management research*. Sage Publications. London.

Klein, M.R., Methlie, L.B. (1995) *Knowledge-based decision support systems with applications in business*. Second edition. John Wiley & Sons. Chichester.

Mallach, E.G. (1994) *Understanding decision support systems and expert systems*. Irwin. Boston.

Rajkovič, V., Bohanec, M. (1991) Decision support by knowledge explanation. In: Sol, H.G., Vecsenyi, J. (eds.): *Environments for supporting decision processes*. Elsevier. Amsterdam.

Rupnik-Miklič, E., Zupančič, J. (1995) Experiences and expectations with CASE technology - an example from Slovenia. *Information & Management* **28**.

Vadera, S., Nechab, S. (1991) Are expert system shells and toolkits too general? In: Singh, M.G., Travé-Massuyès, L. (eds.): *Decision support systems and qualitative reasoning*. North-Holland. Amsterdam.

8 BIOGRAPHY

Marko Bohanec is a researcher at Jožef Stefan Institute, Department of Intelligent Systems, Ljubljana, and assistant professor in information systems at the Faculty of Organizational Sciences, University of Maribor. He obtained his Ph.D. in Computer Science at the Faculty of Electrical Engineering and Computer Science, University of Ljubljana. His research interests are in decision support systems, expert systems and machine learning. He has published in journals such as *Machine Learning*, *Acta Psychologica*, and *Information & Management*.

Bojan Cestnik is the general manager of software company Temida and a researcher in the Department of Intelligent Systems at Jožef Stefan Institute in Ljubljana. He obtained his Ph.D. in Computer Science at the Faculty of Electrical Engineering and Computer Science, University of Ljubljana. His professional and research interests include knowledge based information systems and machine learning. His research work was presented at several international conferences. He has been involved in several large-scale software development and maintenance projects.

Vladislav Rajkovič is a professor of information systems at the Faculty of Organizational Sciences, University of Maribor. He also works with the Department of Intelligent Systems at the Jožef Stefan Institute in Ljubljana. His research interests focus on artificial intelligence methods for supporting decision processes. His works have been published in *IEEE Trans. on Systems, Man, and Cybernetics*, *Acta Psychologica*, and *Information & Management*

4

Misuse and nonuse of Knowledge-Based Systems: The past experiences revisited

P. Brézillon and J.-Ch. Pomerol
LAFORIA-IBP, Case 169, University Paris 6
4, place Jussieu, 75252 Paris Cedex 05, France
Tel.: +33 1 44 27 70 08, Fax: + 33 1 44 27 70 00
E-mail: {brezil, pomerol}@laforia.ibp.fr

Abstract

It is difficult to determine the number of expert systems or Knowledge-Based Systems (KBSs) that really are operational within companies or administrations. It seems that a large number of such systems have never been used in operations and a rich literature stresses this point. We think that most of these references do not address some dimensions that are of paramount importance. In this paper, we provide a review of the literature according to three neglected dimensions: (1) the differences between automatic KBSs and non-automatic KBSs; (2) the types and importance of decisions that are involved; and (3) the types of data acquisition that is required. Keeping in mind these three dimensions, we review the literature about the acceptance of KBS and their use and point out that most of the observations can be interpreted along these three dimensions.Furthermore, these dimensions permit us to explain some failures and difficulties that have already been pointed out in several scientific domains in which interactivity is crucial, such as Decision Support Systems (DSSs). Our approach brings some new insights on the problems of KBS acceptance and leads us to propose some recommendations.

Keywords

Expert systems, knowledge-based systems, decision support systems, user-system interaction

1 INTRODUCTION

We do not know how many Expert Systems (ESs) or Knowledge-Based Systems (KBSs)[1] that are operational within companies or administrations. Durkin (1993) lists about 2500 ESs, but the exact operational status, as regards operational use, is often not precisely stated. However, some clues exist. For instance, each of the top five Japanese companies has from 20 to 30 operating KBSs (Mizoguchi and Motoda, 1995). Many insurance companies also use such systems (Rowe and Wright, 1993; Meyer et al., 1992).

However, a large number of KBSs has never been used in operations as stressed in the literature. For instance, Majchrzak and Gasser (1991) point out that more than 50% of the systems, which are installed in companies, are not used. The given reasons are: (1) KBSs solved 80% of problems, when users mainly need a support for the 20% others; (2) Integration of KBSs in an organization implies interaction of KBSs with classical software and changes in the organization itself; and (3) KBSs were often imposed on users who know little about the technology.

The above rationales are probably true. However, we think that most of the papers do not address some dimensions that are of paramount importance. Among the neglected dimensions, we want to introduce: (i) the differences between automatic KBSs and nonautomatic KBSs that are intended to be manipulated by end-users; (ii) the types of decision that are involved; and (iii) the types of data acquisition that must be made.

Hereafter, we intend to show that these dimensions explain most of the successes and failures of KBS use as confirmed by the large amount of papers that are already devoted to this topic. We thus provide a revisited view of the literature according to the dimensions presented above. We will moreover show that most of the problems are related to interactivity and that these problems are not specific to KBSs but also exist in any non-automatic Decision Support Systems (DSSs).

We begin, in Section 2, with a presentation of the context of our study. We present the literature revisited in Section 3. On this basis, we discuss then the KBS-development problems in Section 4 and the choice between KBS and DSS in Section 5.

2 THE CONTEXT OF OUR STUDY

2.1 A basic distinction

Our interest concerns KBSs in operation within companies and administrations. We can split these systems into two classes, namely automatic systems and nonautomatic ones. The difference between them is that an end-user interacts with nonautomatic systems for solving a problem while automatic ones, obviously, run alone. As discussed below, the intervention of the end-user may occur at different steps of the problem-solving process.

[1] In the following, we will use ES and KBS interchangeably. The main reason is that the term used now is KBS, but most of the criticisms that are applied to ESs, may also be applied to KBSs. We use the term 'system' to cover both of them when possible.

Automatic systems

Initially, one conceived the building of KBSs as a process of acquiring already 'known' knowledge from experts. Therefore, KBSs mimic the human-expert reasoning to solve decision problems (Hatchuel and Weil, 1992). When integrated in an information system, the KBS automatically acquires its data and provides a problem-solution to the information systems that is assumed to be sound. We call such systems, automatic systems. Process control is the main domain of automatic systems, but one can also find such systems in many industrial processes. They work if the decision is directly dependent on the diagnosis of the current state (Pomerol, 1995). Starting from the experts' knowledge, these systems generally evolve towards refined diagnostic systems in which the model is progressively adjusted by the process engineers. Finally, after refinement, automatic systems act as black boxes whose models may be far from the initial human expertise. For instance, in the SEPT project (Perrot et al., 1993), a temporal cutting out has been introduced to analyze long sequences of recorded signals after incidents to facilitate the diagnosis by the system. This aimed to distinguish incidents very close in time. Such a temporal cutting out does not correspond to the operators' experience in the control command room whose decisions rely on a global analysis.

Automatic systems, which are numerous in some branches, are almost never discussed in the literature and seems to be well-accepted within companies.

Nonautomatic systems

The expert knowledge in nonautomatic systems is also initially acquired from human experts, and users update it while using the system. Being un-integrated, the system, besides expert knowledge, needs specific data defining the situation in which the problem to be solved occurs. Such data are acquired either at the beginning of a session or during the problem solving. While automatic systems directly acquire data from the information system, in many application domains the user must provide the data (e.g., when sophisticated vision is needed). This implies that such systems are nonautomatic. Nonautomatic systems can be classified according to application domains such as: consultancy, clerical work (bank, insurance, etc.), medicine, public information, design.

These nonautomatic systems represent the most important part of KBSs. Very often, it is wrongly assumed in the literature that they represent the totality of KBSs. At least, we can find many papers that are devoted to the failures and, sometimes, the successes of this kind of systems. This is the reason we will especially examine hereafter nonautomatic systems.

2.2 Three basic problems

By definition, a nonautomatic system needs some help from humans. It is mostly important to distinguish between the different natures of human interventions. For simplicity sake, we will only distinguish two types of intervention. The first one concerns data acquisition. The system requires (or prompts) the user to provide some data that are essential for system processing either at the start or during the problem solving. The second type of human intervention concerns what is generally called interactivity. In the context of knowledge systems, interactivity corresponds to the control of the system by the user to achieve a heuristic search about the decision at hand (Lévine and Pomerol, 1989 and 1995).

Data acquisition

Even when a KBS possesses expert knowledge, it needs the support of the end-user to acquire data on the situation at hand. Most of the data are acquired at the beginning of the session, but also during the system reasoning. When other data are needed, the system generally prompts the user. The main obstacles to automatic data acquisition are met when performing tasks in which natural language or reading of manuscript or 'good enough' vision capabilities are needed.

In all these three cases, the end-user plays the role of a data gatherer, who need not know why the system needs a specific data, but is only required to provide them. This may result in sequences of questions that appear incoherent for users (Keravnou and Washbrook, 1989; Woods et al., 1990). This is particularly frustrating for end-users and may lead them to reject the system.

Also, the user is very sensitive to the quantity (in term of reduced workload or usefulness) of outputs with respect to the time and the work that is necessary to enter the data. We can summarize the situation by considering the symbolic ratio R:

$$R = \frac{\text{Quantity of outputs}}{\text{Workload necessary to provide data}}$$

A system in which $R < 1$ has very little chance to be accepted, and eventually used. This situation is very frequent in clerical work where users are (still!) either obliged to bridge the gap between natural language or hand writing and the machine. Note that the situation is not symmetrical because once the data are entered into the machine, the system is perfectly able to produce, on its own, various outputs (e.g., a letter, a report or a record). As a consequence, one can improve R by increasing the numerator, which in turn, requests a serious integration of the system within the information system. Also, the time spent during a consultation with a KBS is a determining factor of its acceptance (Pomerol and Retour, 1990). Roughly speaking, this time corresponds to the time spent for data acquisition. Moreover, the end-users may have other sources of information (control boards, telephones, etc.) and wish to direct the machine's attention to different subsets of data, different domain issues, and different hypotheses to help the KBS to refine its understanding of the problem. Generally, the system is not able to accept such additional data.

What type of decision?

The result of the system running is either a diagnosis, a proposal of action or a mere suggestion. In order to anticipate the end-user's reactions, it is absolutely necessary to understand the nature of the intended output of the system. When the expected output is a diagnosis, end-users receive the diagnosis either as a confirmation or as a disagreement of their own diagnosis. In the latter case, the user and the system may enter into a dialogue to solve the conflict. (It is also the case in training.) This is well documented in the literature and leads to questions about explanation, understanding of the output, etc. For instance, several authors mention that users' questions in traditional KBSs do not reflect the end-users' actual needs, e.g., see (Kidd, 1985; Gilbert, 1987). The main problem is that the system reasoning may be quite different from the user's reasoning. Thus, users face both the problem they seek to solve and the logic of the system at the same time. Moreover, the system may not solve the exact problem that the user actually wants to solve or needs help in solving it. For example, present diagnostic systems perform classification procedures to answer the questions: What is the fault? Or What is the remedy? Empirical studies have shown that users, engaged in a range of diagnostic tasks, rarely ask experts either of these questions (Kidd and Sharpe, 1988). More often, to solve their problem, they want answers to questions such as: Why did fault X happen? Will remedy Y cure it? Can I test W without affecting the level of Z? Another point is that users do not want abstracted information, only information in the specific context of their particular problem.

Consider now the case in which the system output is a decision. There are a number of examples in management and consulting: investment choice, different types of underwriting, responsibility assignment, facility location, etc. Three prominent attributes characterize these decisions in an opposite way to control process decision: (1) their consequences are difficult to assess because the results are delayed (we discuss this point later); (2) the results are important in term of return (for example, decide whether or not to build a new facility); and (3) the decision is irreversible (e.g., once the building of a factory has begun, there is no way to stop or modify the process except for details). What is surprising in such contexts is that the system designers may have thought that the system should make the decision alone. These types of decision are far too risky and important to be left to a system. This is the realm of the Decision Support Systems (DSSs). The designer must understand that, in this case, what users need is a help and further information and not an automatic decision making. Thus, we are in a situation in which the user needs to understand the models that are used by the system and have to be confident of the system outputs. Among the prominent questions bothering the decision makers is the link between the possible actions and the results. The answer to this question depends on what will happen in the future. This is the look-ahead problem (Pomerol, 1995). This problem, together with subject preferences, deserves a special subsection.

Incidence of the future and of preferences

When coping with a decision problem, the decision maker faces two complex issues: (i) How to anticipate the results of a given action?; and (ii) How to choose among the possible actions taking into account their uncertain consequences? In the second question, the choice is given by a translation of the decision maker's preferences onto the set of uncertain issues. However, most often, systems address neither of these two issues. It is therefore not surprising that people confronting real decisions do not believe in ES or KBS support.

In most systems, one implicitly supposes that there is a direct link between the current state of nature, the actions and the issues. In other words, the system runs in a certain world and future does not matter (Pomerol, 1995). It is the case in many industrial processes where the time interval between two actions is so narrow that the uncertainty of the environment cannot entail important consequences. We thus discover again one more reason for the success of KBSs in the control process or industrial reactive systems.

The other implicit assumptions generally made by KBS designers is that everybody has the same preferences. Again, it is generally true in industrial processes: one wants to maximize the output of the process. It is also the case in medicine (and more generally in diagnosis) where one wants to cure the system or the patient even if people may disagree on the tradeoff between the expected result and the necessary resources for the tests. In many other cases (e.g., investment choice, location, etc.), it is unlikely that experts, users, or modelers have the same preferences. The decision-maker (or end-user) requirement of introducing his own preferences often surfaces in needs such that those expressed by Kidd and Sharpe (1988):

- Set out his own constraints on an acceptable solution, e.g., 'It must be quick' or 'I can't take the back panel off because I haven't got the tools';
- Put forward his own plans, solutions or explanations for evaluation, e.g., 'Will swapping that component clear it for good?' or 'Did it fail to work because of the sequence I used?';
- Reject or request alternatives to solutions proposed by the expert, e.g., 'I've already tried that and it didn't work' or 'Are there any cheaper options?'.

It is noteworthy that the fundamental requirement of system users of being not deprived of expressing their preferences is generally recognized in DSSs. We have argued that it is one, among the best virtues of DSSs, to permit this expression through heuristic search (Lévine and Pomerol, 1989 and 1995).

According to the three main difficulties of (1) data acquisition, (2) type and importance of a decision, and (3) the role of the uncertainty and of preferences, it is interesting to review the literature to see if our distinctions are relevant and explain, at least partly, the lack of satisfaction of KBS users.

3 THE LITERATURE REVISITED

Not surprisingly, most of the papers focus on the relationships between the system and the end-user. This confirms that automatic systems do not raise many problems. When data acquisition is possible via the information system, and when actions are sufficiently 'continuous' so that the consequences are almost certain, automatic systems acting as sophisticated automata rise no other problem than a good modeling and a good developing team. The literature being almost exclusively devoted to nonautomatic systems, we restrict ourselves to these systems in this section.

3.1 The relationships between the end-user and the system

There are several common arguments about the misuse and nonuse of KBSs. We can classify most of these arguments by using the attributes that we have introduced previously. Many comments are related to data acquisition. It appears that users do not want to be used as data gatherers. Remember that KBSs have been designed initially like oracles for helping users considered as novices--in their tasks (Karsenty and Brézillon, 1995): all the knowledge is within the machine. The noble part of the task (the reasoning) being in the system, the role of the user is to:

- act as an interface between the machine and its environment,

- be a natural language interpreter, the eyes and hands of the machine,
- function as a passive data gatherer for the machine (a data entry clerk (Fisher, 1990)).

Now, it is obvious that no one wants to use a system during a long time if it is for playing the above role. The system then suffers of this irremediable flaw, and is quickly rejected, except for provisional use for training.

It is also mentioned that KBSs are not able to take into account the fact that users become increasingly experienced. This may also be interpreted as a desire to alleviate the data-acquisition burden for experienced users. Very often, one can observe that users cease to use a system because they already have forged the decision in their mind before the end of the data acquisition.

Leaving the data acquisition aspect, we found references in which authors put forward many observations relative to users' wishes. Users would like to have the possibility to: generate partial solutions by themselves; try to explain the problem and identify a solution; provide spontaneously information; come back on the data provided previously; ask their questions; and give their answers in their language. The flexibility requirements involve an interruption device and the expression of a partial explanation. When users have troubles with the system reasoning, they must infer machine intentions, resolve impasses and recover from errors (person or machine) that led the machine expert offtrack, and have a limited set of possible interpretations. One reason is that users generally must follow underspecified instructions, and the unique way to interrupt the system reasoning is to abort it.

The main attempt to convince users was to provide them with explanations. However, it was a pitfall because the explanation was only **from** the system **to** the user, the user does not intervene in the building of the explanation (Karsenty and Brézillon, 1995). Rejection of an explanation may be due to a misunderstanding of the explanation, or the need of another type of explanation, or the inability to use the explanation. Clearly, there is a need for alternative explanations, and a reactive approach to explanation is not sufficient (Moore and Swartout, 1990).

The following step was to tailor explanation to users' needs. Among the various interesting attempts, there are: (i) Adapting the degree of details to the users' knowledge (Wallis & Shortliffe, 1984; Swartout, 1983); (ii) Adapting the explanation types to the users' knowledge through a user model (Paris, 1990; Moore and Swartout, 1990); (iii) Adapting the explanation types to the users' goals (McKeown et al., 1985; Van Beek, 1987). In most of these attempts, explanations are conceived as texts that have to be generated, again from the system to the user.

Most of these common arguments deal with the mostly important capacity of the system to allow end-users exploration, which is at the root of their 'what-if' implicit analysis and of the look-ahead. As already mentioned, one of the main concern of the decision maker is to bridge the gap between the actions and the consequences. The user needs a friendly help to perform the look-ahead that is a crucial movement of decision making. This help includes the understanding of the system reasoning and the need of exploration and explanation capabilities among which we can find in the literature:

- Provide system solutions with concrete examples and convincing arguments;
- Solve problems in a comprehensible way for the user, mainly in the user's semantics, not only in terms of the official norm;
- Provide explanations in the user's terms when no solution is found;
- Offer training functions;

- Allow users to return easily to previous states of their information search.

All these users' requirements for a better control of the system reasoning are more or less similarly expressed in DSS literature. They seem to be very common in any interactive system in which users want to impose their preferences via the control of the exploration. For important decisions discussed in Section 2, the final choice depends on users' preferences, and users try by a number of ways to recover the system control, even to abort it if necessary.

In the context of 'what-if' analysis, the need for approximated data and for a robustness evaluation of the system recommendation is a classical requirement of decision aid in DSS framework. This requirement is very frequent and leads to questions as: How to deal with approximated solutions (e.g., the range of prices is around ...)? Curiously, the question of approximate data is often tackle in KBSs by various means, such as fuzzy logic. However, it is rarely mentioned as a user's requirement. Conversely, the literature on DSSs often points out this question.

The most convincing evidence that users will not give up their right to control a decision is that many rejected systems have been revamped into a training system. The user may deviate from the original goal of the system either for a subuse (e.g., training or 'what-if' question) or another goal (e.g., note ideas in an electronic agenda that becomes a record of the user's history). Not only users may deviate the system function, but also knowledge engineers: The most popular case is those of MYCIN becoming a series of tutoring systems (Clancey, 1986).

Using a system for training acknowledges that the system is valuable within a given context (preferences, implicit assumptions, contextual assumptions, etc.) but, in the practical situation at hand, many extra adaptations and interpretations remain necessary. Users consider therefore that the system is unable to make the decision and that they are unable (or do not worth it) to tailor the system at their needs. Thus, the system is valuable for training in what is considered as a theoretical framework, but the reality, which requires more subtle insights which remain out of the system's grasp. Another definitive argument is that either the system is able to make the decision and users disappear (automatic system) or the system is unusable. Then, we enter into the DSS realm and KBS users' claim joint the usual requirements of DSS users. Designers must acknowledge that there is no alternative way between an automatic systems and human decision. In the latter case, the system is either a training system or a DSS, **not a knowledge-based decision matter**.

3.2 The System and the Organization

Many authors have considered KBSs from an organizational viewpoint and have attributed nonuses or misuses of KBSs to organizational failures. For example, see references in Pomerol (1990). The common statement is that the organization fails to integrate the system. Changes in work is the first cause of conflict when introducing into organization new information technology systems (Agro et al., 1995). The authors often refer to the difficulty of introducing a new technology into an organization that should accept changes (Hatchuel and Weil, 1992). Most organizations prefer to take a low risk position when considering a new technology. As such, projects that require the minimum resources and have the maximum likelihood of success are preferred (Durkin, 1993).

Typical organizational implementation problems include inadequate preplanning for the social as well technology changes concomitant with modernization efforts. Here are some causes of failures that one can find in the literature: inadequate training, workteams not supported by management, failure to anticipate organizational resistance, incongruent pay systems, failure to understand how work is really made, increasing of the workload, etc. Instead of simply modifying some work procedures, entire units may need to be reorganized and appraised in different ways, new cultural behaviors may be to be instilled, and every one in the organization may need to be reskilled (Majchrzak and Gasser, 1991). Another problem in a working environment may concern the possible isolation of users working with KBSs among their colleagues that pursue their work in the usual way.

The problem raised by data acquisition when integrating the system in an information system (see above) is sometimes interpreted as an organizational or software problem. Stand-alone KBSs would move towards systems embedded in other conventional software programs (Durkin, 1993). Commercial tools are black boxes and thus are of little use to companies. Developers have to customize KBSs and to integrate them in existing information systems. Whereas they often prefer to establish their own expert-system building methodologies and think to integrate when the system is completed.

For a large part, the observations about organizational changes are not different from the usual views about introducing changes within organizations and go back to Lewin (1947, quoted by Pomerol (1990)). Any introduction of a new system into an organization either MISs (Management Information Systems), DSSs, EISs (Executive Information Systems), etc., rises the same types of questions. Chandrasekaran (1994) gives some interesting comments on such "smart" systems.

Other views are related to knowledge objectivity in KBSs. Among them, the risk of a possible direct control of the users' work by their chief (Hatchuel and Weil, 1992); a fear of a comparison of the KBS capabilities relatively to the present user; the eventual finding of user's mistakes by the KBS (Ackerman et al., 1992); and the users' fear to be in danger of losing their job (Sakagushi et al., 1987). The transfer of expert knowledge into a system also may be transfer of power (Belanger et al., 1995). For instance, KBSs, which are never tired, can have higher productivity than users. Users may consider to be replaced by KBSs as a danger for them, while experts maintain their power because of their skills and access to special information that is valued by high individual ranking.

However, KBSs may be a way for a top-down transfer of competence and responsibilities in normal condition and, conversely, a bottom-up transfer of competence in critical situation (de Terssac and Chabaud, 1992). This move of responsibility among actors is generally well perceived: users' work is favoured, chiefs are relieved of a part of their routine work (Pomerol, 1990; de Terssac and Chabaud, 1992).

In our opinion, it appears that the users' level of competence does not depend on the intrinsic characteristics of the used technology (a KBS is a tool among other tools for users), but on the specifications and decomposition of the work, and on the modes along which the work is structured in a company. We think that the introduction of KBSs in organization is a step of the computerization process that stretches now from structured to less structured tasks. This modernization may last for many years accompanying the movement of information computerization.

Besides the organizational obstacles related to change, one of the main impediments on the way of KBS integration is data acquisition. In many clerical tasks, people handle manuscript letters, listen people talking natural language, etc. The computer technology does not allow a direct transfer of this information into the machine. Thus, a human operator is necessary to introduce the data. On the one hand, this is the main reason for the relative failure of introducing KBSs in many administrative tasks. When automatic data acquisition is technically impossible, the unique way to integrate the system is to invent work procedures that oblige the end-user to effectively use the system. On the other hand, many systems have been designed to tackle decisions in which the human component is mostly important, e.g., combining human competences (Hatchuel and Weil, 1992) or of the type discussed in 2.2.2. In these cases, it is obviously not surprising that the system may be rejected, and, in the best case, becomes a training system.

For instance, operators in a control room argue that (Huguet et al., 1995):
- they want to avoid the system's control which could be used to check the amount of time spent on each order;
- they intend to protect themselves against a possible load increase as the system will allocate production orders as soon as the resources become available;
- they wish to avoid an additional management task which is little compatible with the production work;
- they have their own doubts about the advantages of the system being fed with data in real time.

Part of experts' knowledge cannot be codified (Hatchuel and Weil, 1992). This concerns the use of the know-how in comunicational contexts where predominates interaction among several actors. Such a meta-know-how is generally described in nonwritten rules. A non-written rule takes into account the real context of the work at a given moment. Such a contextualization of procedures permits the solution to be tailored to the conditions of the task; such "makeshift repairs" permit the executing actors to reach the efficiency that is wished by those that specify the work to do. It is a manner to reach the solution whatever is the path that is followed. The validation of non-written rules is more linked to the result than the procedure to reach it, a logic of the efficiency (de Terssac, 1992). Such knowledge is for a personal use, not to be used by others.

4 KBS-DEVELOPMENT PROBLEMS

4.1 The different actors

Several human actors intervene during the lifecycle of a KBS: the manager who decides the construction of the KBS, the expert whose knowledge and heuristics have to be captured by the system, the knowledge engineer who models the expertise, the end-user who gains practical experience by frequently using the KBS, and the occasional end users (novices, users from other departments that occasionally consult the KBS, etc.). The importance of each human actor varies according to the phase of the KBS design. Some of them only intervene during a small number of phases. For instance, it is frequent that the main user does not intervene in the early phases of the design, and this is generally a problem for the acceptance of the KBS later. This probably implies that users intervene in the KBS design, whereas they are confronted with highly nontransparent systems that are far from easy to use (Oberquelle et al., 1983).

After the system development, some actors are authorized to modify the knowledge base. The authorized actors generally are: the domain expert, the knowledge engineer, and eventually the main user. The user that has to make strategic decisions, is sometimes an authorized actor. Conversely, a user who either follows operating procedures or supervises the process is not an authorized actor. The updating task of the knowledge base is crucial because a KBS that is not maintained is a dead one. When users must intervene in the knowledge base for maintenance, they generally prefer to add rules rather than intervene directly on the structure of the KBS itself. This leads to a complex structure of the KBS that becomes quite unexplainable for other humans (e.g., experts) and for themselves after a while. This situation is particularly crucial when KBSs are developed in an empirical way without any written trace. Maintenance becomes a fastidious task for the user, and added to the task at hand. We also distinguish actors and roles played by actors. Actually, a role is not always held by the same human actor. For instance, the design may begin with a domain expert and finish with another one. The change of main user, for instance, implies a need for training at any phase of the KBS lifecycle. As a consequence, a part of the experience-based knowledge may be lost (e.g., information in the way a KBS is coded). Moreover, a given human actor may play different roles too. For instance, main user and maintainer may be considered as two roles that are played by the same actor. This depends on the relationships between the user and the system in the achievement of the task at hand. The system may play different roles too: tutor, suggestor, advisor, critic.

4.2 Knowledge engineering

"*Knowledge engineers are like priests; They receive the "Word" from experts above, add nothing to the content, but codify it accurately into written rules, and pass it down to ordinary folks as commandments to live by*" (Clancey, 1993).

A missing link is that experts provide knowledge in the context of a given situation. The contextual dimension of the acquired knowledge is generally not taken into account, whereas experts--as, for example, decision makers--heavily rely on information coming from the environment, often in an intuitive or unstructured way (Pomerol, 1993). The decision makers try to identify the current state by reference to their past experience. This means that we can assume that the subject has recorded many situations or states he has already met or has learnt about (Pomerol, 1995). Thus, the humans' expertise must be considered in the context of their action, and that context must be acquired.

The knowledge acquisition comprises various biases due to the interpretation and the way to code knowledge. The Knowledge Engineer (KE)'s interpretation of the experts' knowledge is made in the KE's context, not necessarily in the expert's one, and, moreover, the operating context may differ of the the two previous ones. The KE's context relies on the representation formalism that has generally been chosen for reason others than for the knowledge acquisition (e.g., for using a software already existing in the company). Expert's knowledge is reconstructed by the KE and knowledge acquisition can be analyzed as a process of knowledge creation (Cooke, 1994). When the human expert provides knowledge for a given context of problem solving, this context is generally not totally acquired by the KE.

Moreover, KEs introduce additional pieces of knowledge that obscure the knowledge bases. For example, the rule ordering that has been shown to directly control the firing of rules and may produce incorrect results in the system reasoning. In a system such as GUIDON (Clancey, 1986), screening clauses are added to the rule base to limit the effects of triggered rules. The same conclusion has been reached in the SEPT project (Brézillon et al., 1988). Screening clauses obstruct the facility to change the knowledge base due to the continuous changes required by the domain expert. As a consequence, such a control on the system reasoning, which generally is ignored by experts, implies that experts cannot always follow and validate the system reasoning.

KEs generally have a false understanding of users' needs. When users express their needs in terms of **what** they want, the KE treats the request in terms of **how** to do. This is the well-known problem of the logic of use against of the logic of functioning that leads to a conflict between what the system does and what users' needs are. Users need information that is tailored to **their** psychology **not** to that of KEs (Wood and Wood-Harper, 1993). This leads to a difficulty for implementing a KBS in the organizations and to nonadaptability and misunderstanding during the users' training.

Also, large companies design and develop by themselves KBSs (Mizoguchi and Motoda, 1995). This insures a direct compatibility with existing software in the industry. It is generally a computer engineer that plays the role of the KE (and it is a reason to distinguish actors and roles, mainly because experts often develop KBSs by themselves).

4.3 Partial conclusion

One way to improve the relationships between the user and a KBS is to permit the user to have an active role, be alive to the interest of the KBS and contribute to its coming. However, we must avoid the optimistic view that user involvment is sufficient enough to insure the success of a project (Agro et al., 1995). The user wants to follow easily the evolution of the system reasoning and communicate with the KBS in an accessible language. On the other hand, the KBS must minimize user memory overload, provide feedback (let users know what effect their actions have on the system), provide clearly marked exits and shortcuts, help users ask questions and give an overview of the organization (structure) of the information. The KBS also must take into account: the components forgotten by the user; the components added by the user; the parameter values often used by the user; the ordering constraints not respected by the user (Leviat and Thomas, 1993).

If the target is an operational use of a system, it is unlikely to reach it out of an end-user centered approach. The first step of this approach is a careful analysis of the user's task without, and with the system in the user's working environment. Indeed, many KBSs addressed mythological tasks which are neither interesting for the user nor for the organization. A typical example is given by many ESs intended to help salesmen during commercial transactions. Nobody wondered how, during the fragile dialogue between a buyer and a vendor, the latter could manage an interaction with the computer and on what topic.

Besides the analysis task and its working context, including data acquisition, the designer must understand the issues at stake. Many working situations ask for humanity rather than for expertise (e.g., communication, intention, commitment). If the human component at stake is important, it is unlikely that a system be trusted. The designer must, from scratch, be concentrated on helping the decision maker rather than try to replace him by the system. This is a typical of DSS framework (Keen and Scot Morton, 1978). The same conclusion can be reached when the future or the preferences really strongly matter. One cannot hope either to model preferences of each user or to capture all the subjective probability, this suffices to impede many systems to be used. Designers must reduce their ambition to only model the part of the knowledge which is common to all the users. This implies that the system be highly interactive so that each user can introduce his preferences and subjective anticipations.

5 KBS or DSS?

The main criticisms presented in the previous sections concern the lack of interest for the users, the poor exploration capabilities and the type of work (or decision) that the system is intended to do. To overcome these difficulties, there are only two solutions: integrate and automate, or if automation is not possible or wished, to be more aware of users' needs. In the latter case, the user must be able to intervene at different steps of the system development. Moreover, the user would intervene at various levels: in the design loop, in the problem solving, and in the knowledge base. Moreover social issues like the introduction of the KBS in a company must be prepared.

The designers must anticipate the integration of the user (if any) in the information system, including KBS modules. Furthermore, one must plan the exact role of the user, either data gatherer or interacting actor. In the latter case, the system must help the user to have an active role (Carr, 1992; Woods and Roth, 1988). Indeed, the task must be accomplished interactively by the two interested persons who are the KBS and the user. The active role implies that there is a shared control of: the interaction (e.g., the user may interrupt the system without aborting it), the knowledge base (e.g., to provide spontaneously information or for maintenance purpose), and the problem solving.

The shared control of the problem solving implies a decomposition of the task, some tasks being jointly solved by the system and the user (de Greef and Breuker, 1989; 1992). Indeed, a shared control in the noble part of the task (i.e., the data treatment) may permit to exploit the complementarity of the competences of the user and the system. This is particularly important when alternative solutions appear during the problem solving.

All the recommendations described in this section leads to consider the system and the user as a 'joint cognitive system' (Woods et al., 1990). These views about joint cognitive system are very close to those put forward for years in DSS literature (e.g., Keen and Scott Morton, 1978; Lévine and Pomerol, 1989). We think however that we must go a step further. Indeed the system must be an intelligent assistant system (Boy, 1991; Brézillon and Cases, 1995). For this, we consider three aspects:

(1) Explanation. The role of the explanations in a cooperative problem solving must be revised, because explanation is intrinsic to any cooperation (and, conversely, the system and the user must cooperate to build an explanation) (Karsenty and Brézillon, 1995).

(2) Incremental knowledge acquisition. The system needs to incrementally acquire knowledge from user to after relieve users with the same type of problems (Abu-Hakima and Brézillon, 1994). Note that we have here a kind of explanation from the user to the system, when actually one only considers explanation from the system to the user.

(3) Context. It is necessary to make the context of the user-system interaction explicit in the problem solving to provide relevant explanation and acquire incrementally knowledge (Brézillon and Abu-Hakima, 1995).

All these views simply generalize some common aspects discussed in the DSS community since many years. Apart to stress some topics about knowledge modeling, it now appears that KBSs do not differ from DSSs and encounter the same problems of man-machine integration.

6 CONCLUSION

There is an abundant literature about misuse and nonuse of KBSs. It is mostly important to turn back to this experience and to understand what are the real problems with such systems.

Our analysis shows that most of the failures occur with nonautomatic systems and are related to data acquisition and interactivity weaknesses. The first common pitfall is to confuse data acquisition and interactivity. Users refuse the work overload of introducing data, except if they are convinced that the output really worth it. As a consequence, in domains where data are issued from natural language exchanges or manuscript writing, up to now, it is unlikely to oblige end-users to act as a data provider in front of any computer system, KBSs included.

The second question, which arises similarly in DSSs and other advanced information systems, is the problem of interactivity. It is very difficult to define what interactivity means, and to handle the user integration into an information system. This raises many issues as explanation, contextual information, learning. The main result in this domain is that the user wants to be helped or complemented by the system, but not replaced (Keen and Scot Morton, 1978). It is therefore important to analyze the task and the type of decision that the user is facing. The most important point being to recognize that some decisions are intrinsically human in nature and that the destinity of the system is not to make the decision.

The third point is that organizational problems about changes have already been described with the introduction of many advanced information systems. Again, DSSs provide good examples and guidelines.

Finally, the increasing complexity of systems, devices and organization entails the need for sophisticated training of people. KBSs have an important role as a part of training systems. This, in turn, raises new issues about explanation, trainee's experience, contextual changes. All these problems enter into the general setting of man-system cooperation and joint cognitive systems.

It is more and more difficult to distinguish between DSSs and KBSs. Most of the views on users' involvement during design and development (mainly KBSs) and progressive development (DSSs), understanding of the reasoning (KBSs), confidence and acceptance of the model (DSSs), explanation facilities (KBSs), enhancement of the dialogues capabilities (DSSs), all of these views converge towards some common knowledge related to the design of advanced cooperative information systems. This knowledge focuses on three main issues, namely, the user involment, the careful analysis of the task at the early steps of the design, and the integration of the system in an organization. The design of operational nonautomatic systems requires the control and the adequate answers to these three challenges.

7 REFERENCES

Abu-Hakima, S. and Brézillon, P. (1994) Knowledge acquisition and explanation for diagnosis in context, *Research Report 94/11*, LAFORIA, University Paris VI, Paris, France.

Ackermann, W., Giustina, L.D., Gremion, C., Gremion, S. and Pomerol, J.Ch. (1992) Etude sur les nouvelles technologies et l'aide à la décision, *Rapport de ENA Recherche.*

Agro, C., Cornet A. and Pichault F. (1995) L'implication des utilisateurs dans les projets informatiques : un scénario en quête d'auteurs, *Gérer et Comprendre*, **41**, 33-44.

Belanger, F., Burns, M.B. and Will, R.P. (1995) Transference of power: Shifting expertise to expert system developers, *Proc. of the 11th Conf. on Artificial Intelligence for Applications*, 65-71.

Boy, G. (1991) Intelligent Assistant Systems, Academic Press, London, Knowledge-Based Systems, **6**.

Brézillon, P., Fauquembergue, P. and Hertz, A. (1988) SEPT, an expert system approach for the monitoring of EVH substation control equipment, *Proc. of the Symposium on Expert Systems Application to Power System*, Stockholm-Helsinki, 1988, 6.9-6.13.

Brézillon, P. and Abu-Hakima, S. (1995) Using knowledge in its context: Report on the IJCAI-93 Workshop, *The AI Magazine*, **16(1)**, 87-91.

Brézillon, P. and Cases, E. (1995) Cooperating for assisting intelligently operators, *Proc. of the International Workshop on the Design of Cooperative Systems*, INRIA ed., 370-384.

Carr, C. (1992) Performance support systems: A new horizon for expert systems, *AI Expert*, 44-49.

Chandrasekaran B. (1994) AI, knowledge, and the quest for smart systems, *IEEE Expert*, December, 2-5.

Clancey, W.J. (1986) From GUIDON to NEOMYCIN and HERACLES in twenty short lessons: ORN final report 1979-1985, *The AI Magazine*, 40-60.

Clancey, W.J. (1993) Notes on “Epistemology of a rule-based expert system”, *Artificial Intelligence Journal*, **59**, 197-204.

Cooke, N.J. (1994) Varieties of knowledge elicitation techniques, *Int. J. Human-Computer Studies*, **41**, 801-849.

Courbon, J. Cl. (1992) Expert systems as a methodological step in conventional decision support system, *Economics and Cognitive Science*, P. Bourgine and B. Walliser (Eds.), Pergamon Press, 383-386.

de Greef, H.P. and Breuker, J.A. (1989) A methodology for analyzing Modalities of System/User Cooperation for KBS, *Proc. of the 3rd European Workshop on Knowledge Acquisition for Knowledge-Based Systems*, Paris, 462-473.

de Greef, H.P. and Breuker, J.A. (1992) Analysing system-user cooperation in KADS, *Knowledge Acquisition*, **4**, 89-108.

Durkin, J. (1993) Expert Systems. Catalog of Applications, Intelligent Computer Systems Inc., PO Box 4117, Akron, Ohio 44321-117.

Fischer, G. (1990) Communication requirements for cooperative problem solving systems, *Information Systems*, **15(1)**, 21-36.

Gilbert, N. (1987) Question and Answer Types, In: Moralee D.S. (Ed.) *Research and Development in Expert Systems III*. Cambridge University Press.

Hatchuel, A. and Weil, B. (1992) L'Expert et le Système, *Economica*, Paris, France.

Huguet, M.J., Erschler, J., de Terssac, J. and Lompré, N. (1995) Negociation based on constraints in cooperation, *Proc. of the International Workshop on the Design of Cooperative Systems*, INRIA ed., 109-126.

Karsenty, L. and Brézillon, P. (1995) Cooperative problem solving and explanation, *Int. J. on Expert Systems With Applications*, **8(4)**, 445-462.

Keen, P.G.W. and Scott Morton M.S. (1978) Decision support systems, Addison-Wesley Publishing Company, Readings, MA.
Keravnou, E.T. and Washbrook, J. (1989) What is a deep expert system? An analysis of the architectural requirements of second-generation expert systems, *The Knowledge Engineering Review*, **4(3)**, 205-233.
Kidd, A.L. (1985) What Do Users Ask ? Some Thoughts on Diagnostic Advice, In: Merry M. (Ed.) *Expert Systems 85*. Cambridge University Press.
Kidd, A.L. and Sharpe, W.P. (1988) Goals for expert systems research: an analysis of tasks and domains, In: *Annual Technical Conference of the British Computer Society, Cambridge University Press*, 146-152.
Lévine, P. and Pomerol, J.Ch. (1989) SIAD et systèmes experts, *Hermès*, Paris.
Lévine, P. and Pomerol, J.Ch. (1995) The role of the decision maker in DSSs and representation levels, *Proc. of the 28th Annual Hawaï International Conference on System Sciences*, Nunamaker J.F. & Sprague R.H. (eds.), IEEE Computer Society Press, Los Alamitos, USA, **3**, 42-51.
Levrat, B. and Thomas, I. (1993) Tailoring explanations to the user's expectations: a way to be relevant, *IJCAI Workshop on Explanation and Problem Solving*, 1-10.
McKeown, K.R., Wish, M. and Matthews, K. (1985) Tailoring explanations for the user, *Proc. of IJCAI'85*, 794-798.
Majchrzak, and Gasser, L. (1991) On using Artificial Intelligence to integrate the design of organizational and process change in US manufacturing, *AI and Society Journal*, **5**, 321-338.
Meyer, M.H., Detore A., Siegel S.F. and Curley K.F. (1992) The strategic use of expert systems for risk management in the Insurance Industry, *Expert Systems With Applications*, 5, 15-24.
Mizoguchi, R. and Motoda, H. (1995) Expert systems research in Japan, *IEEE Expert Magazine*, 14-23.
Moore, J.D. and Swartout, W.R. (1990) A reactive approach to explanation: taking the user's feedback into account, In: Paris C.L., Swartout W.R. & Mann W.C. (Eds.) *Natural Language Processing in Artificial Intelligence and Computational Linguistics*, Kluwer Academic Publishers.
Oberquelle, H., Kupka, I. and Maass, S. (1983) A view of human-machine communication and co-operation, *Int. J. Man-Machine Studies*, **19**, 309-333.
Paris, C.L. (1990) Generation and explanation: building an explanation facility for the explainable expert systems framework, In: Paris, Swartout, Mann (Eds.), *Natural Language Generation in Artificial Intelligence and Computational Linguistics*, Kluwer Academic Publishers.
Perrot, L., Brézillon, P. and Fauquembergue, P. (1993) Towards automatic generation of knowledge bases for diagnosis systems in the field of power systems, *ESAP'93*.
Pomerol, J.Ch. (1990) *Systèmes experts et SIAD : enjeux et conséquences pour les organisations*, T.I.S., 3(1), 37-64.
Pomerol, J. Ch. and Retour, D. (1990) L'introduction et l'utilisation des systèmes experts dans le tertiaire, *Bilan d'Etudes*, C3E, 10 rue Saint Claude, 75003 Paris.
Pomerol, J.C. (1993) Multicriteria DSSs: State of the art and problems, *Central European Journal for Operations Research and Economics*, 2(3): 197-211.
Pomerol, J.C. (1995) Artificial intelligence and human decision making, *Proc. of Euro XIV*, Jerusalem, R. Slowinski Ed., 169-196.

Rowe, G. and Wright, G. (1993) Expert systems in Insurance: A review and analysis, *Intelligent Systems in Accounting, Finance and Management,* 2, 129-145.
Sakaguchi, T., Tanaka, H., Uenishi, K., Gotoh, T. and Sekine, Y. (1987) Prospects of expert systems in power system operation, *9th Power Systems Computation Conference*, Cascais, Portugal.
Swartout, W.R. (1983) XPLAIN: a system for creating and explaining expert consulting programs, *Artificial Intelligence*, **21(3)**, 285-325.
Terssac (de), G. (1992) "Autonomie dans le travail", *Série Sociologie d'Aujourd'hui,* Presses Universitaires de France.
Terssac (de), G. and Chabaud, C. (1992) Impact social des systèmes experts. Repères pour une méthodologie de conception, *Technologies, Idéologies, Pratiques*, **X(2-4)**, 7-28.
Van Beek, P. (1987) A model for generating better explanations, *Proc. of the 25th Conference of the Association for Computational Linguistics*, Stanford, 215-220.
Wallis, J.W. and Shortliffe, E.H. (1984) Customized explanations using causal knowledge, In: Buchanan B.G. & Shortliffe E.H. (Eds.), *Rule-Based Expert Systems: The MYCIN Experiments of the Stanford Heuristic Programming Project*, Reading, Mass: Addison-Wesley.
Woods, D.D. and Roth, E.M. (1988) Cognitive systems engineering, In: Helander M. (Eds.) *Handbook of Human-Computer Interaction*. North-Holland: Elsevier.
Woods, D.D., Roth, E.M. and Benett, K. (1990) Explorations in joint human-machine cognitive systems, In: *Cognition, Computing and Cooperation*, Robertson S, Zachary W & Black JB (Eds.), 123-158.
Wood, J.R.G. and Wood-Harper, A.T. (1993) Information technology in support of individual decision-making, *J. of Information Systems*, **3**, 85-101.

8 BIOGRAPHY

Patrick Brézillon is a researcher at the National Center of Scientific Research in France (CNRS). In 1983, he received his These d'Etat in natural sciences at the Pierre and Marie Curie University. The topic of his thesis concerned the mathematical modeling of the calcium metabolism as a self-oscillating nonlinear model. Now, he aims to merge the mathematical modeling with the AI approach and is concerned with topics such as cooperation, context, explanation and incremental knowledge acquisition in the framework of 'intelligent' cooperative systems.

Jean-Charles Pomerol is Professor of Computer Science and the head of the LAFORIA-IBP, a laboratory at University Paris 6 associated with CNRS. This laboratory is entirely devoted to Artificial Intelligence and Speech Recognition. Jean-Charles Pomerol defended his These d'Etat in convex analysis in 1980. Then, he turns to decision theory and decision support systems. His current interests are about the design and development of 'intelligent' decision support systems. He is the author or co-author of many papers and four books, concerning expert systems, decision support systems and multicriteria decision.

5

The effective use of a decision support tool in the area of strategic marketing management.

P.R.Burrell
Knowledge Base Systems Centre,
South Bank University, Borough Road, London SE1 0AA, UK, email: phillb@vax.sbu.ac.uk.

Y. Duan
Faculty of Business,
University of Luton, Luton LU1 3JU, UK, email: duany@vax2.luton.ac.uk.

A. Boskovic
LAFORIA-IBP,
University Paris VI,UPMC, BP 169, 75252 Paris, cedex 5, France.

Abstract

Management at a strategic level involves a high level of risk and uncertainty. These problems are compounded further in the area of marketing due to the fact that firms often face turbulent and unpredictable markets. Expert systems and decision support systems might have a large impact in this area but the development of such systems has proven difficult with less than expected results. This paper provides a description of an effective decision support tool embedded within a hybrid expert/decision support system. This tool is derived from a modified version of an existing operational research technique and is used to introduce structure and objectivity into a largely subjective process of attaching values to a set of decision criteria.

Keywords

Analytic hierarchy process, decision support, expert system, strategic management, marketing

1 INTRODUCTION

Managers at the strategic level are responsible for the "external and future" and long term plans. Such decisions are frequently high risk with a considerable degree of uncertainty attached to the outcomes. The knowledge needed at this level is not as specific as that in the lower level of a company and, by nature, is more unstructured. Beerel (1987) points out that strategic managers are continuously faced with complex and unstructured decisions at a high level of uncertainty and have a lot at stake. The strategic manager mediates the relations between the company and the outside world and they are responsible for the general direction of the company. The relationship of the company to its environment is a central matter of concern and predictions about the future are particularly important. The information required is aggregate information. Both the scope and variety of the information are quite large, but the requirements for accuracy are not particularly stringent.

This level of uncertainty applies, probably more than most, to areas of marketing and as most firms have to face turbulent and sometimes unpredictable markets, their managers have to watch and decide about their product-market strategy. Nobody should doubt the importance of marketing planning in the modern business. However, Kotler (1991) finds that many companies, for various reasons, operate without plans. He stresses that formal planning can yield many benefits for all types of companies. Sound planning helps the company to anticipate and respond quickly to environmental changes, and to prepare for sudden developments.

Although a huge amount of information is available on marketing planning, it is still an area which is less well understood and where there is a lack of a framework which can be easily transferred into a computer system, or directly applicable to build an expert system (ES). As Mitchell *et al* (1991) have found, our understanding of causal structure that relates market factors is relatively loose, at least compared to the engineering domain in which many expert systems have been developed. The development of ESs has revealed the incompetence of our own knowledge of how to analyse marketing problems. Because of these reasons the construction of ESs in marketing is more difficult than in other domains.

The authors (Duan and Burrell, 1995a) believe that these difficulties arise because traditional ES technology is too inflexible to cope with the loose causal structure of information associated with the marketing domain. For this reason, a more flexible approach in the form of a hybrid system combining both expert system and decision support technology was required. Not only was there a need for a hybrid technology but also the need for appropriate decision support tools capable of working within the framework of the marketing domain. This paper presents a brief introduction to HYMS [**HY**brid **M**arketing **S**ystem] in order to provide an understanding of the core model used and the issues related to its use. It then discusses, in more detail, the problems associated with structuring the domain like marketing and how an operation research technique, the Analytic Hierarchy Process was modified, in order to overcome its deficiencies, and used to establish objectivity and structure in the decision hierarchy.

2 INTRODUCTION TO HYMS

The system architecture of the initial prototype is shown in Figure 1. The system consists of several modules, some of which contain knowledge bases, and others, decision support. The system guides the user through the marketing planning process form the pre-diagnostic stage, by establishing goals and supplying information where necessary, to providing advice on the best strategy to adopt. A fuller description of HYMS has been presented by the authors (Duan and Burrell, 1995b, 1996) in other publications.

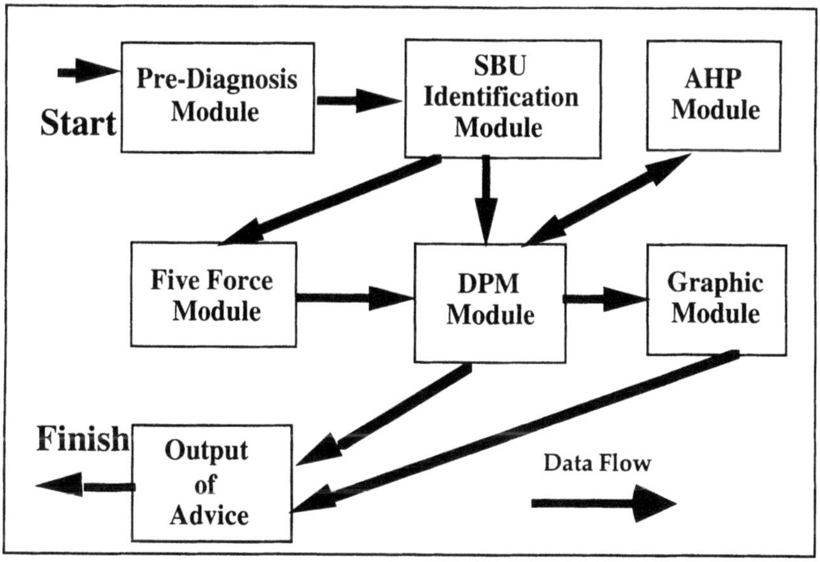

Figure 1 System Architecture of HYMS

The core module of HYMS is the Directional Policy Matrix (DPM) which consists of three components; the Market Strength Evaluator, the Business Strength Evaluator and the Strategy Generator. The DPM is based on McDonald's (1989) and McDonald and Wilson's (1990) nine step marketing planning process model and is implemented as a 3 * 3 matrix where a company's strategic business unit is assessed, based on factors related to the business strength and market attractiveness. The dimensions used for assessing the position on the matrix represent the significant factors of the internal and external environment from which strengths, weaknesses, opportunities and threats arise. Nine boxes are formulated and each of these positions calls for a different marketing strategy. Qualitative analysis is used to assess the business strength as strong, medium or weak and the market attractiveness as high, medium or low.

The qualitative analysis for the DPM is implemented through the Analytic Hierarchy Process (AHP) module by applying a method of pair-wise comparison to the factors related to business strength and market attractiveness. This process results in a set of weights being attached to these factors which is then used by the strategy generator to plot a position on the policy matrix.

3 THE DECISION HIERARCHY

One of the most important aspects governing any decision support is choosing the factors related to the decision process and then arranging them in a hierarchical structure. Once selected, these are arranged in order descending from an overall goal, to criteria, to sub-criteria and to any alternatives at successive levels. Arranging the goals in a hierarchy serves the purposes of providing an overall view of the complex relationships inherent in a situation and helps the decision maker assess whether the issues in each level are of the same order of magnitude.

Implementing this decision hierarchy for decision support in the area of diagnostics is reasonably straight forward, in the way that top down goal decomposition can be applied to a majority of problems. In the area of strategic marketing planning this is not the case, as the task is compounded by the fact that this hierarchy is not a traditional decision tree. Each of the factors may represent a different cut of the problem. Some may represent social factors while another, economic factors. Also, both of these may need to be evaluated in terms of the other. It may also be necessary to insert or eliminate factors as necessary to clarify the task of setting priorities or to sharpen the focus on one or more parts of the hierarchy. Thus a hierarchy representing a general problem can be easily adapted to represent one specific case.

Although the problem of structuring the decision hierarchy for the given application is subject to the constraints mentioned, it transpires that the decision process relies more on the relative importance assigned to each of the factors of the decision hierarchy. This allows a certain amount of flexibility in the design of the hierarchy in that it was not necessary to establish a causal relationship between the factors in the hierarchy, but more to group related factors and sub factors together. The top level factors were dictated by the use of the chosen DPM model and the sub factors relating to these were positioned accordingly. These are shown in Figure 2a, 2b.

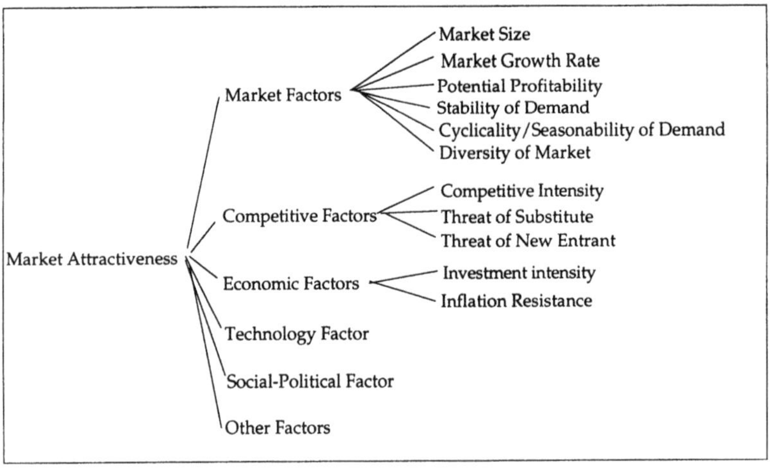

Figure 2a The hierarchies of decision factors for market attractiveness

The decision hierarchy was established from knowledge collected from experts and relevant documents. Using published documents, as a major source of knowledge, is quite common in the marketing area. COMSTRAT (Curry *et al*, 1992) (Mentzer and Gandhi, 1992) and NEGOTEX (Rangaswamy *et al*, 1989) used the relevant academic literature to generate their decision hierarchies and McDonald (1989), and McDonald and Wilson (1990) have published papers and reports about his marketing planning model. Although the knowledge from published documentation is easy to access, it is limited to generalities and is not sufficient to build a specific hierarchy. It was therefore deemed necessary to elicit the help of experts as another major source for knowledge.

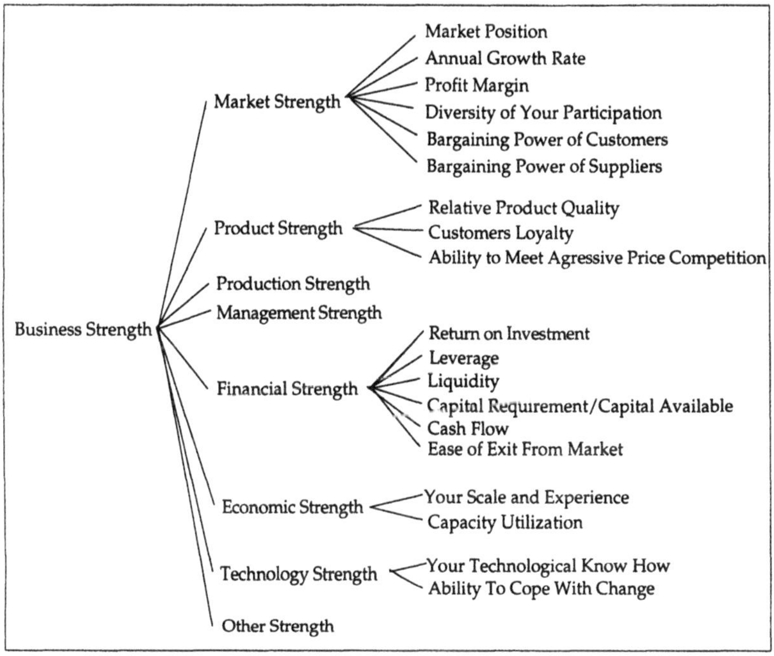

Figure 2b The hierarchies of decision factors for business strength

4 THE AHP PROCESS

Having established a structure for the decision hierarchy it becomes necessary to assign some value of importance to the factors composing the hierarchy. This raises the question as to whether each of the factors/sub-factors should be of equal importance. As Day (1986) indicated, in relation to the marketing domain, there are several problems: first, many of the factors are interrelated; second, a factor such as technological position may be of minor significance in one market while being the dominant determinant of survival in another market swept by a new generation of technology. Assigning values to various factors entirely depends on different circumstance and users' personal judgement. Any decision support capable of satisfying these requirements must be able to introduce structure and objectivity into the largely subjective process of attaching values to a set of decision criteria in a multi-criteria decision making situation.

The chosen model to implement this subjective process was the AHP. This is an Operational Research (OR) technique for applications in diverse decision problem areas (Saaty, 1977, 1978, 1980, 1990) and is concerned with how to derive

relative scales using judgements given in the form of pair-wise comparisons. In this instance, the pair-wise comparisons are carried out between the factors and sub-factors related to the decision hierarchies of both the market attractiveness and business strength.
Solving a decision problem, using the AHP, involves four steps (Johnson 1980):

- Establishing a decision hierarchy.
- The pair-wise comparison of the decision elements.
- Estimating the relative weights of the deciding elements using the "eigenvalue method".
- Aggregating the relative weights of decision elements to be applied at different levels of the decision hierarchy.

It was only necessary to implement the first three of these steps as the complexity of the full AHP was not required. The result of the eignvalue method gives a matrix with the following form:

$$A^*W = n * W$$

where A is the is the matrix of pair-wise comparisons, $W = (w_1, w_2, \ldots\ldots, w_n)^T$ being the vector of relative weights; the eigenvector, and n the number of elements; the eigenvalue. Because the pair-wise values of matrix A rely upon human judgement, matrix A contains inconsistencies and therefore n may only be considered as an approximation. This now becomes:

$$\underline{A}^*\underline{W} = l_{max}^*\underline{W}$$

where $\underline{A}$ is the observed matrix of pair-wise comparisons, l_{max} is the principle eigenvalue and $\underline{W}$ is an estimation of W. The closer l_{max} is to n, the more consistent are the pair-wise values of $\underline{A}$. This has led to the need of a consistency index (CI) Saty (1980) where:

$$CI = (l_{max} - n)/(n - 1)$$

and the consistency ratio (CR):

$$CR = (CI/ACI)^*100$$

where the Average Consistency Ratio (ACI) is the average index of randomly generated weights. Saaty (1980) proposes the rule of thumb, where a CR of 10% or less is considered acceptable. If this is not the case, then the pair-wise comparison of $\underline{A}$ needs to be recalculated. The value of ACI depends upon the size of the matrix and is shown in Figure 3.

	n	2	3	4	5	6	7	8
ACI	0.00	0.58	0.90	1.12	1.24	1.32	1.41	

Figure 3 The ACI for a linear 1-9 scale (Saaty's result)

5 DEFICIENCIES WITH THE AHP

Criticisms regarding the use of the AHP seemed to be levelled at the use of the linear scale of comparisons. This is a standard scale used for establishing the difference of importance between elements in the decision hierarchy. Saaty (1980) describes the scale as linguistic and supports its use through a series of experiments. This scale is shown in Figure 4.

Intensity of importance	Definition	Explanation
1	Equal importance	Two activities contribute equally to the objective
3	Weak importance of one over another	Experience and judgement slightly favour one activity over another
5	Essential or strong importance of one over another	Experience and judgement strongly favour one activity over another
7	Demonstrated importance	An activity is strongly favoured and its dominance is demonstrated in practice
9	Absolute, extreme importance	The evidence favouring one activity over another is of the highest possible order of affirmation
2, 4, 6, 8	Intermediate values between two adjacent judgements	When compromise is needed
Reciprocals	If activity *i* has one of the non zero numbers assigned to it when compared with activity *j*, then *j* has the reciprocal value when compared with *i*	

Figure 4 Saaty's linear scale of comparisons

A review of the major criticisms (Salo and Hamalainen 1994) cited problems in four areas:

- The meaning of the pair wise comparisons.
- The relationship between scores and criteria weights.
- The properties of the 1-9 ratio scale.
- The prohibited complexity of the super-matrix approach.

Davis (1993) also criticised the method as being difficult to use, perhaps because of an unfamiliarity of the scale used. The major concern seems to be the difference between the use of a linguistic scale and the algebraic ratio interpretation of responses implied by its use. A second is the effect of the scale on the inconsistency of the matrix of judgements. In the original version of the AHP the decision maker is presented only with the English language descriptions of the scale. This conceals what is being asked, to estimate ratios of weights for pairs of criteria. A number of experiments (Holder, 1990) (Lund and Palmer, 1986), using the nine point linguistic scale, suggested that, dependent upon the users background, the use of a pair-wise ratio presented a clearer interpretation of comparison process and that the use of the linguistic scale often led to an inconsistency of judgements. It is suggested therefore that the use of this scale leads to violations of the normal usage of the English language, for example: If the decision maker evaluates A as weakly more important than B and B as weakly more important than C this implies that A is extremely (absolutely) more important than C.

6 MODIFICATIONS TO THE AHP

The way to try to overcome these deficiencies was first, to offer the user a linguistic scale, but not to hide the numerical meaning of the points of the scale. It was considered more "user friendly" to assess intangible, non measurable criteria in English than in pure numbers. However numbers give the linguistic scale a more precise meaning and for that reason, we also presented them to the user. In this way, user evaluation can show if the inconsistency of the judgements is significantly inflated by the use of a linguistic scale. The other deficiency is addressed by using a multiplicative (geometrical) scale. This deficiency was also recognised by Lootsma (1989) who introduced the concept of a symbolic scale based on psychological measurements.

This theory was the bases for the development of a multiplicative scale used in our model. We have adopted a scale with the same number of points as Saaty's, consequently exactly the same semantics have been used. This scale is shown in Figure 5.

aij in the matrix of pair-wise comparisons	**Semantic interpretation**
16	factor i is extremely more important than factor j
8	factor i is very strongly more important than factor j
4	factor i is strongly more important than factor j
2	factor i is moderately more important than factor j
1	factor i is equally important to factor j
1/2	factor i is moderately less important than factor j
1/4	factor i is strongly less important than factor j
1/8	factor i is very strongly less important than factor j
1/16	factor i is extremely less important than factor j

Figure 5 The multiplicative scale used in the AHP module

This scale is more satisfactory than the linear 1-9 scale in terms of consistency. Every point of this 1-16 multiplicative scale can be expressed in terms of two other points on the same scale and the "gaps" associated with intermediate values have now been eliminated.

Implementing the 1-16 multiplicative scale as opposed to Saaty's 1-9 linear scale required that the ACI also had to be modified. Saaty's (1980) linear scale integers in the interval 1 to 9 were randomly generated to form a judgement matrix. In our model we are using a multiplicative 1 - 16 scale so the corresponding ACI had to be empirically determined. In order to achieve this, and also to test our empirical approach, we first repeated the Saaty's original method, for the 1-9, scale for matrices of size 3 to 8. For each matrix size the ACI was computed on a sample of 1000 matrices. We found that we had a slight variation in the second decimal digit for some of the points of the scale (Saaty's original scale is shown in Figure 3) but concluded that this was most likely to be due to the distribution of the pseudo-random generator used in the computation. We used the same method to compute the ACI for the multiplicative 1 - 16 scale. The steps of the scale used in the AHP module (1/16, 1/8, 1/4, ... , 8, 16) were randomly generated. The sample size of 1000 was not changed. The results were the following, as shown in figure 6.

	n	3	4	5	6	7	8
ACI	0.70	1.29	1.51	1.79	1.81	2.07	

Figure 6 The ACI generated for a multiplicative 1-16 scale

These results were used for the consistency check in the AHP module when the comparisons were evaluated on the multiplicative scale.

The original implementation of the AHP requires the decision maker to complete a sequence of positive reciprocal matrices by answering n(n-1)/2 questions for each matrix (where *n* is the size of the matrix), each entry being an approximation to the ratio of the weights of two items being compared. Harker (1987) developed an extension to the eigenvector approach of the AHP which allows the decision maker to say "I don't know" or "I'm not sure, I prefer not answering" to some of the questions being asked and shows that non negative, quasi-reciprocal matrices can be used in exactly the same manner as positive reciprocal matrices, for which Saaty's AHP theory was developed. Even the relationship between l_{max} and n remains unchanged. (One still has $l_{max} > n$ for the general case and $l_{max} = n$ iff the matrix A is consistent). This may be useful when the decision maker does not have a good understanding of their preferences between two particular alternatives or if the alternatives represent a sensitive subject so that the decision maker is unwilling to make a direct comparison. This incomplete pair-wise comparison method was incorporated into our AHP model.

7 IMPLEMENTATION OF THE MODEL

The pair-wise comparison of elements is implemented through the AHP module which comprises the AHP Interface Unit and the Eigenvector Computation Unit. The Interface Unit guides the decision maker through the application of the AHP. It presents a graphic display with the hierarchy of factors and sub factors to which the decision maker seeks to assign weights. If necessary, help with the weight assignment can be evoked and is supplied in the form of a sequence of questions to help to evaluate the pair-wise comparisons between all the relevant criteria. The overall view of the evaluations is presented in the form of a triangular matrix. Once the user judges the pair-wise comparisons complete, weights are computed. If all the pair-wise comparisons have not been evaluated, then an incomplete judgement matrix is sent to the Eigenvector Computation Unit which treats it as an incomplete pair-wise comparison. A general model of the module shown in Figure 7.

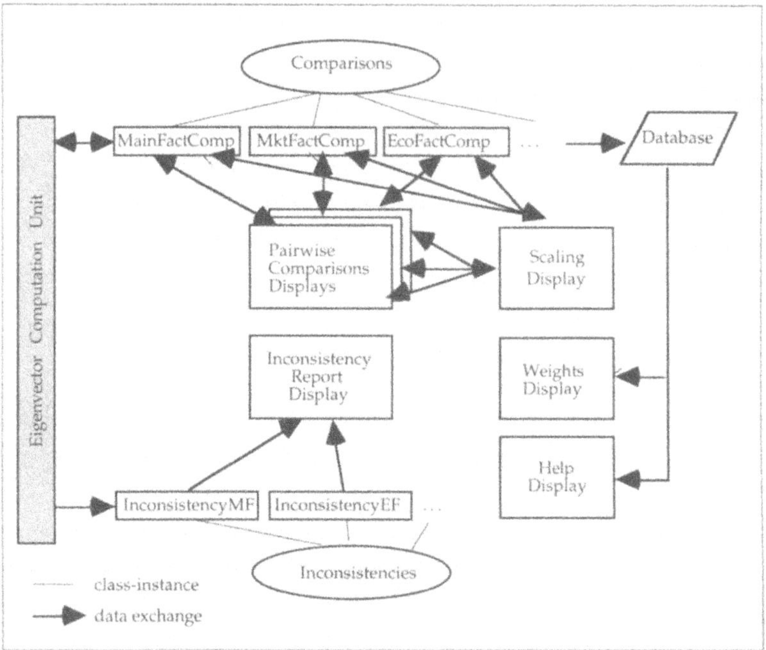

Figure 7 The structure of the AHP Interface Unit

If the user's judgements were consistent, weights are displayed and the user may save them if required. In the case where inconsistencies are detected the AHP Interface Unit generates an Inconsistency Report, from the information provided by the Eigenvector Computation Unit, which gives the details of each triplet of inconsistent comparisons. The inconsistencies are sorted by their magnitudes in a decreasing order and this information can then be used to produce a consistent judgement matrix.

8 CONCLUSION

Marketing provides many opportunities for the application of expert systems and decision support systems, but the progress in this area is still relatively slow. This project has shown that HYMS is an effective hybrid decision support tool, and can demonstrate to marketing executives its capability by helping them make more consistent and better decisions. The system developed combines the advantage of ES and DSS. It provides more systematic analysis using selected marketing techniques and appropriate decision support tools.

The use of the AHP has proven an effective method of assigning strengths to various marketing factors in a variety of different marketing situations.

Although this technique has come under some criticism, these have been largely related to the interpretation of the linguistic used. The modification to this scale have, we believe, have overcome some of these interpretation problems. The use of the 1-16 multiplicative scale now allows the user to express any point on the scale in terms of two other points on the same scale and the qualitative and quantitative values presented to the user provide a method by which more effective judgements can be made for the pair-wise comparisons.

To evaluate the success of such a system as this is a difficult task because there is no objective standard by which any measurements can be made (Wensley 1989). An evaluation of HYMS should cover the system's effectiveness and its usability but the effectiveness and usability of a prototype system, such as this, can really only be evaluated by experts' hands-on experience. The response by a number of experts using the system was generally favourable. The users reported positively on the efficiency and effectiveness of the program. The type, clarity and meaning of conclusions were all deemed acceptable. Furthermore, test conclusions were considered to be accurate "given that this is by nature a fairly inexact science". Most favourable and promising of all was a comment by one user that "the program had proven thought provoking" and had helped him to identify, and challenged him to think about, programmatic areas in his real-life plan.

9 REFERENCES

Beerel, A.C. (1987) *Expert Systems: Strategic Implications and Applications*, Ellis Horwood, Chichester.

Curry, B. Moutinho, L. and Davies, F. (1992) Constructing a knowledge base for a marketing expert system, *Marketing Intelligence & Planning*, **10**, 12-20.

Day, G.S. (1986) *Analysisn for Strategic Market Decisions*, West Publising Company, USA.

Davis, A.P. (1993) How an AHP can facilitate Marketing Decision Making, *Business School Research Series*, Loughborough University, UK.

Duan, Y. and Burrell, P. (1995a) Some Issues in developing Expert Systems for Strategic Marketing Planning, *8th International Symposium on Artificial Intelligence, Monterrey, Mexico*, 78-85.

Duan, Y and Burrell, P. (1995b) A hybrid system for strategic market planning, *Marketing Intelligence and Planniing*, **13**, 5-12.

Duan, Y. and Burrell, P. (1996) HYMS: A Hybrid Marketing System,*Third World Congress on Expert Systems, Soeul, Korea*, Vol. 1, 335-342.

Harker, P.T. (1987) Alternative Modes of Questioning in the AHP, *Mathematical Modelling*, **9**, 353-360.

Holder, R.D. (1990) Some Comments on the Analytic Hierarchy Process, *Journal of the Operational Research Society*, **41**, 1073-1080.

Johnson, C.R. (1980) Constructive critique of a hierarchical prioritization scheme employing paired comparisons, *International Conference of Cybernetics and Society,* IEEE, Cambridge, Mass.

Kotler, P. (1991) *Marketing Management Analysis, Planning, Implementation, and Control,* Prentice-Hall, New York.

Lootsma, F.A. (1989) Conflict Resolution via Pair-wise Comparison, *European Journal of Operational Research,* **40,** 109-116.

Lund, J.R. and Palmer, R.N. (1986) Subjective Evaluation: Linguistic Scale in Pair wise Comparison Methods, *Civil Engineering Systems,* **3,** 182-186.

McDonald, M.H.B. (1989) Marketing planning and expert systems: an epistemology of practice, *Marketing Intelligence and planning,* **7,** 16-23.

McDonald, M.H.B. and Wilson, H.N. (1990) State-of-the-art development in expert systems and strategic marketing planning, *British Journal of Management,* **1,** 159-170.

Mentzer, J.T. and Gandhi N. (1993) Expert systems in industrial marketing *Industrial Marketing Management,* **22,** 109-116.

Mitchell, A.A., Russo, J.E. and Wittink, D.R. (1991) Issues in the development and use of expert systems for marketing decisions *International Journal of Research in Marketing,* **8,** 41-50.

Rangaswamy, A. Eliashberg, J. Burke, R.R. and Wind J. (1989) Developing marketing expert systems: an application to international negotiations, *Journal of Marketing,* **53,** 24-39.

Saaty, T.L. (1977) A Scaling Method for Priorities in Hierarchical Structures, *Journal of Mathematical Psychology,* **15,** 234-281.

Saaty, T.L. (1978) Modeling Unstructured Decision Problems: The Theory of Analytical Hierarchies, *Mathematics and Computers in Simulation,* **20,** 147-157.

Saaty, T.L. (1980) *The Analytic Hierarchy Process,* McGraw-Hill, New York.

Saaty, T.L. (1990) How to Make a Decision: The Analytic Hierarchy Process, *European Journal of Operational Research,* **48,** 9-26.

Salo, A.A, and Hamalainen, R.P. (1994) On the Meassurment of Preferences in the Analytic Hierarchy Process", *Helsinki University of Technology Report,* Finland.

Wensley, A. (1989) Research directions in expert systems, in *Knowledge-Based Management Support Systems*, (ed. G.I. Doukidis, F. Land and G. Miller), Ellis Horwood, Chichester, 248-275.

10 BIOGRAPHY

Phillip Burrell is a Principal Lecturer and Director of the Knowledge Base Systems Centre at South Bank University, UK. He has researched in the area of Artificial Intelligence for many years and has been involved with a number of funded projects over this period. He studied at the University of Leeds, UK, Kings College, University of London, UK and undertook further research at Imperial College, University of London, UK.

Yanqing Duan is a Research Fellow in the faculty of Business at the University of Luton, UK and before that, a Research Fellow at the Knowledge Base Systems Centre at South Bank University, UK. She received her Ph.D. in Expert Systems from the Aston Business School, Aston University, UK. Her areas of research are with decision support systems and expert systems, especially for business applications.

Aleksandra Boskovic was a research student with LAFORIA-IBP, University Paris VI, France and participated in a European research student exchange program with the Knowledge Base Systems Centre at South Bank University, UK where she held a position as a research assistant. She is now pursuing a successful career in industry.

6

Information technology in hypointegrated organizations: communication support versus decision support[1]

Tommaso Cariati
Dipartimento di Organizzazione Aziendale, Università della Calabria
P.zza Roma, 2 - 87040 Castiglione Cosentino (CS), Italy
Tel. No. + 39 984 442554

Gianpaolo Iazzolino
Dipartimento di Organizzazione Aziendale, Università della Calabria
Via S. Allende, 53 - 87030 Roges di Rende (CS), Italy
Tel. No. + 39 984 461478

Anna Tancredi
Consultant of Organizational Psychology
Via Tribunali, 40 - 87100 Cosenza, Italy
Tel. No. + 39 984 21152

Abstract

The tumultuous developments of Information Technology and the organizational revolution, beginning in Japan with the Lean Organization concept, where important keywords are autonomy, empowerment etc., changed radically the strategic and operational conditions of companies. The environment was becoming more and more chaotic and, in this context, *hypointegrated organizations*, characterised by weak structural links and by a dispersed memory where the communication process became the central aspect, emerged.

After discussing the features of the emerging organization forms taking into account the principal theories, our work analyses thoroughly the communication process because

[1] The research was carried out cooperatively, but in particular Cariati wrote section 1, 5, 6, Iazzolino section 2, Tancredi section 3, 4.

communication has become the co-ordinating and integrating instrument, bound to the ability of using the available media in an effective way.

We suggest organizational criteria for integrating available information technology to implement effective, efficient and reliable information systems to support work, decisions and communication in hypointegrated organizations. According to our model, in a learning organization vision, users should define, with the help of technicians, communication, decision and work support requirements.

In conclusion, we present an application of the proposed information technology integration model: the Urban Regional Co-ordination Planning project, still in progress in Calabria.

Keywords

Transactional approach, relational theory, learning organization, network enterprise, hypointegrated organization, decision support systems, empowerment, communication process, decision process, information technology, technological network, distributed systems.

1 INFORMATION TECHNOLOGY AND ORGANIZATIONAL REVOLUTION: BASIC QUESTIONS

Many contributions in the international debate about Management Information Systems at the beginning of the '80s pointed out that information technology applications developed in the past neglected the real organizational and decisional processes (Keen, Scott Morton, 1978).

In fact, much of the research work in the area of Decision Support Systems arose from this observation and adopted Simon's framework of problem solving process, and bounded rationality to design more effective Management Information Systems (Simon, 1977). Moreover, authors focused on implementation problems and argued that information system implementation is a process which requires organizational and social change (Keen, Scott Morton, 1978); so, many of them declared one must be careful and prepare adequately for this change, for example through Lewin's three stages of social change: Unfreezing, Moving and Refreezing (Lewin, 1947).

Later, new concepts like Group Decision Support Systems, Office Automation Systems, Computer Based Co-operative Work, etc. came to underline the need of a richer approach than even Decision Support Systems one for successful information technology introduction in organizations.

Some authors (Ciborra, 1984; Cariati et al., 1989) on the basis of the theory of transactional costs (Williamson, 1975, 1979) pointed out that Simon's decisional, cybernetic approach was not adequate to design effective computer based systems in many organizational situations. In particular, they felt the decisional approach neglected the following aspects: (a) in organizations, collective, co-ordinated problem solving rather than individual is important; (b) complexity depends not only on the generic uncertainty (Galbraith, 1977) but also on transaction, exchange uncertainty; (c) a more realistic view of the co-operative work must take into account also conflictual, opportunistic human behaviour; (d) an organization is a negotiated order in a network of relationships among actors, operating not necessarily within a hierarchy (Ciborra, 1984; Ouchi, 1980).

While the discussion about what an information system should be or should not be was going on, two phenomena recently changed many things.

First of all, the advancement of information technology has been so rapid that the friendliness of software systems and environments has enabled users to build their own systems tailored to specific needs. So, we have systems based on 4th Generation Languages, on Declarative Languages like Query by Example language or easier ones, on Hypertext and Hypermedia systems built by users themselves, making and refining prototypes that are good, even if they are often not very efficient, nor very reliable.

On the other hand, technicians, having perhaps learned the lesson about systems failures, developed some organizational sensibility and built less naive systems than those built in the past. So, we also have systems designed by engineers based on Object Oriented Languages, on Data Base Management Systems, on Client/Server network architecture that are efficient, reliable and effective enough to provide also Decision Support Systems functions and facilities (Saccà, 1995). Moreover, everybody is aware that communication facilities like Fax, E-mail, Computer Conference Systems, etc. are all very important in present organizations.

The second phenomenon is the revolution in organizational forms. In fact, new competitive requirements, a more dynamic environment, even new information technology have induced important changes in company behaviour. Thus, concepts like Lean Organization (Womack et al., 1990), Network Organization (Miles, Snow, 1996; Thorelli, 1986), Business Process Reengineering (Hammer, 1990), Learning Organization (Nonaka, Johnson, 1985), etc. have emerged. Perhaps now wc have good information technology but we do not have organization any more; organization, also because of or thanks to information technology, it is becoming more and more virtual (Davidow, Malone, 1992). But even so organizations continue to be defined through at least three important attributes or dimensions which characterise any company: the economic dimension, the social dimension, and the legal dimension. So researchers have to focus their attention on both the organizational dimension and the other ones.

The transactional cost theory highlighted the crucial question: why does an organization exist? (Williamson, 1975,1979; Ouchi, 1980; Milgrom, Roberts, 1992). Perhaps it is centred too much on a purely economic exchange concept (Migliarese, Ferioli, 1994, 1995) and neglects symbolic interpersonal transactions which always take place in any social interaction, as pointed out by psychologists, linguists and educators (Watzlawick et al., 1967; Bruner, 1986), but it provides a paradigm for understanding many present innovative organizational forms. But now we probably need a more powerful framework to explain every complex organizational phenomenon; this framework may be defined by the integration of different paradigms that till now have operated separately, such as the transactional, relational (Ferioli, 1994; Migliarese, Ferioli, 1995), linguistic, and others.

Returning to Decision Support Systems, in the early '80s their conceptual scheme included a Data Base, an adequate User Interface and, to underline the importance of suitable data processing models, a Model Base (Keen, Scott Morton, 1978). But in time it has evolved significantly to incorporate a Knowledge Base, an Expert System and, lastly, a Text Base "for providing not only quantitative but also qualitative information to the decision makers" (Hwang et al., 1995); see Figure 1.

We ask: is it really necessary to point out in a paper written for this purpose that text handling in Decision Support Systems is important too? Did not Hypertext Systems stress this need for any Management Information Systems at least from mid '80s (Conklin, 1987), with this term coined in the late '60s (Nelson, 1967)?.

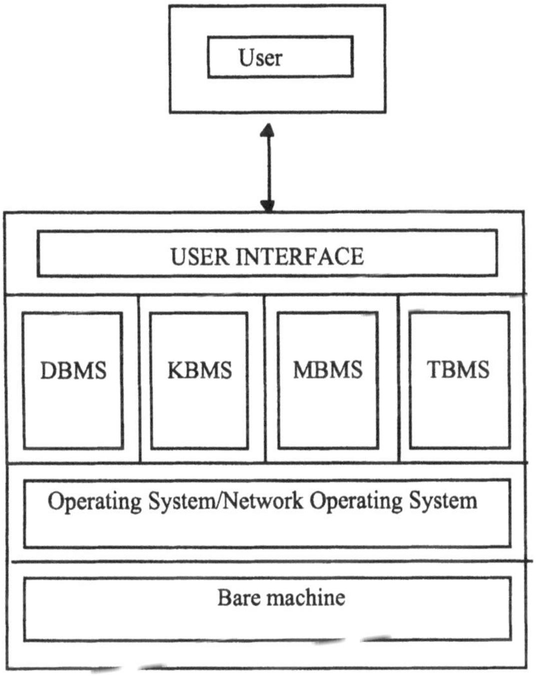

Figure 1 DSS conceptual scheme

However, the crucial question, even after so much work has been done, is still: have we understood properly the decisional process, especially when it takes place in the new organizational forms? Many problems are still open, such as:

1. Actors preferences are developed dynamically during problem resolution and during processes of interpretation construction, not before (March, 1987).

2. Rules come normally to code historical experiences that otherwise can not be made useful (March, Olsen, 1976).

3. Ambiguous problems are often better solved through exploratory resolution methods, not through quantitative models (Lindblom, 1959).

4. The meaning of a message, a problem, a symptom is defined through evocative exploration of the deep structure of the language (March, 1987).

5. Maybe we do not have to make decisions but just to wait for solutions to come to us (Harrigel, 1975).

Paradoxically these problems are particularly important in current virtual, magmatic, hypointegrated, quasi-market/quasi-clan (Ouchi, 1980) organizational forms.

Nevertheless, the discussion and the research work must go on. But one day perhaps we will find out that the really important question is: why do people enter organizations? Then the answer may be too complex and too simple at the same time... an ontological answer: people enter organizations because, they unconsciously hope, organized work permits them to go beyond space and time. But when we find this out, we will be able to say with Pessoa: "One day, when time is finished, our lives will meet again, but free from Places and Names".

2 FEATURES OF EMERGING HYPOINTEGRATED ORGANIZATIONS

The principal causes of the process of change that have been noted in the last decade show a wide-spread instability due to internal and external turbulence of organizations, and also to the rapid acceleration of change.

In order to be able to move within such a complex and heterogeneous context, some researchers consider it useful to refer to the theories based on chaos, which are becoming more and more popular even in study of management.

The main challenge in a firm is to generate competitive advantages within chaotic conditions of discontinuity, even by modifying the organization.

The change that seems relevant to the above aim is in the learning ability of the organization, this means the flexibility and the ability to continuously review strategic choices and to give attention to all signals especially those coming from the external environment (Nonaka, Johnson, 1985).

In order to create an environment oriented towards action learning, it is necessary to act on: the forms of management behaviour, going beyond the concept of uniformity, but evaluating the differences and disagreements, and the forms of relationships at the interpersonal and interfunctional level, by paying attention to real relationships between people and groups, leaving behind those tools of integration which seem too structured and procedural (Miggiani, Scilletta, 1992).

The element of "disorder" in the organization may be important and in some cases it's necessary to include it in the planning phase, in order to develop a system in which there is overflowing information, activities and management responsibilities (Nonaka, 1991). In fact, only in this way we can have the creation of common schemes and languages with major effectiveness in communication and in the distribution of information.

As an example, we might underline the difference between handbooks about organization existing in western companies, USA and Europe, and those existing in Japanese Companies (Nonaka, Johnson, 1985): while operating handbooks in the western world prescribe activities and responsibilities in detail, in Japan they focus on behaviour and values, and training is left to managers and to their ability to transmit competence and motivation and also to stimulate continuous improvements (Womack et al., 1990).

Learning is generated not only by internal relations, but also by the external ones and such relations are not only related to buying and selling, but also to "co-operation in generating/acquiring knowledge" (Miggiani, Scilletta, 1992).

The *network enterprise*, which any pushes organization towards learning and therefore towards innovation, is the suitable answer to the turbulence and instability of the environment. The model of the structured firm is characterised by stability in relations. Here the behaviour produces the structure, and vice-versa: the structure generates the behaviour but this also takes on a corrective value for structural evolution (Pilotti, 1990).

The elements that remain invariable are the rules which define the process of co-production: such rules take on the connotation of linguistic-communicative rules and in this context the new information technology assumes a central role.

The network enterprise doesn't have a permanent strategic and operating centre: it is changeable and determined from time to time according to the strategy adopted.

The term network enterprise, or network of companies, or organizational network indicates different classes of organizational forms. One class concerns the processes of activity decentralisation towards firms that are sub-suppliers. A second class concerns the enterprises connected to a particular area, for example the called "industrial districts" or "scientific and technological parks". A third type seems to be formed by associations - the Confederation of Agriculture, production co-operatives, or by special contract agreements.

However, a tendency that is worth underlining is the fact that many big companies organise themselves internally into independent units, i.e. business units, teams, project groups on the border of market and hierarchy.

This process of weakening structural connections produces new organizational forms, that we call *hypointegrated*.

These organizational forms present problems of control and observation because their memory is dispersed and their parts are connected in a very weak relations network, similarly with the territorial systems (Ciborra et al., 1977; Ciborra et al., 1982).

This leads to the need for an efficient co-ordination of the activities of all single sub-units, and also for some variables that have become essential for competitiveness: (a) the globalization, which brings the need of finding a compromise between a unitary management and an adequate perception of local situations; (b) the need to reduce the "time to market", which requires a better integration between functional units; (c) the necessity of better service to client; (d) the need to control and reduce costs.

The main problem of hypointegrated organizational forms is not decision support, but communication support, which has also important implications for individual or group decisions.

Of course, information technology has a key role for its capacity of co-ordinating different levels and different sub-units, connecting people of one organization or between different organizations (Rockart, Short, 1989).

3 COMMUNICATION SUPPORT VERSUS DECISION SUPPORT

In the past researchers' attention was directed mostly to the problem solving aspects, especially on individual levels, this was due to organizational models that used to concentrate the decision power in specific subjects, inside some organizations and arranged in certain hierarchic levels.

Decisions have been, and sometimes still are, characteristics of high level and intermediate management and the importance of the decisions then corresponds to the recognised power of a decision maker.

One of the models of problem solving maintains that during the process detailed instructions are carried out at an unconscious state, like computer programs, that organise in a sequence the complex myriad of information contained in our mind.

The decisional process is highlighted as a way of reacting to problems. In fact, in this process there are not only logical and analytic components that can run by means of analytical instruments, but also creativity, critical judgement and general ability that can be called "intuition".

Many researchers lead in the attempt to create operative models that can be used in practice and Lang, Dittrich and White (1978) gave us a wide review.

An important aspect in the decisional processes is that which examines the nature of the problem; this problem can be considered as a deviation from the rule - problem in its strict sense - or as a research into the best choice for the future.

In the first case, it deals with correcting or eliminating an undesired effect, in the second we face undefined situations, free from any exact solution, but rather with many possible results characterised by a different level of pleasure of the decision maker. It is this second aspect that characterises the actual corporate problems.

Faced with these questions, traditional schemes and structures seem to be old-fashioned, while other organizational forms develop solutions by co-operative activities.

The processes that become active in this case aren't analytical or quantitative, but holistic and qualitative and are based on the relation and communication ability of the same group.

The decision support or group decision support systems must demonstrate the capacity to integrate actively in the managerial decision process and to integrate actively in the group. This means we should elaborate models, valid for the different knowledge approaches that characterise the different decision makers.

Thus, the internal events require an adequate strategy of inference, for example the construction of a model. Whoever creates the model must mention explicitly the rules linking the sub-units (Kleinmuntz, 1966).

In the decisional process it is necessary to have at one's disposal information that, because of nature and complexity, will never be complete and exact. It is therefore necessary to have a correct definition of the information needed and an efficient data acquisition.

This data are necessary for the production/elaboration of products and services, distributed in the field and not located in the office.

The information requirements are often not well defined and therefore there is an information overload or it becomes unusable. Information requirements must consider opportunity, punctuality, availability and comprehensibility.

In fact, these characteristics are rarely found, especially in weak structures or in professional working groups, whose components can be also very distant geographically or structurally.

In these cases, the decisions belong to the group and have effects not only on the vertical structure, but mostly on a number of "cells" of collateral work, that can be defined as a group of persons whose energies are directed to common objectives, that operate well together, harmoniously and with good results (Francis, Young 1979).

These cells can be composed of people with different skills and coming from various working, geographic, cultural backgrounds, usually without formal leadership.

The use of technology must allow people to meet with unlimited time, place or presence, realising, when necessary, a sort of permanent meeting.

It is important to point out the emergence of new concepts of "space" and "information/product", when space isn't only real, but virtual, because of information technology. The information/product must have in this virtual space different representations; it is necessary therefore to articulate the information as "public", "shared" or "private".

As an example, we mention the demonstration system DICUN (Distributed International Communications Using Networks - 1990) which was developed in the ambit of the European RACE project to study international interactions of a groupware between different multimedia workstations. It shows that the interpersonal relation between the components of those virtual groups seem to become friendly and that the groups seem to be steadily "oriented towards work".

During the realisation of a new product/service, we note in these groups the constitution of "cells" of independent work from the traditional hierarchy, with an acceleration of useful exchanges.

In fact hypointegrated organizations are often made by actors having equal power and the same rights and generate "bossless" organizational situations.

4 THE COMMUNICATION PROCESS IN BOSSLESS SITUATIONS

It has become necessary to develop the interfunctional collaboration, operating deeply on the mechanisms that establish the connective tissue of the firm (Milana, 1991).

While the control systems and management by objective are fundamental instruments to orient, value and control the firm's and the individual's actions and results, the internal communication plays an important role in supporting and diffusing the culture of the service and the total quality and information systems can facilitate notably the intersection.

In fact, the structure of company communication models can influence, by it self, the way of being and behaving in terms of safety, responsibility and independence. The same structure can also influence the way of operating of a group in terms of speed, exactness and adaptability.

If we consider two schemes of communication as in Figure 2, where the arrows represent bi-directional communications, we notice how the star scheme shows the presence of a leader that determines and manages the transactions. It is therefore an autocratic organization where the decisional power is concentrated in the hands of one subject. The circular scheme instead is typical of an open and democratic organization, where the whole group participates in the decisions, because communication between the subjects is free to flow in every direction.

It seems also that the models of communication of this type are more functional in the introduction and consolidation of the firm transformation phases (Bavelas, Strauss, 1962) and that co-operation is the best way of managing hypointegrated situations (Greiner, 1972).

It is evident, then, how the ability to establish efficient interpersonal relations and therefore to develop effective communication transaction is the critical knot of the new organization forms. In fact communication services create the "nervous tissue" of the firm.

As regards this, in a communication process, not only the "text" but the following four aspects are fundamental (Kjolseth, 1972):

1. the *background knowledge*, i.e. the knowledge people possess;
2. the *foreground knowledge*, i.e. the knowledge of the communication rules regarding different situations;
3. the *emergent grounds*, i.e. specific rules necessary during communication process;
4. the *transcendent grounds*, i.e. what determines the bounds of relevance in a specific situation.

It is well worth underlining that communication is more or less important in every organizational situation: in the bossless ones, however, it assumes a central role in co-ordinating and integrating activities and also in the decision making process that becomes collaborative.

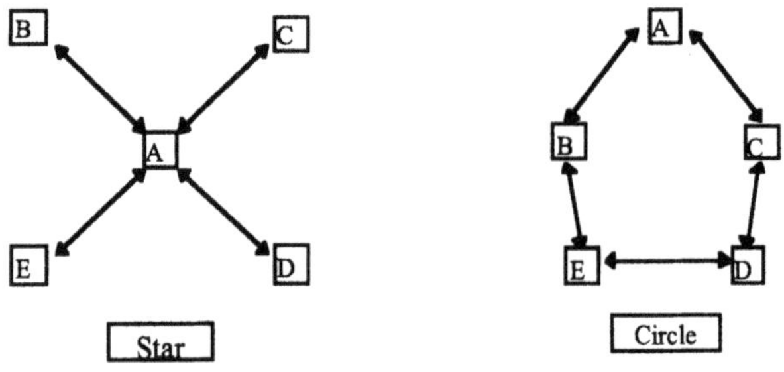

Figure 2 Two schemes of communicational process

5 CRITERIA FOR USING AVAILABLE INFORMATION TECHNOLOGY

After considering the central role of the communication process in emerging organization forms, especially in the hypointegrated and bossless ones, we'll focus our attention on the importance of using the available information technology in an effective way.

We'll suggest organizational criteria for the implementation of effective, efficient and reliable information systems to support work, decisions and communication.

The dream of software systems designers remains interoperability, i.e. the possibility to integrate in one system different devices, processors, Operating Systems, software platforms, application packages, etc.

Waiting for this dream to become reality, maybe across the realisation of a software portable layer integrator, that works as interface between basic platforms such as operating systems, Database Management Systems, etc. and external application packages - hoping it isn't a "Waiting for Godot" - we must integrate what is available on the market in the best possible way.

In the market, besides powerful and sophisticated operating systems and network operating systems, we have Hypertext Systems, productivity tools and Project Management systems; enhanced database management systems, even multimedia or multidimensional, whose technology is already mature; packages of Product Data Management and Engineering Document Management, Work Flow Management systems, middleware for the development of applications centred on firm processes; all these software systems are waiting to become appropriately integrated.

The integration of instruments and environments can happen on a work flow management platform that permits a co-ordination of information and people engaged in work groups. Work flow management systems that rely on special relational databases embedded in developing environments, possibly object oriented, give a first answer to problems of interfunctional integration by means of the *vault*, a common database system where data, documents, etc. are stored and managed as in Figure 3.

The integration of the virtual organizational parts can be based on a technological infrastructure client/server to which it is easy and possible to join, even temporarily with a portable personal computer, possibly extracted from a special chassis.

The nodes of technological infrastructure don't coincide with the organization units or people, i.e. with the nodes of the organizational network; they are only doors, entrance points to the network. The technological infrastructure is a hyper-network where it is possible to define many different organizational networks.

Every project group, team, task force, etc., in which empowerment is one of the most important keywords, must define the requirements of the technological system it wants to use. The users, in a learning organization perspective, must take the initiative and define their needs in terms of information, decision support, communication, external interface, connection to network functionalities.

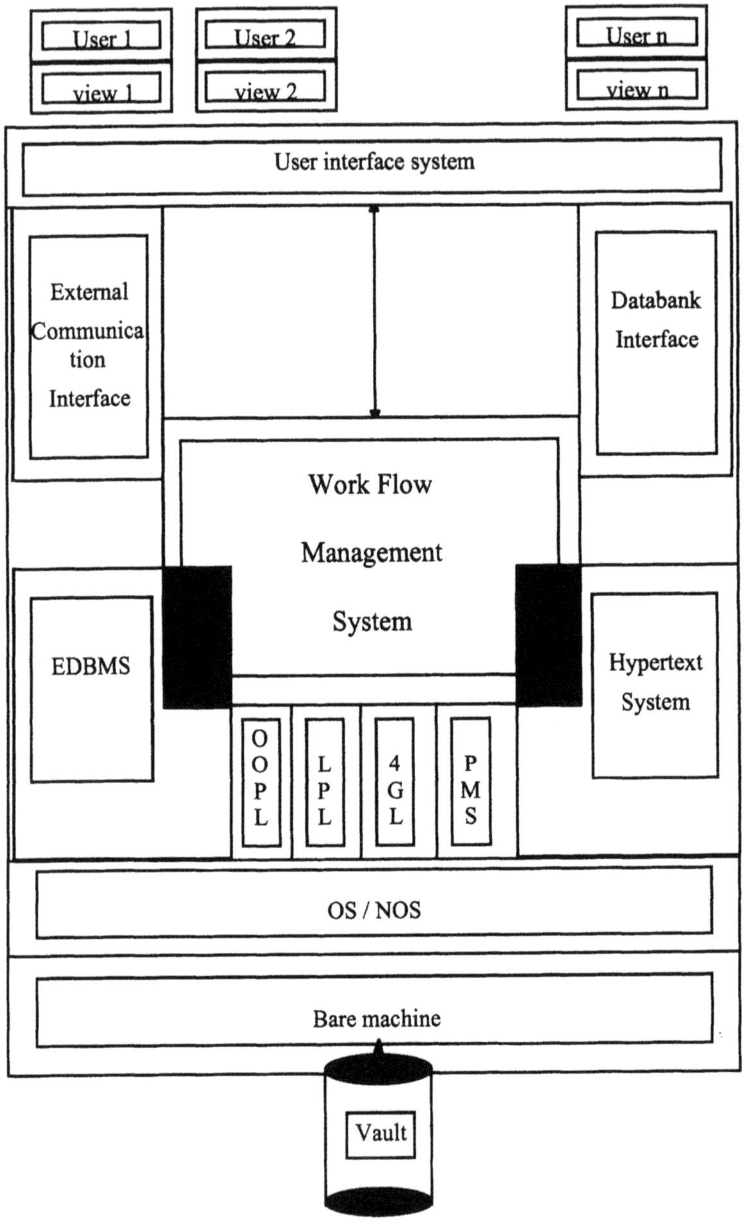

Figure 3 Information Technology integration model

In this phase the users must be helped, according to the dimensions of the group, from one or more information technology-organizational consultants, coming from management information systems unit or function. These consultants operate similarly to the maintenance employees and have a particular professional skill: they have good knowledge of computer science and a certain sensibility for business and organization problems.

The first thing to be done is to define correctly the nodes of the organization network - single person or group or organizational unit - and the relations between these nodes. This work has to be done co-operatively and will be defined across an hypertext software system: on the relative hyper-graph nodes, relations, functions, tasks, working instruments will be defined. A copy of this organizational model could be installed in every node of the technological network which corresponds to a node of the organizational network.

Much attention must be dedicated to system security and reliability, even though the importance of this problem differs from case to case. In particular, we must consider the problems of data integrity and consistency; they must be treated carefully in the definition of the data scheme and in the analysis of the redundancies (Date, 1986). The problem is particularly critical when data are distributed. In this case, in order to avoid too many data transfers and too many break downs and recovery of the system for the execution of complex protocols, it is worth making some duplicate copies of data in different sites. In this way, if a place has all the data it needs, the only transfer of data necessary is when we must carry out remote updates.

Other technical problems regard the incorrectness of data that happens when we have the execution of concurrent transactions and when we have the failure of the system; these problems must be administrated with accurate lock and unlock clause, with special log transactions and adequate recovery protocols. Finally we have problems that stem from

the distribution of transactions, these must be managed with two phase commitment protocols (Ullman, 1982).

Moreover in the distribution of data the problem of location of fragments of relations in different nodes of the network becomes critical. An accurate assignment of horizontal fragments - only some lines - or vertical fragments - only some columns - can reduce significantly the transfer of data from one node to another of the network. It is always possible to reform data across ordinary or special SQL clauses like union, intersect, except, not in, join.

6 INFORMATION TECHNOLOGY IN A PLANNING PROJECT

To realise the urban regional co-ordination plan of Calabria, the most southern region of the Italian peninsula, a working group formed by many skilled people who operate in the Universities of Cosenza and Reggio Calabria was established. This working group identified the first instrument of co-ordination in the regional periodic conferences which were attended by the interested parties, even only as suppliers or users of the information of the plan. The territory is an hypointegrated system so the plan and the planning process required particular attitude from the operators involved.

The working group was divided into subgroups formed by interdependent units that require continuous information exchange, besides a support for the decisions or for projection, such as Geographical Information Systems, Computer Aided Design systems, etc.

The information system design, conceived together with the project group, proposed to use information technology as communication, co-ordination, decision support for users, information sources and project groups, in the phase of realisation of the plan as well as in the phase of putting the plan into operation. The information system project examined three principal aspects (Cariati et al., 1993): (a) definition of the technological infrastructure - hardware, software and communication networks - necessary to collect, store and communicate information; (b) definition of the organizational structure in terms of behaviour, resources, tasks, competencies, responsibilities for efficient management of the technological infrastructure and the information; (c) definition of standards, methodology, and instruments that make sure the information system doesn't become, once the plan becomes reality, a "cathedral in the desert".

For this purpose we proposed a guide scheme that consists of an "informative contract" among people that operate in the region and are therefore interested in the project as information users or suppliers; this was to avoid obsolescence and inconsistency of the managed information, which is the principal resource of the system.

As regards the technological infrastructures, technicians together with main users realised a system based on three principal nodes, located near the three principal centres involved in the planning processes and in the realisation of the plan itself, i.e. the "Office of Plan", University of Calabria and University of Reggio Calabria.

To these three principal points all those people involved in the plan and those interested in the information system must be connected, for example institutions - Chamber of Commerce, Professional Associations, etc. - as users and as information sources. The emerging system is a computer network providing also sectorial data banks created on the base of the information collected or produced by the system, to which the extemporaneous users of the system will derive, i.e. those users not directly involved in the planning work or in the realisation process of the plan.

The principal nodes of the system have a general structure that includes:

1. Multimedia database that organises in a unique conceptual scheme all the information regarding the region and the plan;

2. Information sources interfaces across which the system acquires the information coming from the area;

3. User interfaces and work support tools across which the users retrieve information from the system and submit elaboration, simulations, evaluations, etc. Among these we have:
   - interface to data-banks from extemporaneous users;
   - plan user interface;
   - decision support environment;
   - work support tools;

4. Management module for the information system.

7 CONCLUSIONS

In this research we started by considering the dynamic and changeable nature of modern companies in the face of environmental turbulence.

In fact, the environment was becoming more and more chaotic and, in this context, hypointegrated organizations, characterised by weak structural links and by a dispersed memory where the communication process becomes the central aspect, emerged.

After discussing the peculiarities of the emerging organization forms, even taking into account the principal theories, our work analyses the communication process because communication becomes the co-ordinating and integrating instrument, bound to the ability of using the available media in an effective way.

We have suggested organizational criteria for integrating available information technologies to implement effective, efficient and reliable systems to support work, decisions and communication in hypointegrated organizations. According to our model, in a learning organization vision, users should define, with the help of technicians, communication, decision and work support requirements.

Finally, we presented an application of the proposed information technology integration model: the Urban Regional Co-ordination Planning project, an ongoing project in Calabria.

Further developments of this research would be: (a) the definition of an interpretation theory of the new organization forms that seem to have the characteristic of hypointegration, that is able to integrate relational, transactional, linguistic-communication approaches that usually operated independently; (b) the realisation of applications of the information technology integration model in different organizational context to test its validity further; (c) the definition of a training model for users to also develop the appropriate response to organizational needs.

8 REFERENCES

Bavelas, A. and Strauss G. (1962) Group Dynamics and Intergroup Relations, in *The Planning of Change* (eds K. Benne and R. Chin), New York, Holt, Rinehart & Winston.

Bruner, J. (1986) *Actual Minds, Possible Worlds*. Harvard Univ. Press, Cambridge, Mass.

Cariati, T. and , G. and Saccà, D. (1993) Sistema Informativo per il Piano di Coordinamento Regionale della Calabria, in *Report at the Regional Government*.

Cariati, T. and Ciborra, C. and Maggiolini, P. (1989) Office Information Systems Planning: the Transactional Perspective, in *Organization and Information Systems* (eds Z. Kaltuekar, J. Gricar), Bled, Slovenia.

Carta, G. (1989) Innovazione e Cambiamento Organizzativo. *L'Impresa*, **4**, 78-84.

Ciborra, C. (1984) Management Information Systems: a Contractual View, in *Beyond Productivity: Information Systems Development for Organizational Effectiveness* (ed Th.M.A. Bemelmans), North-Holland, Amsterdam.

Ciborra, C. (1989) *Tecnologie di coordinamento*. Franco Angeli, Milano.

Ciborra, C. and Gasbarri, G. and Maggiolini, P. (1977) Systèmes d'information et systèmes d'organisation hypointégrés. *Modelisation et maîtrise des systèmes*. Editions hommes et techniques, Paris.

Ciborra, C. and Maggiolini, P. and Migliarese, P. (1982) Regional Information Systems: Alternative Models and Design Strategies, in *Evolutionary Information Systems* (ed. J. Hawgood), North Holland, Amsterdam.

Conklin, J. (1987) Hypertext: an Introduction and Survey. *IEEE Computer*, September 1987.

Date, C.J. (1986) *Introduction to Database Systems*. Addison Wesley, Reading, Mass.

Davidow, W.H. and Malone, M.S. (1992) The virtual corporation. *Harper Business*, New York.

Ferioli, C. (1994) La relazione come modello di legami nelle reti organizzative interne, in *Le relazioni interorganizzative*, Workshop AiIG, Bologna.

Francis, D. and Young, D. (1979) *Improving work groups; a practical manual for team building*. University Associates, San Diego, California.

Galbraith, J.R. (1977) *Designing Complex Organizations*. Addison Wesley, Reading, Mass.

Greiner, L.E. (1972) Evolution and Revolution as Organizations Grow. *Harvard Business Review*, July-August, 37-46.

Hammer, M. (1990) Re-engineering Work: Don't Automate, Obliterate. *Harvard Business Review*.

Herrigel, E. (1975) *Lo Zen e il tiro con l'arco*. Adelphi, Milano.

Hersey, P. and Blancherd, K. (1982) *Management of Organizational Behavior*. Prentice-Hall Inc., Englewood Cliffs, N.J.

Hwang, C. and Conlon, S. and Gillenwater, E. (1995) *Incorporating a Text Base into Decision Support Systems*. (not yet published report).

Keen, P.G. and Scott Morton, M.S. (1978) *Decision Support Systems: an Organizational Perspective*. Addison Wesley, Reading Mass.

Kjolseth, R. (1972) Making Sense: Natural Language and Shared Knowledge in Understanding, in *Advances in the Sociology of Language* (ed. J. Fishman) The Hague, Mouton.

Kleinmuntz, B. (1966) *Problem Solving: Research, Method and Theory*. John Wiley & Sons, New York.

Lang, J.R. and Dittrich, J. and White, S. (1978) Managerial problem solving models: a review and a proposal. *Academy of Management Review*, October.

Lewin, K. (1947) Group Decision and Social Change, in *Readings in Social Psychology* (eds T.M. Newcomb and E.L. Hartley), Holt, New Jersey.

Lindblom, C.E. (1959) The Science of Modelling Through. *Public Administration Review*.

March, J.G. and Olsen, J.P. (1976) The uncertainty of the Past: Organizational Learn Under Ambiguity. *European Journal of Political Research*.

March, J.G. (1987) Ambiguity and Accounting: the Elusive Link between Information and Decision Making. *Accounting, Organization and Society*.

Miggiani, F. and Scilletta, V. (1992) Progettare l'apprendimento organizzativo. *Sviluppo & Organizzazione*, **133**, Set/Ott.

Migliarese, P. and Ferioli, C. (1995) Strumenti organizzativi ed informatici di collaborazione nell'impresa innovativa, in *Organizzazione, risorse umane, e processi innovativi nello sviluppo del sistema delle imprese*, Workshop AiIG, Torino.

Milana, P. (1991) Service management e interfunzionalità. *Harvard Espansione*, **52**, settembre, 89-96.

Miles, R. and Snow, C. (1986) Network Organizations: New Concepts for New Forms. *California Management Review*.

Milgrom, P. and Roberts, J. (1992) *Economics, Organization and Management*, Prentice Hall Inc., New Jersey.

Nelson, T.H. (1967) Getting it out of our System, in *Information Retrieval: A Critical Review* (ed. Schechter), Thompson Books, Wash.

Nonaka, I. (1991) The knowledge-creating company. *Harvard Business Review*.

Nonaka, I. and Johnson, J. K. (1985) Organizational learning in Japanese companies. *California Management Review*.

Ouchi, W.G. (1980) Markets, Bureaucracies and Clans. *Administrative Science Quarterly*, October 1980.

Pilotti, L. (1990) Dall'impresa-struttura all'impresa-progetto: dalle transazioni ai linguaggi nelle forme di impresa a rete. *Economia e politica industriale*, **65**.

Rockart, J. F. and Short, J. E. (1989) It in the 1990s: Managing Organizational Interdependence. *Sloan Management Review*, Winter.

Saccà, D. (1995) *Sistemi evoluti di basi di dati*. Franco Angeli, Milano.

Simon, H.A. (1977) *The new Science of Management Decision*. Prentice Hall, New Jersey.

Thorelli, H. (1986) Networks: between markets and hierarchies. *Strategic Management Journal*.

Ullman, J.D. (1982) *Principles of Database Systems*. Computer Science Press Inc.

Watzlawick, P. and Blavin, J.H. and Jackson, D.D. (1967) *Pragmatic of Human Communication*. W.W. Norton & Co, New York.

Williamson, O.E. (1979) Transactional-cost Economics: the Governance of Contractual Relations. *Journal of Law and Economics*, October 1979.

Williamson, O.E. (1975) *Markets and Hierarchies: Analysis and Antitrust Implications*. The Free Press, New York.

Womack, J.P. and Jones, D.T. and Roos, D. (1990) *The Machine that Changed the World*. Rawson.

9 BIOGRAPHY

Tomasso Cariati graduated in Management Engineering from University of Calabria, Italy, in 1984. Later he attended a post graduate course of Software Engineering and started to carry out research in Management Information Systems and Organizational Systems, areas in which he is currently involved. He also worked as a consultant for several companies. At present he is lecturer of Economics and Management in the Faculty of Engineering at the University of Calabria, Italy.

Gianpaolo Iazzolino graduated in Management Engineering in 1993. Since graduating he has continued his research into new forms of organization, both internal and external, and their link with innovation processes. He has taught in the Engineering faculty of the University of Calabria. He is currently involved in a research project, "Innovative organizational models", in the Department of Business Organization.

Anna Tancredi has a degree in psychology from the University of Roma. At present she is working as an educational consultant for several companies. She has also participated in designing educational multimedia products.

7

Individual and organizational effectiveness: Perspectives on the impact of ESS in multinational organizations

Sven A. Carlsson
Department of Informatics
School of Economics and Management, Lund University, Ole Römers väg 6
S-223 63 Lund, SWEDEN
sven.carlsson@ics.lu.se

Dorothy E. Leidner
Information Systems Department
Hankamer School of Business, Baylor University, P.O. Box 98005
Waco, Texas 76798, USA
Dorothy_Leidner@baylor.edu

Joyce J. Elam
Department of Decision Sciences and Information Systems
Florida International University, University Park Campus
Miami, Florida 33199, USA
elamj@servax

Abstract

Individual and organizational effectiveness are foundations of Information Systems' theory, research, and practice. In this paper, Quinn and associates' competing values approach (CVA) of organizational effectiveness is used for discussing and assessing the impacts of Executive Support Systems (ESS) on managerial behavior and leadership. It is suggested that an ESS is effective to the extent that it supports top-level managers and executives in promoting organizational effectiveness and that the ESS should effectively support the managers in their different managerial roles. A CVA-based analysis of data from interviews with ESS users in Mexico and Sweden suggests that ESS can support managerial behavior and leadership in different ways. Based on the empirical study and CVA, four archetypes of ESS use are suggested. The study has implications for: 1) ESS theory and research in that it links ESS use to behavioral complexity, and 2) ESS design and implementation in that it suggests a complementary view of the purposes of ESS.

Keywords

Executive Support Systems, Executive Information Systems, Implementation, Effectiveness, Assessment, Leadership, Behavioral Complexity

1 INTRODUCTION

Executive Support Systems (ESS) and Executive Information Systems (EIS) are computer-based information systems that purport to support top-level managers in their work. A growing number of organizations and managers are using ESS/EIS (Fitzgerald, 1992; Watson et al., 1992; Nord & Nord, 1995). ESS and EIS are Information System (IS) products that are applied to the administrative core of organizations for business administrative process innovations (Swanson, 1994). When such systems are used by top management, their impacts on strategic decision making have the potential of being significant (Rockart & De Long, 1988; Elam & Leidner, 1995; Leidner & Elam, 1995; Leidner et al., 1995; Molloy & Schwenk, 1995). Research that examines ESS use and the impacts of ESS use is needed.

Research suggests that two requisites of effective leadership are cognitive complexity and well-developed mental models (Bartunek et al., 1983; Streufert & Swezey, 1986; Weick, 1979; Lord & Maher, 1991; Isenberg, 1994). The relationship between ESS use and mental models has been addressed. Rockart and DeLong (1988) suggest that ESS by improving access to internal and external data, by combining data from multiple sources, by presenting data in meaningful formats, and by providing analytical capabilities, may enhance senior managers' mental models. An empirical study of roughly 100 EIS users examining the effects of EIS use found that the length of use and/or frequency of use were positively related to mental model enhancement (Leidner et al., 1995). Vandenbosch and Higgins (1995) found in a survey of 73 executives that perceptions of competitive performance resulting from ESS use were strongly related to mental-model building. Mental-model building is the process of changing mental models either to handle disconfirming information or to fit with new environments. Vandenbosch and Higgins did not find any relationship between competitive performance and mental-model maintenance.

Although research suggests that cognitive complexity is a necessary condition for effective leadership, more recent research has questioned whether it is a sufficient condition (Hooijberg & Quinn, 1991; Hart & Quinn, 1993; Denison et al., 1995). These researchers suggest that the sufficient condition is "...behavioral complexity which connotes action as well as cognition; that is, effective leadership must be the ability to both conceive and perform multiple and contradictory roles." (Denison et al., 1995). Building in part on these researchers' results and suggestions, this paper will address the linkages between ESS use and executive behavior and leadership.

The competing values approach (CVA), developed by Robert Quinn and associates, provides a comprehensive framework of organizational effectiveness and suggests linkages between managerial behavior and organizational effectiveness. A premise of this paper is that an ESS is effective to the extent that it supports top-managers and executives in promoting organizational effectiveness by providing support for the various managerial roles of managers. This study investigates how top managers in multinational corporations utilize ESS in their management activities. In discussing and assessing the impacts of ESS, the competing values approach is used. This study thus aims to shed some light on the relationship between ESS use, managerial behavior, and organizational effectiveness.

The remainder of the paper is organized as follows: the next section briefly discusses ESS research. It is followed by a section that presents the Quinn et al.'s competing values approach (CVA). Section 4 presents the study and the research methodology. The section following uses the CVA to discuss and assess the effects of ESS use on managerial behavior and suggests four archetypes of ESS use. The final section discusses limitations, conclusions, and suggestions for further research.

2 EXECUTIVE SUPPORT SYSTEMS AND ESS RESEARCH

Executive Information Systems (EIS) and Executive Support Systems (ESS) are sometimes used interchangeably, but some researchers refer to ESS as systems with a broader set of capabilities than EIS (Rockart & De Long, 1988). For example, ESS can include modeling and analysis capabilities (e.g., trend analysis, decision support systems and query capabilities) and provide capabilities like electronic communication (e.g., e-mail, computer conferencing, and word processing), and other office information systems capabilities (e.g., automated roledex, tickler files, and electronic calendars). Vandenbosch and Higgins (1995) found that the type of analysis that had a positive impact on executives' mental-model building included: "determining which data will be seen together and hence, which will be compared; selecting presentation formats; manipulating rows, columns, and sort order of reports; and 'mucking around in the data,' calculating single ratios or differences depending on what strikes them as important when they see the numbers." This suggests that the use of analysis capabilities in ESS is rather simple compared to what can be found in advanced Decision Support Systems. In this paper we use the term ESS instead of EIS for the following reasons: 1) it refers to a broader set of capabilities, and 2) the computer-based systems we studied can best be categorized as ESS, i.e., they had ESS capabilities.

Our view of ESS is that it is not a particular type of information technology (IT) in a restricted sense, but primarily a perspective on executives and executive work and on the role of information technology and computer-based systems as executive support tools. There is room for different perspectives on ESS and therefore also room for different ways to assess the effects of ESS use. A problem with ESS theory and research is that the construct ESS implies no specific role or purpose, solely that the ESS supports whatever role the executive follows or has chosen. Other types of systems have clearer roles and purposes -- see, for example, the discussion and definition of Decision Support Systems in Keen and Scott Morton (1978) and Silver (1991). Executives play many different roles and the importance of the roles changes over time. An alternative is to view ESS as support by design. Taking a support by design perspective means that the context where an ESS is to be used has to be understood. It also means that issues of how and when an ESS is to be used have to be raised as well as discussions of impact measures. This will be addressed in Sections 3 and 5.

Past ESS research consists of descriptions of ESS implementations in organizations (Applegate & Osborn, 1988; Rockart & De Long, 1988; Osborn & Applegate, 1989; Houdeshel & Watson, 1987; Simons, 1992), frameworks for the study of ESS (Millet & Mawhinney, 1990; Carlsson & Widmeyer, 1990), development issues (Volonino & Watson, 1990, 1990-91; Watson et al., 1991; Houdeshel, 1990; Rockart & De Long, 1988; Walls et al., 1992; Carlsson & Widmeyer, 1994), and more recently, theory-based studies that examine the impact of ESS from the users' perspective (Leidner & Elam, 1993-94, 1995; Molloy & Schwenk, 1995; Vandenbosch & Higgins, 1995; Leidner et al., 1996; Watson et al., 1995) A general goal when designing and implementing an ESS is that it should lead to effective use. The construct "effective use" forces attention to the dependent variable(s), that is, it forces attention to performance. Discussing, defining, and applying performance variables is essential if the ESS field is to make further inroads into understanding the phenomena involved in designing, building, implementing, using, and assessing ESS. Using DeLone and McLean's (1992) IS success framework, one finds that most empirical EIS/ESS studies use as success measures: ESS quality, ESS information quality, ESS use, and/or user satisfaction -- for more extensive reviews of ESS research, see, for example, Sprague and Watson (1996) or Leidner et al. (1995, 1996). Based on reviews of EIS/ESS studies, we suggest that more exhaustive studies focusing on individual impact and organizational impact are needed as well as studies that are grounded in management and organization theories.

The study reported in this paper is part of an on-going project on ESS which aims to enhance existing ESS knowledge. In the first phase a survey study in the U.S., Sweden, and Mexico was conducted. It was based on a decision making perspective and hence the generalizations might be limited to that area (Leidner et al., 1996). In the second phase, reported here, a field study was done in several corporations in Mexico and Sweden. One of the purposes of the field study was to focus on factors not covered in the survey study. Carlsson and Widmeyer (1994) have suggested that the competing values approach can be used as one way to conceptualize ESS as well as being a reference theory for an ESS design approach. In this paper we use recent CVA studies as a foundation for discussing and assessing the impact of ESS use.

3 THE COMPETING VALUES APPROACH AND ESS ASSESSMENT

Organizational effectiveness is one of the foundations of management and organization theory, research, and practice (Lewin & Minton, 1986) and it is also central in the IS field (De Lone & McLean, 1992). Effectiveness is a dependent variable that lies at the very center of all organization theory (Lewin and Minton, 1986). In recent years we have seen different efforts in developing organizational effectiveness constructs. The competing values approach (CVA) was, in part, developed to clarify effectiveness (Quinn, 1988; Quinn and Rohrbaugh, 1981, 1983).

CVA perceives organizations as paradoxical (Cameron, 1986; Quinn & Cameron, 1988) and it suggests that to achieve high performance requires an organization and its top-managers to simultaneously perform paradoxical and contradictory roles and capabilities (Hart & Quinn, 1993). The competing values model of organizational effectiveness incorporates three fundamental paradoxes acknowledged in the literature: flexibility and spontaneity vs. stability and predictability (related to organizational structure); internal vs. external (related to organizational focus); and means vs. ends (Quinn & Rohrbaugh, 1983; Quinn, 1988) -- see Figure 1.

Quinn and Rohrbaugh (1983; Rohrbaugh, 1981) found that most measures of effectiveness reflect one of four organizational models: human relations model, internal process model, rational goal model, or open systems model. The four quadrants in Figure 1 provide competing views on the meaning of organizational effectiveness. The human relations model is characterized by a focus on internal flexibility to develop employee cohesion and morale. It stresses human resource development and participation. The internal process model is characterized by a focus on internal control and uses information management, information processing, and communication to develop stability and control. The rational goal model is characterized by a focus on external control and relies on planning and goal setting to gain productivity and accomplishment. The open systems model is characterized by a focus on external flexibility and relies on readiness and flexibility to gain growth, resource acquisition, and external support.

The competing values model points out the simultaneous opposition in the criteria that organizational members use to judge effectiveness. An organization does not pursue a single set of criteria. Instead an organization pursues competing, or paradoxical, criteria simultaneously. Organizations are more or less good in pursuing the criteria, and, according to the CVA, organizations differ in their effectiveness.

The CVA has been used by some researchers in the IS field. McCartt and Rohrbaugh (1989, 1995) have used it to assess GDSS and to explain failure and success in implementing GDSS. Carlsson and Widmeyer (1990, 1994) have used it to develop a conceptualization of ESS and to discuss how different technological building blocks can be used in building ESS. Stein and Zwass (1995) have used it to suggest how to support organizational memory with information systems.

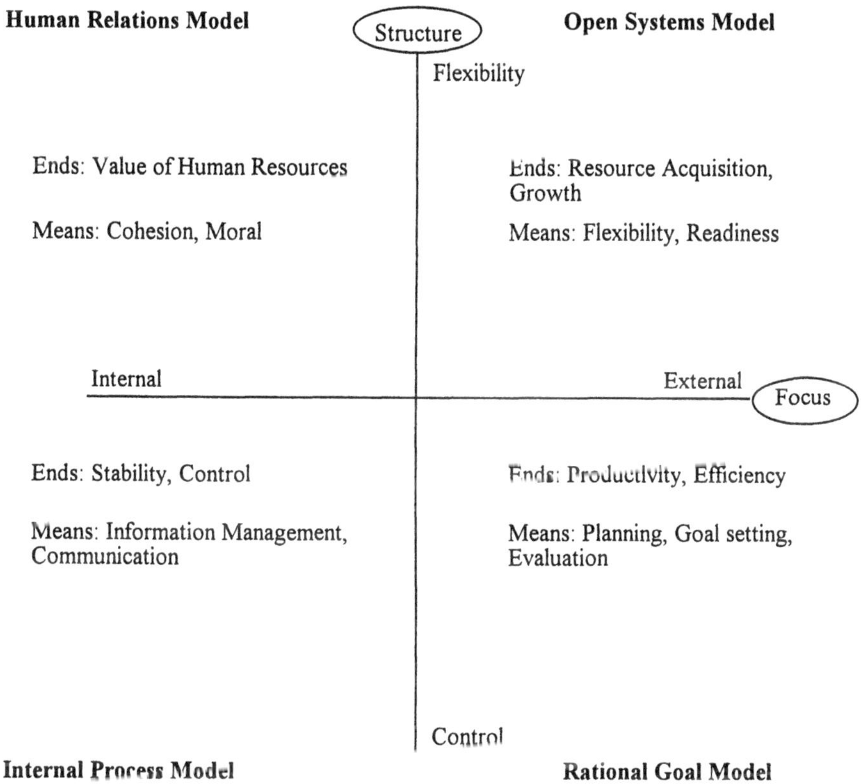

Figure 1 The competing values model of organizational effectiveness. Adapted from Quinn and Rohrbaugh (1983).

3.1 Managerial roles

Quinn (1988; Quinn et al., 1990) translated the construct of effectiveness into managerial roles (Table 1). Table 1 presents the four organizational models and the associated managerial roles.

INTERNAL PROCESS MODEL: Emphasizes measurement, information management, and information processing; historical and present times oriented; focuses on analyzing static data, cross-sectional data, and giving snapshot views.

- Monitor Role: In this role a manager collects and distributes information (mainly internal and quantitative information), checks performance using traditional measures, and provides a sense of stability and continuity.
- Coordinator Role: In this role a manager maintains structure and flow of the systems, does scheduling, organizes and coordinates activities (logistic issues), solve house keeping issues, and sees that standards, goals and objectives, and rules are met.

RATIONAL GOAL MODEL: Task clarification; goal and objectives setting; decision making; decision implementation (action); achievement oriented.

- Director Role: In this role a manager clarifies expectations, goals and purposes through planning and goal setting, defines problems, establishes goals, generates and evaluates alternatives, generates rules and policies, evaluates performances.
- Producer Role: In this role a manager emphasises performance, motivates members to accomplish stated goals, gives feedback to members, and is engaged in and supports the action phase of decision making.

OPEN SYSTEMS MODEL: Future oriented; analyze cues and information from a dynamic and longitudinal view (a "moving picture" view); multiple focuses; influencing and being influenced by the environment; adaptability and flexibility.

- Innovator Role: In this role a manager interacts with the environment, monitors the external environmental (environmental scanning), identifies important trends, is engaged in business and competitive intelligence (relying on induction and intuition), develops mental models, convinces others about what is necessary and desirable, facilitates change, and shares "image and mental models."
- Broker Role: In this role a manager obtains external resources, is engaged in external communication, tries to influence the environment, and maintains the unit's external legitimacy through the development, scanning, and maintenance of a network of external contacts.

HUMAN RELATIONS MODEL: Process-oriented; stresses cohesion, consensus and healthy conflicts, and teamwork; human resources and the development of commitment; information sharing and participative decision making.

- Facilitator Role: In this role a manager fosters collective effort, tries to build cohesion and teamwork (building the trustful organization), facilitates participation and group problem solving and decision making, pursues "moral" commitment, and is engaged in conflict management.
- Mentor Role: In this role a manager is engaged in the development of people by listening and being supportive, is engaged in the development of individual plans, and gives feedback (for individual development).

Table 1 Key characteristics of the four organizational models and the associated managerial roles -- adapted from Quinn (1988), Quinn et al. (1990), and Denison et al. (1995).

The descriptions of the organizational models and the associated managerial roles focus on aspects related to managerial behavior and information and knowledge work.

After Quinn and Rohrbaugh's initial studies, work on CVA has proceeded. The CVA model has been validated (Quinn, 1988), and used to study executive leadership (Quinn, 1988; Hart & Quinn, 1993) and overall organizational effectiveness (Hart & Quinn, 1993). Recent research suggests that effective executives are capable of balancing and performing contradictory and complex roles (Hart & Quinn, 1993; Hart & Banbury, 1994) such as being both opportunistic and strategic. The focus of some studies has been on explaining why some executives are considered more successful than others (Quinn, 1988). More recent research suggests that it is possible to link executive behavior to firm performance; for example, Hart and Quinn's (1993) study suggests that executives that have the ability to play multiple and competing roles produce better firm performance, especially with respect to organizational growth and innovation (business performance) and organizational (stakeholder) effectiveness. In a recent study, Denison et al. (1995) empirically tested the CVA model and the associated roles. They found support for the model and the roles, especially for managers that were considered high performing. Denison et al.'s (1995) work has led them to define effective leadership as "*...the ability to perform the multiple roles and behaviors that circumscribe the requisite variety implied by an organizational or environmental context.*" (Denison et al., 1995)

From our point of view, the CVA model and the research derived thereof have several characteristics fruitful to explore from an ESS perspective. First, they are related to a critical construct: organizational effectiveness. Second, they have a paradox and complexity perspective on effectiveness and managerial roles enabling an explanation of contradiction deemed necessary in recent research (Robey, 1995). Third, the effectiveness construct has been translated into managerial roles, problem orientations, and managerial behavior. This makes it possible to discuss how ESS can be used to support top-level managers in their different roles. Lastly, they point out that not all ESS are equally effective.

Based on the CVA, we suggest that an ESS is effective to the extent that it promotes organizational effectiveness by supporting managers in their varied managerial roles. Our definition of effective ESS use has implications for how learning is perceived. Several researchers have defined learning as being primarily cognitive. Huber says that "An entity learns if, through its processing of information, the range of its potential behaviors is changed." (Huber, 1991). This definition of learning was used by Vandenbosch and Higgins (1995). They said that an ESS user had learned if system use had led to the potential for change in performance. Based on our definition of effective ESS use we suggest that learning is both cognitive and behavioral, that is, an ESS user learns if system use leads to the potential for change in performance (cognitive) as well as actual behavioral change.

4 RESEARCH METHODOLOGY

As said, this paper reports on an on-going study of ESS. In the first phase a survey study was carried out. Data was collected from approximately 300 ESS users in the U.S., Mexico, and Sweden -- approximately 100 users from each country. The questionnaire collected data on personal decision making styles, reasons for ESS development, ESS use, and the users' perceptions of the benefits gained from using ESS (Leidner et al. 1995, 1996). In the second phase, ESS users and developers were interviewed. This paper is based on interviews done in four Mexican and four Swedish organizations. Typically, at least three persons were interviewed in each organization including at least one top-level manager and the IS manager responsible for the ESS. We used open-ended, semi-structured questions. Each interview was conducted by at least two interviewers. The interviews were tape recorded and transcribed. Secondary data like annual reports, company presentations, and EIS project descriptions and evaluation were also collected.

The transcribed interviews, personal notes from the interviews, and secondary data provide the data that were analyzed -- the main source was the transcribed interviews. An interview transcript is a text. There are different text analysis methods. Lacity and Janson (1994) suggest that IS researchers could use positivist approaches, linguistic approaches, and interpretive approaches in analyzing texts. We chose an interpretive approach. Given a text, several different interpretations, based on different approaches, can be made (Wolcott, 1990). Our intention is to do several analyses and also to examine what the different interpretations give. The next section presents and discusses our first interpretation.

Although the methodology is most appropriately labelled field study as the data were not collected longitudinally, we followed procedures suggested for case study research in designing the study. Following Sanders (1982), the three components in our study design were: 1) determining the limits of what and who is to be investigated, 2) data collection, and 3) analysis of the data. In the analysis we followed the four levels described by Sanders (1982): 1) description of the phenomena, 2) identification of themes or invariants, 3) development of noetic/noematic correlates -- the what (noema) and how (noesis) of experience, and 4) abstraction of essences or universals from the noetic/noematic correlates. We used Sanders′ four levels although our approach differed on one important aspect: the use of theories. Sanders approach is in line with traditional phenomenological approaches which say that theories should be developed directly from field data. The difference in approaches is related to a key question in empirical research: the role of theories. Eisenhardt (1989) discusses the use of theories in case studies. She suggests three ways to use theories: (1) as a guide in designing a study and data collection; (2) as a part in an iterative process of data collection and analysis where the first theories are enhanced, expanded, and modified -- in same cases even abandoned altogether; and (3) as a final product of the study. This final product can be in the form of constructs, conceptual frameworks, or mid-range theories.

In designing the survey study, we borrowed heavily from management theories of executive work with a special focus on decision making. We also used Huber′s (1990) propositions on the effects of IT on organizational design, intelligence, and decision making. In designing the field study, we used the results of the survey study and added other theories, for example, Mintzberg′s (1973, 1994) activity view with its ten executive roles, Kotter's (1982) process view with the two key processes -- agenda setting and network building -- and the competing values approach′s managerial roles. One reason for incorporating and expanding the theories is that we assumed they would be useful in directing our questions and explaining things found as surprises in the survey study. For example, the survey study suggested that Mexican executives perceived benefits not addressed in the study since they continued to use the ESS despite no significant relationships between perceived benefits and length of use. The benefits perceived by the Mexican executives could have been of a different nature than was addressed by the survey.

The use of theories in interpretive studies, as discussed above, can be compared to Glaser and Strauss′ (1967) grounded theory. Glaser and Strauss say that the discovery of theory should be directly from field data and strongly warned researchers against the first type of use of theories (in designing a study). They are more comfortable with the other two ways to use theories. Grounded theory has lately been criticized: Layder asserts that researchers can and should use theories in all three ways. He says that the grounded theory must "...break away from its primary focus on micro phenomena. The very fixity of this concentration is a factor which prevents grounded theory from attending to historical matters of macro structure as a means of enriching ... research on micro phenomena" (Layder, 1993).

5 RESULTS AND DISCUSSION

A central question in this study is: Are there archetypes of effective ESS use? To investigate this question, we looked for patterns of different ESS use in relation to managerial roles. We concurrently strove to assess the organization's situation, for example, if it was trying to change its vision and strategy or if it had a fairly clear and stable strategy and vision. Our field study data indicated two distinct visions of ESS: one, as a personal productivity tool; the other, as an organizational change tool. The personal productivity vision coincided with a fairly clear and stable organizational culture and strategy whereas the organizational effectiveness vision coincided with a view to change the organization's culture and strategy. Within each of these two visions, we found examples of systems that supported a great many managerial roles as well as systems that supported very few organizational roles such that the following grid of ESS effectiveness emerges:

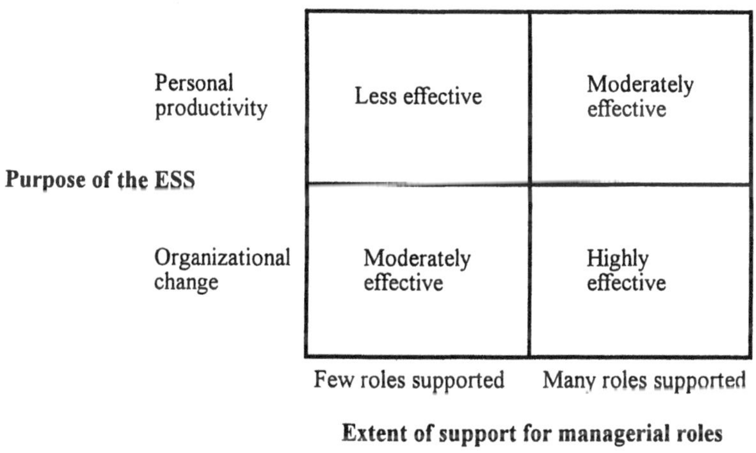

Figure 2 Grid of ESS effectiveness.

5.1 Organizational ESS: A view to change

Organizational ESS were those built in response to a perceived need to enable the organization to cope with environmental uncertainty and turbulence. ESS were seen as a way of inculcating a new organizational vision and as a way of shaping organizational culture. Three of the systems in Mexico and one of the Swedish systems are classified as organizational ESS.

Of the four organizational ESS, two were highly effective in that they addressed virtually every managerial role presented in Table 1. These two systems had very widespread use across divisions and downward in the organization and showed a balance of information in the four quadrants. Both organizations with organizational ESS were large multinational manufacturers. The average number of users in each of the two companies was 200.

In terms of the monitor role, these systems provided finance and sales information as well as daily production and inventory information. This helped the managers maintain control over their organizations and focus individuals on the success factors important to them. One of the systems was organized around ten critical success factors that could be viewed in terms of a selected product by a selected region across a selected time frame. The data was gathered real time from the chosen region, be it in South or Latin American, or Spain where the organization had divisions, and displayed graphically in less than ten seconds. It is felt in these organizations that managers will focus on the success factors that are being monitored closely by top managers.

In terms of the coordinator role, the uniformity of reports in the systems facilitated coordination across functions. For example, one manager stated that "if we need to present information to stockholders we can sometimes have a view ahead of what is going to happen in the next month like maybe the flat division's plant is thinking about having maintenance so maybe in the next month it is going to be lower in sales so he deals with that and informs our CFO. So if we are trying to ask for some loans or some other thing then we need to take into account that situation." Thus, the information contained in the system assisted in coordination not only within divisions and departments, but across divisions and departments. Furthermore, according to one division President, the ESS helped reduce the need for coordination. He stated that "if you leave a problem out of hand, then you have a lot of coordination and a lot of conflict among the functions. If you tackle the problem when it is just marginal, then hopefully it is also easier to solve. So, in a way, the ESS also helps you avoid the conflict." The attitude in both organizations with organizational ESS was that the more users in the more divisions worldwide, the better the coordination. Said one of the controllers in one of the organizations: "It is very difficult to have some uniformity in reports with a lot of divisions if we don't have a system that is for everyone." The goal from the inception of the ESS was to provide information to as many managers worldwide as possible. In addition, electronic mail was seen in both organizations as a means of improving coordination. One of the two organizations had 2000 employees using electronic mail. They hoped to shift from an autocratic management style to a more consultative style and were using the shared vision provided by the ESS as well as the electronic communication provided therewith to encourage this change.

In terms of the director role, the ESS was seen to help the organization achieve quality leadership objectives. The ESS provided planning and budgeting information as well as marketing and price information for use in strategic planning. In terms of the producer role, the ESS helped in that it gave feedback to subordinates concerning whether or not they were meeting goal performance. In one of the organizations, the CEO had a monthly "direction" meeting in which all the people who reported directly to him attended. He explained during this meeting his assessment of organizational performance during the past month and presented the main indicators he was examining as well as his interpretation. He used the ESS during the meeting to display his thoughts and encourage the subordinates to make necessary improvements in the coming month.

In terms of the broker and innovator roles, the ESS provided external information about the industry, business cycles, and the purchasing profiles of customers. In one of the organizations, the CEO was attempting to make the company a publicly traded company in the US. For this reason, he wanted to "know every single movement that is happening in the company each month" so as to enable him to have explanations for potential lenders. One of the CEO's subordinates stated his view that the CEO's "main target for using the ESS is to be well prepared to answer the questions of the lenders." The ESS was also used to assist with important decisions such as deciding on whether to close a plant, whether to implement price increases or decreases, and what type of product mix to produce each month. The other organization with an effective organizational ESS was growing by acquisition. Each time an acquisition was made, the systems in the acquired organization were immediately replaced with the systems of headquarters and the acquired company's information was incorporated into the ESS for monitoring. This allowed the newly acquired organization to be quickly initiated to the vision and style of headquarters (though not always without some resistance over the massive and sudden changes introduced by headquarters). The company is currently pushing to include more information about customers and even linking certain modules of the ESS to customers so that major customers themselves will be able to check the status of their orders.

Lastly, in terms of the facilitator and mentor roles falling under the Human Relations Model, the organizational ESS were designed to provide human resource information. The human resource information was used, for example, when the Director of Personnel needed to consider whether to eliminate positions or relocate individuals within the organization to another position. One of the director's of planning was having to considerably downsize the organization. He stated that before he had the ESS, he was unable to obtain information about employees without word rapidly spreading concerning whom he was considering for the layoff. The ESS greatly facilitated his role by enabling him to search for employee information without having to ask for it. In one of the organizations, employee satisfaction surveys were conducted each year. The survey had been developed by industrial psychologists for this organization. The responses were included in a human relations module in the ESS. Each manager could see his subordinate's responses as well as the satisfaction of the subordinates of other managers. The other organization had an holistic view of the ESS as engendering a certain management style which endowed the organization with a competitive advantage. Human resources were viewed in this organization as the basis on which the organization competed. The ESS was viewed as a means of inculcating the desired management style.

In summary, two of the organizations comprising the field study exhibited ESS with a view to organizational change. Both of the ESS supported a wide variety of managerial roles and were widely used in the organization.

Two other organizational ESS were noted but these were not yet able to support a wide variety of managerial roles but were rather concentrated on only a few roles. Both systems, though, demonstrated great potential for radical organizational influence. The Mexican organization, with 10 users, is part of an organization with 100 divisions worldwide. The Swedish organization, with 70-80 users, has operations in over 20 countries. The Mexican organization clearly viewed the ESS as a part of their turnaround strategy. A manager here described the organization's environment before NAFTA as follows: "before NAFTA was like a kid riding a bike with training wheels -- it was hard to fall down." The removal of the training wheels brought many a Mexican organization to their knees. In this organization, the goal was to spread a new culture, one that emphasized profits rather than volumes sold. This company found that they were unable to eliminate unprofitable product lines after the opening of the market because they did not have information available on which products were generating profits and which were not. The only information available was volumes sold. It comes as no surprise then that this organization began with a focus on measuring profitability of products in support of the monitor role. The system had not yet spread to lower levels but the President of one of the divisions stated that a goal was to begin getting information downward in the organization in order to encourage subordinates to become more proactive in responding to the increased competition.

The second of the organizational ESS we classify as moderately effective was found in one of the Swedish organizations. This organization had many users -- 70 to 80 -- who used the system primarily to access and review external information, reflecting the goal of improving the organization's competitive response with the ESS. The organization had a link to several external databases. In addition, the organization distributed yearly customer satisfaction surveys the responses to which were entered into the ESS. These surveys were considered an important tool in improving customer service in an increasingly competitive industry. This company had adopted a strategy of growth by acquisition. To facilitate this strategy, a computer-based Du Pont model was incorporated into the ESS and used by the executives for assessing the effects of potential company acquisitions. The system was used to assess several acquisition decisions per month. A positive effect of this type of use is that the ESS can be used for generating and evaluating alternatives, running simulations, and conducting quantitative analyses. Interestingly, in this organization, internal information was less widely used and only available in monthly figures perhaps reflecting a less time pressed management philosophy.

In summary, the two moderately effective organizational ESS were both viewed as important tools in helping the organization respond to a demanding environment, but were both vary narrow in their support of managerial roles which limited the ability of the ESS to facilitate change. However, both systems had widespread top management support and were well-positioned to become highly effective in the future.

5.2 Personal ESS: A view to personal productivity

The ESS classified as personal ESS were built for the primary reason of making information available to managers. These systems tended to change very little over time. Several of these systems provide information in support of most of the managerial roles proffered earlier but the systems are not used in such a manner as to inculcate or force organizational change but rather as a means of remaining stable.

Of the four organizations with personal ESS, one demonstrated a good balance of information across the managerial roles. This system contained market information, competitor information, and annual competitor reports. In addition, the system contained internal accounting and financial figures for all divisions in their worldwide operations. However, with only 15-20 users in a company of 9000 across 50 countries, organizational impacts are unlikely. The users interviewed widely agreed that the ESS was a "tool to increase personal work" and nothing more. Indeed, the purported aim of the ESS in this organization was "standardization and structuring of information, coordination of information, and increased knowledge of markets and competitors." This purpose in fact supports several managerial roles and the system as a personal productivity tool was very effective. The users concurred that the "rationalization and coordination of work had improved" and that they were "better informed" about the business than before. However, there was no apparent vision to spread the system either down or across in this organization. They felt the system was there to support a few individuals and it did that very effectively.

The remaining three systems classified as personal ESS were less effective in that they failed to support a variety of managerial roles. Two of these systems were found in multinational Swedish manufacturing organizations; the third, in a multinational food and products company in Mexico. One of the Swedish organization and the Mexican organization had both experienced failure with an initial ESS. Managers in both of these organizations felt intuitively that the ESS should help them respond to competition in their industry. However, in both cases the original ESS fell into desuetude shortly after its inception. Reasons given for the failure included the difficulty of integrating information from the worldwide operations and lack of support from the top managers. The Swedish company was in the process of building a new system focused on customer information, factory information, and product quality information. A prototype was being used by 15 users. The Mexican organization still had some marketing managers using the ESS but had halted any plans to improve the ESS.

The third system labelled less-effective personal ESS was found in another Swedish manufacturing organization. In this company, the system had not experienced failure but had not experienced tremendous use either. Among the ten managers using the ESS, the only perceived change in the availability and quality of information with the ESS was that, after the ESS was built, managers did not have to wait as long to have questions answered. There was no external information or human resource information in the system and only monthly internal information was included. The developer stated that the ESS was not developed in "response to a problem but as a way to make information available to people." When asked whether the ESS provided new information, one manager responded that "it is the same information but maybe you look at it a bit more just because it is easily available." This organization demonstrated little vision for the future of ESS other than it would continue to provide the same information to top managers that before was available only in printed form.

In summary, for the personal ESS, it seems that the distinction between effective ESS use and less effective ESS use is related to provision of modules in support of the majority of the managerial roles. Although we did not gather information on the cost of developing and maintaining the ESS in each of the organizations, it is proposed that personal ESS that require large amounts of human or capital resources are likely to be difficult to justify over the long-term and may consequently fall into desuetude. An extreme case of less effective personal ESS can also be found. non-using managers. This group did not surface in the study since we only interviewed ESS users. The ESS literature has several example of ESS failures where in some cases managers never start using the system or stop using the system (Sprague & Watson, 1996).

6 CONCLUSION AND FUTURE RESEARCH

Rockart & De Long (1988) suggested that ESS researchers should review the descriptive and prescriptive management and executive literature because "...the views we hold of executive work greatly influence how we think about executive support systems" and "...reviewing the literature can help ESS researchers, developers, and users become more conscious of the implicit models they have of the executive function. Only by making these beliefs explicit can we begin to reflect on their influence on ESS design." In this paper we have used Quinn and associates' competing values approach to examine the effectiveness of ESS in organizations. We have suggested that an ESS is effective to the extent that it is used by a manager in such a way as to support the manager in his different managerial roles, and support managerial behaviors that circumscribe the requisite variety implied by an organizational or environmental context. The presented view can be contrasted to the common view of ESS: "the purpose of ESS is to provide an executive easy on-line access to to current information about the status of the organization and its environment". We have explored how the CVA of organizational effectiveness and its associated managerial roles can be used for discussing and assessing the impacts of ESS on managerial behavior. We identified four archetypes of ESS use that were related to effective and less effective managerial behavior. The results and suggestions, although tentative, are promising but further research on Executive Support Systems (ESS) on managerial behavior and leadership is needed.

7 REFERENCES

Applegate L., and Osborn, C.S. (1988) Grumman Corporation: business information system. Harvard Case (9-188-061), Harvard Business School, Boston, MA.

Ashby, W.R. (1952) *Design for a brain*. Wiley, New York, NY.

Bartunek, J.M., Gordon, J.R., and Weathersby, R.P. (1983) Developing "complicated" understanding in administrators. *Academy of Management Review*, 8(2), 273-284.

Cameron, K.S. (1986) Effectiveness as paradox: consensus and conflict in conceptions of organizational effectiveness. *Management Science*, 32(5), 539-553.

Carlsson, S.A., and Widmeyer, G.R. (1990) Towards a theory of executive information systems. *Proceedings of the Twenty-Third Annual Hawaii International Conference on System Sciences*, (ed. J.F. Nunamaker, Jr.), Vol III, 195-201.

Carlsson, S.A., and Widmeyer, G.R. (1994) Conceptualization of executive support systems: a competing values approach. *Journal of Decision Systems*, 3(4), 339-358.

Denison, D.R., Hooijberg, R. and Quinn, R.E. (1995) Paradox and performance: toward a theory of behavioral complexity in managerial leadership. *Organization Science*, 6(5), 524-540.

De Lone, W.H., and McLean, E.R. (1992) Information systems success: the quest for the dependent variable. *Information Systems Research*, 3(1), 60-95.

Eisenhardt, K. (1989) Building theories from case study research. *Academy of Management Review*, 14(4), 532-550.

Elam, J.J., and Leidner, D.G. (1995) EIS adoption, use, and impact: the executive perspective. *Decision Support Systems*, 14, 89-103.

Fitzgerald, G. (1992) Executive information systems and their development in the U.K.. *International Information Systems*, 1(2), 1-35.

Glaser, B., and Strauss, A. (1967) *The discovery of grounded theory: strategies for qualitative research*. Aldine, Chicago, IL.

Hart, S., and Banbury, C. (1994) How strategy-making processes can make a difference. *Strategic Management Journal*, 15(4), 251-269.

Hart, S.L., and Quinn R.E. (1993) Roles executives play: CEOs, behavioral complexity, and firm performance. *Human Relations*, 46(5), 543-574.

Hooijberg, R., and Quinn, R.E. (1991) Behavioral complexity and the development of effective managers. In Hunt, J. and Phillips, R. (Eds.), *Strategic management*, Texas Tech University, Lubbock, TX.

Houdeshel, G. (1990) Selecting information for an EIS: experiences at Lockheed-Georgia. *Proceedings of the Twenty-Third Annual Hawaii International Conference on System Sciences*, (Ed. J.F. Nunamaker, Jr. and R.H. Sprague, Jr.), Vol III, 178-185.

Houdeshel, G., and Watson, H.J. (1987) The Management Information and Decision Support (MIDS) system at Lockheed-Georgia. *MIS Quarterly*, 11(1), 13-30.

Huber, G.P. (1990) A theory of the effects of advanced information technologies on organizational design, intelligence, and decision making. *Academy of Management Review*, 15(1), 47-71.

Huber, G.P. (1991) Organizational learning: the contributing processes and the literatures. *Organization Science*, 2(1), 88-115.

Isenberg, D.J. (1994) *Managerial thinking: an inquiry into how senior managers think*. Book manuscript.

Keen, P.G.W., and Scott Morton, M.S. (1978) *Decision support systems: an organizational perspective*. Addison-Wesley, Reading, MA.

Kotter, J.P. (1982) *The general managers*. Free Press, New York, NY.

Lacity, M.C., and Janson, M.A. (1994) Understanding qualitative data: a framework of text analysis. *Journal of Management Information Systems*, 11(2), 137-155.

Layder, D. (1993) *New strategies in social research*. Polity Press, Cambridge.

Leidner, D.E., and Elam, J.J. (1993-94) Executive information systems: their impact on executive decision making. *Journal of Management Information Systems*, 10(3), 139-156.

Leidner, D.E., and Elam, J.J. (1995) The impact of executive information systems on organizational design, intelligence, and decision making. *Organization Science*, 6(4), 645-664.

Leidner, D.E., Carlsson, S.A., and Elam, J.J. (1995) A cross-cultural study of executive information systems. *Proceedings of the Twenty-Eighth Hawaii International Conference on System Sciences*, (Ed. J.F. Nunamaker, Jr. and R.H. Sprague, Jr.), Vol. III, 91-100.

Leidner, D.E., Carlsson S.A., Elam, J.J., and Corrales, M. (1996) Executive information systems in Mexico, Sweden and the United States: the effects of culture on EIS use and benefits. Working Paper, Baylor University, Waco, Texas.

Lewin, A.Y., and Minton, J.W. (1986) Determining organizational effectiveness: another look, and an agenda for research. *Management Science*, 32(5), 514-538.

Lord, R.G., and Maher, K.J. (1991) *Leadership and information processing: linking perceptions and performance*. Unwin Hyman, Boston, MA.

McCartt, A.T., and Rohrbaugh, J. (1989) Evaluating group decision support system effectiveness: a performance study of decision conferencing. *Decision Support Systems*, 5, 243-253.

McCartt, A.T., and Rohrbaugh, J. (1995) Managerial openness to change and the introduction of GDSS: explaining initial success and failure in decision conferencing. *Organization Science*, 6(5), 569-584.

Millet, I., and Mawhinney, C.H. (1990) EIS versus MIS: a choice perspective. *Proceedings of the Twenty-Third Annual Hawaii International Conference on System Sciences*, (Ed. J.F. Nunamaker, Jr. and R.H. Sprague, Jr.) Vol III, 202-209.

Mintzberg, H. (1973) *The nature of managerial work*. Harper & Row, New York, NY.

Mintzberg, H. (1994) Rounding out the manager's job. *Sloan Management Review*, 36(1), 11-26.

Molloy, S., and Schwenk, C.R. (1995) The effects of information technology on strategic decision making. *Journal of Management Studies*, 32(3), 283-311.

Nord, J.H. and Nord, G.D. (1995) Executive information systems: a study and comparative analysis. *Information & Management*, 29(2), 95-106.

Osborn, C.S., and Applegate, L.M. (1989) Xerox Corporation: executive support systems. Harvard Case (N9-189-134), Harvard Business School, Boston, MA.

Quinn, R.E. (1988) *Beyond rational management: mastering the paradoxes and competing demands of high performance*. Jossey-Bass, San Francisco, CA.

Quinn, R.E., and Cameron, K. (Eds.) (1988) *Paradox and transformation: toward a theory of change in organization and management*. Ballinger, Cambridge, England.

Quinn, R.E., and Rohrbaugh, J. (1981) A competing values approach to organizational effectiveness. *Public Productivity Review*, V(2), 122-140.

Quinn, R.E., and Rohrbaugh, J. (1983) A spatial model of effectiveness criteria: towards a competing values approach to organizational analysis. *Management Science*, 29(3), 363-377.

Quinn, R.E., Faerman, S.R., Thompson, M.P., and McGrath, M.R. (1990) Becoming a master manager. John Wiley & Sons, New York, NY.

Robey, D. (1995) Theories that explain contradictions: accounting for the contradictory organizational consequences of information technology. *Proceedings of the Sixteenth International Conference on Information Systems*, December 10-13, Amsterdam, The Netherlands, 55-63.

Rockart, J.F., and De Long, D.W. (1988) *Executive support systems: the emergence of top management computer use*. Dow Jones-Irwin, Homewood, IL.

Rohrbaugh, J. (1981) Operationalizing the competing values approach. *Public Productivity Review*, V(2), 141-159.

Sanders, P. (1982) Phenomenology: a new way of viewing organizational research. *Academy of Management Review*, 7(3), 353-360.

Silver, M.S. (1991) *Systems that support decision makers*. John Wiley & Sons, Chichester, England.

Simons, R. (1992) Asea Brown Boveri: the ABACUS system. Harvard Case (9-192-140), Harvard Business School, Boston, MA.

Sprague, R.H., Jr., and Watson, H.J. (1996) *Decision support for management*. Prentice Hall, Upper Saddle River, NJ.

Stein, E.W., and Zwass, V. (1995) Actualizing organizational memory with information systems. *Information Systems Research*, 6(2), 85-117.

Streufert, S., and Swezey, R.W. (1986) *Complexity, managers, and organizations*. Academic Press, New York, NY.

Swanson, E.B. (1994) Information systems innovation among organizations. *Management Science*, 40(4), 1069-1092.

Vandenbosch, B., and Higgins, C.A. (1995) Executive support systems and learning: a model and empirical test. *Journal of Management Information Systems*, 12(2), 99-130.

Volonino, L., and Watson, H.J. (1990) The strategic business functions approach to EIS planning and design. *Proceedings of the Twenty-Third Annual Hawaii International Conference on System Sciences*, (Ed. J.F. Nunamaker, Jr.) Vol III, 170-177.

Volonino, L., and Watson, H.J. (1990-91) The strategic business objectives method for guiding executive information systems development. *Journal of Management Information Systems*, 7(3), 27-39.

Walls, J.G., Widmeyer, G.R., and El Sawy, O.A. (1992) Building an information system design theory for vigilant EIS. *Information Systems Research*, 3(1), 36-59.

Watson, H.J., Rainer, K., Jr., and Koh, C. (1991) Executive information systems: a framework for development and a survey of current practices. *MIS Quarterly*, 15(1), 13-30.

Watson, H.J., Rainer, K., Jr., and Houdeshel, G. (Eds.)(1992) *Executive information systems: emergence, development, and impact*. Wiley, New York.

Weick, K.E. (1979) *The social psychology of organizing*, Second edition. Random House, New York, NY.

Wolcott, H.F. (1990) *Writing up qualitative research*. Sage, Newbury Park, CA.

8 BIOGRAPHY

Sven A. Carlsson, assistant professor at Department of Informatics, Lund University, Sweden. He has a Ph.D. in Informatics from the School of Economics and Management at Lund University. His research interests include the use of information technology to support both individual and group decision making, strategic information systems, and organizational transformation through information technology. He has been a visiting scholar at University of Arizona, Tucson, and University of Southern California. His articles have appeared in *Journal of Management Information Systems*, *Information & Management*, *Journal of Decision Systems*, *Scandinavian Journal of Information Systems*, and international conference proceedings.

Dorothy E. Leidner, assistant professor at Baylor University in Waco, Texas, received her Ph.D. in information systems in 1992 from the University of Texas at Austin where she also received her Master's and Bachelor's degrees. Her research interests include executive information systems, international IS issues, and electronic classroom technologies. She has published in *Information Systems Research*, *Journal of Management Information Systems*, *Decision Support Systems*, *MIS Quarterly*, *Organization Science*, and international conference proceedings.

Joyce J. Elam is the James L. Knight Eminent Scholar in Management Information Systems in the Department of Decision Sciences and Information Systems, College of Business Administration, Florida International University, Miami, Florida. Before joining the faculty of Florida International University in 1990, she was an associate professor in the College of Business Administration at the University of Texas at Austin, and a Marvin Bower Fellow at the Harvard Business School. Dr. Elam earned her Ph.D. in operations research from the University of Texas. Her research deals with the competitive use of information technology, the management of the information services function, and the use of information technology to support both individual and group decision making. Her articles have appeared in such journals as *Information Systems Research*, *Decision Sciences*, *Operations Research*, and *Decision Support Systems*. She is co-author of the book, *Transforming the IS Organization*, published by ICIT Press, Washington, D.C. She has served as associate editor for *MIS Quarterly* and is currently on the editorial board for *Information Systems Research*.

8

User-centered DSS design and implementation

Jean-Claude Courbon
Institut National des Télécommunications
9 rue Charles Fourier 91011 Evry-Cedex, France
Tel (33 1) 60 76 45 77 Fax 60 76 44 93 Email courbon@int-evry.fr

Abstract

Methodologies for DSS design have traditionnally put the emphasis on the Decision, or the System, or the Support part of these systems. Illustrating it with two opposite case studies, this article tries to propose a rationale for a User-centered approach to DSS design and implementation. It stresses the importance of considering design, development and user participation as strongly related activities because DSS projects are change as well as learning processes, and communication is becoming paramount in a view of decision making taking place in more group-oriented and informal settings.

Keywords

Decision Support Systems, Design, Methodologies, Users

1 INTRODUCTION

Since the emergence of the first DSSs in the early '70s (Scott-Morton 1971, Gerrity 1975), researchers and practitioners have been working in various directions which could be summarized by the three letters composing the name of these new tools.

The Decision path was originated by Gerrity (1975), and later on by Keen and Scott-Morton (1978) and Stabell (1988) among others. The interest in the Support aspect of DSS was linked with interactivity and dialogue which were investigated early on by Carlson et al (1977) and then by Sprague and Carlson (1982). This path culminated with the explosive development of microcomputing and spreadsheeting software in the '80s which made all these ideas commonplace and taken for granted. The greatest research line was in the System track and culminated with the emergence of the notion of DSS generators. The artificial intelligence field added to the emergence of so-called knowledge-based DSS (Bonczek et al, 1981) and recently software engineering development in the object-oriented direction have come into the DSS field too.

However, and readily from the start, the question about the methodology to design and implement DSSs immediately arose when building the first systems. As a computer application, there was something special about DSSs : they were aimed at managers instead of clerical workers. It followed that the methods used for conventional information systems were not adapted to final users who had the status in the organization to reject something they felt not useful or convenient enough. Designers and DSS project managers were not in a position to impose use of their developed systems, be it through compulsory measures, or training, or whatever means toward implementation and use of systems vital for the organization. This problem was first addressed by Ness (1975) and opened a line of research on methodologies adapted to this specific type of computer systems.

This paper will first look at the various methodologies which have been proposed for DSS. It will then focus on the idea of user-centered design and implementation by first looking at two case studies illustrating the outcome of opposed approaches to this user-orientation paradigm. In a third part, we will explore the rationale for this paradigm, and see how it fits into the foreseeable evolution of the DSS field.

2 DSS DESIGN AND IMPLEMENTATION METHODOLOGIES

2.1 Decision-centered design methodology (Gerrity)

Along with the development of an early DSS in the field of portfolio management, Gerrity came up with the first proposal for a design methodology adapted to decision support. Figure 1 summarizes this. Without going into details, this method emphasizes a sequence of phases somewhat similar to the systems analysis approach used in the information system field where the entry point is the analysis of the decision process for which a DSS is to be built.

The original aspect of this methodology is the early focus on obtaining both a descriptive and a normative model of decision making. The idea here is to grasp a good understanding of the decision behavior of the future users in order to provide them with the useful tools for supporting their decisions as they make them. But, at the same time, Gerrity insisted on arriving at a normative model of decision making, deriving it from the theory of the problem domain of the "good" way to take decisions. As an example for the portfolio management system, managers tended to make their investments and divestments in the portfolios managed by looking principally at the behavior of particular stocks or bonds. But the theory said that a change in a portfolio was to be considered in the perspective of the portfolio as a whole. The preferred information for the descriptive model was a graph of stocks, but the theory said that a graph of the content of a portfolio (growth vs revenues) had to be the primary information taken into account to make a decision. It follows that the DSS designed has to include tools for both models in order to induce future users to evolve toward the "good" decision making process.

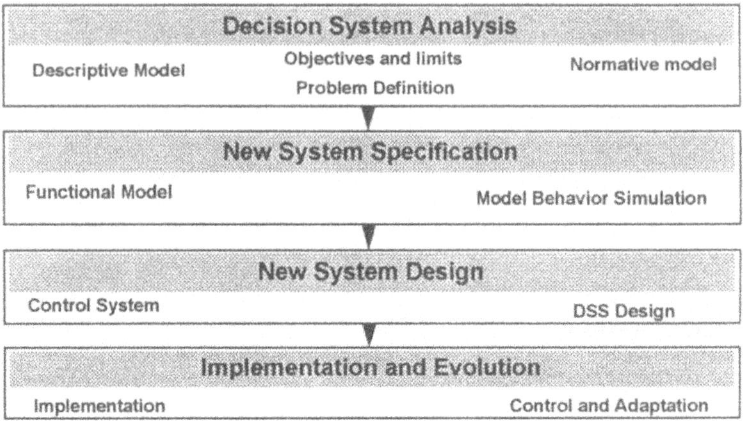

Figure 1 Gerrity decision-oriented methodology.

2.2 System-centered design methodology

Another approach to DSS design comes from the software engineering field. At first, DSS design was viewed as the interconnection of a model base and a data base through a monitoring system to interpret user commands, mix the adequate data/model combination and present generated information. The question was at that time the efficient integration of software and communication .

With the arrival of artificial intelligence techniques applied to decision support, the architecture of DSSs became more a mix of rules and facts with an inference engine. The design of knowledge-based DSS was the process of knowledge acquisition, with many proposals to this difficult (in fact unsolved) task such as, for example, KADS.

More recently, object orientation in programming, method development and software engineering techniques has lead to new design methods like, for example, the vision of DSS as the assembly of component software (see Becker, 1993, for example).

2.3 Support-centered design methodology (Sprague)

Realizing that interactivity was a central part of DSS functionalities, Sprague (1982) proposed his ROMC approach. The design paradigm here is that dialogue design is the paramount task of the designer : thorough dialogue design, and its early implementation and testing, will be the basis to a clearer view for an eventual set of specifications for the future DSS.

More precisely, good dialogue design implies answering several questions. First, *Representations* have to be identified ; they are the mental images which the decider uses when following his decision process. These representations have to be put directly on the screen in order to provide the necessary support to the user. The second phase lies in the identification of *Operations*. They correspond to all the actions which the user carries out on the representations, and they have to be implemented directly in the context of the previous representations. They are verbs of the application, and they will become functions to be coded later. The last two phases refer to *Memory* – what the DSS should do to minimize the memorizing mental load of the user – and *Control*, which is the set of all the features which will allow the user to easily engage, wherever he/she may be in the dialogue, in any type of use of the system. Control should also be symetrically exerted by the system.

2.4 User-centered design methodology (Ness, Courbon, Keen)

As early as the mid '70s, Ness (1975) had shown that the question of DSS design was that of having it really used by organizations, not a trivial task for practitioners seeking an effective contribution of their DSS efforts. He proposed what he called the "middle-out" or "inside-out" approach, as opposed to traditional "top-down" or "bottom-up" approaches. Later, Courbon et al (Evolutive approach, 1979, 1980) and Keen (Adaptive design, 1981) went further in this direction.

The main principles of these appoaches are :

- Begin with the "crucial" decision problem, and try to provide quick help. The idea here is that the designer should engage as soon as possible in a dialogue with the user. Instead of formulating a grand plan based on agreed on specifications, the designer should come up with a quick solution to a limited aspect of the problem to be tackled in order to build trust into the designer/user relationship.
- *Shorten as much as possible the life cycle* of each version of the system being built. The traditional view of the life cycle of a system is a sequence of phases going from analysis to evaluation through design, coding, implementation and use. Instead of several months or years to go through these phases, the approach here claims that it should take only one month, one week, even a few days between analysis and evaluation.
- *Evolve the system through multiple cycles*. Obviously, such short life cycles cannot result in very much work done in a single life cycle. Therefore, the approach proposes a design and implementation strategy where the system evolves through several or many cycles. The assumption is that the user, being constantly present in the design process, at the use and evaluation phases, will probably come up with a clearer view of what he wants, or what he can expect.
- *Evaluate constantly*. This is a consequence of the strategy, where each version of the system being built is evaluated at the end of any cycle. The advantage is that more or less implicit objectives of the user become more obvious, his expectations are quickly visible, and he can envision new possibilities on a practical basis. The initial "crucial" problem can then be put in perspective (maybe it was not really that important, something else might then appear as more valuable in terms of decision support), and in the worst case, the system may abort quickly before too much work, money, time and energy have been put into a dead-end system.

The rationale behind such a user-centered approach to DSS design is that it is difficult to draw precise specifications for a DSS. Managers often do not have a "need" for a DSS, they just have a "desire". Moreover, they do not have a clear idea of what they really want, they just have a feeling that a DSS might help them. The challenge, for the designer, is then to built a system for people who just have a fuzzy idea of what they want. Therefore a methodology should refrain from targeting early on for specifications, these will appear progressively thanks to the prototype being progressively built.

It is interesting to note that such an approach has been advocated for DSS, whereas traditional business data processing systems needed more well-established methodologies based on systems analysis. However, a few years ago, even specialists of MIS have been promoting approaches close, in some respect, to the ideas presented above. Rapid Application Development, or RAD (Martin 1991) has become a buzzword outside of the DSS field.
Before going further into analysing the user-centered approach to DSS design, and looking at its implications in the evolving field of decision making in organisations, we will try to illustrate with two opposed case studies the difference between the user-centered approach and system- or decision-centered appoaches.

3 CASE STUDIES

3.1 Case 1 : Planning of airline pilots stand by/training.

In this case (Zarate 1991) the decision support needed was for the administrative staff in charge of distributing over a monthly timescale a given number of days for pilots to be assigned to stand by periods (being ready to take over sudden shortage of on-duty pilots) or for training. More precisely, this staff was given, at the beginning of the month, a certain number of 2-day to 6-day/pilot periods to schedule over the month. A representation of the total number of pilots either on duty, on holidays or on stand by/training is given in the following graph, where the "slack" on top of these cumulated assignments is the number of pilots in excess compared to the total number of available pilots (which varies depending on retirements, recruiting or long-term leaves of absence).

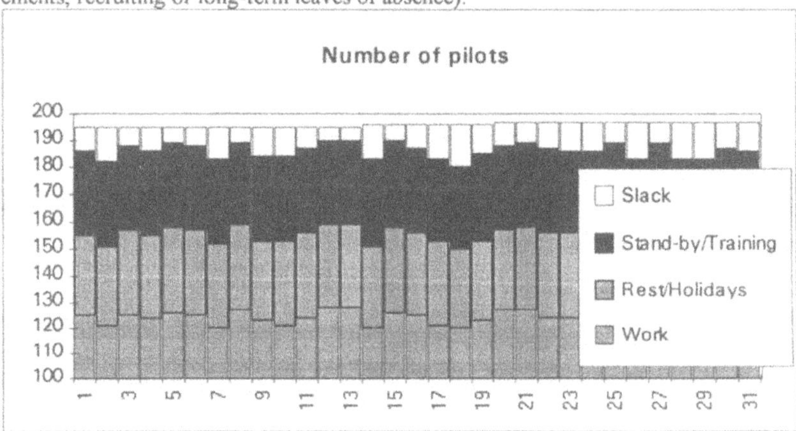

Figure 2 Various levels of pilots assignments

The challenge for the planner was clearly to allocate these 2 to 6-day periods so that the slack would be as evenly distributed as possible over the 30 days of the month. The next graph shows the top of the preceding one, with a normalization of the total number of available pilots by making it flat at its level of the beginning of the month. Here the ideal result is shown where the slack is constant for the whole month. However, it is not an easy task (nor a totally feasible one depending on the numbers) to fill the black area with 2 to 6-days horizontal periods to attain this optimum result. The problem is also slightly more complicated because there are, at the beginning of each month, some remaining scheduled days left over from the previous month, and in the same way, some of the remaining load can be assigned to the next month.

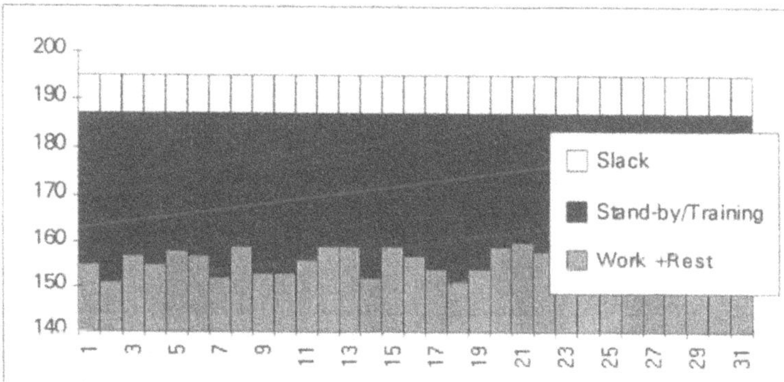

Figure 3 An ideal distribution of stand by/training load.

The DSS which was built considered the problem as an integer linear programming model with an objective function minimizing each day's difference from a constant slack. The planner was then able to adjust various parameters affecting constraints to generate more or less acceptable solutions.

This approach to decision support is somewhat far from the user's own understanding of the problem, and his/her interaction with the LP model parameters not very natural. Implementation and most notably, use of this system, were revealed to be problematic.

One can argue that building a DSS for this problem might have been more successful if the designers had tried to look at the problem from the decider's point of view. If they had followed Sprague's ROMC approach, they might have tried to discover the most familiar representation of the problem from the user's standpoint, and maybe found that the most powerful metaphor for this problem was actually similar to the well-known Windows game "Tetris". Indeed, the task appears as an intelligent game where the user "drops" blocks (here horizontal ones, 2 to 6 units large) onto the floor of a "lake" (in the above graph, the line "Work + Rest") in order to end up with a horizontal surface. Strategies could be devised (for example, begin with small "blocks" and fill the bottom of the lake), and support might have taken various forms (like filling the leftover "holes").

Although such a "user playing a game" approach might not have been so rewarding "scientifically" speaking from the designer's point of view, it is clear that it might have been more fruitful in terms of DSS success, user adoption and, in the end, effectiveness.

However, if we look more globally into the chain of actors in this decision support problem, from management, which gives directions, to pilots who inherit the output of the system through designers of the DSS and their users, the reasons for the approach taken stems partly from an obvious Operations Research culture of the designers group. But more importantly, the approach followed illustrates a political struggle between the management and the pilots. Actually, the DSS has to show, in the end, that the total number of pilots in the company is too high (a constant slack is in fact the demonstration of this excessive slack). A solution buried in an O.R. setting is, from the administration's point of view, easier to use as an argument than a more simple (or simplistic) DSS that even pilots, or their representatives, could work with.

3.2 Case 2 : Scheduling nurses in an hospital.

In this case (Esaki 1995, Courbon and Esaki 1992), the DSS built was for the scheduling of nurses for a 4-week period across the various shifts in a ward. The head nurse's planning task was very cumbersome, due to the combinatorial nature of assigning nurses of different skills to night, afternoon and morning shifts and, at the same time, to the necessity of satisfying multiple constraints. It took several hours, even days, to build such a schedule and later on to adapt it to disturbances. The constraints come from different sources. Some of them are linked to union contracts, some others depend on the load of the ward which can change from season to season affecting the minimum requirements per shift. Moreover, nurses can be full-time or part-time employees and the head nurse tries to satisfy nurses' wishes in terms of days of work and/or type of shifts they prefer.

Without going into detail on the DSS which was built, it can be said that 1) design and implementation followed an "evolutive approach" – as exposed in 2.4 –, 2) object programming was the development environment (using Smalltalk), 3) the support given was based on the expertise of the head nurses in their decision processes and was incorporated into a knowledge-based system and, 4) interactivity and dialogue design were the early and central focus of the development process.

Figure 4 shows an example of a schedule generated by the DSS on which the head nurse could make changes and build alternatives interactively. Horizontally, the pool of available nurses (senior and junior) and assistants is represented, plus three lines for checking the scheduled vs required level of nurses per shift. The columns indicate the daily assignments of each employee over the 4-week period, coded by a number (type of shift) or a letter (V for holidays for example).

Contrary to the previous case, the system developed here proved a success, and its use spread rapidly throughout the hospital, mainly thanks to its user-centered orientation from the beginning. Among many observations which were made in this case, we will present briefly some of the most interesting ones.

One of the first issues from the start was to elicit from the head nurse some kind of objective function which could measure the quality of a schedule in order for the DSS to be somewhat goal-oriented. It was almost impossible to get a response from the head nurse, and similarly she was very hazy when trying to explain why one version of a schedule might be better than another. Therefore, the designer began with the limited objective of building feasible schedules, and left it to the decider to improve it interactively toward an elusive evaluation of schedule quality. If the designer had insisted on getting clear evaluation measures (even qualitative ones) of schedule quality, he would probably have missed the point. Because, later, it appeared when observing the head nurses behavior with the DSS that what they looked for in a schedule was an expected "robustness", i.e. a schedule which would require minimal adjustments against foreseeable disturbances the ward was used to, like a nurse falling ill for example.

May June	1992	25	26	27	28	29	30	31	1	2	3	4	5	6	7	8	9	10	11	12	13	14	15	16	17	18	19	20	21
BALDI Corinne	Infirm 100	1	1	2	O	O	4	2	1	1	3	O	O	4	3	2	2	4	1	O	O	4	1	4	1	2	4	O	O
BAMBERGER	Infirm 100	4	2	3	4	1	O	O	V	V	V	V	V	O	O	1	O	O	4	1	3	2	2	O	O	4	2	2	O
BOULLIN Nathalie	Infirm 100	3	2	4	1	2	O	O	4	3	2	4	2	O	O	O	4	2	O	4	1	1	4	2	2	O	O	4	1
BRENON Barbara	Infirm 59.38	O	O	5	5	5	O	O	O	O	O	O	V	O	O	V	V	V	V	V	O	O	V	O	O	O	5	5	5
EUGENE Carole	Infirm 100	O	O	4	3	3	1	1	O	4	1	2	4	3	O	4	3	3	4	1	O	O	5	5	5	5	O	O	O
GALLARD Annelie	Infirm 100	4	3	O	4	4	3	O	O	O	4	3	3	1	4	3	O	O	5	5	5	5	O	O	O	4	1	3	2
JAUFFRED Helene	Infirm 100	O	4	3	2	4	P	O	2	2	O	O	4	P	1	4	1	1	O	O	4	3	3	1	O	O	4	P	3
PETITJEAN Chantal	Infirm 100	2	4	1	1	O	O	4	3	O	5	5	5	5	O	O	O	4	2	2	O	O	O	O	4	3	3	1	4
POLASTRI Florence	Infirm 100	5	5	O	O	O	2	3	O	O	4	1	1	2	2	O	4	1	2	4	2	O	4	3	3	1	1	O	O
ROSSIER Denise	Infirm 71.25	O	O	O	O	O	5	5	5	5	O	O	O	O	5	5	5	5	O	V	O	O	V	V	V	V	V	O	O
CALDAS	Aide II 100	O	O	7	7	6	6	6	O	6	7	7	1	O	O	6	6	1	1	1	O	O	6	6	1	O	O	1	1
CARRO Amparo	Aide II 100	7	7	1	1	6	O	O	6	6	6	1	V	O	O	V	V	V	V	V	O	O	V	V	V	V	V	O	O
FERNANDES-DO-V	Aide II 100	6	6	O	O	1	1	1	1	1	7	O	O	7	7	7	7	1	O	O	1	1	1	1	6	6	6	O	O
RODRIGUEZ	Aide II 80	7	1	6	6	O	O	O	O	O	O	6	6	6	1	O	O	O	7	7	1	6	O	O	O	1	1	7	7
REGUEIRO Maria	Employ 100	2	2	2	2	2	O	O	2	2	2	2	2	O	O	2	2	2	2	2	O	O	2	2	2	2	2	O	O
Night		1	1	1	1	1	1	1	1	1	1	1	1	1	1	1	1	1	1	1	1	1	1	1	1	1	1	1	1
Afternoon		2	2	2	2	2	1	1	1	1	2	1	2	1	1	2	2	2	2	2	1	1	2	1	1	2	2	1	1
Morning		3	4	4	4	3	3	3	3	3	3	3	3	3	3	3	3	4	3	3	3	3	3	3	3	3	4	3	3
Aides		3	3	3	3	3	2	2	2	3	3	3	2	2	2	2	2	2	2	2	2	2	2	2	2	2	2	2	2

1 = 7:00am - 3:30pm
2 = 7:00am - 12:00am and 2:30pm - 5:00pm
3 = 7:00am - 12:00am and 6:00pm - 9:00pm
4 = 1:30pm - 10:15pm
5 = 9:45pm - 7:15pm
6 = 7:00am - 11:30am and 2:30pm - 6:00pm

O = day-off
V = holiday
P = problem

Figure 4 A 4-weeks schedule (taken from Esaki, 1995).

Another observation had to do with the effort made to fill the DSS with as much expertise from the head nurses as possible in order to provide better support. Looking into the way they interactively modified solutions generated by the system under construction, the designer was able to put forward some rules they applied and that were included in the knowledge-based system. But in this process, it was discovered that a lot of this "expertise" had to do with what has to be called "private" knowledge. What should be done with remarks like "Mary already dodged Christmas and New Year, she has got to be on duty for Easter" or "Jane and Ann's relationship has deteriorated, better not put them on the same shift" ? Going too far into capturing the expert knowledge, especially the private one, most of the time can be a never-ending quest, and in some cases, an unjustified pursuit. A DSS has to leave room for personal input from the decider, otherwise, he/she will feel constrained, which is not the best way to gain acceptance of the system.

This remark is further confirmed by another strange observation, at least from the designer's point of view. If one looks carefully at Figure 4, one can see cells in the schedule containing the letter "P", which stands for "Problem". This appeared in the early versions of the system, whenever the program was not able to find an assignment for the day and the employee concerned. This "P" indicated that the solution proposed was not complete and that the programfailed somewhat . What was considered by the designer as a flaw, to be corrected as soon as possible, turned out not to be a nuisance for the user. Actually, the head nurses did not mind having to solve local problems by themselves, it even gave them a feeling of usefulness : a system proposing a schedule in a matter of seconds where a manual solution needed hours of pencil and eraser work was less intimidating if it needed, itself, some help. A DSS is a system supporting the decider, here it was also becoming symmetrically a system supported by the decider, therefore a cooperative system. Without going as far as saying that the "bug" becomes a "feature", it should be realized that allowing incomplete solutions, even unfeasible ones (but interactively improvable) is not always a flaw (a point of which the designer should be ashamed) and in some cases, it might be the difference that facilitates adoption and use.

4 A RATIONALE FOR USER-CENTERED APPROACHES

4.1 DSS should be usable, useful and used

Research in the DSS area always addresses decision problems, or decision processes, and aims at giving an answer in the form of a computerized artifact to support decision making. In doing so, systems proposed or developed have first to be *usable*, which means that a dialogue understandable by anyone provides ways of getting added value with respect to a decision to be made. However, a DSS might be the answer to a non-problem, or give answers based on assumptions that do not correspond to reality, or, more frequently, potential users discard it because it lacks important aspects of the decision situation that deciders consider unavoidable. Therefore, however usable, some systems might not be considered *useful*, whether for good or bad reasons. But most DSSs built can be considered useful, or potentially useful. In the latter case, a last hurdle is to have them really *used* in the day-to-day organizational context.

The fact that a DSS is really used is actually the "acid test" of the power of a DSS design methodology. A designer cannot blame users, managers, executives or the organization for their inability to understand how useful a system might be. He has to put this social context in the design methodology from the beginning, and not only during a short period early on when getting data on their needs or behavior. If we regroup under the term "users" the set of people and groups for whom the designer works, a constant reference to and participation of users in the whole design process is a necessary, although not sufficient, requirement if use is a measure of success.

4.2 DSS Design cannot be separated from implementation

Design to some extent refers to the intellectual process of conceptually building up a map of the system which will be "physically" built later on, the way an architect "thinks" and "paints" a future house or apartment complex. It is obviously common for designers (or architects) to take into account the context which might include the organizational setting, the financial limits, on the technological possibilities for example. But very often, these contexts are considered to be constraints to be fulfilled in the end rather than input and components of the design work. If designers aim at producing a DSS which will ultimately really be used, then the implementation phase should be planned early on in the design. Methodologies based on paradigms like "design the dialogue first" as in Sprague ROMC approach, or the "evolutive" approach which puts users in the driver's seat during the implementation and evaluation phases of the succeeding life cycles of the system being built, have therefore a good chance of ending up with systems which will really be used.

4.3 DSS design is a change process

Like many applications of technology to business management, DSS must be seen as the careful planning of the interactions between the technology introduced, organizational structure, activities carried on and behavior of the actors, as was emphasized by Leavitt et al (1973). Success in DSS design and implementation means that, in this socio-technical context, the coupling of the social and the technical processes which take place has been carefully managed.

Courbon and Bourgeois (1980) summarized the various approaches identifiable when trying to couple these two processes, the social one and the technical one. Figure 5 shows these two processes. The technical process can be summarized as a first phase in the analysis of the decision situation and ends up ultimately with the evaluation of the system designed, built and used. The social side is a process starting with an "awareness" phase were users come to know that some new computerized system is being studied, whether the initiative for such a system was taken by the organization or following a request they themselves made. Some social discussions will take place, and somehow, they will progressively freeze into some attitudes or expectations regarding the final delivered system.

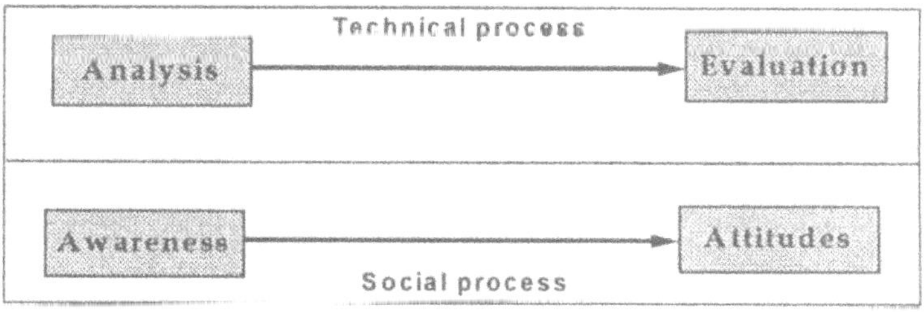

Figure 5 DSS design and implementation as a socio-technical process (Courbon and Bourgeois, 1980).

The main question for the designer is therefore to manage and couple these two processes in order to end up with a final situation where *evaluation* of the system (result of the technical process) is as close as possible to *attitudes and expectations* of users.

Coupling these two processes can be done in several ways, and Figure 6 tries to illustrate four main approaches, in a slightly caricatural and simplified way.

The *technocratic approach* consists in a sequential coupling beginning with the technical process. Here, the designer somewhat "knows" what is good for the users and builds his/her system before any of them knows what is going on. The challenge is then to later manage the social process by having users informed about a new system and discuss it so that they come to expect a system with the characteristics of the one already available. There are cases where this approach can work, but chances are that users do not go follow the direction the project manager would like them to take.

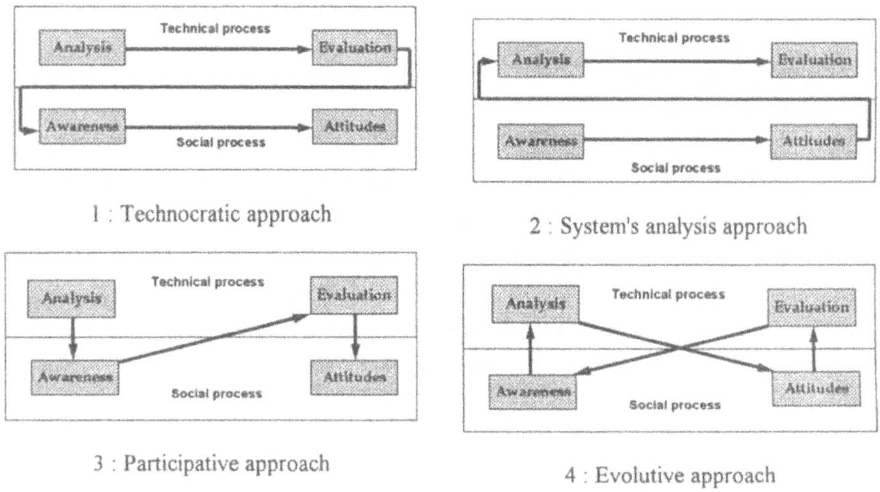

Figure 6 Various approaches for coupling the technical and social change processes.

The *system's analysis approach* recognizes that user input is necessary, and couples the two processes sequentially, but does it the other way around. Here users are present early on and actually no technical process takes place before users come to an agreement on what the system should do. When the social process is completed, then the designer gets a set of system specifications and he/she tries to get some signature from the users on what the system should look like. Then, he/she expects the users to quietly wait for the specialists to then go into their technical process of analysis up to delivery and use. The question in this case is how to freeze this social process, especially if the technical life cycle is long : will not users continue to discuss, or change their expectations and attitudes ?

A third approach is the *participative* one. Here there is a recognition that this two processes have to be managed parallelly rather than sequentially, that users have to be present at each stage, and that the life cycle of the technical process will permanently be enriched by participation and feedback from users (or from theirrepresentatives). The chances of a correspondance between the evaluation of the system and users' expectations are often increased.

The *evolutive approach* is an extension of the participative one. Here the iterative process is expressed by the loop through the four stages of the technical and social processes, which are therefore coupled in a continuous fashion rather than sequentially or in parallelly. Hopefully, the recurring phases of the active user's participation at each cycle will close the gap between his/her expectations and the final stabilized system delivered.

4.4 Decision and DSS design are both learning processes

A closer look at the last approach in the preceding section points to an interesting aspect of what a user-centered approach really is. Each cycle or interaction in prototype building is in fact a sequence of 1) *action* – whenever the designer implements a new version and the user works with it – and 2) *reflexion*, i.e. the feedback where the user and the designer think about what should be done next based on the preceding active use.

But action and reflexion are the two basic components of learning. In Piaget's terms, we acquire knowledge, starting from the date of our birth, by a first mechanism – *accommodation* – where we learn from "objects" we interact with and from which we empirically build adapted responses, or routines, to them ("schemes" as Piaget call them). Then, a second mechanism takes place – *reflective abstraction* – which happens when a mental reconstruction of all the schemes at a new level of abstraction becomes necessary. Indeed, there are situations where new "objects" cannot fit anymore with the available routines. The human being must then reconstruct and rearrange in his/her brain all his/her routines at a new level of abstraction to deal with these new, unmanageable situations.

User-centered design approach, as it has been described, therefore becomes a dual learning process. On one side, it allows the designer to learn about the user, his/her problem and behavior ; this gives the designer the opportunity to more clearly understand the nature of the decision support to be provided. On the other hand, the user, through his/her repeated use and analysis of it comes to learn about the system progressively built, thus increasing the probability of appropriation of the DSS by the user. Moreover, during this process, the user will also learn about his/her own decision making abilities and/or shortcomings. Often, being implicated in the design and implementation of the DSS will be, for the user, as valuable as the finished product.

One of the reasons why a user-centered approach to DSS design increases the chances of success comes from this implicit nature of user-centered DSS design as a shared learning experience.

4.5 Decision processes are a lot more than intelligence, design and choice

The DSS field has long been influenced by Simon's model of decision process. Departing from the view of a decision maker as a rational person who optimizes some objective function, he introduced the notion of *bounded rationality*. Here, decision is viewed as a sequence of, and iteration through, three phases : *intelligence* – problem finding and identification –, *design* – where alternatives are generated and evaluated – and *choice* – which takes place in a process where the decision maker merely tries to arrive at a *satisficing* solution. Indeed, such a vision appeared to be very fruitful and in part justified the emergence of DSSs themselves which found their legitimacy in the support they tried to provide in these three phases, and not only in the choice one.

But there is a limit to what this model can account for when looking at decisions as they are made in an economy and in organizational settings as they are evolving nowadays. We will refer here to a challenging view of managerial decision making recently proposed by Langley, Mintzberg et al. (1995). They contend that, up to now, decision making has been considered either as a *sequential process, driven by diagnosis* (Simon's classic model), or as *anarchical, driven by events* as in the so-called "garbage-can" model, or, a mix of both of them, as an *iterative process, driven by diagnosis and interrupted by events.*

The authors consider that the mainstream thinking about decision making suffers from three limitations, 1) *reification* because decision is in fact a "construct" reflecting the observer bias, 2) *dehumanization* because actually "decision makers play a central role as creators, actors and carriers, and organizational decision processes are often driven by the forces of affect, insight and inspiration", and 3) *isolation* because decision analysts tend to address well identified decision processes whereas "[strategic] decision processes are characterized more by their interrelations and linkages than by their isolation".

Looking at these three criticisms from the DSS designer's point of view can lead to a new understanding of what DSS are useful for when opening up the concepts of decision, decision maker and the decision making process.

The first criticism, *reification,* warns us against trying too hard to identify problem diagnosis and solution seeking by suggesting that commitment to action, which we tend to consider as concrete and real decision to be supported, is more a construct of the outside observer and is more diluted and evasive than we would like it to be. In most cases, decision is in fact the exploration of issues which, sometimes, progressively converges toward a problem and an action. Decision support here is more an information and communication environment which helps this issue thinking and "toying". If one considers, for example, the field of EIS (Executive Information Systems), a clear type of DSS, it is easy to observe that an EIS does not contain much hard decision support. Usually, an EIS is a platform which presents synthetic indicators and allows easy exploration of them. Indeed, it has been summarized as a "What is ?" tool rather than a "What if ?" one. In this case, the user-centered approach is obvious and testimonied by the usual existence of a few EIS designers working directly with executives to build them "screens" following their questioning and issue concerns. Often, the real value of these EISs lies in the focus on issues that executives want the organization to deal with by "showing" managers which strategic directions concern top management.

"Opening up the decision maker", as Langley et al. invite us to do, means that a decider is more than a rational, even a limited one, or a "cerebral" as they call it, human being. The authors propose an alternative model of decision making as an *insightful, driven by inspiration* process. Intuition is a very difficult phenomenon to understand, but it probably plays an important role any time a decision maker gets a sudden grasp of a whole situation and somewhat cristallizes or orients in a specific direction his/her, and others, thinking about an issue or a problem. What can information systems and DSSs do regarding this elusive behavior to support it ? Probably not much, but any contribution, however limited, is likely to generate important added value.

Let us propose here some research tracks along the idea of investigating the useful metaphors (in the sense of Sprague's ROMC approach) that, for a decider, might trigger intuition and insight. We suggest that the "network", "battlefield" and "chaos" metaphors are prospective candidates for decision support in this line of research. Executives tend to think in terms of ***networks***, for example in the field of financial links among companies of interest, of experts from various origins, of power people or university alumni, of logistics and flows of cash and goods, or of company organizational charts. Maintenance and exploration of these computer supported networks might be a base for this intuitive reasoning. *Battlefield* animation relates to the fact that executives are usually involved in several strategic projects (competitor take-over, subsidiary creation with other companies, big contract negotiation, technology adoption, etc.) which develop over months and interact with each other. Visualization of selected information pertaining to these undertakings might be of some help, and multimedia DSS is probably part of the answer. The *chaos* metaphor is even more speculative, because it rests upon a theory of the shape of evolution, of trends, of discontinuities and irreversibilities which, intuitively and implicitly, corresponds to an executive struggle with the vision of the future to forecast, prevent or build. Here also it is obvious that any investigation depends on a thorough user-orientation in DSS design and implementation.

4.6 Decision support is becoming communication support

The last criticism of Langley et al concerns the tendency of researchers and practitioners to isolate decision making processes, whereas they rightfully consider that in reality they are characterized by numerous linkages between interrelated issue streams. These linkages can be sequential, conditional or coordinating ones, and providing a support locally may lead to the significance of the overall intricacies of these dependencies being lost. However, broadening the scope of decision support has a good chance of ending up with overly complex systems, or unmanageable ones, or ones having an unreasonable cost.

But if one considers that the overall picture of decision making processes linkages is to be taken into account for decision support, we have to put it in the perspective of managers communicating between themselves and among issue streams. This means that, not surprisingly, decision processes such as related issue streams monitoring are actually a collaborative activity, and therefore group-oriented. It follows that decision support will evolve toward communication support. The field of Group-DSS has already brought valuable results, although most of them fall into the category of interactive Electronic Meeting Support (EMS). However, issue streams extend over lengthy periods and EMSs leave a lot of activity in-between formal meetings.

It is our belief that DSS has a lot to gain from incorporation of groupware functionalities to feel this gap. In fact, we can argue that more and more, traditional decision support will appear as complements, even software components, indeed very useful ones, of systems deeply rooted in the groupware category. Technologies in this field are numerous, for example shared document data bases, conferencing, workflow applications, application sharing and videoconferencing besides electronic messaging, group scheduling and project planning. But here again, technology only comes second to organizational development issues and user participation in system design and implementation.

5 REFERENCES

Becker, K. (1993) Reusable frameworks for Decision Support Systems development, unpublished PhD Thesis, *University of Namur*, Belgium.

Bonczek R.H., Holsapple C.W. and Whinston A.B. (1981), *Foundations of Decision Support Systems*, Academic Press, Orlando.

Carlson E.D., Grace B.F. and Sutton J.A. (1977) Case studies of end-user requirements for interactive problem solving systems, *MIS Quarterly*, Vol 1, No 1, March.

Courbon, J-C., Grajew, J. and Tolovi, J. (1979) L'approche évolutive dans la conception et la mise en œuvre des Systèmes Interactifs d'Aide à la Décision, *Informatique et Gestion*, Janvier-Février.

Courbon, J-C. and Bourgeois M. (1980) The information System Designer as a Nurturing Agent of a Socio-Technical System, in *The Information System Environment*, H. Lucas et al. Eds, North Holland.

Courbon, J-C. and Esaki, J-C. (1992) User-driven Functional Specifications for Decision Support Systems : the Case of a Nurse-Scheduling DSS, in *Economics/Management of Information Technology*, CEMIT/CECOIA3 Conference Proceedings, Tokyo.

Esaki, J-C. (1995) Conception et réalisation de systèmes interactifs d'aide à la décision orientés-objet : cas d'un planning infirmier, unpublished PhD Thesis, *University of Geneva*, Switzerland.

Gerrity, T. (1975) Design of man-machine decision systems : an application to portfolio management, *Sloan Management Review*, Vol 12, No 3, Winter.

Keen, P.G.W. and Scott-Morton, M.S. (1978) *Decision Support Systems : an organizational perspective*, Addison Wesley, Reading.

Keen, P.G.W. (1981) Adative design, ACM Transactions, *Data Base*, Winter.

Langley, A., Mintzberg, H., Picher, P., Posada E. and Saint-Macary J. (1995) Opening up Decision Making : The View from the Black Stool, *Organization Science*, Vol. 6, No. 3, May-June.

Leavitt, H.J., Dill, W.R. and Eyring, H.B. (1973) *The organizational world : a systematic view of managers and management*, Harcourt Brace Jovanovich.

Martin, J. (1991) *Rapid Application Development*, Mac-Millan.

Ness, D. (1975) Interactive systems : theories of design, Joint Wharton/DNR Conference on *Interactive Information and DSS*, The Wharton School.

Piaget, J. (xxxx), *L'abstraction réfléchissante*,

Scott-Morton, M.S. (1971) *Management decision systems : computer-based support for decision making*, Harvard University Press, Cambridge.

Srague, R. and Carlson E. (1982) *Building effective decision support systems*, Prentice Hall.

Stabell, C. (1988) Towards a theory of decision support, in Proceedings of *DSS-88*, Weber S. Ed.

Zarate, P. (1991) Conception et mise en oeuvre de Systèmes Interactifs d'Aide à la Décision : application à l'élaboration des plannings de repos du personnel navigant, unpublished PhD Thesis, *University of Paris IX Dauphine*, France.

6 BIOGRAPHY

Jean-Claude Courbon has been Professor of Information Systems at the Institut National des Télécommunications (Evry, France) since 1992. He got an engineering degree from Ecoles des Mines de St Etienne (1964) and a PhD in Business Administration from the University of Texas at Austin (1974). After working as an engineer in the oil business for 6 years for Total, he taught at the University of Grenoble, HEC in Montréal before becoming Professor at the University of Geneva for 12 years. His research has long been in the DSS field, end-user computing and Computer Assisted Learning. More recently, his interests moved to EIS (Executive Information Systems) as well as Group DSS and Groupware.

9

Co-decision within Cooperative Processes: Analysis, Design and Implementation Issues

Giorgio De Michelis
Laboratory for Cooperation Technologies, Department of Information Sciences, University of Milano
Via Comelico 39, 20135 Milano, Italy; tel: +39 2 55006 311; fax: +39 2 55006 276; email: gdemich@hermes.dsi.unimi.it
and
RSO SpA
Via Leopardi 1, 20124 Milano, Italy

Abstract

This paper analyzes group decision making from a pragmatic point of view, as a sub-process of a cooperative process. It shows how group decision making is carried on through two different co-decision forms (namely co-decision with equal and distinct roles) depending on the positional relations of its participants. Since the position (client or performer) of a participant in a co-decision is highly context dependent, co-decision support systems must enhance the awareness of their users with respect to the cooperative process and the positional relation where they are situated.

Keywords

CSCW, DSS, GDSS, Co-Decision, Cooperative Process

1 INTRODUCTION

Decision Support Systems (DSS) appeared in the seventies as an evolutionary advancement beyond earlier philosophies of EDP and MIS (Keen, Scott Morton 1978; Sprague, Carlson, 1982). Rather than merely processing and delivering information on the basis of a previously defined schema, DSS are designed to actively interact with the decision maker, to assist her with information processing in arriving at better decisions.

The process of decision making (Simon, 1960) is made up of four major phases (Sprague, Carlson, 1982):

1. the intelligence phase, which consists in problem recognition and definition;

2. the design phase, which encompasses the generation of (alternative) problem solutions;
3. the choice phase, which is characterized by the selection of an appropriate solution;
4. the implementation phase, which deals with justifying and executing the chosen solution.

The rationality of decision making processes depends therefore on the quality of the chosen solution with respect to possible alternatives, i.e. on the completeness of the space of possible solutions taken into account together with the adequacy of the criterion through which one solution is chosen with respect to the problem to be solved (Simon, 1960).

Most DSS are characterized by the fact that they support primarily individuals instead of groups, while almost all important managerial decisions are the results of group activity. Any individual decision by a member of a group (decisions are always made by individuals) is in fact a moment of the process through which the latter deliberates something defining and/or influencing the future behaviour of the group and the process under its responsibility. Boards, committees, teams, councils etc. are typical names of groups where decisions are taken.

The quality of the deliberation process of a group is not the sum of the qualities of the decisions of its members: any different member of the group may in fact define the problem in a different way either because she has different information or because she has different aims, and any therefore may choose a different solution. Moreover, since the final decision of the group is the result either of a combination of the individual decisions of its members or of the selection of one of them, it cannot be rational in the above sense (it cannot be the best combination or the best choice). The social dimension of the group decision process affects its rationality defining new requirements for the sytems supporting it, which are not taken into account by traditional DSS.

Ever since the late seventies, early eighties awareness of the fact that major organizational decisions are never taken by individuals in isolation has grown. This has brought forth the need for systems supporting the group where they are taken, its deliberating capability, rather than the rationality of its members' decisions. The focus has shifted therefore from the four-phase model of rational decision making (Sprague, Carlson, 1982) to other views of group decision making (Kraemer, King, 1986) enlightening its social nature (interest conflicts, influences, power relations, ...), its multiplicity (different views and different solutions foreseen by different actors, ...), its complexity (forthcoming problems and opportunities, changing contexts, ...).

New support systems have been conceived from this perspective, namely Group Decision Support System (GDSS - Kraemer, King, 1986; Lee et al., 1988), which, instead of supporting the rationality of the decision as in the case of DSS, provide support: for the communication between members of a group, in particular for contexts of direct contact like decision rooms (Dennis et al., 1987) and collaboration laboratories (Stefik et al., 1987), and distant synchronous communication like teleconferencing facilities; for the access to relevant information and information sources (in particular to those characterizing the decision to be taken and the dynamic context where it is taken); and, finally, for the use of qualitative and quantitative decision- and/or argumentation models (Conklin, Begeman, 1988; Lee, 1990).

We must mention that the first empirical studies on the effects GDSS use on group work had contradictory results: the quality of decisions, group confidence and satisfaction, the number of comments, the level of conflict are some of the issues on which different studies reported inconsistent observations (Vogel et al., 1988). These studies seem to suggest, if they can suggest anything given their limitations, that the use of the first GDSS has no direct appreciable effect on the group decision process, and that therefore the development of new systems must follow a different orientation. In the late eighties, also in connection with the emergence of the new field of Computer Supported Cooperative Work (CSCW; Ellis et al., 1991; Schmidt, Bannon, 1992) confidence grew relative to the idea that supporting group decision making cannot be separated by supporting its other relevant cooperative activities, like communication and information processing (Kraemer, King, 1986), since group decision making is generally embedded in a more general cooperative process.

New GDSS are therefore expanding the set of services they offer users or embedding them in more general CSCW platforms (Malone, Crowston, 1991).

In this paper I take a slightly different view: both although and because I agree with the mainstream of GDSS research (Kraemer, King, 1986) that group decision processes have a social and processual nature, that communication and information processing activities play an important role in them and, finally that they require systems supporting any form of group work, including but not limited to decision making. I think that decision making as a group cooperative process (let me call it co-decision to distinguish it from individual decision) can and must be analyzed, out of the rationality paradigm lying at the basis of most of the DSS (Keen, Scott-Morton, 1978) and of some of the GDSS (Conklin, Begeman, 1988; Lee, 1990), from a purely pragmatical point of view as a form of cooperation where participants do nothing but take decisions. I also think this analysis can offer new insights on the support it needs and on the support that can be given to it through information and communication technologies.

This paper proposes the approach to cooperative processes under development from more than ten years in Milano (De Michelis, 1994, 1995, 1996) as the theoretical framework where two types of co-decision - respectively, co-decision with equal and with distinct roles - are distinguished and characterized from the viewpoint of positional relations binding their participants within a cooperative process. Afterwards, the requirements which systems supporting the two forms of co-decision must satisfy are briefly discussed and, finally the issues raised by their implementation within an organization are surveyed. An HBR case study (Rothstein, 1995) is recalled in the next section; it is also discussed occasionally in the other sections to give some empirical evidence to the findings they propose.

2 A CASE HISTORY

Each issue of the Harvard Business Review (HBR) contains a case study, where various scholars and practitioners of management sciences and related disciplines discuss a case history prepared by one member of the HBR editorial staff.

In the January-February 1995 issue the HBR case study (Rothstein, 1995) proposes the discussion of the failure of an empowerment project at SportsGear.

The story begins (my rather short summary focuses on the events I consider most relevant) with a board of directors meeting where under the sponsorship of the CEO an empowerment program is launched to revitalize 'SportsGear'; the board also agrees to start it with a project in the manufacturing area. After a seminar where a consultant explains what empowerment is and how it has to be implemented, an empowerment team is created with people from the manufacturing, marketing, IT, and retail departments under the direction of the manufacturing vice-president. They make a commitment to define an empowerment program enhancing the performances of the manufacturing process with respect to customer satisfaction, delivery times, design innovation, information sharing, and so on. The team works together with great enthusiasm for the fixed period and finally comes out with a report proposing some main changes in the manufacturing process: "permit a manager to follow a product from design through sales to customers, allow salespeople to refund up to $500 worth of merchandise on the spot, make information available to salespeople about future SportsGear products, swap sales and manufacturing personnel for short periods to provide insights into one another's jobs, and establish a hot line so that salespeople could keep manufacturing informed about how SportsGear products were selling". The story ends with another meeting, where the report is presented to the board of directors but fails to convince all the department directors and is rejected: in particular, the directors of the personnel, financial, legal and strategic planning departments form "a wall of resistance".

The reaction of the board of directors "stunned the team members... they had felt confident in their sound research and thoughtful presentation." They did not expect the story to have this unhappy ending.

The case is well articulated and has many features that can be considered representative of many true change management projects: the CEO has great ideas but does not pay attention to the implementation of his ideas; various department managers show opportunistic behaviour and do not exhibit any opposition to the project until they have the chance to reject it; the empowerment team is enthusiastic but unable to win direct involvement on the part of all the department managers; ....

The comments of the experts (ranging from professors of management sciences and organizational psychology to consultants and top managers) offer various insights and explanations about the factors which caused the failure of the project: all the actors made several tactical errors; empowerment was not grounded on a radical change of the fundamentals of human resource politics; the CEO did not assume responsibility for the project; the empowerment team was not representative and did not involve all the department managers in its activites; the empowerment initiative was not led by the managers but by the consultants.

The comments of the experts are all plausible and meaningful, but they leave me with the impression that they are strongly biased due to the simple fact that they are given after the failure of the empowerment project. This impression is supported by the fact that they are supported by single principles of good change management and not by a theory of organizational decision processes where change management can be taken into account.

The theory of cooperative processes introduced in the next section offers a coherent language for analyzing the SportsGear case study and discussing its negative outcomes showing that they were generated by the way the decision process was conducted. I will come back to it in the next section.

3 CO-DECISION FORMS AS COOPERATION FORMS

As I claimed in the Introduction the decisions taken into consideration in this paper are co-decisions, i.e. decisions that are not taken by isolated individuals but are the outcome of a group of persons and are generally part of larger processes, e.g., those processes that are frequently called business (with external focus) and/or organizational (with internal focus). It is well known, in fact, that managerial decisions are generally (co-) decisions of this type, since managers' work has the role of influencing, orienting, controlling the business processes of the organization they manage and of developing organizational processes focused on improving performance. From this point of view, co-decisions have a process nature: they are subprocesses of the process within which they are taken.

This delimitation of the study field opens two complementary research issues: on the one hand, since co-decision is a cooperative subprocess of a larger process, it is necessary to analyze the latter as a cooperative process (it is not important here to distinguish between the two types of processes mentioned above, but to understand their common cooperative nature) and to distinguish the forms cooperation assumes within it (reducing cooperation to a generic and contingent combination of communication and action it is not sufficient, since it does not help in analyzing and evaluating real cooperative processes); on the other, it is necessary to understand the role co-decision plays within cooperative processes and how it is practiced, i.e. to analyze co-decision forms as cooperation forms.

I couple the neutral and general meaning of cooperation to indicate people doing something together (Schmidt, Bannon, 1992) with a relational view on human activities embedding them within the communication flow of its participants (Flores, 1982; Winograd, Flores, 1986). The pragmatic dimension of human communication, in fact, relates the actions of its participants with their expectations, as first, defining the conditions of satisfaction they should meet, as second, declaring if the latter have been met. Every activity, therefore, has at least one client, who has a need and requests its satisfaction, and one performer, who performs to satisfy the request: both the client and the performer contribute to the value of the performed activity, respectively, requesting it and performing it. Human activites have a social nature, they are rooted in the social relations of their participants. They are processes of communication and action, they are cooperative processes.

The primary form of cooperation within a cooperative process is just the collaboration between clients and performers: a cooperative process develops a partnership between them.

Collaboration is performed through the communication between the performers and the clients from which the activity performed by the first ones receives its value. Within collaboration, in fact, perfomers and clients create a common understanding of what has to be done, shape the performance under execution and evaluate it. The coupling of a performance and its value within a cooperative process depends on the collaboration of its clients and performers: if it fails this may very easily be because the performers do something that does not satisfy the clients and therefore has no value. Collaboration creates a common *language* and a common understanding between the clients and the performers through mutual listening. Collaboration is the form of cooperation through which the relationship between clients and performers is carried on successfully. The idea that clients and performers are not competitors but partners and the idea that a project manager is the coach of her team are both captured in the above concept of collaboration.

The plural form for client(s) and performer(s) above is not casual: cooperative processes have, generally, more than one performer (only trivial activities can be performed by one unique actor; in all the other cases several performers cooperate to perform them) and, frequently, more than one client (in an organizational structure, as an example, a requested performance impacts several persons, who all are, sometimes without knowing it, its clients). A cooperative process can be represented in graphical form as in Figure 1.

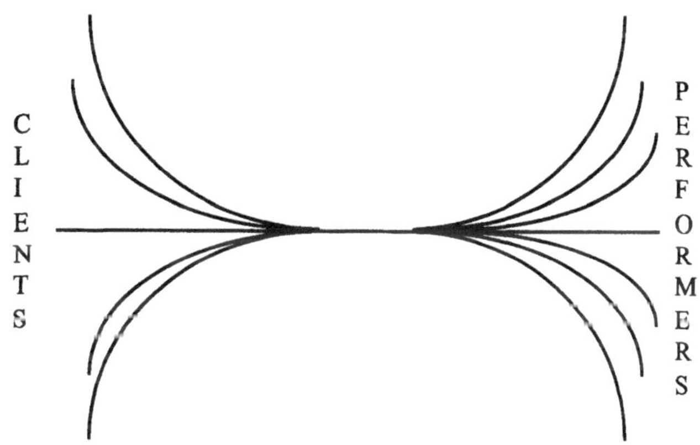

Figure 1 A cooperative process as a relation between clients and performers.

In the HBR case study (Rothstein, 1995) recalled in section 2 several actors participate to the organizational process that should lead to the empowerment of SportsGear: the CEO; the members of the empowerment team, including the manufacturing vice-president and people from the manufacturing, IT, marketing and retail departments; the external consultant, the directors of all the other departments (personnel, financial, legal and strategic planning). The positions they occupy with respect to the performance of the process (designing and implementing an empowerment program) are well defined for the CEO (he is a client), the empowerment team and the external consultant (they are all performers) while those of the department directors exhibit a serious ambiguity, that is a relevant indicator of a major problem in process. It is possible to give two different interpretations of the above mentioned ambiguity:

1. they are clients, since, as members of the board, they are the requestors of the empowerment program to the team led by the manufacturing vice-president. The bitter surprise of the empowerment team during the final meeting is therefore generated by its wrong expectation that they would act as performers. The CEO has also some responsibility on the failure of the program because he did not play adequately his role of *primus inter pares* among the clients;
2. they are performers, since the CEO is their client with respect to the plans discussed at the meetings of the board of directors. This is frequently the case in today enterprises, where managerial meetings are organized to operationalize strategic plans transforming them into departmental action plans. In this case the failure of the empowerment program is due to the lack of responsibility assumption by the directors of the personnel, financial, legal and strategic planning departments. During the final meeting they act as clients, while they are performers.

As it has been claimed above, the collaboration between clients and performers is the main form of cooperation within a cooperative process. But it is not the only one, when the process is not a trivial one. The coordination of the performances of the many performers of a complex cooperative process so that they can result in the satisfaction of the request of its clients, as well as the harmonization of the conditions of satisfaction of its many clients are performed through different cooperation forms, deserving a particular attention.

On the one hand, the activities of the performers are interrelated in a partial order of causal dependencies, characterizing the flow of actions that conducts to the completion of the cooperative process. Disregarding the normative means (procedures, roles, plans, ...) through which this partial order is defined and maintained, whose analysis is out of the scope of this paper (De Michelis, 1996), it can be observed that any activity in the partial order is embedded by its causal dependencies within a cooperative (sub-) process, whose clients include some of the performers of the main process themselves. Every performer of a cooperative process is generally, also, client within some of its sub-processes. A similar observation can be made also with respect to its clients, that sometimes are performers of some of its sub-processes. Within a cooperative process, every participant switches from one position to another one (e. g. from performer to client) collaborating in different moments with a different sub-group of participants.

On the other hand, between the many clients of a cooperative process there is a mutual relation that is not a client - performer collaboration, but it is based on their being all clients within the same cooperative process. The client - client relation is not associated with a cooperative sub-process, it does not embed any activity: it is a purely communicative relation, developing in time, where the clients harmonize their conditions of satisfactions and agree on one common unique request to be satisfied, i.e they co-decide it. All the clients are equal with respect to the request they co-decide: every one of them, in fact, has a condition of satisfaction that must be met by the unique performance of the cooperative process. They play equal roles within the co-decision.

Co-decision with equal roles occurs when two or more people participate in a decision process where all of them share full responsibility for the decision to be taken. Co-decision with equal roles is a process where the opinions of all the participants converge towards a common decision. Convergence may be enhanced either through persuasion or through mediation. Co-decision with equal roles, logically precedes the action: if it is carried on successfully, it fixes the common *expectations* with respect to the outcome of a cooperative process; it defines the condition of satisfaction shared by all its clients. Co-decision with equal roles is carried on by the clients of a cooperative process. If a cooperative process has several clients, each can be considered as intermediating a different relationship with the environment in which the cooperative process is performed: the cooperative process has a complex relationship with its environment; it has a complex environment. Co-decision with equal roles is the means through which the cooperative process is protected from the complexity of its environment.

Finally, between the many performers of a cooperative process there is, also, a mutual relation that is not a client - performer collaboration, but it is based on their being all performers within the same cooperative process. The performer - performer relation is not associated with a cooperative sub-process, it does not embed any activity: it is a purely communicative relation, developing in time, where the performers maintain the coupling between their performances, so that their integration is possible and effective. Also in this case, the participants are involved in a co-decision process, but the latter has a rather different nature with respect to co-decision with equal roles. Every performer, in fact, has only responsibility on her performance and on its fitting with the performances of the other performers; every one of them has a different responsibility in the decision to be taken. The performers play different roles in the co-decision.

Co-decision with distinct roles occurs when two or more persons participate in a decision process, where each has her own responsibility on a particular issue related to the whole decision to be taken. Co-decision with distinct roles is a process where the individual decision of any participant takes into account the constraints defined by the decisions of the other participants, so that overall the individual decisions constitute a sound collective decision. Successful co-decision with distinct roles creates a non void intersection among the decisions the participants take on the issues under their responsibility. Through successful co-decision with distinct roles the participants in a cooperative process recognize and maintain the mutual *interfaces* between their respective performances. Co-decision with distinct roles is carried on by persons which are all performers of the same activity.

From this short summary of the three main cooperation forms (more can be found in: De Michelis, 1994) many aspects of co-decision emerge deserving a closer attention in order to analyze the requirements the systems supporting co-decision should meet.

'Client' and 'performer' do not define roles, rather they define relative positions: a participant in a cooperative process is neither a client nor a performer. At any moment, she is in a client or performer position depending on the activity she is currently engaged in and on her responsibility on it. At any moment, she is in a client (performer) position in one specific (sub-) process where other persons (not necessarily all the participants of the cooperative process) are involved either in client or in performer positions. Whenever she switches from one activity to another one she changes her position accordingly. Positions are relative because they are context dependent: they depend on the past history of the cooperative process, on the partial order of causal dependencies of its action flow, on its participants, on their mutual positions, on its communication flow. The way people cooperate within a cooperative process is also highly context dependent: to perform effectively a person must know not only what is her task but also where she is situated (Suchman, 1987).

The participants in a cooperative process, from this viewpoint, are members of a social community, of a community of practice (Seely Brown, Duguid, 1991): the concept of position is not superposing to it any formal organization but offers a means to analyze the complexity of its cooperative processes and how it impacts their performances (De Michelis, 1994, 1995, 1996).

Cooperation forms are strictly coupled with positional relations: collaboration occurs between clients and performers; co-decision with equal roles between clients; co-decision with distinct roles between performers. A form of cooperation is not a style of behaviour a person can choose: it is a matter of practicing a social relation. A person can not choose the form of cooperation she engages herself in, nor a group of persons can do it: the form of cooperation they engage in depends on the positional relations where they are situated.

Moreover, whenever a group of persons is engaged in a particular cooperation form, then they are in the correspondent positional relationship: if they are collaborating, then they are in a client - performer relationship; if they are co-deciding with equal or distinct roles, then they are, respectively, in a client - client or performer - performer relationship. From the way people are cooperating the observer can induce some information about the cooperative process to which they participate. Since cooperation occurs only within cooperative processes, group decision making is always part of a cooperative process.

There are two rather different forms of co-decision where participants interact in rather different ways: a behaviour which is effective in one of them is not effective in the other. Both the rational decision approach and the managerial common sense (the former has deeply influenced the latter) have paid a great attention to one of them - co-decision with equal roles - disregarding the other one. GDSS are either supporting synchronous communication, like decision rooms and collaboration laboratories, or supporting co-decision with equal roles (Conklin, Begeman, 1988; Lee, 1990). Only in the software engineering field some tools have been designed taking into account co-decision with distinct roles and the problem of the consistency of the interfaces between concurrent activities.

The pragmatical approach presented here allows to make one step further with respect to the garbage can model of group decision making (Kraemer, King, 1986), enriching its capability of taking into account the diversity decision processes may exhibit, with some insights in the forms of their diversity.

In the HBR case study presented in section 2 (Rothstein, 1995), the 'wall of resistance' of the directors of the personnel, financial, legal and strategic planning departments shows without any doubt that they are behaving in accordance with co-decision with equal roles: they reject the program with highly general remarks, underlining the dangers to which it exposes SportsGear rather than the problems they think their departments will individually encounter if it is implemented.

From the rational decision viewpoint the ambiguity of their position is not relevant: the only interesting evaluation is if they are right rejecting the empowerment program prepared by the team or not. It is only from the pragmatic point of view that emerges the question of their position with respect to the empowerment plan and it makes sense asking if their cooperation has been coherent with their responsibility. What can be evaluated in terms of rationality from one viewpoint is characterized in terms of responsibility from the other.

4 COMPUTER SUPPORT FOR CO-DECISION

As it has been recalled in the Introduction of this paper, there is a substantial agreement today that systems supporting group decision making can not be effective if they are not supporting also any other cooperative activity of its actors. The analysis carried on in the previous section allows to go further in the characterization of the requirements they must satisfy, avoiding the generic call for systems supporting any form of communication, cooperation and information processing.

In the previous section it has been shown that human beings are situated in the cooperative process in which they currently participate and, furthermore, that at any moment their situatedness is characterized by their positions in it and by their mutual positional relations.

The complexity of cooperative processes makes particularly difficult for participants remaining aware of the context where they are situated. On the one hand, they have difficulties to understand what is going on, what they should do, how they should behave, what the other participants are doing and should do, and the resolution of these doubts to move to action becomes time and resource consuming affecting their performances and stressing them; on the other, sometimes they feel that they didn't do the right thing, or that someone else didn't do it, causing problems, again, that have negative effects on the cooperative process, i.e. affecting their performances and stressing them.

In both cases, the problems are generated by a lack of awareness of the context where they are situated. Systems supporting the actors of a cooperative process, while they are co-deciding or, more generally, while they are engaged in any form of cooperation, should therefore enhance their awareness of the context where they are situated, taking into account of the different dimensions of that context.

First, they should enhance user awareness of the cooperative process where she is situated. Remaining in the spatial metaphor a cooperative process is performed in a work setting with a physical and an electronic component. While the former is characterized by the arrangements of the work space where its participants are located, the electronic component of the work setting is its virtual augmentation generated by the interface allowing the access to computer-based tools and systems: productivity tools, information repositories and, mainly, communication media. The quality of a system supporting cooperative processes depends, therefore, both on the richness of the tool set it offers to its users and on the way its interface makes them available in their work setting. Its interface must reflect the ongoing cooperative process offering services to the cooperation form its participants are engaged in, so that they can access transparently or in a visible way (Agostini et al., 1996) the tools allowing her to cooperate appropriately.

The groupware platforms already available in the market offer some services from this point of view, while new more powerful prototypes are currently under development: the BSCW system at GMD (Bentley et al., 1995) and the Milano system at the Cooperation Technologies Laboratory of the University of Milano (Agostini et al., 1995, 1996b). The Milano system couples the work center concept of Anatol Holt (Holt et al., 1983; Holt, 1988) with the relational view of cooperative processes proposed in this paper, so that its user interface mirrors the cooperative process where its user is situated in her work space.

Second, they should enhance user awareness of the positional relation binding her with the persons with whom she is cooperating and of the cooperation form associated to it. The question here is to support the awareness of a user not only with respect to the cooperative process where she is situated but also with respect to its sub-process where she is currently active. The user interface of the system should, therefore, at any moment make available to its user the tools that are needed in the form of cooperation and/or in the activity in which she is engaged. Moreover, when the user moves from one cooperation form to another one, the system should switch accordingly. The Milano system offers some hints on how this level of awareness can be supported (Agostini et al., 1995, 1996b).

Third, they should enhance user awareness of the cooperative form where she is currently acting, with a particular attention to co-decision forms. Let us have a closer look at the type of support we can envision for the two forms of co-decision.

- Whenever a cooperative process has more than one single client, then co-decision with equal roles is the cooperation form through which the clients share their expectations with respect to the process outcome, so that the performers know what they have to do. The main co-decision problem is generated by the fact that those, who should take a decision together, do not cooperate properly during the process. If, when a breakdown occurs, each of the clients reactivate the collaboration with the performers without taking into account the opinions of all the other clients, the performers can not understand which are the conditions of satisfaction of their performance, and the cooperative process can fail to reach a successful completion. Making expectations visible, helping the participants to understand each other and allowing to change expectations, within the space of possibilities of the performer is what supporting systems should do with respect to co-decision with equal roles. Systems like CM/1™, the industrial derivation of gIBIS (Conklin, Begeman, 1988), are particularly well suited to support co-decision with equal roles.
- Whenever a cooperative process has several performers who concurrently act to satisfy the same client, co-decision with distinct roles is the cooperation form through which the performers maintain the integration conditions of their respective performances. If they are able to define together the interfaces mutually constraining their respective performances, then their performances will be able to meet the condition of satisfaction of their common clients. As with co-decision with equal roles, also co-decision with distinct roles may become critical, because those, who should take a decision together, do not cooperate properly during the process. If, when a breakdown occurs, each of them looks for the best

general solution able to fit the condition of satisfaction of the client, instead of looking to the changes she can afford in her specific task, redefining its interfaces with the tasks of the other performers, then the cooperative process can enter in crisis, as its participants relinquish their own responsibilities of performers to play mutually as clients. Co-decision with distinct roles is, generally, badly understood and badly supported within cooperative processes. For particular types of activity - e.g. software engineering - the methods and tools used to guide the development process embody a discipline for the definition and maintainance of the interfaces between subtasks, but no general tools have been designed to support co-decision with distinct roles.

The three types of awareness are presented in order of relevance, since a person can not be aware of the form of cooperation she is practicing if she is not aware of the cooperative process wher she is engaged and she can not be capable to co-decide properly without being aware of the position she occupies.

The problem, therefore, is not to switch from GDSS to more general groupware systems supporting any form of cooperation, but to embed GDSS in a groupware platform supporting user awareness and open to modularity (Agostini et al., 1996). GDSS, in fact, like any other cooperative and/or individual tool, are resources for action (Suchman, 1987) that the user needs within the context where she is situated.

5 IMPLEMENTING CO-DECISION SUPPORT

The implementation of a co-decision support system within an organization is not a technical matter: it is a complex change management process impacting all the dimension of the socio-technical system characterizing that organization. The quality of the system is not a sufficient condition for granting its success.

In the following some major aspects of the above claim are briefly recalled.

Before implementing a co-decision support system it is necessary to foresee the performances it should improve within the organization, so that every involved person can understand its importance. From this point of view, the rational decision approach is often misleading, since it focus on the abstract dimension of the optimality of the decisions to be taken, rather than on the performances of the processes where they are taken. Decision making, generally, is not important per se, out of the context where it occurs.

When implementing a co-decision support system it is also necessary to analyze carefully the current practices of the involved persons. A realistic look at them will help to avoid technological innovations that are not usable in the context of the organization where the implementation will take place. Real case studies show, for example, that paper is still in many cases the most acceptable document support for managers involved in decision making. One important guideline is therefore to implement the new system in such a way that it supports in an integrated way both paper and electronic wok.

Like any change management process, the implementation of a co-decision support system impacts dramatically its users. A particular attention must be paid to their empowerment so that the users can fully exploit the services offered by the new system while improving their performances. Moreover, the implementation itself must be conceived as part of this empowerment program. The effective use of co-decision support systems is, in fact, impossible if its users do not abandon the rational decision common sense to share the new pragmatic viewpoint characterizing decision making in terms of responsibility.

Improving group decision making within an organization is not possible if organizational roles and structures remain unchanged, since co-decision forms can be obstacled by organizational rules. Implementing a co-decision support system must either be an occasion for a global rethinking of the organization or, at least, be accompanied by those organizational changes that are necessary for the full exploitation of the system to be implemented.

Finally, the implementation of a co-decision support system is not instantaneous: it is a cooperative process (an organizational process, in accordance with the definitions given in this paper). As such, it needs to be supported by cooperative process support systems and by co-decision support systems.

6 CONCLUSION

The pragmatic approach to cooperative processes within which co-decision with equal and with distinct roles have been distinguished, constitutes the conceptual basis of the prototype of the Milano system for supporting cooperative processes, under development at the Cooperation Technologies Laboratory of the University of Milano (Agostini et al., 1995, 1996b).

The characterization of the two co-decision forms proposed in this paper will be tested and improved, so that it can offer the guidelines for the specification and the design of the co-decision support modules of the Milano system.

7 ACKNOWLEDGMENTS

I thank Alessandra Agostini and Maria Antonietta Grasso for the many discussions we had about the issues raised in this paper and Monica Divitini for her careful reading and correcting it. This paper presents a research that has been conducted with the financial support of the EC within the IMPACT project of the COST-14 Action, and of the Italian National Research Council (CNR) within the coordinated project "Environments for Supporting the Design of Information System".

8 REFERENCES

Agostini, A., De Michelis, G. and Grasso M. A. (1995). The Milano System, in *A Computational Model of Organizational Context, COMIC Deliverable 1.3*, 163-92 (Available on request from the Computing Department, University of Lancaster, Lancaster LA1 4YR, UK, e-mail: tom@comp.lancs.ac.uk).

Agostini, A., De Michelis, G., Grasso, M. A., Prinz, W. and Syri, A. (1996) Contexts, Work Processes and Workspaces. *Computer Supported Cooperative Work (CSCW). An International Journal*, (to appear).

Agostini, A., De Michelis, G. and Grasso M. A. (1996b) *Cooperative processes in the net.* Technical Report CTL-DSI Milano University, Milano.

Bentley, R., Horstmann, T., Sikkel, K. and Trevor J. (1995): Supporting Collaborative Information Sharing with the World Wide Web: The BSCW Shared Workspace System, in *Proceedings of the 4th WWW Conference*, Boston.

Conklin, E. J. and Begeman, M. L. (1988) gIBIS: a hypertext tooling for exploratory policy disucssion, in *Proceedings of the 2nd Computer Supported Cooperative Work Conference 1988*, ACM, New York, 140-52.

De Michelis, G. (1994) From the analysis of cooperation within work-processes to the design of CSCW Systems, in *Proceedings of the 15th Interdisciplinary Workshop on Informatics and Psychology: Interdisciplinary approaches to system analysis and design*, Schaerding, May 24 - 26.

De Michelis, G. (1995) Computer Support for Cooperative Work: Computers between Users and Social Complexity, in *Organizational Learning and Technological Change* (eds. C. Zucchermaglio, S. Bagnara and S. Stucky), Springer Verlag, Berlin, 337-330.

De Michelis, G. (1996) Work Processes, Organizational Structures and Cooperation Supports: Managing Complexity, in *Proceedings of the 5th IFAC Symposium on Automated systems Based on Human Skills - Joint Design of Technology and Organization*. Elsevier International, Oxford, (to appear).

De Michelis, G. and Grasso, M. A. (1994) Situating conversations within the language/action perspective: the Milan Conversation Model, in *Proceedings of the 5th Computer Supported Cooperative Work Conference 1994*, ACM, New York, 89-100.

Dennis, A. R., Joey, F. G., Jessup, L. M., Nunamaker, J. F. and Vogel, D. R. (1988) Information technology to support electronic meetings. *MIS Quarterly*, **12**.4, 591-619.

Ellis, C. E., Gibbs, S. J. and Rein, G. L. (1991) Groupware: some issues and experiences, *Communications of the ACM*, **34**.1, 38-57.

Flores, F. (1982) *Management and Communication in the Office of the Future*, Hermenet San Francisco.

Holt, A. W. (1988) Diplans: A New Language for the Study and Implementantion of Coordination. *ACM Transactions on Office Information Systems*, **6**.2, 109-25.

Holt, A. W., Ramsey, H. R. and Grimes, J. D. (1983) Coordination System Technology as the basis for a programming environment. *Electrical Communication*, **57**.4, 307-14.

Lee, J. (1990) Sibyl: a tool for managing group decision rationale, in *Proceedings of the 3rd Computer Supported Cooperative Work Conference 1990*, ACM, New York, .

Lee, R. M., McCosh, A. M. and Migliarese P. (1988) *Organizational decision support systems*. North Holland, Amsterdam.

Keen P. G. W. and Scott-Morton M. S. (1978) *Decision support systems*. Addison-Welsey, Reading.

Kraemer, K. and King, J. L. (1988) Computer-based systems for cooperative work and group decision making. *ACM Computing Surveys*, **20**.2, 115-46.

Malone, T. W. and Crowston, K. (1991) *Towards an interdisciplinary theory of coordination* (TR#120), Centre for Coordination Science, M.I.T., Cambridge.

Rothstein, L. R. (1995) HBR Case Study. The Empowerment Effort that Came Undone. *Harvard Business Review*, **73**.1, 20-31.

Schmidt, K. and Bannon L. (1992) Taking CSCW Seriously: Supporting Articulation Work. *Computer Supported Cooperative Work. An International Journal,* **1**.1/2, 7-40.

Seely Brown, J. and Duguid, P. (1991) Organizational Learning and Communities of Practice: a unified View of Working, Learning and Innovation. *Organization Science*, **2**.1, 40-56.

Simon, H. (1960) *The New Science of Management Decision*. Harper & Row, New York.

Sprague, R. H. and Carlson, E..D. (1982) *Building effective decision support systems*. Prentice-Hall, Englewood Cliffs.

Stefik, M., Foster, G., Bobrow, D. G., Kahn, K., Lanning, S. and Suchman, L. (1987) Beyond the chalkboard: computer support for collaboration and problem solving in meetings. *Communications of the ACM*, **30**.1, 32-47.

Suchman, L. A. (1987) *Plans and Situated Actions*. Cambridge University Press, New York.

Vogel, D. R., Nunamaker Jr., J. F., George, J. F. and Dennis, A. R. (1988) Group decision support systems: evolution and status at the University of Arizona, in *Organizational decision support systems* (eds. R. M. Lee, A. M. McCosh and P. Migliarese). North Holland, Amsterdam, 287-304.

Winograd, T. and Flores, F. (1986) *Understanding Computers and Cognition*. Ablex, Norwood.

9 BIOGRAPHY

Giorgio De Michelis teaches Theoretical Computer Science at the University of Milano, where he has been working since 1972.
His research covers the models of concurrent systems (Petri Nets) and Computer Supported Cooperative Work, where he has developed and is developing prototypes of support systems for cooperative processes (CHAOS, UTUCS, MILANO).
He is responsible of the Cooperation Technologies Laboratory at the Dipartimento di Scienze dell'Informazione of the University of Milano; he is Chairman of the Management Committee of the European Community COST 14 Action, CO-TECH.
He is author of more than eighty papers in the areas of his interest.

10

Using the Internet to implement support for distributed decision making

A. R. Dennis
Terry College of Business, University of Georgia
Dept of Management, Athens GA 30602, USA, Tel:+1 (706) 542 3743, Fax:+1 (706) 542 3743, Email: adennis@uga.cc.uga.edu

F. Quek
London School of Economics and Political Science
Dept of Information Systems, Houghton Street, WC2A 2AE, UK, Tel:+44 (0171) 955 7403, Fax:+44 (0171) 955 7565, Email: f.k.quek@lse.ac.uk

S. K. Pootheri
Dept of Mathematics, University of Georgia
Athens GA 30602, USA, Email: sridar@math.uga.edu

Abstract

This paper addresses implementation from the point of view of DSS construction and installation, and highlights the challenges faced when developing DSS in light of rapidly changing business environment and technological advances. In view of the tremendous interest in the Internet, the paper suggests that the Internet has inherent characteristics that are well-suited to supporting distributed work and distributed decision making. The paper then presents TCBWorks as a first generation DSS built for the Internet, and hopes that through sharing the experiences and lessons learnt, the potential and pitfall of this technology and its fit to distributed decision making can be explored, thereby guiding further research in this area

Keywords

Internet, Distributed Decision Making, TCBWorks, Web-based Groupware, DSS Implementation, Web-based technologies, Communicative Competence

1 INTRODUCTION

Decision Support Systems (here taken in the broadest sense) are technological artifacts which are created from and with computer-based technology (Silver, 1991). As software engineered systems, they draw heavily upon the wide range of computer science and management science technologies. DSS developers, not unlike any software developers, will use programming languages, development tools, specialised designed tools or "DSS Generators" (Sprague, 1980), or embed other technologies such as graphics, dialog management, and model management. This paper focuses on DSS technologies for ***the implementation**** of the designed solution, that is the construction and installation of such systems (Silver, 1990; Fenton & Hill, 1993). Though the choice of the development tool or system plays a key role in determining the success of any system such as a DSS (Silver, 1990), their implementation has become ever more difficult.

The world we live in today is in constant and rapid change, reflecting the dynamism on the one hand, and the chaos and confusion that they create on the other. These rapid changes in business and technological advances mean that DSS need to be developed and implemented quickly enough to respond to decision maker's changing needs. DSS as a class of computer-based solutions have their own unique characteristics (Kivijarvi and Zmud, 1993) which neccesitate their development being different from traditional system development life cycle (SDLC) approach used for transaction processing systems. Because of the semistructured or unstructured nature of problems addressed by DSS, managers' perceived needs for information will change and so the DSS must also change (Turban, 1990, p. 158). This has the inadvertent effect of resulting in systems with short life-spans that lose their utility quite rapidly, and may actually become a competitive disadvantage by locking organizations into decision processes that cannot change to meet new requirements.

Traditional SDLC approach has given way to Prototyping and Rapid Application Development (RAD). Also, unlike in the past where a programming language or development tool can have a shelf life of n years, technological advances have in effect, introduced newer versions rapidly. These days, a version difference can mean a total reskilling and retooling. Big tools developers like Microsoft even introduces the policy that version support is limited to just 1 year from the introduction of the new version. As such, developers constantly have to deal with the dilemma of deciding whether revisions to systems (maintenance or enhancements) should be completely rewritten in the latest version, or with another tool or language. This dichotomy of innovation on one end and continuity on the other, highlights the challenges faced when developing DSS in a rapidly changing business environment and technological advances (Benamati et al, 1995). For DSS to be viable and popular (i.e., cost, speed of development, scalability and ease of maintenance), the choice of the right development strategy and tool become ever more important to determine their success.

There is no doubt that the Internet, and in particular, the World Wide Web, has become an important form of communication technology. It is threatening to invade our homes just like what personal computers, telephones and televisions have already done. While personal computers offer computing power, the Internet offers online computing and access to information on a scale unimaginable even a few years before.

From the point of view of technological advances, the Internet technology is compelling. It seems to be going from strength to strength, and looks like being the backbone of a whole new way of computing. Web-based applications are sprouting out everywhere, and we are beginning to see a new generation of systems built for the Internet, with major hardware and software companies pledging support and jumping onto the Internet bandwagon.

---

*For a fuller discussion on Implementation, see Daellenbach (1994)

From the point of view of organisational decision making, the Internet is also compelling. *"Almost every time there is a genuinely important decision to be made in an organization, a group is assigned to make it -- or at least to counsel and advise the individual who must make it."* (Hackman and Kaplan, 1974). Much research on organisational decision making has examined the role of computer-based systems in supporting group decision making, not only the traditional DSS-style decision support function, but also the communication needs of groups, whether they meet together in the same room at the same time, or are distributed groups whose members work in different locations at different times (Jessup and Valacich, 1993; Johnson-Lenz, 1992; Nunamaker et al, 1991). The Internet, and the Web in particular, may be the ideal technology to support the communication needs of distributed groups.

Our goal in this paper is to share our experiences in developing and using TCBWorks, a first generation Web-based groupware system that can support distributed decision making. TCBWorks is designed to be used in any place, at any time, whether participants meet together in a special purpose computer-supported meeting room or work across the Web from different locations in different organisations.

2 THE INTERNET

The Internet is basically one big global network of computer networks. Once you connect your PC to the Internet, it can talk to any other computer in the world that is also connected with. Synonymous with the Information Superhighway, the Internet came into existence in 1969 as ARPANet, a US Defense Department network supporting military research (Krol, 1992). It was developed to satisfy the need for researchers at different geographical locations to be able to communicate with each other on a more rapid basis than before (Uhlig, Farber and Bair, 1979). However, connection only became more easily available and open to a wider audience in 1982 when the National Science Foundation developed NSFNet which was the precursor to finally enabling everyone access to the network.

There are two directly opposing views of the Internet. As stated in an article in Personal Computer World (Jan, 1996): *"One is that it is full of junk and porn, stuffed full of useless information no-one needs and a hang-out for losers and perverts. The other is that it offers people a new golden age of information that will liberate them from industrial slavery"*. Both of these views are somewhat distorted to the extreme. The Internet certainly is a mass media distribution mechanism for a variety of information, software, entertainment and commerce. Not only can it open up the world where you can be put in touch with people around the world, but it has the potential to bring a richer medium of communication that can contain audio, video, text, graphics, modelling etc.

The Internet holds the promise of a technology that can rival the significance of the telephone and television that connects the world. The advent and availability of personal computers in the mid 1970s, once strictly in the domain of government agencies, researchers and scientists, have been the major factors in changing the way we work today and in the future. Their pervasiveness in homes and offices today, across all age groups and occupational levels, have certainly influenced the development of interactive systems like DSS as prior to this, many of the office applications of computers lie in non specialist uses (Newman, 1987).

Telecommuting, the technology of bringing the work to the workers (Kelly and Gordon, 1986) is already widespread, especially with doctors, lawyers, sales people and researchers. And there is also the emergence of Groupware technology, and CSCW as a field of study. In essence, we are seeing the convergence of a number of technologies which are heralding in an era of distributed technology for distributed work. Despite all these potential and possibilities, there are still a number of major issues to be addressed: security, electronic payment protocols, bandwidth constraints, standards, governance etc. Until they are dealt with effectively, the hype and the scepticism will continue to cast a shadow of doubt over the Internet.

Existing office computer systems do not always offer the flexibility required to meet the needs of today's user. The problem is that people need to have access to organisational information in a relatively unstructured manner, access from any location. Noam (1995) highlighted a reversal in the historic direction of information flow: *"In the past, people came to the information, which was stored at the university. In the future, the information will come to the people, wherever they are"*. And this is where the authors believe that the Internet can hold the key in revolutionising the way businesses are conducted, offices communicate, workers interact and systems are developed and use (Quek and Tarr, 1996)

By far, one of the best example of using distributed technology to support distributed work is e-mail. It has not only become popular in the academic and research world, but is fast becoming a standard practice in the business world (Crawford, 1982). It is the choice of managers (Markus, 1994) and even the home as it is much faster and cheaper than faxing or snail mail (conventional mail). It is also capable of sending documents together with the mail, providing a much richer medium (Rice and Shook, 1990; Lee, 1994).

3 SUITABILITY OF THE INTERNET FOR DSS IMPLEMENTATION

Technological advances and the myriad of development tools available today are still beset with issues of incompatible machines, platforms and operating system, on top of costly proprietary systems. The Internet has offered a new dimension of appreciating and evaluating the opportunities for completely new ways of doing things. As researchers, the authors feel that it is important to explore this technology to frame and extend the discussion about the role of the Internet in the future of DSS, and identify some meaningful and effective use.

3.1 Addressing Implementation Challenges

The construction and installation of DSS are not everyday occurrences that organisations and individuals can commit themselves to easily. They can not only be costly undertakings but are also highly specialised applications. The Internet has the potential to address some of these implementation challenges. Not too long ago, client-server technology was touted as the technology of choice for distributed organisations as a means to improve productivity, reporting and decision making. Likewise, Groupware technologies were held in the same breath to provide the mechanism for co-ordination and control of group work. Today, both of these are seriously under threat by the Internet development, and may not face up to the more open Internet which provides an inexpensive alternative. The following are some implementation challenges that can be addressed by using Internet technology:

- **Distributed technology** - Because the Internet was borne out of a US military project to address the concern of a nuclear strike wiping out a single-site computer system, it can be a very secure and reliable way of providing distributed working.
- **"Open" Technology** - Development tools and languages such as Java, provide development of applications which are independent of platform and operating system, and be able to run client application no matter where you are or what machine is being used. Unlike previous "Open" systems ventures such as those between IBM and Apple (1991) to create Taligent, an operating system built on object oriented technology, the push for "Open Systems" has not seen the kind of success that the Internet has achieved in a relatively short period of time. In effect, it is becoming the catalyst for vendors, developers and users to work towards more "open" technology.
- **Promote reuse** - SunSoft's Java scripting language promises a new generation of Internet applications that is an example of a true application of object technology. This promotes reuse of objects like assembly blocks when constructing applications.
- **Accessibility** - Even though the Internet has been around since 1969, it did not exactly take off until 1992 when the World Wide Web (WWW) came about, a collection of servers working together to form a graphically-based hypertext network. It is through this user interface that the Internet suddenly become accessible to a global community without barriers of language, culture or geographical distinction.
- **Availability** - Today, the Internet is often quoted as being made up of 50,000 networks, four million computers and 20-40 million users. Its exponential growth is expected to continue, with office networked computers expected to have Web access, people buying affordable Internet boxes, and home computers hook up via Internet Service Providers.
- **Distributed Resources** - There is no need to rely on dedicated resources from one single source. The Internet technology actually addresses the problem of different platforms and operating systems, and had successfully developed protocols to enable different networks to communicate with each other. One example of an overwhelming success of this technology is e-mail.
- **Development of Intranet** - The private use of Internet technology within organisations are known as Intranets, which will provide a seamless application platform for users both inside and outside the organisation.
- **Distribution of System/Installation, Version Upgrade and Maintenance** - Unlike groupware or other current technologies which have the problem of availability of client program, the right version for a platform and operating system, and keeping it up-to-date, Internet programs such as Java applets need little client-side maintenance. Because applets are downloaded from the server before executing on the client, the current version is automatically downloaded. They are also highly portable, thus reducing both maintenance and time-to-market for multiplatform applications.

3.2 Current Research Interest

There has been a growing interest in distributed systems such as distributed GSS/GDSS, and this can be seen as a natural progression from earlier work in GDSS/GSS and their applications such as Decision Conferencing and Electronic Meeting Systems (EMS) in the late 1980s and early 1990s (Jelassi et al, 1992). Most of these research focus on decision room environment where a group of participants meet face-to-face in the same room, working on a common task (Dase et al, 1995; Dennis et al, 1990/91; and Stohr and Konzynski, 1992).

Dase et al (1995) thus suggested that current research framework developed for GSS/GDSS (McGrath 1984; Dennis et al, 1988; and Nunamaker et al, 1993) must be extended or adapted to deal with new issues in contrast to co-located participants/decision makers (Gallupe and DeSanctis, 1988). As such, DGSS/DGDSS is relatively new and there is little theoretical or empirical research on this topic. In short, the multiple decision maker aspect (Huber, 1984), the geographically dispersed aspect (Hiltz and Turoff, 1992) and the enabling technologies aspect (Fellers et al, 1995 and Bhargava et al, 1995) raise many new questions, challenges and opportunities in research and application areas.

DGSS/DGDSS is gaining popularity not because of advances in long distance communication systems and satellite transmissions, but because of the Internet's mass appeal. Fellers et al (1995) argues that the innovation in using systems (technologies) comes not from their existence, but from their increasing availability to the general public. The Internet growth points to a new application development trend which provides exciting possibilities for distributed applications. Despite its early days, the Internet technology can and should be exploited to further the goals of DSS (Bhargava et al, 1995). One such implementation is DecisionNet (Bhargava et al, 1995), a repository of decision support and modelling technologies that also allow these technologies to be used interactively over the WWW. Another example is the research at Humboldt University on developing "method servers", WWW-based servers of computational services such as algorithms and solvers (Krishnan et al, 1995). DecisionWeb is a system designed to be a "front-end" for traditional problem-solving meetings to enable a group to list, categorize and prioritize ideas asynchronously via the Internet prior to a meeting (Danyi, 1994). Other uses of the Web include providing web pages of topic specific information and resources which have proved to be popular, for example ISWorld Net DSS (Power et al, 1995) and Groupware Central (http://www.cba.uga.edu/group ware/groupware.html).

3.3 Addressing Systems for providing Decision Support

It can be said that much of the mainstream research into DSS tend to be technologically focused, and still lacks the promise that remain true to what DSS aims to do, that of providing support for ill-structured problems (Sprague and Carlson, 1982). Humphreys and Nappelbaum (1995) argued that there is still an almost complete absence in practical applications at top management level of interactive computer-based systems based on traditional DSS and IS design methodologies (Lederer and Sethi, 1988). A decade earlier, Humphreys (1984) had already raised this concern, and advocated for the development of "*techniques for the psychological validation of the decision makers' own problem structuring language than to try to invent a universal problem structuring language that will have to be taught from scratch to high level decision makers*". Alter (1979) perhaps provides the best explanation for this state of affairs: simple DSS are easier to understand, implement, control and modify than complicated DSS. The advent of personal computing had led to the natural application of computing power and technology to managerial needs such as in decision making, by making new discoveries in decision methods or decision technology and applying them through creating tools that decision makers might find helpful. Most of these efforts have been in decision analysis and other forms of decision modeling and human information processing through interactive use of computers, electronic storage media, and electronic communications and information display.

This evolution of DSS, which focuses on the development of technologically supported means of collecting, managing, and displaying information that might be useful in decision situations (Sprague, 1980; Steeb and Johnston, 1981; Stodolsky, 1981; Turoff and Hiltz, 1982; Vogel and Nunamaker, 1988), sadly, also reflected the failure of the traditional DSS/IS approach with complex DSS (Ginzberg, 1975; Manley, 1975; Lucas, 1976; Alter, 1979). GDSS soon came into the limelight, stemming in part from the rise of interest in the area of technological support for groups. Much of GDSS research has taken the view that the most fundamental activity of group decision making is interpersonal communication and hence, to improve group communication activities (DeSanctis and Dickson, 1987), resulting in the development of computer-based workbench environments which facilitate group communication.

But this popular form of DSS/GDSS research did not actually address what Kraemer and King (1988), and Phillips (1989) identified as the other approach to DSS/GDSS, of studying the decision making itself both at individual and group levels (cf. DeSanctis and Gallupe 1987), on *"discovering psychological or cognitive processes of individuals and groups involved in reaching conclusions and on the sociology of small-group interaction"*. This second approach of providing *" a problem solving environment that is group centred and is primarily intended to help managers consider uncertainty, form preferences, make judgments and take decisions"* claimed Phillips, is a more superior approach. Clearly the first approach seems more feasible and less problematic to undertake research than the second, and understandably reiterates Alter's point about dealing with creating simple DSSs. It is easier to build technical aids for decision making than to paint a clear picture of what decision making is. These new technologies are widely adopted and used, but it still is not always clear whether they really improve the condition of those who use them.

3.4 Addressing Support for Distributed Decision Making

The body of research in DSS/GDSS and their conception of "group" may not be relevant or appropriate to study about the growing interest in supporting distributed decision making and cooperative work activities. Groups are not always small, participants come and go, their goals are neither shared nor existing, their tasks can be ambiguous, and decision making may occur in a distributed fashion (Lyytinen et al, 1994; Bannon, 1994). In their CSCW-related research, Schmidt and Bannon (1991) find "cooperative ensembles" (instead of the word "groups") are either large, or are embedded within larger ensembles. They are also often transient formations, emerging to handle a particular situation after which they are dissolve again, and their work is distributed logically, in terms of control, and involve incongruent strategies and discordant motives. There is also the notion that there is no omniscient agent in many of these situations. As such, decision making is inevitably distributed among the decision making agents who have unique situations to face, and their own sets of perspectives, goals and interests to take into account. The question is how then do we address the support for such distributed decision making?

One approach is the integration of CSCW work into GDSS research. The former's strength is in its detailed investigation of exactly how work gets done in organizations, with a particular focus on cooperation, co-ordination and communication in work. For example, in CSCW research, attention has been turned towards the development of an understanding of how to support distributed decision making and cooperative work activities where people are working at "arm's length", without direct communication and without necessarily even knowing each other or knowing of each other. In such cases, people must cooperate via a more or less shared or common information space, such as a 'space' comprising data, personal beliefs, shared concepts, professional heuristics etc. (Bannon & Schmidt, 1991), which is typical of a distributed organization.

Decision makers in a distributed environment should still have the benefit of equal time and opportunity to participate and influence the decision task at hand. Habermas's (1990) theory of communicative action advocates taking informed action through an ideal process of *"a forum of speakers exhibiting communicative competence"* (Jackson, 1991), as opposed to reducing the stakeholders from the role of active participants to that of mere "witnesses" (Ulrich, 1988). As a basis of communicative action all participants will ideally, need to provide information about "what they know best". It is also necessary to organize, and feedback, on a distributed basis, an enhanced understanding of this collective knowledge, given that a suitable vehicle of communication could be found for this purpose.

It is the identification of this suitable vehicle of communication to support Habermas' theory which the authors believe the Internet to be the potential contribution in supporting decision making in a distributed environment. Having an effective vehicle of communication means an orientation towards the discourse within an interpretive framework where each participant's assumptions about what is (or assumed to be) commonly known within the organization can surface (McCaskey, 1988). Therefore, it is not apppropriate to presume the hegemony of the interpretations and assumptions of any particular group or stratum (Humphreys et al, 1995). We are only at the stage of dealing with the efficiency of the vehicle of communication. In this light, the authors introduce TCBWorks as an example of how using web-based technology can potentially help improve the communicative competency of distributed decision makers.

4 USING THE WEB TO SUPPORT DISTRIBUTED DECISION MAKING

The technology for supporting group work (on-site or distributed) has spawn the emergence of groupware and groupware technology. Many groupware systems use proprietary software and architectures running over local area networks or proprietary wide area networks to distribute information among participants. Until recently, there have been few alternatives. The recent explosion of the Web presents a new opportunity as we can now build systems and architectures that take advantage of widely adopted open standards that are available to most potential users of groupware.

4.1 Groupware

Groupware is a term that is commonly used, but lacks a commonly accepted definition. In general, it is a set of hardware and software designed to help groups work together. Vendors, consultants, users, and university researchers all have used the term to refer to many different types of software, each of which support very different types of group work. This form of groupware provides two key functions to groups. First, it enables group members to generate, read, and organise information in a structured manner (Nunamaker, 1991). A weak form of this type of groupware is the usenet newsgroups, which are very good at enabling many people to generate information, but are seriously lacking in the ability to organise it. Groupware enables groups to edit, move, delete, and structure information so that it is presented in a hierarchy or map that is easy to analyse and can evolve as new information is added.

The second key function of this form of groupware is the ability for group members to rank, rate, or otherwise quantitatively analyse the relative merits of alternatives (i.e., to vote) (Nunamaker, 1991). Most groupware systems enable users to vote by ranking or rating alternatives. Some support multicriteria decision making, so that a set of alternatives can be evaluated by all members on a series of criteria (e.g., rating cars on gas mileage, acceleration, etc.). Others support more elaborate decision analysis processes. In any case, each participant enters his or her ratings, analyses, or votes, which are then combined with those of all other participants and presented to the group as a whole for further discussion.

Many companies now use this form of groupware in special purpose meeting rooms, as well as using it to enable groups to "meet" from different geographic locations. This form of groupware has also been the subject of much academic research. While it can improve the quality of group decisions in some cases, its primary benefit is time savings: research with more than 40,000 participants suggests that it can reduce the time needed to make decisions by 50-90% (Groupware Central, accessed 1995; Jessup & Valacich, 1993; Nunamaker, 1991).

4.2 TCBWorks: A first generation Web-Groupware system

TCBWorks (http://tcbworks.mgmt.uga.edu:8080) is different from the "typical" discussion-oriented tools now available on the Web. It is designed to enable people to interact, discuss issues, and make decisions. It can support both structured discussions and multicrieria decision making. The principal organising object in the TCBWorks is the ***project***. A project contains all the data and processes needed to perform most group tasks. Projects are organised in a hierarchy, so that projects can contain sub-projects, sub-sub-projects, and so on. All projects contain the knowledge to be added, deleted, modified, and moved, among other functions. Each project in turn contains a set of ***topics***. Topics contain many of the same properties as projects. They are also organised in a hierarchy (with a series of topics, sub-topics, etc. within each project), and can be added, deleted, modified, and moved.

Topics in turn contain ***comments*** (short paragraphs of text) that can be added, deleted, and modified. Comments can also contain HTML tags, enabling participants to specify formatting (e.g., bold, italics, bullet lists), as well as taking advantage of all the other benefits of the web. It becomes simple to embed a graphic in a comment (provided, of course, you know the HTML syntax and the web address of the graphic). It is also simple to put a link to other web documents as part of a comment or a reference to more information. Comments can be anonymous or identified by the name of the contributor.

Each topic can be rated (i.e., ***voted on***) using a set of criteria defined by the group. There are a maximum of ten criteria, each with user-defined ranges (i.e., minimum and maximum values). Each participant can enter a rating for each topic for each criterion and the system provides the mean value of the group's ratings. The topics can then be viewed in order based on their mean rating across all criteria, or on the mean rating for any one criteria.

There are four categories of users in TCBWorks:

- ***System Administrator:*** the super user can perform any function, such as to create and delete other users;
- ***Project Organizer:*** the user can create new projects and perform any function to the projects created, and also grant access to other users, delete the project, move it, etc;
- ***Participant:*** the user can only access those projects to which he or she has been granted access by a project organizer, and perform those functions permitted by the organizer;
- ***Observer:*** the user has read-only access to the projects specified by an organizer.

4.3 Interface and Technical Design

When the user first connects to the web server, it presents a login screen that requests for the user's name and password. Once successfully logged on, the user is presented with the ***Project Screen***, which displays the list of projects available to the user (all projects to which the user has access). The ***action buttons*** displayed on the left of the screen change depending upon the type of user. A project organizer would have all of the buttons, except the ***Controls*** button, which is used to control access to the database (e.g., create new users). A participant has no ability to create or change a project, and therefore only have the ***Open*** and ***View*** buttons (as well as help, refresh, and exit). Not all of the buttons available to an organizer may be valid for a specific project. For example, an organizer of one project may only grant participant rights for that project (not organizer rights) to another organizer, meaning that he or she could not delete the project.

Once a project has been selected, the user clicks the Open button, and the ***Topic Screen*** is displayed. This screen displays all the topics that exist for the project and enables the user to discuss topics and add new ones. Once again, the buttons that are displayed depend upon the type of user and the rights granted by the project owner. System administrator(s), the project organizer, and any user to whom the organizer has granted organizer rights can perform any function. Participants will only have those buttons to which the organizer has granted rights.

The Topic Screen enables users to perform two major functions (aside from editing and adding topics): discussing the topics, and voting. The discussion screen displays all the comments entered under a topic, and provides an input box for participants to enter their comments. There are typically many comment from different participants under the same topic. Comments are normally displayed in the order in which they are entered, but participants also have the option to insert comments after a specific comment, simply by changing the number in the comment number box. The organizer can specify whether participants can ***Insert, Delete*** or ***Replace*** comments, as well as specifying whether comments will be anonymous or identified by the name of the contributor.

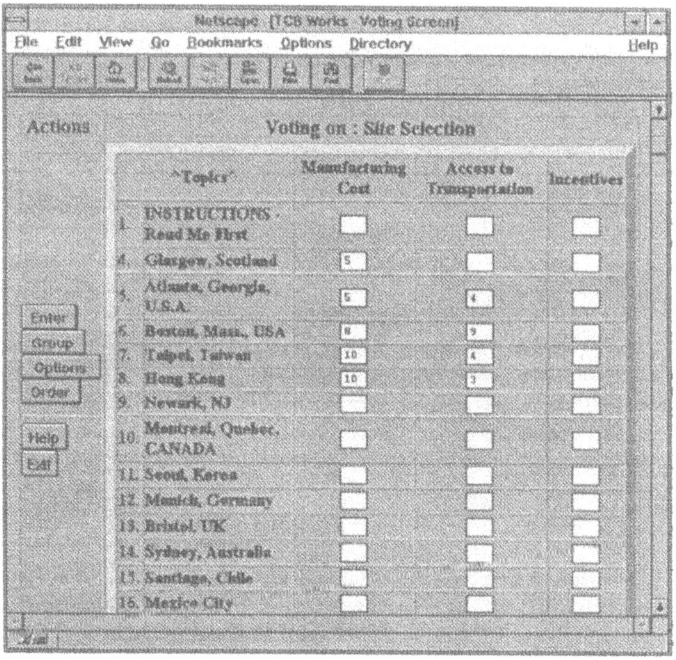

Figure 1 Voting Screen

The last major function is voting (see Figure 1). The organizer first defines the criteria that will be used (anywhere from 1-10 criteria are possible) and the scale that will be used for each (any integer range; the default is 1-10). Once these have been defined, participants can enter their opinions on each of the topics in the project in the boxes provided. Votes can be easily changed at any time and participants can move back and forth between the screen where they type their votes and the screen that displays the average vote of all participants.

The technical design of the system consists of using a series of 28 C programs (about 30,000 lines of code) working on data in an SQL database to generate the HTML forms. These forms capture the user's commands and present information in response, and are generated on the fly. Each program in the system first generates an HTML form by reading the parameters passed by the previous program and by accessing data from a MiniSQL database. Since groupware is inherently a multi-user environment, the use of a database engine greatly simplifies programming by handling the potential concurrency problems, such as the ability to lock records to indicate to other users that someone is making a change.

The HTML forms collect the user's commands through the use of push buttons such as "add a new project". We found this approach to be very efficient. It is modular so it also reduces the complexity of the system. The Web server does not remember the previous states that it took to reach any given screen. Each transaction is a separate request. The user can get into any screen (sometimes using a bookmark) and exit at any state. Therefore, the HTML form that is returned with each request must contain sufficient information to tell the system all choices made by the user in the previous screen, in addition to the current request.

4.4 Experiences using TCBWorks

TCBWorks is currently in use by more than 100 organisations around the world. Most are headquartered in North America, followed (in order) by Europe, Australia-New Zealand, Asia, South America, and Africa. There are many ways of examining the ways in which TCBWorks is being used. One is to consider distance and time. TCBWorks was designed to be used by people working in different places and times across the Internet. However, more than half the organisations are also using it in intranets (intranets use the same network standards as the Internet e.g. TCP/IP, but are designed primarily for private use). The most common use is to support different time and place discussions within a campus or corporate office park, but it has also been used to support same time and place meetings in decision room settings and those where some meeting participants are at remote locations.

Another way of examine its use is to look at the nature of the groups and tasks. One classification is a loosely connected electronic community of users that share the same interests and many of the same goals. An example here is the Executive Operating Committee of ISWorld Net which will be elaborated in the next section. Similarly, a variety of student groups at the University of Georgia and elsewhere are using the software within their campus (i.e., an intranet) to discuss issues of interest to the students. Job-hunting, and course evaluations are typical applications. The key benefit here and in the ISWorld Net example, is the ability to hold formal and informal discussions and to share information and opinions among a groups of individuals with common interests in a more structured form than a newsgroup, listserv, or mailing list would provide.

Task forces and project teams are more tightly connected examples. The Modelling and Simulation community has a variety of Standards Groups, each of which must work together to design, propose, and formally approve sets of standards. Standards Group members are drawn from organisations all over the world and must represent the interests of their members in developing the standards. Members hold regular face-to-face meetings, but use TCBWorks to plan meeting agendas, and discuss issues outside of the face-to-face meetings to reduce the need for meetings. Several U.S. Air Force bases are also using the software to support distributed teams whose members are drawn from different sections within the same base (again, an intranet). In this cases, members also hold regular face-to-face meetings, but use the software to extend the meetings. The key contributions for these distributed project teams are the ability to extend *focused* discussions beyond the face-to-face meetings. Face-to-face meetings (and telephone calls) are used to co-ordinate work and clarify issues requiring "richer" discussions than is possible using the electronic media.

About a quarter of TCBWorks installations have been in special purpose decision rooms, either instead of or in addition to more powerful groupware systems designed specifically to support face-to-face meetings (e.g., GroupSystems, VisionQuest). The rationale is that TCBWorks provides a simpler user interface, enables a common tool to be used in the meeting room and on the desktop, more easily enables remote group members to participate, and costs less. *Creative Loafing*, an Atlanta-based "alternative" newspaper with circulation of 180,000 uses TCBWorks in their decision room for strategic and operational planning, and employee feedback. In the next few months, the system will be opened to enable access from their four satellite offices outside of Atlanta, so that managers at these locations can participate in planning meetings over the Web combined with simultaneous conference telephone calls. Another application area that is somewhat surprising to us is the use of the software in education. About a quarter of the users are using the software to support education, either distance education across the Internet or to support class discussions in decision rooms or outside of regular class time.

4.5 ISWorld Net Example

The ISWorld Net example which is introduced here, is an interesting look at how TCBWorks was used by its Executive Operative Committee as a mechanism for distributed decision making. ISWorld Net (http://www.isworld.org/isworld.html) is a worldwide virtual organization and its mission is to *"provide information management scholars with a single entry point to resources related to information systems technology and to promote the development of an international information infrastructure that will dramatically improve the world's ability to use information systems for creating, disseminating, and applying knowledge"*. Some of its founders include the Academy of Managements' Organization Communications and Information Systems Division, the Association for Information Systems, the International Conference on Information Systems and the International Federation for Information Processing: Technical Committee 8.

The members of this committee are individuals who are actively involved in helping to build and/or promote ISWorld Net. Each member is involved in developing a set of web pages to support the world-wide community of information systems faculty, with each member typically managing and developing one sub-area (e.g., DSS, groupware etc.). The committee as a whole develops strategic objectives, and operating standards, and also advise on a day-to-day basis the chairperson and, through him or her, the officers of the ISWorld Net Governance Committee. Because members of this committee are individuals who represent their own institutions all over the world, and their contributions are entirely voluntary, the committee requires a communication medium which is accessible to all its members to communicate and coordinate their activities. Using e-mail via setting up discussion lists was the best choice under such circumstances since most universities would have e-mail facilities.

However, when it comes to ocassions for decision making, the committee has been faced with a lack of a proper mechanism to facilitate this type of distributed virtual organizational decision making. Also, the bigger problem is the actual lack of a formal decision making process within this committee. Revisiting Habermas' (1990) theory of Communicative Action, due to the distributed nature of the committee's members, the "turn taking" (Bannon, 1994) more often is mistimed, the discussion may not be in the right sequence, and not everyone who wants to contribute can have equal time and opportunity to participate in this process. Often, in order to push through certain decisions, the chairperson will adopt the policy that no response means no objection, and will be accepted after a predetermined time has elapsed. Clearly, there is a need to address the members' and the committee's communicative competence in this respect.

Decisions to be made range from strategic decisions such as the choice of marketing strategy to promote ISWorld Net to the more mundane and time consuming discussion about design guidelines for page formatting. And using the email is deficient in supporting such decision making activities. The availability and accessibility of TCBWorks to this committee was welcomed and on the outset, looked very promising to suit its needs. By far, the biggest advantage is that there is little set-up time, little maintenance and all its members who are already active on the Web can use their web browsers to use this tool. A few years earlier, this scenario would not have been possible as proprietary groupware software would have been cost prohibitive and to get the client software to the distributed members (each with their different platform and operating system) would almost be an unsurmountable challenge.

Over a two-week period, the committee actively experimented with this tool. As the material is to be organized by projects, the chairperson set up a number of projects, and the members contributed the topics of interest in the various projects. Using TCBWorks, comments on each topics are archived in the sequence that they are posted and can be viewed by everyone. This is a particularly useful feature as it created the shared "collective memory" of the committee. Most members who used it genuinely felt that it has a lot of potential and promise. Also, this feature can add value by letting others see the issues that are debated (if necessary).

However, since this initial two-week period, the committee had not used TCBWorks. One of the authors of this paper sent an email to this committee to solicit for feedback about its use, with which the following replies were received:

- the committee as a whole did not really give it much of a test, maybe we should try again
- the tool did not fit the way the committee operates
- the committee does not have that many issues and when they do, email will suffice
- getting into it requires about 5 steps (what page is it on, what is the password, what is the account name, how does this work?)
- not everyone participated

The responses revealed a certain degree of expectation of TCBWorks (in comparison with other groupware products) in terms of its deficiency in interface design, interaction and ease of use. It did not however, reveal the greater problem of a lack of a decision making process. TCBWorks neccessitates that the *"discussion agendas are clearly defined by the project leaders who shape and guide the discussions to reach the project objectives. Objectives and timetables are clearly defined and work assigned to various members"*. Though TCBWorks requires no facilitators, facilitation is still neccessary via the project leaders to make sure that participants understand and observe the requirements and constraints. In the case of the ISWorld Net committee, it was a "free for all" situation. Of the several projects that were set up, each project never achieved the critical mass of getting all the members to be involved, or the topics to be debated and decided upon.

There was a successful outcome though, on the project that was set up to test the tool. The chairperson had suggested that everyone should at least post a comment under this project, and as a result, generated the most comments. One of the discussion topic was on the choice of day to meet at the ICIS conference in Amsterdam in 1995. Another topic was to vote on this. Everyone did meet up with each other at the conference on the right day. Ironically, this date also coincided with the last use of this tool. There was no momentum to use TCBWorks again.

This brief example of the use of TCBWorks by the ISWorld Net committee highlights both the failure and the potential of its use. The failure can be seen in terms of being an example of a good technological support for a non-relevant task at hand. The committee lacks a decision making process in the first place, and therefore, to introduce a decision making mechanism like TCBWorks will not help the situation. The potential can be seen in terms of helping to improve the communicative competence of distributed groups or communities. If there is a process, if everyone participates, if everyone who want to participate can participate, then TCBWorks stands as a good prospect of achieving just that. Already the ISWorld Net committee is considering having another go, this time with a decision making process in place.

5 LESSONS LEARNT

We learned a host of lessons from developing and using the system, both technical and user-based. The first major technical lesson we learned was that it is possible to develop a major application system using the Web. The use of a Web browser such as Netscape as the client environment offers some distinct advantages and disadvantages over traditional system development.

First, because the Web browser provides many built-in functions, development proceeds much faster than it would in a traditional development environment. Traditionally, 80% of any DSS is the user interface. With Web-based development, much of the interface is automatically provided by the browser; you only need to specify what functions to use. It is very much like building with children's blocks -- or objects. Interface coding is reduced to about 40% of the application, saving a significant amount of programming time. The disadvantage is that you are limited to the capabilities of the browser. For example, traditional interface concepts such as drag-and-drop are not (yet) available, so you cannot use them.

A second technical lesson was security; security concerns were expressed by a significant percentage of our users. One level of security is in the web server itself. Most servers can restrict access to only certain Internet addresses, (e.g., within one company or set of companies). The problem occurs if users regularly use CompuServe or other commercial access provider, because one must grant access to all users of those services -- not a very satisfactory solution. Using the security built into the web server was not as good an option as we initially believed. To make the software more secure, every time a user successfully logs in with a correct userid and password, the user is assigned a randomly generated authentication code that is valid for at most 12 hours, without it no access is granted. This prevents the editing scenario described above. It also prevents someone from placing a bookmark in the middle of the system to bypass the login process. You can still bookmark a screen, but the authentication code granting access will be useless after 12 hours, and the system will require you to login. The system also has a logout option, which removes the authentication code from the system and prevents anyone walking by your computer from using the Go Back option to gain unauthorised access to the system. However, logging out is not normally expected of Web-based systems, so this may not be as secure as we would like.

Learning about the software, and making an informed decision about its fit with a specific organization's needs is simplified by using the Web. Since it is Web-based, anyone with a Web browser can experiment with it. About 20 organizations have established databases on our server at Georgia as a trial period before deciding whether to install it on their server.

Distribution and installation on a remote server is relatively straightforward. TCBWorks and the web server and database server can be downloaded from the Web via FTP or a Web browser. The rollout of the second version of the software was rather simple from a technical perspective, illustrating one of the benefits of the Web. To upgrade the approximately 20 organizations using databases on our server, we simply added a link from the home page of version 1.0 to the home page of version 1.1. No changes were required to any client computers. Users simply added a bookmark to the new version to their browser. Likewise, the organizations using our software on their servers simply downloaded the software to a new directory and added a link from their home page.

We also learned several important lessons about user expectations. Most users have been quite enthusiastic about the software. It is a novel Web application and also provides clear value to their work groups and project teams. However, some users have been less than enthusiastic. Rather than viewing the system as a Web application, they see it as a regular desktop application and hold it to the same standards. They expect to use all the standard interface concepts such as double-clicking to open, dragging-and-dropping to move and using pull-down menus with multiple windows. These simple operations are beyond the capabilities of DSS built with today's Web browsers. Until the next generation of browsers become more common, we will not be able to satisfy users with these needs.

A second issue deals with response time. In general, every request issued by the user results in a request sent to the Web server. Response times vary depending upon network traffic. Though most intranet users have reported response times of 1-2 seconds, or less, it varies tremendously across the Internet. North American and Asian users have reported response times of 1-2 seconds, but most response times are considerably longer. Even moderately longer response times (3-4 seconds) can prove extremely frustrating, because they occur after *every* command. Several potential users have discontinued use of the software because the response times proved too frustrating.

Depending upon your viewpoint, the limitations of bandwidth and response times will either be a fundamental issue, or a minor one. Bandwidth will grow rapidly as new technologies are deployed (e.g., wavelength division multiplexing across fibre optic cable). However, demand will also grow as more users join the Internet and as existing users place more demand from new applications. Predicting effects becomes difficult, although we anticipate that supply will rise to just keep pace with demand, making bandwidth a continuing issue.

Finally, the experiences gained from understanding the use of TCBWorks, particularly examples like the ISWorld Net committee's use, can provide invaluable insight into justifying an orientation towards research on this new environment of distributed work and distributed collaborators, on understanding the task to be performed and less on "homogeneous groups" type research.

6 CONCLUSIONS

Much of our present groupware research has focused on the one-time use of groupware for special organisational decision-making or in laboratory settings with student groups. We have far less field-based research with on-going project teams and task forces, and far less with distributed teams and task forces. Understanding the long-term effects of the use of web-based groupware becomes critical.

One key issue may centre on the role of a facilitator, a specially trained individual who assists the group in using the technology to make decisions. Current LAN-based groupware designed to support decision making in decision rooms tend to require a facilitator (e.g., GroupSystems). These system are typically complex and are designed around the presumption of the facilitator to minimise the amount of effort that regular participants must take to learn the software (Nunamaker, et al. 1991).

TCBWorks takes a different approach. It is designed to provide an extremely simple user interface that requires no facilitator. The trade-off, of course, is that it lacks some of the functionality of the complex systems. Several of the organisations now using TCBWorks in decision rooms no longer use facilitators. The facilitator was important in the initial few times that TCBWorks was used, to help in training the users on both the software and good groupware-supported decision process, but now that users have some experience, they no longer want the facilitator. The question is whether we will see this trend continue. With hindsight, this may an obvious outcome. Single-user DSS does not require facilitators, so why should group DSS? And if single-user DSS had required the use of the facilitator, would their use be cost effective, and would they have enjoyed the rather widespread use they receive today?

A limiting factor in the use of web-based groupware is the user interface. The interface is limited by the use of web-browsers, which place huge constraints on what is and is not possible. One potential solution to some of the user interface issues may be Java, although its ultimate value is unclear at this point. With Java, one can write mini-programs that could provide many of the interface characteristics desired by users, and also enable the user to work isolated from the server and only connect periodically (e.g., every few minutes) to issue updates to and receive updates from the server Java may also permit background work, so that updates can be sent immediately, but the browser does not pause and lock the user from continuing to work. Also, we could explore web initiatives such as ISWorld Net which can provide a platform for experimentation and research. We could see how TCBWorks works for the committee the next time round after learning from their earlier experience which was not a particularly good test of it due to a lack of intellectual involvement.

We believe that we are the edge of a revolution in DSS development. We expect that within two years, most companies will realise that the Web is not only a means of electronic publishing, but can be a full-scale system development environment. Rather than developing systems for Windows, UNIX, or Apple, companies will begin developing for the Web. Even systems that are designed solely for internal use (and do not access the Internet) will use Web browsers as the client. Of course, the Web will need to mature, and there will still be the need for traditional DSS applications, but more and more applications that require networking will use the Web, rather than proprietary operating systems and networks. Those who get to the Web first, learn its intricacies, and push its limits will have a distinct advantage. But we must remember the context of the application as shown in the ISWorld Net example. We do not want to end up with having sophisticated systems and tools looking for decisions to make and problems to solve.

7 REFERENCES

Alter, S (1979) Decision Support Systems; Current Practice and Continuing Challenges. Addision-Wesley, Reading, Massachusetts.

Bannon, L.J (1994) CSCW - Challenging (G)DSS Perspectives on the role of Decisions, Information, and Technology in Organizations in B.Mayon-White, S.Ayestaran and P.Humphreys (Eds), Decision Support in Organizational Transformation. San Sebastian. Universidad del Pais Vasco Press.

Benamati, J., Lederer, A.L. and Singh M. (1995) The Impact of Rapid Change in Technology on the Information Systems Organization, in *Proceedings of the First Americas Conference on Information Systems*, August 25-27, Pittsburgh.

Bhargava, H.K., Krishnan, R. and Muller, R. (1995) On Sharing Decision Technologies over a Global Network, in *Proceedings of the First Americas Conference on Information Systems*, August 25-27, Pittsburgh.

Crawford, A. (1982) Corporate Electronic Mail - A Communication-Intensive Application of Information Technology. *MIS Quarterly*, **6**, 1-13.

Daellenbach, H.G. (1994) *Systems and Decision Making: A Management Science Approach.* John Wiley and Sons, Chichester, 189.

Danyi, P. (1994) *Groupware '94 Conference and Exhibition.*

Dase, M.A., Tung, L. and Turban, E. (1995) A Proposed Research Framework for Distributed Group Support Systems, in *Proceedings of the 28th Annual Hawaii International Conference on System Sciences*, IEEE Computer Society Press, Los Alamitos, California.

Dennis,A.R. (1995) Groupware Central, *http://www.cba.uga.edu/groupware/groupware.html*

Dennis, A.R. and Nunamaker, J..F., and Vogel, D.R. (1990/91) A Comparison of laboratory and field research in the study of electronic meeting systems. *Journal of Management Information Systems*, 7 (3), Winter, 107-135.

Dennis, A.R, and Nunamaker et al (1988) Information Technology to support electronic meetings. *MIS Quarterly*, December , 591-624.

DeSanctis, G. and Dickson, G.W. (1987) GDSS software as "shell" system in support of a programme of research. In Proc. of 20th annual Hawaii conference on systems sciences.

Fellers, J.W., Clifton, A. and Handley, H. (1995) Using the Internet to Provide Support for Distributed Interactions, in *Proceedings of the 28th Annual* Hawaii *International Conference on System Sciences*, IEEE Computer Society Press, Los Alamitos, CA.

Fenton, N. and Hill, G. (1993) *Systems Construction and Analysis: A Mathematical and Logical Framework.* McGraw-Hill, Maidenhead, 18.

Gallupe, R.B. and DeSanctis, G. (1988) Computer-Based Support for Group Problem-Finding: An Experimental Investigation. *MIS Quarterly* **12** (2).

Ginzberg, M.J. (1975) A Process Approach to Management Science Implementation. PhD dissertation, Massachusetts Institute of Technology.

Habermas, J. (1990) The theory of communicative action. Volume 1: Reason and the rationalisation of society. Polity Press, London.

Hackman, J.R and Kaplan, R.E. (1974) Interventions into Group Process: An Approach to Improving the Effectiveness of Groups. Decision Sciences, 5, 459-480.

Humphreys, P.C. (1984) Levels of representation in structuring decision problems. Journal of Applied Systems Analysis, **11**, 3-22.

Humphreys, P.C. and Nappelbaum, E.L. (1994) Structure and communications in the process of organizational change: Eastern European experience and its general relevance. B.Mayon-White, S.Ayestaran and P.Humphreys (Eds), Decision Support in Organizational Transformation. San Sebastian. Universidad del Pais Vasco Press.

Humphreys, P.C., Berkeley, D. and Jovchelovitch, S. (1995) Organizational Psychology and Psychologists in Organizations: Focus on organizational transformation. Forthcoming in the Interamerican Journal of Psychology.

Hiltz, S.R. and Turoff, M. (1992) Virtual Meetings: Computer Conferencing and Distributed Group Support, in *Computer-Augmented Teamwork: A Guided Tour* (ed. R.P. Bostrom, R.T. Watson and S. Kinney), Van Nostrand, Reinhold, New York.

Huber, G.P. (1984) Issues in the Design of Group Decision Support Systems. *MIS Quarterly* **8**

ISWorld Net (1994), *http://www.isworld.org/isworld.html*, November 28.

Jackson, M.C. (1991) Systems methodology for the Management Sciences, Plenum, N.Y.

Jelassi, T., Klein, M.R. and Mayon-White, W.M. (1992) Decision Support Systems: Experiences and Expectations, *IFIP Working Group 8.3 Conference Proceedings*, North-Holland, Amsterdam.

Johnson-Lentz, P. and Johnson-Lentz, T. (1992) The process and impacts of design choices, in *Computer-Mediated Communication Systems: Status and Evaluation* (ed. Kerr, E.B. and Hiltz, S.R.), Academic Press, New York.

Kelly, M.M. and Gordon,G.E. (1986) *Telecommuting: How to make it work for you and your Company*. Prentice-Hall, New Jersey.

Kivijarvi, H. and Zmud, R.W. (1993) DSS implementation activities, problem domain characteristics and DSS Success. European Journal of Information Systems, **2** (5).

Krishnan,R. et al (1995), *Method Servers.*

Krol, E. (1992) *The Whole Internet User's Guide and Catalog*. O'Reilly and Associates, CA.

Lederer, A.L. and Sethi, V. (1988) The implementation of strategic information system planning methodologies. MIS Quarterly, **12**, 445-461.

Lee, A. (1994) Electronic Mail as a Medium for Rich Communication: An Empirical Investigation Using Hermeneutic Interpretation. *MIS Quarterly*, **18** (2), 143-157.

Lucas, H.C. (1976) The Implementation of Computer-Based Models. National Association of Accountants, New York.

Lyytinen, K., Maaranen, P. and Knuuttila, J. (1994) Groups are not always the same: An analysis of group behaviours in electronic meeting systems. CSCW: An International Journal, **2** (4), 263-286.

Manley, J.H. (1975) Implementation attitudes: a model and a measurement methodology. In Implementing Operations Research/Management Science (Schultz, R.L and Slevin, D.P, eds), American Elsevier, New York, 183-202.

Markus, M.L. (1994) Electronic mail as the medium of managerial choice. Organization *Science*, **5** (4), 502-527.

McCaskey, M.B. (1988) The challenge of managing ambiguity and change. In L.R. Pondy, R.L. Boland, Jr and H. Thomas (Eds), Managing ambiguity and change. Wiley & Sons, Chichester, 1-15.

McGrath, J.E. and Hollingshead, A.B. (1994) *Groups Interacting with Technology: Ideas, Evidence, Issues and an Agenda*. Sage Publications.

Noam, E. (1995) What then is the role of the university?. *Science* **13**, October, 247.

Nunamaker, J.F., Dennis, A.R., Valacich, J.S., Vogel, D.R., and George, J.F. (1993) Group Support Systems Research: Experience from lab and field, in *Group Support Systems: New Perspectives* (ed. Jessup, L.M. and Valacich, J.S.), Macmillan Publishing Company.

Nunamaker, Jr., J.F., Dennis, A.R., Valacich, J.S., Vogel, D.R., and George, J.F. (1991) Electronic Meeting Systems to Support Group Work. *Communications of the ACM*, **34**.

Phillips, L.D. (1989) People-centred group decision support. In G. Doukidis, F. Land and G. Miller (eds) Knowledge based management support systems. Chichester, Wiley & Sons.

Power, D., Bhargava, H. and Quek, F. (1994) ISWorld Net Decision Support Systems, *http://power.cba.uni.edu/isworld/dss.html.*

Quek, F. and Tarr, I. (1996) An Example of the Use of the WWW as a tool and environment for Research Collaboration, in *IFIP Working Group 8.4 Conference Proceeding* (ed. Glasson, B. et al), April, Arizona. (in press)

Rice, R. and Shook, D. (1990) Relationships of Job Categories and Organizational Levels to Use of Communication Channels, including Electronic Mail: A Meta-Analysis and Extension. *Journal of Management Studies*, **27**, 195-229.

Schmidt, K. (1991) Riding a Tiger, or Computer Supported Cooperative Work. In L.M. Bannon and K. Schmidt (Eds) Proceedings of the 2nd European Conference on CSCW. Kluwer, Dordrecht, 1-16.

Schmidt,K. and Bannon, L. (1992) Taking CSCW Seriously: Supporting articulating work. Computer Supported Cooperative Work, **1** (1-2), 7-40.

Shonk, J.H. (1992) *Team-Based Organizations*. Homewood, III., Business One Irwin.

Sprague, R.H. (1980) A framework for the development of group decision support systems. MIS Quarterly **4** (4), 1-26.

Sprague, R. H and Carlson, E.D. (1982) Building Effective Decision Support Systems. Prentice-Hall, Englewood Cliffs, New Jersey.

Steeb, R. and Johnston, S.C. (1981) A computer-based interactive system for group decision making. IEEE Trans. Syst., Man, and Cybern. **11** (8), 544-552.

Stodolsky, D. (1981) Automatic mediation in group problem solving. Behav. Res. Methods *Instrum*. **13** (2), 235-242.

Stohr, E.A. and Konzynski, B.R. (1992) *Information Systems and Decision Process*, IEEE Comuter Society Press, Los Alamitos, California.

Turban, E. (1990) *Decision Support and Expert Systems: Management Support Systems.* Macmillan, New York.

Turoff, M. and Hiltz, S.R. (1982) Computer support systems for group versus individual decisions. IEEE Trans. Commun. **30** (1), 82-91.

Ulrich, W. (1988). Systems thinking, systems practice and practical philosophy: A programme of research. Systems Practice, **1**, 137-163.

Vogel, D. and Nunamaker, J.F. (1988) Group decision support system impact: Multimethodological exploration. In Proceedings of Conference on Technology and

Cooperative Work, J. Galegher, R. Kraut, and C. Egido, (Eds). National Science Foundation, Bell Communications, University of Arizona, Tucson.

8 BIOGRAPHY

Alan R. Dennis is Associate Professor of Management in the Terry College of Business at The University of Georgia. He received a Bachelor of Computer Science from Acadia University, an M.B.A. from Queen's University, and a Ph.D. in Management Information Systems from the University of Arizona. His current research interests include group brainstorming and decision making, and the design of web-based technologies to support collaborative work. His research has appeared in MIS Quarterly, Information Systems Research, Academy of Management Journal, Management Science, Communications of the ACM, Organizational Behavior and Human Decision Processes, and J. of Applied Psychology.

Freddie Quek is an Information Systems Manager at Electronic Press Ltd (UK), which is an electronic publishing arm of the Current Science Group of medical publishing company. He received a Masters of Science from the London School of Economics, and is currently pursuing his Ph.D. in Information Systems at the same institution. He is also the Professional Activities Division Editor of ISWorld Net. His current research interests include decision support systems, electronic publishing, databases and the use of web-based technologies to support collaborative work.

Sridar K. Pootheri is a Ph.D. candidate in the Dept of Mathematics at The University of Georgia. He received a Bachelor of Math from the Vivekananda College at the University of Madras, and a Masters of Math from the Ramanjuan Inst. of Advanced Study in Mathematics at the University of Madras, India. His current research interests include Graph Theory and Combinatorics and the design of web-based technologies to support collaborative work.

11

A DSS design method based on organizational change

Claudio Ferioli
Dpt. of Economics and Production - Politecnico di Milano
P.zza Leonardo da Vinci, 32 - 20133 Milano - Italy
Fax +39.2.2399.2720
E-Mail ferioli@mail.ecopro.polimi.it

Piero Migliarese
Università della Calabria e Politecnico di Milano
P.zza Leonardo da Vinci, 32 - 20133 Milano - Italy
Fax +39.2.2399.2720
E-Mail migliare@mail.ecopro.polimi.it

Abstract

The paper proposes a DSS design approach based on three organizational aspects: (i) the analysis of decisional requirements of managers, (ii) the changes the DSS causes in users work habits and (iii) the changes the DSS causes in organizational power equilibrium. The aim of the proposed approach is to save the implementation from failure and to foresee reasons why organization components might reject the DSS. For each of the three aspects the paper describes the main problem the DSS designer has to face with and some solutions are proposed. In particular, as regards the analysis of power equilibrium changes, the paper proposes a new method based on the analysis of the network of relations existing in the organization. The relational method overcomes some of the limits of the two classical organizational approaches to political analysis of IT system introduction in organizations: i.e. the transaction cost perspective and the organization power theory. The paper describes an application of the proposed design approach, regarding the DSS introduction in a public health agency.

Keywords

DSS design, organizational change, network analysis, relational analysis.

1 INTRODUCTION: THE GAP BETWEEN DSS AND ORGANIZATIONS

Research on DSS has been conducted for more than 15 years in the international scientific community (Angehrn and Jelassi, 1994; Gorry and Morton, 1971) and has obtained several important results, such as the development of decisional theories and software tools for individual preferences modeling, for finding single or multi-attribute functions, for decomposing such functions, etc. (Radermacher, 1994). DSS topics have been extended from individual decision support to Group decision support (GDSS) (Nunamaker, Vogel and Konsynski, 1989; Gallupe, Bastianutti and Cooper, 1991; Poole and De Sanctis, 1992; Migliarese, 1992) and to Organizational decision support (ODSS) (Lee, McCosh and Migliarese, 1988; George, Nunamaker and Valacich, 1992). Decisional support tools have been commercialized by several software houses, even if under different labels (DSS, EIS, MIS, etc)

In spite of the important theoretical results some authors underline that there is a gap between the DSS technical potentiality and their (limited) use in organizations; this gap exists for most of innovative IT application too (Ciborra, 1993). At large, Information Technologies are not playing the expected central role in organization developments and in emerging competitive changes (Land, 1995).

This gap may be explained from different points of view. It may be underlined that organizations and persons have a natural inertia. The speed of technical development is greater than that of organizational and personnel changes. Existing DSS (as well as other innovative IT applications) are useful tools for management to achieve their ends (Bariff and Ginzberg, 1982): at present they are scarcely used because of managers' psychological resistance, but they will be completely adopted in the future, when new decision makers will take the place of those who are now managing organizations.

A second perspective explains the gap through technical reasons (Radermacher, 1994; Bell, 1992). DSS are not used because they don't provide real help to decision makers. According to some authors, current decision support systems provide only low level support, based on data organization and on an enormous amount of computations of an easy but tedious nature. Instead it is necessary to design more powerful DSS that are able to support complex and sophisticated decisional processes. New technical solutions are to be discovered, for example in the field of Artificial Intelligence.

A third point of view considers mainly organizational problems (Mumford, 1979). The gap is due to a mismatching between DSS and organizations: some innovative IT applications are implemented without considering social and organizational constraints (Whitaker, 1994). A socio-technical approach is then required: DSS design should comprise also the analysis of DSS impact on organization and the introduction of a new decision tool should be coupled with planned organizational changes (Keen, 1980).

This paper proposes a design approach for managerial DSS that embraces mainly the third perspective: this choice is due only to the obvious need to set limits on the field of research. As a matter of fact each of the three points of view may be correct for some situations and wrong for others. The designing of decision support tools should take into account suggests from the three of them.

The proposed design approach links DSS design to the social and technical analysis of the organization. Three interdependent aspects are considered as relevant for managerial DSS design:
(1) the **decisional requirements** of managers,
(2) the changes the tool requires in users' work habit, that may cause resistance to the new tool introduction and even lead to its failure (**work habit changes**),
(3) the changes in power equilibrium of organization, that may cause a resolute opposition to the system (**political changes**).

In the following the paper will refer to managerial DSS requiring an "ad hoc" and continuous data entry process (i.e. following considerations are not valid for DSS that use already existing data bases, created for example for accounting purposes, customer order collection, etc.).

On one hand the design of these managerial DSS needs to satisfy the requests of managers and to provide effective help for their decision taking .

On the other hand the designers must prevent opposition to the tool by the users who are required to enter the data even if they gain no direct benefits from the tool (Grudin, 1989). Refusals may derive from unwelcome or misunderstood changes in work habits (**work habits changes**) as well as from the defence of the actual role and power in organization (**political changes**).

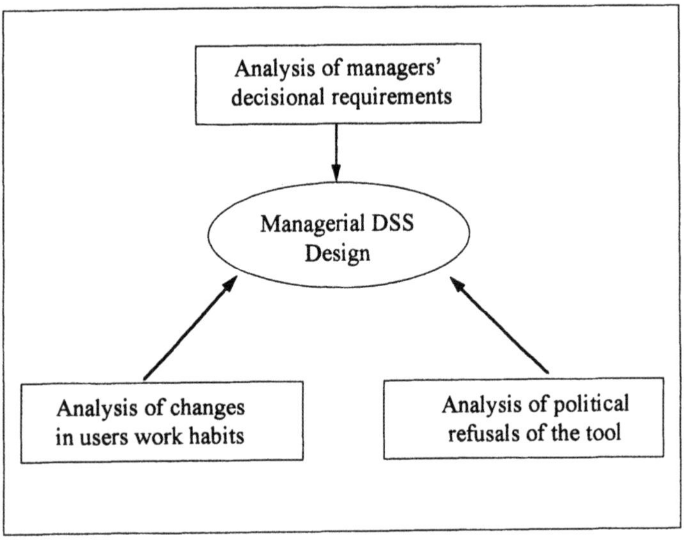

Figure 1. The proposed design approach.

The next paragraphs will examine these three aspects and will provide an approach for designing managerial DSS introduction in organizations.

The proposed approach is partially based on existing literature, mainly as regards the analysis of manager decisional requirements (section 2) and of work habits changes (section 3).

For the political change problem, the paper proposes instead a new method based on the analysis of the **network of relations** existing in the organization (section 4.3).

Organizations are described as networks composed of nodes (individuals, groups, organizational units, etc.) linked through complex relations of several types (economic relations, hierarchical relations, interpersonal relations, etc.). The set of existing relations influences the behavior of each node towards the other ones: friendship, collaboration, competition, hostility, etc. In particular the level of opposition against a managerial DSS is due to the relations linking the managers (who will benefit from the system and decide its introduction in the organization) and the other employees, who won't receive direct benefits from the system.

This method is proposed for overcoming some of the limits of the two classical approaches in the analysis of political opposition to new technical system: the transaction costs theory (section 4.1) and the organization power perspective (section 4.2).

As an example, the paper will describe the application of the proposed designing approach in a real organization (section 5).

2 THE ANALYSIS OF MANAGERS' REQUIREMENTS

The first aspect considered in the design of a managerial DSS is discovering of the decision requirements of managers (Rockart, 1979).

Organizations are considered as the result of decisions taken by persons at different levels in the hierarchy. The decision maker is supposed to act in an intentionally rational way (Thompson, 1967): the problems he has to face concern limitations of the human mind and complexity of the external environment. A DSS has to facilitate the decision process and support the decision actors. This perspective is focused on the decision maker: the design of an IT tool begins with the analysis of the decision needs of the end user; the data model and the whole system are then designed in order to satisfy the discovered requirements (structured analysis) (McMenamin and Palmer, 1984).

The classical analysis of decisional requirements of managers considers problems in DSS design deriving from "intrinsic" limitations in the human decision making process (Simon, 1976).Those problems affect not only the decision processes of organizational actors but also the design of IT based support. Some of the main problems concern for example: the bounded rationality of the decision actor, the presence of uncertainty, differences in individual preferences, the tacit knowledge, the feature of adaptive rationality (Table 1).

Limits deriving from non collaboration of other organizational actors, opportunistic use of information, social impact of information technology, etc., are not taken into account (DeMarco, 1978).

The **bounded rationality** affects the analysis of decision requirements of managers: the human mind of design team members is unable to discover all the decision needs that a DSS has to satisfy (Hewitt and De Jong, 1984). A prototyping approach partly solves this problem, by enabling a cycle of interaction with the end user that facilitates the emerging of decision needs (Ives and Olson, 1984).

High levels of **uncertainty** affect several aspects of an IT based support systems (output required, input collected, use of the system, etc.) as this may produce situations that never existed before (Ciborra, Migliarese and Romano, 1984; Heiner, 1983). The design of IT systems should realize flexible or easy-to-modify tools in order to cope with unexpected changes (Davies, 1992).

Differences in end users individual preferences are problematic mainly for multi-user support systems and for commercial (non custom) tools. A possible solution (used mainly in GDSS) regards the possibility for user preference specification; another solution (used in some commercial tools) is provided by the production of easy-to-tailor systems (Gardner, Paul and Patel, 1995).

The **tacit knowledge** indicates that not all knowledge is formalisable and so can be included in IT based decisional support. Parts of an individual's knowledge and an organization's knowledge are not transparent and accessible to the designer (Polany, 1966; Sternberg and Wagner, 1986) This problem enlarges the use of design techniques that are based on end-user participation in order to extract the superior knowledge of end-users (Briefs, Ciborra and Schneider, 1984).

The **adaptive rationality** concerns the process of individual and organizational learning (Argyris, 1982; Piaget, 1974; Weick, 1979; Norman, 1983). The expertise of DSS users increases through a learning-by-using process (Rosenberg, 1982): users get progressively more keen on DSS use and discover new possible area of application. This increasing expertise changes the decision needs: some of the old functions became superfluous and new ones are requested. Two solutions may be adopted: the first is the use of prototyping techniques for system development; the second is to implement easy-to-redesign and easy-to-upgrade systems (Mumford, 1991).

Table 1. Main problems and classical solution for the analysis of DSS user requirements

Main problems	*Classical solutions*
Bounded rationality	Prototyping approach
Uncertainty	Flexible and easy-to-modify systems
Differences in user preferences	Possibility for preferences specification. Easy-to-tailor systems.
Tacit knowledge	Design techniques based on end user participation
Adaptive rationality	Prototyping approach Easy-to-upgrade and/or easy-to-redesign tools

According to this perspective, the designer's efforts are concentrated on the development of an IT system able to satisfy the users' decision requirements and to cope with intrinsic constraints of the human mind and of the external environment. The challenge facing the system designer is to produce the best technical solution for supporting the end users. High technical expertise is required, both in software implementation and in software engineering for providing the best decisional support and for reducing the effects of underlined problems (Table 2).

Table 2. A synthesis of the analysis of decisional requirements of the manager.

Key actors	*Considered Constraints*	*Role of the designer*
the manager as a decision maker	• technical problems; • "intrinsic" limitations in decision making.	Technical Expert

3. THE ANALYSIS OF WORK HABIT CHANGES

The described analysis of manager decisional requirements is not enough for designing effective DSS. Frequently, decision support systems fail when they are introduced in organizations, even if they satisfy all the decision requirements of the managers (Keen, 1980; Ginzberg and Ariav, 1986).

This paragraph will analyze some causes of failures of DSS introduction from the perspective of changes in work habits. The introduction of a DSS changes the work habits of several people apart from the manager gaining direct benefits from the application. Those changes cause problems in DSS introduction and may lead it even to a complete failure.

One of the most important problem in the introduction of managerial DSS is the disparity between benefits for managers and additional work for other employees.

On one hand, there are great benefits for the managers who decide on the introduction of the decision support system. On the other hand, a DSS often requires that some people do additional work (for example for data entry processes), while those people are not the ones who perceive a direct benefit from the application (Grundin, 1989).

This extra work is extremely important for the success of the DSS, as it ensures the correctness of the data that form the basis of the decisional support. But employees may have a low motivation to do it well, as it is an additional work that doesn't produce direct benefits for them (Ehrlich, 1987).

The search of an appropriate solution for this problem has to be one of the central aims in designing decision support. Two classical solutions are proposed in literature: changing job description (**mandatory solution**) or enlarging benefits of the DSS to everyone uses it (**involvement solution**).

The **mandatory solution** is based on a top-down logic of organizational change: it supposes that organizations have to adapt to a well-designed technical system. Job description and personnel characteristics are changed in order to cope with new IT system.

The costs of this change may be very high and are mainly due to personnel qualification. new job descriptions require skills improvements, training periods, new criteria for personnel evaluations, changes in labour contracts. The costs of this solution may be justified if the introduction of the new decision support system affects the whole organizational information system, for example when the new managerial DSS is part of a new information system that involves the whole organization. (Cherns, 1980; Rowe, 1985)

Otherwise the second solution is generally to be preferred (Grudin, 1989). The **involvement solution** follows the logic of modifying both the system and the organization to adapt each other.

The designer has to modify the decision support to enlarge its benefits also to other employees (apart from the manager). This means building in additional features, changing the system architecture, etc. New benefits partially change work activities, for example, with the reduction of routine tasks or the facilitation in doing the job. Even if a training period is always required, the personnel costs are generally lower than in the mandatory solution. Technical costs instead increase, because the application gets more complex to implement and more difficult to manage.

A second problem in introducing decision support regards the match between user capabilities and technical requirements of the application (Phillips, 1992). On one hand, some users (also managers) have low expertise in computer usage and are not accustomed to use complex IT tools. On the other hand decision support complexity is difficult to reduce and to hide to the end-user.

Two classical solutions to this approach regard the design of easy man-machine interfaces (changes in the system) and the planning of effectiveness training period (changes in the organization).

The design of man-machine interfaces should produce DSS which are easy to learn and to use, so as to obtain user satisfaction and prevent failures of the system due to the handicap of complexity (Alter, 1990; Keen and Scott-Morton, 1978; Rockart and DeLong, 1988).

Interface design includes also the implementation of different facilities for improving user friendly features of the system, such as possibilities for user customization (choice of colours, system driven process versus user driven process, ...), help on line, etc.

The training period is equally important for reducing the gap between user expertise and DSS capability requirements. This phase is effectively made if it is aimed not only at explaining system function but also to promote the use of the system. It has to make the users appreciate the advantages deriving from the system, in order to motivate them to use the system and to reduce the fear of the new tool.

The problems deriving from changes in work habits sometimes are objective and due to real small revolutions, but sometimes they may be only due to wrong perceptions and/or wrong images of the tool.

Users and designers often describe an IT system through metaphors (DeSanctis, Snyder and Poole, 1994) that are generally influenced by previous experiences and/or by personal attitudes and preferences. People with low expertise on computer usage may develop an unjustified fear of using new tools and so refuse to face up to and to solve the real problems. The use of design techniques based on user participation (for example prototyping) correct wrong metaphors of the system and reduce the possible fear of the users against the new technical tool (Hirschheim and Klein, 1989; Madsen, 1989).

The work-habits-changes perspective requires from the DSS designer the capability of facilitating the user in adopting the new tool. The designer has to play the role of technical facilitator, the one who modifies the tool in order to adapt it to organizational and personal characteristics (for example in designing easy man-machine interfaces), as well as the role of organizational facilitator, when he modifies the organization to adapt to the system (for example with dealing with job redesign, training the users, controlling emergent metaphors of the systems, etc) (table 3).

Table 3. A synthesis of the analysis of work habits changes

Key actors	*Considered Constraints*	*Role of the designer*
• organizational decision maker • non-expert users • employees with no direct benefits from the DSS	• additional work for data entry and background activities; • gap between capability required by the DSS and expertise of its users • wrong metaphors of the system	• Technical Facilitator • Organizational Facilitator

4 THE ANALYSIS OF POLITICAL DSS REFUSAL: A RELATIONAL APPROACH

Some DSS introductions fail even if they're well designed according to technical perspectives as well as in relation to work organization impact. Some of the users may boycott the tools, as they are afraid of losing part of their power in the organization. In fact, the introduction of a new DSS for providing a particular user (the manager) with an enlarged amount of information and expertise might change the existing organizational power equilibrium (Markus, 1983; Grover, Lederer and Sabherwal, 1988; Scarbrough and Corbett, 1992). Those organizational actors, who are penalized by the system, will try to defend their position with several strategies, from incorrect communication of data to an attempt to make the tool fail entirely.

The effective design of a managerial DSS requires a third point of view regarding the possibility of opportunistic and strategic behavior of organizational actors (March, 1991).

This phenomenon is generally studied through two classical perspectives from organization theory: the transaction-cost perspective and the power perspective.

4.1 The transaction costs perspective

The transaction cost perspective describes every link between two (or more) organizational actors through the concept of economic "transaction". Four phases compose a transaction: the research of the counterpart, the negotiation of contractual conditions, the control of the exchange and the maintenance of the link (Williamson, 1975).

Organizations are designed in order to minimize the transaction cost (i.e. the sum of the costs for the four phases): the best solution is chosen among three pure organizational forms (market, hierarchy, clan) or among mixed forms (Williamson, 1979; Ouchi, 1980).

IT tools generally modify transaction costs: in this way a DSS introduction may change the best organizational form (for example from hierarchy to market).

According to the transaction cost perspective, IT tools may fail because of opportunistic behavior of (some) organizational actors: those who have not economic interest in reducing transaction cost (and in moving to a new organizational model) will not collaborate in designing the new information system and in its introduction in the organization.

The focus on economic costs only is the main limit of the transaction cost theory. This approach doesn't consider social and psychological aspects, technical constraints, interpersonal links, etc., that are as important as economic transactions in IT design. The transaction costs perspective application needs to be completed with the analysis of other dimension involved in organizational interaction, apart from the economic one (Ferioli and Migliarese, 1995).

4.2 The power perspective

A second classical organizational theory is the power perspective: with respect to the transaction cost theory, the centre of the analysis is extended from the concept of economic transaction to the larger concept of organizational power.

The power perspective analyzes how the introduction of an IT based system may modify the distribution of power among organizational actors (Keen, 1981; Newman and Noble, 1990). Those changes determine the extent to which organizational actors promote, accept or refuse the system (the rule is that everyone tries to maintain or to augment his own power).

The difference of interest in using the system might cause a conflict between the organizational actors in favor of the tools and the ones against it (Bariff and Galbraith, 1978). The resulting force field will determine the success or the failure of the new Information System: the difference of power will decide the game.

The power perspective foresees the use of power every time there is a difference of interest between two organizational actors (Pfeffer, 1981). This analysis of organizations is only partially true: as a matter of fact, in some cases power is exerted even without diverging interests, in other cases contrasting interests don't cause power conflicts. The predictability of organizational behavior and conflicts is the main problem of power perspective use in DSS design, when it's necessary to foresee the power reaction a new IT system may cause.

For this reason the use of the power perspective has to be coupled with a deeper analysis of the reasons that may lead to or prevent organizational conflict.

4.3 The proposed Relational Perspective

The two previous sections have underlined some limits in the two classical perspectives for the analysis of DSS political refusal (the transaction costs theory and the power perspective). In the following the paper proposes a third approach, based on the analysis of the **network of organizational relations** existing among organizational actors, that overcomes the described limits. This Relational Perspective is presented here as alternative to the two classical perspectives (and in this sense it is used in the application described in par. 5); nevertheless it could be used also together with the transaction cost theory and/or the power perspective, for completing and enriching the analysis.

The word "relation" was firstly introduced in organization theory by Elton Mayo and his Human Relations school. Even if nobody can deny the importance of this school in organization studies, the concept of relation is used here with a limited meaning: (1) only interpersonal relations are considered; (2) the analysis is centered on the organizational climate, whereas the relation remains only on the back.

Some authors (Gabarro, 1990; Granovetter, 1992; Ferioli and Migliarese, 1994) have proposed the concept of relation as the basis for organizational analysis. The relation describes the link between two organizational actors according to several dimensions (Donati, 1991): it may be considered as an extension of the economic transaction to include also interaction of other types (such as social links, technical interdependencies, psychological interactions, etc.) (Migliarese and Ferioli, 1995).

Examples of organizational relations are:

- an internal market mechanism, with an internal price system for regulating exchanges among organizational units (economic relation);
- interpersonal contacts (social relation);
- an IT based network linking two offices (technical relation);
- the authority link between a supervisor and his subordinates (hierarchical relation)
- the esteem of a young employee toward an old expert (psychological relation)
- etc.

In the analysis of the network of organizational relations, organizations are considered as networks composed of **nodes** and of **relations** linking the nodes.

Several criteria may be defined for the location of **nodes**: formal borders of organizational units, similarity in technical activity, equality in hierarchical position, similarity in professional qualification, etc. For the purposes of relational analysis, the best criterion is the relational homogeneity of nodes: this defines the nodes so that all the components of a node have the same set of relations with every other organizational actor (Baker, 1992).

The width of the nodes varies in relation to the size of the analysis (Ferioli and Migliarese, 1994). For example, if the analysis concerns a whole organization with many divisions located in several countries, a local factory may be considered a node; whereas if the analysis is limited to a shop floor the size of nodes is restricted to the individual employee.

Each node is linked to the other nodes through a set of **relations**. For example a subordinate may be linked to his supervisor through: (1) a hierarchical relation, (2) a psychological relation (esteem of supervisor expertise), (3) a technical relation (interdependencies in work activities), (4) a social relation (due to friendship).

The analysis of the sets of relations linking the nodes (i.e. the analysis of the network of relations) enables prediction of the behavior of each node toward the other ones: for example the previous subordinate-supervisors relations will be generally characterized by trusting and collaborative behavior and will refuse opportunistic behavior and/or conflictual use of power.

In this way, the analysis of existing network of relation explains the political reaction that a DSS introduction may cause in an organization. For example, opportunistic behavior on the part of the users and attempts to boycott the tool will be expected whenever there are conflictual relations between the managers (the nodes gaining direct benefits from the systems) and the employees who are requested to entry the data.

But, specifically in the Relational Perspective proposed when talking about nodes and relations, we are referring to a structural perspective of organizational units, nodes and relations **combined** with a personalistic view: when referring to nodes, the Relational Perspective implies an organizational unit and a specific employee. So the Relational Perspective combines a structural organization analysis with an individual, social and psychological perspective. Social determinism and functionalism are avoided.

The Relational Perspective requires the DSS designer to understand the existing network of relations and to prevent organizational "nodes" from engaging in opportunistic behavior and from disruptive power conflicts. For this goal he has to modify both the tool and the organization.

Changes in the tool could reduce the causes of conflict and restore the original power equilibrium (technical facilitation).

Changes in the organization could vary from forcing new power equilibrium (dismissal of nodes against the system) to modifying the network of relations in order to facilitate a painless conflict solution (mediating solution).

The analysis of the existing network of relations as well as the proposal of good organizational solution requires from DSS designer also political competence (Table 5).

Table 5. A synthesis of the analysis of political oppositions

Focus	Considered Constraints	Role of the designer
• organizational decision maker • opportunistic organizational actors • self-interest behavior	• non collaborative/boycotting behavior • attempts to maintain/augment individual power • existing network of relations	• Technical Facilitator • Political mediator

5 AN APPLICATION: THE DSS DESIGN FOR A HEALTH AGENCY

In this section we will describe the application of the three indicated perspectives for implementing managerial DSS in an Italian public health agency. The case regards the psychological and social division of the health agency. This division provides a town of about 120,000 persons with psychological services and social work.

An expert psychologist is the manager of the division: his task is very broad and covers, for example, the technical supervision of other employees, the institutional deputation of the division, psychological consulting, planning and control of the division's activities. This psychologist is one of the four top managers of the health agency: so he's always very busy with his work.

The other psychologists and social employees of the division are organized in nine teams. Three teams deal with child patients (from 0 to 14 years old), three with adolescent patients (from 14 to 18 years old) and three with senior patients (more than 18 years old). Each group of three teams has a sector-head psychologist and each team a team-head psychologist (Fig. 2).

Moreover the division is composed of some administrative employees, working in a central office under the direction of an administrative boss.

At the beginning of 1994, the division manager asked a consulting-team (composed of the authors of this paper) for the design and the implementation of a managerial DSS.

The introduction of a managerial DSS in this psychological and social division required a complex process of organizational change and political mediation in the organization. The initial decisional user requirements were modified and complemented with other features in order to make the organization accept the new system.

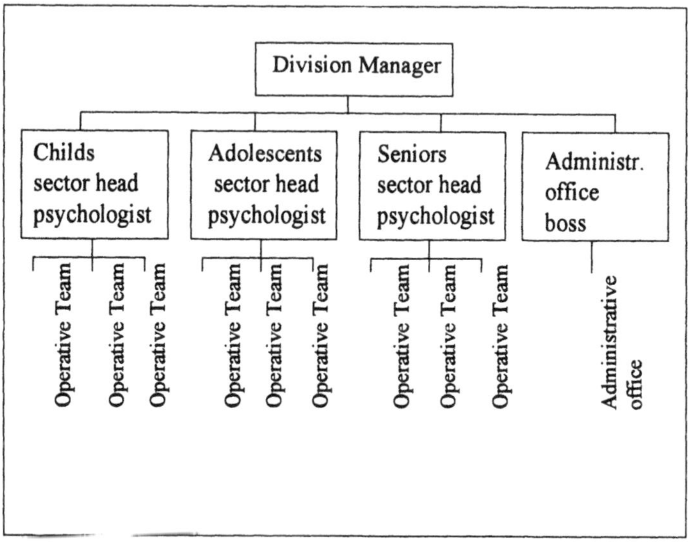

Figure 2. The social and psychological health division.

5.1 The manager's decision support requirements

The division manager asked for a managerial DSS for supporting his planning activities. He wanted an IT based tool providing help for decision taking in annual plan formulation as well as in three-year long plan activity. The manager needed an accurate and synthetic description of the past activities of his division (data such as: the number of patient with certain diseases, the frequency of certain psychological treatments, the correlation between external conditions and certain diseases, etc.) in order to formulate a good organizational plan for the future.

A DSS was designed, based on data collected about the teams' activities. At least once a week, each psychologist and social employee would have provided data about his own patients (diagnosis, therapy, results, etc.), through structured interfaces for computer data entry. Through the tool, the manager would have extracted the required statistical information from data collected.

Uncertainty about which data to collect was one of the main problems in this design phase: information required by the manager may vary in relation to new planning needs. Attention was paid in designing a flexible system: the possibility for new user-defined queries was introduced and the data base was built in order to be easy to modify.

When the news of the introduction of the new DSS circulated in the organization, psychologists and social employees expressed their strong opposition against the new IT system. Some causes of opposition were easy to foresee while others were less clear. For preventing system failure, the division was analyzed according to the work-habits-changes perspective and the relational perspective.

5.2 The work habits perspective.

The DSS introduction would have changed the work habits of the psychological and social employees.

First, most of the psychologists and social employees did not have any expertise in computer usage. Even if the data entry interfaces were user friendly and easy to use, the DSS would have required a minimal amount of computer learning. In most employees the need for a training process caused an "a priori" refusal of the system: some employees refused to have to learn a new subject.

Second, the DSS was designed for managerial planning activities. Psychologists and social employees would have obtained no direct benefits from the system, whereas they would have taken on the data entry activity. Even if interfaces were designed in order to minimize the time required for data entry, psychologists and social employees had to modify their work organization for maintaining the data base. This caused a diffused refusal of the new DSS.

5.3 The Relational Perspective.

The analysis of the network of relations in the division revealed a third cause of opposition against the DSS. Four nodes were detected with the criterion of relational homogeneity:

1) the manager.
2) the administrative employees
3) the team head psychologists and a few other social employees
4) the remaining psychologists and social employees.

The relations discovered among the four nodes are complex and composed of several dimensions. In the following the paper provides only a synthetic description, sufficient for understanding the case (Figure 3 and Figure 4).

Relations among node 2 and nodes 1, 3, 4.

Node 2 is linked with similar relations to all the remaining nodes.

First, there is a technical relation based on the work flow of documents from/to administrative office to/from psychological teams.

Second, there is an important social relation. Psychologists appreciate administrative employees, because they relieve psychologists from all the fastidious bureaucratic problems and duties. Administrative employees esteem psychologists and social employees, because of their professional preparation and their ability to deal with patients. The emerging social relation is characterized by a mutual liking that enables a good work collaboration.

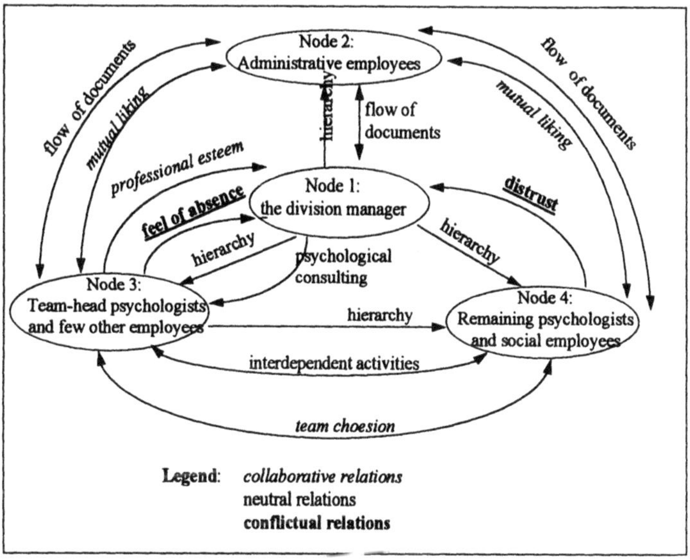

Figure 3. The network of relations in the social and psychological division.

Relations between node 1 and node 3.

The link between node 1 and node 3 is based on four main relations:

(a) hierarchical relation: node 1 is the supervisor of the components of node 3;
(b) technical relation: the division manager (node 1) gives psychological consulting to team head psychologists (node 3);
(c) psychological relation of esteem: the psychologists and social employees of node 3 recognize the professional capability of the division manager and his psychological expertise.
(d) psychological relation of absence: the division manager is very busy also with his institutional task (he is one of the top managers of the health agency). This causes frequent small conflicts with head team psychologists, as they perceive him as far from the division.

The resulting relation may be defined "neutral": there is a mutual professional trust that enables an effective work collaboration (relations "b" and "c"). Nevertheless, interpersonal relations remain quite cold, because of relation "d".

Relations between node 1 and node 4.

The relation between node 1 and node 4 is based (i) on the hierarchical authority of the manager (hierarchical relation) and (ii) of a relation of mistrust of node 4 toward node 1.

Because of work load problems, the division manager gives direct psychological consulting only to the team head psychologists: the remaining psychologists and social employees have few opportunities for working together with him. Consequently members of node 4 don't appreciate the professional capability of the division manager: they see him only as a hierarchical boss.

Moreover the feel of division manager absence - see previous relation "d" between node 1 and node 3 - is perceived also by components of node 4.

In the resulting relation, work collaboration is very difficult and many psychologists mistrust the manager.

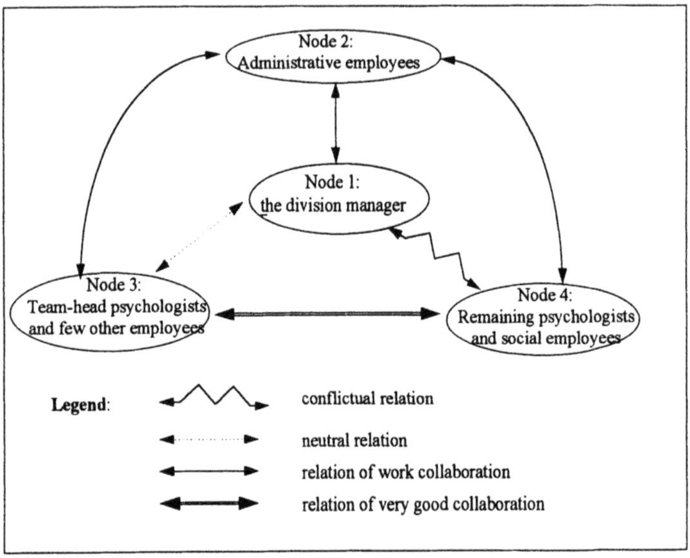

Figure 4. A synthesis of the network of relations in the social and psychological division.

Relations between node 3 and node 4.

The link between node 3 and node 4 is based on:

(a) hierarchical supervision of members of node 3 toward components of node 4
(b) technical relations. Between the activities of the two nodes there are complex interdependencies as they work together in the teams caring for patients.
(c) social relations: the team based organization and the particular task (the care of social and psychological disease) has developed a strong cohesion among team members. Interpersonal relations are characterized by trust, commitment to mutual help, friendship. These teams may be correctly defined as "clans" (Ouchi, 1980).

The resulting relation is very warm and it enables a strong work collaboration.

Conclusions on the network of relations analysis

The managerial DSS was perceived as a relational instrument. Existing relations influenced the "political" judgment to its introduction in the organization.

Psychologists and social employees of node 4 were particularly against the DSS. Because of the existing relation between node 4 and node 1 (Fig. 4), they saw the new IT tool as an instrument of control of their activity imposed by the manager.

The opposition of other psychologists and employees (belonging to node 3) was less strong, and limited to work habits change reasons. Nevertheless the warm relation linking node 3 to node 4 prevent psychologists belonging to node 3 from taking sides in favor of the DSS.

5.4 Case Solution.

The design and system implementation strategies were modified for solving the three problems which had emerged as causing the initial refusal of the DSS:

PROBLEM 1: psychologists and social employees were afraid of the DSS because of their low expertise in computer usage;
PROBLEM 2: psychologists and social employees had to change their work habits without obtaining any direct benefits from the DSS;
PROBLEM 3: the components of node 4 perceived the DSS only as a tool for hierarchical control.

Four solutions were adopted (Table 6).

First, the design team adopted design techniques based on user participation: several meetings with employees (belonging both to node 3 and to node 4) took place for explaining the future functions of the DSS and for understanding their oppositions. This reduced the fear of an unknown system that caused an initial "a priori" refusal of the system (PROBLEM 1).

Second, the data base of the DSS was modified. Some suggestions of the employees belonging to node 4 were accepted, in order to eliminate the fear of a system designed only for controlling their activity (PROBLEM 3).

Third, the functions of the DSS were changed: a lot of new features were added so to make the system useful to all the psychologists and social employees. The DSS was transformed from a statistical tool to an IT based psychological chart. Everybody (and not only the manager) obtained benefits from the new system (PROBLEM 2). Moreover the new DSS was no longer seen as a tool for hierarchical control, but as an instrument useful for all the employees (PROBLEM 3)

Fourth, also the administrative employees were trained in using the system. Administrative employees were expert in computer usage so the training for using the DSS was very cheap. The benefits instead were great: thanks to their collaborative relations with psychologists and social employees, administrative employees provided an important technical help to psychologists and social employees in using the DSS and in assuring a continuous training on the field (PROBLEM 2).

Table 6. The solution for the DSS introduction in the social and psychological health division

Discovered Problems	*Adopted Solutions*
1. poor expertise of psychologists and social employees in using PC systems that caused an "a priori" refusal	• several design meetings with user participation • administrative employees' support
2. psychologists and social employees didn't obtain direct benefits in using the system	• the DSS was changed from statistical tool to IT based psychological chart
3. some social employees feared of more hierarchical control	• the DSS data base was modified and several social employees suggests were introduced. • the DSS was changed from statistical tool to IT based psychological chart

The resulting tool was quite different from the one initially designed. Software implementation was more complicated and more expensive, but the design team solved the emergent problems and the tool was successfully introduced in the organization.

Moreover the DSS introduction changed the existing network of relations. The relations between node 2 (the administrative employees) and node 3 (the team head psychologists) and the ones between node 2 and node 4 (the remaining psychologists and social employees) were enriched by the continuos training in the field that administrative employees provided to psychologists and social employees concerning DSS use (Figure 5).

The resulting relations have become strongly oriented to work collaboration (Figure 6).

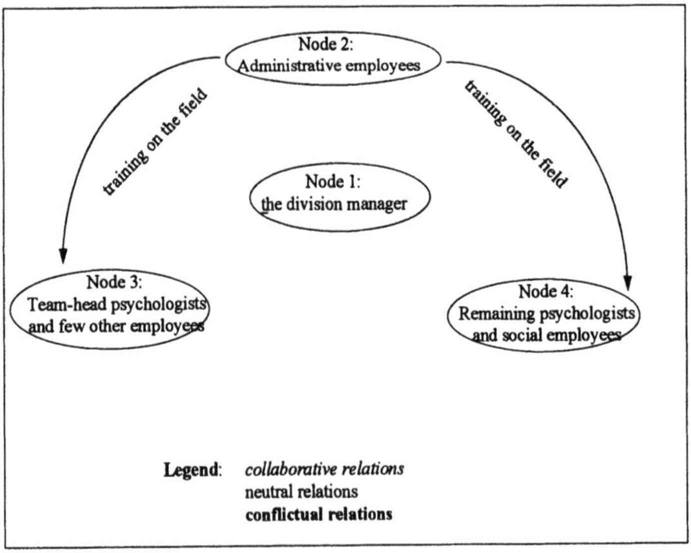

Figure 5. The **new** relations due to the DSS introduction.

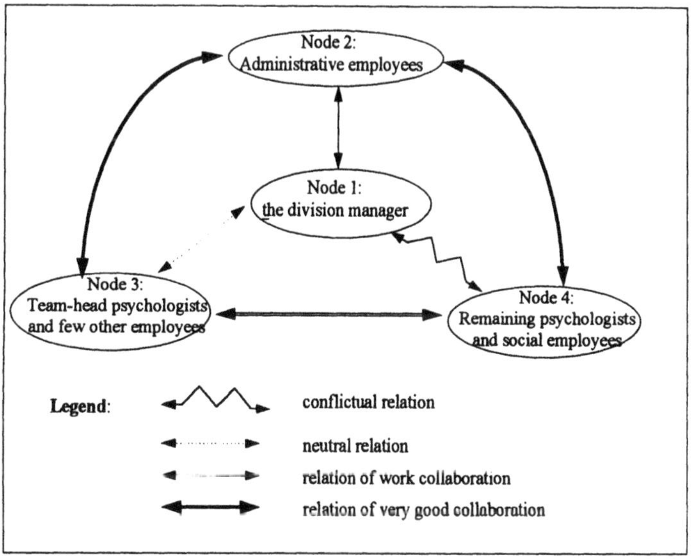

Figure 6. A synthesis of the network of relations in the social and psychological division, after the DSS introduction.

6 CONCLUSIONS AND REMARKS FOR FUTURE RESEARCH

The introduction of a new DSS in an organization is similar to the introduction of every new technical system in a socio-technical environment. Apart from technical problems, social and organizational aspects are also important for deciding the success or the failure of the tool

The design approach proposed in this paper underlines three aspects as relevant for preventing DSS from failure:

- the analysis of the decision needs of the manager
- the analysis of changes in users' work habits caused by the tool
- the analysis of (possible) political opposition against the DSS.

This approach has been tested on a particular class of DSS: those requiring a continuos data entry activity by some employees, who are different from the manager and don't receive direct benefits from the tool.

Future researches should be conducted to provide further validation of the proposed approach and for its extension also to other kind of DSS.

The paper has also proposed a new method of analysis, based on the study of the network of organizational relations. This relational method provides the basis for the analysis of the political problems caused by the introduction of DSS in organizations.

The relational analysis of organizations is the subject of research that is now being conducted about the use of innovative IT applications in organizations and in new models of organizations (for example: Ferioli and Migliarese, 1994; Ferioli and Migliarese, 1995).

Some real applications (such as the health agency described above) have proved the validity of the relational analysis method: for this reason the paper indicates that relational analysis is a promising area for future research on DSS design and introduction in organizations.

7 REFERENCES

Alter, S.L. (1990) *Decision Support Systems: Current Practice and Continuing Challenges*, Addison-Wesley, Reading, MA.

Angehrn, A.A. and Jelassi, T. (1994) DSS research and practice in perspective. *Decision Support Systems*, 12, 267-275.

Argyris, C. (1982) *Reasoning, Learning and Action*. Jossey-Bass, San Francisco

Baker, W.E. (1992) The network organization in theory and practice. In *Networks and Organizations*, (ed. Nohria N. and Eccles R.G.), Harvard Business School Press

Bariff, M. and Ginzberg, M. (1982) MIS and the behavioural sciences. *Data Base*, 13, 1, 19-26

Bariff, M.L. and Galbraith, J.R. (1978) Intraorganisational Power Considerations for designing Information Systems. *Accounting, Organizations and Society*, 3, 25-27.

Bell, P.C. (1992) Decision Support Systems: Past, Present and Prospects. *Journal of Decision Systems*, 1, 2-3, 127-137.

Briefs U., Ciborra, C. and Schneider L. eds. (1984) *System Design for, with and by the Users*. North-Holland, Amsterdam

Cherns, A.B. (1980) Speculations on social effects of new microelectronics technology. *PC/Computing*, September 1988, 21.

Ciborra, C. (1993) *Teams, Markets and Systems*. Cambridge University Press, Cambridge.

Ciborra, C., Migliarese, P. and Romano P. (1984) A methodological inquiry of Organizational Noise in Socio-technical Systems, *Human Relations*, 37, 8, 565-88.

Davies, W.S. (1992) *Operating Systems, A Systematic View*. Benjamin Cummings, New York.

DeMarco, T. (1979) *Structured Analysis and System Specification*. Yourdon Press, New York.

DeSanctis, G., Snyder, J.R. and Poole, M.S. (1994) The meaning of the interface. *Decision Support Systems*, 11, 319-335.

Donati, P.P. (1991) *Teoria relazionale della società*, Franco Angeli, Milano.

Ehrlich, S.F. (1987) Strategies for encouraging successful adoption of office communication systems. *ACM Transactions on Office Information Systems*, 5, 340-357.

Ferioli, C. and Migliarese P. (1995) Opportunities and drawbacks of information technology in the emerging forms of organization. In *Proceedings of the Third European Conference on Information Systems* (ed. Doukidis G., Galliers R., Jelassi T., Krcmar H. and Land F). Athens.

Ferioli, C. and Migliarese P.(1994) The role of IT and GDSS in internal network organizations. In *Proceedings of IFIP WG 8.3 Working Conference "Decision Support in Organisational Transformation* (ed. B. Mayon-White, S. Ayestaràn and P. Humphreys), San Sebastian.
Gabarro, J.J.(1990) The Development of Working Relationships. In *Intellectual teamwork,* (ed. J.Galegher, R.E.Kraut and C.Egido), Lawrence Erlbaum Associates, New Jersey.
Gallupe, R.B., Bastianutti, L.M., Cooper, W.H. (1991) Unblocking brainstorms. *Journal of Applied Psychology,* 76.
Gardner, A.L., Paul, R. and Patel, N.V. (1995) Moving beyond the fixed point theorem with tailorable information systems. In *Proceedings of the Third European Conference on Information Systems* (ed. G. Doukidis, R. Galilee's, T.Jelassi, H.Krcmar and F.Land).
George, J.F, Nunamaker Jr, J.F. and Valacich, J.S. (1992) ODSS Information technology for organizational change. *Decision Support Systems*, 8, 307-315
Ginzberg, M.J, and Ariav, G. (1986) Methodologies for DSS Analysis and Design: a Contingency Approach to their Application. In *Proceedings of the 7th International Conference on Information Systems,* San Diego, CA.
Gorry, A. and Morton, S. (1971) A Framework For Management Information Systems, *Sloan Management Review,* 13, 1, 55-70.
Granovetter, M.(1992) Problems of Explanation in Economic Sociology. In *Networks and Organizations,* (ed. Nohria N. and Eccles R.G.), Harvard Business School Press.
Grover, V., Lederer, A.L. and Sabherwal R. (1988) Recognizing the politics of MIS. *Information and Management,* 14, 3, 145-156.
Grudin, J. (1989) Why groupware applications fail: problems in design and evaluation. *Office Technology and People*, 4, 3, 245-264.
Heiner, R. (1983) The origin of predictable behavior, *American Economic Review*, 73, 560-95.
Hewitt, C. and De Jong, P. (1984) Open systems. in *On Conceptual Modeling* (ed. M.L. Brodie, J. Mylopulos and J.W.Schmidt) Springer, New York.
Hirschheim, R. and Klein, H.K. (1989) Four Paradigms of Information Systems Development. *Communications of the ACM,* 32, 10, 1199-1216.
Ives, B. and Olson M.H. (1984) User involvement and MIS success: a review of research. *Management Science*, 30, 5, 586-603.
Keen, P.G.W. (1981) Information Systems and Organizational Change. *Communications of the ACM,* 24, 24-33.
Keen, P.G.W. (1980) Adaptive Design For Decision Support Systems. *Data Base*, 12, 1-2, 15-25
Keen, P.G.W. and Scott-Morton, M.S. (1978) *Decision Support Systems: An Organizational Perspective*, Reading, MA.
Land, F. (1995) The new alchemist: or how to transmute base organizations into corporations of gleaming gold, in *Proceedings of the Third European Conference on Information Systems* (ed. G. Doukidis, R. Galliers, T.Jelassi, H.Krcmar and F Land).
Lee, R.M., McCosh, A.M. and Migliarese P., eds.(1988) *Organizational decision support systems*, North-Holland.
Madsen, M. (1989) Breakthrough by breakdown. In *Information Systems Development for Human Progress in Organizations* (ed. H.Klein and K.Kumar), North-Holland, Amsterdam
March, J. (1991) How decisions happen in Organizations. *Human-Computer Interaction.*

Markus, M.L. (1983) Power, Politics and MIS Implementation. *Communications of the ACM*, 26, 6, 430-444.

McMenamin, S. and Palmer, J (1984) *Essential Systems Analysis*. Yourdon Press, New York.

Migliarese, P. (1992) Sistemi di supporto per i processi decisionali. In *Progettare e gestire l'impresa innovativa* (ed. R.Filippini, G.Pagliarani, G.Petroni), ETAS Libri, Milano

Migliarese, P., Paolucci, E. (1995) Improved communications and collaborations among tasks induced by Groupware. *Decision Support System Journal*, 14, 237-250.

Migliarese, P. and Ferioli, C. (1995) Strumenti organizzativi ed informatici di collaborazione nell'impresa innovativa, in *proceedings of the workshop AiIG: Organizzazione, risorse umane e processi innovativi nello sviluppo del sistema delle imprese*, Torino, Italy.

Mumford, E. (1979) *Computer Systems In Work Design: The ETHICS method*, Associated Business Press.

Mumford, E. (1991) Decision Making And The Organizational Environment: Today's Problems And Tomorrow's Needs. In *Environment for Supporting Decision Processes* (ed. H.G.Sol and J.Vecsenji), North-Holland.

Newman, M. and Noble, F. (1990) User Involvement as an Interaction Process: a Case Study. *Information Systems Research*, 1, 89-113.

Norman, D.A. (1983) Some observations on mental models. in *Mental Models* (ed. D. Gentner and A.L. Stevens) Lawrence Erlbaum, Hillsdale, N.Y.

Nunamaker Jr, J.F., Vogel, D. and Konsynski (1989) Interaction of Task and Technology to Support Large Groups. *Decision Support Systems*,5, 2, 139-152.

Ouchi, W.G. (1980) Markets, Bureaucracies, and Clans. *Administrative Science Quarterly*, 25.

Pfeffer, J. (1981) *Power in organizations*. Ballinger, Cambridge, MA.

Phillips, L. (1992) Gaining Corporate Commitment to Change. In *Executive Information Systems and Decision Support* (ed. C.Holtman), Chapman & Hall.

Piaget, J. (1974) *Understanding Causality*. Norton, New York

Polany, M. (1966) *The Tacit Dimension*. Doubleday, Garden City-N.Y.

Poole, M.S., DeSanctis, G. (1992), Microlevel structuraction in computer supported group decision making, *Human Communication Research*. 19.

Radermacher, F.J. (1994) Decision support systems: Scope and potential. *Decision Support Systems*, 12, 257-265.

Rockard, J.F. (1979) Chief Executives Define Their Own Data Needs. *Harvard Business Review*, 57, 2, 81-93.

Rockard, J.F. and DeLong D.W. (1988) *Executive Support Systems*, Dow-Jones, Irwin, Homewood, IL.

Rosenberg, N. (1982) *Inside the Black Box: Technology and Economics*. Cambridge University Press, Cambridge.

Rowe, C.J. (1985) Identifying causes of failure: a case study in computerized stock control. *and Information Technology*, 4, 63-72.

Scarbrough, H. and Corbett, J.M. (1992) *Technology and organization. Power, meaning and design*. Routledge, London

Simon, H.A. (1976) *Administrative Behavior*. The Free Press, New York

Sternberg, R.J. and Wagner R.K. eds. (1986) *Practical Intelligence*. Cambridge University Press, Cambridge.

Thompson, J.D (1967) *Organizations in actions*. McGraw-Hill.

Weick, K.E. (1979) *The Social Psychology of Organizing*. Random House, New York.

Whitaker, R. (1994) GDSS' Formative Fundaments: An Interpretive Analysis. *CSCW: An International Journal*, 2, 4, 241-262

Williamson, O.E. (1975) *Markets and Hierarchies: Analysis and Antitrust Implications*, Free Press, New York.

Williamson, O.E. (1979) Transaction-Cost Economics: The Governance of Contractual Relations, *Journal of Law and Economics*, 22.

8 BIOGRAPHY

Claudio Ferioli participates in a number of research projects about the emergence of new organizational models and the role played by information technologies in implementing organizational changes. He collaborates with public health organizations on management consultancy and software implementation. He is an assistant in the class of Economics and Company Organizations and of Organizational Systems at the Politecnico of Milan.

Piero Migliarese is a full Professor of Business Economics and Organizational Systems. He teaches courses at University of Calabria - Italy and at Politecnico of Milano-Italy. He is a member of IFIP Working Group 8.3 on Decision Support Systems. His research interests are regarding innovative organizational models, information systems, group support systems. At present he proposed conceptual models regarding coordination and cooperation supports coming from Information Technologies. He has authored various papers on these subjects at national and international levels.

12
Change process implementation: a collective analysis and management procedure

E. Francardi and M.F. Norese
Dip. Sistemi di Produzione ed Economia dell'Azienda - Politecnico di Torino. C.so Duca degli Abruzzi, 24 - 10129 Torino, Italy, tel. 011-5647279, fax 011-5647299

Abstract
Operational tools may be introduced in change processes to facilitate actual change activation and succesful implementation. The adoption of a conceptual framework from literature, and its operationalisation, by means of a system of structured Schemes in a procedure of collective analysis and management, may supply appropriate "tools" for structuring problem situations and their evolutions and may be suitable for being inserted into communication contexts. The integrated use of Schemes and different techniques in a collective process of change analysis, planning and control is described in this paper. The main Schemes are presented in detail, together with some results that have arisen from the application of the system to a change process now in progress.

Keywords
Change process, multicriteria approach, cooperative decision support systems.

1 INTRODUCTION

Change process is defined as the development and implementation of new ideas by people who over time engage in transactions with others within an institutional context. Inventing and implementing new ideas is a collective achievement of pushing and riding those ideas into good currency (Van de Ven, 1986). The actors in this process learn, i.e. invent and fix, new models of integration for the organized action (Crozier, 1977). This consists of both the discovering or, in certain cases, the creation and acceptance of new relational models, new reasoning modalities and a new collective capacity of solving the problems of the collective action. 'Policy formulation and implementation are processes that have not to be viewed as discrete or chronological but as interactive and muddled' (Pettigrew, 1990).

Change is a complex situation in which communication plays a predominant role. Recognizing elements of complexity and originating relevant cognitive and operational actions, in an interactive context, are the basis for activating a change process and for supporting and controlling its implementation. A technical support to the organizational change process should help the involved actors to identify the specific level of complexity and consistent activities in order to transform new ideas into a concrete reality and to communicate, by relevant and formalized structures, in each phase of the change process

(Mucci and Norese, 1989). This paper describes a system developed to support the work of face-to-face groups on organizational change. Formulating and implementing changes within organizations implies the employment of techniques and tools which can work to various degrees of precision in conceptual model building, as and when necessary, according to the needs of the analysis (Humphreys and Berkeley, 1992), facilitating discussion and explicit negotiation of the significant problem elements, enabling the structuring of different courses of action and their assessment and control.

The system proposes a set of structured Schemes to support identification and analysis of the change process key elements, and their integration with different tools, that have been proposed in literature, in a procedure of collective analysis and management. Schemes and procedure have been tested in relation to some change processes that have already been concluded, in order to redefine the steps and global evolution as though the process management were a formal collective action. The system and its Schemes are now used, as a support for the initial stages of two technological and organizational change processes.

The integrated use of Schemes and different techniques in a collective process of change analysis, planning and control is described in the second section by a tool of structural modelling. The main Schemes are presented in detail in the third section. Some results arising from the application of the system to a change process now in progress allow the procedure to be analysed in the last section.

2 CHANGE ANALYSIS AND MANAGEMENT PROCEDURE

The starting point of the procedure application is the definition of a collective context of Change Analysis and Management (CAM Team or simply The Team). An initial problem formulation, mainly of a colloquial or textual nature, should define all the significant elements that characterize the problem situation (the team's role, the nature and freedom of action, organizational change situation, actor situation at least in terms of role and the resources of the involved individuals, groups and organizations and so on). These elements are essential to recognize the situation complexity and elaborate possible inquiry actions. Different courses of action may be activated and techniques and tools may be called; a system of structured Schemes connects the sequence of actions to increase the efficiency and effectiveness of change analysis and management meetings (Huber, 1984).

A Map has been used to describe the system and the main procedure passages. This 'Map' has been proposed in Lendaris (1980) as a tool of structural modelling which consists of 'elements' and 'connections'; the 'elements' are, either intermediate or final, states of knowledge; the 'connections' are refinement processes (called steps) which lead one from one state to the next. In Lendaris (1980) three kinds of activity may occur in each step:

- an additional assumption is made (!),
- further information is added (?), and/or
- an algorithm or operation is carried out (*).

The Map organizes states of knowledge (the different Schemes) which are essential at the different change process structuring stages (see figure 1).

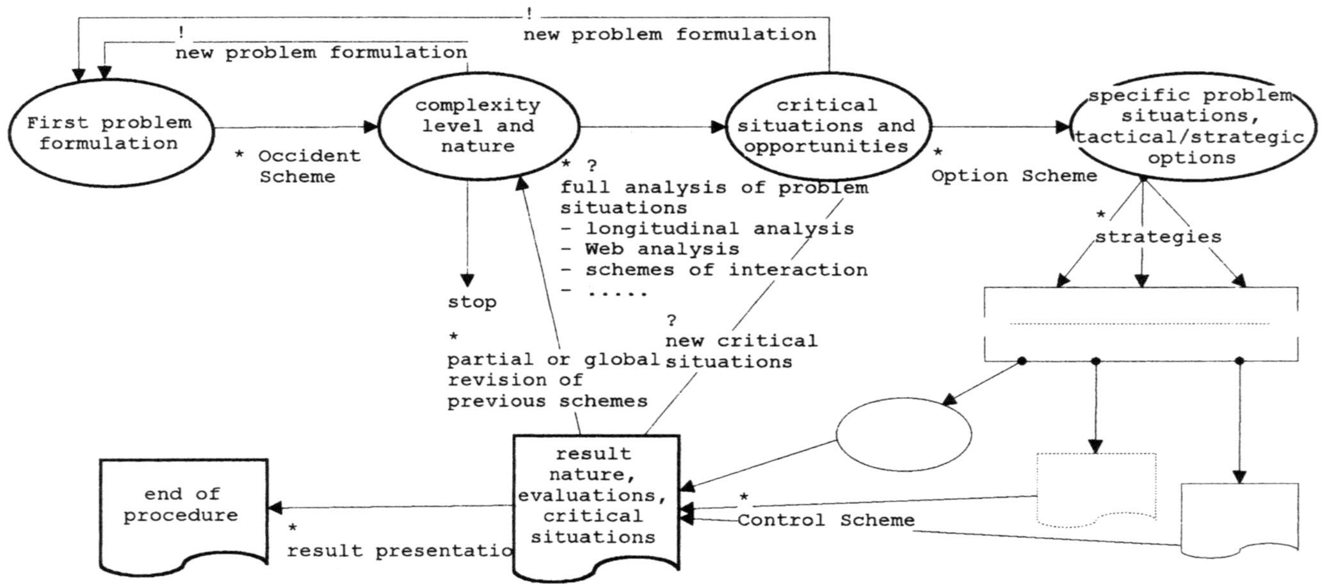

Figure 1 The sistem and the main procedure passages.

From the first problem formulation the team proceeds *to recognizing the level and class of complexity* to be faced by the first Multidimensional Scheme of Organizational Change Complexity Identification (OCCIDENT Scheme). A collective definition of the Scheme elements helps verify whether the team presents the necessary competences, which includes all the key roles and functions, and, whether it can operate cooperatively.

Some typical classes of complexity are related to specific methodological approaches and techniques. If the situation appears too complex to face the team may ask to interrupt the procedure; in some other cases, when the situation is not sufficiently characterized, a new problem formulation may result to be essential to reduce ambiguity, incoherence or incompleteness.

When the recognized complexity is acceptable and clearly characterized, a full analysis, using the support of specific techniques, may reduce the identified critical conditions.The Occident Scheme can evolve in relation to the analysis results and may require a new problem formulation or induce the passage to a second Scheme, called the Option Scheme. This tool is applied to a *collective and detailed definition of specific problem situations* and then to consistent *development of tactical/strategic options*, for a collective assessment and /or selection.

The results from cognitive, tactical and strategic activities are integrated and evaluated using a Control Scheme which concludes a procedure cycle. This Scheme allows the *verification* of time and resource constraints, the *examination* of process development and actor involvement, and the *assessment* of prefigured results. The control nature is closely related to the choosen and implemented strategy; a Control Scheme has to include all the significant elements in a formal structure that is easily readable and suitable for transformation into an evaluation model.

New steps are activated in relation to the collective analysis of the previous results by the Control Scheme. They may require the partial or global revision of the previous Schemes to collectively identify ill-judged elements of complexity and problem situations and to explain strategies that have resulted to be not operative, not effective enough or problematic. New critical situations may be proposed as the object of a new Option Scheme development.

Final or temporary evaluation and acceptance by the team leads to result presentation and can cause the end of the procedure.

3 SCHEMES AND SUPPORTING TOOLS

3.1 The Occident Scheme

The Multidimensional Scheme of Organizational Change Complexity Identification is a tool that is applied to recognize change as being multifaced and to express different actor's points of view about change complexity (Le Moigne, 1985; Pettigrew, 1990), to identify these complexities collectively, at least in general terms, and to characterize the main elements of risk which have to be analysed and reduced before any new change process step.

Multiple elements concur to define organizational change complexity. The main points of view proposed in literature and here recognized as significant and sufficient to elaborate a complete and operative framework are synthesized in the Scheme. They are related to three dimensions, *change nature*, *complexity characteristics* and *problem situation*, which are articulated in nine criteria, each of which joins to different qualification states (Roy, 1985;

Vincke, 1992). In figure 2 nine axes represent the criteria and their qualification states. Combinations of these states (one for each criterium or attribute) identify change profiles at different complexity levels.

Change nature
Organization change form and diffusion and temporal and spatial characteristics globally define the change nature. Different forms are identified, as in Van de Ven (1986), in relation to the main involved organization variables; the types of diffusion are expressed in functional and contextual terms, as analysed in Kling (1987); processual structures and spatial characteristics are defined in relation to the distinction between drastic and incremental, strategical and peripheral change; between the outer and inner context of the organisation; between the contextual situation and the focal situation (see for instance Pettigrew, 1990; Kling, 1987 and Le Luarn, 1989).

Complexity characteristics
Different complexity forms (orientation, understanding and decision complexity) characterize the change process. Elements of a reference system (points, coordinates and catagories) allow the course of action to be oriented; the nature and conditions of this reference system induce different complexity states. Information elements on the organization and specific change can be globally or partially lacking and may require specific inquiry activities. The decision system nature and uncertainty of the involved actor's behaviour must be identified, at least in order to compose an operative management group that is consistent with the decision complexity level.

Problem situation
The nature of the environmental stimuli to change and the perspectives on action in organization characterize the problem situation that develops in relation to change. External and internal critical factors can generate a crisis situation, positive stimuli and internal interests can generate opportunities (Mintzberg, 1976; Pettigrew, 1990). In the "situational control" perspective external factors or events constrain or force people and organizations to behave in certain ways; in the "rational actor" perspective, people and organizations evaluate alternative courses of action and exercise free rational choices. In the "emergent" perspective on action, the behaviour of people and organizations emerges from a dynamic interaction of external circumstances and internal motives of interests (Pfeffer, 1982; Markus and Robey, 1988).

3.2 Supporting techniques

When the change complexity is recognized by the Occident Scheme as being globally acceptable, a full analysis can reduce critical marginal conditions and allow more detailed characterizations. Specific techniques may be activated in an approach which is contextualist and processual in character, 'to draw on phenomena at vertical and horizontal (processual) levels of analysis and the interconnections between those levels through time' (Pettigrew, 1990).

Methodological approaches and tools have been proposed in literature, to operationalise these concepts in actual change processes (Walsham, 1990) They consist above all of the Kling's Web Model (1987), for the analysis of the social and technological change context, methods of longitudinal field research (Van de Ven and Huber, 1990), to analyze and interpret process patterns in longitudinal data collected in the field, schemes of interaction between the

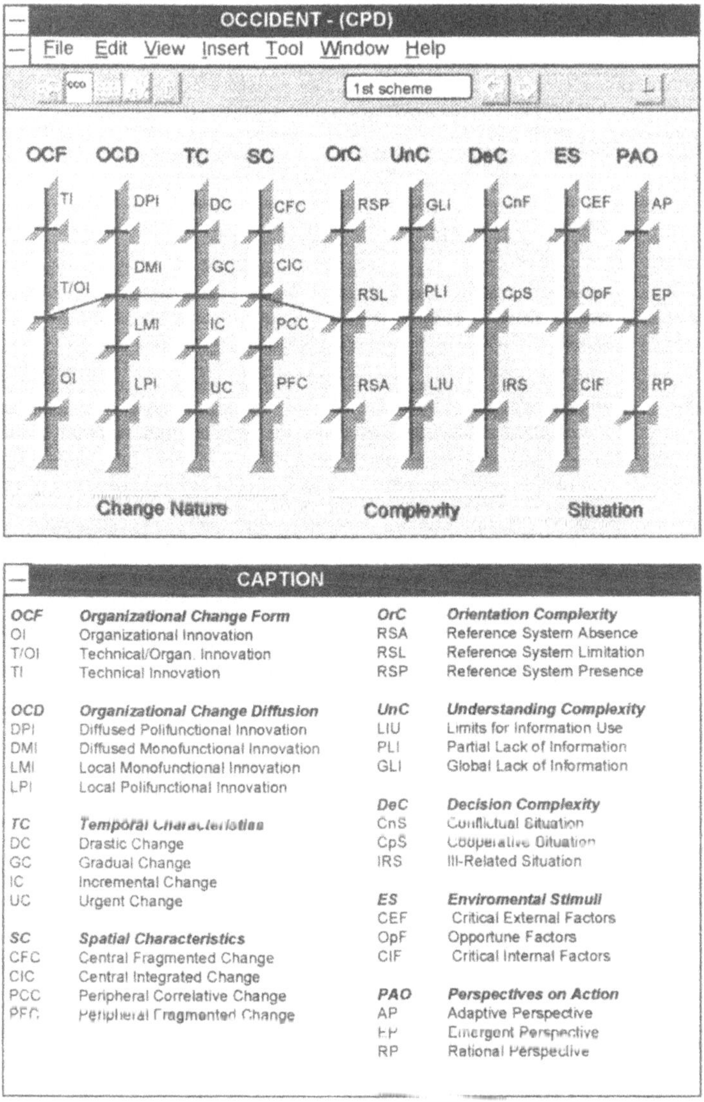

Figure 2 Occident Scheme.

level of action/process and the level of context/structure, suggested by Orlikowski and Robey (1991) as a framework based on Giddens' structuration theory (Giddens, 1984), methods of problem structuring (Bowen, 1983; Rosenhead, 1989), to reduce difficulties in problem formulation and to help members of the team to negotiate their views of the problem and a consensus for action (Eden, 1988). Classical Operations Research techniques can be used in relation to more structured problem elements. These tools have to be integrated into the system and activated in relation to specific profiles/classes of change complexity.

3.3 Option Scheme

The Option Scheme proposes a more detailed analysis of identified critical situations and translates the knowledge of specific problem and the team's action context into operative terms. It helps reduce the tendency to examine too few points of view and scenarios (Huber, 1984), both in the initial phases of the change process and then when specific problem situations become evident.

This scheme presents a bipolar structure which allows both the problem situation to be described in detail and the problem solving options to be collectively identified, or elaborated, and examined. The same modular structure characterizes and integrates the two technical actions. The problem situations can be described in the first part by two dimensions, the *political-organizational* and the *technical-organizational* dimensions, which are able to synthesize knowledge from the Occident Scheme development and results from specific inquiry and structural analysis actions (see 3.2). *Operative* dimensions, in relation to the previous problematic dimensions, define the structure of the suitable courses of action in the second part of the Scheme. One or more tactical and strategic option can be identified in the organization memory (Mintzberg et al., 1976) and/or elaborated by the team's competences. The Scheme operative dimensions support the option structuring in formal, operative and instrumental terms and, if necessary and significant, allow a multicriteria evaluation and selection of multiple options (Vincke, 1992). Attributes and criteria are developed, in relation to the significant dimensions and qualify specific difficulty situations, in the first part of the Scheme, and local solutions, in the second part. The multidimensional structure makes a collective definition of possible options more complete, easier and analytical. The team's negotiating activities can be oriented towards specific elements of problem and/or option definition, that is, towards attributes-criteria or specific qualification states instead of global alternatives, to find terms of agreement and to reduce ambiguity and conflictuality.

The Option Scheme component parts are strictly related to the specific change process step and to its critical situations and possible solutions. Some qualification attributes and criteria are frequently proposed in literature and recognized as often being useful in the analysed cases, but a general structure, that is able to face different situations, does not exist. An example of Option Scheme use is described in the next section.

3.4 Control Scheme

A Control Scheme concludes each procedure cycle, integrates results from all the different activities, validates and evaluates them. Control nature changes together with the process development and is oriented towards a collective analysis of previous results in conceptual, logical, experimental and operational terms (Landry et al., 1983).

A Control Scheme should include all the significant elements of a procedure cycle in a formal easily readable structure that can be transformed into a multicriteria evaluation model (Roy, 1985; Vincke, 1992). This model presents the same structure, during each process phase, and different specific criteria, such as consistency, accuracy and completeness, reliability, compliance with requirements and usefulness, timing, economics and resource consumption, outcome nature, process nature and organizational effectiveness, and so on.

4 AN APPLICATION

A new organism (CPD) was created at the Politecnico of Torino in 1993 and definitively installed in 1994 to coordinate different activities and improve educational services. CPD consists of sixteen members who represent three faculties and are equally divided into eight teachers and eight students. In the first year four committees are appointed for special functions: Statistical study of secretery service data, Questionnaire on the courses, Quality parameters and Student information.

The introduction of this organism into university contexts may be seen as an element of organizational change which, using Mintzberg (1983) terminology, is oriented towards an evolution from a *professional bureaucracy* to a mixed model, with elements of *adhocracy*, *divisionalized form* and mainly *machine bureaucracy*.

Change complexity has been analysed with the president of this new organism. The first analysis took place at the beginning of 1994 and mainly dealt with institutional documents. An Information Technology change process is also in progress at the Politecnico and the two processes are inevitably interconnected. A Web Analysis (Kling, 1987) has been developed to identify the essential elements of these change contexts and some critical elements have been identified in the CPD access to data, mainly from a technical point of view. An Occident Scheme which characterizes the initial complexity as being very limited is presented in figure 2. The profile is in fact nearly 'flat' and the medium positions on each axis represent the less crucial states.

In 1994 CPD became a valid interlocutor for the university governing organisms but some conflictual actions had been developed against CPD. Change complexity may be underestimated both in the Occident Scheme and in reality.

The previous Web Analysis was brought up to date in 1995 and a longitudinal study of the first years of work detailed actions, at individual and institutional levels and their interactions.

In the up-to-date Web Analysis some relationships between CPD and other actors changed. Some of these were lost, while some became very strong; there were some new involved actors and the roles and functions of others changed. Technical problems concerning access to data were also present but some possible solutions were preliminary being tested.

The situation seems to be evolutive from a historical point of view; CPD role and main functions were not fully understood at the Politecnico during the first explorative and explicative phase in 1993; when CPD looked for resources some involved actors recognized the change process nature and reacted at an institutional level as they were afraid of losing autonomy, and at an individual level by refusing access to parts of the global Information System. As a consequence CPD orients towards a wide information diffusion of its actual functions, to reduce the negative impact of the reaction.

The global situation is now more critical than the first Occident Scheme represents. The evolutions in the global situation require a new complexity analysis. The second Occident Scheme (see figure 3) presents a more irregular profile in relation to the *Decision complexity* (*conflictual* and not *cooperative*) and to the *Spatial characteristics* (the change is *central*, that is, it includes vital functions in the organization, but is *fragmented and not integrated*, because the key areas at the Politecnico are poorely correlated in relation to the involved functions).

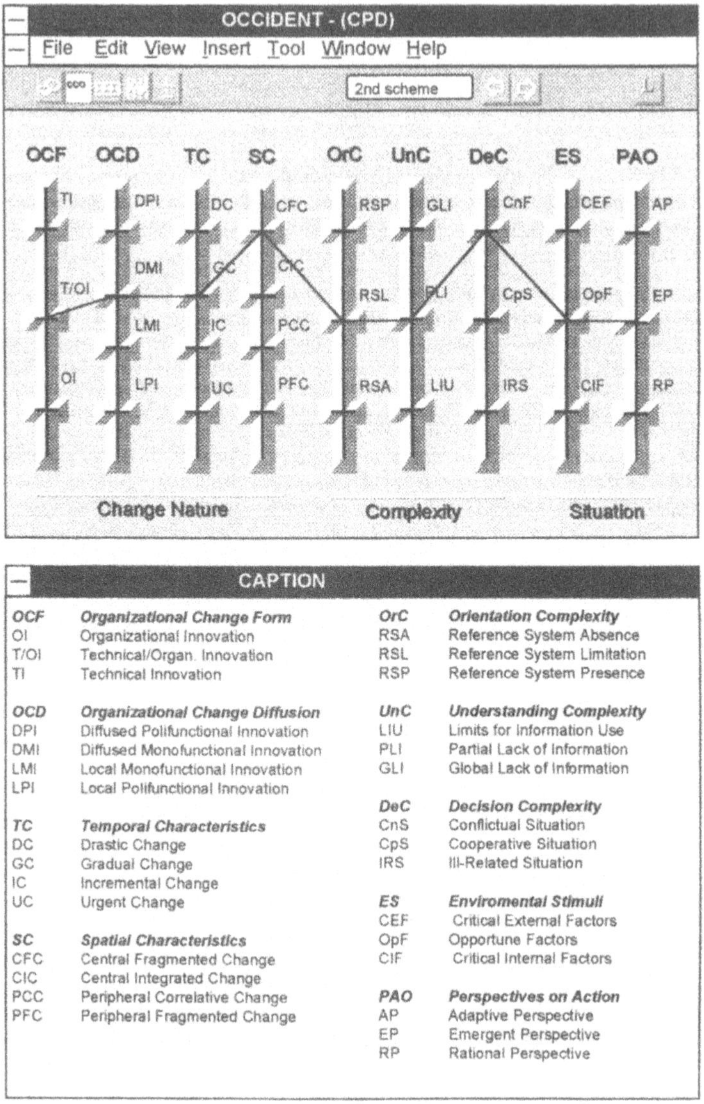

Figure 3 The second Occident Scheme representing the situation at 1995.

Results from the different analyses allow an Option Scheme elaboration. Three problem situations are described, by attributes, in the first part of the Scheme. "Data aquisition and interchange" is the first problem, which is mainly of a technical-organizational nature; two attributes formalize the Web Analysis identification of this critical situation: *code difficulties* and *Data Base typologies*. In relation to this problem, the second part of the Scheme proposes an operational dimension, through three attributes/criteria, to analyse and evaluate (if necessary) the different possible solutions in terms of *cost, timing* and *effectiveness* (see figure 4).

The other two problem situations, "Organizational relationship" and "Results from CPD actions", are mainly of a political-organizational nature. Three attributes describe the level and nature of the difficult internal relationships (*full relationship activation, contact activation, collaboration between CPD and local commitees)* and four attributes/criteria allow some operational solutions to be defined and analysed, in terms of *new cooperative context need, action operational level, structuration modalities* and *problem disaggregation level*. The results are described through four attributes (*detailed structuring of course programmes, programme documentation, exam coordination and activation of local didactic commitees*) and four attributes/criteria allow some options to be formally elaborated and assessed, in terms of *user involvment* and, as for the previous problem situation, *new cooperative context need, action operational level* and *problem disaggregation level*. Possible solutions to these two problem situations have to be analysed separately and then they may be integrated by a collective action of structuring (Friend, 1989).

The Option Scheme is now under examination in the CPD Commitees as only the president has been involved in the Scheme elaboration and analysis. A collective context of Change Analysis and Management must be created inside the CPD.

5 CONCLUDING REMARKS

Ill-structured problems, such as multiactorial and multiorganizational problems connected with the management of new ideas, procedures, technologies and so on, require specific emphasis on the activities of conceptualisation and problem definition (Sol, 1985). Change complexity knowledge, in terms of context, process and content of change, creates greater communication and collective action possibilities, oriented to the detailing of problem situations, making decisions, implementing them and to controlling their implementation.

Different methodological and conceptual indications have been proposed in literature to reduce project failure risks and to create an actual change culture. This knowledge implementation requires a global framework to guide human and institutional action without limiting the process development.

The framework proposed in this paper, tries to include all the main indications from literature in a system of structured Schemes which adopts a Multicriteria approach (de Montgolfier and Bertier, 1978), that connects the possibility of using methods (mainly multicriteria methods) with a specific way of acting on the representations and allows courses of action and procedures that are sufficiently elaborate to deal with complex situations and sufficiently free from structural limits. These procedures help actors translate facts, proposals, points of view and preferences into formal models where mental, written and numerical data, from different sources, are organically synthesized and easily "linkable" to the proposing actors and context and process conditions. These models can be activated and used in different phases of the process without a substantial change of structure; they evolve, induce different results and can be combined in several ways, always using the same language.

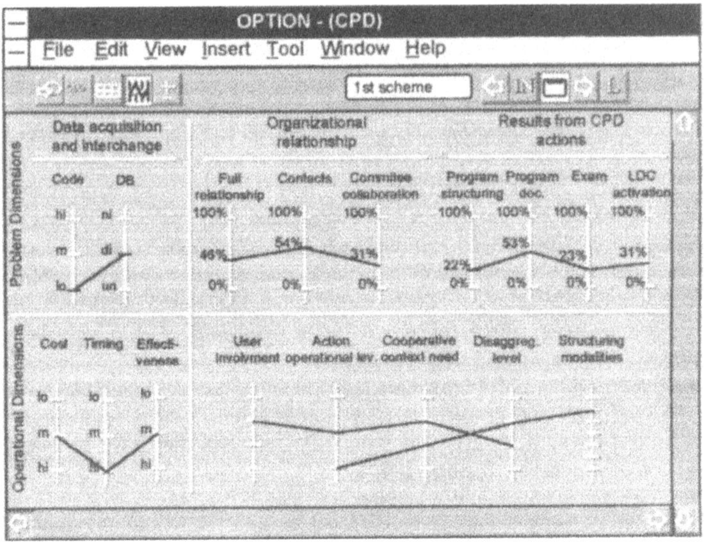

Figure 4 Option Scheme.

The system and its Schemes are now used as a support for two technological and organizational change processes. The essential target for the future is to test Schemes and procedures in actual different situations. The basic structure of a prototype system, designed by the same approach adopted in (Buffa et al., forthcoming), is now being implemented. Using QuerySys, a new generation windows-based full text retrieval environment (Marzano et al., 1993; INSIEL, 1993), the system can integrate three different paradigms of data management: DBMS for processing structured data, information retrieval for processing full text data and hypertext for browsing and linking different *chunks* of information. The experience acquired by manually using the procedure, when data and human knowledge are limited, will improve both the change support possibilities and data base and the model base management by a system, when manual use becomes difficult and time-consuming.

6 REFERENCES

Bowen, K. (1983) An experiment in problem formulation, *Journal of Operational Research Society*, 34, 685-694.

Buffa, F., Marzano, G. and Norese, M.F. (1996) MACRAME: a modelling methodology in multiactor context, accepted for pubblication on Decision Support Systems.

Crozier, M. and Friedberg, E. (1977) *L'acteur et le systeme*, Editions du Seuil, Paris.

De Montgolfier, J., and Bertier, P. (1978) *Approche multicritere des problemes de decision*, Editions Hommes et Techniques, Paris.

Eden, C. (1988) Cognitive mapping, *Eur.J.Opl. Res.*,36, 1-13.

Friend, J. (1989) The strategic choice approach, in *Rational analysis for a problematic world: problem structuring methods for complexity, uncertainty and conflict* (ed. J. Rosenhead), Wiley, Chichester.

Giddens, A. (1984) *The constitution of society: outline of the theory of structure*, University of California Press, Berkeley.

Huber, G.P. (1984) The nature and design of post-industrial organizations, *Management Science*, 30, 8, 928-951.

Humphreys, P. and Berkeley, D. (1992) Support for the synthesis and analysis of organisational Systems in deciding on change, in *Decision Support Systems: Experiences and expectations* (eds T.Jelassi, M.R. Klein, W.M. Mayon-White), IFIP North-Holland, Amsterdam.

INSIEL (1993) *Querysys Document Retrieval System - Manuale operativo*, Extralito, Pasian di Prato.

Kling, R. (1987) Defining the boundaries of computing across complex organizations, in *Critical issues in Information Systems Research* (eds. R. Boland and R. Hirschheim), Wiley, Chichester, 307-362.

Landry, M., Malouin, J.L., and Oral, M. (1983) Model Validation in Operations Research, *Eur.J.Opl. Res.*, 17, 207-220.

Le Louarn, M (1989) How intervention procedures may be related to different kind of change, in *Operational Research and the Social Sciences* (eds. M.C. Jackson, P. Keys and S.A. Cropper), Plenum, New Jork, 343-348.

Le Moigne, J.L. (1985) Progettazione della complessità e complessità della progettazione, in *La sfida della complessità* (eds. G. Bocchi G. and M.Cerutti), Feltrinelli, Milano, 84-102.

Lendaris, G. (1980) Structural Modeling - A tutorial guide, *IEEE Trans. Syst., Man, Cybern.*, 10/12, 807-830.

Markus, M. and Robey, D. (1988) Information technology and organizational change: casual structure in theory and research, *Management Science*, 34, 5, 583-598.

Marzano, G., Franzin, S., Gregori, G., Silli, E. (1993) Visual Information Retrieval: verso la definizione generale di un approccio operativo, in *Informatica e Diritto*, Edizioni Scientifiche Italiane, Firenze, 83-105.

Mintzberg, H., Raisinghani, D. and Theoret, A.(1976) The structure of the unstructured decision process, *Administrative Science Quarterly*, 21, 246-276 .

Mintzberg, H. (1983) *Structures in fives. Designing effective organizations*, Prentice Hall, Englewood Cliffs.

Mucci, L. and Norese, M.F. (1989) Intervention and change process. Interaction between communication and formalization, in *Operational Research and the Social Sciences* (eds. M.C. Jackson, P.Keys and S.A. Cropper), Plenum, New Jork, 297-304 .

Orlikowski W.J., and Robey, D. (1991) Information technology and the structuring of organizations, *Information Systems Research*, 2/2, 143-169.

Pfeffer, J. (1982) Organizations and Organization Theory, Pitman, Marshfield.

Pettigrew, A.M. (1990) Longitudinal field research on change: theory and practice, *Organization Science*, 1, 3, 267-292.

Rosenhead, J. (ed.) (1989) *Rational analysis for a problematic world: problem structuring methods for complexity, uncertainty and conflict*, Wiley, Chichester.

Roy, B. (1985) *Methodologie Multicritere d'Aide a la Decision*, Economica, Paris.

Sol, H. (1987) Conflicting Experiences with DSS, *Decision support Systems*, 3, 203-211.

Van do Ven, A.H. (1986) Central problems in the management of innovation, *Management Science*, 32, 590-607.

Van de Ven, A.H. and Huber, G.P. (1990) Longitudinal field research methods for studying processes of organizational change, *Organization Science*, 1, 3, 213-219.
Vincke, P. (1992) *Multicriteria Decision-Aid*, Wiley, Chichester.
Walsham, G. (1990) Implementation of Operational Research: some lessons from Organization Theory, Paper presented to IFORS 90, Athens.

7 SHORT BIOGRAPHY

Maria Franca Norese is an assistant professor of Operational Research in the Faculty of Engineering at the Politecnico of Torino (Technical University of Turin). She has been involved with direct analyses of organizational change processes for ten years. Her current research interests focus on the use of classical and new OR tools in organizations, to support individual and collective problem structuring and modelling.
Her papers have been published in the *European Journal of Operational Research, Decision Support Systems* and *Multi-Criteria Decision Analysis*.

Enrico Francardi is a graduate in Industrial Engineering from the Politecnico of Torino (Technical University of Turin) who undertook a period of applied research in development of information systems at the Politecnico Central Unit for Data Elaboration.

13

Are your business and your IT strategy in phase ?

P. J. Georges
Director of Quality Management, Transpac
Tour Montparnasse B 13, 33 avenue du Maine
75755 PARIS Cedex 15 - FRANCE
Tel: +33 1 45 38 41 98 Fax: +33 1 45 38 71 47
E-mail: georges@transpac.atlas.fr

Abstract

Business success does not come from advances in Information Technology (IT). True, IT has helped companies to produce more, but the only effect has been to bring prices down to their marginal value. Further, some have profited solely by the rapidity of information flow to gain an "opportunity" advantage over competitors. However, real business success can be traced back to new ideas or new ways, not new computers. A winning strategy for every business must therefore address, with the help of IT, the production of content as opposed to volume and speediness.

Information in the large is the prime material that companies process in their business. A company's information system can be used to build a valid model of its activities. Application of simple information theory measurements to this model yields the intrinsic value and cost of all activities. These measurements can equally be applied on the corresponding software systems and therefore produce a relative measure of how well the computer systems in place support the business activities.

With such a model it is possible to measure the goals and capabilities of any organization. Hence its capacity to elucidate the strategy and the relevance of decisions concerning the products, the organization, and the company's computer system.

Keywords

information theory, reengineering, systems, strategic management

1. INTRODUCTION

Companies choose their own goals. One of their objectives is to deliver goods to the market (at least for business enterprises). A century ago, the capability to deliver decided the price. Later, with mass production the price could no longer be fixed at will, hence the costs had to be part of the economic equation. Today, the only sure fact is that the price of any product or service will be driven downward to its production cost by the market pressure, companies having to abandon one after the other any given market depending on their individual cost structure.

In the field of Information Technology, 50 years of technological breakthrough seem to bring no real gain in either productivity or returns. The paradox is that technological progress should bring productivity and economical gains and it doesn't. This is known as the Solow paradox, after Robert Solow, Nobel prize in Economics in 1987, who demonstrated that there is an ever increasing gap between technological progress and economical gains.

Economical gains are generally measured as the difference between the price of the product or service on the market, and the costs to bring it to the market: customers are the independent and supreme judge for each product. This method of measuring gains suffers from the major drawback that gains are only known after the sale. The value of products is therefore felt only through their market value tomorrow on decisions made today.

These two aspects, technological progress and value, must first be brought together before the Solow paradox is explained: economical gains have been lagging behind technological progress because they are tied, not to the latter, but to the value of use. In our Information Technology world the difficulty is to measure the value of use of Information.

2. ON WHAT TO DECIDE

Some 20 years ago, many organizations went through a fitness program, in which consultants helped to make the production more "lean": in vain, the lower the price at which they were able to sell, the leaner they had to be. Companies were then told that in fact they hadn't been listening carefully enough to their customers, i.e. what customers were ready to buy and at which price they would buy today, and (hopefully) tomorrow. That meant that organizations not only had to be leaner, but also more flexible, forcing companies into Business Process Reengineering (BPR, the now famous management fad).

Since it is well known that BPR programs do not seem to provide any real sharp edge on competition, the alternative is to launch a good Total Quality Program: it is then discovered that the real goal of the company is to serve some evolving (human) need (forever): Quality is Eternity.

Anticipation must be taken into account. Hamel and Prahalad's book (1994) hits the point in this respect. A company's survivability must be built into its genes. However, one must add Senge's (1990) therapy to Hamel and Prahalad's diagnosis: in order to survive one must possess the right learning tools to adapt. But neither one of them show the path to be followed.

The flaw in this never-ending quest of the holy grail is that companies are not able to measure their business against (1) its goals, (2) its market, (3) its organization and people. This stems from the fact that no strategic model or Total Quality program can measure whether the organization of the enterprise is in phase with its objectives. The first decision that a company must make is to equip itself with the right measuring tools.

3. INFORMATION MODEL

The value of decisions, of product use, of knowledge itself is explicit in the existence of certain elements of information. The cost of gaining such information is directly linked to the diversity of meaning and represents in a valid way the cost of operation of the equipment and organization for which such information is needed. A measure of the quantity of information is a valid measure of the processes themselves. Information content becomes a controlling factor of the company's strategy since it represents both today's capabilities and tomorrow's possibilities and shortcomings.

The method developed by Michel Vicarini (1992) measures the activity of any company or service through measuring its information system. The method first measures an objective value (intrinsic) of the products and services, in other words its added value. It is used at the same time to measure the effort needed to produce such products and services, in direct relation with the actual operating costs.

The measures taken at the industrial activity level can be linked directly with the measures made at the Information System end, in particular but not exclusively in its computer system component. The software process can therefore be monitored through exogenous metrics, giving it the credibility needed to participate in the company's strategic decisions:

- does the intrinsic value of a given activity justify a computer system ?
- will the investment and exploitation costs of such a system leave room for profitability ?
- which architecture and capacity are needed for the computer system ?

The foundation of the method is that the value of any activity is carried by the data-elements or "views" describing the various "objects" (be it a product in the company, a customer, a procedure) in their relation to each other in participation in the activity. Every single view carrying the meaning of an object is a valid representation of that object: the semantics of any reality is derived from its structured expression. Measuring the information content of the data-elements of an activity is the measure of the activity itself.

Three types of objects characterize the activity, and define its context:

- products and services, at their various steps of development
- procedures used to manage the production of products and services
- partners responsible for the processes delivering the products and services.

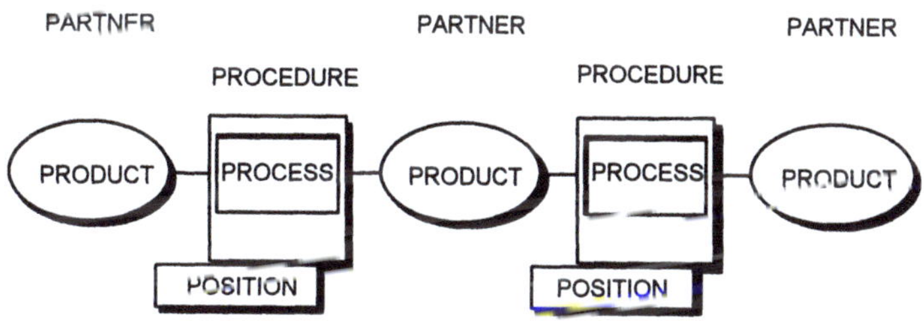

Figure 1 - Activity Model

A view is therefore the situation within which a given object of an activity is referenced. To obtain a valid measure of any activity, data-elements must be expressed in a structured fashion with a normalized vocabulary, so as to have a standard. Activity is therefore described by structured views attached to every object participating in the activity. The underlying model of activities that support the method gives the context of interpretation of the messages.

A view is described by its 3 ordered parts:

- a LITERAL, the etymological meaning of the data-element (e.g. date, name...),
- a *situation*, the meaning of the literals in the context,
- the **object** (or context) to which the view is attached.

Examples of views are:

DURATION *minimum* of **loan**
AMOUNT *desired* of **loan**
ADDRESS of **customer**

4. INFORMATION METRICS

The metrics used to measure the business activity are the mean information content and the quantity of decision applied to the formal description of the said activity. These metrics were formalized by Shannon and Weaver a few years ago (1949).

The mean information content is computed as the entropy, in the Information Theory sense, of the formalism used to describe the objects of the activity.

$$\text{Mean Information Content} = -\sum_{i} \frac{n_i}{N} * \log_2\left(\frac{n_i}{N}\right)$$

with n_i the number of occurrences of word i , and N is the total number of words used to describe the reality. As an example, mean information content of a uniformly random text written with an alphabet of 32 characters is 5 (the maximum).

Information value is derived by multiplying the Mean Information Content by the number M of distinct views built with the given alphabet.

Information Value = M * Mean Information Content

Quantity of decision is the logarithm of the number of distinct elementary decisions necessary to choose one outcome among a finite number of mutually exclusive events. This is called Complexity of use. For the activity, it corresponds to the number of distinct words used to describe it, i.e. the number of distinct literals, situation and objects. The formula is:

$$\text{Complexity of use} = (N_l * N_s * N_o) * \log_2(N_l * N_s * N_o)$$

in which N_l, N_s, N_o are respectively the number of distinct literals, the number of situations and the number of distinct objects.

For software this can be read as the measure of the difficulty to assemble the code: the complexity of use in this case is computed from the number of distinct verbs (instructions or modules depending on the point of view), user functions and distinct literals of the activity. It is clear that a correspondence can be established between the complexity of the activity, and the complexity of the system used to support that activity.

Equating complexity with cost on one side, and complexity with processing power on the other, two rules of thumb are important at this level:

1. There is a diseconomy if the complexity of the supporting information system goes over 75% of the value of an activity. This departs radically from the use of function points where for every user change request a qualified estimate expressed in function points is produced. If it fits the budget it is accepted; if not it is rejected or postponed until next year. Now a much more efficient decision making process can be put to work: complexity in software can be accepted only if it stays within 75% of the complexity of the supported activity. That complexity itself can only be accepted if it corresponds to an adequate increase in the intrinsic value of the activity (adequate may mean to maintain or to improve on the efficiency measured as the ratio of intrinsic value to complexity).
2. The capabilities of the computer system necessary to handle a given level of complexity for an activity must match: complexity of the order of 30,000 can be handled on the desktop; 100,000 requires a client-server architecture; 300,000 a mainframe or a special purpose computer system. The question of what can be developed at the desktop level, what should be maintained as a client-server application, or what justifies the investment of a (still) multi-million dollar piece of equipment, rests in the hands of decision makers but not working solely from IS department decrees.

5. DECISION MAKING: AN APPLICATION

The example is taken from a loan acquisition process in a large French banking institution. The activities were modeled after the meta-model presented in Figure 1, the identification of the various objects being obtained from the views describing the loan acquisition process. The results of the analysis are shown in Figure 2. Values for the different activities are cumulative at each position, they are not the individual values corresponding to the views of the corresponding activity. Hence, the values of Information value and complexity of use increase from one position to the next. Moreover values computed for each object type (product, procedure, partner) are not additive. The values on the ACTIVITY line are computed from all the views on all the objects considered for all positions up to the current one.

The interpretation of data in Figure 2 is derived from some formal mathematical results on the activity model, and also from experimental data collected over some ten years in production and service industries.

Information values around 500 (loan identification position for ACTIVITY in Figure 2) are representative of common management activities: identification and indexation of the objects of the activity. Values around 1,000 are representative of management and resource planning: it is the Information value for the overall process described here. Control and forecast activities would have produced values up to 1,500.

Information value for a procedure should not go over 25% of the Information value for a product. The measures obtained are compatible with that limit.

Information value

	Loan Identification	Loan Schedule	Borrower Profile	Offer Delivery
Product	47	223	223	223
Partners	436	436	464	473
Procedure	47	47	47	73
ACTIVITY	598	844	870	919

Complexity of use

	Loan Identification	Loan Schedule	Borrower Profile	Offer Delivery
Product	1 944	15 108	15 108	15 108
Partners	67 064	67 064	77 939	86 375
Procedure	1 349	1 675	1 675	4 018
ACTIVITY	157 040	237 666	243 247	297 541

Figure 2 - Loan process measurements

For an Information value of 1,000; Complexity of use should not be over 100,000. The reason is clear in the partners values (essentially the borrower in the present case) that are far too high. This can be interpreted in two different ways, as far as the strategy of the company is concerned:

- given the intrinsic values of the product (the loan), identification of the borrower is overly complex, i.e. unnecessary; or,
- with such detailed knowledge on the borrower, more sophisticated loans can be offered.

It should be noticed that these results can be produced specifically and systematically only because it is possible to attach a measure to each activity and to each object of the activity. You can control only what you can measure.

As for the organization, one can notice that all the intrinsic values for the product are reached at the scheduling position (223), and that the borrower's value is practically known at the first position (436 over 473). Adequate organization of the process (smooth operation without bottlenecks), requires that the value be accumulated in equal steps throughout the process. The BPR gurus could work on this.

The software application for the loan process is composed of some 40,000 lines of COBOL, made up of 14 transactions in 231 modules. The application needed restructuring in order to improve its reliability (the same controls were not applied consistently across the transactions) and its evolutivity (the backlog of evolution orders was more than 3 months).

The analysis of the software program showed that the number of distinct data-elements was equal to 167, due to the lack of a data dictionary. The Information value derived from the views of the activity as processed in the software is 4,085. The complexity is 10,028,602 (231 modules * 14 functions * 167 data-elements * $\log_2$ of the same product).

We have found experimentally that the Information value of the software (4,085) must be at most equal to 25% of the Information value of the product (844): the present software program is not in phase with its purpose (in other words it does too many things for what it is used for).

As pointed out before, the complexity of the software (>10,000,000) should stay within 75% of the complexity of the product (≈240,000): gains in the present situation can only be found by mass-production of the product to offset the operating cost, not a likely occurrence here. The software must therefore be drastically reorganized to reduce its complexity of use under 180,000.

6. CONCLUSION

It is always very difficult in any business situation to reach optimal decisions with respect to the conduct of business. Intimacy with the organization, its goals and its market, help managers to make, most of the time, the right decision. Nevertheless, everybody tends to be dissatisfied with such a process, in the sense that hard facts can very seldom be pinpointed as the rational element behind the decision.

Modeling the activity from the information system point of view makes it possible to measure the goals and capabilities of the organization. The interpretation of the measurements for the various processes allows managers to elucidate the strategy and the relevance of decisions concerning the products and the organization. Moreover, adequate allocation of resources, in particular for the company's computer system, can be justified directly in terms of their value to the organization, as opposed to their cost.

7. ACKNOWLEDGEMENT

The method exposed has been developed by Michel Vicarini, PhD in Physics from the University of Paris. He has successfully been applying his method as a consultant with various French institutions and companies, and is the author of several publications on its application, both in the field of information systems and in strategic management.

8. REFERENCES

Hamal, G and Prahalad, C.K. (1994) Competing for the Future, Harvard Business School Press, Cambridge, Mass.

Senge, P. M. (1990) The Fifth discipline, Century Business Press

Shannon, C. E. and Weaver, W. W. (1949), The mathematical Theory of Communication, University of Illinois Press, Urbana, IL.

Vicarini, M. and Georges, P. J. (1994) Information et Business Process Engineering, Flux n° 162, revue des ingénieurs supélec ISSN 0766-3536

Vicarini, M. (1992) La Théorie de la réalité, Processeurs n° 1

9. BIOGRAPHY

Patrick J. Georges is Director of Quality Management of Transpac, a subsidiary of France Télécom for switched data networks. Prior to joining Transpac, he was at SESA, then ARM Conseil, both French software consulting firms, where he held several positions as project leader, company manager for large software projects in control and telecommunications, and consultant in management of information systems for both private and government companies. Georges holds an engineering degree from Ecole Supérieure d'Electricité, France and an MS in Electrical Engineering from Carnegie Mellon University.

14

Executive information systems development in Thailand

W. Jirachiefpattana, D. R. Arnott and P. A. O'Donnell
Department of Information Systems, Monash University
Level 7, 26 Sir John Monash Drive, Caulfield East, Melbourne, 3145, Australia, Phone +61 3 9903 2208, Fax +61 3 9903 2005, Email darnott@is.monash.edu.au

Abstract

This paper examines EIS development in Thailand. Thailand is a newly industrialised country, typical of other developing countries. First, the paper discusses the nature of the Thai economic and political systems. Four case studies are explored to examine how EIS are developed and to explore the influence of the economic and political environment on EIS development. Only one of the four systems examined can be considered highly successful. The factors behind EIS success and failure in a developing country are discussed. The paper concludes by suggesting that to develop an EIS successfully in a developing country and evolutionary approach with strong user participation should be followed. It is also suggested that outsourcing EIS development to foreign consultants is unlikely to be successful.

Keywords

Executive information systems, developing country, systems development, evolutionary development, outsourcing

1 INTRODUCTION

Executive information systems (EIS) are a class of information systems which support the work of senior management by providing effective access to timely internal and external information (Houdeshel and Watson 1987, Rockart and DeLong 1988, Wallis 1989, Armstrong 1990, O'Leary 1990, Paller and Laska 1990, Volonino 1992).

Most of the studies of EIS development and use have been of organisations in Western industrialised countries. Many developing countries are investing heavily in information technology. In particular, the newly industrialised countries of South-East Asia depend upon information technology to support rapid economic growth and their position in an extremely competitive commercial hemisphere. It follows that many large organisations in developing countries will have implemented or are considering implementing EIS to support their senior executives. "Are these systems successful? Are they different to Western EIS? Are they developed differently?" are three fundamental questions that have not been addressed by previous studies but are the subject of this paper.

In this paper we describe EIS development in Thailand. Thailand has been used as a representative developing country for this study. It has a population of 60 million with a per-capita income of $US2040 compared to the USA with US$24 750. Economic growth is around 8.5% per annum. First, we present the research method used in this study followed by a discussion of the nature of the Thai economic and political systems and summary descriptions of EIS in four large organisations. The EIS development processes are discussed in terms of political and economic pressures, development strategies, EIS teams and technical constraints. Finally, some general observations are made regarding EIS practice in developing countries.

2 RESEARCH METHOD

The research described in this paper is exploratory in nature and is aimed at discovering how EIS are developed in a developing country. A case study method was used for the project with the systems development process being the subject of study. A case study captures greater detail than a survey (Galliers 1992, Yin 1989) especially in terms of identifying the nature and important characteristics of the systems development process (Benbasat et al 1987). This approach is consistent with other studies of EIS development (Sundue 1986, Volonino, Robinson and Watson 1989, Armstrong 1990a and 1990b, Gunter and Frolick 1991, Moynihan 1993, Suvachittanont, Arnott and O'Donnell 1994, Pervan and Meneely 1995, Hasan and Gould 1995).

One of the researchers is a Thai national with many years industry experience in information technology. Personal contacts were used to identify Thai organisations that had implemented EIS for at least one year. Four organisations were identified and formal approaches were made to the chief executive officers; all agreed to take part in the research. The four cases are thought to representative of EIS in Thailand especially given the early stage of information technology adoption in the country. The Thai researcher performed field data collection during January and February 1995.

Different questionnaires were developed for EIS developers, the EIS co-ordinator and executive users. The questionnaire for each group was distributed to the subjects by the EIS co-ordinator. The co-ordinator determined which executive users would receive the questionnaires. The executives users were asked about the success of the EIS, while the developers were questioned about the development process. The questions for the co-ordinator focused on system initiation as well as the general nature of the development of the EIS over the life of the system. In most cases the co-ordinator was also a developer.

The questionnaires were left with the organisations for a week. Once returned the responses were analysed and detailed follow-up questions were prepared. These questions were answered in structured interviews that ranged in length one to two hours. Two organisations did not return the questionnaires by the due date and the respondents were personally interviewed using the questions presented in the questionnaires. Follow-up questions were also asked. Published information about the organisations (eg annual reports) and system documentation was also consulted. Similar methods have been used to study EIS development in Western organisations (Suvachittanont, Arnott and O'Donnell 1994).

One aspect of the research that is different to Western studies is the reluctance of executive users to answer questions that relate to the impact of the systems on organisations and individuals. Only two executives (from different organisations) answered these questions, despite each CEO having agreed to take part in the research. This may reflect a Thai cultural bias where managers, no matter how senior, are uncomfortable with criticising the initiatives of their organisations. This lack of executive user response means that no detailed analysis of system success from a user perspective is possible. Some managers did provide anecdotal comments on system performance.

3 THE ECONOMIC AND POLITICAL ENVIRONMENT

This section provides an overview of Thai economics and politics as well as a description of the industry environment of the organisations that provide the case studies.

3.1 Thai economics and politics

Porter (1990) argues that government influences many, perhaps all, aspects of a nation's industry structure. The most direct affects are the development and enforcement of regulations for entry to the industry, competitive practices, and profitability. Regulations of product quality and safety, and environment quality are less direct forms of a government's influence. Government regulations can influence the behaviour of firms as suppliers or buyers, and can also affect the position of a company in an industry. The industry environment can have a major influence on the nature of information systems that are developed to support senior executives.

The Thai economy is perhaps more influenced by politics than those in the West. Political leaders must be accepted by the military; indeed, most political leaders are senior military officers. If politicians' policies and actions strongly conflict with the Thai military, they are usually removed from office. In the 1991 military coup, the coup leaders, Generals Kraprayoon and Kongsompong asserted that the reason for their action was the corruption of the Chatichai government. Others have argued that the real reason was that the Chatichai government had excluded the top military leaders from the benefits of economic growth (Warr 1993). Although there have been elected governments in Thai history, none have survived for a full term. In addition to direct military intervention this instability is due to the inability of any political party to command a majority of seats in the Thai Representative Parliament and successive governments have been unable to balance the interests of the coalition parties. The collapse of the Chuan government is a recent example.

Regardless of the reason for political change (military coup or election) government policy can change rapidly. Thai business analysts attempt to anticipate the economic future by analysing the background and affiliation of members of the new cabinet. Government administration tends to favour firms which support the coalition parties or firms in which leaders of the government parties are involved. In Porter's terms, this is the most direct political influence on the economy possible.

Thai government industry policy is implemented through the Board of Investment which uses a combination of investment promotion schemes, tariff and tax policies, and trade and price controls to direct the pattern of private investment. The trade regime in Thailand also includes a number of restrictive measures, for instance, quantitative import and export controls (Warr 1993). These government intervention and protection policies may change radically with a change in government.

Throughout Thai history, economic activity has been dominated by the Royal Family and other wealthy families. In the past, commerce was considered a low status occupation in Thailand. As a result many commercial activities were conducted by Chinese immigrants. Today, many companies are operated by people of Chinese descent. It is common for Chinese companies to invite members of the Royal Family and other wealthy families, politicians and the military to be on their board of directors. The political power of these non-executive directors acts to provide privilege and protection for these companies.

3.2 Commercial banking in Thailand

Many Thai commercial banks are owned by Chinese-Thai who belong to the same dialect group (Chaiyasoot 1993). The Sophonpanich family is the largest shareholder in the Bangkok Bank, while the Lamsam and Ratanarak families control the Thai Farmers Bank and the Bank of Ayudhya, respectively. Among the 16 commercial banks incorporated in Thailand, the government is a major shareholder of the Krung Thai Bank and the Siam Bank, while the largest share of the Siam Commercial Bank, the first bank established in Thailand, is owned by the Royal Family. This concentration of bank ownership is uncommon in Western countries.

To reduce the concentration of ownership in the banking industry, the Thai monetary authorities adopted policies to encourage the entry of more finance companies and introduced capital divestiture requirements for existing shareholders. The first policy failed because Thai banks were the major shareholders of many of the new finance companies; nine of ten largest finance companies are associated with the four major banking groups and the Siam Commercial Bank. The second policy also did not achieve its goals. There are now more individual shareholders but the patterns of control within each bank have not substantially changed. Small shareholders have been unable to unify in order to exert influence on the company and large shareholders have used other people and related companies to buy new shares.

Although Thai bankers dictate the cost and the allocation of domestic credit, the government does influence the operation of the banks through the regulations of the Bank of Thailand, the central bank. The main features of these regulations include the specification of interest rate ceilings for loans and deposits, control of new entry, agricultural credit policy, compulsory bond holding for branch expansion, and specification of minimum capital funds to risky assets ratio. These measures are designed to prevent excessive expansion of credit and to ensure that the banking system is reliable. They are similar to Western central banking practices.

3.3 State enterprises

State enterprises are involved in many areas of business including infrastructure, manufacturing, transport, tourism, services, trade and finance. Most state enterprises are monopolies. These state enterprises are the major sources of income for many military officials and civilian politicians. The management of a state enterprise comes under the authority of a parent ministry and according to state enterprise regulations, only the supervising minister, with the approval of the cabinet, can appoint the state enterprise's chairman, CEO and deputies. The appointment of a CEO to a state enterprise by the supervising ministry is often decided on the basis of requests and pressure from politicians and the military and most appointees are former bureaucrats and military officers. As a result, they can lack the background needed to manage an efficient commercial business (Dhiratayakinant 1993). This system of patronage means that the political parties strongly influence economic decision making through their indirect control of state enterprises.

State enterprise management lack flexibility and autonomy in developing strategic and operational plans. State enterprises are responsible not only to their supervising ministries, but also to a number of boards and committees. If a state enterprise develops new projects, they must be reviewed by the National Economic and Social Development Board (NESDB). Capital budgets and annual investment plans are screened by the Capital Budget Committee, while the National Debt Policy Committee reviews all investment projects which require loan financing. Any significant changes to the mission and operation of a state enterprise must be approved by the National State Enterprise Committee. All subsidy requests made by state enterprises are reviewed by the Budget Bureau and their annual operating reports must be submitted for examination. The Auditor General's Office audits the financial statements of the enterprises. Standard methods and procedures of accounting are set up by the Comptroller General's Office principally to supervise the legality of expenditure disbursement. The recommendations of these regulatory organisations are finally decided on by the Cabinet, which may overrule any lower decision (Dhiratayakinant 1993).

In summary, the Thai political system is extremely volatile as compared to most Western democracies. Further, Thai governments are more interventionist with respect to the economy than in the West and many senior managerial positions change frequently in response to changes in government. As a result of these political and economic forces the organisational environment of EIS development is also volatile. To the extent that Thailand is representative of developing countries it follows *ceteris paribus* that the development of EIS in a developing country is likely to be significantly more difficult than in an industrialised country.

4 THE CASES

In this section, the general background of each case is described, together with an overview of each EIS. Table 1 illustrates the characteristics of these organisations and their systems. The organisations are all large by international standards. All have successfully computerised their operational data processing systems. They have used a variety of development approaches for their EIS and the systems vary widely in terms of success.

Case 1: The Transportation Company

The "Transportation Company" is a state enterprise which employs almost 20 000 staff. In its 1994 annual report, profits before tax were US$168.49 million. Its stated strategies for maintaining its market share and profitability are total quality, cost advantage and external competence. The Transportation Company aims to support these strategies with motivated and unified staff, financial strength, strong information systems and a simplified fleet.

Developing an EIS was part of the overall Management Information Systems Plan. The objective of the EIS is to provide top executives with rich management information to monitor organisational activities, and to provide support for planning and decision making. The EIS project was initiated by the President of the company in January 1994 immediately after he was appointed. The non-information system executive sponsors were the Vice President of Corporate Planning and the Vice President of Accounting.

The EIS development commenced without formal cost-benefit analysis and was approved by the Executive Management Committee. The initial cost of hardware, software and personnel in the EIS development were US$130 370, $92 592 and $74 074 respectively. The company spends around US$74 000 annually for maintenance and operation of the system. The technical environment is client/server in nature with Pilot's Lightship as the main software.

Currently, the implemented EIS is the first production version and covers production, finance and accounting, marketing, and human resources. Its general features include key indicator tracking, exception reporting and drill down. The information is presented in tabular, graphic, and text formats on request. The EIS also provides personal tools to support executive work including e-mail, diary, calculator, and staff directory. The first version was delivered within 12 months and comprised 181 screens. Fifteen senior executives, including the CEO, were the initial users. The EIS is considered successful by both developers and users.

Case 2: Bank A

"Bank A" is a major commercial bank with 12,000 employees and significant state shareholding. Net profit was US$119 million for the first half of 1994. The bank has 331 branches in Thailand and 6 branches abroad. The Bank aims to expand its branch network, both within Thailand and throughout the Asian region.

The EIS project was initiated by the President and Chief Executive Officer in 1992. Instead of receiving hard copy management reports, he wanted an interactive system which could provide both an overview of the bank and detailed information about the performance

Table 1 An overview of the systems

Issues	***Case 1*** *Transport-ation Company*	***Case 2*** *Bank A*	***Case 3*** *Bank B*	***Case 4*** *Energy Company*
Characteristics of the organisation				
Strong international focus	✔	✗	✗	✗
State enterprise	✔	✗	✗	✔
Controlled by one family	✗	✔	✔	✗
Initiation of the EIS				
Year	1994	1992	1991	1986
Initiated by top management	✔	✔	✔	✗
Sponsored by top management	✔	✔	✔	✔
Sponsor involved in systems development	✗	✗	✗	✗
Development time took more than 6 months	✔	✔	✔	✔
Cost-benefit analysis before development	✗	✗	✗	✗
# of initial executive users	15	18	15	16
# of screens of the initial system	181	10	60	12
# of current executive users	15	18	15	16
# of screens of the current system	181	80	60	20
Technical features of the EIS				
E-mail	✔	✔	✔	✔
News service	✔	✗	✗	✔
Word processing	✗	✗	✔	✔
Electronic calendars	✔	✗	✔	✔
Key indicators tracking	✔	✗	✔	✗
Drill down	✔	✗	✔	✔
Exception reporting	✔	✔	✔	✔
Graphical presentation	✔	✔	✔	✔
Tabular presentation	✔	✔	✔	✔
Textual presentation	✔	✔	✔	✔
Colour presentation	✔	✗	✔	✔
External data accessibility	✔	✔	✔	✔
Easy to learn and use	✔	✔✗	✔	✔
Applications Supported				
Marketing	✔	✔	✔	✔
Finance	✔	✔	✔	✔
Manufacturing	✔			✔
Personnel	✔	✔	✔	✔
Distribution	✔			✔
Corporate planning	✔			

of the branches. The executive sponsor was the Executive Vice President, Technology Group. The EIS project was approved by the Board of Directors. No formal cost-benefit analysis was performed.

The EIS was developed on an existing IBM mainframe and personal computer network using the Personnel Assistance Systems (PAS) software package and general purpose software such as COBOL. Existing hardware and software was used because the developers were both comfortable and experienced in the use of the technology. The first EIS application, finance, was delivered within eight months and was based on existing reports; it comprised 10 screens. The initial users were three Senior Vice Presidents. The number of screens and executive users has increased to 80 and 18, respectively. The completed system provides support for finance, personnel and marketing.

The design of the personnel and other EIS applications are totally different. The personnel application was developed on a personal computer using the PAS software package. This allowed the analyst/programmers to develop "user friendly" interfaces. The other applications were written in COBOL and have a non-graphical interface.

Bank A's EIS project can be regarded as relatively unsuccessful. The poor user interface of most applications has led to a low usage rate among executives. The system has not been updated due to internal regulatory constraints and an inflexible technical architecture.

Case 3: Bank B

The third case, "Bank B" is a leading commercial bank in the South East Asian region. The bank employs 25,000 employees and according to its 1993 annual report, profit after tax was US$556 million. The Bank operates 427 branches: 407 domestic and 20 foreign. The board and senior management of the bank is dominated by one family. Prior to the development of the EIS, Bank B had attempted to use information technology to support management. This proto-EIS involved the creation and transmission of daily trial balance sheets to Head Office, in order to provide both operational units and senior management with detailed accounting information and the overall status of all branches on the next working day.

The EIS development project commenced in September 1991 under the sponsorship of a Senior Vice Executive President. The aim of the EIS was to provide information to top executives to help them make better and faster decisions. Moreover, the Bank also wished to provide a continuity of information during the transition to a new management team. The project proceeded without cost-benefit analysis and the approximate initial cost of hardware, software and personnel was US$300 000, $100 000 and $200 000, respectively. Annually, the Bank spends about US$60 000 for maintenance and operation of the system. The technical environment was client/server with high-end Apple Macintosh computers used as the executive workstations. The data-base product 4th Dimension was the primary development tool.

The first EIS was delivered after 12 months and comprised 60 screens. The current EIS supports 15 senior executives and their staff and covers the marketing, finance and personnel areas. The system comprises three main functions: executive summary reports, business performance analysis, and support tools. The information is presented in tables, graphics, and text. Colour is used to highlight information and to produce attractive screens.

The EIS of Bank B can be considered to be a relative failure. According to anecdotal evidence the system has not been used by executives for some time. Executives continue to receive verbal reports on business unit performance from their support staff each morning. The EIS was largely developed by a foreign consultant who did not adapt his design strategies to Asian management styles.

Case 4: The Energy Company

The final case, the "Energy Company" is a state enterprise whose mission is to create a fully integrated business to support the energy, and therefore economic, stability of the country. The main business units are downstream oil, natural gas, central services and petrochemical. In 1993 the organisation generated a net profit of US$309 million on income of $3.43 billion.

The Energy Company's EIS has evolved to its third version. The first version was created in 1986 on the initiative of the Head of Information Systems Department at Head Office. He hoped that senior executives could receive information faster if management reports were provided electronically. His concept was approved by senior management. The Head of Information Systems also acted as the project manager while the Deputy Governor, Policy and Planning was the executive sponsor. The first version comprised 12 screens and was used by 16 senior executives. It was developed on networked personal computers using the C language.

The second version of the EIS commenced in 1990 due to significant changes in the business of the corporation. This version was not based on the first EIS; it was a new

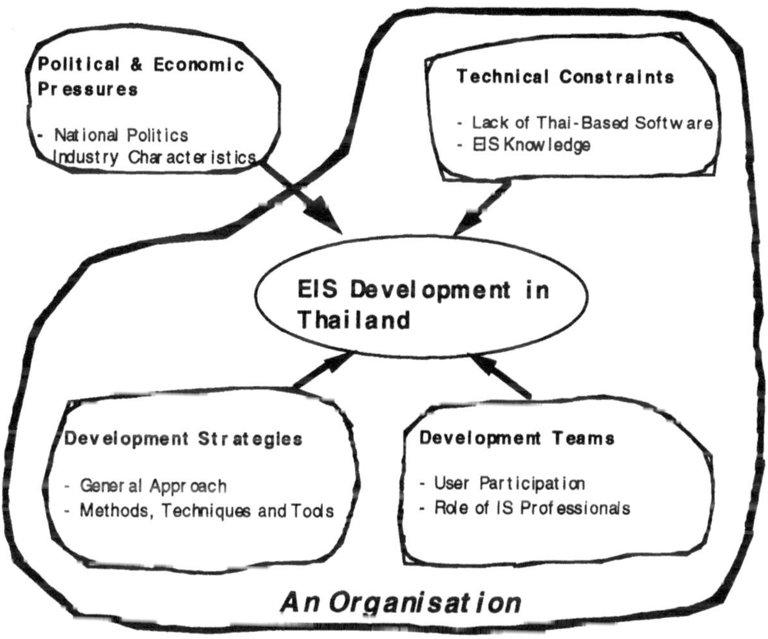

Figure 1 Major factors affecting EIS development in Thailand

development using a client/server architecture, programmed in Visual Basic and a relational database management system, INGRES. Currently, 16 executives use the second version of the EIS while the third version is being developed.

The current, second version of the EIS has two major modules: applications and office automation. The EIS provides information related to the petroleum business, personnel, subsidiaries and joint ventures. It covers the marketing, finance, manufacturing, personnel and distribution departments. Management information is presented as exception reports in the forms of text, graphs and tables. These reports were designed by the staff of the IS Department and they are not customisable. When they want to retrieve information, executives click the icon which represents the required report. The other module of the system, office automation, includes word processing, e-mail, and electronic scheduling.

This EIS can be regarded as a qualified success. The third version of the system is under-development and the previous versions have been used by executives and their staff. There is some anecdotal evidence that the project has been dominated by the information systems department and that the system requirements and designs have not been determined or confirmed by the executive users.

5 FACTORS IN EIS DEVELOPMENT

Figure 1 illustrates some of the major factors involved in EIS development in Thailand. These factors are grouped into four broad classes: political and economic pressures, constraints, development strategies, and development teams. The following sections discuss these factors in detail.

5.1 Political and economic pressures

As outlined in Section 3, the Thai political environment is more volatile than in most Western countries. Also mentioned in Section 3 are the processes whereby the Thai Government intervenes and influences. The combination of a volatile political system and greater direct influence on industry means that the environment for EIS development is much more uncertain and complex than is assumed in most EIS research. One result of this development environment is that Thai executives strongly focus on short term planning.

Senior executives of private corporations pay close attention to any kind of formal and informal information delivered from the Cabinet or Government agencies. The greater the rate of political change, the greater is the need for anecdotal information by Thai executives. It is difficult for EIS to serve this need. Where data is available the monitoring functions of EIS are particularly relevant. A similar focus exists in state enterprises. The political environment affects state enterprises to a much greater extent than private corporations. The tight controls on management and operations and the frequent change of Board membership, as well as CEOs and other senior executive appointments means that EIS development is even more uncertain. EIS for Thai state enterprises need to address frequent changes of user population and frequent changes in policy direction.

All four case studies were subject to the influences of this environment. One important consequence was that the information technology group or manager tended to take a much greater control of the project than in the West; some even acted as the source of system requirements.

5.2 System development strategies

The four Thai cases exhibit major differences in the approaches adopted for the development of EIS. Table 2 compares these differences in the categories of requirements elicitation, analysis and design techniques, and development tools. Three distinct development approaches were used: evolutionary, traditional or linear systems development life cycle (SDLC) and outsourcing. The use of systems analysis techniques and the selection of hardware and software was strongly influenced by the development approach. The organisation which used the traditional SDLC approach applied large scale information systems methods and tools while the one which employed the evolutionary approach used methods and tools common to Western EIS cases. Two cases used outsourcing to some degree; the methods and tools which they used varied according to which vendors were used and which parts of the development process were outsourced.

Evolutionary development

The Transportation Company is the only case which clearly applied an evolutionary approach to EIS development (Suvachittanont, Arnott and O'Donnell 1994). By using this approach, the EIS development team started with a small system which offered enough substantial information to gain top executives' attention. This initial system involved management information about traffic, production, finance, marketing, competitive position and customer service quality. It was also a vehicle for EIS developers to understand the way that the executives managed the business. At the same time the executives learnt about the nature and possibilities of EIS. Meanwhile, the team continued the development of applications for every management information group including operations and performance, technical, human resources and corporate overview.

The development process of this company involved the iterative non-linear performance of the following processes: planning and research, requirements analysis and logical design, physical design, construction and testing, implementation, and maintenance. Planning and research involved the identification of organisational mission and objectives and the assessment of executive needs. The second phase involved requirements analysis and logical design, including the specification of critical success factors (CSF), key performance indicators (KPI), required management information and information presentation standards. The availability of hardware and software was assessed, and the resources required for the project were proposed, approved and acquired. Technical staff were trained to use new EIS software especially in relation to the multi dimensional database concept. After design standards were developed, databases and screens were designed. Finally, construction, testing, implementation and maintenance took place.

Table 2 Comparison of EIS development

Features	*Case 1* *Transportation Company*	*Case 2* *Bank A*	*Case 3* *Bank B*	*Case 4* *Energy Company*
Development approach	Evolution	SDLC	Outsourcing	Outsourcing
Hardware platform	LAN-PC-Mainframe	LAN-PC-Mainframe	LAN-PC-Mainframe	LAN-PC
Requirements identification methods				
Critical Success Factors /KPI	✔	✔	✔	✔
Strategic Business Functions	✔	✖	✖	✖
Synthesising from the existing systems/reports	✔	✔	✔	✔
Discussion with support personnel	✔	✔	✔	✔
Interview with executives	✔	✖	✔	✔
Informal discussion with executives	✔	✖	✔	✖
Examination of strategic plan	✔	✖	✖	✖
Consultation	✔	✖	✔	✖
Prototyping	✔	✖	✔	✖
Questionnaire	✔	✖	✖	✔
Matrix and affinity analysis	✔	✖	✖	✖
Brian storming (Group discussion)	✔	✔	✔	✔
Analysis & design techniques				
Data dictionary	✔	✖	✖	✖
Normalisation	✖	✔	✔	✔
Modular design	✔	✔	✔	✔
Structured flow chart	✖	✔	✔	✔
Structured walkthrough	✔	✔	✔	✔
Structured English	✖	✔	✔	✔
Pseudocode	✖	✖	✔	✔
Decision trees	✖	✔	✖	✔
Data flow diagrams	✖	✔	✔	✔
Functional decomposition	✔	✖	✖	✖
Rapid application development	✔	✖	✖	✖
Tools				
EIS software	Lightship	✖	✖	✖
Image capture and scanning	✔	✔	✔	✖
Disk backup and recovery	✔	✔	✔	
DBMS	Lightship	DB2	Sybase	INGRES
4GL	dBase, Excel	PAS	4th-Dimension	Super-NOVA, Lotus, Excel
Desktop publishing	✖	✖	✔	✖
Query languages	Focus	SQL		MS Access
Traditional programming languages	COBOL, PL1	COBOL		C Language
Other				
One-to-one training	✔	✔	✔	✔
Training material	✔	✔	✔	✔

The operation or application of these phases was not isolated. Phases overlapped in time and where conducted in different sequences. For some tasks the development phases were repeated several times and the cycles only slowed when the task was relatively well understood. The major forces behind the general iterative process were the difficulty of identifying the requirements of executives and a lack of knowledge about this relatively new information technology. Put simply, the users could not articulate what they wanted and the systems analysts were uncertain about how to proceed.

Several existing methods, techniques and tools were used to help the EIS developers elicit executive requirements and create a working system. The requirement identification methods included critical success factors (CSF), strategic business functions (SBF), synthesis from existing systems, discussion with support personnel, informal discussion and interviews with executives, prototyping, examination of the strategic plan, and consultation with an EIS expert from the United Kingdom. Other development techniques included functional decomposition, modular design, structured walkthroughs, matrix analysis and rapid application development.

The development tools used were the EIS package Lightship from Pilot Inc, image capturing and scanning and in-house software, such as COBOL, PL1, FOCUS and Lotus 1-2-3. While Lightship was used for presenting information to executive users and managing the EIS database, in-house software was used for capturing data from the corporate database, converting it into text files and then transferring it to the Lightship Server. External data was also keyed into the EIS via a simple data entry system developed using in-house software.

A traditional information systems approach

Bank A employed a traditional waterfall development approach to direct and manage the EIS development project. The development process involved a largely linear execution of requirements analysis, system development, user acceptance, system installation, use and maintenance. Requirements analysis was conducted with each executive's support personnel. An initial definition was provided in written form. The systems analysts reviewed these reports and sought clarification in interviews with the support staff. They identified the possible sources of the required information. The system analysts also examined the existing key performance indicators and management reports. They proposed additional or alternative reports which they thought would be of interest to the executives.

Following requirements definition, the database was designed and created and application programs coded and tested. The developers used a variety of techniques including normalisation, modular design, structured flow charts, structured walkthroughs, structured English, data flow diagrams and decision trees. The EIS was implemented using image scanning, DB2, SQL, COBOL, and IBM programming languages.

When system construction was completed, it was demonstrated to the executive users. The system was refined after comments from the executives particularly regarding the user interface. The system was tested by internal auditors before release to the users in order to ensure the system worked properly and was secure.

Outsourcing

Lacity and Hirschhiem (1993) define information systems outsourcing as applying to a wide range of contractual arrangements from contract programmers to third party facilities management. They argue that the three most meaningful classification of these contracts are: body shop, project management and total outsourcing. Body shop is the use of contract programmers/personnel who are managed by company employees. Project management is outsourcing for a specific project or portion of the information development work while total outsourcing is the total provision by a vendor of a significant information system. Fitzgerald (1994) further categorised the reasons for outsourcing by an organisation under three broad factors: technical, financial, and strategic and organisational. The development of EIS in Bank B and the Energy Company were to some extent outsourced. However the activities that were outsourced and the rationale behind the adoption of outsourcing differ between the two cases.

In case of the Bank B, a major US-based consulting company was contracted to provide requirements identification, general system design, system architecture design and construction by working closely with the internal project manager and business system analysts of the Bank. This is close to total outsourcing according to Lacity and Hirschheim. The formal reason for employing the consultant was that the internal staff lacked experience in the conceptual design of data presentation for executives. Even though the Bank has strongly invested in information technology, the installed systems are focused on the operational services rather than management support. It is surprising that such a large bank by world standards did not recruit staff with management support skills. Two programmers from the Bank's IS department were involved in the construction phase under the supervision of the consultant. We believe that internal political conflict rather than professional inexperience was the major reason for the outsourcing of this particular EIS development.

A proprietary development methodology supplied by the consultant was used for the EIS development. Although the methodology used terms like prototyping and module delivery, it can best be termed a variant of the waterfall model. This reflects its development from the consulting firm's large scale operational systems methodology and also reflects the one-shot nature of many consulting interventions. The process of the initial EIS development life cycle covered planning, business requirements definition, prototyping and system development, system installation, and maintenance.

The planning phase involved hardware and software selection, preliminary business requirements review and project organisation. During requirements identification, the EIS team examined existing reports, talked with support personnel, and interviewed the senior executives. KPI were identified and a prototype was developed. This prototype was reviewed by management. Further modules were audited by the auditor of the Bank before delivery to the executive users. The techniques used in systems development included data modelling, normalisation, structured flow charts, modular design, pseudocode, structured testing and walkthroughs. The 4th Dimension package was the major software tool used to develop applications and user interfaces. Once the system was installed, one-to-one training was conducted. A "quick reference" brochure was produced.

In the Energy Company, outsourcing is the standard development policy of the Information Systems Department. The department believes that this is the way to increase its productivity with limited personnel. Rather than allocating all to one development project, the department can allocate professional IS staff to manage and co-ordinate several projects with different vendors. However, the department requires that requirements analysis, and the specification of input, process and output formats are the responsibility of its own staff. This is "bodyshop" outsourcing for strategic reasons.

The EIS development approach of the Energy Company is best classified as waterfall development rather than evolutionary even though the EIS is approaching its third version. Each version has been a completely different system with different technical and application environments. Development followed the stages of requirements analysis and design, physical system development, system testing, system installation, training, and system evaluation. The internal IS staff prepared the formal requirements and design specification and database design and construction were performed by a contractor. In requirement and design specification, system flow charts and data flow diagrams were used to improve the understanding of the consultant about the organisation and data flows. Questionnaires and interviews were used to identify executive's requirements. However, the IS staff were not able to access all the executives. The Head of the IS Department reported that "the executives could not sacrifice their time". As a result the requirements specification was prepared from an IS rather than an executive's perspective.

In addition to data flow diagrams and system flow charts, modular design, normalisation, structured walkthroughs were cited as useful techniques. BASIC, Microsoft Windows, C, Lotus 1-2-3, Microsoft Excel and Microsoft Access were used to develop the applications. To maintain the EIS database, IS staff gather data from business units, enter it to Lotus 1-2-3 or Microsoft Excel on a diskette, and use the diskette to update the data stored in the executive LAN. This process was not automated as only consolidated data was required and the hardware platform of each business unit differs from the one provided to executives. After the contractor delivered the system, the IS staff tested every screen using walkthroughs. To train the executives, a one-to-one training strategy was used where two IS staff were assigned to explain how to operate the system when the executives requested. An summary document of the user manual provided by the contractor was prepared. When the system was used for six months, system evaluation via a was conducted in order to get feedback and problems.

The experiences of these organisations calls into question the use of outsourcing for EIS development. EIS, especially in a developing country, need frequent revision to accommodate changes in the organisation's environment and the wishes of individual executives. In both cases, system evolution has been seriously constrained by the absence of the primary developer after initial development. In both cases there has been no transfer of skills and knowledge to the host organisation. For outsourcing to be effective for EIS we hypothesise that client IS personnel must be trained and motivated to provide on-going support and system development.

5.3 Technical constraints

Lack of Thai language software

Unlike other South East Asian countries such as Malaysia, Singapore and Hong Kong, which use English as an official language, Thai is the only official language in Thailand. Only highly educated Thais read and understand the English. Virtually all corporate and government data is kept in Thai text. The only exceptions are data collected for international organisations (eg UN) and where a company has a significant foreign share-holding or performs most of its work outside Thailand. The Transportation Company is the only such organisation in this study.

This dependence on the Thai language could be a major obstacle for EIS development as all major computer software is English-based. If an EIS software vendor wants to promote its product in Thailand, it must modify the software to manage the Thai language data. Not many companies have developed Thai versions because of complicated structure of the language, the cost of development relative to the market size and until recently the lack of any intellectual property law. At present most EIS data must be translated from Thai to English on input and English to Thai on output. This can reduce the currency of information; it definitely adds to costs and could be the reason that some organisations in this study used non-EIS specific software which was able to manage Thai characters and grammar.

By using non-EIS specific software Thai organisations loose the major benefit of EIS software, the ability to create multi-dimensional data bases that more accurately reflect the structure of the organisation than a relational data-base. The ability to quickly consolidate data across time periods, business units and other data categories and to "drill down" through a data aggregation hierarchy are perhaps EIS's greatest contribution to information systems practice. The use of conventional software for language reasons means that Thai organisations cannot exploit these processing features.

EIS development knowledge

EIS is a relatively new information technology for Thailand. Few IS professionals understand the concept and there is a lack of experience in developing such systems. Most senior management lack IT knowledge and are not as aware of EIS as their Western counterparts. The EIS team of the Transportation Company addressed executive EIS knowledge by asking vendors to demonstrate a prototype of a mini-specification and informed the executives that their system could look similar to this prototype. This gave the executives a clear idea of the potential of EIS.

Many Thai IS professionals are also unaware of EIS theory and practice, especially client focused evolutionary development. Bank A and the Energy Company used traditional large-scale methods of IS development. However, in the Transportation Company the EIS developers understood that EIS is an evolutionary system and they improved their knowledge about EIS by studying international research. Additionally, the Transportation Company allowed the team to consult an international expert who had experience in developing EIS in the same industry.

5.4 Development teams

The structure of EIS teams in Thai organisations is very different to that reported in Western studies (Rockart and DeLong 1988, Armstrong 1990, Watson *et. al* 1990, Barrow 1988, Paller *et. al* 1990). Whereas Western EIS teams are responsible for the actual development of the system and often include users and IS professionals, in the Thai cases the teams acted more like steering committees and the actual developers were removed from their user constituency. This may account for the (reported) strong technical focus of EIS development.

Table 3 presents the organisation of the formal EIS team of the four cases. With the exception of the Energy Company, technical staff were excluded from formal membership of the team. These technical staff (programmers, system analysts, and technical support staff) were assigned to working groups under the supervision of members of the EIS development team.

The EIS project of the Transportation Company was announced as a major policy by the President and he personally appointed the members of the EIS team. The team reported progress of the project to the President and Executive Management Committee. This EIS team incorporated a project manager, a group of IS managers and a group of functional managers. The project manager was the Deputy Vice President of Corporate Planning, a very senior appointment for an EIS project. The functional group involved managers of the Finance and Accounting Information Services Department, and the Revenue Analysis

Table 3 Organisation of EIS team

Characteristics	*Case 1* *Transportation Company*	*Case 2* *Bank A*	*Case 3* *Bank B*	*Case 4* *Energy Company*
Number of key members	• 6	• 4	• 5	• 3
Team leader (skills)	•Deputy Vice President of Corporate Planning (Corporate vision and objectives)	• Chief of Business Information Services (Correctness and completeness of information)	• Vice President of office of president (MIS and MBA)	• Head of IS Department (Computer and management)
Other members (skills)	• Deputy Director of Data Services • Mgr of the Dpt. of IS Devel. • Mgr of the Dpt. of IS Planning (Analysis of mgt. info.; Facilitation skills; Hardware & software evaluation; System analysis, design & devel.) • Mgr of the Dpt. of Revenue Analysis (Mgt. info. analysis & research) • Mgr of the Dpt. of Finance & Accounting Info. Services (Mgt. Info. Services)	• Chief of the Corporate Business IS Section (System construction) • Vice President of Research & Planning Dpt. (Data provider) • Vice President of Accounts Dpt. (Data provider)	• Vice President of Accounting and Costing Dpt. (Business Analysts) • Vice President of Operation and Planning Dpt. (Business Analysts) • 2 External consultants (MIS design; Technical architecture)	• Systems Analyst (System analysis and info. providers) • Contractor (System development)

Department. These managers normally provide statistical data, including some external data, to top management and directors every month. The IS group included the Deputy Director of Data Services and managers of Information Systems Development, and Information Systems Planning. This group was responsible but not personally involved in technical development having several technical working groups to perform the actual system development.

The organisation of the EIS team of the Bank A indicates that the Technology Group dominated the project. Even though its team structure was similar to the Transportation Company, the project manager held a much lower position. The project manager was the Chief of Business Information Services which is a section of Retail Banking Information Systems Department while other two members were Vice President of Accounts Department, and Vice President of Research and Planning Department. Interestingly, the project manager was much more junior that the other members of his own team.

The EIS team of the Energy Company consisted only of Head Office IS staff. There were no users involved in this level of the project. This is because the Head of the IS Department believed that he knew what information executive needed. He related "if any one wants to know what the requirements of executives are, I can identify. It is unnecessary to interview executives; just ask me" (*sic*). Because of the outsourcing strategy used the EIS has not been able to evolve to meet executive requirements and executive have no voice on the EIS team.

Although the EIS team of Bank B involved three Vice Presidents and two international consultants, the evolution of its EIS has also been constrained. The foreign project manager resigned after the initial EIS was installed. As the IS Department was not involved in the project they are both unable and not motivated to provide ongoing support. Staff have been made available to maintain the data in the system. However, no one is actually responsible for the ongoing development of the project.

The nature of the Thai EIS teams may be responsible for some of the differences in development patterns to Western EIS that have observed in this study. In particular there appears to be a separation of the EIS "team" from actual development. User participation seems largely confined to steering committee meetings. Thai executives play a passive role in ongoing system development.

6 CONCLUDING COMMENTS

This paper has examined the development of four EIS in Thailand. The Transportation Company's system can be regarded as a success; the Energy Company, a qualified success; Bank A, relatively unsuccessful and Bank B, a failure. To the extent that Thailand is representative of developing countries and the cases are representative of large organisations in such countries some general observations on the nature of EIS development in developing countries can be made.

EIS development is likely to be more difficult in a developing country than in the West. The relatively volatile political environment and a greater degree of both direct and indirect government intervention in the economy act together to produce an extremely difficult systems development environment. System are likely to require fundamental revision more frequently than in the West. System development methods must be able to cope with rapid evolution at both the applications level and of functionality within applications.

In this study only one organisation used an evolutionary development approach that is favoured by Western organisations. It was also the most successful. In such a volatile environment we suggest that traditional operational development approaches are not relevant. Further, they are antithetic to system success and the standing of IT within the organisation. The first step in transferring EIS technology to organisations in developing countries should be an education program for both IS professionals and management.

A special concern raised by this study is the relative failure of two common outsourcing strategies to deliver successful system. In both cases the provider was a foreign consulting firm. These consultants did little to adapt their practice to the customs and management processes of the client organisations. We believe that the system would have been more successful if a transfer of skill had been part of the contract as once the initial system was developed the local IS personnel were unable to further develop or maintain the system.

Another problem for EIS development in developing countries is the tendency for the project to be driven by the IS department with relatively low level of user participation in design and development. The initial education program recommended above may help overcome this problem. However, if the local culture of management means that involvement in system development is "beneath" a manager then EIS may not be an effective information technology for that organisation. Further, if language and other constraints mean that EIS-specific software cannot be used then many of the potential benefits of EIS may not be realised.

If the above mentioned problems with EIS development cannot be overcome for a particular implementation then we see little benefit in pursuing the development. The results of this study should enable this decision to be made early in the life of the project. However, EIS is not the only information systems approach to supporting management activities. If EIS is inappropriate then the decision support systems (DSS) approach may have merit. In DSS the focus is normally on supporting one manager to perform one task. The systems are much smaller and user involvement is often easier to achieve. It may also be a much easier technology to transfer to developing countries especially in terms of staff training. DSS is a much cheaper and less risky management support strategy than EIS. It may also be more successful.

Despite the problems identified in some of the cases in this study it is possible to develop effective EIS in large organisations in developing countries. The prescription is clear and similar to early cases in the West. Organisations is developing countries should be able to benefit from Western experience of failure and success. An EIS is likely to be more successful if an evolutionary development approach is used. Systems are subject to greater change than in the West and the design should cater for this volatility. Users should be genuinely involved in development especially in requirements specification. Development should be performed by local information systems professionals who understand the local management culture and customs.

7 REFERENCES

Armstrong, D. (1990a). 'How Rockwell Launched Its EIS'. *Datamation*, 30:8, 69-72 (Mar.).

Armstrong, D. (1990b). 'The People Factor in EIS Success'. *Datamation*, 30:7, 73-79 (Apr.).

Benbasat, I. Goldstein, D.K. and Mead, M. (1987). 'The Case Research Strategy in Studies of Information Systems'. *MIS Quarterly*, 11:3, 369-386 (Sept.).

Chaiyasoot, N. (1993). 'Commercial Banking' *The Thai Economy in Transition*, (ed.) Peter G. Warr. Hong Kong: Cambridge. 226-164.

Dhiratayakinant, K. (1993). 'Public Enterprises' *The Thai Economy in Transition*, (ed.) Peter G. Warr. Hong Kong: Cambridge. 265-324.

Fitzgerald, G. (1994). 'Outsourcing of IT in the United Kingdom: A Legitimate Strategic Option?' *Proceedings: 5th Australasian Conference on Information Systems*, (eds.) Graeme Shanks and David Arnott. VIC.: Monash University Printing Services. 27-40.

Galliers, R.D. (1992). 'Choosing Information Systems Research Approaches' *Information Systems Research: Issues, Methods and Practical Guidelines*, (eds.) Robert D. Galliers. London: Blackwell Scientific. 144-162.

Gunter, A. and Frolick, M. (1991). 'The Evolution of EIS at Georgia Power Company'. *Information Executive*, 4:4, 23-26 (Fall).

Hasan, H. and Gould, E. (1994). 'EIS in the Australian Public Sector'. *Journal of Decision Systems*, 3:4

Houdeshel, G. and Watson, H.J. (1987). 'The Management Information and Decision Support (MIDS) System at Lockheed-Georgia' *Executive Information Systems: Emergence • Development • Impact*, (eds.) Watson, J. Hugh; Rainer, Kelly R.; Houdeshel, George. New York: John Wiley & Sons. 13-31.

Lacity, M. and Hirschheim R (1993). *Information Systems Outsourcing*.. Chichester: Wiley.

Laothamatas, A. (1994). 'From Clientelism to Partership: Business-Government Relations in Thailand' (ed.) Andrew MacIntyre. NSW., Australia: Allen & Unwin Pty Ltd. 195-215.

McFarlan, E.W. (1984). 'Information Technology Changes the Way You Compete'. *Harvard Business Review*, 62, 98-103 (May-Jun.).

Mintzberg, H. (1979). 'An Emerging Strategy of "Direct" Research'. *Adminstrative Science Quarterly*, 24:4, 582-589 (Dec.).

Moynihan, G.P. (1993). 'An Executive Information System: Planning for Post-Implementation at NASA'. *Journal of Systems Management*, 44:7, 8-31 (July).

Muscat, R.J. (1994). *The Fifth Tiger: A Study of Thai Development Policy*.. New York: The United Nations University Press.

O'Leary, M. (1990). 'Putting Hertz Executives in the Driver's Seat' *Executive Information Systems: Emergence • Development • Impact*, (eds.) Watson, J. Hugh; Rainer, Kelly R.; Houdeshel, George. New York: John Wiley & Sons. 343-347.

Paller, A. and Laska, R. (1990). *The EIS Book: Information Systems for Top Managers*.. Illinois: Dow Jones-Irwin.

Pervan, G.P. and Meneely, J. (1995). 'Implementing and Sustaining Executive Information Systems: Influencing Factors in a Mining Industry Context' *Proceedings of the 28th Annual Hawaii International Conference on System Sciences Vol III: Information Systems—Decision Support and Knowledge-Based Systems*, (eds.)

Jay F. Nunamaker, Jr and Ralph H. Sprague, Jr. CA.: IEEE Computer Society Press. 101-109.

Porter, M.E. (1990). *The Competitive Advantage of Nations.*. London: The Macmillan Press Ltd.

Porter, M.E. and Millar, V.E. (1985). 'How Information Gives You Competitive Advantage'. *Harvard Business Review*, 63, 149-160 (Jul.-Aug.).

Rockart, J.F. and DeLong, D.W. (1988). *Executive Support Systems: The Emergence of Top Management Computer Use.*. Illinois: Dow Jones-Irwin.

Sundue, D.G. (1990). 'GenRad's On-Line Executives' *Management Information Systems: Readings and Cases- A Managerial Perspective*, (eds.) Boynton, C. Andrew; Zmud, W. Robert. Glenview, Illinois: Scott, Foresman. 162-170.

Suvachittanont, W. Arnott, D.R. and O'Donnell, P.A. (1994). 'Adaptive Development in Executive Information Systems : A Manufacturing Case Study'. *Journal of Decision Systems*, 3:4

Tambunlertchai, S. (1993). 'Manufacturing' *The Thai Economy in Transition*, (eds.) Peter G. Warr. Hong Kong: Cambridge. 118-150.

Volonino, L.; and Drinkard, G. (1989). 'Intergrating EIS into the Strategic Plan: A Case Study of Fisher-Price' *Proceedings of the Ninth International Conference on Decision Support Systems Providence, R.I., The Institute of Management Science* , (eds.) Widmeyer, George. 37-45.

Volonino, L.; Robinson, S.; and Watson, H.J. (1992). 'EIS and Organizational Change' *IFIP Transaction A (Computer Science and Technology)*, (eds.) T. Jelassi, M. R. Klein and W.M. Mayon-White. Amsterdam: North-Holland. 309-321.

Wallis, L. (1989). 'Power Computing at the Top' *Executive Information Systems: Emergence • Development • Impact*, (eds.) Watson, J. Hugh; Rainer, Kelly R.; Houdeshel, George. New York: John Wiley & Sons. 301-314.

Warr, P.G. (1993). 'The Thai Economy' *The Thai Economy in Transition*, (eds.) Peter G. Warr. Hong Kong: Cambridge. 1-80.

Watson, H.J. Rainer Jr., R.K. and Koh E. Chang (1991). 'Executive Information Systems: A Framework for Development and a Survey of Current Practices'. *MIS Quarterly*, 15:1, 13-30 (March).

Whymark, G.K. (1991). 'Development of the EIS Concept and Its Implementation in the RAN'. *The Australian Computer Journal*, 23:3, 110-118 (Aug.)

Yin, R.K. (1989). *Case Study Research: Design and Methods*. (2 ed.). CA.: Sage.

8 BIOGRAPHY

Ms Waraporn Jiracheifpattana

Ms Waraporn Jiracheifpattana (nee Suvachittanont) is a doctoral candidate in the Department of Information Systems at Monash University, Australia. before she commenced her PhD program, she worked as a system analyst at the Information Institution for Education and Development (IPIED), Thammasat University, Thailand. her major works include the creation of the Provincial Management Information System and the Departmental Management Information System which assists government officers allocate budget to villages. As well, she has worked as a researcher to develop Human Development Indicators under United Nations sponsorship.

Professor David R. Arnott
Professor David R. Arnott is the Head of Department of Information Systems at Monash University. He is also Associate Dean of the Faculty of Computing and Information Technology. Professor Arnott commenced his computing career in 1970 and worked during the 1970's as a systems analyst and consultant, specialising in the support of management rather than the automation of clerical processes. He became an academic in 1980. Professor Arnott's teaching area is the managerial use of information systems, and his principal research area is the use of psychological theories of human judgement in the development of decision support systems.

Mr Peter A. O'Donnell
Peter O'Donnell is a Lecturer in Information Systems at Monash University. He received a Bachelor of Applied Science from the Ballarat College of Advanced Education and a Master's of Computing from Monash University. His current research interests include the design of multi-dimensional data structures and the use of influence diagrams in decision support.

15

Business patterns: reusable abstract constructs for business specification

H. Kilov I.D. Simmonds
Insurance Research Center
IBM T J Watson Research Center
30 Saw Mill River Road, Hawthorne, NY 10532, U S A
{kilov, isimmond}@watson.ibm.com

> 'Alice had never been in a court of justice before, but she had read about them in books, and she was quite pleased to find that she knew the name of nearly everything there. "That's the judge," she said to herself, "because of his great wig." ...
>
> "And that's the jury-box," thought Alice; "and those twelve creatures," (she was obliged to say "creatures," you see, because some of them were animals, and some were birds,) "I suppose they are the jurors."'
>
> Lewis Carroll. *Alice's Adventures in Wonderland.*

Abstract

Business patterns are powerful, high-level constructs that provide a natural and well-structured way of both understanding and specifying businesses and their rules. To be of use, business specifications have to be presented in an abstract and precise manner, and this paper shows how to do just that. Key concepts include business invariants and operations, and a higher level notion of "business pattern". Specifications built in this way can be parameterized and reused in various business contexts. Business patterns in particular promise to be extremely helpful as a basis for systematic business analysis and subsequent implementation of the results of this analysis. We have successfully used these concepts and constructs in our engagements with (insurance) customers (Kilov et al., 1996).

The motivation for our work is to allow the production of complete, rigorous business specifications understandable by both business users and system developers. These specifications require rigorous expressions of semantics — that is, assertions — rather than loose, "intuitive," descriptions. We present different kinds of reusable and abstract specification fragments — patterns — such as "action" and "module" patterns, which have different characteristics. We include examples of both elementary patterns — such as "composition" — and nonelementary patterns — such as "information gathering" and "joint ownership". Unlike typical programming constructs, instantiations of business patterns are inherently interactive and so must adapt to their changing environment.

Keywords
Precision, abstraction, reuse, change, business pattern, generic relationships, collective behavior

1. INTRODUCTION

1.1 Motivation

There are countless examples showing that system development almost inevitably fails in the absence of complete, clear and rigorous specification of the business in business terms. For example, "The [US] Treasury Department has acknowledged that its decade-long effort to modernize the Internal Revenue Service's [...] computers is 'badly off the track' and must be rethought from top to bottom. [...] The Deputy Secretary of the Treasury, Lawrence Summers, told a House appropriations subcommittee that the [$20 billion] project [...] was driven by what technology was available rather than what would make the best tax collection system." (*International Herald Tribune*, March 16-17, 1996, page 3).

When a customer wishes to address a business goal with a partially automated solution, specifications are required of fundamental business needs (the "problem specification" or "business specification"), of a desired business strategy (the "business design"), of a system providing appropriate functionality (the "system specification"), and of how this system is to be produced (the "system implementation"). Whilst these four concerns are naturally and clearly separated in activities other than information management (eg in traditional engineering (Parnas, Madey, 1995; Parnas, 1995)), the practice of information management often fails to separate them, leading to excessive complexity, inconsistency, incompleteness, and therefore to failure of the development project.

The goal of a business analyst is similar to the goal of a traditional architect when understanding and eliciting a customer's wishes: it is to provide a business (rather than software) specification that will be unambiguously understood by both business users and system developers. The business specification can then be used as a basis for projects that enhance or put in place new business processes or products, some of which are to be partially automated; it is also a sound basis for defining the scope of such a project. In order to be useful for these purposes, the business specification must be abstract (with no implementation details), complete (having no gaps for developers to fill), precise (requiring no guesses over ambiguities), simple and concise (so that it will be read and understood by all).

Swatman (1994) and others have noted that the strengthening of the analysis-design boundary will be of increasing importance as companies outsource more and more of their software and system development and maintenance. Each participant — service consumer and provider — in the outsourcing relationship should have well-defined (contractual (Meyer, 1988)) obligations and responsibilities. The business specification and business design are a natural responsibility of the service consumer.

Our general goal is to ensure the widespread production and use of rigorous business specifications that can be **unambiguously understood and used** by subject matter experts (SMEs), business analysts, and system designers and developers. We believe that business specifications are an essential, and alarmingly undervalued, basis for the development of solutions to business problems. They are undervalued because too often they are not produced, and when they are, they are incomplete and insufficiently rigorous. Alternatively they are presented in terms of possible solutions and system constructs which, for reasons of lack of conceptual familiarity, may be difficult for business users to understand and thus check for completeness or accuracy. Finally, they may be too complex due to artificial restrictions imposed by using constructs based on current implementation technology.

More specifically, we have the feeling that fragments of business specification are often reinvented. Consider, as a specific example, the description and thus implementation of insurance underwriting for different kinds of insurance (life, health, etc) which have important non-trivial concepts and constructs in common, such as the insurance application folder which itself is a composition of insurance application, requests for changes to insurance application, and an underwriter's decision. (The concept of a composition is defined below.)

We want to understand and precisely and unambiguously capture these fragments, and make them available for reuse. This has been done elsewhere — and successfully — by "Real Engineers" (for example, Ohm's Law of electrical resistance[1] (Parnas, 1995a)), architects (in Alexander's "Pattern Language" (Alexander, 1979)) and even programmers (Backus-Naur form for specifying context-free grammars). As can be clearly seen from the previous sentence, formulating such a pattern ranks like a scientific discovery (and the discoverer's name is assigned to the pattern)!

A first level of generic reusable business specification fragments is presented in (Kilov, Ross, 1994; ISO, 1995a; ISO, 1995b). Experience of using these fragments — generic relationships — is presented in, for example (Kilov et al., 1996; Redberg, 1996). This paper is our first attempt at achieving a second — and perhaps more business-specific — level. Therefore the paper points to areas of future research, and contains only a few ready-made and reusable solutions.

Specifications exist at all stages of information management and, therefore, there is an opportunity to find patterns at all stages. In particular, our first level generic patterns have been successfully applied to the specification of both entire domains of business (eg medical insurance) and details of technological infrastructure (eg long transactions).

1.2 Patterns elsewhere

One definition of "pattern" given by the Concise Oxford Dictionary, is a "regular or logical form, order, or arrangement of parts". The value of a pattern when used in a specification or design is that someone familiar with it may either recognize an occurrence of it (and so better and more quickly understand the overall design), or recognize that a pattern is applicable within a particular situation (and so reuse the pattern as a known and proven specification or design strategy). The same pattern is encountered in many different contexts, and therefore can be invented once and reused afterwards rather than being separately reinvented for all contexts it is encountered in. To be reusable, a pattern must be specified in a precise, explicit, and unambiguous manner, so that it should be immediately clear whether or not it is applicable in a particular situation.

[1] "No Electrical Engineer confuses the "dot" notation for derivatives with the fact that an ideal resistor obeys Ohm's law. They also understand that the existence of resistors that are not ideal does not mean that the mathematics they have learned is irrelevant."

At the time of writing, the notion of design pattern has come to be considered as a key element of good software implementation practise, and especially when using an object-oriented programming language. A catalogue of generic and widely reusable design patterns has been published (Gamma et al., 1995) and others seek to find more specific patterns for application to more specific software design and implementation problems, such as for achieving data persistency or concurrency control.

Design patterns for software were themselves inspired by Christopher Alexander's work in architecture and civil engineering (Alexander, 1979). Alexander noted many common patterns that had been frequently reused in architecture, many over millennia and across several continents. Alexander's patterns are rigorously defined and make explicit use of specification notions such as invariants. In particular, Alexander states that "... a pattern defines an invariant field which captures all the possible solutions to the problem given, in the stated range of contexts"; that "the task of finding, or discovering, such an invariant field is immensely hard..." and that, nevertheless, "anyone who takes the trouble to consider it carefully can understand it". Our goal in discovering and formulating business patterns is to do just that, while being at the appropriate level of precision, so that "these statements can be challenged, because they are precise"! For example, "each room has light on two sides"; "establish ... marketplaces... made up of many smaller shops that are autonomous and specialized"; "traffic accidents are far more frequent where two roads cross than at T junctions" (Alexander, 1977).

Even within architecture, Alexander's work on patterns remains controversial. Nonetheless his work has originated in a mature and ancient discipline. Both his work and that of patterns for software design satisfy another (reuse-related) definition of pattern from the Concise Oxford Dictionary — "a model or design [...] from which copies can be made."

2. REUSABLE BUSINESS SPECIFICATION FRAGMENTS

2.1 Basic concepts and approach

Business analysis should be done before, and separately from, the design of any imagined automated support, with coding of such a system a distant third. Business analysis involves understanding the business: elicitation of all written and unwritten business rules, and ensuring that rules are documented precisely and in a manner that will be both read and unambiguously understood by all interested parties. It tames complexity by identifying only pure business "things", relationships, rules and constraints, and the behaviors of collections of these "things". It does not refer to computers, screens, databases, tables, etc., because these are both unnecessary details and may confuse many (non-specialist) readers. It relies upon explicitly defined concepts and semantics rather than meaning presented only implicitly, either in names or informal descriptions. Implicit semantics result in the need for each reader to "interpret" — that is, invent a meaning for — the named or described concepts; each reader inevitably invents a different meaning, and the resulting system fails to meet the needs of the business, which were never explicitly captured. The major part of a business specification — the deliverable of business analysis — is a structured representation of all rules that govern the business.

Our analysis approach insists on being simple, abstract and concise. Its concepts address primarily: collections of related things (objects); what you can do to these collections (operations); and what is always true, no matter what you do to them (invariants). Most operations and invariants involve several interrelated things (example: milk a cow, buy a house, take money from customer's account). A contract for an operation (elsewhere called a use case) should state: what "things" are relevant (signature), when you have to do it (triggering conditions), when you can do it (preconditions), what is achieved (postconditions), and what doesn't change (relevant invariants only). Contracts do not say how they are to be fulfilled: this will be specified during their refinement, ie design and development.

2.2 First level - basic reusable patterns

As mentioned above, a business specification consists primarily of **operations** (specifications of changes to collections of things) and **invariants** (specification of unchanging properties of collections of things). Most invariants are about constraints on the properties of collections of several objects rather than constraints on individual objects. Given this, it was natural to look for powerful, reusable and abstract constructs — patterns of invariants, as it were — for expressing invariants (and their properties) in the relationships between objects. It appeared that a very small number of generic relationships — such as composition (see below) and dependency — are encountered in all applications and thus — if and when precisely defined — provide an excellent basis for reuse. As noted in (Mac an Airchinnigh, 1994), "abstractions are, of course, the ultimate in reusability!"; thus abstractions such as generic relationships (and invariants!) are essential for saving intellectual efforts, time, and money.

Most high-value reusable patterns are likely to refer to collections of objects since most of business is about **collective behavior**: that is, properties that are not about a single "thing" but, rather, about a "set of related things". A pattern defines a collection of interrelated things together with available operations (like the **module** described more formally in an object-oriented extension of Z (Alencar, Goguen, 1992)), so that these things are not considered in isolation. Therefore, in specifying a business pattern it will not be necessary — as implied by many legacy OO languages and thus many OO "analysis and design" methods — to overspecify and make unnecessary choices by attaching the collective state (invariant) or collective behavior (operation's pre- and postconditions) to a particular object referred to in the invariant or in the operation. An emphasis on collective-behavior-oriented (rather than isolated-object-oriented) approach has been used in such ISO standards as (ISO, 1995a, ISO, 1995b) and is essential for successful business specifications; in particular, the constructs available to the subject matter expert and the business analyst are not restricted to the ones available in a particular family of implementations.

Specifications whose invariants are expressed in terms of generic relationships can be extremely compact and readable when compared to other specification approaches, while remaining complete and precise (several examples are shown later in this paper). Nevertheless, there still remains a need to present summary views of each specification on a small number of pages, covering both operations and invariants. An important international (ISO) standard — the Reference Model for Open Distributed Processing (ISO 1995b) — provides concepts for doing just that. Moreover, certain business-specific aspects of such concepts are referred technically as the enterprise viewpoint, and, at the time of writing, are a research topic for an ISO standardization technical committee. Our hope is that business patterns will be a (however partial) contribution to providing an enterprise viewpoint for business specifications.

The generic relationships of (Kilov, Ross, 1994; ISO, 1995a) can be seen to be "elementary molecules" or "elementary business patterns", in the sense that some or all of them are encountered in all business specifications. They may be considered as building blocks from which both complex and complete business specifications, and higher-level, reusable yet still generic "nonelementary business patterns" can be constructed. Some simple nonelementary patterns were shown in (Kilov, Ross, 1994a). A "notification" is a typical example widely used in telecommunications and elsewhere: it results in the creation of an instance of a thing (such as a "traffic violation ticket") only if a triggering condition ("notification criteria") is satisfied for a particular state of a particular instance of a "monitored object". A notification is composed out of two elementary generic (reference) relationships. Another example of a nonelementary pattern — a composition of symmetric relationships — will be used in the joint ownership pattern below.

2.3 Second level

First level, basic, reusable patterns, like the generic relationships mentioned above, can be used not only for business specifications, but also for specifying their refinements, including business design and system design and development. Moreover, they can be used (and have been successfully used) to specify a "meta-model" of the information management lifecycle itself. This can happen because concepts underlying generic relationships — such as invariants and collective behavior — are encountered at all stages of information management lifecycle. Thus, these concepts are of (re)use at all stages of information management; they provide a great help as powerful generic constructs used to understand the business and specify this understanding. Composition is a good example of a first-level basic construct. Interestingly enough, others have already termed these generic relationships "patterns" (Ayers, 1996).

In moving to a second level of reusable constructs, we must formulate these patterns in terms of the solid and powerful foundation provided by the basic patterns. In particular, the patterns must continue to promote abstraction and precision, and therefore both their discovery and formulation should be free from unnecessary and irrelevant — at this level of abstraction — details, to "enhance understanding" (ISO, 1995b)

When we try to identify "second-level" concepts and constructs for business specifications, they will inevitably define and refer to common business notions. As such they will not immediately be useful in implementation, for example, although we will indicate that many business patterns may have components relevant at other stages of information management lifecycle. While a second-level pattern may refer to business notions, it will still be generic enough to be of (re)use for all kinds of businesses. Obviously, first level, basic constructs can and should be used to specify the second-level ones. Information gathering is a good example of a second-level construct.

2.4 Composing patterns to form a specification

To quote Alexander, "each pattern helps to sustain other patterns [...] the individual configuration of any one pattern requires other patterns to keep itself alive" (Alexander, 1979).

When creating a business specification, we want to construct a unified view of a business by composing fragments, specified as viewpoints (Harrison et al., 1996) each of which is a composition of patterns. An entire viewpoint (eg Underwriting) may itself follow a pattern.

Composition is essential both laterally and vertically. Laterally, different — peer — parts of a specification which refer to some common "things" must be brought together, at which point the invariants of these components must be conjoined (and reconciled, as necessary). This is a highly non-trivial problem (outside the scope of this paper); however, we want to note that business patterns provide at least a good way to specify the problem. Vertically, a high-level and, of necessity, less detailed component must be composed with its details, again requiring a conjoining of invariants. Correspondingly, at a software level, we must learn how to compose software frameworks which operate at differing levels of abstraction. Indeed, we expect that business patterns — and, correspondingly, software frameworks — may be instantiated at different levels of abstraction within a single business specification, and so may need to be composed both laterally and vertically with other instances of themselves! This most certainly happens with abstract patterns like invariants and generic relationships.

2.5 Where to look for business patterns

It seems reasonable to presume that we can identify and develop business patterns more or less on paper, at least for the early stages of the information management process such as business specification and business design. Thorough understanding of business specification and design concepts can be — indeed, is best — achieved without resort to software design considerations. After all, businesses existed and flourished for a long time without any software implementation, and business specifications existed and were even taught (eg for banking, insurance, accounting, law, etc.) without any reference to computer systems. As an example, consider a complex specification for life insurance including parameterizable contracts with customers published in 1835 (Proposals, 1835). Probably, it was not the first such specification (it appears that the concept of life insurance dates back to the 16th century, and insurance for merchant voyages goes back over millennia).

There may be a substantial amount of work in designing and implementing each business pattern. Typically, each business pattern permits several refinements depending in part upon the business and system environments; and these refinements may also be precisely formulated as reusable patterns. In this way we will incrementally build up an asset base of business patterns with corresponding software frameworks.

2.6 A more technical foundation

As mentioned earlier, our approach is concerned with collections of things ("objects"), what you can do to these collections of things ("operations" specified in terms of a "signature", "precondition", "postcondition" and "triggering condition"), and what is true about the things no matter what you do to them ("invariants"). Careful consideration of (dynamic) triggering conditions will probably require dealing with obligations (Meyer, Wieringa, 1993) and related issues which may be better discussed in the framework of a workflow specification (and thus provide precise specifications of important fragments of the workflow framework). It is common practice to factorize out system invariants — conditions that cannot be violated at any time except, perhaps, as an intermediate step in an operation passing between two valid states.

A number of highly reusable "generic relationships" (Kilov, Ross 1994; ISO, 1995a) greatly simplify the specification of many, if not most, invariants. These include "composition", "dependency", "symmetric" and "reference", some of which appear in the examples given below. Each generic relationship has been formally defined (in terms of its invariant) for reuse, and comes with specifications of associated basic CRUD (Create, Read, Update, Delete) operations applied to its participants. Specializations of the generic relationships (Kilov, Ross, 1994) (such as different mutually orthogonal kinds of composition) augment the invariants of the most generic relationships. These specializations are still generic.

Quite a few things are known about each pattern. Some of these things are captured as invariants, which are typically expressed in terms of generic relationships. Many of the things included in these invariants represent formal parameters — "slots" to be filled as the pattern is instantiated. A "slot" is a "parameter", "formal" (in the generic specification) or "actual" (in its instantiation). For example, in the generic Composition pattern below, the formal parameter (see below) "composite type" may be filled by the type "Underwriting case folder", and the formal parameter "component types" may include "Application for insurance" (with exactly one instance), "Changes to application" (with a possibly empty set of instances) and "Underwriting decision". For a perhaps more often encountered example of a Composition, the "composite type" formal parameter may be filled in by the type "Croque Monsieur", with the "component types" formal parameter filled in by an (ordered!) set {"Toasted white bread", "Mustard", "Ham", "Melted Swiss Cheese"} (with at least one instance of each of these component types).

3. FROM A WARM AND FUZZY FEELING TO A PRECISE SPECIFICATION

3.1 An example of a first-level (business) pattern: Composition

Even for very abstract and generic patterns, such as composition, it is possible to say very many things — the invariant for a composition tells a lot, and reusable CRUD (Create, Read, Update, Delete) operations are very well defined, taking several pages (Kilov, Ross, 1994). Let us consider this pattern (a generic composition) in more detail.

Firstly, "everyone knows what a composition is", thus having a warm and fuzzy feeling about this construct. A car is a composition of an engine, a body, and four wheels; a book is a composition of pages; and an insurance contract is a composition of "contract components", right?

Secondly, we observe that using examples is not sufficient: a new construct may not **exactly** correspond to any existing one; and we need to abstract away from details specific only to particular examples.

What do these constructs — presented by examples above — have in common? There exists a "composite" and "components"; and there may be several components of different types in the same composition (in Alexander's example of a marketplace composition above, the autonomous and specialized shops — components — are certainly of different types). Also, not all component instances may be present in the composition (is a car without a wheel still a car? probably, yes). Moreover, a composite and a component in the same composition should be of different types, that is, they should have distinguishable properties. We may also observe (or reuse the observation of others (Wand, 1989)) that a composite has two kinds of properties: independent of properties of any component in a composition (eg the author(s) and title of a book) and those determined by properties of components (eg the number of pages of a book, or —more interestingly — the book's abstract, or the price of Croque Monsieur in the example above).

After some effort we discovered (abstracted out) the **invariant of a composition** (Kilov, Ross, 1994): a composite type corresponds to one or more component types, and a composite instance corresponds to zero or more instances of each component type. The application-specific types for the composite and each of its components should not be equal. There exists at least one resultant property of a composite instance (determined by the properties of its component instances), and at least one emergent property of a composite instance (independent of the properties of its component instances)[2].

The composition and its invariant have thus been expressed in terms of formal parameters: composite type, composite instance, set of component types, sets of component instances for each component type, set of resultant properties of the composite, and set of its emergent properties. This list of formal parameters constitutes the signature of a composition.

Even with all this we had not captured everything interesting about a composition. We noticed that there were several different generic kinds of composition, and specified them. Indeed, a composition may be:

- ordered or not
- hierarchical or not
- fixed or not (an example of a fixed, ordered, hierarchical composition is the composite layering of a highway)
- and, finally, it is possible to determine whether a composite or a component can exist independently of the existence of a composition.

Thus, we described four **mutually orthogonal generic subtypes** of composition. These subtypes are defined in a more precise manner, using invariants, in (Kilov, Ross, 1994). Moreover, we may and probably should define generic operations (like "add a new component of this type to that composition") for each of these subtypes. Such an operation will be defined precisely, just as any other operation, by using pre- and postconditions, etc., as noted above; some of these conditions are implied by the invariant of the appropriate subtype of the generic composition (eg ordered composition).

When we (re)use composition or its subtype, we do not need to repeat its invariant: it is quite sufficient to refer to it by using the name, as in:

```
Fast French Food: Ordered composition (croque monsieur,
{Toasted white bread, Mustard, Ham, Melted Swiss cheese}),
```

or, graphically, as in:

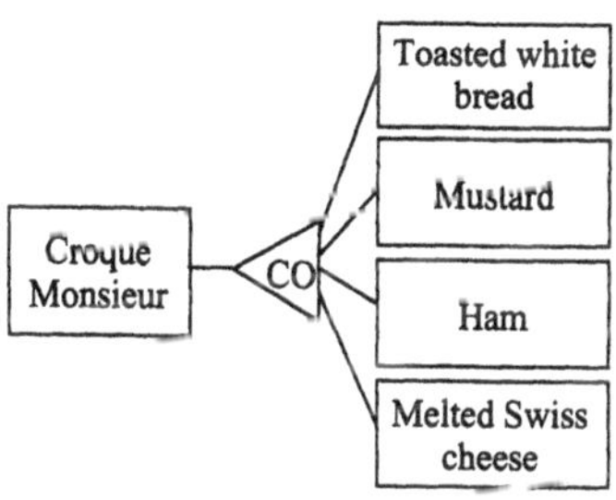

[2] It is interesting and instructive to note that this invariant corresponds to Alexander's description of an invariant (see above).

If we are still concerned about the precision of this specification (and we may well be), the next step will include using a *formal* specification language such as Z (Nicholls, 1995), perhaps with extensions. If we do that (Kilov, 1993) and translate the result back into stylized English — such as the one used above in the specification of the invariant — then this result will provide important insights and perhaps will point at still existing omissions and ambiguities, as indicated, for example, in (Mac an Airchinnigh, 1994).

Do you still think that "everyone knows what a composition is"?

3.2 An example of a second-level business pattern

As with many patterns that we have noticed reoccurring and have subsequently explicitly abstracted, described and "named," information gathering is an abstraction of a wide variety of incredibly common business operations performed in many, if not all businesses. Moreover, and frustratingly, we know that we have reinvented this pattern many times over the years, without having ever before explicitly preparing it for reuse. Examples of information gathering include: get a credit report, establish birthdate, interview candidates for a job opening, find a job, find a spouse, find a divorce lawyer.

Informally, the information gathering pattern is about obtaining some information from some environment. Gathering the information may be a non-trivial task, requiring several requests from several external sources. The information eventually obtained may not be what was originally requested, and the expectation of the requester may change over time. In general there should be a set of "quality" criteria specified in the information gathering operation's postcondition stating whether an obtained value is acceptable. There may be several sufficiency criteria, with a relation "is better than," and a way to decide when to "stop" in requesting more and more acceptable information, perhaps based on some cost-benefit assessment. This description is better than "everyone knows what a composition is," but still too imprecise to be of substantial practical use. Let us make it more precise.

Less informally, the overall operation to request information starts with some source information, some desired information (eg type of resulting value) and some sufficiency criteria, together with believed sources of further information (if any). After the operation, a result has been obtained and is deemed acceptable, although the result may not be what was originally desired. However, this obtained result will (have to) have at least some of the properties (that is, be a supertype) of the desired result. Moreover, the sufficiency criteria may be changed between the start and the end of the operation.

Inherent in information gathering is the fact that you may not receive what you requested, at which point you must resort to suboperations that decide the need for better information, seek to obtain that better information, change sufficiency criteria, and even change assumptions about what result may be the best obtainable in the situation.

Note that already we have considered aspects of both business specification — what outcomes we will accept — and business design — how we might change our sufficiency criteria based on successive responses to our requests (however, the definitions of these "change" operations belong to the business specification). Additionally in business design, we might want to assign each operation and suboperation to a particular job role within the enterprise, or decide what parts of the information gathering process may be wholly manual, wholly automated, or supported interactively, and so on.

4. TECHNICAL DETAILS

4.1 Naming of patterns and their components; precision

We have been using the term "business pattern" to cover that concept which includes "slots" for all information management stages. Alternatively, we could — probably should — choose separate stage-specific names for those fragments of a pattern that are fully instantiated at the end of each stage. Since we have yet to fully comprehend all relevant concepts, find satisfactory names for these specific notions, or fully define the boundaries between these "stages", it seems a little premature to finalize (or even suggest) names. This approach of using viewpoints, or stages, is consistent — in intention if not in name — with the ISO Reference Model for Open Distributed Processing (ISO 1995b).

Patterns and their slots must themselves be given names. These names should be carefully chosen to help people build an intuition — a "correct" warm and fuzzy feeling — as to when and how to consider applying the patterns. For example, we feel that minimal explanation and documentation can render both "information gathering" and "composition" sufficiently plain and intuitive that the potential applicability of these patterns to appropriate situations will be evident. Here we are more fortunate than our colleagues who are seeking names for design patterns, since the language and abstractions of business and society with the corresponding "intuitive understanding" have emerged together over centuries if not millennia rather than the few decades of mostly isolated maturation of the computer industry. But even for business patterns, **names and feelings are certainly not sufficient**.

Inventing names — for patterns, slots, and so on — does not, by itself, define these things. This is because however intuitive they may seem, different people will interpret the same, however "meaningful" or "natural," names in different ways. In contrast, the usage of precise specifications, including invariants and pre- and postconditions, does define things, their relationships, behavior, and so on, in a complete and unambiguous way.

4.2 Completeness/ instantiation

The (re)use of a pattern is termed instantiation. A complete pattern instantiation has to provide values for all formal parameters. However, at any one time only some of the formal parameter slots may have been filled. It is a very deliberate decision, on our part, to allow this, making explicit our concern to enable rigorous capture of incomplete knowledge and, more generally, to enable independence in decision making; that is, to actively encourage separation of concerns when capturing business knowledge. Note that a formal specification language Z (Nicholls, 1995) permits the specifier to do just that, but in a formal — rather than just rigorous — manner. For example, it permits specifying abstract, generic, and often incomplete constructs of open distributed processing, thus leading to better understanding and reuse (Kilov, Johnson, 1996).

A parameter may be, and often is, a nonelementary thing, such as a set, a relation, a sequence, and so on (as shown above in the composition examples). As such, and in the same vein as the previous paragraph, a slot may be partially filled (for example, only some members of the set may be provided), and an explicit decision must be made that the slot is complete. For example, as noted above, a composition may be "fixed", implying that all components have been enumerated and there will be no more additional components; or, more often, a composition may be variable. Note that making a decision that something is "complete" is a different concern from declaring that the decision will not be changed at some time in the future.

4.3 Stages of completion / instantiation

As suggested above, the instantiation of a pattern usually occurs in a number of stages, during business specification, business design, system design and implementation.

For each slot we can state in which (possibly many) stages it is possible to add (or refine existing) values to the slot. For example:

- most information specifically related to business processes, job roles, organizations and so on must be supplied during business design
- only those job roles (for example) that are mandated by laws, regulations and so on should be considered part of business specification

No processes, job roles or organizations should be either invented or modified during system design and system implementation, whose goals are simply to produce a system that satisfies a specification and scope of automation as identified in business specification and business design. However, a stage-specific (for example, implementation-specific) refinement may be required, probably resulting in a (for example, implementation-specific) predicate being conjoined to an existing pattern's invariant.

Some patterns may be primarily used to complete slots of other patterns at a stage beyond business specification. As such, they have no slots that are completed during business specification. An example might be a pattern to specify relationships between a business's sub-organizations; since internal structuring of a business — even if subject to external regulation — is a matter of business design, this pattern would probably have no business specification-level aspect.

5. GENERAL FORM OF PATTERNS

This section is concerned with the content and documentation of patterns. We discuss generic aspects of the "form" of patterns. In documenting a pattern, we seek to ensure that the pattern is rigorously expressed and both easily taught and appropriately presented for reference when applied in a particular situation. Also, it should be clear whether a particular business pattern is or is not applicable in a particular situation, and thus an understandable and unambiguous definition of each pattern is essential.

Inventing (discovering) a new pattern is hard, and does not need to be done by everyone involved. As reading and thus reusing is substantially easier than writing, reusing existing patterns is substantially easier than discovering new ones; and leads to reuse with substantial savings of intellectual effort, and thus time and money.

All patterns "exist" in some context. Obviously, providing all details about a context will lead to a substantial, often unacceptable, increase in the size and complexity of the specification. Therefore, only the top-level information (resultant properties of the "composite", see "composition" pattern above) about the context should be provided — and referred to — in a business pattern specification. This information (as well as any other) should be provided explicitly.

5.1 Classification of patterns into "modules" and "actions"

We have broadly classified all patterns that we have so far encountered as being either "actions" or "modules". This classification is related to the overall intent of the pattern. If the intent is to provided a reusable structuring of an operation and its suboperations, albeit with reusable invariants for the values of its slots, the pattern is an "**action**" (like "information gathering"). If the intent is to provide a reusable way of expressing a complex invariant, albeit with related operations consistent with and supporting the invariant, the pattern is a "**module**" (Alencar, Goguen, 1992) (like "composition" or "joint ownership").

We would like to follow our intuition and believe that many or even most patterns are either "modules" or "actions". Modules can be seen to be predominantly about high-level, reusable invariants. Actions are predominantly about high-level, reusable pre- and postconditions. In other words, a module describes constructs that exist "all the time", whilst an action — constructs that "start" and "end" (eg "repayment of mortgage"). This description is quite informal. Sometimes it is difficult (and may not be necessary) to distinguish between modules and actions: a marriage, for example, has a start and an end, but, unlike a mortgage repayment, is not about one particular operation. This should not prevent us for specifying a marriage as a business pattern — after all, both an action and a module exist in some context and have an invariant! In a similar vein, other possible broad categories could conceivably be those that are predominantly about "obligations", "triggering conditions", or "permissions". This classification of business patterns may thus be somewhat arbitrary; but the specification of a business pattern should in any case be precise, explicit, and therefore unambiguous.

Example actions might include: assessment, information gathering, negotiation, receipt of a communication and transfer of ownership. Example modules might include: ownership, joint ownership, officially registered event, bill of materials and, more abstractly, composition (see above) and reference from (Kilov, Ross, 1994; ISO, 1995a). Another example of a module has been discussed at some length by Wegner in (Wegner, 1995) — a marriage contract. This example includes obligations and permissions of the kind described in (Meyer, Wieringa, 1993), and often includes operations leading to the change of some invariants — quite typical for an open (externally interacting) system. In fact, as noted in (Wegner, 1995), this distinguishes an open system from a closed one.

Note that all of these patterns — and particularly the actions — may be applicable at several levels of granularity, while still remaining at the business specification stage of information management. For example, "in verifying the correctness of the transfer of ownership of a house I must: verify that the purported seller is the current owner (which may require that I gather information about the present ownership of the house ...) and verify that funds are available for the transfer (which may require that I gather information about the availability of funds for the transfer ...) ..." and so on. Here the actions verification — which is a special case of assessment — and information gathering are each used several times, with verification being applied and composed with itself at different levels of granularity. Both interact with module patterns related to ownership. The phrases written in brackets could have been omitted to present a high-level view of the overall verification action.

Let us describe the invariant for a general (business) pattern.

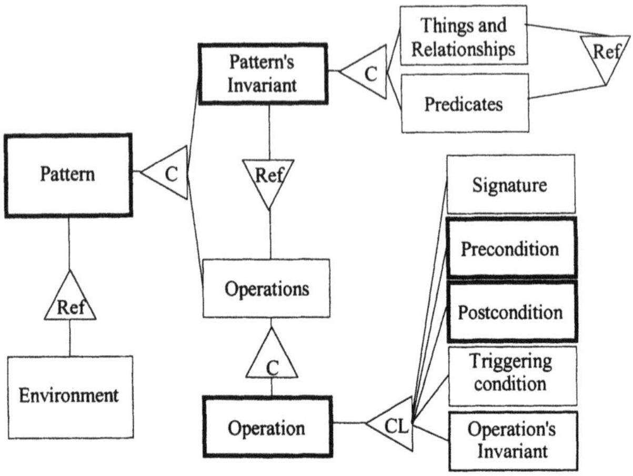

This picture is a graphical representation of the invariant of a pattern (in other words, it represents a substantial part of the precise specification of a pattern). It uses the composition pattern described above, as well as reference — another generic relationship pattern. It shows that any pattern is composed of the pattern's invariant and a composition of operations. Every operation, in turn, is composed of its signature, precondition, postcondition, triggering condition, and the operation's invariant. This composition is a list (Kilov, Ross, 1994), meaning that neither the composite, nor the components may exist independently of the composition. An invariant is composed of things and relationships, and predicates (about these things and relationships). The reference relationships show that some properties of "maintained" things — such as Operations in the `Pattern's Invariant - Operations` relationship, or Pattern's Invariant in the `Environment - Pattern's Invariant` relationship — are determined by the properties of their "reference" things — such as Pattern's Invariant in the former, or Environment in the latter relationship.

Obviously, this specification may be considered partial. It does not include, for example, such informal but useful pattern components as the description of the goal, the name of the author, etc. Also, we may refine this specification and show, for example, that there are two different subtypes of an operation — one that does not change the environment, and another that does (eg an operation in an open system may change the pattern's invariant, see below). There are other, equally interesting and important, ways to refine this specification.

For an action pattern (that defines an interesting and potentially reusable operation applied to a collection of things), the composition of operations ("subactions") shown in the picture above will be partially ordered (some operations may be executed in parallel). For a particular kind of action you may reuse many typical subactions (eg "assessment" typically involves "information gathering" subactions).

For a module pattern, usually no ordering of operations is defined. Also, new operations may be typically added (especially for modules); and operations themselves may be considered as parameters.

6. CHANGES

6.1 Inevitability

Business pattern instantiations are often interactive. In other words, they exist in an open world which permits unpredictable inputs during the "lifetime" of an instantiation of the pattern. As a result of these inputs, the environment of the pattern instantiation may change, resulting in changes of its invariant, as well as pre- and postconditions of its operations. Usually only fragments of a pattern may be considered "closed" and "atomic" and so considered to have an unchanging environment as in conventional "short" transactions (Wegner, 1995).

We have seen that these considerations apply to a module pattern, such as a marriage contract. The same, however, is true for an action pattern, for example, a mortgage repayment contract. In the United States (an environment), a mortgage repayment contract includes in its invariant the existence and properties of an escrow account held by the mortgage company to settle possible changes in taxes and insurance. When the laws and regulations about the maximum possible amount of the escrow account changed (thus providing some help to mortgage holders who did not want to have excessive amounts of money on their escrow accounts), new operations were added to the business pattern (eg "credit" — another business pattern of a particular action). Some old, existing, operations in the business pattern for a mortgage repayment contract were also changed as a result in this change of laws and regulations.

6.2 Changes to invariants

A pattern's invariant is relatively stable, but can change, especially when laws and regulations change. We have seen a marriage contract example above. As another example, "joint ownership" — perhaps of shares — may have tax consequences. When tax laws change, the invariants that model the laws — and the concepts in terms of which they are expressed — will change. Again, for example, there is currently a notion of "capital gains tax" in the US; if a proposal to restructure the tax system as a "flat tax" were adopted then the notion of "capital gains tax" may disappear completely, leading to changes to (fragments of) the invariants modeling taxation and joint ownership. These changes will imply appropriate changes to operation definitions: some operations will become unavailable because their preconditions will not be satisfiable (they even may refer to concepts no longer available!), and some other operations will have to change their pre- or postconditions.

Why will operations have to be changed? As shown above, an invariant of a pattern is referenced by (in a reference relationship (Kilov, Ross, 1994) with) all operations of that pattern. The invariant of a generic reference relationship states that some properties of the maintained object (in this case, the pre- and postconditions of the module's operations) are determined by some of the properties of the referenced object (the module's invariant). As such, when the invariant changes, all operations of that pattern must be reassessed because the precondition for each operation assumes that the invariant is also satisfied, as does its postcondition.

An example of an invariant that is, at the time of writing, changing for many businesses is: `actual year=1900+system year, where 0≤system year≤99`, be it within the business's information systems or preprinted forms (including cheques). This invariant will soon be invalidated, at which point many operations will be invalidated and will need to be changed to satisfy the new invariant (stating how "century" will be captured and affect the outcome of operations). As the pre- and postconditions of most of these operations are at best implicit in the code of some system, many billions of dollars may be spent in more or less successful attempts to resolve this problem, either in advance or as part of a cleanup.

Note that when such changes to invariants occur, they are first formulated as a change proposal before being adopted, and on adoption both old and new formulations must be maintained, at least for some time. In particular, this allows processing errors to be corrected when, for example, a letter containing a cheque arrived but "fell behind the back of a filing cabinet". In such a situation a correction must be calculated in terms of the rules in effect at each point in time between error occurrence (losing the letter) and error discovery and correction, implying the availability of each **version** of the rules. It is obviously essential to have an explicit and precise specification of the operations to be executed in such erroneous situations.

6.3 Changes to pre- and postconditions of operations

As for invariants, in most cases we assume that the pre- and postcondition stated when an operation "starts" do not change during the operation. For atomic, short-lived, non-interacting operations this is true, because there is simply no opportunity for the postcondition and invariants to change. However, for prolonged business operations — for example, some kinds of assessment such as the underwriting of a nonstandard insurance application, or selection of an appropriate treatment for a medical condition — obviously the definition of an operation (including the pre- and postcondition as well as the invariant) may change.

Once an operation has started, we lose all interest in its triggering condition and whether or not it continues to be satisfied. However, we are interested in the pre- and postcondition and the invariant until the operation is concluded, and should not (and cannot) assume that they remain constant throughout the operation.

We have already seen examples of changes to operation specifications triggered by changes in invariants (new laws and regulations about mortgage escrow accounts; or eventual changes in capital gains tax laws). Examples of changed pre- and postconditions for a (long) operation are common in a bureaucracy (an organization that tries to make the lives of its "subjects" more difficult). If a subject needs to obtain a permission from the bureaucracy and satisfies the preconditions for doing so at the moment of requesting the permission, and if the process (operation) of obtaining this permission is lengthy, then it is quite possible for the bureaucracy to change — "on the fly" — the pre- and postconditions of "obtaining permission" in such a way that the new preconditions would be more difficult to satisfy. As another example, in the midst of underwriting a particular application for health insurance, new regulations may appear stating that an underwriter must approve health insurance for persons with some specific preexisting conditions.

7. EXAMPLE OF AN ACTION PATTERN: INFORMATION GATHERING

This and the following section present examples of second-level business patterns. These examples show both the content (semantics) of the patterns, and illustrate how patterns might be presented for reuse. The language and layout used for presenting the patterns are perhaps nearer to those suitable for inclusion in a patterns catalogue (Alexander et al., 1977) than in a general introductory text about (business) patterns (Alexander, 1979). We tried to be as precise as possible, and already see some ways of improving the presented patterns.

7.1 Informal introduction

Information gathering is an action to obtain some information using some environment (eg an applicant for insurance seeks to determine whether his application will be approved, declined, postponed, approved with substandard conditions; or a bureaucracy wishes to determine a person's birthdate supported by acceptable evidence).

The pattern recognizes that requested and obtained information are often different (indeed, are of different types; in the birthdate example above, it may be impossible to provide any birth certificate for an immigrant, and other supporting evidence could be used). An operation to obtain information of a particular type may retrieve less rich information (a supertype) or, conceivably, better information (a subtype). In cases where less good than requested information is received, the obtained value should be of a supertype of the requested type of the requested value.

Also, as the action proceeds there may be a change in expectations on what results can be retrieved at a reasonable cost to the requestor. Consequently, a gathering action may consist of one or more operations that request information, together with operations for making decisions to obtain more information or to change expectations for the gathering action. The pattern's invariants refer to expectations (sufficiency criteria) and types of resulting (ie requested and obtained) values.

7.2 Invariant

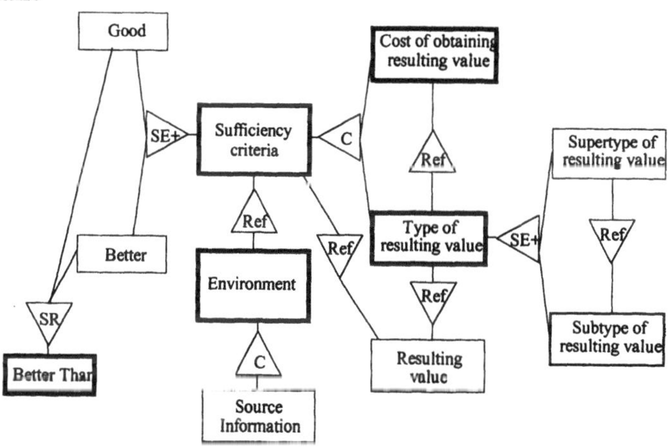

7.3 Operation: request for information

Signature

The signature of this operation consists of the things highlighted in its pre- and postconditions, together with the things referred to in the pattern's invariant above (which is this operation's invariant).

Precondition

- `source information` exists
- requested `type of resulting value` exists
- `environment` (element of the set of environments) together with corresponding `sufficiency criteria` exists.

Postcondition

- `resulting value` exists and satisfies one of the `sufficiency criteria` for the `environment`
- the `type of resulting value` is one of the `supertypes of resulting value`
- `cost of obtaining resulting value` is known

Note: sufficiency criteria may be changed between the start and the end of the operation.

7.4 Sub-operation: obtain better information ("further request")

Precondition

The following exist:

- `source information`
- old `resulting value`
- old `type of resulting value`
- requested `type of resulting value`
- old `environment` with corresponding `sufficiency criteria` one of which has been satisfied by the old `resulting value`
- sum of old `costs of obtaining resulting value`
- `environment` to be used to obtain better information.

Postcondition

- new `resulting value` exists and satisfies one of the `sufficiency criteria` for the new `environment` which is a `sufficiency criterion`, `better than` the old one
- new `type of resulting value` is a `subtype` of the old type `of resulting value` and a `supertype` of the requested type `of resulting value`
- new `cost of obtaining resulting value` is known.

7.5 Sub-operation: change sufficiency criteria

Precondition

- old `sufficiency criteria` for the `environment` exist.

Postcondition

- new `sufficiency criteria` for the `environment` exist and are different from the old `sufficiency criteria`.

7.6 Sub-operation: change relation "is better than" for sufficiency criteria

Precondition

- old relation `is better than` exists.

Postcondition

- new relation `is better than` exists for the same set of `sufficiency criteria` and is different from the old `is better than`.

7.7 Sub-operation: decide need for better information

Precondition

The following exist:

- `source information`
- old `resulting value`
- old `environment` with its `sufficiency criteria` one of which has been satisfied by the old `resulting value`
- sum of old `costs of obtaining resulting value`
- new `sufficiency criteria`.

Postcondition

For the given sum of old `costs of obtaining resulting value` and old `environment`, one of the following:

- `resulting value` satisfies new `sufficiency criteria` (information has been obtained)
- `resulting value` does not satisfy new `sufficiency criteria` (triggers "obtain better information")

Note: this assessment may be done by a human; and may include "override criteria" (compare with the considerations below).

7.8 Possible extension

We may also consider the nonmonotonic case where it will be discovered that something that you thought was true is in contradiction with the newly established information — in other words, that the "current" state of the system is about to become inconsistent. This situation is analogous to the one with mutually inconsistent obligations, or with mutually inconsistent viewpoints that nevertheless need to be composed (Harrison et al., 1996). One way of dealing with these problems is provided by explicit partial ordering of the importance of information (obligations, viewpoints), so that the "less important" information will be overridden by "more important" one.

7.9 Informal guidelines on how to instantiate

Information to be gathered — and the procedure for gathering it — may be arbitrarily simple or complicated. For example, a telephone number is relatively simple while a medical history of a candidate for health insurance (and her ancestors) may be extremely complex. Some businesses (such as a credit bureau) may exist simply to gather and supply information.

We suggest that the pattern is instantiated in roughly the following order:

- types of gathered (requested and obtained) values
- source information and environment(s)
- relative acceptability of gathered values in different circumstances
- sub-operations for obtaining better information
- sub-operations for deciding need for better information

• other sub-operations
• costs associated with obtaining a resulting value

The values to be gathered should be specified first since it is difficult to understand how to gather something that is itself not understood. Likewise, it is useful to understand the environment from which the information is being gathered sooner rather than later. Since it is often the case that the value actually obtained in an initial attempt may not be the value requested (perhaps the requested value is simply unobtainable as in the birthdate example above), it is important to specify all possible sources of information and the different kinds of information obtainable from each source.

We specify relative "quality" of value types in terms of subtyping relationships:
• a value is strictly "richer" than another value if it contains more information
• that is, it has all of the properties of the "less rich" value plus some additional properties (which is precisely the definition of a subtyping relationship)

In general, an operation to obtain information of a particular type may retrieve less rich information (a supertype) or, conceivably, better information (a subtype). In defining the post-condition of a specialized "obtain better information" operation, you must state what types of resulting value the operation must recognize, perhaps including a value of "unacceptable". In cases where less good than requested information is received, the obtained value should be of a supertype of the requested type of the resulting value.

For example, instead of obtaining a birth certificate for a person, it may be possible just to establish a date (or even the year) of birth from some other documental sources: thus, "obtaining a birth certificate" will have a type "establish a birthdate using the best possible document", and its supertype will be "establish some birthdate information using a documental source". The invariant includes a (partial) ordering of acceptability criteria, with a relation "better than", and a way to decide when to "stop" in requesting more and more acceptable information should be provided.

Additional details, such as job roles, precise ordering of requests, and what types of gathering to outsource, are considered to be beyond business specification and best handled during business design.

8. FRAGMENTS OF A MODULE PATTERN — JOINT OWNERSHIP

8.1 Informal introduction

The joint ownership pattern is about most kinds of property ownership. It deals with several owners of a property, leaving the property itself atomic (ie ignoring its composition). It is applicable in many cases, including situations when a property typically has only one owner, but may conceivably have several.

Examples are well-known: joint ownership of a company (shareholding), of a house, of a car (by the bank and the owner), of a racehorse (by the members of a syndicate), and so on. Another interesting example is "joint tenancy", which happens when the composition in the invariant is fixed, and can be changed only with the death of a co-owner.

At least two specializations of joint ownership exist (but will not be considered here): one in which a co-owner can dispose of his share in the property without consulting other co-owners, and the other in which this is not allowed.

We have not included all possible operations. For example, in addition to the operations presented below, there are also such operations as "redistribute the shares of interest in property" (with the operation invariant "the collection of owners is unchanged"), "transfer share of interest in property to a new party", and so on. The specification of these operations is probably straightforward.

8.2 Invariant

The `property` belongs to a non-empty `collection of owners`; and a `share of interest in property` for each `owner` has been established. (A composition of symmetric relationships, a generic molecular pattern described in (Kilov, Ross, 1994a), can be used to rigorously formulate this invariant).

Note: If the share of interest has not been established (ie it is not yet known to the business), in most cases the only operation that can be applied for this pattern is "establish the share of interest"; this operation involves information the pattern of which was presented above.

8.3 Acquire interest in property

Invariant

`Property` exists

Precondition

- `joint ownership` is not a `joint tenancy`
- the (old) `collection of owners` has been established
- it has been established that `co-owners` of the old `collection of owners` agree to the acquiring `interest in property` by the `collection of parties` to acquire `interest in property`
- the `collection of parties` to acquire `interest in property` has been established.

Postcondition

- the `collection of owners` is equal to the union of the old `collection of owners` and the `collection of parties` to acquire `interest in property`
- the new `share of interest in property` for each `co-owner` has been established.

8.4 Lose interest in property

Invariant

`Property` exists

Precondition

- the (old) `collection of owners` has been established
- the party to lose `interest in property` has been established.

Postcondition

- the `collection of owners` is equal to the difference between the old `collection of owners` and the `owner` to lose its `share of interest in property`
- the new `share of interest in property` for each `co-owner` has been established

- the share of interest in property of the owner to lose interest in property has been extinguished.

9. CONCLUSION AND FUTURE RESEARCH

The existence of many business patterns can be inferred from the language of business. Generic business concepts — "negotiation", "ownership", "receipt" and so on — are a rich source of relatively abstract patterns. However, to be of value, these patterns have to be(come) precisely specified. Some of them probably are precise — in economics and other professional texts such as (Alexander et al., 1977) — but are perhaps incomplete. Requirements for specification completeness are quite different for different audiences: business analysts and developers of information systems are not experts in the subject matter of the business they will partially automate, and thus require explicit specification of all "common knowledge" of subject matter experts. As this common knowledge may (and usually does) rely upon quite different default assumptions for different subject matter experts, the value (and understandability) of business patterns can be substantially improved by specifying these common-knowledge assumptions explicitly. Indeed, often a pattern can only be used once these assumptions have been made explicit. Such specifications will also lead to the discovery of different specializations (subtypes) of these patterns, and of additional parameters essential for successful pattern reuse and instantiation.

More specific language — "term life insurance policy" — will lead to more concrete, although still generic, business patterns of more focused reuse value. Given this assertion, we expect there to be considerable reuse value in action patterns that capture common business actions such as "negotiation", "assessment", "information receipt", "information recording - solicited" and "information recording - unsolicited", and module patterns such as "ownership", "joint ownership", "liability", and so on. Having said this, we intend to construct and refine a catalogue of patterns as they are encountered and reused — by us and others — during business analysis.

Note that we (almost) did not use the buzzword "Object-Orientation"in this paper. The most important of the concepts we use are **abstraction** and **precision** (leading, for example, to understanding and reuse), which have been around a lot longer than OO, and were warmly embraced and emphasized by the best OO advocates. These concepts may be used both for understanding the business and for providing technical solutions based on this understanding. Moreover, our approach yields business specifications that can form the basis for system development in a variety of paradigms including both OO and the more "traditional" ones.

An interesting test of the validity of patterns with common language roots is whether their "natural" value appears to be preserved when their documentation is (carefully!) translated into languages and cultures other than, for example, American English. It may even be that some patterns have limited applicability, being tied to specific cultures.

10. REFERENCES

Alencar, A.J., and Goguen, J.A. (1992) OOZE. In: *Object orientation in Z* (Workshops in Computing), ed. by S.Stepney, R.Barden and D.Cooper. Springer Verlag, 79-94.

Alexander, C., Ishikawa, S., Silverstein,M., Jacobson, M., Fiksdahl-King, I., Angel, S. (1977) *A pattern language*. Oxford University Press.

Alexander, C. (1979) *The timeless way of building*. Oxford University Press.

Ayers, M. (1996) Book review of "Information modeling — An object-oriented approach" by Haim Kilov and James Ross. *Software Engineering Notes*, Vol. 21, No. 2, 91-92.

Gamma, E., Helm, R., Johnson, R., Vlissides, J. (1995) *Design patterns: elements of reusable object-oriented software*, Addison-Wesley.

Harrison, W., Kilov, H., Ossher, H., and Simmonds, I. (1996) From dynamic supertypes to subjects: a natural way to specify and develop systems, *IBM Systems Journal*, Volume 35, Number 2, to appear.

ISO (1995a) ISO/IEC JTC1/SC21, Information Technology - Open Systems Interconnection - Management Information Systems - Structure of Management Information - Part 7: General Relationship Model, ISO/IEC 10165-7.

ISO (1995b) ISO/IEC JTC1/SC21/WG7, Open Distributed Processing — Reference Model: Part 2: Foundations (IS 10746-2 / ITU-T Recommendation X.902, February 1995).

Kilov, H. (1993) Information modeling and Object Z. In: *Proceedings of the Conference on Next Generation Computer Technology and Systems*, Haifa, Israel (June 1993), 182-191.

Kilov, H., Johnson, D.R. (1996) Can a flat notation be used to specify an OO system: using Z to describe some RM-ODP constructs. In: *Proceedings of FMOODS'96: IFIP WG 6.1 Conference on Formal Methods in Open Object-based Distributed Systems*, Paris, March 1996, 407-418.

Kilov, H., Mogill, H., Simmonds, I. (1996) Invariants in the trenches. In: *Object-oriented behavioral specifications*, ed. by H.Kilov and W.Harvey, Kluwer Publishers, to appear.

Kilov, H., Ross, J. (1994) *Information Modeling: an Object-oriented Approach*. Prentice-Hall, Englewood Cliffs, NJ.

Kilov, H., Ross, J. (1994a) Generic concepts for specifying relationships. In: *Proceedings of NOMS'94 (IEEE)*, Orlando, 207-217.

Mac an Airchinnigh, M., Belsnes, D., and O'Regan, G. (1994) Formal methods & Service specification. In: *Towards a Pan-European Telecommunication Service Infrastructure* (Lecture Notes in Computer Science, Vol. 851). Ed. by H.-J.Kugler, A.Mullery, N.Niebert, Springer Verlag, 563-572.

Meyer, B. (1988) *Object-oriented software construction*. Prentice-Hall

Meyer, J. J.Ch., Wieringa, R.J. (1993) *Deontic logic in computer science*. John Wiley & Sons.

Nicholls, J., ed., (1995) *Z Notation, Version 1.2*, The University of Oxford, September 1995.

Parnas, D.L. (1995) Teaching programming as engineering. In: *ZUM '95: The Z Formal Specification Notation* (Lecture Notes in Computer Science, Vol. 967). Ed. by J.Bowen and M.Hinchey, Springer Verlag, 1995, 471-481.

Parnas, D.L. (1995a). Language-free mathematical methods for software design. In: *ZUM '95. The Z Formal Specification Notation* (Lecture Notes in Computer Science, Vol. 967). Ed. by J.Bowen and M.Hinchey, Springer Verlag, 1995, 3-4.

Parnas, D.L., Madey, J. (1995) Functional Documents for Computer Systems, Science of Computer Programming, Volume 25, 1995, 41-61.

Proposals of the Massachusetts Hospital Life Insurance Company, to make insurance on lives, to grant annuities on lives and in trust, and endowments for children (1835), James Loring printer, Boston.

Redberg, D. (1996) *The search for the linking invariant: behavioral modeling versus modeling behavior.* In: *Object-oriented behavioral specifications*, ed. by H.Kilov and W.Harvey, Kluwer Publishers, to appear.

Swatman, P. (1994) Management of Information Systems Acquisition Projects, in *Proceedings of OzMISD'94, First Australian Conference on Modelling and Improving Systems Development*, Lilydale, Victoria, 3-4 February 1994, 115-131.

Wand, Y. (1989) A proposal for a formal model of objects, in *Object-oriented concepts, databases and applications*, edited by W. Kim and F. Lochovsky, Addison-Wesley, 537-559.

Wegner, P. (1995) Models and paradigms of interaction. *ECOOP'95 Tutorial Notes*, July 1995, Aarhus, Denmark (Brown University Department of Computer Science Report CS-95-21).

11. BIOGRAPHIES

Haim Kilov has been involved with all stages of information management system specification, design, and development. His approach to information modeling, widely used in telecommunications, financial, document management, and insurance areas, has contributed clarity and understandability to enterprise and application modeling, leading to specifications that are demonstrably better than "traditional" ones. It has been described in "Information modeling: an object-oriented approach" (Prentice-Hall, 1994). Haim Kilov is using and extending his approach in customer engagements. He is a member of and active contributor to several international standardization technical committees. He has been a speaker and a program committee member at numerous national and international conferences. His interests are in the areas of information modeling, business specifications, and formal methods.

Ian Simmonds has worked on techniques and tools for developing systems. He was a leading participant in the PACT and ATMOSPHERE ESPRIT projects and the EAST EUREKA project. In these and other projects his work focussed on the specification and systematic use of technical frameworks for CASE tools and integrated software engineering infrastructures. In particular, he was an active participant in the international (ISO) standardization of the Portable Common Tool Environment (PCTE). Since joining IBM's Insurance Research Center, he has been studying the application of object-oriented techniques to the development of business systems for the insurance industry, with an emphasis on reuse of both techniques and content. His interests include rigorous specification of business requirements, the use of these as a basis for systematic development of business systems, and the transfer of these techniques for use by IBM's customers and consultants.

16

System For Preparing Management Decisions: A Gas pipeline siting case study

O.I. Larichev, E.N.Andreyeva, M.Y. Sternin.
Institute for System Analysis
Russia,117312, Moscow, pr. 60 let Octjabrja, tel. (095)-135-85-03;
Fax : (095)-938-22-09
E-mail: larichev @glas.apc.org

Abstract

The paper describes the analysis of an important problem: the choice of a gas pipeline route on the Yamal Peninsula in the North of Russia[1]. It is a real case of a difficult and controversial real-life decision. The authors were in the position of consultants, helping to decision makers to develop and justify a new and promising variant of the decision. The result of the utilization of verbal(categorical) decision analysis and a decision support system are given .

Keywords

Multicriteria choice, decision support system, active groups.

1 INTRODUCTION

The preparation of strategic and complex decisions is a long and time-consuming process. Two aspects are especially important: the exploration of the positions of different active groups participating in the solution of the problem and the invention of new, promising decision variants, acceptable to the problem to theactive parties.

The goal of the paper is to present a case-study describing the application of the DSS called ASTRIDA to the solution of a new and difficult problem in the development of the gas industry in Russia. This case involves major uncertainties and the necessity of making a difficult choice. We shall describe below the problem and our experience in applying the DSS.

---

[1] The research is partly supported by the Russian Fund for Fundamental Research N 95-01-00083 and NSF grant DPP9213392.

2 BACKGROUND

According to expert estimations, gas extraction in Russia will decrease in the next few years. To compensate for this reduction and to keep the gas supply to Europe, the Government of Russia is pushing the exploration of new gas fields. The Northern regions of West Siberia are famous for the great deposits of natural gas discovered there during the last 10-15 years. The most outstanding gas fields, with reserves of more than 20 trillion cubic meters, are situated on Yamal Peninsula, which has severe climatic conditions and a vast expanse of permafrost soils.

For the Central Government of Russia and the institutions responsible for energy, the issue of gas development on the Yamal peninsula is clear: the resources should be developed. The logic of such a decision is easy to understand: gas reserves elsewhere are exhausted and gas exports can noticeably increase Russia's national income. There are many unsolved problems within the framework of the initial decisions on Yamal development. One of the most essential is the choice of route for that part of the gas pipeline from the gas fields to the existing gas pipeline system. During the elaboration of the gas pipeline project, the idea of straightening the pipeline received strong support. The point was to make the line shorter by crossing the Baidaratskaya Bay, an inlet of the Kara sea. A second land-based option would cross the Yamal Peninsula to the east of Baidaratskaya Bay. The choice of option has been the subject of bitter discussion between two institutes involved in the project during the last two years. Both have arguments for and against the sea and land routes. The decision point and the start of pipeline construction has been recently postponed, partly due to the complexity of this choice.

Thus the task addressed here is one of decision-making with two alternatives. As we shall see, this problem concerns the interests of various different groups who are able to influence the choice. It also depends on unknown natural conditions, and on contradictory appraisals of the alternatives on various criteria, etc. In the following, we consider these options in detail.

3 TWO OPTIONS

The two options are: a sea route, crossing the Bay, and a land route. The following distinguishing characteristics have been included in analysis: 1. Length of the route. The sea option is shorter than land route. 2. Terms of construction. The conditions of construction are very difficult for both options: a large expanse of permafrost and enormous rivers and lakes. But there is an essential difference: the need to cross the bay (about 68 km length). 3. Time for construction. Construction for both the options depends on how the work is organized. There is no appropriate technology in Russia for pipeline construction at the bottom of the sea. Some foreign firms have offered their help in constructing the sea segment of the pipeline. 4. Cost of construction. This factor is of great importance but very difficult to estimate. In principle, it is possible to evaluate the cost of the land route from knowledge of the necessary quantity and prices of tubes for pipeline, technological and building equipment, fuel and labor cost. 5. Impact on the environment. As noted above, the land route will cross many ecologically valuable areas, including reindeer pastures, wildlife refuge, hunting lands as well as rivers and lakes famous for their very high productivity and fishing resources. 6. Risk of pipeline rupture accidents. The probability of a land route accident may be assessed on the basis of existing data on pipeline operations in the North. Statistical information on gas pipe line accidents in mountain regions can help to make this assessment more precise and adapted to the Polar Ural region. On the other hand, risk assessment for the sea route is rather difficult. World experience includes no statistic data on the operation of an underwater pipeline under such severe arctic conditions. The situation with Baidaratskaya Bay is unique with specific features which could cause an accident. Namely:

- instability of the shore sites with permafrost processes and impact of sea ice.
- rupture of or damage to of the pipeline by underwater ice.
- experts on ice conditions in the Kara sea confirm the probable appearance of iceberg sections capable of reaching Baidaratskaya Bay.

7. Consequences of pipeline rupture accidents. In the land route case an accident on the pipeline is associated with explosion and fire. As a result, the impact on the natural environment is very high: complete destruction of the vegetation cover and thermal regime of permafrost soils, and the death of all wild animals. An underwater accident has less environmental impact: the gas will dissolve in water and is not toxic. The ice cover is not solid and gas can come out through cracks into the atmosphere. 8. Time to recover from accident. This factor determines gas supply reliability. There is much experience of repair operations in the case of land laid pipelines in the Russian North. As for the underwater part of the sea option, repair of a destroyed segment is limited to the 2-2.5 months a year when the Bay is free of ice. Furthermore these operations require special techniques and equipment (barge, caisson apparatus, etc.) 9. Uncertain and unknown factors. Any choice of option has some circumstancesabout which not enough is known at the time of decision-making. Most of these unknown factors would need long-term observations and prolonged investment in scientific research before uncertainty about them could be reduced. Thus, the decision must be made under conditions of major uncertainty, given that the construction start date has been set in the immediate future.

4 ACTIVE GROUPS

Before comparing the two options we must analyse who will make the choice and how. It is not likely that the choice of option will be made by a single decision-maker, because of the high cost of this project. On the contrary, several institutions and organization are taking part directly or indirectly in the decision. We will call them the "active groups". They are the following:

1. Russian joint stock company "Gasprom" (RAO Gasprom), which ordered the development of the project, and will evaluate and confirm it.
2. The two project research institutes who developed the two options (sea route and roundabout land route): each institute supports a different option.
3. Nadymgasprom - the operational division of RAO Gasprom in the North Siberia region, which is responsible for the construction and exploitation of the gas pipeline system.

4. Ministry of Economy - evaluates the economic considerations and economic efficiency of future project, and approves the design.
5. Ministry of protection of environment and natural resources - evaluates the ecological impact and ecological security of the project, gives the permit for construction.
6. Local authorities in the Yamal region, who must give their agreement to one option for the pipeline.
7. Local communities (or representatives of native peoples),whose territory and resources will be impacted by the construction of a very large pipeline system.

The active groups have different motivations concerning the choice in question. Actually we face different orientations and contradictory opinion towards the criteria. One might expect that they would support different options.

To understand better the attitude of all the active groups in this great project, it is worthwhile noting that the idea of its development appeared more than 15 years ago. During the intervening period much has happened in the life of Russian society: transformation from centralized governance and planning to new market relations accompanied by high inflation, assessment of the efficiency of the northern mining and oil activities under new economic conditions, establishment of new relations between federal and regional authorities, increase of the role of local communities in the decision-making regarding the use of resources or territories which traditionally were inhabited by the people of these communities. All these factors impacted on the opinions of the active groups involved in this project of exploration of Russia's richest gas reserves in the most complex geographic region, famous for its strong traditional economy of yamal-nenetz people based on biological resources.

All the societal processes in Russia were still in flux while the situation with Yamal project started up very rapidly in 1984 but was frozen after 1989 for a while. The freeze was connected with very strong opposition to the operational activity of the construction firms from local authorities, from the indiginous people of the peninsula and from a group of scientists - members of National Commission of Experts who made the evaluation of the feasibility study: the basic document for this development.

The leadership of the RAO Gasprom had to agree to the temporary suspension of the activity at the peninsula in accordance with the commission's conclusions. It had become clear that there were too many unsolved technical and environmental problems which couldn't be avoided or neglected: they required fundamentally new decisions. Among those problems was that of the choice of the main pipeline route from the mother gas fields - Bovanenkovo-Harasavey to the European part of Russia and western countries.

First the experts of the RAO Gasprom submitted for consideration 6 different routes, which combined some options for routes through land and sea. After long discussions in which many specialists were involved (in accounting for all expenditures, assessing of advantages and disadvantages of each route, etc.) only two options were left: the short route involving the crossing of Baydaratzkaya Bay and a longer route, taking a roundabout way, crossing the western part of Yamal peninsula and Polar Ural.

Each route crossed very complex sites and needed additional investigations under field conditions. It was necessary to determine which industrial company (Russian or foreign) would be able to carry out this work. During the initial discussions of the two options, the leadership of RAO Gasprom had already stated its preference in favor of the sea route. The process of searching for a foreign company who could take on the laying of pipeline on the sea bottom was already very active while the preparation of the feasibility study was only just getting underway.

Nevertheless, a serious investigation, involving the comparison of the two options, had to be made. This work had been entrusted to two project design institutes which already had considerable experience in the development of pipeline systems in Western Siberia. One of them, GIPROSPECGAS (St.Petersburg), started first and from the very beginning was a strong supporter of the land route. The staff of the Institute conducted investigations comparing the two options and confirmed again that the land route was more preferable.

In explaining this choice they gave the following arguments. There are no firms in Russia, not even in the world, who have experience in construction of gas pipelines under such complex permafrost conditions and under the persistent impact of active sea ice. This option needs special and very expensive equipment for working in the sea the while Russia has a difficult financial situation and it would mean creating new debts to foreign countries.

The risk of accidents during exploitation of the pipeline system is very high while the period for repair works is limited by the period of only three to four months of\ open water in Baydaratzkaya Bay. This factor reduces the general reliability of the gas supply system.

As for the land route option, any breakdown of the pipeline could be restored within 72 hours regardless of the season and using only domestic technical means.

The other institute, YUSNIIPROGAS (in Donetzk), is a supporter of sea route and made its own comparison of the two options. They accepted the concern that sea route needs a quite new technology for pipe laying (the depths of the bay varies from 6 to 29 metres), has many uncertainties which are usual for the Arctic. But Russia is opening a new stage of gas field development - in the exploration of the arctic shelf zone. So it is high time to begin to obtain some new experience - new for the whole world - and thus to be ahead. This idea was very popular among the leaders of RAO Gasprom and very soon this Institute received the leading position in the development of this project. As a foreign partner, the Dutch company "Haarema" was selected to construct the first two lines of the underwater part of the pipeline system.

The feasibility study was ready in summer 1994, but the start of the construction depends on the readiness of other parts of the project - preparation of gas fields for exploitation, not to mention the financial and organizational problems. It is worth noting that the famous and very powerful Ministry of Pipeline Construction, which had previously existed in the Soviet Union and which provided the resources for creating numerous pipelines all over the country, had now been transformed into several holding companies. This means that now there is no single strong construction company which could carry out the whole range of construction works. RAO Gasprom has to deal each time with a different company regarding different parts of the whole project. Also, the extraordinary permafrost conditions required additional experiments searching for quite new technological solutions. This work is not finished yet.

Throughout all this period RAO Gasprom, the final decision-maker, returned back to the two options for the Yamal gas pipeline route many times and in spite of contradictory views, stuck to the sea route. Moreover, the Board of Directors examing the feasibility study made by YUSNIIPROGAS in 1994, came to the final conclusion that the sea route was the only acceptable option. The complex situation in regard to energy policy in Russia nevertheless didn't change the attitude to natural gas as priority number one in the fuel balance. But the attitude to different gas fields changed, depending on the readiness of technological decisions, success in cooperation with foreign companies and the investment climate. Due to these factors, preference in time of development was given to gas-condensate and gas-oil fields located in the shelf of Barentz sea, while Yamal gas fields were supposed to be involved in activity afterwards. It was reported recently by officials of RAO Gasprom that the start of the construction of the Yamal gas pipeline system has been postponed until 1997, while the preparation works in the Pechora sea and adjacent coastal zone are already under way.

Another active group, Nadymgasprom (a division of RAO Gasprom in Western Siberia), was in charge of realising the plans to develop the most Far North gasfields in the Yamal Peninsula. During the period of preparation for exploration, this organization is monitoring the field work which has been conducted specifically to increase knowledge about the geographical and engineering peculiarities of the future construction under severe arctic conditions. It is clear that the political strategy of this department reflects the attitude of its patron organization, RAO Gasprom, although, as a technical executive division, it has its own interests related to enhancing its influence in the region, the more complete use of the personnel at its disposal (they had to cut back operational works in accordance with general decrease of activities of the gas industry during the last period).

Therefore this active group is interested in speeding up the start of development, but the land route provides more employment with the use of domestic experience in pipeline construction in permafrost regions, including laying pipes on the bottom of the Ob river.

A new active group, which began to take part in the decision-making process only during the last 8-10 years, comprises the local communities of the indiginous population, more precisely, representatives of them in local administrations or regional associations. For the Yamal peninsula, the relevant organization is a regional association called "Yamal - for future generations". Since the beginning of the geological and other exploration activity, this group has been in strong opposition to the industrial development of the territory. It is worth noting that the yamal-nenetz ethnic group is rather stable and is well versed in social and political science. It had a well developed traditional economy based on reindeer breeding, commercial and domestic fishing, hunting on land and marine wild animals.

The ecological state of the territory where the yamal-nenetz group lived traditionally for many centuries is a crucial factor in their survival and development as an ethos in the future. Namely, these territories appeared to be under obvious ecological danger from the large scale development of gas deposits, construction of many engineering projects, of a railroad and a pipeline system. The methods of industrial development employed in other places in the North-West of Siberia have demonstrated its destructive character from the ecological point of view, and the danger for northern yamal-nenetz population has actually become obvious. They have started a long and hard struggle for their rights, which is continuing up till now.

The transformation of the northern traditional economy is proving to be particularly painful and difficult. The need to resist waves of Russian unstable conditions and maintain market requirements, placed the local communities, with their low profit branches of the economy, in particularly hard situation. Most of the collective farms are in a state of decay, new individually owned farms try to find their way in this cruel financial world, many people have lost their jobs and even the very low income they had before. The perspective of the new events, related to gas development, became a new alternative which could impact on their life, not only in a bad way, but perhaps which could offer some new opportunities.

RAO Gasprom tried to use this mood of change in its own interest, making a very successful attempt to change the general negative attitude of the indiginous population regarding industrial development. The aboriginal population was given an opportunity to be an active participant in this development, distributing shares of the new objects within the local communities, with preferencial treatment for indiginous people. This measure actually had a positive effect and there are a lot of people who now support the Yamal gas development project as offering a new hope for this administrative region. The delay in the start of the construction is a question of even more vital interest than the question of development itself. Nevertheless, the indiginous people have more real imagination about their rights and the responsibilities of "developers" so this problem of mutual understanding is not simple and needs more time to form a compromise in the decision-making.

The obligatory participant in this decision-making game is the State Ministry for Natural Resources and Protection of the Environment. Its role is rather standard: to make an assessment of the future impact of the project on the environment and to give the permit, or not, for its realization. This Ministry had rejected the Yamal feasibility study in 1989. although the new (corrected) variant of the feasibility study on the construction of the main pipeline system from Yamal to the Centre is ready, it has not yet been submitted to the Ministry for consideration. This will be the final decision-making step before the actual action, so RAO Gasprom will try to do its best to avoid a new failure. In December 1995 a new State Law on ecological expertise was passed in the Russian parliament (the State Duma) which further strengthens the position of this Ministry in its relationship with the Government Departments for industrial branches of the economy.

5 THE EVALUATION OF OPTIONS

Many reports were prepared by the two project organizations, containing calculations based on different models and assumptions. Those reports were taken as the base for the analysis given in the paper. Let us note that the evaluations of options on criteria given by the two organizations are different and sometimes contradictory. The analysis was done for RAO Gasprom by a team from the Russian Institute for Systems Analysis including the present authors.

Multi-criteria utility theory requires deterministic or probabilistic evaluations of options. But how could we get them in this case? We look at the options through "a fog of uncertainty" deriving partly from the difficulty of measuring options in terms of the criteria. How could we evaluate the cost in a period of massive inflation? How could we compare the probability of an accident in the absence of information, reliable models or data of long-term observations?

The essential difference between the options consists in crossing the Baidaratskaya Bay (option A) and in the construction of an additional 160 km. of pipeline (option B). It is logical to take into account only the criteria where we can find an essential difference between the options in terms of those criteria. In other words, we take criteria where one can see something really different through "the fog of uncertainty". For example, the preliminary estimation shows that the time required is 5-7 years for both options. The unstable internal economic situation can impact on the starting time.

1. Cost. The cost of crossing Baidaratskaya Bay (Ca) is determined by a foreign firm which is ready to construct this part of the pipeline. The initial approximate estimations show that the cost of option A is a little bigger than the cost of option B.
2. Ecological impact. Both options have a negative impact on the environment. But for option B this influence is much larger: it occupies a lot of land and crosses many rivers, though there is some uncertainty about the influence of option A on marine life.
3. Probability of accident. Due to unstable shores and heavy blocks of undersea ice the probability of an accident is larger for option A.
4. Consequences of the accident. In the case of option B, an accident is usually connected with an explosion and destruction of the environment. In the case of option A, there would not be an explosion. The gas would rise through the water and cracks in the ice. Option B is clearly worse.
5. Reliability of gas supply. The repair of the pipeline after an accident requires much more time for option A, particularly since the bay is free from ice only 60-70 days per year. Option A is clearly worse.
6. Uncertain and unknown factors. There are many uncertain and unknown factors connected with the realization of the unique project of crossing the Baidaratskaya Bay. Option A is clearly worse.

So, we have the comparative evaluations of options in the qualitative form. These are practically all that we can measure. It is difficult to get more than comparative measurements. How could we draw conclusions with such weak measurements?

6 THE COMPARISON OF TWO OPTIONS

In the framework of categorical or verbal decision analysis (Larichev, 1987,1992) special methods for comparison of alternatives described in terms of verbal evaluations upon criteria have been developed (Moshkovich,1991; Berkeley et al., 1990; Larichev and Moshkovich, 1996). One of these is the method of pair-wise compensation. In using this method, one is trying to find a condition when the disadvantages of one option are dominated by the disadvantages of the other.

First, the decision maker ranks the disadvantages of two options separately. In our case he or she ranks the disadvantages of Options A and B from the point of view of his or her preferences. Then, special "reference options" are created, which are constructed from real ones in the following way: each has the best (or worst) evaluations of two options on all criteria, except for one or two on which real disadvantages are given. When comparing the two reference options, the decision maker finds the partial compensation of some disadvantages of one alternative by the disadvantages of the other one. If it is possible to find such compensation for all disadvantages of one alternative the problem is solved. When comparing the two reference options, the decision maker performs a psychologically valid operation involving the comparison of two objects which differ only on two or three criteria (Larichev, 1992). It is possible to prove (Moshkovich, 1991) that the operation of the compensation is mathematically true in the condition of preference independence (Keeney and Raiffa,1976). The check of the condition of preference independence is the coincidence of results of comparisons for two pairs of reference options which differ only in best or worst evaluations on all criteria except one or two (on which real disadvantages are given).

But it is not always possible to find pair-wise compensation of disadvantages of two alternatives. By making only qualitative comparisons, one can receive noncomparability, when some evaluations are better for the first option and some better for the second, which was the case in the comparison of the two options for Yamal pipeline. The greater uncertainty and lower reliability of gas supply for option A are worse than ecological impact for option B. But the negative consequences of an accident for option B is worse than the larger probability of an accident for option A. In such case it is necessary to undertake an attempt to develop a new, more promising option on the base of existing ones.

7 THE DEVELOPMENT OF A NEW OPTION

In this case, as in many others, the practical value of decision analysis consist not only in the comparison of existing options, but in the creative invention of new ones. A method for aiding strategic choice, ASTRIDA (Berkeley et al., 1991) has been developed which permits not only the comparison of several options, but also the definition of the requirements of a new, desirable and potentially best option. ASTRIDA uses verbal evaluations of the options on each criterion, and calls for the decision-maker to make pair-wise comparisons. Such comparisons can be made from the points of view of different active groups. We shall give below the analysis corresponding to the interests of RAO Gasprom.

In the case of incomparability, the method ASTRIDA proposes is to make a modification of one existing option. That is, the method asks the question: what needs to be changed in one option to make it equal to or better than the other option? Thus, ASTRIDA defines the characteristics of a potentially best option that was not initially on the original list of preferred alternatives.

A new sea route option resulted from a search for ways to change these characteristics. (Larichev et al., 1995). Discussions with the experts suggested ways in which the negative comparisons of the sea option could be removed:

- To eliminate the influence of seashore instability, special shafts could be constructed at a safe distance from the sea, and the pipeline put through them. This construction will incur additional costs: *Cshafts*.
- To avoid damage to the pipeline from ice scouring, the pipeline can be laid in special trenches 1.5 - 2 meters deep. They would be deeper than the project plan calls for, so the costs, *Ctrenches*, will also be additional.
- Icebergs are a very rare but dangerous event in the bay. A special observation service and a special ship to drag the iceberg away would eliminate this problem. Let us denote the cost of the service and ship by *CIce*.

Adding these features to the old sea alternative creates a new option with an element of uncertainty approximately equal to the traditional land option. The probability of an accident for the new sea option is not very different from that for the land option. With the development of a special repair service for the underwater tubes, the reliability of the gas supply could be made equal. Thus, no significant differences now exist between the sea and land routes, except cost and ecological impact. The cost of the new sea option, *Csea+ Cshaft+ Ctrenches+ Cice,* will clearly be more expensive. The land option will still create greater environmental destruction. Now the comparison can be considered as one between higher costs and better environmental protection.

8 THE ANALYSIS FROM THE POSITIONS OF THE ACTIVE GROUPS

The analogical analysis was made from the positions of the active groups. The development of the new option was useful in this case too. Concerning the two initial options only, the positions of the local authorities and the local population were clear: they supported the sea option. (the projects research institutes obviously supported the options developed by them). The new sea option was more attractive for the Ministry of Ecology and Nadymgasprom. The positions of RAO Gasprom and the Ministry of Economy in the final, crucial choice presented above were influenced by the financial situation in Russia. In recent years this situation has been rather difficult.

9 THE INFLUENCE OF RECOMMENDATIONS

The report, with the recommendations presented above, was given to RAO Gasprom. At that moment the first sea option was the more attractive one for the majority of managers. That why they were expecting that analytical report prepared by the consultants from Institute for Systems Analysis would be positive on this option. But the report created doubts about the possibility of acceptance of this option. At that moment the intention to begin the construction of the pipeline was strong enough.

In spite of the government's desire to make practical steps in regard to pipeline construction, there were some grounds for postponing this decision. We can say that one of them was the uncertain and unknown factors shown by the report. There was an objective conformation of this fact: during the delay in the beginning of construction, new investigations were undertaken on the problem of instability of the seashore that was presented in our report.

Recently the start of the Yamal pipeline construction was postponed yet again due to several important factors. From our point of view, the most important one is the uncertainty in the problems connected with the conditions of the construction. Unfortunately, it is impossible to remove this uncertainty completely. That is why the next decision (based on new data) is to be taken again under conditions of uncertainty.

Uncertainty exists in either option. That is why consideration must be given only to the factors for which essential differences truly exist. In other words, we must look at only the bright lines and broad brush strokes. The decision analyst tries to reduce the problem to one where the crucial choice could be evident. In our case, the comparisons of two options (land option and new sea option) revealed the necessity of crucial choice between the great cost of the construction of a safe pipeline in the difficult Arctic conditions and the huge damage to the unique nature of Yamal. The value of the analysis consists in the possibility to help people (decision makers and experts) to develop a new, promising decision variant which could be the best one under some conditions.

10 CONCLUSION

The implementation of the results of the analysis required repeated meetings with experts and decision makers. The questions discussed were very sensitive from organizational point of view due to necessity to begin the pipeline construction. But finally a delay was accepted in order to study in detail the main sources of uncertainty indicated by the analysis. For the analysts this was a demonstration of the influence of the analysis on real decisions.

11 REFERENCES

Berkeley D., Humphreys P., Larichev O., and Moshkovich H. (1991) Aiding Strategic Decision Making: Derivation and Development of ASTRIDA. In *Environments for Supporting Decision Processes* (Eds. J. Vecsenyi and H. G. Sol), North Holland, Amsterdam

Larichev O., Brown R., Andreyeva E., and Flanders N. (1995) Categorical decision analysis for environmental management: a Siberian gas distributing case. In *Contributions to Decision Making* (Eds. J.-P.Caverni, M. Bar-Hillel, F.H. Barron & H. Jungermann), North Holland, Amsterdam

Larichev, O. (1992) Cognitive validity in design of decision-aiding techniques. *Journal of Multi-Criteria Decision Analysis* **1**, 127-138.

Larichev O. (1987) *Objective models and subjective decisions.* Nauka Publishing House, Moscow. (in Russian).

Larichev O. and Moshkovich H. (1996) *Qualitative methods of decision making*. Physmatlit Publishing House, Moscow. (in Russian).

Moshkovich H. (1991) Qualitative methods in multiattribute decision making. *Proceedings of 13th Research Conference on Subjective Probability, Utility and Decision Making,* University of Fribourg, Switzerland.

12 BIOGRAPHY

Professor O. Larichev is head of a department of the Institute for System Analysis of Russian Academy of Sciences. His fields of interest are psychology, decision making, multicriterial mathematical programming, decision analysis, nonlinear programming. He is an author of seven books and 170 papers in the fields of decision making and artificial intelligence.

Doctor E. Andreeva is the leader of the Geoinformational and Analytical Centre of the Russian North, Institute for System Analysis of Russian Academy of Sciences. Fields of interest are resource and environment management in the Arctic and the North; Impact of oil and gas industry on ecological and social system. Dr. Andreeva is an author of one book and 45 papers in the fields regional policy in the North, analysis of ecological and social consequences of the industrial activity in polar regions.

Michael Sternin is a senior scientific researcher in the Decision Support System department of the Institute for System Analysis of Russian Academy of Sciences. His field of interest is Decision support systems. He is an author of 35 papers in various areas of the field of decision making

17

Design and testing of a DSS to help reduce bias in judgemental forecasting

Michael Lawrence
School of Information Systems
University of New South Wales
Sydney 2052 Australia
Telephone: (02)385.4417 Fax: (02)662.4061
e-mail: M.Lawrence@unsw.edu.au

Abstract

One of the most widely occurring management decision tasks is preparing the monthly forecasts. This execution of this task requires the application of management judgement to combine contextual knowledge with the time series historical data. The task would appear well suited to the application of a DSS. Yet surveys in the USA, UK and Australia show very low penetration of any direct computer support in the estimation of forecasts. This paper gives some clues as to the reasons for this state of affairs and explores a tool, potentially more acceptable to forecasters which is designed to help reduce the human bias present in extrapolating a time series. The tool which is behaviourally rather than mathematically based, is shown to improve estimation accuracy over a purely judgemental alternative and to be significantly better than the naive forecast.

Keywords

Forecasting, decision support, DSS, judgement, bias

1 INTRODUCTION

Surveys of forecasting practice in Australia, USA and the UK indicate the continuing high use of judgemental and opinion based methods in preference to quantitative methods (e.g. Sparkes and McHugh, 1984; Dalrymple, 1987; Tarranto, 1989; Sanders and Manrodt, 1994). These studies of business (mostly sales) forecasting practice reveal that only around 10% of the firms surveyed use quantitatively based forecasting techniques and that the number of firms who have tried and subsequently abandoned these techniques is about double the number currently using them. This situation cannot be blamed on lack of supply of forecasting technology - there has been an enthusiastic response by system developers and there is a wide range of inexpensive and user-friendly PC windows and main-frame based software to choose from. These systems benefit from the great volume of forecasting research conducted over the last 25 years. As might be expected, this lack of use has been a cause of concern to researchers and management educators who believe that valuable technology is remaining under-utilised (Makridakis, 1988; Armstrong, 1994).

Improvements in forecasting could have a significant impact on business. Most businesses are involved in regularly developing forecasts and losses through inaccurate forecasts can be high (Makridakis, 1988). For example, organisations involved in warehousing and distribution incur holding and obsolescence costs on their inventory which can be around 25% per annum. In addition lost business from stockouts may be even more damaging. But the preference revealed in these studies for judgemental methods cannot be dismissed as the action of a business community unconcerned by forecast errors. The surveys cited show that business does keep records of forecast accuracy and that they are unlikely to continue to use a method which does not perform (Dalrymple, 1988). Nor can the preference be attributed to lack of knowledge of quantitative forecasting technology. Armstrong (1994) comments that an increasing exposure to forecasting technology has not increased its use.

The barriers to information systems implementation success theorised and explored in the literature include (Hirschheim and Newman, 1988):

User reasons (e.g. lack of felt need, conservatism),
technology and implementation reasons (e.g. poor system quality, inappropriate design, poor user training), and
organisational reasons (e.g. inadequate management support).

Before we apply this model to computer based forecasting systems we need to briefly present the current paradigm which structures and underpins forecasting research and software products. The current paradigm of forecasting research and software products decomposes the forecasting task into the following steps

a) Develop an extrapolation on the basis of the time series data.

b) If necessary, modify the extrapolation using contextual data. This contextual data may reflect marketing plans, macroeconomic expectations, competitor intelligence or microeconomic factors such as labour disturbances.

Forecasting research for the last fifteen years has been dominated by the pursuit of step (a) above with the search for the best forecast model that generates the most accurate extrapolation. This activity has lead to a number of laboratory based forecasting competitions (e.g. Makridakis et al, 1982; Makridakis et al, 1993) which have acted as a significant focus for further research. However there is not universal acceptance of step (b) with some authors cautioning against modifying the extrapolation except under the most exceptional circumstances such as what are called "broken leg cues" (Armstrong, 1985). Furthermore step (b) is often difficult to perform because it may not be clear the extent to which recent exceptional phenomena have been incorporated into the quantitative forecast or have been left out (being treated as a random event) and therefore need to be incorporated judgementally.

These problems with step (b) have generated the feeling that the forecast should not be manually modified, leading to the situation where the forecasting system replaces rather than supports the business forecaster. We thus suggest that an important reason for the lack of use of forecasting technology is its inappropriate design and the lack of appeal of its underlying paradigm.

An alternative paradigm for forecasting was pioneered by Edmundson (1990) with the DSS tool GRAFFECT, later incorporated into some commercial forecasting systems (e.g. foreGraph). These systems are not based on the two steps given above nor are they based on a fitting a mathematical model to the time series history. Rather they allow the forecaster to develop the forecast judgementally. The task decomposition used in these tools breaks the time series into its trend, seasonal and randomness elements. The forecasting user, sitting before a graphical representation of the series on the computer screen, has a choice of various forms of statistical support and also can judgementally intervene to modify or dictate the seasonal and the trend terms. As seasonals and trend are generally far from stationary, this is often a very desirable facility. The forecast is then made on the de-trended and deseasonalised series either judgementally or using a quantitative forecast model. Edmundson (1990) showed that the judgemental forecast made using his GRAFFECT tool was more accurate than that made using a pencil and paper judgemental approach and was also more accurate than deseasonalised exponential smoothing, the most accurate quantitative method for the time series used in his experiment.

However there would appear to be further gains in accuracy possible. Lawrence and O'Connor (1995) showed that a judgemental extrapolation was subject to a number of biases which reduce its accuracy. Their experiment suggested that subjects forecasting a time series tended to be too extreme in their estimates. This result can also be viewed as a reversal of the usual anchor and adjustment bias in which subjects anchor on a value already known and arrive at their estimate through making an adjustment (generally too small) from this anchor point (Tversky and Kahneman, 1974). In the case of time series forecasting, subjects appear to adjust too much from the anchor point of the most recent observation. Harvey (1995) also observed this same phenomenon and argued it may be due to the subjects seeking to estimate a forecast which "looked like" the original observed series in both its trend and its randomness. Lawrence and O'Connor (1995) argued it may be due to the subjects not discounting their estimates for the uncertainty of the direction of the movement from the anchor point. They demonstrated that if the error in picking the right direction (up or down) was taken as the uncertainty, and the amount of adjustment discounted by the uncertainty, then the estimates were effectively debiased. Thus if this approach could be incorporated into the procedure, it would appear that the resulting forecast could be improved. This paper examines this approach to improving the estimation of a judgemental forecast when the time series has been deseasonalised.

2 RESEARCH QUESTIONS

In a laboratory setting Lawrence and O'Connor (1995) found that subjects were biased in their forecast estimates by adjusting too far from the anchor point (taken to be the last observation). Lawrence and O'Connor suggested that subjects employed a two stage process for estimating their forecast. In the first stage the direction of change was picked and in the second, the size of the adjustment from the anchor point was estimated. They argued that the subjects did not reflect in the second stage the likelihood of error in the first stage. When the subjects' results were discounted for their probability p of picking the correct direction of the change (from the last observation) the forecast accuracy was significantly improved. The discounted adjustment *DADJ* can be shown (Lawrence and O'Connor, 1995) to be given by the formula:

$$DADJ = (2p - 1).ADJ \qquad (1)$$

where *ADJ* is the adjustment from the anchor point in which no allowance has been made for uncertainty in the direction in the adjustment. One can see if the probability p is 0.5 (indicating no belief about whether the time series will go up or down) that $DADJ = 0$, while if $p = 1$, (perfect confidence) then $DADJ = ADJ$. In this paper a DSS was developed and tested which decomposed the task into the two stages and discounted the size of the adjustment for the ambiguity of picking the direction. Such a DSS would be able to be incorporated into a tool like GRAFFECT to improve the core extrapolation task.

3 RESEARCH METHODOLOGY

A DSS was developed which presented a graph of a time series to a subject and asked that a one step ahead forecast be developed in two stages:

Stage 1. Estimate the direction of the change from the last observation and the likelihood of the chosen direction being correct (only the rounded percentages 50%, 60%, 70% ...100% were available for choice).

Stage 2. Estimate the amount of change from the last observation *conditional on the direction being correct.*

Thus the major feature of this DSS is the structuring of the task and the detailed decomposition of the estimate into the above components.

The subject had presented to him on the computer screen a graph showing the time series at an appropriate presentation scale (Lawrence and O'Connor, 1993). Via a mouse and the numeric keypad the subject entered the information shown above following definitions of what to enter displayed on the screen. The screen then displayed both the initial estimate (i.e. undiscounted), the discounted estimate and after the subject indicated he was satisfied with the estimates in that round, the actual was displayed. Colour was used to differentiate these different data points. The cycle was then repeated with each subject estimating 24 forecasts for the one time series. A total of 30 time series were used in the experiment. These time series were drawn randomly from the real-life monthly series in the M-Competition (Makridakis et al., 1982) and deseasonalised using the same seasonal factors as used in the M-Competition. Feedback was provided to subjects by the following means: (a) screen display of the original and discounted estimates and the actual value; (b) the progressive score of the percent correct for direction of change.

A reference group of subjects estimated the forecasts without the benefit of the decomposition based DSS using instead a computer presentation of the time series graph similar to that in the DSS. The subject indicated his estimate of the forecast using a mouse to position a cross hair on the screen.

The subjects were undergraduate and graduate students at the University of New South Wales majoring in Information Systems. No monetary or other compensation was paid to the subjects.

4 ANALYSIS METHODOLOGY

The metric used to assess forecast accuracy and compare the DSS with the reference was the Mean Absolute Percentage Error (MAPE), defined as the mean of APE where

$$\text{APE} = |\text{ACTUAL} - \text{FORECAST}| / \text{ACTUAL} \qquad (2).$$

This metric was selected for several reasons. First it is less affected than squared measures by extreme errors, and thus is a good measure for comparisons across techniques. Second, the metric is independent of scale, enabling a comparison to be made across a number of different time series. Perhaps most importantly it is the dominant metric used in practice to measure forecast accuracy.

In addition to the reference forecast of subjects using the simple (non-decomposition) graph based DSS, the forecast accuracy of a naive forecast was calculated. The naive forecast (the last actual) has been shown to be a surprisingly accurate forecast and has been often used as a reference to measure forecast accuracy (e.g. Lawrence and O'Connor, 1992).

5 RESULTS

The MAPE accuracy results for the DSS group are shown in Figure 1 along with the results for the reference group (called Graph) and the naive forecasts. When paired t-tests were run, the DSS accuracy was better than both Graph and Naive above the 0.06 significance level. Naive and Graph were not significantly different in accuracy as was expected from the results reported in Lawrence, Edmundson and O'Connor (1985). Thus while the differences in accuracy between the DSS and the reference group may not appear to be exceptional they are nevertheless significant and suggest an important direction in improving forecast accuracy.

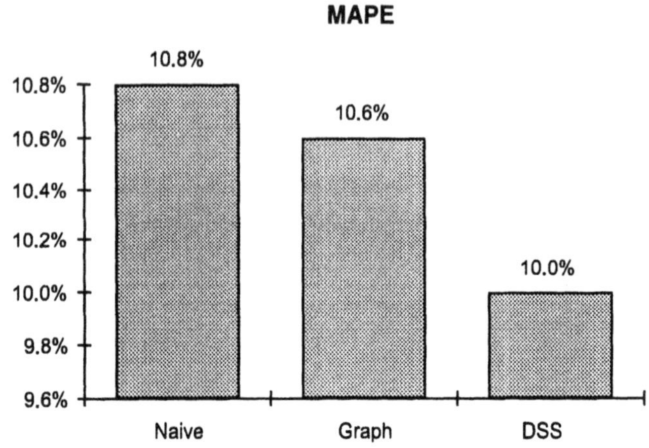

Figure 1. Comparison of DSS, Graph and Naive forecast accuracy

6 DISCUSSION

A more detailed examination of the results indicated that although the DSS users did exhibit superior performance, they were not learning from their experience and improving their estimation skills. When the 24 months of each subject's trials were split into two groups (months 37-48 and months 49-60), there was no improvement in estimating the probability of picking the direction of change. The usual metric for judging the accuracy of a subjective probability estimate is the calibration of the estimate in the light of subsequent events. The results in Table 1 below give the average expectation of being correct in the chosen direction and the actual percent correct. This shows that the expectation was about 10% higher than the actual realisation indicating overconfidence in the judgements. Furthermore the overconfidence was not adjusted in the light of the worse than expected performance despite a display which presented as a running score the percentages for picking correctly the direction of change.

	Expected	Actual
Months 37-48	65.4%	56.5%
Months 49-60	65.6%	55.6%

Table 1. Expected and Actual probability of forecasted direction.

If the confidence in the direction had been correctly estimated the performance of the DSS users would have been even better. This opens the question as to how the forecasters can be helped through a modification to the DSS to improve their estimation skills. We see more vividly the calibration errors when the calibration diagram presented in Figure 2 is inspected. This diagram presents for each stated confidence level the actual percentage of times the chosen direction was correct and the number of estimates (n) falling into that interval. For example when the 41 subject estimates claimed 100% confidence they were correct 75.6% of the time. Apart from at the 50% level, (for which there could hardly be any overconfidence) they were consistently overconfident. The worst result is at the 80% stated confidence level where only 50.1% of the direction predictions were correct. This general overconfidence has been observed in numerous studies in other task areas (Tversky and Kahneman, 1974) but rarely is the calibration curve so flat as in Figure 2. This figure reveals little skill in correctly estimating confidence and indicates substantial opportunity for improving performance.

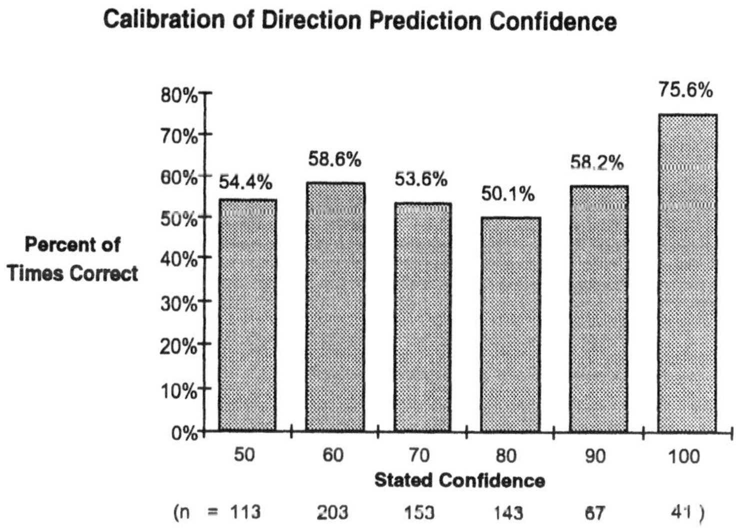

Figure 2 Calibration of direction prediction confidence

7 CONCLUSIONS

This study has suggested that the reason for the low penetration of computer based support for forecasting is the lack of user acceptance of a paradigm which places too much emphasis on the extrapolation of the time series and too little on the judgement and expertise of the forecasters. A new paradigm focused on supporting the judgements of the forecasters in all stages of the forecast preparation was introduced and the problem of reducing persistent human bias in extrapolation was defined as the task of this study. Based on earlier work by the author a two stage forecast decomposition embedded in a DSS was used to improve human judgement. This was shown to be significantly better than unaided judgement. However there was seen to be still a significant overconfidence bias in the judgements which suggests there is considerable further scope for improvement in the process. This work demonstrates a behaviourally based DSS in contrast to the usual mathematically based tools.

8 REFERENCES

Armstrong, J.S. (1985) *Long Range Forecasting: From crystal ball to computers.* 2nd Edition. Wiley, New York.

Armstrong, J.S. (1994) Review of Sanders and Manrodt. *International Journal of Forecasting,* **10,** 471-472.

Dalrymple, D. J. (1987) Sales forecasting practices: Results from a US survey. *Journal of Forecasting* **3,** 379-391.

Edmundson R. H, Lawrence M. J. & O'Connor M. J. (1988) The use of non-time series data in sales forecasting: a case study. *Journal of Forecasting,* **7,** 201-212.

Edmundson, R. (1990) Decomposition: a strategy for judgemental forecasting. *Journal of Forecasting,* **4,** 305-314.

Harvey, N. (1995) Why are judgements less consistent in less predictable task situations? *Organisational Behaviour and Human Decision Processes,* **63,** 247-263.

Hirschheim, R. & Newman, M. (1988) Information systems and user resistance: theory and practice. *The Computer Journal,* **31,** 398-408.

Lawrence, M. J. and O'Connor, M. J.(1995) The anchor and adjustment heuristic in time series forecasting. *Journal of Forecasting,* **14,** 443-451.

Lawrence, M. J. and O'Connor, M. J. (1992) Exploring judgemental forecasting. *International Journal of Forecasting,* **8,** 15-26.

Lawrence, M. J. and O'Connor, M. J. (1993) Scale, randomness and the calibration of judgemental confidence intervals", *Organisational Behaviour and Human Decision Processes,* 56, 441-458.

Lawrence, M. J. Edmundson, R. H. and O'Connor, M. J. (1985) An examination of the accuracy of judgemental extrapolation of time series, *International Journal of Forecasting,* **1,** 25-35.

Makridakis, S, Anderson, A, Carbone, R, Fildes, R, Hibon, M, Lewandowski, R, Newton, J, Parzen, E, and Winkler, R, (1982) The accuracy of extrapolation (time series) methods: results of a forecasting competition. *Journal of Forecasting,* **1,** 111-153.

Makridakis, S, Chatfield, C, Hibon, M, Lawrence, M, Mills, T, Ord, K, and Simmons, L, (1993) The M2-Competition: A real time judgementally based forecasting study, *International Journal of Forecasting,* **9,** 5-22.

Makridakis, S, (1988) Metaforecasting *International Journal of Forecasting* **4,** 467-491.

Sanders, N, and Manrodt, K. (1994) Forecasting practices in US corporations: survey results, *Interfaces,* **24,** 92-100.

Sparkes, J. R. and McHugh, A. K. (1984) Awareness and use of forecasting techniques in British industry, *Journal of Forecasting,* **3,** 37-42.

Tarranto, M. (1989) *Sales forecasting practice in Australia.* Unpublished B Com honours thesis. University of NSW, Kensington NSW.

Tversky, A and Kahneman, D (1974) Judgement under uncertainty: Heuristics and Biases *Science,* **185,** 1124-1131.

9 BIOGRAPHY

Michael Lawrence is Professor of Information Systems at the University of New South Wales, Australia. His major area of research is support for managerial decision making where judgement and quantitative analysis need to both play a part. He has a particular interest in time series forecasting and his publications include *Management Science, International Journal of Forecasting, Organisational Behaviour and Human Decision Processes, MIS Quarterly* and the *Journal of Forecasting.*

18

Designing and implementing DSS with System Dynamics: Lessons learned from modeling a Global System of Mobile Communication (GSM) market

C. Loebbecke
University of Cologne, Bern University
Wilh.-Backhaus-Str. 23, 50931 Koeln, Germany
Tel./Fax:+49/221/444 900,
e-mail: claudia.loebbecke@uni-koeln.de

and

T. X. Bui
Naval Postgraduate School, Department on Systems Management
Monterey, Ca 93943-5000
Tel.:001/408/656/2630, Fax ext.: 001/408/656/3068,
e-mail: tbui@nps.navy.mil

Abstract

This paper proposes an integrative approach for the design and implementation of systems to support market-related decisions in a dynamic environment. It outlines various design issues relevant to a dynamic decision environment and introduces system dynamics as an implementation-oriented DSS design methodology. A real-life case study from the German "Global System for Mobile Communication" (GSM) market briefly investigates basic design principles of a successful implementation, describes design and implementation experiences, and shows selected results. Lessons learned from the case study provide a critical assessment of the proposed approach. The paper closes with a brief summary and some suggestions for further research.

Keywords

DSS design, DSS implementation, System Dynamics, Cognitive feedback

1 INTRODUCTION

To help managers deal with strategic decision making and planning, research in management science and operations analysis traditionally offer a number of forecasting methods. A large, but not very recent body of literature (e.g., Makridakis, Weelwright, 1973; Roberts, 1978; Fourt and Woodlock, 1960; Mahajan and Peterson, 1978 and 1985; Lewandowski, 1974) reports on various quantitative and qualitative forecasting methods focusing on problem-tailored extrapolations from the past. These methods have been integrated into (what today would be called) a DSS to support strategic decisions. Most of them were designed to help managers understand themselves and their organization by studying and explaining the past. However, as Makridakis pointed it out (1990), any attempt to derive normative theories based on observation of the past, and to use such theories for predictive purposes runs the risk of misrepresenting the reality, as the future conditions will in all likelihood be changed.

Given the lack of historical data in complex in highly dynamic environments, simulation offers a valid alternative to support strategic decisions. In a simulation, all assumptions are required to be stated explicitly. They are translated into a set of equations to show the interdependence of the various assumptions and the resulting consequences. However, simulations can only show the consequences of the assumptions entered by the model users, regardless if these assumptions are correct or false (Forrester, 1972).

Forrester proposes Systems Dynamics (SD) as an alternate solution. System dynamics has been successfully applied in a broad variety of economic and social settings, including market simulations. Due to its main characteristics and strengths, it has proven to be especially appropriate for modelling

- decision environments driven by a high degree of dynamic feedback loops between intervening forces (Homer, 1987; Morecroft, 1986; Baills and Olivier 1993), and
- situations with a large amount of implicit expertise (usually at the best available in form of 'soft information' on the practitioners' side).

System dynamics based systems provide a framework for understanding the dynamic interrelationships between system elements (Senge, 1990). Hence, system dynamics go beyond the strict decision support metaphor, and should be applied as a tool conducive to support thinking, group discussion and learning in management teams (Morecroft, 1992).

The system dynamics approach to design and implement decision models emphasizes intuitive understanding of the mathematics underlying dynamic systems (Radzicki, 1993) by providing an integrated dynamic modelling approach that combines quantitative and qualitative aspects to simulate a phenomenon over time (Forrester, 1971; Lyneis, 1980). Based on the basic principles of cybernetics, according to which the behavior of the system elements is endogenous and necessarily dependent on that of other elements (Roberts, 1978), the methodology allows the representation of feedback loops and their underlying assumptions. Finally, system dynamics permits the integration of information cues that foster cognitive feedback (Bui and Loebbecke, 1996) as described in the following section.

Beyond the traditional aim to improve 'often subjective' decision quality, Forrester suggests the following questions, by which to judge system dynamics based systems (Forrester, 1972):

- Are the underlying assumptions more transparent than in mental models?
- As assumptions change over time, are their consequences adequately re-assessed?
- Is the model structure transparent and easy to understand in comparison with verbal texts or purely mathematical representations?

The main objective of this paper is to advocate the use of SD to model dynamic processes in a computerized DSS environment without resorting to complex mathematics. SD can be used as an iterative and on-line modeling approach that progressively helps the decision makers build an decision and simulation model. Once built, the computerized system can be implemented as a DSS that serves not only as a simulation tool for those users who are just interested in simulating outcomes, but also as a knowledge extraction and learning engine for those who prefer to appreciate the consequences of their own assumptions built into the system.

2 DSS DESIGN AS A MODELING PROCESS

The literature in DSS advocates the use of prototyping as the appropriate approach to building DSS. Iterative as well as interactive design and incremental development have proved to be critical in eliciting users requirements, improving systems functionalities, and enhancing user acceptance. However, prototyping, as an iterative process is not sufficient in helping DSS developers capture and model the dynamics of a problem.

Independently of the model adopted, modeling implies that assumptions must be explicited represented, 'soft' variables be taken into consideration, and cognitive feedback be used to enhance the quality of decision making as well as the decision processes.

2.1 Explicit representation of assumptions

Each strategy and each behavior is based on certain assumptions, which are often implicit and not tested. In case these assumptions contain internal contradictions, the latter are transferred to the resulting strategy, making its implementation difficult or even impossible. Dynamic simulations surface the underlying assumptions and show inconsistencies. At the same time they open discussions about diverging assumptions and their consequences can contribute heavily to 'better' decisions (Bui and Loebbecke, 1996).

2.2 Integration of 'soft' variables

Without any doubt, 'soft' variables like 'confidence' or 'motivation' are intrinsic decision making elements. By omitting such variables one would run the risk of failing to capture something essential to the relevant processes. Since parameter values of 'soft' variables are often arbitrary, strong sensitivity analyses are necessary to assure their internal consistency.

2.3 Provision of cognitive feedback

Recently there has been a growing body of research evidence from cognitive science suggesting that cognitive feedback can be used to enhance the quality of decision making as well as the decision processes (e.g., Balzer et al., 1989; Sengupta and Te'eni, 1993; Sengupta and Abdel-Hamid, 1993; Paich and Sterman, 1993; Bui and Loebbecke, 1996).

Cognitive feedback can be defined as information provided to decision makers for them to gain a better understanding of the decision processes. This information includes the relations in the decision environment, relations perceived by the decision maker about that environment, and relations between the environment and the decision maker (Balzer et al., 1989; Bui and Loebbecke, 1996). A number of researchers (e.g., Forrester, 1987; Milling, 1990; Senge, 1990; Morecroft, 1992, Paich and Sterman, 1993; Radzicki, 1993; Bui and Loebbecke, 1996) identify several types of information cues that could be used as feedback, the main ones being 'time navigation', 'space navigation', 'problem determinants', 'holistic view', and 'institutional memory'.

The reason for providing cognitive support is to offer decision makers information that allows them to learn more about the problem and its environment. In a dynamic setting, Newell et al. (1989) argue that providing cognitive feedback to decision makers helps them

- construct an appropriate model of the reality,
- operate in a real-time, rich and complex environment requiring a vast amount of knowledge,
- learn from the environment and from experience by simulation, thus enhancing the decision makers' ability to comprehend the dynamic changes of the underlying assumptions, and
- adapt quickly to the changes dictated by the users as the environment changes over time.

3 A CASE STUDY: MODELING THE GERMAN MARKET OF THE GLOBAL SYSTEM FOR MOBILE COMMUNICATION (GSM)

3.1 The problem

In most countries, operators of the Global System for Mobile Communication (GSM) face outstanding business opportunities in a young market. Due to the complex and dynamic nature of the telecommunication sector, it is difficult to establish a strategic business plan taking into account all intervening factors and their interdependencies.

In this context, the proposed system dynamics based design and implementation approach has been successfully applied with senior executives in Hong Kong and Vietnam (Loebbecke and Bui, 1994) and in Germany (Loebbecke, 1996). This section briefly discusses a particular

DSS designed and implemented in Germany to support GSM operators' strategic decisions related to the growth of the national demand for GSM in a ten-year time span.

3.2 Modeling objectives

In spite of the dynamics in the telecommunications sector almost every operator around the globe applies a selected set of forecasting methods - these days commonly incorporated into a DSS - to predict various output variables such as 'number of users', 'volume', 'price', 'profit', etc. (e.g., Altobelli, 1991; Phan, 1993; EMCI, 1993; Commission of the EC, 1990, Jagoda and Villepin, 1993). Nevertheless, forecasting in telecommunications has been always problematic due to the high number of variables that can act upon the market. Predicting demand for new telecommunication markets such as GSM is even riskier due to the lack of parallel development of products compared to that of mature systems (Commission of the EC, 1992; Loebbecke, 1996). In this context, the objectives of the DSS illustrated in this section (Loebbecke, 1996) , refer to three different levels (see Figure 1):

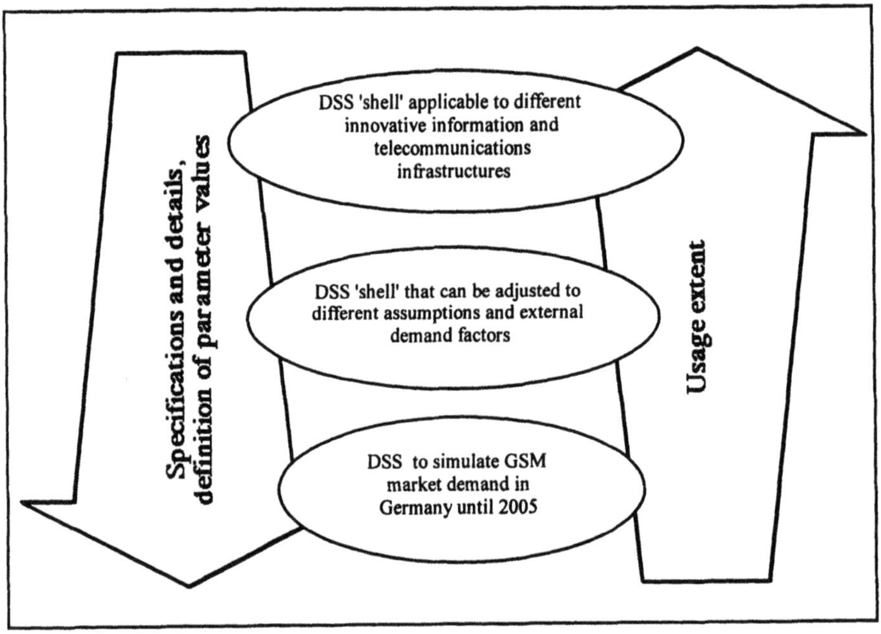

Figure 1 Development and implementation objectives.

The first objective of the DSS is to simulate market demand for GSM (in Germany) presenting the interrelationships of various demand driving factors. The DSS aims at estimating the total demand for mobile communication measured by the number of users and at predicting the relative relevance of the GSM demand driving factors. Based on various simulation results, GSM-operators, users, and regulators should gain adequate support in their different strategic planning decisions. The main goal of our DSS is not to offer precise quantitative predictions of the future, but rather to uncover the trends of key decision elements where many of them are interrelated in complex fashions.

The second level refers to a DSS 'shell' that can be adjusted to different assumptions about various demand driving forces or different external factors. For example, a single user of the DSS can enter his/her personal assumptions about selected demand driving factors. We consider a good intelligent DSS as one that can be adapted to new contexts as it evolves with its users over time. Furthermore, the system should provide the flexibility to be customized to simulate the national GSM demand in any country of the world.

On a third level, the system should be robust and flexible enough allowing to simulate the demand for other innovative telecommunication infrastructures, such as individual satellite communication, fax, or future infrastructures such as the Universal Mobile Telecommunication System (see, for example, Buitenwerf, 1994).

3.3 Design concept

The DSS to be illustrated in this paper considers GSM as an aggregated product offered by the various network operators. Its overall design logic (Loebbecke, 1996) follows two main ideas:

- A country's population is divided into four main user groups depending on the average number of their outgoing GSM minutes per months. These four groups are called 'non-users', 'small users', 'average users', and 'large users'. Based on these four groups, twelve different 'flows' among the user groups (users changing from one group to another) can be distinguished (see Figure 2).

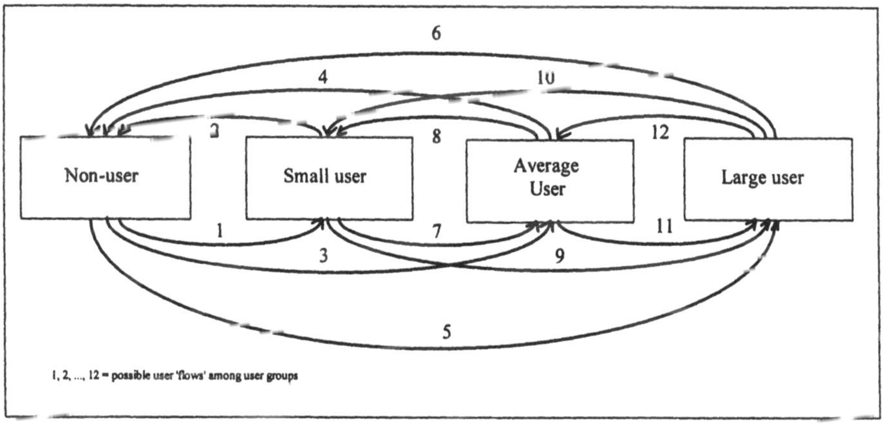

Figure 2 Four user groups.

- The demand for GSM, and more precisely each of the twelve flows in Figure 2, depends on seven main demand factors (Figure 3), each of which consists of several subfactors (Figure 4). Each subfactor is composed out of one or more factor components. The factors and subfactors show the impact that certain components have on the demand development. For example, the value of the component 'security needs' may rise progressively over time, while the impact of the component 'security needs' on GSM-demand, i.e., the value of the component 'security needs factor' decreases. Figure 5 conceptualizes to two step modelling and data gathering approach.

  Most subfactor components depend on the number of GSM users, and thus lead to an enormous density of feedback loops within the whole system: The number of users drives the value of most components, while the value of the component - translated into the according factor - drives the number of users. These feedback loops represent the mutual dependence between technological infrastructures and services on the one hand and social usage of these technologies on the other hand.

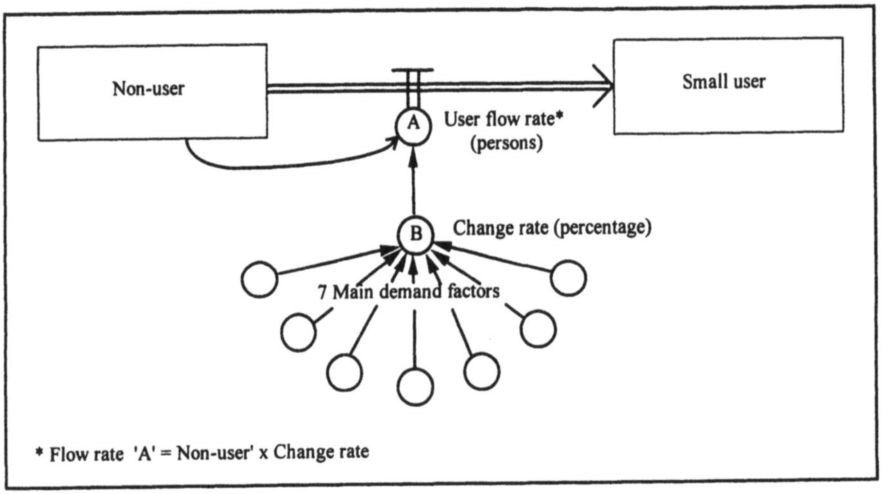

Figure 3 Relationship between user groups and demand factors.

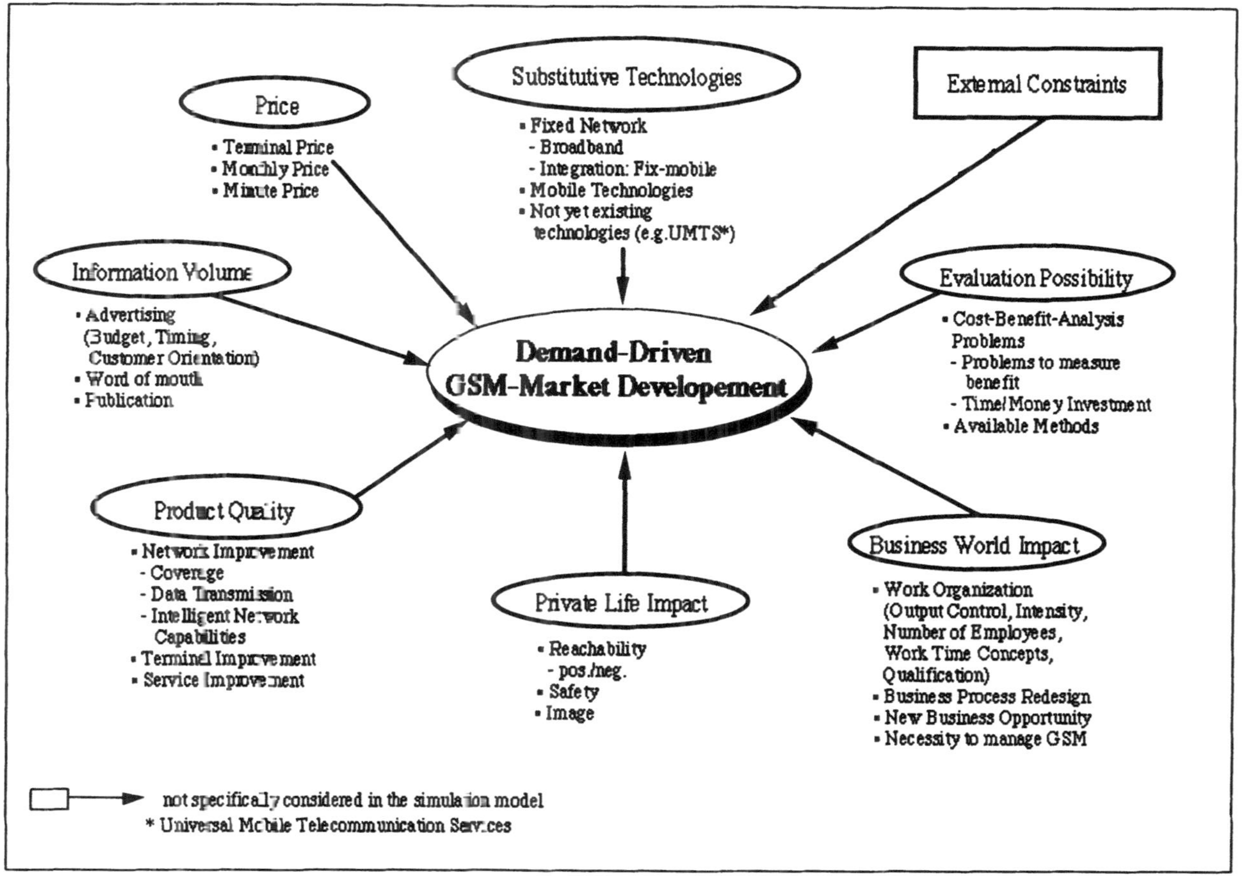

Figure 4 GSM demand factors and subfactor

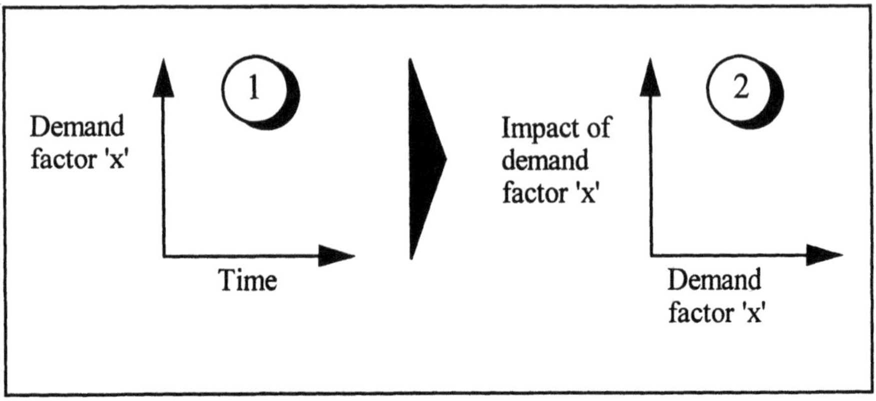

Figure 5 Two-step data gathering and modelling.

The complexity and richness of the DSS (21 stocks[1], more than 80 functional relations defined as graphs, and altogether more than 425 system variables) do not permit a comprehensive illustration and discussion, neither of the detailed modelling principles nor of the input data.[2]

3.4 Selected results

The simulation output could be displayed on various levels: (1) the relationship between any component (e.g., 'security needs') and the subfactors of that component (e.g., the impact of the 'security needs' on each of the twelve flows among user groups), (2) the comparative presentation of the importance of the seven main demand factors for any specific flow, and (3) the resulting overall number of users in each user group as well as the according GSM usage volume.

Figure 6a and 6b show the relative weight of the seven main demand factors for the 'flow' from 'non-users' to 'small users' over 54 quarters representing the years 1992 to 2005. In addition to the trends for each factor, the numbers attached to the vertical axis showing the minimum, maximum and mid-point values for each factor have to be taken into account.

1 Variables modeled as accumulations over time.

2 For a detailed description, see Loebbecke (1996) as well as for a shorter version Loebbecke and Bui (1994).

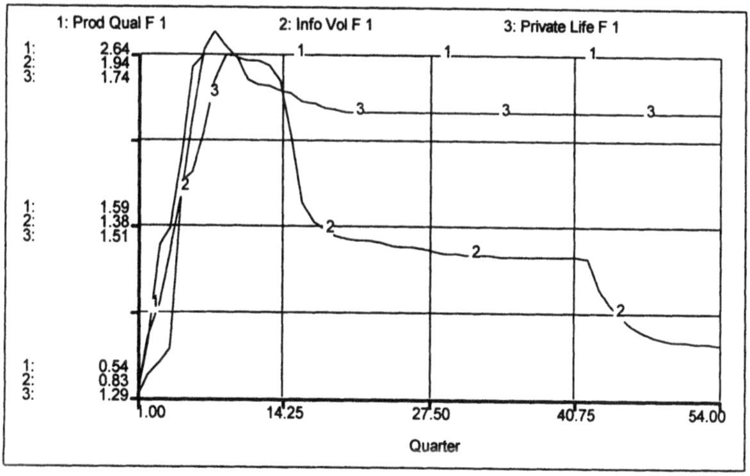

Figure 6a Basic Scenario: GSM main demand factors (1) - Germany 1992-2005.

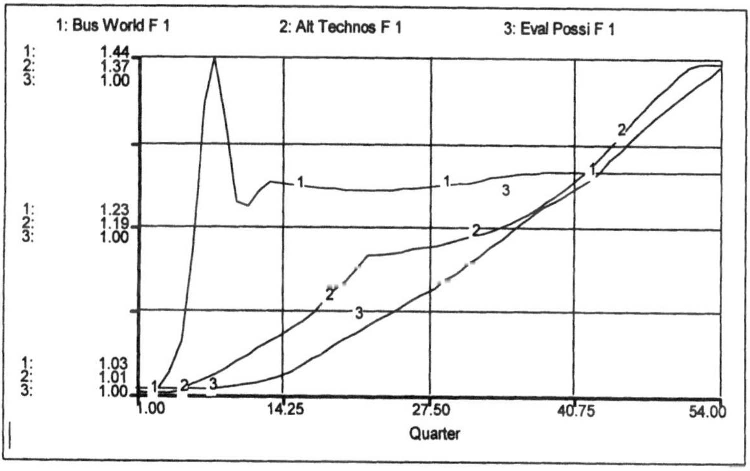

Figure 6b Basic Scenario: GSM main demand factors (2) - Germany 1992-2005.

The basic scenario developed for the German market predicts almost 20 million GSM users for the year 2005. It reveals a clear correlation between the number of users and the GSM monthly and minute price (see Figure 7a). The split of the users among the four groups and the resulting GSM usage is displayed in Figure 7b.

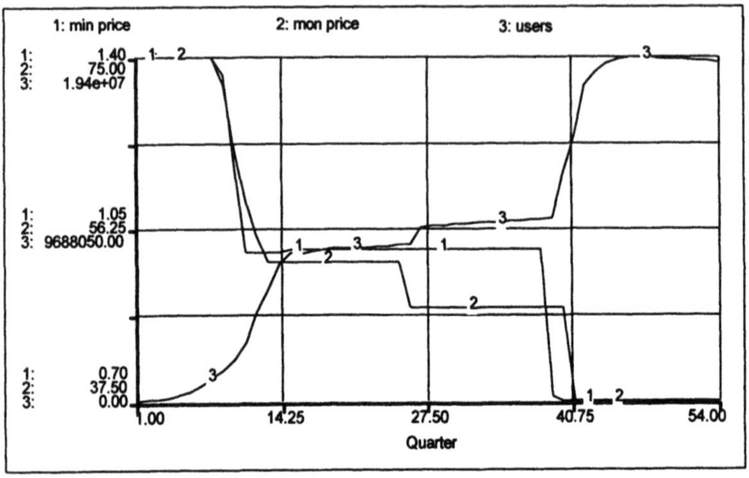

Figure 7a Basic Scenario: Minute price, monthly price, and number of users - Germany 1992-2005.

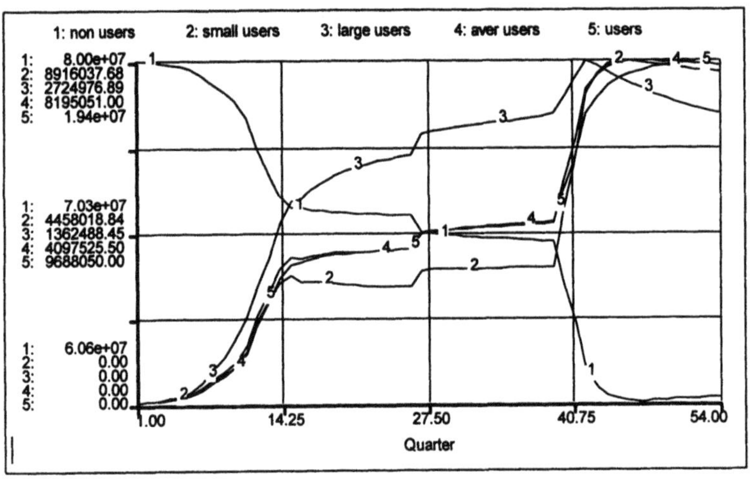

Figure 7b Basic Scenario: Number of users per user group - Germany 1992-2005.

To illustrate some of the dynamics explored and discussed during the design iterations, Table 1 lists four main scenarios and their results in terms of the total GSM user number.

Scenario 1a and 1b: Concerning the overall number of GSM users, reduced average prices for GSM lead to two main results: (1) the number of users reaches its maximum earlier than in the basic model, and (2) the overall maximum lies with 18.8 million people roughly 0.6

million users below the basic version. This second phenomenon certainly shows a counterintuitive outcome to be explained by the price sensitivity of the demand: Since both the minute and the monthly price reach their minimum values earlier, and thus do not allow for further price reductions, less 'upward steps' in the 'user curve' lead to a lower maximum number of users. However, as shown in the base case, these price reductions are even more important for pushing the GSM demand than the absolute price.

Scenario 2: Originally, the executives considered a growing use of alternative technologies (e.g., fixed network, individual satellite communication, DECT, etc.) to lower the demand for GSM. After several iterations and scenario discussions, they completely changed this structural assumption and assessed an increase in the use of alternative technologies to be complementary to an increase in the demand for GSM (embedded in the basic scenario). By totally neutralizing the factor 'alternative technologies', scenario 2 illustrates the impact of 'alternative technologies' for the overall number of users (and for all other demand factors).

Scenario 3: The last scenario in Table 1 depicts the possibility to consider more than the seven demand factors built in the basic DSS structure. It reflects on the political discussion in Germany to measure driving speed on highways and to charge drivers automatically (either for driving too fast, or for driving at all - as mentioned, it is a political discussion) and it illustrates the impact of such a political decision on the demand for GSM.

Table 1 Overview of Scenario Results (Loebbecke, 1996)

Scenario	*Conceptual focus*	*Main change versus basis version*	*Quarter with max. user number*	*Max. user number (million)*
Basic version	---	---	54	19,4
1	Main demand factors, GSM prices			
1a		Slightly lower average prices	31	18,8
1b		Even lower average prices	15 and 54	18,8
2	Basic factors (impact of demand components)	Neutralization of 'alternative technologies'	45	16,2
3	Additional external demand factor	Collection of traffic fees via GSM as additional demand factor	54	34,6

4 EXPERIENCES REGARDING DESIGN AND IMPLEMENTATION

At the beginning of the development and implementation efforts, the executives were briefed on the underlying DSS design concept and the computerized version of system dynamics functionalities. In particular, tools to test various assumptions and to reach a common mental model were introduced in an interactive manner. Each of the experts received a one-hour tutorial on a sample simulation based DSS focusing on the built-in system dynamics functionalities.

To facilitate the knowledge extraction process, DSS designers based their questions on the seven GSM demand factors shown in Figure 4. Knowledge extraction was conducted by protocol analysis using Forester's system dynamics graphical representation scheme. Due to the limited customization with the computer screen, model section and simulation results requested by the experts were printed and posted on the wall to support observation, reflection, design, and action (see also Loebbecke and Bui, 1994).

During the DSS design phases, the application of the system dynamics approach turned the meeting room into an active learning environment, where managers got engaged in the process of constructing and redefining their understanding of GSM demand. Experts began very early to simulate less complex real world problems. Thus, they got a better feel for the system dynamics approach and gained confidence in the design approach and its results.

Several progression tests were conducted. They began with the 'whole' system, and then systematically 'took the model apart'. The tests helped the executives understand how individual processes and interdependencies work, and why the processes interact in the way they do to generate market growth.

System dynamics proved to facilitate straight-forward thinking about processes involved in the generation of dynamic market behavior patterns without requiring high-level expertise in mathematics. Therefore, the DSS was easily accessible to most GSM executives that participated in the development effort.

After modelling their view of the evolution of GSM demand, subsequent exploration and experimentation helped the executives to develop a deeper, more critical understanding of the seven main factors involved, their interdependencies, and the consequences of their 'behavior patterns'. The various analyses provided by system dynamics during the DSS design led to a shared mental model for the group to collectively enhance its modelling perceptions of the dynamic decision situation.

A total of 59 iterative design sessions led to the 'final' version of the DSS structure. Within this structure, the executives ran about 100 simulation resulting in an evenly high number of scenarios. In many cases, however, a set of 'main scenarios' was derived after several iterations based on rather similar changes in the basic assumptions.

5 LESSONS LEARNED

The main benefits of the use of computer-based system dynamics as a modeling approach are (1) to derive a dynamic, operational model for decision support, and (2) to capture qualitative knowledge from a group of experts.

- The overall advantage of using system dynamics to analyze complex market interdependencies has become evident: Executives need not become proficient in solving differential equations in order to gain insight into the dynamic processes that permeate market cycles and the diffusion of innovative products.

  A difficulty of designing DSS in a dynamic environment lies in the modellers' inability to infer sufficient operational knowledge. With the built-in simulation capability, system dynamics allows to respond in new contexts that helps experts refine their view of the problem. As such, the output of a simulation run becomes the input to another one until a satisfactory DSS structure is achieved. The process of graphical and/or numerical presentation encouraged and supports the integration of various capabilities and the broad know-how of different group members (see also Bui and Loebbecke, 1996).
- Based on the assumption that 'two experts are better than one', opinions from more than one expert, whenever possible, contribute to 'better' decisions (Senge, 1990; Kaplan and Norton, 1992). The use of multiple opinions not only helps revealing different views of a given problem, but can eventually consolidate expert consensus. Together, the views can provide a comprehensive and holistic description of the problem (Bui and Loebbecke, 1996).

  By making the assumptions which constitute certain market forecasts etc. explicit, system dynamics allows to rigorously examine the thinking which underlies these assumptions. Once an executive's assumption has been rendered explicit, the thinking of other executives usually can be incorporated by modifying the initial specification. Among other advantages, this enables to determine whether executives are disagreeing about the existence of a particular relationship, or whether they are disagreeing about the strength of a particular relationship that they agree exists.

The experiences from implementing our DSS confirm that the development of a shared mental model and the provision computer-based cognitive aid, especially cognitive feedback, contribute to more accurate model assumptions and a higher degree of acceptance regarding the generated scenarios (Simon, 1991).

Finally, our work has proven two-level feedback to be valuable for the DSS users during their design and implementation efforts. First, feedback about the consequences of assumptions shows how accurate these assumptions are. Thus, outcome feedback allows decision makers as to adjust their assumptions and judgements (e.g., Hogarth, 1981; Tindale, 1989). Secondly, cognitive feedback fosters the awareness regarding the quality of decision processes. Hence, our research confirms the work by Doherty and Balzer (1988) who state that cognitive feedback is effective in improving the quality of decision processes by clarifying decision makers' intentions and by controlling the implementation.

6 SUMMARY AND FUTURE RESEARCH

The purpose of this paper is to advocate the use of computer-based system dynamics as an iterative modeling approach to integrate DSS design and the implementation for decision making in a dynamic context. The proposed approach has been successfully applied to the design and implemention of a system that supports strategic decisions related to the growth of national demand for GSM in Germany. It allowed us to take advantage of the opportunity to work with an interdisciplinary group of high-level experts from different GSM operators. Their know-how and views on the GSM market collectively promised a valuable source of knowledge. However, their expertise is still limited by the complexity and uncertainty of the telecommunication demand in the future and by the lack of historical data due to the infancy of the new technology.

This opens a number of research possibilities. Additional work is needed to explore the medium-term relevance of the designed DSS. To what degree will the actual use of the system depend on continuous mediation by external modellers? Furthermore, more research is needed to understand the relative importance of the different features embedded in system dynamics based DSS design (i.e., the different forms of graphical representation, the development towards a shared mental model, the provision of cognitive feedback through different information cues).

So far, the approach proposed in this paper was tested in a stand-alone computer environment. More design work is required if this approach is to be applied in a distributed network: How do decision makers develop shared mental models in a distributed and interactive environment? It will also be important to investigate the opportunities for system dynamics based DSS designs and the applicability of the resulting systems in different cultural and inter-cultural environments.

In spite of the intensive involvement of GSM experts, the proposed approach implies strong responsibility on the modellers' side (Szyperski, 1974). Further investigations are necessary to fully understand the impact of those development team members who come from outside the considered business sector (e.g., GSM), and, ideally, to find ways to neutralize their impact regarding the resulting decisions taken by the executives.

Responses to the research questions outlined here should allow further fine-tuning of the system dynamics based approach to design and implement DSS in complex and dynamic decision environments.

7 REFERENCES

Altobelli, C. F. (1991) *Die Diffusion neuer Kommunikationstechniken in der Bundesrepublik Deutschland - Erklaerung, Prognose und marketingpolitische Implikationen*, PhD thesis, University of Tuebingen, Heidelberg.

Baills, G. and Olivier, C. (1993) MIRZA, *Un Modèle Dynamique du Marché de l'Automobile*, Presentation to the Congrès AFCET (Association FranÁaise pour la Cybernétique Economique et Technique).

Balzer, W., Doherty, M. and O'Connor, R. (1989) Effects of Cognitive Feedback on Performance, *Psychological Bulletin,* 106, 410-433.

Boland, R.J., Jr., Trenkasi, R.V. and Te'eni, D. (1994) Designing Information Technology to Support Distributed Cognition, *Organization Science*, 5, 456-475.

Bui, T. and Loebbecke, C. 96) Supporting Cognitive Feedback Using System Dynamics: A Demand Model of the Global System of Mobile Communication, *Decision Support Systems*, forthcoming.

Buitenwerf, E. (1994) Third Generation Mobile Telecommunication Systems, *Mobile Communications International*, 18, 72-75.

A Study of the Analysis of the Introduction of GSM in the European Community (1990) Commission of the European Union, Brussels.

Mobilise - PSCS Concept: Definition and CFS - Preliminary Version (1992) *First Deliverable of the Mobilise Consortium, RACE Project Mobilise*, Brussels.

Doherty, M. and Balzer, W. (1988) Cognitive Feedback, *Human Judgement: The SJT View*, (eds. Brehmer, B. and C. Joyce), North-Holland, Amsterdam, 163-197.

Economic and Management Consultants International, Inc. (1993), *Digital Cellular: Economics and Comparative Technologies*, Washington, D.C..

Forrester, J. (1969) *Industrial Dynamics*, MIT Press, 6th ed., Cambridge, Mass.

Forrester, J.(1970) *Urban Dynamics*, MIT Press, 3rd ed., Cambridge, Mass.

Forrester, J. (1971) *World Dynamics*, MIT Press, Cambridge, Mass.

Forrester, J. (1972) *Grundzuege der Systemtheorie*, Gabler Verlag, Wiesbaden.

Forrester, J. (1987) Lessons from system dynamics modeling, *System Dynamics Review*, 3, 136-149.

Fourt, L. A. and Woodlock J. W. (1960) Early Prediction of Market Success for New Grocery Products, *Journal of Marketing*, 25, 31-38.

High Performance Systems Inc. (1994), Stella II - An Introduction to Systems Thinking, Hanover, NH.

Hogarth, R. (1982) On the Surpise and Delight of Inconsistent Responses, *Question Framing and Response Consistency*, (ed. R. Hogarth), Josey Bass, San Francisco.

Homer, J. B. (1987) A Diffusion Model with Application to Evolving Medical Technical Technologies, *Technological Forecasting and Social Change*, 31, 197-218.

Jagoda, A. and de Villepin, M. (1993) *Mobile Communications,* Wiley, Chichester.

Kaplan, R.S., and Norton, D.P. (1992) The Balanced Scorecard ñ Measures that drive Performance, *Harvard Business Review*, 70, 71-79.

Lewandowsky, R. (1974) *Prognose- und Informationssysteme und ihre Anwendungen*, Springer Verlag, Berlin.

Loebbecke, C. (1996) *Evolution innovativer Informationstechnologie (IT)-Infrastrukturen - Dynamische Simulation des deutschen Mobilfunkmarktes*, Metzler-Poeschel, Stuttgart.

Loebbecke, C. and Bui T. (1994) *A Comparative Study of GSM Demand for Germany, Hong Kong, and Vietnam*, Working Paper, The Hong Kong University of Science and Technology.

Lyneis, J. M. (1980) *Corporate Planning and Policy Design: A System Dynamics Approach*, MIT Press, Cambridge, Mass.

Mahajan, V. and Peterson, R. A. (1978) Innovation Diffusion in a Dynamic Potential Adopter Population, *Management Science*, 24, 1589-1597.

Mahajan, V. and Peterson R. A. (1985) *Models for Innovation Diffusion*, *Sage*, Beverly Hills.

Makridakis, S. (1990) *Forecasting, Planning, and Strategy for the 21st Century*, The Free Press, Macmillan, New York.

Makridakis, S. and Weelwright S.C. (1973) Quantitative und technologische Methoden der Prognosen und Planungssysteme, *Vortraege zur Marktforschung, 20/ 21*, (eds. K. Holm and A. Haeger), Bundesverband deutscher Marktforscher e.V., Hamburg.

Milling, P. (1990) Time - A Key Factor in Corporate Strategy, *System Dynamics '90,* (eds.D. Andersen et al.), *Proceedings of the 1990 International System Dynamics Conference*, Boston.

Morecroft, J. D. W. (1986) The dynamics of a fledging high-technology growth market: Understanding and manging growth cycles, *System Dynamics Review*, 2, 36-61.

Morecroft, J. D. W. (1992) Executive Knowledge, Models and Learning, *European Journal of Operational Research*, 59, 9-27.

Morita, A. (1985) *Made in Japan, Akio Morita and Sony*, E.P. Dutton, New York.

Newell, A., Rosenblum, P.S. and Laird, J.E. (1989) Symbolic Architectures for Cognition, *Foundation of Cognitive Science*, (ed. E.D. Posner), MIT Press, Cambridge, Mass.

Paich, M. and Sterman, J.D. (1993) Boom, Bust, and Failures to Learn in Experimental Markets, *Management Science*, 39, 1439-1458.

Phan, D (1992) The Diffusion Process of Value Added Services on a Telecom- munication Network: The Example of French Videotex Services on 'Kiosque Teletel', *9th International Conference 'Telecommunications Bridge to the 21st Century*, Sophia Antipolis, France.

Radzicki, M. J. (1993) Dyadic processes, tempestuous relationships, and system dynamics, *System Dynamics Review*, 9, 1993, 79-94.

Roberts, E. B. (1978) System Dynamics - An Introduction, *Managerial Applications of System Dynamics*, (ed. E.B. Roberts), Cambridge, Mass.

Senge, P. M. (1990) *The Fifth Discipline, The Art and Practice of the Learning Organization*, Doubleday, New York.

Sengupta, K. and Abdel-Hamid, T. (1993) Alternative Conceptions of Feedback in Dynamic Decision Environments: An Experimental Investigation, *Management Science*, 39, 411-428.

Sengupta, K. and Te'eni D., (1993) Cognitive Feedback in Group Decision Support Systems, *MIS Quarterly*, 87-113.

Simon, H. (1979) *Models of Thought*, Yale University Press, New Havwen, Conn..

Sprague, R. and Carlson, E. (1982) *Building Effective Decision Support Systems*, Prentice Hall, New York.

Sterman, J. D. (1989) Modelling Managerial Behavior: Misperceptions of feedback in a Dynamic Decision Making Experiment, *Management Science*, 35, 321-339.

Szyperski, N. (1974) Forschungsstrategien in der Angewandten Informatik, Konzepte und Erfahrungen, *Angewandte Informatik*, 16, 1974, 148-153.

Tindale, R.S. (1989) Group vs Individual Information Processing: The Effects of Outcome Feedback on Decision Making, *Organizational Behavior and Human Decision Processes*, 44, 454-473.

Veit, K. P. (1978) System Dynamics and Corporate Long Range Planning, *Managerial Applications of System Dynamics*, (ed. E.B: Roberts), Cambridge, Mass.

8 BIOGRAPHY

Claudia Loebbecke received a Master in Business from the University of Cologne, Germany, an M.B.A. from Indiana University, USA, and a Ph.D. in Business from the University of Cologne. She was an Associate Consultant with McKinsey & Co. in Germany, as a Research Assistant at the European Institute for Business Administration (INSEAD) in Fontainebleau, France, and as a Research Consultant at the Hong Kong University of Science and Technology (HKUST).

Tung Bui currently holds joint appointment at the U.S. Naval Postgraduate School, Monterey, California and the Hong Kong University of Science and Technology. He earned his PhD in Managerial Economics from the University of Fribourg, Switzerland and a PhD in Informations Systems from New York University. Dr. Bui is currently the Director of the PRIISM (Pacific Rim Institute for Research in Information Systems Mangement) consortium.

19

Ethical imperatives in Decision Support Systems design

Andrew McCosh
Department of Business Studies, The University of Edinburgh, William Robertson Building, 50 George Square, Edinburgh EH8 9JY Scotland. Tel: 0131 650 3801, fax: 0131 668 3053. E mail: a.mccosh@ed.ac.uk

Abstract

The paper addresses the need to build ethics into the process of designing decision support systems. Two examples are offered, in which the essential concept of a DSS is changed considerably when the priniciples of ethics are applied, taking the decision models far beyond the basic quantitative and economic variables customarily employed. Ethical concepts are described first, and their applicability to DSS design is then demonstrated.

Keywords

Ethics, Decision Support Systems, Investment Appraisal Theory

1 INTRODUCTION

The tradition in DSS design work has always been to ensure that the quantitative aspects of the problems are handled with care and correctness, and to ensure simultaneously that the user groups and other affected personnel within the organisation are satisfied by the services which it enables them to provide. This paper contends that there is need to go beyond this. In some instances at least, it is necessary to go beyond getting the sums right, and beyond ensuring the supportiveness of the insiders who have to work it, to the stage of establishing that the system gives answers which are morally sound.

2 WHAT IS A SYSTEM?

The word system has had the misfortune to become fashionable, and it is therefore used to mean all sorts of things. The word is in decline as a precise scientific concept. This is a shame; it is a very useful word to describe certain specific combinations of people and of artefacts. I shall define it below; this definition is very similar to other cybernetic definitions.

A system has a series of attributes. These include (1) its membership list, (2) its purposes or functionality, (3) its self-controlling procedures, and (4) its mechanisms for finding out what is going on around it. We shall look at each of these in turn.

A system has members, and therefore also has non-members; it is possible, at any given moment, to list the members. There may be a mechanism for new members to join, and there may be a mechanism for existing members to depart, but this is not essential in all systems. In the present paper I shall be confining myself to that subset of systems in which some of the members are human: at the same time, it should be appreciated that the theory of systems does not require this attribute.

A system has functionality. A system is created in order to fulfil some need. Hobbes has shown (Hobbes, 1898, and also Kavka, 1986) how primitive humans in a 'state of nature' create a communal system for their own protection and to reduce the number of people they have to fight. The Apollo system, which had computer, rockets, and people as principal components, was created to land a man on the moon. A church (in the sense of a denomination) is created to enable like-thinking worshippers to promote their views and to worship the way they want to. It is sometimes convenient to look at a church as a system. A market is certainly a system, and each market is itself a component in a larger system of interacting markets. The functionality of a market is to enable people to enhance their material welfare by gaining access to goods and services they cannot make (or make as well) themselves. In each case, there is a goal to be fulfilled.

It is not unusual for a system's functionality to change, especially when it is new. There may be an initial formal goal for the system, which moved people to set it up, and perhaps to pay for setting it up. There may be a significantly different official or formal ultimate goal for the system, which is what it is officially trying to do when it reaches its stable state. Almost certainly, there will be an array of by-product consequences of the system's operations, which may be helpful to the fulfilment of its main goals, may hinder them, or may totally obstruct.

The World Bank and IMF, for instance, were set up by men of the highest integrity and the best of intentions, to assist less developed nations in catching up economically with the remainder. It actually became an economic 'body shop', into which wrecked economies were towed, to be hammered back into something resembling the right shape. This process works quite well for advanced and basically sound 'Mack Truck' economies, which have got into temporary difficulties. The hammering process is not so appropriate for inherently weak 'Trabant' economies, which just cannot absorb the structural adjustment blows. The hammerees generally are unhappy about this process, mainly because they had previously had a perfectly workable (albeit horsedrawn) economy before the salesman came along with the new supercharged model, but failed to tell them it could not be expected to stay on the road with a learner driver. The stated goal was to push progress into locations where market forces would not have pushed it, and to promote growth where the markets would not have promoted it. It appears the market was right, in that the side effects have (in some instances) caused more damage than the intended goals have caused benefit.

It is important to note that the functionality of a system is not a permanent and unchanging one. A true cybernetic system contains, within itself, procedures for monitoring how it is getting along, and how far it is fulfilling its function. The monitoring subsystem will have the capacity to make adjustments to the way the system operates. Above the monitoring system, there will be a metasystem which monitors the viability of the present set of objectives, with powers to amend these if need be.

This hierarchy of control systems can be carried to any level one may desire, but it is unusual for any system containing humans to have less than three to five layers, and it is similarly unusual for a system without humans as members to have more than two or three layers. (Beer, 1979)

In every important instance, there is a cyclical process in a system. The activity of the system takes place. The amount that has been achieved is appraised. The monitoring system considers whether this is good enough, or whether changes are needed. The changes, if any, are put into position. The activity of the system takes place again. And so it goes on.

The sensors through which a system checks its environment are the fourth set of attributes mentioned above. These may perhaps be best illustrated by a conspicuous failure. The IBM company was so hierarchical, so ponderous, so inwardly focused, and so committee-bound that it took twelve years after it had successfully entered the microcomputer market before it worked out that these little but powerful devices would affect its mainframe business. They are only just beginning to recover from this severe sensor failure now.

A number of important theories have been developed about systems. The most important, at least for the present purpose, are those developed by Ashby (1957) and by Beer. Ashby, especially, has shown that the system you need to control another system has to be at least as complex as the system it is supposed to control. This point is vitally important, as we shall see below.

When we discuss a Decision Support System, I take that to be a special case of the general man-machine system discussed above. The combination of the people and the machinery has functionality, as all systems have, but this functionality is especially designed to enable a particular class of decisions to be taken. The literature on DSS design and development is well developed, and there are many effective models for the design process and for the proper implementation of the resulting systems. The papers by Ferioli and Migliarese, by Berztiss, and by Brezillon and Pomerol, all in this book, are good examples of the processes involved. The mission of the present paper is to suggest that, for some situations, it is not quite enough to tackle the problem this way. We need, in some but not all cases, to take formal account of ethical issues if we are to provide a genuine and enduring support to the decision makers we are seeking to serve and to the publics which they, in turn, are trying to help.

In most instances, it will be shown that the ethical dimension of DSS design and implementation will involve us in a deeper search for the people who will be affected by the decision we are about to construct and to implement. It is not enough just to take account of the manifestly affected. We must consider the people, and the environmental dimensions, which are less directly involved at the outset, but who may be affected ethically as the implications of the decision unfold.

3 WHAT DOES 'ETHICAL' MEAN?

There are at least five topics within the overall task of being ethical. To be ethical, we must be fair, we must look after our own interests, we must guard the interests of others, we must meet our obligations, and we must be willing to be subject to the same rules as we seek to apply to everyone else. There are other aspects of morality, but they seem less likely to impinge on problems of DSS design.

3.1 The dimension of fairness

The dimension of fairness has been at the forefront of ethical writing since the earliest days. In the Nicomachean Ethics (Aristotle, Ross ed, 1980) the great man, writing about 350BC, devotes half of book five to the topic of justice, and it is clear that he holds justice, lawfulness, and fairness to be close relations. The task of a judge, in cases of rectification, is often one of restoring to the aggrieved party a 'fair' share of whatever was in dispute. Indeed, the word for judge and the word for 'bisect' are nearly the same; that is the task the judge performs. A hundred and fifty years earlier, Confucius (Fung, 1948) had addressed the same kinds of problem, and had arrived at a very similar answer.

There have been contributions on fairness from a large number of writers since then, but we will 'fast forward' to the present. John Rawls ideas seem very mechanistic, in general, but he does offer a useful definition of a fair system (Rawls, Bedau ed, 1969) when he states that it ought to be based on a pair of rules under which (1) each person has the most extensive liberty compatible with the same liberty for everyone. This seems very reminiscent of Kant's universal principle of justice. Rawls second rule (2) requires that social and economic inequalities be arranged to be for everyone's advantage, and attached to positions everyone could aspire to. Midgley has complained (Midgley, Eliott ed, 1966) that Rawls' ideas are insufficiently humane, by simply omitting anything resembling compassion from his writings. This criticism seems valid; the Rawls items I have read are seriously too legalistic. At the same time, his idea of granting rights of aspiration to, and access to the routes toward, prosperity is a good example of what the word fair means in its financial manifestation. Rawls might also argue that compassion is inherently unjust. If we give someone something out of compassion, they have no right to it (presumably), so justice is not being done. Love or brotherhood, perhaps, but not justice.

On the intensely practical side, for many years now, company auditors have reported that an account showed a 'true and fair' view of the firm's financial condition. Until it fell into the hands of the lawyers, and was reduced to being the summation of an assortment of pronouncements by very variable judges, 'true and fair' was a very clear concept. In addition, it was clear that it was not a precise concept. The profit reported was one of a range of numbers within which range all competent evaluators would agree the true profit lay. If the firm tried to report a profit outside that range, the report would be qualified. The principle was based on prudent judgement and fairness to all parties, and, as Kavka points out 'Rules of conduct grounded in prudence and reciprocal in form, connect with two of the most ubiquitous and reliable of human motivations, rational self-interest and a sense of reciprocity or fair play'. (Kavka, 1986, P310)

In discussions with people in the business communities, Barry (1979) established that the concept of fairness was the central essence of what they thought business ethics was all about. When pinned down, the business people tended to formulate their interpretation of fairness in business in terms very like the silver or golden rule.

In building a DSS, it is surely a vital element to look ahead, to see what conflicts might arise, to consider whether we might be deemed, by public opinion, to have dealt unfairly with people. There are situations in which this is a definite risk, and it is then essential that we should design our DSS so that it will flag a warning of a possible future difficulty, whether of public relations, or employee relations, or even of law.

3.2 The dimension of self

There is considerable agreement that everyone has an obligation to look after himself. This is different from being selfish, a word which is never used in English without a negative connotation which implies that you have failed to contribute your fair share to some common activity. The self is a very important creature to the majority of ethicists, and is to be looked after with considerable care and thoughtfulness. The idea of self-love has been in use at least since Aristotle, but the name seems to have been introduced by Bishop Butler, and comes in a range of available temperatures.

The Bishop (Butler, Darwall ed, 1983) proposed a 'cool and settled selfishness' from which interested actions could proceed, and contrasted this with a 'passionate or sensual selfishness' which resembled a desire amounting to lust for power, honour, or the good or ill of another person. Butler points out that the people need to have love for themselves and also to have love for others. He uses the word benevolence for that, and we will consider it further below. A man will follow courses which will do him good directly in himself, and also that will do good as a citizen, and by the first he will benefit the public by being a more useful contributor and by the second he will benefit himself by increasing society's regard for him. We need both, in his lordship's view. We have an obligation to think ahead and to behave with reasonable caution, because God gave us (but not the other animals) a brain to do that with and we deserve censure if we fail to make good use of it {Sermon 2. Para 10}. God also supplied a conscience in each person which governs and over-rules (if need be) all the other appetites. This is perhaps most explicitly set forth in another book, the Dissertation on the Nature of Virtue (Butler, Carlsson ed, 1964), where the Bishop defines prudence as a 'due concern about our own interest or happiness, and reasonable endeavour to secure and to promote it.'

Thomas Hobbes was active before Butler, and was rather more of an enthusiast for self-love. If Butler favoured a cool version, Hobbes' was too hot to touch. 'The right of nature, which writers commonly call jus naturale, is the liberty each man hath, to use his own power, as he will himself, for the preservation of his own nature; that is to say of his own life; and consequently, of doing anything, which in his own judgement, and reason, he shall conceive to be the aptest means thereunto.' (Hobbes, Sneath ed, 1898, Of Man, Chapter 13).

A third version of self-love is offered by Immanuel Kant, who serves it up on ice. According to Sullivan (1994), he instructs us to regard ourselves as a valuable human being, with capabilities to be developed, just like everyone else. We should not treat other people any better than we treat ourselves. We have a strong moral obligation to build up our own capabilities. This is what he means by treating our abilities with dignity, which means we have to work hard to enhance and to develop them as far as they can be made to go.

The categorical imperative, which is the fundamental ethical instruction Kant issued, is provided in three forms. The second of these, which is the one favoured by Pope John Paul II (La Barge, 1990), states that we have a moral obligation to act so as to treat humanity, whether in the form of our own person or of any other person, always as an end, not as a means. (Sullivan, 1994). The instruction appears to instruct us to treat everyone with respect, which may seem uncontroversial, but also to treat everyone equally, which could easily be interpreted in a misleading way.

The concept of self-love is therefore considered carefully by a number of important writers in the ethical field, and it is clear that we are expected to pay attention to our own welfare as well as to that of others. It must be admitted, as a matter of practice, that the problem of under emphasising our own interests has not been a very major problem in DSS design problems I have been involved with, or have observed over the years. All too often, the idea of self-love, in some kind of corporate format, has been the only explicit goal.

3.3 The dimension of unselfishness or humaneness

Every document calling itself ethical has a prescription in it somewhere that encourages the reader to think of other people besides himself. There have been a range of texts, and a wide variety of recommendations on the importance of this dimension of ethicality. It is the aspect of ethics which is the most controversial in business situations.

The controversy is not confined to business situations. There is a very broad range of opinion among philosophers on this matter. At one end of the spectrum, there are the universal love advocates, led by Mo Ti (Jochim 1980) and Jesus Christ, both of whom would have us love our enemies as well as our friends. At the other end, there are the earthier philosophers like Hobbes, Machiavelli (1993), and Mandeville, who take the whole idea of self interest very seriously indeed. As tends to be true with most spectra, there is a very large group in between, who offer an almost infinite variety of options.

It is contrary to the nature of a business negotiation to adopt the universal love principle. The executive who tried to do unto others as he would like them to do unto him will wind up giving away his shareholders' entire company.

The views of Hobbes and Mandeville are much more likely to enable a business negotiation to occur. Their views involve sympathy to those in need or in distress, but a powerfully self-orientated approach in other cases.

Bernard de Mandeville alleges that all the apparently virtuous actions we take are actually prudential or selfish actions in disguise. In a rather marvellous doggerel saga-poem accompanied by some hilarious but occasionally scurrilous notes, (Mandeville, 1989), suggests that the unselfish actions of people are nothing more than cunningly manipulated acts of self-interest. The manipulators are 'dextrous and skilful politicians', who manage to turn the vices of the citizens to the public benefit. To my view, the important bit is that he says a person should get no credit for virtuous action, because he has only engaged in that action because of some selfish motive. The man who gives to charity in public, the soldier who is brave from fear of shame, and others are really the victims of a vast conspiracy by the powers that be to achieve the goals of unselfishness from a totally selfish company.

Hobbes had a rather minimalist view of unselfishness, which Kavka (1986, p347) called the 'Copper Rule' to emphasise that it was neither Gold nor Silver. 'Do unto others as they do unto you' he suggests. By all means extend the right hand of fellowship to the other side. You must sincerely try to maintain a moral covenant. But if the other lot back out, you are free to hit them with all the ammunition available. You are certainly not under any obligation to continue to abide by a covenant the other side is obviously not going to stick to.

Thomas Hobbes, despite his apparent role as bete noir of ethical philosophy, had a characteristically robust view about what to do to people who refused to help the needy (Hobbes, Leviathan, Ch15). 'A man that by asperity of nature, will strive to retain those things which to himself are superfluous, and to others necessary, and for the stubbornness of his passions, cannot be corrected, is to be left or cast out of society, as cumbersome thereunto. For seeing every man, not only by right, but also by necessity of nature, is supposed to endeavour all he can to obtain that which is necessary for his conservation; he that shall oppose himself against it for things superfluous, is guilty of the war that thereupon is to follow'. He goes on to say that the state is responsible for making sure that those in need are looked after; they should not be left to the charity of individuals.

In building a DSS, and indeed in handling many other kinds of business transactions, it is the comment of Hobbes which should be in our minds. It is just not good enough to harm those who cannot defend themselves by means of a routine business transaction, in which we simply did not think through the problem enough to realise the damage we were doing. It seems reasonable enough to be fairly tough in business-to-business dealings, subject to obligations (see below), but we ought not squash people who cannot fight back. As DSS designers, the adoption of this moral requirement adds a serious additional item to think about to our already well-laden list.

3.4 The dimension of obligation

In philosophy, an obligation is something we ought to do, but may refuse to do. Ross (1970) suggests we may upset a few people, or even quite a lot of people, by failing to meet our obligations, but the choice to refrain from fulfilling them remains totally in our own hands, and failure to meet them need cost us nothing, not even a sleepless night. Individuals acquire obligations from their roles. As father, I ought to take my son to a football match. As a company director, I ought to give clear guidance to my various managers. As a bishop, I ought to encourage my vicars in their ministries. I acquire the obligations by having accepted the status. In the case of a company, obligations are acquired by signing contracts, but also by making informal promises. A company may even acquire obligations by the simple passage of time. If a firm has financed the village brass band for the last sixty years, it has an obligation to go on financing it.

It is not uncommon for people to feel more strongly bound by an obligation than they feel bound by a legal contract. There is a substantial difference in behaviour among nationalities here. The real issue is communitarianism. If I am a part of a community, I will conform to its rules. Moreover, if I fail to conform to the rules of the community, I will expect to be ostracised or penalised in some other way. This is a powerful conformative force.

Every person, and every entity, needs to be part of at least one system each and most of us are part of dozens. It is partly a matter of prudence. Loners get "picked off", while herds and tribes live on, and so do most of their members. It is partly a matter of foresight. A co-operator will get system help in time of need, a whinging isolate will be left to whinge even as he failed to help the rest. Long-term far-sighted egoism entails trust in other system members. Long-term far-sighted egoism may even entail occasional heroic suicidal action, where the "self" being preserved is "man's own nature". Hobbes set that equal to his life, but it could be his progeny. Or her progeny. The best way to look after number one is to persuade others to behave in a long-term far-sighted egoistic fashion, and to do the same yourself. Some will be persuaded on grounds of duty, some on grounds of benevolence, some on grounds of prudence. Use whatever will work to promote system loyalty, obligation, and support. On historical evidence, egoism is the easiest to "sell", and long-term far-sighted egoism is only slightly harder.

As DSS designers, we are at a disadvantage on this topic. The problem is that we do not, in general, know what obligations the company or person we work for has taken on. Sometimes these are phrased very loosely, and this can come across in incredibly loose terminology when the instructions are being drafted for a new DSS. The only way to cope with this is by means of a series of questions to try to ensure that we do not miss anything large.

3.5 The dimension of universality

Immanuel Kant's famous categorical imperative (Kant, Abbot Translation, 1946) required universalisability before a maxim was allowed. We are prevented from using a maxim unless we would be prepared to require everyone else to stick to it too. Universalisability is a reasonably straightforward, rather stringent, screening system for weeding out policies which fail in some way to support the mission of not making the inequality situation worse.

4 EXAMPLE (A) A DSS FOR FACTORY RELOCATION:- EXPANDING OUR HORIZONS THROUGH SPACE

We have now looked at the essential ingredients of ethicality, and it is time to try to show how this new dimension can be employed in the typical DSS situation. We will look at a capital expenditure model for factory location in this section, and then at a capital expenditure model for natural resource management in part five. It will be shown that we must expand our horizons. In part four the horizon expansion is through space as we consider the impact of the change on communities in many places. In part four the horizon expansion is through time, as we consider the impact of the natural resource exploitation activity on future generations.

The DSS models we use in handling capital expenditures are very well defined. Unfortunately, because they are highly quantitative in character, they usually miss out some very important parts of the computation. We know quite well how to carry out the net present value calculations, and how to determine the cost of capital and how to estimate the cash flows. There are a few minor controversies on these issues, but by and large the finance community considers the problem pretty completely solved. It is not a contention of this paper that the finance community does these sums wrongly in the mechanical sense. Instead, it is my contention that they forget several important elements of the computation completely.

It is a common occurrence for a multinational company nowadays to consider moving a factory from one country to another, or perhaps moving the production of a product group, so that an old factory is no longer required. When we are working out whether this would be a good move or not, the usual computations show certain labour costs as being discontinued (usually involving a redundancy payment), certain other labour costs as commencing, and various other costs being incurred for the physical movement of various tools from one site to the other. The normal computation would also show that the material costs, being drawn now from a different source, have changed, and that the costs of transportation of the final product have changed. Obviously, the expectation is that the proposed move will only take place if the net present value of the differential cash flows of the project after tax are positive when discounted at the company's after-tax cost of capital. This process is well understood.

The problem is the omissions. I have had an opportunity to examine quite a number of these DCF computations in several companies (45 in 8). The cash flows as stated above are shown, but the cash flows associated with the true costs of winding down the old plant in a humane and ethical fashion are definitely not estimated well. The only recognition that the employees are being laid off is the budgeted figure for a legally required redundancy payment. In some cases, even this is omitted. There is, typically, nothing in the sum which talks about the costs associated with the outplacement service. There is not likely to be any mention of the costs incurred by the company in helping the community to attract new employers. The costs of assigning a good, and rather expensive, manager to the community to help it get over the shock is not included in the DCF sum either.

The reader may say that it is quite in order, mathematically speaking, for these items to be missed out. If the company was not planning to incur these costs, and was really planning to head for the foreign site without taking any of these steps to alleviate the problems caused by the move, the sums they are doing, as described in the last paragraph, are a true and fair reflection of what is going to happen. That point is certainly accepted. We may not like them much, but at least they are doing their sums aright.

My ethical complaint is different. What is usually happening is that the multinational actually goes to quite a bit of trouble on these matters. A good down-sizing manager is sent in to help out. The local outplacement industry is mobilised at the company's cost. Extensive costs are incurred at the site being left which were not included in the capital budgeting analysis. Why do I complain about this, then? Surely if the company is being as helpful as this, there is nothing to get excited about, and we should all be rather grateful that the company is doing its best to help?

The problem is that the omission of these costs from the budget on which the decision was based biases the decision in favour of moving. The costs of moving out of the old site are systematically underestimated. In some instances, the costs of opening up the new site are even more seriously underestimated. I took the trouble to work it out in one instance, the only instance where I could get any figures for these items. The result in that particular instance was to reduce the decision to move to a net present value of zero from a net present value of (about) a quarter of the cost of the machinery being moved across. A zero NPV still indicates that the action should be undertaken, but it would be very hard to justify the move in view of the management time and trouble that had to be expended to obtain such a minimal reward.

Do I then have any ethical complaint on this topic? I believe so. Case (1) is where the company does not carry out these remedial tasks, and does not budget for them, in which instance it is getting its sums right but is failing seriously in the morality of its actions, as discussed earlier when we looked at the moral injunctions, for instance, of Kant (1954). The company may be said to failed on humaneness and on meeting its moral obligations. It is difficult to tell whether it can be criticised for unfairness; this rather depends on employment alternatives in the community they are leaving. Case (2) is where the company does carry these tasks out, but does not budget for them, and therefore exposes itself to the risk that it has made the wrong decision. This is less likely, but is an even more agonising situation. The firm in this case has failed to look after the dimension of self-love, and may have violated its obligations to its own shareholders. Only in Case (3), when the company takes the actions after budgeting for them, is the situation in ethical balance.

My specific request is that the DSS models which are so commonly deployed for capital investment decision support, especially for evaluating situations in which employment levels will be changed, perhaps simultaneously in several different points in space, should be augmented to take account of the ethical realities. A company which takes its decisions on one set of criteria and actually behaves according to another set is taking serious ethical risks, and also serious prudential risks.

5 EXAMPLE (B) A NATURAL RESOURCE MANAGEMENT PROBLEM:- EXPANDING OUR HORIZONS THROUGH TIME

The second DSS example we will look at is another capital expenditure analyser, which carries out the same computation as the one we have just looked at, but which is normally written to a different design to deal with the special situation of a natural resource company such as a forest products group or a mining concern.

In this situation, the problem of disrupting the lives of people and indeed of entire communities is commonly present in mining projects, but we will not consider this again as it has been covered well enough in the discussion of section four. Instead, we will consider the need to cope with the demands of morality by expanding our planning horizons through time. Far too often, in this kind of situation, the DCF sum is carried out over a very short planning horizon, and this can have an appalling effect on the environments, both physical and human.

It would be helpful to consider an example of this problem. The general corporate tendency, and even more generally the governmental tendency, is to assume that the period of time over which a project should be assessed is the length of time the machine will last. If we are going to buy a computer to perform a particular task, and the machine will be useable for six years, then the cash flow computations are done over the six year period. Occasionally, the decision may be taken to assume that we will get another machine after the first one fails, in which case the decision is computed over twelve years, but that is done so seldom that it could almost be ignored. If the project is going to generate sales revenues which increase steadily over time from a low base to a stable state in year ten, which is not an uncommon pattern, the futility of stopping the analysis in year six becomes obvious.

Table 1 - Illustrative figures for Example B

Year	*Machine*	*Net Sales* 14%	*Net Cash*	*DCF Factor* 12%	DCF	*Total DCF* to date
0	-7500		-7500	1.00	-7500	
1		1000	1000	0.89	893	
2		1140	1140	0.80	909	
3		1300	1300	0.71	925	
4		1482	1482	0.64	942	
5		1689	1689	0.57	958	
6		1925	1925	0.51	975	-1898
7	-7500	2195	-5305	0.45	-2400	
8		2502	2502	0.40	1011	
9		2853	2853	0.36	1029	
10		3252	3252	0.32	1047	-1211
11		3252	3252	0.29	935	
12		3252	3252	0.26	835	558

In this table, we can see that the total net present value to the end of year six is -1898, which suggests that we should not engage in the project. By the end of year twelve, the net present value has gone positive, which suggests that we should engage in the project. Obviously, I have concocted these numbers to make them come out that way, but the problem is very real. Time and again the procedures manuals and the decision support models in use for capital projects have been based on the wrong time horizon, and I have to report that in 35 years of looking at this kind of issue I have not yet seen a British company or an American company use a time horizon that was too long.

In the case of decision support systems, the usual error is that the model is constructed with a fixed format, so that everything has to stop at an arbitrary date, which is often at the end of year ten. In the example above, the project would still have been looking negative (npv =-1211) at that stage. This DSS defect is, however, not my main concern. It is an error, and a serious one, in terms of evaluating the economical situation soundly. In this paper we are concerned about the ethical situation to a greater extent.

The ethical problem is very nearly the same in appearance, in that it depends on the use by the DSS of too short a time horizon. The essence of the problem is different, though, because a large proportion of the ethically important items get missed out altogether because of this.

The morality issue which usually arises in a mining situation is morality through time. If we sink a shaft, drive tunnels hither and yon, and extract non-renewable natural resources then we are obviously making a choice which will affect all future generations. The oil, or the coal which we take out will not be available to them. If we are mining for gold or diamonds, the assets are more permanent, and the assumption may fairly be made that no restitution needs to be made for the actual product. In both instances, however, the territory surrounding the mine may be permanently damaged, and we have an obligation to repair that or to render the mine safe in some other way. There are parts of the tin mining areas of Cornwall which have had to be permanently sealed off because a millennium of digging has left the land in a completely lethal state.

If the natural resource company is dealing with renewable resources, the situation is potentially less devastating, but we still need to handle the DSS design problem very carefully. If a timber stand is felled, and the timber is put to sound economic uses, the territory can be either left to regenerate or it can be actively replanted. There is controversy as to how this should be done. Active replanting immediately after a felling has been criticised as likely to damage the land for a very long time. Leaving the land for a couple of years and then replanting was the favoured option when last I had the change to discuss the matter with a Forestry specialist.

The consequence of this, of course, is that the DCF calculation must be done with a very long time horizon indeed. The entire production cycle varies from one species to another, but let us suppose a stand matures in fifteen years. The planting takes a year, growing takes fifteen, felling takes one, two years fallow, and restart. A grand total of nineteen years. There is no point in doing the DCF computation for any smaller period than that. If we fail to take these reconstitutive charges into the account, the chances are that someone will simply try to walk away at the end of the felling, leaving the place to do its own regeneration. It is little short of miraculous how well nature has hitherto managed to cope with this behaviour, but there are limits.

If we are going to handle the situation ethically, we need to recall the need to be fair, and to meet our obligations. In this instance, the obligations are to the next generation, or the one after that. As a general rule, in renewable natural resource DSS design, it would make sense to establish a regulation that the time horizon must equal the growth interval plus five years.

In the case of non-renewable natural resources, the time horizon is extremely hard to predict. The mining company will be hoping the mine will last forever, and most people will completely agree with them. The only way to handle the need to build a restitution fund in this situation is by means of a levy on the cost of the mine, which is used to build a capital sum which can be used by the local government to put the land back to its original format after the mine stops. If the mine is a failure, there may not be enough in the kitty to restore the land, but there will at least be something to alleviate the situation.

Although this section has been written in the context of mining companies, there is reason to believe that DSS designers working for routine manufacturing or service businesses should think in terms of long horizons as well. It is only necessary to look around the derelict buildings which clutter every city to appreciate that the termination sequence of a plant, or project, or company was not taken into consideration.

There are very strong practical reasons why this was so. The man who started the business had no intention of ever stopping. The company, in his dream, would go on for ever, and would eventually be a mega-business managed by his great-grand children. Making provision for cleaning up the mess after it folded would never enter his head. Also, when, at some future date, the business got into difficulties, and when it became increasingly obvious that there was a serious risk of collapse, the capacity of the firm to make an provision for cleaning up would be very seriously impaired. In the last few years before a corporate collapse the managers usually engage in all sorts of rather desperate manouevres to keep the show on the road, each of which consumes a portion of the ever-shrinking resource base. Closing the place down while there is still enough to give everyone a decent payout happens very rarely indeed. Accordingly, it is suggested that there is a need for the local authority or some similar government agency to take a role, building a fund for each business out of revenues raised from it, which will enable the restoration of the status quo ante.

From the point of view of our main concern, the ethical aspects of DSS design, the issue is one of fairness from one generation to the next, and of meeting obligations. We may not have a legal obligation to restore the land on which our factory has been sitting for fifty years, but there is a very strong case to be made for a moral obligation. It is a contention of this paper that DSS designers have a professional obligation to consider, in each instance, whether issues like this are applicable to the DSS they are working on.

6 CONCLUSIONS AND ACTION RECOMMENDATIONS

In moving toward the formulation of my conclusions I would like to introduce two more powerful authorities to set the scene. They are Adam Smith (1969) and W Ross Ashby (1957). Everyone knows about Adam Smith, as the inventor of economics and especially of the "invisible hand" which makes markets operate. However, my reason for citing him is the other major work he wrote, which makes clear that the invisible hand cannot work unless the society in which it is placed is stable and humane. Ross Ashby contributed the separate but valuable insight that a system cannot be controlled except by another system possessed of the requisite variety, which normally means the control system will be as complex as the original one.

Adam Smith wrote two books which should be read together. Too often the only work of his that is quoted is the single paragraph about the invisible hand which guides the butcher and others to serve up dinner. In fact his two main books were his lecture notes for two of the four segments of the same university course, and ought to be taken as a totality.

Smith's Wealth of Nations is one of the most famous texts ever written. His Theory of Moral Sentiments (Smith 1969) is less well known, probably even less often read, but it has a very powerful message too. You really cannot understand the picture in the Wealth of Nations unless you place it in the frame of the Moral Sentiments. This is a long book, because it explores, most elegantly, the byways of all the meanings which the virtuous words and the vicious words can take on, and explains why one is more or less meritorious than another. The role of conscience, the authority of the general laws of morality (3.5), and the importance of self-control (4.2) are all discussed at sufficient length that even the slowest of his undergraduate students would probably have got the general idea.

The main point is that he was setting forth a very coherent and detailed set of assumptions about the kinds of behaviour that he expected people to engage in. The invisible hand which appears in the Wealth of Nations to serve up dinner, appeared also (fifteen years earlier) in part 4 of Moral Sentiments, this time in the role of sharing the landlord's crops out equally amongst the population. Those criticising Smith's writings seem to be founding their complaints on a single paragraph, and ignoring the very specific, interpersonally ethical, relationships which he consistently promoted, and within which setting the business operations in Wealth of Nations were to be assumed to be set.

It seems to me that we have a comparable situation now, a quarter of a millennium later. The technically elegant scheme (Smith's economics) could only work reliably in the defined social context (described in Smith's book on morality). In our own day, we have to set our technically elegant DSS designs and plans in as sound a framework of the total social context as can be arranged, or they may well give us strange, and perhaps shocking, results.

The second topic is on the dimension of control. A very important work in cybernetics was the pair of books by William Ross Ashby on the design specifications for a brain. In this he drew up an effective proof of a most significant theory of cybernetic control which is a rather complex concept, but which has a very simple result. He called it the 'Law of Requisite Variety'. If you have a complex system with N dimensions to its complexity, you cannot control its behaviour unless you have a control system which also has N dimensions to its complexity. As a simple example, consider a car. It can travel at a speed from (let us say) -30 to 110 miles per hour, where a minus speed entails reversing. It can be aimed, at any given moment, a few degrees to the left or to the right of its existing course. There are two dimensions of complexity, and you therefore need two dimensions of control. Obviously, these are the accelerator/brake/gearchange system and the steering wheel respectively.

When you consider more complex systems, the problem of creating a control system becomes much more serious. A system which resembles a company has a very large number of dimensions of control. Attempts to list them have never been very successful, but they would include product line range, production methods, region serviced, region from which supplies are drawn, people employed, and customer groups sought. Each of these may be subdivided in certain instances where this becomes important. The task of creating a control system is made more complex because the firm has to ensure that there is a control system for each of these dimensions, and also that there is a control system which achieves co-ordination among them. The task is probably solvable in most cases at the level of a company, though there are many instances where the task has not actually been solved at that level. When we try to add the attainment of ethical standards to the list of dimensions, there will be need for a further set of control measures to help the system understand whether it is meeting its own standards or not. Very few company level systems have even tried to deal with this dimension so far.

With that introduction to the conclusion, let us move to its statement. It is shown in figure 1. Across the top are to be found the features which systems, including DSS, all possess or ought to possess. Down the side are aspects of ethics, which are dimensions I am contending we, as DSS designers, ought to be thinking about in some situations, and certainly in a lot more situations than we actually do think about them. Diagrams are always somewhat blunt instruments, but the main point is that the area of our normal concentration of effort in DSS design work is the small, tadpole-shaped area in the middle.

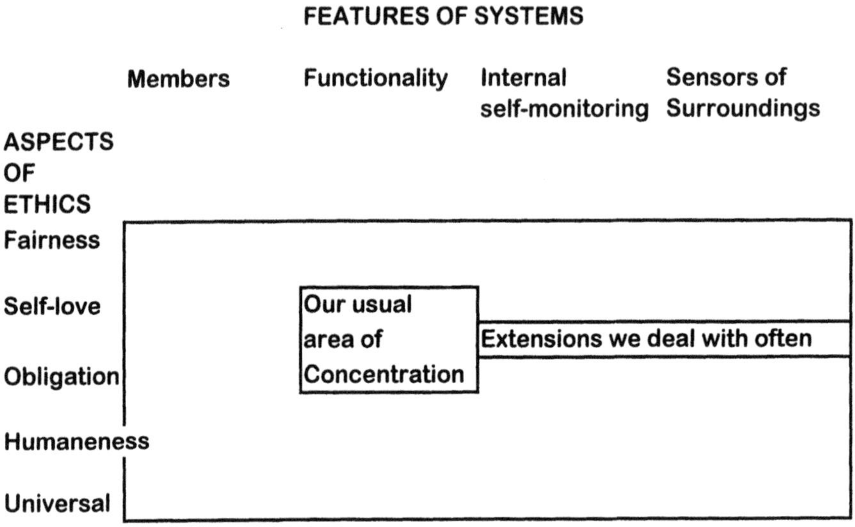

Figure 1 - The Features of Systems and The Ethical Aspects which we typically handle well, and which we typically handle badly.

I think we can reasonably claim to do a good job of handling the functionality of our models, and that we are doing a good job of coping with the ethical requirement to be prudent and look after our own interests. We also do a good job, if the corporate bosses remember to tell us about them, of dealing with the obligations which our company may have to other firms. We also, I am suggesting, do a good or at least fair job of handling self-love and obligation as ethical aspects of our design work of the monitoring systems we build into DSS for their internal cybernetic management, and we spend a lot of effort on data-gathering and on extracting knowledge from experts to enhance our designs.

There is a large territory in the diagram which we do not often deal with. I am prepared to believe that, if we worked at it for a while, we would be able to find instances of DSS which dealt with almost every box on the chart. At the same time, I feel secure in claiming that much of this territory is severely under-explored. The column about membership is conspicuously empty. We deal with membership from a rather narrow viewpoint, counting ourselves, our fellow employees, our company's customers, and perhaps our company's suppliers as the universe of discourse. What about the people we do not or will not sell to? What about the people we do not or will not hire? Sometimes, I concede readily, these are irrelevancies, but I hope I have shown earlier that they are not always.

The other areas in the diagram which are under-explored are the rows labelled by the ethical terms "fairness", "humaneness", and "universality". Taking the first two together, I am suggesting that we just do not have a way of handling these dimensions at the moment. It would be theoretically possible to write a DSS which exhibited justice if you could tell it what was just in its particular milieu. It might even be possible to write a DSS to support the same decision which exhibited humaneness. However, a DSS that tried to do both would probably develop symptoms which could be anthropomorphised as executive stress. To be humane, it would have to give at least one person more than their entitlement, which is unjust (Rawls 1991). It is not suggested here that the handling of these dimensions of ethics needs to be included within the DSS itself, but that these dimensions of morality should be considered during the design process in order to meet the point made by Adam Smith above, that there is a context within which the system will work, and it probably will not work in a different one.

The last point is universality. Immanuel Kant instructs us to adopt rules of behaviour only if we would be satisfied that they should apply to everybody. At the present time, it would be only very slightly unfair to suggest that our maxim for the production and design of decision support systems is that "we will undertake to make systems which work well in functional terms, which can be adapted to new circumstances, which incorporate sensitive sensors about environmental change, and which are orientated towards our corporate profits and meeting our obligations, especially legal ones, and which do not take any account of what this does to the rest of the world's population of people, plants, or animals or their successors into the future". Is that really what we mean? Is it really what we want to mean? I am contending that it is what we are actually doing, by default.

7 REFERENCES

Aristotle (1980) *The Nicomachean Ethics.* Oxford UP, Oxford.

Ashby, W.R. (1957) *An Introduction to Cybernetics.* Chapman & Hall, London.

Barry, V.E. (1979) *Moral Issues in Business.* Wadsworth, Belmont, California.

Beer, S. (1979) *The Heart of Enterprise.* Wiley, New York.

Butler, J. (1983) *Five Sermons preached at the Rolls Chapel and a Dissertation upon the Nature of Virtue,* {ed. Darwall, S.L.}. Hackett Co, Indianapolis, USA.

Carlsson, P.A. (1964) *Butler's Ethics.* Mouton and Co, Hague.

Fung, Y. (1948) *A Short History of Chinese Philosophy.* Macmillan, New York.

Hobbes, T. (1898) *The Ethics of Hobbes, as contained in selections from his Works.* Ginn & Co, Boston, USA.

Hutcheson, F. (1971) *Illustrations on the Moral Sense.* Mass Belknap Press, Cambridge.

Jochim, C. (1980) Ethical Analysis of an Ancient Debate:- Moists versus Confucians. *Journal of Religious Ethics* **8** (1): pp 135-147. Univ of Tennessee, Knoxville, TE, USA.

Kant, I. (1954) *Kant's Ethical Theory.* Oxford, London.

Kant, I. {Abbot, T.K., translator} (1946) *Fundamental Principles of the Metaphysic of Ethics.* 10th edn. Longmans Green, London.

Kavka, G.S. (1986) *Hobbesian Moral and Political Theory.* Princeton UP, Princeton, NJ, USA.

La Barge, J. (1990) Economic Systems and the Sacramental Imagination. In: Gower, J.F. (Ed.) *Religion and Economic Ethics*, pp. 151-172. University Press of America, Lanham, Maryland, USA.

Machiavelli, N. (1993) *The Prince.* Wordwort Reference, Ware, Hertfordshire, UK.
de Mandeville, B. (1989) *The Fable of the Bees.* Penguin Books, London.
Midgley, M. (1966) Duties concerning Islands. In: Elliot, R. (Ed.) *Environmental Philosophy*, pp. 171-185. Univ Queensland Press, St Lucia, Queensland, AU.
Rawls, J. (1969) The Justification of Civil Disobedience. In: Bedau, H.A. (Ed.) *Civil Disobedience*, pp. 240-255. Pegasus, New York.
Rawls, J. (1991) Definition and Justification of Civil Disobedience. In: Bedau, H.A. (Ed.) *Civil Disobedience in Focus*, pp. 103-121. Routledge, London.
Ross, R. (1970) *Obligation: A Social Theory.* Univ Michigan, Ann Arbor, MI, USA.
Smith, A. (1969) *The Theory of Moral Sentiments.* Arlington House, New Rochelle, NY.
Sullivan, R.J. (1994) *An Introduction to Kant's Ethics.* Cambridge Univ Press, Cambridge UK.

8 BIOGRAPHY

Andrew McCosh has been a member of IFIP since 1984. He was professor of management accounting at Manchester Business School from 1971-1985, and Dean of the Faculty for part of that time. He was professor of finance at Edinburgh University from 1986-1995, and Head of Business Finance, Accountancy and Economics for part of that time. He has published forty papers and seven books on systems and on finance.

20

Towards Active Management Information Systems

P. Mertens, J. Hagedorn, M. Fischer, N. Bissantz, and M. Haase

Bavarian Research Center for Knowledge-Based Systems (FORWISS), Am Weichselgarten 7, 91058 Erlangen-Tennenlohe, Germany, Tel.: ++49-911-5302-264, Fax.: ++49-911-536634, E-mail: mertens@wiso.uni-erlangen.de

Abstract

With Active Management Information Systems (Active MIS) we delegate more responsibility to the system. Different types of Active MIS are arranged in a framework that is defined by two scales. We focus on one of the scales, namely the intensity of user interaction, which also serves as the guideline of the paper. At the same time we give examples to illustrate how Active MIS can contribute to the solution of a user's problem.

Keywords

Active Management Information Systems, Data Mining, Critiquing, Navigation, Addressee-Orientiation, Automatic Reporting

1 INTRODUCTION

Computer-assisted management information originally meant printing masses of paper ("number cemeteries"). Analyzing the sales department of a company producing ballbearings we found that each manager received an average of 23 reports a day. Their Management Information Systems (MIS) were totally system-driven.

Meanwhile we have mastered dialogue, hypertext, and hypermedia systems. Vendors of EIS offer the features shown in Figure 1 (left). From their customers they expect the characteristics listed on the right hand side which seems to be far from reality, at least as far as top managers are concerned.

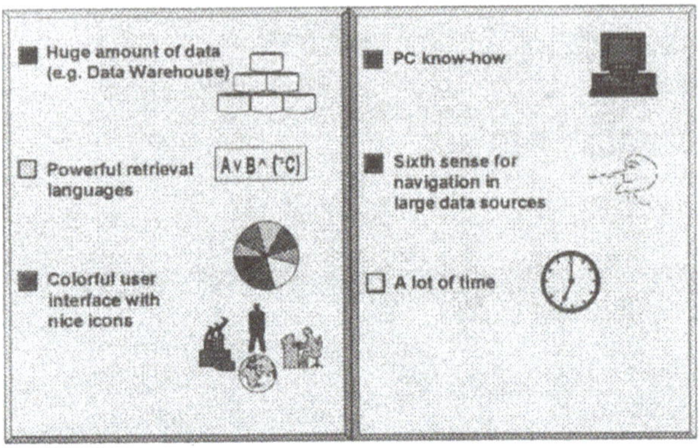

Figure 1 Features and requirements of MIS software

This kind of MIS is fully user-controlled and often result in very time-consuming dialogues, e.g. with a lot of windows opened, menu-entries selected, hotwords clicked, etc., and finally the user might end up being "lost in space".

For that reason we need another paradigm called Active MIS which means that we delegate more responsibility to the system. The ultimate goal is to get reports where

- the selection of critical information from huge databases and data warehouses is the task of the system, not that of the manager,
- the presentation of this information is automated as well, and
- the presentation style considers the decision tasks and the personal preferences of the addressee.

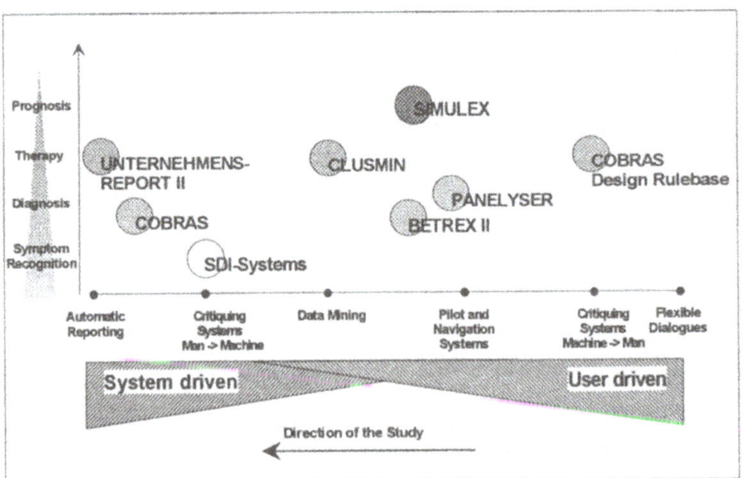

Figure 2 Overview

Figure 2 shows the structure of this paper. Starting from the state of the art, which is interactive MIS, at the right end of the scale we will go back step by step to the goal on the left hand side. We will pass several "stations" which at the same time mark the chapters of our paper. Some innovative examples of Active MIS (prototypes and running systems) that we have developed with German companies from several industries will be outlined. Moreover we will try to overcome techniques where only facts are presented in order to diagnose weaknesses: we want to progress to a stage where we can give therapy suggestions, and then even forecast the impact of the means chosen. Some hints to actual research tasks ("white spots on the map") are given.

2. CRITIQUING SYSTEMS (MACHINE > MAN)

Critiquing Systems offer many degrees of freedom to the user. They only interact when a mistake occurs. They can be compared to an observer with special domain knowledge who is able to give a decisive hint at the right time.

The example we describe below was developed in cooperation with the Bavarian Research Center for Knowledge-Based Systems (FORWISS) and GfK AG, Nuremberg, the leading German market research institute.

Besides other kind of research results the institute provides retail audit data to track the market development, especially the analysis of time series, such as the sales volume of a product line in varying distribution channels. After the comprehensive survey of the data, the latest research results must be presented to the clients of the institute in a few days. Therefore, more automation is welcomed.

System Description: COBRAS

There is a new system now, called COBRAS (Client Oriented Branch Reporting and Analysis System), that supports the market researcher making presentation slides. It simulates the market researcher's working methods and provides know-how about many different analysis types, presentation structures, the design of graphical representation, the preferences of user and client. With the help of that knowledge the Active MIS is able to generate a presentation - automatically or interactively.

At this point we want to draw attention to the critique-component of the system that advises the user when selecting the right visualization technique.

The knowledge consists of general guidelines for business graphics, Corporate Identity recommendations and expert know-how of the market researchers. For example the following rules are part of that knowledge:

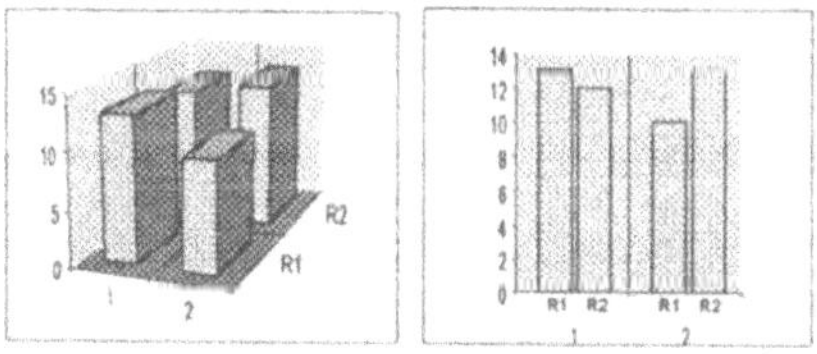

Rule example 1:

If a third axis is needed, it should be integrated in the x-axis using groups (Figure 3).

Figure 3 Rule example 1

Rule example 2:

If the diagram consists of more than 16 columns, its type should be changed into a line diagram (Figure 4).

The rule base gets active as soon as a presentation chart form is filled with new data. For each form a default value is given, especially because it helps to understand the user's intention. Based on this the design component of COBRAS checks, if the default value is adequate, criticizes if necessary and takes on the task of fine formatting, such as labeling axes and data items with the appropriate letter size and position.

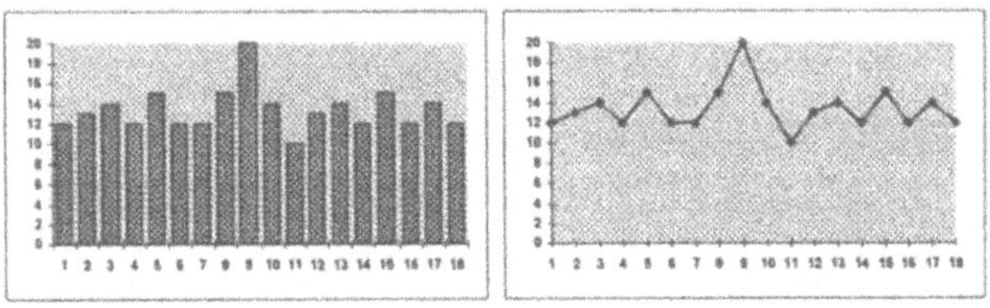

Figure 4 Rule example 2

3 PILOT AND NAVIGATION SYSTEMS

At the International Conference on Economics / Management and Information Technology 1992 in Tokyo Nobel prize-winner Herbert Simon was the keynote speaker. He pointed out the following aspect:

"Information is not scarce. What is scarce is manager's time to attend to all the information that is available."

It may seem trivial, but the following speakers picked up these words again and again - symptom enough that there might be an existing drawback of information systems. The escape attempt to inform managers only on basis of aggregated data is dangerous because of possible compensations at low or medium aggregation levels. But these have to be recognized. Therefore, we'd like to quote Simon again:

"Information systems are best viewed not as providers of information, but as filters for information."

What we really need are systems which support us to filter the enormous data sources, help to navigate or pilot through the data floods, and to cover the information needs of the addressee.

PANELYSER is an example for a pilot system that has been developed in cooperation with the GfK as well. This application acts as an intelligent front-end system that supports the market researcher in accessing the GfK databases and creating a management report.

System Description: PANELYSER

Like COBRAS the system PANELYSER focuses on retail audit data, but also considers data about promotion activities. A multitude of retail outlets supplies the market research institute with information concerning sales, purchases, stock levels, prices, and promotions. The extrapolated data provide more concise information through different aggregation levels and through calculated ratios such as market share or numerical distribution. Therefore, the analyzer is able to run detailed analyses of the market "success" of special product variations in different market segments.

The knowledge of a product group's structure that is necessary to aggregate the retail audit data is stored implicitly in the database. PANELYSER analyzes product group by product group (e.g. Color TV). The short-term analysis always deals with the current period like February/March 1996 in comparison to the corresponding period of the year before. In contrast, the long-term analysis usually handles periods of the last four years.

The whole application combines an expert system for the data analysis with a graphical user interface.

By a top-down analysis, PANELYSER attempts to locate the most interesting market segments, such as brands, retail channels, product segments, regions, etc. PANELYSER looks for the causes and compensating effects on every level of the analysis path. The central focus of the market analysis is based on the absolute change of sales units. To find out the objects that are most responsible for the market development, the system applies an algorithm using the "ABC"-analysis.

Once PANELYSER has found where the market development has occurred, it continues the top down analysis (Figure 5). The system starts with objects that have influenced the examined development most and arranges them in a descending order (Step 1). Step by step the system now accumulates the values for the objects until the sum of sales value rate surpasses a threshold (Step 2). A second threshold further reduces the objects to those that are truly significant. In addition, the system selects objects with considerable relative changes of sold units, so that the market researcher's attention can be directed as well to "small" brands that enter the market (Step 3).

For every "significant" object the analysis path is continued. The result is a widely branched analysis tree that mirrors all important changes in the market from the top to a special product or even a variant of it.

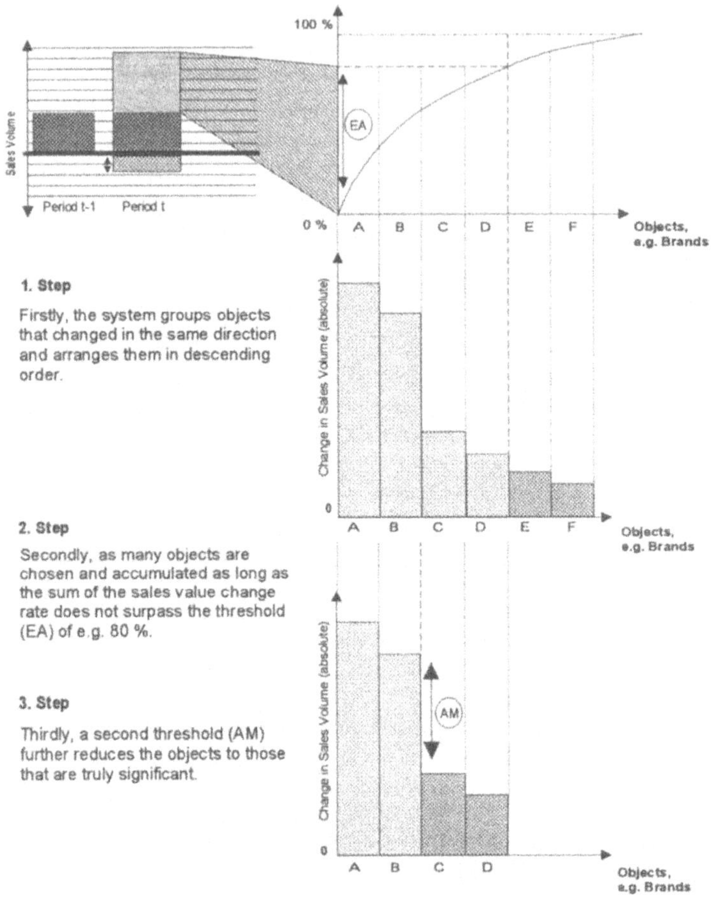

Figure 5 Significance thresholds of PANELYSER

Only the significant objects found in the short-term analysis are further examined. It is very interesting whether the development is subject to a trend or whether it happened to be a "blip". The visualization of the market share development includes hints to special events. A hyperlink (Δ-sign) draws the user's attention to promotion campaigns, etc.

The market researcher normally wants to find *why* sales have shifted. A database that combines retail audit and consumer panel data provides a substantial amount of information to answer those questions. For example, the reason for an increase of a product's market share can be attributed to a decrease in product price, a better distribution ratio, more promotion campaigns, or a combination of several marketing instruments. The system has to analyze whether more households buy a special product for the first time and how many households buy only that product. One method to assist the analysis is the Parfitt-Collins-algorithm (Parfitt, 1968).

The results are presented in a verbal report, by hypertext and dynamically generated business charts.

Figure 6 shows how PANELYSER generates varied text by a lot of different components like the random text generator, the grading functionality, the product group-specific definition database, and the analysis results.

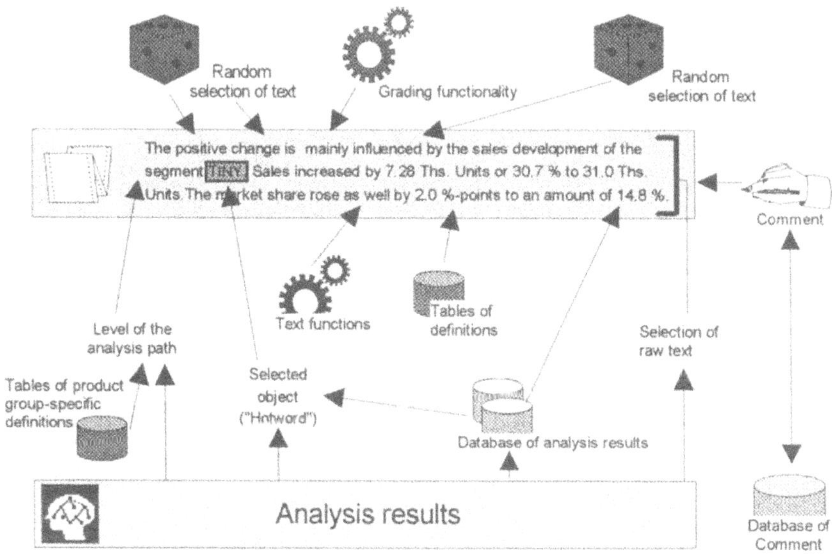

Figure 6 Text components

PANELYSER shortens the time necessary for the analysis of a product group from two or three days to a few hours.

Analysing Profitability Data

Modern software packages for accounting and controlling provide extremely large databases that can be queried on-line and in an ad hoc manner. To facilitate data analysis, available software tools support simple querying and multi-dimensional views. Managers, however, are left alone with detecting the most interesting data constellations.

In the statement of operating results a short-term analysis on profit or loss is completed to discover profit contributions of objects, such as individual departments, customer groups or products. Imagine a company that sells three product groups in several regions to different groups of customers. While product managers for example want to know the actual sales by product in each region, they also need to compare actual sales to projected sales. As examination of performance continues, perspectives may change, and additional views are required. Figure 7 shows example reports and the multi dimensional model they are based on. For thorough examination controllers must navigate through vast and complex hierarchies which may hide important facts deep in the data.

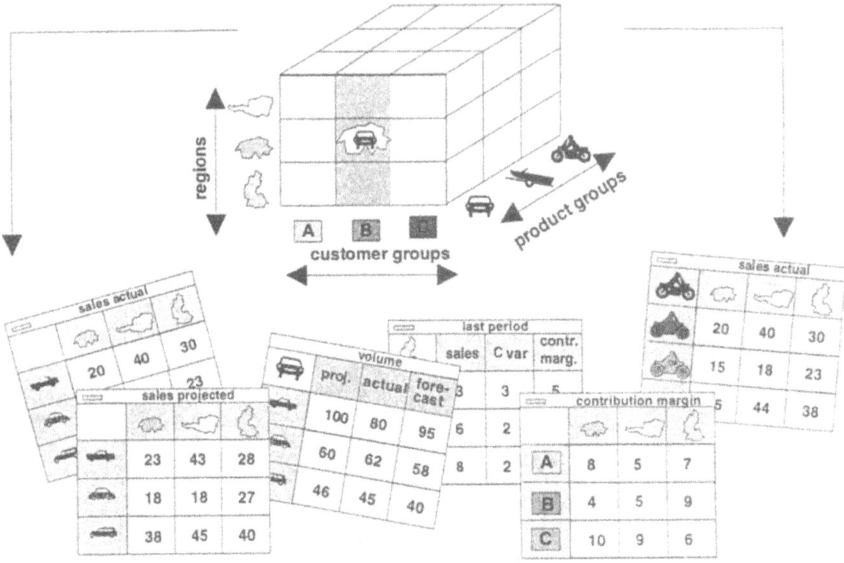

Figure 7 Operating results reports

As a consequence, sweeping changes could remain undetected for a long time. Therefore, we see two important challenges for IS research. First, tools are needed that help controllers to cope with the traditional task of finding the best way through results hierarchies. Second, algorithms may be useful that are capable of automatically extracting meaningful patterns in an unprecedented way. The latter is also known as the task of knowledge discovery, a new and promising research field that has attracted a lot of interest in recent years (Stonebraker et al., 1993).

System Description: BETREX

In the BETREX project, we incorporated algorithms attacking both problems in one system. The research was done in cooperation with the Technical University of Dresden, Germany, (Prof. Dr. W. Uhr). BETREX is designed to generate management summaries from operating results data.

The evaluation of the operating performance is based on key figures referring to objects which are described by classifying criteria. There are basic figures, such as quantities, sales, costs, computed ratios (profit contribution, sales per agent, etc.) and nominal attributes, such as region, product, or salesperson. The structure of a database is defined by the existing criteria and attribute values. Figure 8 depicts items of operating results accounting. Each item of the database represents one order item of a customer invoice, plus additional information, for instance from master data. This organization allows multi-dimensional views and reports. To give an example, a report about sales per customer group would require sorting by the criterion "customer group" and aggregating of the according figures.

characteristics 1-7							values 1 - 5				
mountain	mounty star	south	WS	Abele	900	5.1.93	1000	80	100	150	670
mountain	summit pro	north	Re	Frank	5000	9.1.93	3000	150	110	450	2290
mountain	summit pro	south	WS	Keller	800	8.1.93	1000	50	80	240	630
street	turing machine	south	Re	Maier	1100	7.1.93	1000	50	100	250	600
street	city star	south	WS	Abele	2300	5.1.93	1250	82.5	180	300	707.5
product line	product	region	customer group	customer	order no.	date	gross sales	sales deductions	commissions	prime cost	contribution margin
criteria							key figures				

Figure 8 Operating results data

Navigation Method

The navigation filter of BETREX, as mentioned above, imitates how human controllers would try to find their path through operating results hierarchies. Analysis typically starts with some variance on a highly aggregated level and continues with examinations on different disaggregated levels.

Figure 9 depicts the mode the filter works with example data of a company selling bicycles.

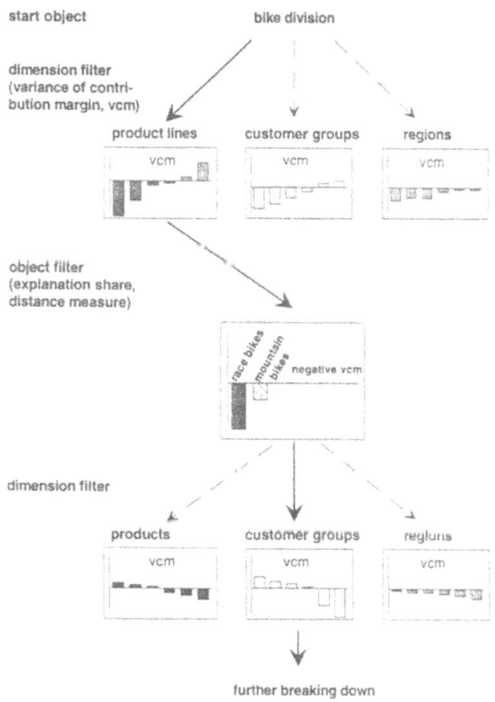

Figure 9 Navigation filter

First, the controller chooses a start object. If none is selected, the system itself selects a start object based on the report addressee's area of responsibility. The objects which are the main cause for the out-of-line situation can be hidden in every dimension available. Therefore, the system must decide on one of three possible hierarchies for the first step of analysis: products, customers, regions.

$$\sigma = \sqrt{\frac{1}{n}\sum_{i=1}^{n}(x_i - \bar{x})^2}$$

Figure 10 Navigation measure

Every bar in the picture represents the variance of a single object in the next subordinated hierarchy, for instance product line one. Generally speaking, the fewer objects cause the variance, the more likely it is that the dimension is responsible for the out-of-line situation in business reality. Accordingly the hierarchy selection is based on a measure that is similar to statistical standard deviation and increases over the objects of every dimension with rising deviation (Figure 10).

In our example, the dimension product lines is selected as the divider. Next, we must decide on which objects the analysis is to be continued. This is done by using a so-called object filter that works with an explanation share and a distance measure. Basically, the system traces a pre-defined explanation share of the variance (e.g. 80 %) of the higher level in each case. However, to avoid analyzing too many objects, the list is pruned when the difference between two objects falls below the threshold determined by the distance measure (e.g. 50 %). This process continues until the variance is explained sufficiently, or no further hierarchies are available.

The system analyzes both the causing and the compensating objects. Furthermore, each object on the navigation path is examined. The system detects changes in product and customer structure, important differences between objects on the same level, and effects on objects on higher levels of the hierarchy.

Case Study

We tested our algorithms with data from a pharmaceutical company for example. The data represented sales of two periods for a certain division of the company. The data volume was about 10,000 records. We will concentrate on the most interesting finding that is achieved in dialogue with the system in about 15 minutes.

The system starts with proposing to look at the dimension product groups. This proposal is made due to the deviation over the elements of this dimension. As a matter of fact, the element product group FBM explains 87 % of the profit contribution deviation on the division level. (In the picture several steps of analysis are omitted for better understanding.) The system searches its way through the hierarchies and stops after four iterations telling the user that 70 % of the profit contribution deviation are caused by the object customer group 10/article 99938.

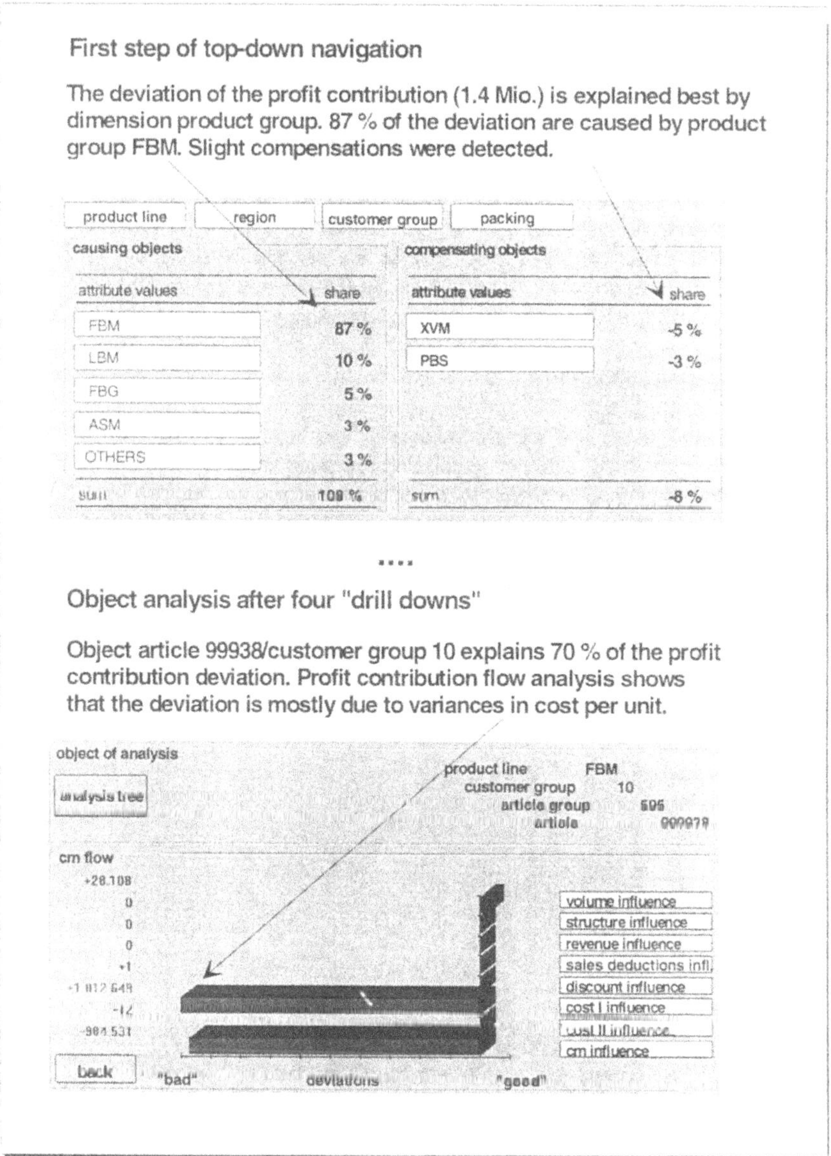

Figure 11 Case Study

Incidentally in the meantime a FORWISS project was to integrate a large part of the top-down navigation concept into the module CO (**Co**ntrolling) of the SAP-System R/3. The functionality will be available in the latest release 3.0.

System Description: SIMULEX

SIMULEX will just be mentioned in this context since - within our framework (Figure 2) - it is an example for an MIS that has some capabilities to recommend an action and to forecast its impact. So we make some progress on the path from symptoms to diagnosis, therapy, and prognosis. If the production control detects a disturbance (symptom), because a bottleneck machine broke down (diagnosis), our system simulates a large number of rescheduling strategies. SIMULEX has an experimental design module to configure a reasonable set of simulation runs. By analyzing the vast simulation output using special statistical procedures the system deducts some recommendations, e.g.: *"If you split the orders A, D, and H and give the highest priority to order B you'll come back to the original schedule on day 144. The additional operating costs are 12 500 DM."* SIMULEX will rank the recommended policies according to a goal which is based on the turnpike scheduling philosophy.

4 DATA MINING SYSTEMS

A totally different approach to analyze accounting data unlike the drill-down heuristic of BETREX works bottom-up. The non-aggregated operating result records are grouped into clusters which are described by their characteristic criteria and key figures. This tool called CLUSMIN is an application of Knowledge Discovery in Databases (KDD) also known as Data Mining. The goal of KDD is the nontrivial extraction of implicit, previously unknown, and potentially useful information from data (Frawley, 1991; Bissantz, 1993; Hagedorn, 1994). To understand the notion of this research field, it is helpful to view the operating result items as points in a multidimensional search space (Figure 12). The dimensions forming the space refer to the criteria and key figures inherent in the profit data. Thus, every single record can be considered a point in space.

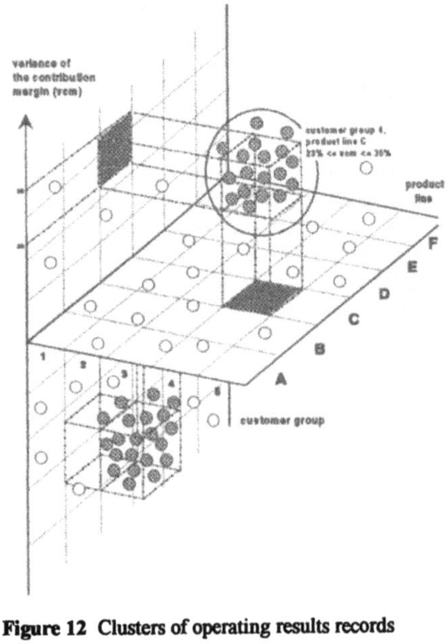

Figure 12 Clusters of operating results records

As can be seen in Figure 12, obvious accumulations of similar records reflect interesting regularities. The notion of similar records enables the system to search for patterns in terms of sets that are meaningful to the user, in effect focusing the search.

System Description: CLUSMIN
CLUSMIN has been implemented to search for those patterns in profit data (Figure 13).

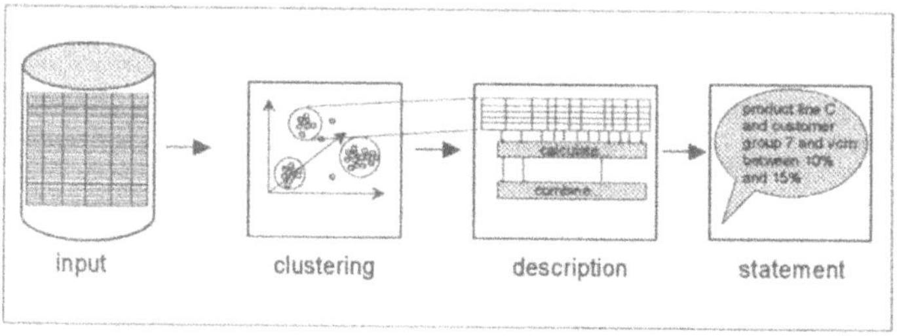

Figure 13 Architecture of CLUSMIN

The discovery procedure of CLUSMIN involves two processes: identifying useful patterns and describing them in a meaningful manner. The pattern extraction uses the statistical technique of cluster analysis to group similar records into subclasses. The ability to use statistical standard techniques is important given that the data is often inherently noisy and the patterns are therefore statistical. For our purposes, we adapted two different methods of clustering known as average linkage and sequential heuristic clustering. The existence of both numeric and non-numeric attributes in operating results data required a particular measure for calculating dissimilarity. Moreover, the clustering has to be influenced according to a user bias. This called for implementation of a module that allows the attributes to be weighed individually. Figure 14 shows the user interface.

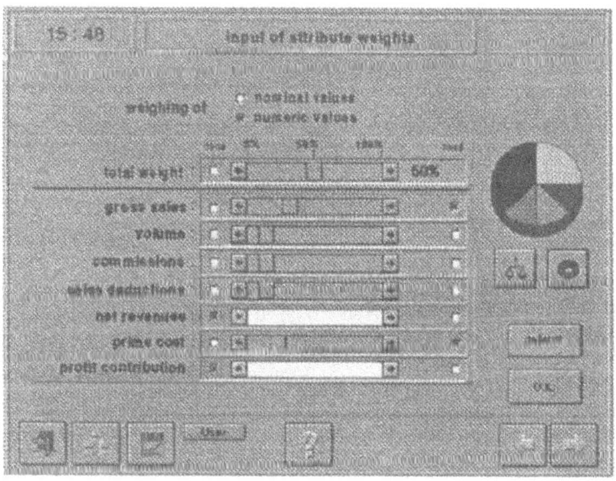

Figure 14 CLUSMIN screen for attribute weighing

Once identified, the groupings have to be described, rather than simply enumerating them. Our procedures for pattern description use a heuristic model based on different ratios which reflect the dispersion of attributes. To put it in simple terms, the algorithm selects those key figures and attributes for description that are statistically far less dispersed within the grouping than within the complete data. With systems like CLUSMIN, there is always the danger that the generated rules are of a trivial nature. So we are looking for ideas to suppress such statements, but up to now we did not find adequate solutions for this rather difficult problem.

Case Study
CLUSMIN was employed to analyze SAP data of a pharmaceutical company.

The system for example detected autonomously that the product groups 595 and 598 were often sold with no sales deduction at all. Please note that such a rule does not necessarily represent all sales of this product group. We look at those rules generated by CLUSMIN as an electronic suspicion. The controller him- or herself has to decide whether this suspicion is worthwhile additional analysis or not. In this example, we decided it would be worthwhile and used a graphical representation to see, if the suspicion is due to a more or less important exception or if the suspicion holds for the product group in total. We found that the detected rule was global and therefore, all the more interesting.

As well the system found some "organizational" lacks. The company had made some mistakes in the maintenance of the complicated tables of the SAP system. So we regard our data mining system as an "instrument to control the controlling".The pharmaceutical company has decided to implement CLUSMIN and transfer it from prototype to a running system.

5 CRITIQUING SYSTEMS (MAN > MACHINE)

In opposite to the critiquing systems that we discussed earlier in this chapter we now deal with a technique where instead of a computer criticizing a person, the person influences the future behavior of the computer. As an example we mention adaptive SDI-Systems (Selective Dissemination of Information), like they were implemented in the IBM Technical Retrieval Center (ITIRC) already in the 1970s.

These systems have the task to keep the researchers and developers informed and to "pilot" them through the vast number of scientific publications. The interested user creates a "permanent profile of information needs" by some key words.The SDI-System checks new documents, chooses supposedly interesting documents and shows them on the display of the researcher's computer. In the case of adaptive SDI-Systems the user returns his or her satisfaction or dissatisfaction by judging the document's value. The application adapts the information profile, especially by modifying the weight of the descriptors.

Systems based on intelligent agents may offer a considerable potential to refine these techniques, e.g. when surfing in the Internet.

6 AUTOMATIC REPORTING SYSTEMS

At the end of the business process that derives management information stands the "finished product", in our case the presentation. A quite realistic vision is the fully automatic presentation that is transported via net.

System Description: COBRAS
At this point we turn back to the system COBRAS that is designed as an intelligent analysis and presentation software for retail audit data with a focus on automation in the client service.

Our aim is to simplify the preparation of presentations. We collected the existing design ideas and tried to capture the expertise of the market researchers and stored that knowledge in the information system. Every market researcher has access to the GfK presentation know-how, thus ensuring a high service quality. The system consists of the basic components shown in Figure 15.

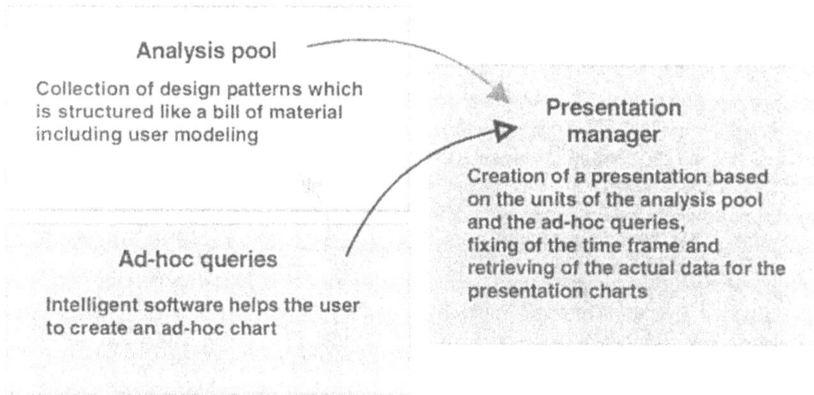

Figure 15 Basic components of COBRAS

The analysis pool represents the design patterns that were collected during the knowledge acquisition. The smallest logical unit of the analysis pool is a single chart. It consists of a diagram and/or a table, some context information, the GfK logo, copyright, and further elements. A chart shows information about a specific subject, for example the model concentration curve of a single brand (Figure 16).

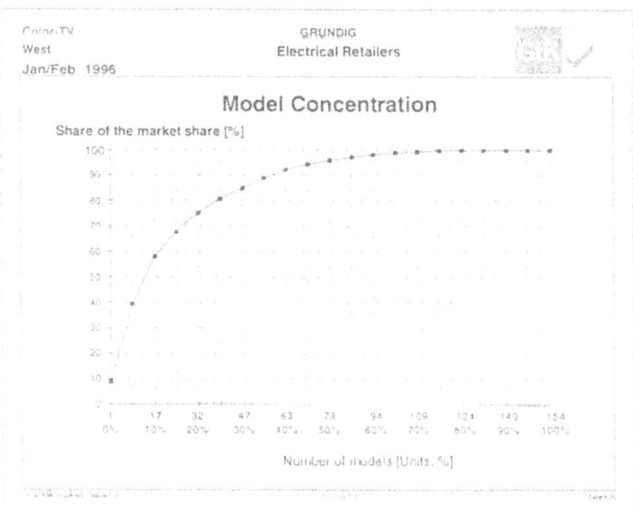

Figure 16 Model concentration

Usually several charts belong together: the first one explains the underlying basics, another one shows the analysis results and yet another one draws conclusions or summarizes the matter. They are arranged in frameworks like the position analysis of brands in a market. The user of the system may change these analyses and save them as standards that are valid for special product groups or clients. So the GfK standard can serve as an extensive chart catalogue that also allows individual presentation profiles. Several retrieval methods enable the user to easily handle the large amount of charts in the catalogue.

Another possibility to access the database of COBRAS is to generate and process ad-hoc queries. The system offers different views on the data depending on the user's preferences (professional or inexperienced user). The design rule base again helps to choose a suitable business graphic type that is generated by the output module.

The user only interacts with the Presentation manager that helps to arrange the charts of the upper components in form of a hierarchical structured presentation. The system saves the chart patterns as well as the matching database queries, so that the user is able to "refill" an automatically generated presentation structure with the actual data in a new reporting period.

Process of the Presentation Workout

If the user wants to create a new presentation, he or she chooses several suitable analysis concepts and structures the presentation hierarchically (Figure 17, 1). This phase can start before the new data is available. Mostly the client's questions are known before, such as: *"How well was our new product distributed?"* The Presentation manager offers the possibility to assign time frames to analyses so that the presentation can be scheduled.

Using descriptors, such as Product, Place, Price, or Promotion, the system generates a ranking of the suitable charts (Figure 17, 2). The degree of a chart's suitability is measured by the fitting of the given descriptors as well as the occasion, such as a presentation for the board of directors. Now the user may choose some of the proposed charts, their order and the underlying data.

Until step 2 the system does not need the actual data. In the following phase the system retrieves the data and checks the necessary presentation time (Figure 17, 3). Then the user may cancel some charts or add new ones (Figure 17, 4).

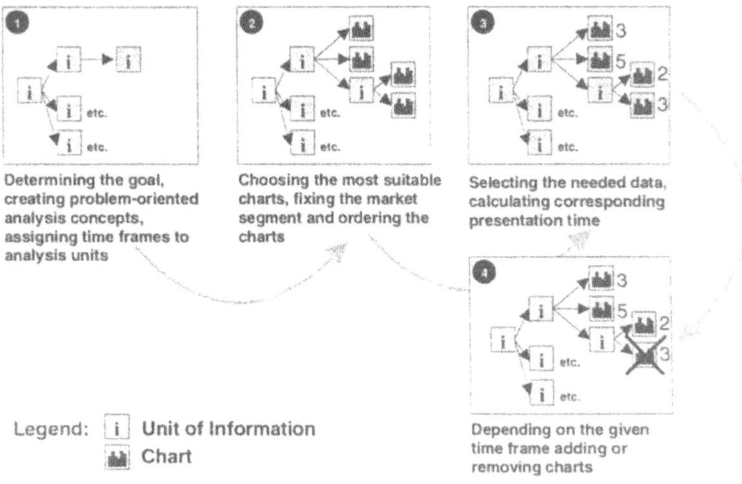

Figure 17 Process of the presentation configuration

Automatic Analysis of Financial Statements
Our last example leads us to the automatically generated report on the left-hand side of the scale (Figure 2). In connection with that we would like to touch user modeling. In the field of business administration the term addressee modeling might be more appropriate because the reports often are addressed to institutions rather than to persons (see below). The existing work of Theoretical Computer Science in this field is respectable, but - as far as we can see - there are not many actual implementations. We think that it is the job of the Information Systems research community to close this gap.

In order to be able to measure the economic success of a business as an outsider, one only has access to information contained in public financial records. This data is mainly drawn from the balance sheet and the profit and loss statement.

Furthermore it is important to realize how other external partners (such as banks, shareholders, etc.) view the business. The creditor's decision is mainly affected by the results of a balance sheet analysis (Hamm, 1994, p.132). The company's desire to continuously know its credit rating and financial standing therefore demands a continuous financial analysis.

System Description: UNTERNEHMENSREPORT
The knowledge-based system described here, UNTERNEHMENSREPORT II (Haase, 1995), was created in cooperation with FORWISS and DATEV e.G., Nuremberg, a large German cooperative association. This association supports German tax consultants with information technologies. The typical clients of the tax consultants are small to medium-sized companies. The existing (running) system UNTERNEHMENSREPORT I which is able to analyze only two consecutive years is used in some 14 000 tax consultants' offices. This system generates an expertise of 20 to 30 pages referring to a company's economic performance. Table 1 gives an output example (translated into English, DATEV, 1992, p. 8).

Table 1 Output example of UNTERNEHMENSREPORT I

...
OPERATING RESULTS
THE OPERATING RESULTS WERE MADE UP OF THE TOTAL OUTPUT REDUCED BY THE COSTS OF MATERIAL AND THE REMAINING COSTS WHICH WERE COMPOSED OF THE PERSONNEL EXPENSES, THE NORMAL DEPRECIATIONS, AND THE REMAINING EXPENSES.
THE CLEAR DETERIORATION OF THE OPERATING RESULTS IN 1994 CAN BE ATTRIBUTED TO THE INCREASE OF GOODS COST PRICES. THE TOTAL OUTPUT ALSO ROSE WHILE THE REMAINING COSTS DECLINED.
FOR THIS REASON THE OPERATING RESULTS BECAME NEGATIVE IN THE REPORTING PERIOD. ...

UNTERNEHMENSREPORT II will offer a lot of additional features. It examines time series on a yearly basis from two to ten consecutive years and on a monthly basis up to 24 months. Moreover, the application analyzes the individual client's industry averages and data which is projected up to five years into the future. It is left up to the tax consultant to choose the time horizons. At DATEV average ratios are available for a substantial number of industries. The system is refined in a way to even distinguish differences between very small, small and medium-sized companies within a single industry.

Figure 18 offers an overview of the dimensions that are integrated into the analysis of UNTERNEHMENSREPORT II (the analysis models will be described below).

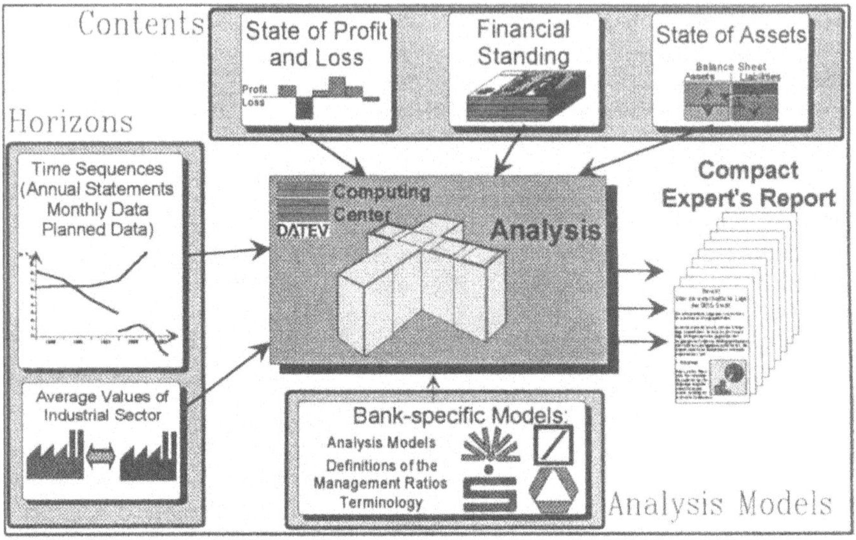

Figure 18 Integrated dimensions in UNTERNEHMENSREPORT II

Addressee-Orientation

An important factor enabling a system to produce high-quality reports automatically is to employ models about the addressee. The report may be for the tax consultant who could use it as a basis for a discussion with his or her client. If the consultants want to give the expertise directly and unchanged to their clients, then the addressee may be the entrepreneur or a manager. A potential external recipient is the company's house bank, for example to apply for a credit.

Depending on the addressee, the user can select whether the report should contain tables or not and whether it will include diagrams and if so, which kind of graphical representation should be preferred.

Especially if the report is intended for a top manager of the client's organization, recommendations how to react to a specific situation may be useful. It is not advisable to use evaluations and risky formulations for all addressees (especially the external ones). The recommendation and judgment problem was solved by providing the respective pieces of text with a special attribute. The default choice for a report is expertises without these marked passages.

Another option is the possibility to choose the level of detail of the expertise. For this reason we implemented a hierarchical design for the expert system. It consists of different layers. The higher the layer, the more consolidated the included information. The top layer, for example, produces text concerning the supreme goal of the analysis, the economic situation of the company. So UNTERNEHMENSREPORT II is able to produce an expertise that only contains the levels of consolidation down to a user-specified layer (Figure 19). The standard report will include the upper four layers (of five). A brief executive summary will be cut off between layer two and three. The long version of the report with all its details, for example for the book-keeper's assistant, consists of all layers.

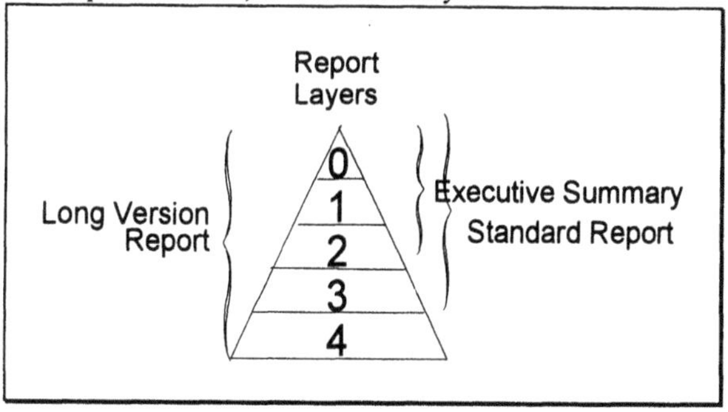

Figure 19 Level of detail

If the addressee of the expertise is a bank, then it is important to follow the bank's guidelines of carrying out credit investigations. Those guidelines partly vary with regard to the definitions of ratios and business terms. That leads to difficulties with the so-called surface text-generation that deals with syntax problems and lexical choice (Rankin, 1993). The German language creates a range of problems here that are not existing in other languages like English.

The system cannot use a fixed business vocabulary, since it has to follow the internal vocabulary of the banks. It holds lists with the special terms and their gender, genitive ending syllable and more. In German, not only the indefinite and definite articles (indefinite article: masc. "ein", fem. "eine", neut. "ein", definite article: masc. "der", fem. "die", neut. "das") depend on the gender of the subject but also the pronouns and many word endings.

E.g., the term "Teilbetriebserfolg" used by the DEUTSCHE BANK for "Operating Results" has another gender than the BAYERISCHE VEREINSBANK's synonym "Betriebsergebnis", which is a neutral noun, but also has a different ending for the genitive case, where "Teilbetriebserfolg" gets the ending "s", while "Betriebsergebnis" will read "Betriebs-ergebnis<u>ses</u>".

Of course, the banks are free to modify their evaluating procedure (e.g. the ratios) without regarding the consequences for UNTERNEHMENSREPORT II. To deal with these modifications we separated this part ot the knowledge base and created special lists. So the knowledge structure is independent of the bank's decisions. Those separated lists contain information concerning the algorithms to compute the ratios and the reliability of the resulting figures. Following Davis and Buchanan we might call that "meta-level knowledge" (Davis and Buchanan, 1984).

7 CONCLUSION

A higher degree of automation in management information assumes that the system knows the user very well. To become more general we want to pick up Negroponte's thesis, saying we are just converting from the information society into the post-information society. The latter is characterized by a turn away from mass communication towards individual communication.

This is one reason why we should pay much attention to Active MIS including user or addressee modeling.

8 REFERENCES

Beys, O. (1994) PANELYSER - Ein Beitrag zur effizienten Analyse von Paneldaten mit Hilfe wissensbasierter Elemente. PhD thesis, Nürnberg.

Beys, O. and Müller, S. (1992) Analysis of Retail Audit Data with Expertise Systems, in *Do New Technologies Help or Hinder Marketing Decisions?* (ed. ESOMAR), Proceedings of the ESOMAR Conference, Rotterdam, 113-123.

Beys, O., Fischer, M., Tripmaker, S., and Mertens, P. (1992) Wissenbasierte Analyse von Handelspaneldaten. *Marketing ZFP,* **3(14)**, 157-166.

Bissantz, N. and Hagedorn, J. (1993) Data Mining (Datenmustererkennung). *Wirtschafts-informatik,* **5(35)**, 481-487.

Bissantz, N., Hagedorn, J., and Mertens, P. (1995) Top-down Navigation and Knowledge Discovery in SAP Operating Results Data: The BETREX System, in *Managing Information & Communications in a Changing Global Environment* (ed. M. Khosrowpour), Proceedings of the 1995 Information Resources Management Association International Conference, May 21-24th, Atlanta, Georgia USA, 420.

DATEV e.G. (ed.) (1992) UNTERNEHMENSREPORT - Produktinformation mit Anwendungsbeispiel. Nürnberg.

Davis, R. and Buchanan, B.G. (1984) Meta-Level Knowledge, in *Rule-Based Expert Systems* (ed. B.G. Buchanan and E.H. Shortliffe), The MYCIN Experiments of the Standford Heuristic Programming Project, Reading, Massachusetts, 507-530.

Frawley, J.F., Piatetsky-Shapiro, G., and Matheus, C.J. (1991) Knowledge Discovery in Databases: An Overview. *AI Magazine,* **3(13)**, 57-70.

Haase, M. (1995) Wissensbasierte Jahresabschlußanalyse mit Unternehmensreport. *Theorie und Praxis der Wirtschaftsinformatik HMD,* **182**, 37-44.

Mertens, P. (1992) An Expert System for Analyzing the Profit and Financial Situation of Small and Medium-Sized Companies, in *Proceedings on World Congress on Expert Systems*, Orlando, 1269-1276.

Mertens, P. (1989) Derivation of Verbal Expertises from Accounting Data, in *Expert Systems in Economics, Banking, and Management* (ed. L.F. Pau, J. Motiwalla, Y.H. Pao, and H.H. Peh), Amsterdam, NewYork, Oxford, Tokyo, 341-350.

Parfitt, J.H. and Collins, B.J.K. (1968) Use of Consumer Panels for Brand-Share Prediction. *Journal of Marketing Research,* **5**, 131-145.

Rankin, I. (1993) Natural Language Generation in Critiquing. *The Knowledge Engineering Review,* **4**, 329-347.

Stonebraker, M., Agrawal, R., Dayal, U., Neuhold, E.J., and Reuter, A. (1993) *DBMS Research at a Crossroads: The Vienna Update,* in *Proceedings of the 19th VLDB Conference* (ed. R. Agrawal, S. Baker, and D. Bell), Dublin, 701.

9 BIOGRAPHY

Prof. Dr. Dr. h. c. mult. Peter Mertens

Peter Mertens, born 1937, is director of the Department for Information Systems Research at the University of Erlangen-Nuremberg, Germany. He is the deputy-spokesperson of the executive committee at the Bavarian Research Center for Knowledge-Based Systems (FORWISS). He is also the editor-in-chief of WIRTSCHAFTSINFORMATIK, the leading German journal dedicated to Information Systems Research.

Professor Mertens graduated from the Technical University of Darmstadt, Germany with a degree in industrial engineering. He worked at several universities, before joining a major IT-consulting firm, at first in a management position, later as managing director.

His main research interests are: IS in marketing, production, logistics, and controlling; MIS; Expert Systems; Data Mining; Workflow Management Systems; Industry-specific application architectures; Virtual enterprises.

Dipl. Inf. Jürgen Hagedorn, Dipl.-Kfm. Margit Fischer, Dipl.-Kfm. Nicolas Bissantz, and Dipl.-Kfm. Michael Haase

They all belong to Mertens' research staff at the Group for Information Systems Research of FORWISS.

21

A case study of EIS development by an experienced EIS developer

P.A. O'Donnell, D. R. Arnott and W. Jirachiefpattana
Department of Information Systems, Monash University
Level 7, 26 Sir John Monash Drive, Caulfield East, Melbourne, 3145, Australia, Phone +61 3 9903 2295, Fax + 61 3 9903 2005, Email peter.odonnell@is.monash.edu.au

Abstract

This paper describes the development of an EIS in an Australian-based subsidiary of a multi-national firm. The EIS development team was lead by an experienced EIS developer seconded from the U.S.-based parent company. The structure of the EIS team and the nature of the system development process are described. Many of the problems that are normally confronted by EIS developers were avoided by the EIS team. The leader of this team was able to use his experience to ensure the smooth progression of the system development effort. The system is now the official management information source in the organisation. A survey of the system's users confirmed that the users find the system useful and the EIS team responsive to their needs.

Keywords

Developer experience, executive information systems, HOLOS, OLAP, system development

1 INTRODUCTION

Executive information systems (EIS) are computer based information systems that provide executives with the ability to monitor various aspects of their organisation. EIS normally provides a multi-dimensional view of data and a high quality graphical interface. The EIS data base includes extracts from the organisation's operational data base and specially acquired internal and external data. The tasks or problems that are supported by an EIS are likely to be strategic and recurring (*ie* they occur frequently enough and are important enough to justify the expense of EIS development).

A common theme of EIS is that the systems should be developed using a prototyping, adaptive or evolutionary approach to development (Courbon, Grajew and Tolovi 1978, Houndeshel and Watson 1987, Rockart and DeLong 1988, Wallis 1989, Paller and Laska 1990, Watson, Rainer and Chang 1991, Waston, Rainer and Frolick 1992, Fitzgerald 1992, Suvachittanont, Arnott and O'Donnell 1994). The number of development cycles becomes less frequent as development staff and users become familiar with EIS technology and the nature of the tasks they are tackling. A common observation in case study research is that the development staff know little about EIS when the project is initiated (Sundue 1986, Armstrong 1990, Watson 1992, Fitzgerald 1992, Watson, Rainer and Flolick 1992, Suvachittanont, Arnott and O'Donnell 1994). This is understandable when a technology is new, but EIS could now be considered a mature information technology after many years of successful systems development. The level and nature of developer experience with the process of EIS development may effect the number of evolutionary cycles, the applications developed, the speed of development, the nature of user involvement, the overall success of the system and many other aspects of the project.

Developer experience in EIS has received little research attention. This paper presents a case study of a successful EIS whose development was co-ordinated by an experienced developer/project manager who was seconded from one part of a large multi-national corporation to another.

2 METHOD

The case study data was collected using questionnaires and structured interviews. The purpose of using questionnaires was to obtain fundamental information about the EIS development and to generate questions for further interview. The subjects were 22 EIS users, the EIS co-ordinator or team leader and three EIS developers. This represents 40% of the user population and 100% of the developer population of the organisation. The users were asked about the outcomes of the EIS from both organisational and individual perspectives, the developers were questioned about the technical details of the development process, and the co-ordinator questioned on system initiation and the general nature of the development of the EIS over the life of the system. The procedure and instruments used have been used in other studies (for example Suvachittanont, Arnott and O'Donnell 1994) and is described in detail in Jirachiefpattana (1996). After the co-ordinator and developer questionnaires were analysed, detailed questions for each of the developers were designed. These questions were answered in structured interviews that ranged in length from 1 to 2 hours.

The EIS co-ordinator, whose experience in EIS development forms the focus of this study, was not one of the researchers and no special relationship existed between the EIS co-ordinator and the researchers. The researchers were not involved in any way in the development of the system.

3 OVERVIEW OF THE EIS PROJECT

The organisation that is the focus of this paper is a manufacturer and distributor of advanced office equipment. The company is a multi-national corporation based in the United States. The Australian subsidiary of the firm employs 700 people and has a network of over 300 retail dealerships. Senior management is spread across five Australian states. It has for many years been widely regarded as an innovator in the use of technology. The organisation has a corporate mission and culture strongly oriented towards the satisfaction of customer needs using a total quality philosophy.

The U.S. based parent company has had for many years a mature and well publicised EIS. The development of an EIS for use by the Australian subsidiary was initiated by that company's General Manager. Another senior manager, the Manager of Business Planning and Development, acted as the executive sponsor of the system. Both believed that important decisions about product strategies were being made without appropriate information. The information provided by the existing intensive manual reporting system was often of poor quality. The information was often not timely and some information was difficult, if not impossible to obtain. The reports produced within different organisation units often was contradictory. The aim of the development of the EIS was to resolve these problems and, in particular, to assist the analysis and understanding of equipment sales.

Within six months of the commencement of the EIS project the first version of the system, with 11 different screen based reports, was installed. This initial system provided information about sales revenue (within the organisation this is refered to as 'Sold Equipment Revenue'). The system sources data from the corporate billing system and other internal financial systems.

4 STRUCTURE OF THE EIS DEVELOPMENT TEAM

A development team of three full time information systems professionals was formed to construct the EIS. This team reports directly to the Chief Financial Officer (CFO). The team leader was seconded from the U.S. based parent company. He had previously been involved in the development of the EIS system in the U.S. and usually works in the finance arm of the firm as a decision support systems analyst. The other members of the development team, whose previous appointments were in the Information Systems Department as applications programmer and systems analyst, were recruited and appointed by the EIS team leader and the Financial Controller (who reports to the CFO). The applications programmer's major skills were in mainframe applications development. The systems analyst's major skills were database development with the Oracle system and PC applications development. The team's offices are located within the Information Systems Department. The EIS team was also, on occasion, supported by a data-base administrator from the Information Systems Department who provided advice and technical support related to the acquisition of data from existing data-base applications in the organisation.

The EIS team leader devised a structure for the control of the EIS development based upon the one used in the U.S. company. Each EIS application (the Sold Equipment Revenue is an example of an EIS application) has a official application owner and a data owner. The application owner for the Sold Equipment Revenue system is the Finance Manager. All changes to the functionality and reports of this application are approved and prioritised by the application owner before they are handed over to the EIS development team for implementation. The data owner represents the functional area that is the major provider of the data for the EIS application. For the Sold Equipment Revenue application the data owner, a member of the finance department, helped the EIS team investigate and resolve inconsistencies and discrepancies in the source data. As a result of this formal ownership structure, relating to both the application and the source data, the EIS has obtained status as the 'official' source of data on Sold Equipment Revenue in the organisation.

5 AN OVERVIEW OF THE SYSTEM

The EIS was constructed using an OLAP compliant (Codd, Codd and Salley 1993) development tool called HOLOS (from Holistic Systems plc.). The server component of the software resides on an Hyundai AXIL 320 computer. The client component of the software runs on IBM compatible PCs running the Windows operating system. Each end-user's PC has approximately 8mb of RAM and has either a 386 or 486 based processor. The connection between the client software on the PCs and the server software on the AXIL 320 computer is made via TCP/IP over an ethernet based network.

The basis of the OLAP architecture is the ability to create multi-dimensional data structures (Frank 1995). Each item of data in a structure, or cell, represents the intersection of a number of dimensions. For example, the data stored in a cell might represent the sales of product number 1102 in the State of Victoria in the 3rd Quarter of 1995. In this case the dimensions describing the data item are product, location and time. The dimension called

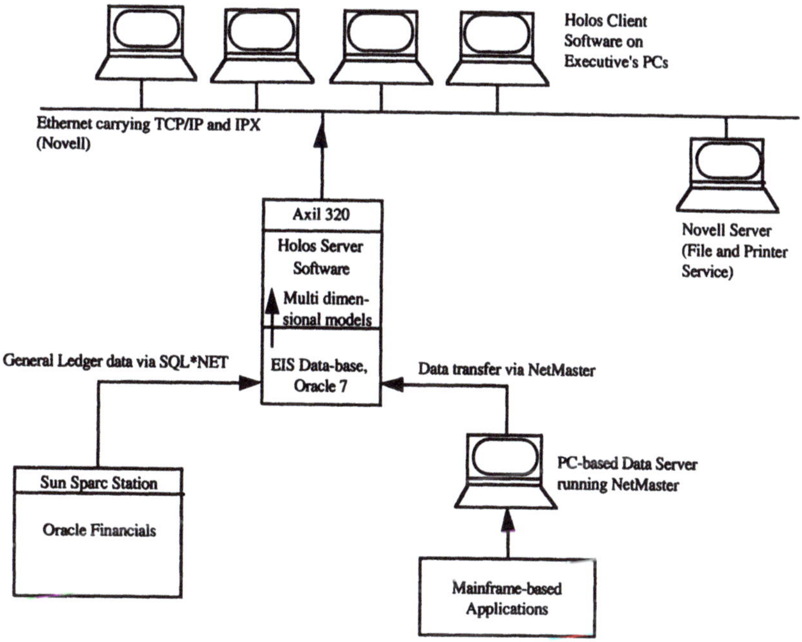

Figure 1 An overview of the architecture of the EIS.

product might contain other attributes, each representing a different product. The location dimension may contain the attributes representing other States or geographic regions. A data structure containing the dimensions of product, state and time is considered as three dimensional data and it can be viewed as any combination of these dimensions.

The data for the system is held in a relational data-base constructed using the Oracle 7 database management software. Using the terminology currently in vogue in trade-related publications on OLAP and EIS this database would be classified as a data-mart (Demarest 1994). This EIS data-base is the source of the data that populates the multi-dimensional models contained in the EIS. The HOLOS product directly queries the Oracle data-base using SQL. Until an update is required the multi dimensional models are stored on disk on the AXIL 320 by the HOLOS system to help facilitate speedy access by end-users of the EIS. The major source of data for the EIS data-base is an existing financial system, developed using the Oracle Financials software package. Some data is also sourced from other applications running on the organisation's mainframe computer systems. The Netmaster product is used to facilitate this transfer. Figure 1 provides an overview of the architecture of the EIS. The AXIL 320 was purchased specifically for the EIS as it was felt that the capacity of the existing computer hardware could not handle the data and query processing associated with the EIS.

The initial version of the system was used by 4 senior executives, 3 middle managers and 3 other users. Currently, the number of users has increased to 55 across all levels of management as shown in Table 1. Table 2 shows the number of users by the business units. Similarly, the number of EIS screens has increased from 11 to 60.

The interface of the system and the reports and screens are typical of that which is expected of an EIS (Martin and Clarke 1989). The major characteristics of the EIS are the display of key performance indicators, exception reporting, the ability for users to 'drill-down' from summary reports to detailed information, color coding of reports, and a mix of graphical

Table 1 The number of users classsified by management levels

Level of management	*Number*
Top management	10
Middle management	15
Operational management	15
Other	20
Total	55

Table 2 The number of users classifed by business units

Business unit	*Number*
Marketing	20
Finance	15
Personnel	10
Supplies/Service	10
Total	55

and tabular display formats. The EIS has been designed to be easy to use; the users control the system using a mouse.

The Sold Equipment Revenue application provides reports on based upon financial and non-financial information. The basic system functions are as follows:

Financial Functions

Sold Equipment Model: This model is primarily concerned with the profitability of the sold equipment. Information in the model includes equipment costs, sales revenue, cost of sales, and related overhead expenses.

Commercial Marketing Model: This model takes information from the Sold Equipment model and provides profitability analyses of the retail dealerships.

Rate Variance Reports: These examine the relationship between volume and price.

Daily Reporting Model: Presents the quantity of machines sold daily (up to the current day).

Service Model: This model shows the number of machines manufactured, associated revenues and costs, and service related labour-hours.

Cost Centre/Human Resources: This provides financial information about cost centres and other organisational divisions.

Non Financial Functions

Technical Service Model: This model enables analysis of the use of parts for the on-site service of equipment.

Stock Model: This model shows the stock levels in various warehouses.

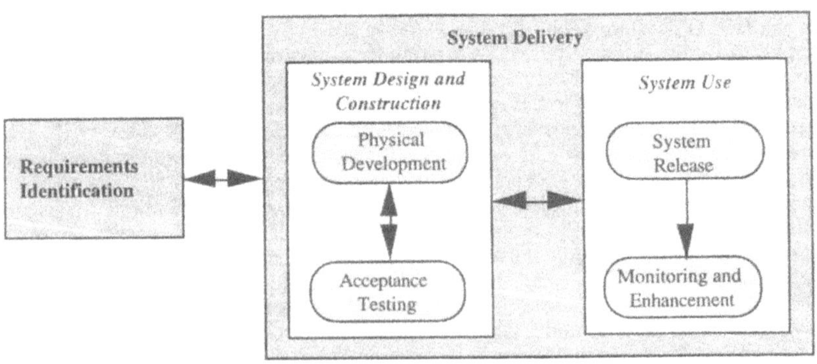

Figure 2 A Model of the System Development Process.

6 THE EIS DEVELOPMENT PROCESS

The initiation phase of the system development progressed quickly. The sponsor provided direction that the first EIS application developed should be one that reported on Sold Equipment Revenue. After this decision had been made and the EIS team leader had arrived from the U.S. an informal cost/benefit analysis was undertaken. The benefits and costs of the new system were projected; the conclusion of this analysis was that development of the system would be worthwhile. The approximate start-up costs for the EIS for the hardware, software and personnel required was AUS$ 178 000, 180 000 and 265 000 respectively. The organisation spends about $245 000 annually for on-going development, maintenance and operation of the system.

A model of the development of an EIS, changed slightly from that used by Suvachittanont, Arnott and O'Donnell (1994), is shown in Figure 2. This model can be used to explain the development of this EIS. The model contains two major phases, requirements identification and system delivery. Development activity interates between these two phases. Within the system delivery phase, there are two major activities: system design and construction, and system use. As with the major phases, the development activity iterates between these two actitives. Table 4 provides a summary of the major tasks, information required, methods used and people involved during each of the development activities.

6.1 Requirements identification

The functionality required in the system was directly determined by the users. They created their own high-level requirements and then provided a requirements specification document to the EIS team. This requirements specification was mostly a set of reports which the users would like to receive. After formal approval of the specification by the application owner the EIS development team undertook the following tasks:

Data Analysis. The EIS team analysed the reports presented in the specification. The users were consulted to help to clarify what data was actually required to produce the reports.

Information Identification. The EIS team, in consultation with the data-base administrator attempted to identify sources for the required data.

Software Selection. The EIS team leader decided, that in order to facilitate timely system delivery, an EIS development tool would be required. A formal package selection process was followed before the HOLOS system was chosen. The formal assessment involved identifying and weighting the required package attributes, identifying candidate tools and then evaluating each tool according to the desired attributes. Table 3 shows the criteria used for the selection of the EIS development tool. It is interesting to note that the tool selected for the project is different to that used for EIS development in the parent company.

6.2 System design and construction

The system design and construction activity comprises two further sub-activities: physical development and acceptance testing.

Phyiscal Development. The physical development activitity consisted of two further sub-tasks, the construction of the EIS data-base and the construction of the EIS itself. The data administrator from the IS Department constructed data loading routines using the IDEAL language. The Oracle EIS database was created to hold this data. The Finance department has responsibility for ensuring that current data is up-loaded into the system when available. Mostly new data becomes available on a monthly basis. However, this does vary from time to time so the data update is initiated manually rather than by some automatic method.

Table 3 Criteria used for EIS package selection

Category	*Criteria*
External product support	Supplier expertise
	User base
	Availability of expertise
Development/maintenance	Quick and easy development
	Separation of data and logic
Value for money	Up front cost
	On-going cost
System environment	Novel compatible
	Windows compatible
Product features	High speed
	Drill-down capability

The initial task faced by the development team in actually coding the system was to learn how to develop applications using the HOLOS system. After the team underwent basic HOLOS training a prototype system was constructed. This prototype served three purposes: to help the team further develop their HOLOS coding skills, to confirm the teams understanding of the user's requirements and to test a proposed standard format for on-screen reports. It had been decided that a standard format for each the interface was required to help provide a consistent and easily understood system. For example this standard included rules for the use of on-screen colours. The background to each screen was grey. Any number could be double clicked to provide more detail. Colour coding was used to highlight exceptions. Numbers in a range that indicated poor performance were coloured red whilst black or green was used for good numbers.

Acceptance Testing. Once the prototype system was made available to users an acceptance testing programe was undertaken. This testing ensured that the system performed its functions in an acceptable manner and also that the data presented were accurate. Interviews of key users were used to collect information during this phase.

6.3 System use

The system use phase consists of the release of the system to user community and then the ongoing maintenance and enhancement of the system.

System Release: After the initial prototype had been modified in light of the feedback obtained as a result of the acceptance testing phase the system was released for use by the wider user community. The numbers of users of the system increased dramatically. The EIS team employed with each new user individual one-to-one training of about one hour duration to make sure that the users understood the basic principles of the system. To train new users in the future, the EIS team has plans to train a group of around 8 specially selected users who will be responsible for the basic training of new users.

To assist users of the system a help function has been included. When users require an explanation of how to use one of the functions of the system, they can activate this function and get (at least) some of the information that they require. A paper-based document describing the use of the system from the user's perspective has been developed by the application owner.

Monitoring and Evaluation: The purpose of this activitiy is to monitor use of the system and identify changes that are required. To implement the identified changes the devlopment process cycles back to the system design and construction activity.

Table 4 Summary of the characteristics of the EIS development process

Activities	*Major tasks*	*Required information*	*Methods/ techniques/ tools*	*Deliverables*	*People involved*
Requirement Analysis	• Data analysis • Information identification • Software selection	• User needs • Information about desired functions • Timing of data • Features of software	• Interview • Critical success factors • Prototyping • Discussion with support personnel	• Functional specification	• Functional area management • Programmers • Data Providers
System Development	• Language training • Model specification development • Functionality coding • Database development • Data loading	• Functional specification	• Prototyping • HOLOS • Oracle • MS-Access • System flow chart • Normalisation • Data flow diagrams • Decision Trees • Pseudocode	• Prototype model • 1st release model	• Programmers • Vendor
Acceptance Testing	• System testing • System modification	• User feedback	• Interview	• Final model	• Programmers • Functional users
System Release	• System installation • Training		• One on one training	• Interactive help	• Programmers • Functional users
System Maintenance and Enhancement	• Functionality Improvement	• User feedback		• Enhanced system	• Programmers • Functional users

Once the system was available to the wider user community, requests for changes and extra functions were received by the EIS team. There were two causes for these requests. One was that with experience, the users came to a better understanding of what the system could do. They were able to understand and describe functions and reports that the system could provide that would be of use to them. Further, as the system was released it obtained status as the 'official' source of information within the organisation. As a result of this 'official' status, changes to the organisation's operations or changing environmental conditions, necessitate (often urgent) changes to the system.

Each system modification request has to be authorised by the EIS owner, the Financial Planning manager. He considers each enhancement request and determines its relevance and importance. Prioritised approved requests are passed onto the EIS team who them work to incorporate the requested change within the system by cycling back to the system design and construction activity.

Table 5 The difficulty of activities related to system development

Activity	*Avg. Score*	*SD.*	*Range*
Identifing executive requirements	3.33	0.58	3-4
Identifying data	2.67	1.15	2-4
Sourcing data	3.33	1.15	2-4
Desigining the system	2.33	0.58	2-3
Constructing the system	2.33	0.58	2-3
Getting feedback from the users	4.33	1.15	3-5

To help monitor the performance and use of the EIS, a monitoring system was developed and added to the system. This monitoring system records information such as how many modules were loaded, which reports were retrieved and how often, and how many people used the EIS. This information has allowed the EIS owner and the development team to remove some unused modules from the system.

7 THE DEVELOPERS' VIEW OF THE DEVELOPMENT PROCESS

In order to better understand the EIS team's feelings about the development of the system, a simple questionnaire was administered to identify the difficulty associated with various activities during the system development. As previously noted, the questionnaire used is the same as used by Suvachittanont, Arnott and O'Donnell (1994). The questions were answered using a scale which ranged from 1 (not difficult) to 5 (very difficult) for each activity specified in the questionnaire. Table 5 presents the mean score, standard deviation (SD) and the range of the responses of the 3 members of the EIS team. The results show that in general, the developers thought that EIS implementation was of reasonable difficulty as the average scores of identifying requirements and data, getting the data, designing and constructing the system is less than 3.5. This indicates that the development, from the perspective of the developers, progressed smoothly.

The only aspect of system development that the developers indicated that they had difficulty was obtaining feedback from users. The developers related that once users had seen the system they were inundated with requests for changes and other feedback.

8 THE USERS' VIEWS OF THE SYSTEM

8.1 Measurement technique

In order to obtain some insight into users' feeling about the system a questionnaire was administered to the system's users. The short questionnaire presented the users with a series of statements. They responded to each of the statements using a 5-point Likert scale. A response of 1 meant that the user thought that the statement was incorrect in regard to their perception of the system while a response of 5 represented very high agreement. For each statement, an average score below 3.0 indicated that the respondents disagree more than agree with the statement about the EIS. As previously noted, the relevance of each statement can be related to trends identified in the general EIS literature and is discussed in Suvachittanont, Arnott and O'Donnell (1994) and Jirachiefpattana (1996).

The executive user questionnaire was sent to 60 users and 22 (36.67%) were returned. Table 6 shows the managerial level of the respondents. More than 27% of the returned questionnaires were completed by the most senior management of the organisation. This

Table 6 Distribution of respondents by position

Position	*Number*	*%*
Senior mgt.	6	27.27
Middle mgt.	8	36.36
Operational mgt.	3	13.63
Others	5	22.73
Total	22	100

Table 7 Distribution of respondents by business unit

Business unit	*Number*
Marketing	12
Finance	7
Supplies/Service	3
Total	22

Table 8 Period of working in the organisation

Years	*Number*
0-5	6
5-10	4
10-15	3
15-20	7
20+	2
Total	22

indicates that, whilst the system is the official source of information in the organisation and as such is used by managers of all levels that it also has a significant number of executive users. Table 7 presents the distribution of the respondents by business units. The highest number of the subjects came from Marketing area. The length of time that of subjects had worked for the organisation ranged from 1 to 23 years as shown in Table 8.

8.2 Primary Purpose of Using the EIS

The primary purposes of using the system were categorised into five groups as illustrated in Table 9. The functional area most frequently addressed by the EIS use was Finance. Here the users accessed the EIS to obtain information about profitability, revenue of various products and cost centres.

Table 10 shows the distribution of the period that users have used the EIS. The majority of the subjects have used the system less than 2 years. The mean time of each user spent using the EIS per day was 50.24 minutes. (Note that the distribution shown in Table 10 the

Table 9 Primary purpose of using the EIS

EIS Functional Area		*Number*
Sales	Sales results/Monitoring/Analysis Product performance Order and installation tracking Identifiying areas of concern	11
Finance	Costs of Centres/Sales/Services/Products Budget Information/Tracking/Trend Revenue and trends Profitability analysis Margin movement/Analysis Actual spending vrs. budget analysis Forecast/Plan comparision Financial figure monitoring	27
Overall managment	Business performance/Planning Problem analysis Planning and control Identifying areas of opportunity Management decision	10
Customer service		1
Other	Data extraction Source data	7

Table 10 Period of time using the EIS

Year	*Number*
0-2	14
2-4	5
4 +	3
Total	22

Table 11 Time spent on the EIS per day

Minutes	*Number*
0-15	2
15-30	9
30-45	0
45-60	7
60 +	3
Total	22

calculation of the mean time spent on the EIS per day excluded one response for which the answer was 1 day.) Table 11 presents the distribution of time spent on the EIS, which varies from 5 to 150 minutes per day.

8.3 Organisational Success

The seven organisational satisfaction measures are shown in Table 12. The total average score was 25.59 out of 35 (73.11%). This score indicates that the users were relatively appreciative of the way that the system supports their work. In general, most measures received high scores which supported the trend observed in the general literature. Only the average score of decreasing paper flow was lower than 3.0.

Table 12 Mean scores and standard deviations for the organisational satisfaction measures

Measure	*Avg. Score*	*SD.*
Important to the organisation	4.36	0.79
Improve the planning process	4.09	0.75
Improve organisational communication	4.00	0.53
Improve operational control process	3.82	1.05
Gain commitment of all managers	3.41	0.80
Improve the image of the IS. Department	3.18	1.05
Decrease paper flow	2.73	1.12

Table 13 Mean scores and standard deviations for the individual satisfaction measures

Measure	*Avg. Score*	*SD.*
Save time	4.14	0.83
Can do more	4.05	1.09
Easier to obtaining information	3.82	1.00
Quicker decision making	3.82	1.14
Better decision making	3.77	0.87
Rely on the EIS	3.59	0.96
Improve thinking about problems	3.45	1.22
Gain more knowledge about IT	3.00	1.23
User involvement in development	2.36	1.47

8.4 Individual Success

The measures of individual satisfaction are shown in Table 13. In supporting individual users work, the EIS can be considered relatively successful with a total average score of 32.0 from 45 (71.11%). The measures that received an average score less than 3 were most interesting as they indicate potential problem areas for this EIS, particiularly "user involvement in development" at 2.36. However, its standard deviation was relatively high (1.47) meaning that there is little consensus among the subjects about the correctness of the statement.

Even though the average score of the EIS facilitating quicker decisions was high (3.82), there was little consensus among users (SD. 1.14). In contrast, there was relatively high consensus about "making better decisions" and "relying on the EIS".

Further insight into the relatively high success rating of this EIS from both the organisational and user perspectives can be gained from unprompted comments about the EIS in general. These comments are produced verbatim in Table 14.

9 CONCLUDING DISCUSSION

The culture of the corporation in this case study is such that executives expected and wanted to use an EIS, in contrast to other EIS development environments where a significant level of user resistance is encountered. The EIS team leader's experience and skills in dealing with executive users helped, no doubt, to ensure that this positive attitude was made to contribute to the success of the system development. Specification of the information requirements of executive users is often considered to be one of the most difficult aspects of EIS development. However, in this case a formal project structure created by the team leader, gave ownership of the requirements definition aspects of the system development to a representative from the user community. This helped to ensure that the initial prototype of the EIS system was useable and performed functions of use and interest to the wider user community. Once the system was installed and users trained they were able to envisage extra functions and reports that the system could produce that would help them in their work. The now mature system has entered and ongoing cycle of maintenance and refinement. It will be important for the developers, if the system is to remain successful, to be able to correctly interpret and also to keep up with these user requests for changes.

Many other problems that are normally confronted by inexperienced EIS developers were avoided by the EIS team. The leader of this team was able to ensure the smooth progression of the system development effort. He ensured that a formal package selection process was undertaken to select an appropriate development platform. An OLAP tool, called HOLOS was chosen. IS professionals when they first use a complex multi-dimensional modelling tool like HOLOS face a steep learning curve and are unproductive for a long period of time while they learn to use the tool to full advantage. In this case the team leader ensured that all the members of the development team were full trained in EIS development with the HOLOS tool. This allowed full advantage to be taken of the flexible modelling and reporting facilities offered by the OLAP architecture.

The EIS team leader has now returned to the U.S. This has not had any adverse effect on the ongoing performance of the system. The remaining members of the development team are now quite expeirenced at working with executive level users and have the required technical skills to continue to enhance and refine the system.

That the system achieved status as the 'official' data source in the corporation was due in part to the willingness of the executives to accept it. However, no matter how willing the user community was to want to use the system as a supply of information, if the data the system reported was inaccurate, untimely or unreliable the EIS would not have retained its status.

Table 14 General comments about the EIS

- Empowerment relies on information - the real facts. They made a great decision when EIS was put in - Total support from me.
- We are firstly to browse-put an issue and then quite quickly analyse the issue-it necessary down & transaction level. Also resolve a lot of disputes- the general rule is that "the system is right". In this way if the system is helps people identify the causes quickly
- The EIS is new and is a customised package. It will evolve into what it should be as it must be a base system by its introductory nature. As deficiencies are found, its performance value will increase. However, it is the first adjustable management microscope useable by individual managers and as such has encouraged previously unseen corporate views.
- Ability to analyse problems from different angles to test assumptions; What if analysis; Developing monitoring mechanisms for approved capital spend/ process changes; Early identification of problems.
- The EIS at this company is still in relative early stage of development. Certain 'modules' are complete and have been available for up to 2 years. However, other modules still in development.
- [The]'EIS' has given all of us much needed fact based data. It is not yet totally perfect but it's also helping us identify the imperfections in our base systems. [The EIS] is only as good as the base data.
- EIS is a continuous process. In a dynamic market place, such as information technology and communications, accurate and timely information is critical, EIS must enable managers to deliver to the market they are targeting with effective communication i.e. market share etc. EIS should be able to be able to be updated easily and keep pace with a dynamic environment, that is present in so many businesses today.
- The effectiveness of EIS is a function of the other systems which are feeding it with information. If EIS is fully integrated at the planning stage to other front-end systems, it will provide the greatest benefits. When EIS has to depend on obsolete system for data, its usefulness is very low.
- Most companies and myself struggle with EIS and DSS. Where should we implement these systems, what level of information should be available. Ultimately, the user will drive the implementation and deployment. However, the IS department must drive the first stages and show what can be done.
- The existence of SQL tables used to feed the HOLOS structures has tangible benefits on the other aspects of accounting work. I recommend that more of our accounting staff learn to write SQL "Select" statements and use SQLLOAD to facilitate their work.

In summary, the positive attitude toward the EIS project from the executive user community along with the skills and leadership of the EIS team leader contributed significantly to the success of this system. Studies of EIS development often disregard these aspects of system development. Future research into EIS should investigate the relationship between the culture and expectations of the executive users and the experience and skill of the development team as they are likely to be major determinants of success and failure in other EIS developments.

10 REFERENCES

Armstrong, D. (1990). 'How Rockwell Launched Its EIS'. *Datamation*, 30:8, 69-72 (Mar.).
Codd, E.F., S.B. Codd, and C.T. Salley. (1993) *Providing OLAP to User-Analysts: An IT Mandate*. E.F.Codd & Associates.
Courbon, J.C., Grajew J. and Tolovi J. (1978) 'Design and Implementation of Interactive Decision Support Systems' *Institute d'Aminisittarion des Enterprises*, Grenoble, France: Unpublished.
Demarest, M. (1994) 'Building the data mart' *DBMS: Database and Client/Server Solutions* 7:8 (July), pp 44-52, 71.
Frank, M. (1995) 'A Drill-Down Analysis of Multi-Dimenional Databases' *DBMS: Database and Client/Server Solutions* 7:8 (July), pp60-71
Fitzgerald, G. (1994). 'Outsourcing of IT in the United Kingdom: A Legitimate Strategic Option?' *Proceedings: 5th Australasian Conference on Information Systems*, (eds.) Graeme Shanks and David Arnott. Monash University, 27-40.
Houdeshel, G. and Watson, H.J. (1987). 'The Management Information and Decision Support (MIDS) System at Lockheed-Georgia' *Executive Information Systems: Emergence • Development • Impact*, (eds.) Watson, J. Hugh; Rainer, Kelly R.; Houdeshel, George. New York: John Wiley & Sons. 13-31.
Jirachiefpattana, W. (1996) *Methdological Issues in EIS Development in Australia and Thailand: A Case Study Approach* Unpublished PhD Thesis. Department of Information Systems, Monash University, Melbourne, Australia.
Paller, A. and Laska, R. (1990). *The EIS Book: Information Systems for Top Managers..* Illinois: Dow Jones-Irwin.
Rockart, J.F. and DeLong, D.W. (1988). *Executive Support Systems: The Emergence of Top Management Computer Use..* Illinois: Dow Jones-Irwin.
Sundue, D.G. (1990). 'GenRad's On-Line Executives' *Management Information Systems: Readings and Cases- A Managerial Perspective*, (eds.) Boynton, C. Andrew; Zmud, W. Robert. Glenview, Illinois: Scott, Foresman. 162-170.
Suvachittanont W., D.R. Arnott and P.A. O'Donnell (1994) 'Adaptive Development in Executive Information Systems : A Manufacturing Case Study'. *Journal of Decision Systems*, 3:4.
Watson, H.J. (1992). 'How to Fit an EIS into a Competitive Context'. Information Strategy: The Executive's Journal, 8:2, 5-10 (Winter).
Watson, H.J. Rainer Jr., R.K. and Koh F. Chang (1991). 'Executive Information Systems: A Framework for Development and a Survey of Current Practices'. *MIS Quarterly*, 15:1, 13-30 (March).
Watson, H.J.; Rainer Jr., R.K. and Frolick, M.N. (1992). 'Executive Information Systems: An Ongoing Study of Current Practices'. International Information Systems, 1:2, 37-56 (Apr.).
Wallis, L. (1989). 'Power Computing at the Top' *Executive Information Systems: Emergence • Development • Impact*, (eds.) Watson, J. Hugh; Rainer, Kelly R.; Houdeshel, George. New York: John Wiley & Sons. 301-311.

11 BIOGRAPHY

Mr Peter A. O'Donnell

Peter O'Donnell is a Lecturer in Information Systems at Monash University. He received a Bachelor of Applied Science from the Ballarat College of Advanced Education and a Master's of Computing from Monash University. His current research interests include the design of multi-dimensional data structures and the use of influence diagrams in decision support.

Professor David R. Arnott
Professor David R. Arnott is the Head of Department of Information Systems at Monash University. He is also Associate Dean of the Faculty of Computing and Information Technology. Professor Arnott commenced his computing career in 1970 and worked during the 1970's as a systems analyst and consultant, specialising in the support of management rather than the automation of clerical processes. He became an academic in 1980. Professor Arnott's teaching area is the managerial use of information systems, and his principal research area is the use of psychological theories of human judgement in the development of decision support systems.

Ms Waraporn Jiracheifpattana
Ms Waraporn Jiracheifpattana (nee Suvachittanont) is a doctoral candidate in the Department of Information Systems at Monash University, Australia. before she commenced her PhD program, she worked as a system analyst at the Information Institution for Education and Development (IPIED), Thammasat University, Thailand. her major works include the creation of the Provincial Management Information System and the Departmental Management Information System which assists government officers allocate budget to villages. As well, she has worked as a researcher to develop Human Development Indicators under United Nations sponsorship.

22

Decision support in marketing

Zita Zoltay Paprika
Budapest University of Economic Sciences
Budapest V. Veres Pálné st. 36.
H-1053. HUNGARY
Telephone: +36 1 1183 037, facsimile: +36 1 1172 959,
e-mail: paprika@mercur.bke.hu

Abstract

This paper takes the example of one of the most important Hungarian banks to show the requirements that a marketing information system must meet under the current Hungarian economic conditions to support the decision making implementing the marketing strategy in the increasing market competition.

Keywords

Decision support, marketing, data base marketing, computer implementation.

1 INTRODUCTION

At present **data base marketing** is the magic word in the international technical literature in relation to which views have been published that by the end of the millennium, according to more than 85% of the American firms, its application will be indispensable to remain competitive. These assumptions involve the obvious business consideration that costly mass marketing should be replaced with data base marketing which also allows for target marketing and thus marketing expenses may actually be targeted at customers who are worth it.

Without arguing with the adequacy of the above logic, it should be supplemented at several points. The majority of marketing decisions affect areas outside the firm, primarily the market and the participants in the market, consumers and competitors. However, the data base of a firm contains very little information about them especially if data are collected in relation to transactions. For example, it is absolutely sure that data base marketing can give no information at all about the satisfaction of customers. This is why a lot of information about consumers and competitors must be collected in different forms and from different sources and it must be classified according to the requirements of the given firm.

A marketing information system must reflect consumer orientation, competitor orientation and the service management concepts in its contents as well. In general the acceptance of the information system within a firm primarily depends on whether it is capable of meeting the information requirements. Very often decision makers are reluctant to state their exact requirements and then the developers of the system have to try to simulate the possible requirements. This is an extremely difficult task in a turbulent business atmosphere which requires frequent strategic adjustments from the players of the economy. Briefly, in such cases a solution should be found according to which the newly developed information system should be able to support basic decision making situations assuming more than one strategies.

The decision supporting nature of a marketing information system should not only be obvious in its contents but also in the structure in which information is stored and presented which should directly assist the decision making process. The classification of information according to subjects and inquiry options based on various marketing orientation may make the system suitable to support more complex, so called ill-structured decision making tasks too.

2 PRECEDENTS TO THE ASSIGNMENT

I took part in the development of the marketing information system, which is the subject of this analysis, as an external consultant. The assignment resulted from a former analytical study prepared for the client by the consultant firm where I am employed. The study reviewed the possibilities of developing a marketing strategy at the client's company. This study indicated that although the client was still a market leader in Hungary with many of its products and services, his position was heavily threatened and therefore there was an obvious need to develop a marketing strategy.

Having considered many other conditions, including immediate privatisation and reorganisation, the management of the company decided that it was not time yet for developing a marketing strategy. However, they supported the idea of developing a good marketing information system with the involvement of the employees of the company to create a basis for a future project and to strengthen the marketing aspects within the company.

So they accepted the idea that in increasing competition they could achieve a significant competitive advantage if they created an information base which they could rely on in making marketing decisions. It was interesting and therefore should be mentioned that the top managers supported the project better as they learnt that with the marketing information system they could set tasks more accurately for the marketing management for which the marketing management would be accountable. The marketing information system aimed at the collection, classification, analysis and evaluation of information related to marketing. We set the goal of providing accurate, up-to-date and fast information to the marketing decision makers. According to our views this is feasible if both the contents and the structure of the information system are consumer-oriented, competitor-oriented and reflect the service management concept.

It was clear already at the beginning that, similarly to marketing, a marketing information system can work well in an organisation only if it is not owned and used by a limited number of specialists but affects the everyday activities of the organisation. Naturally when the system is created and operated there is a need for a co-ordination team, but successful operation is subject to contributions from everybody who is involved in marketing. It is important that people should recognise that the information system is assisting them and that they can also promote its better operation. At the beginning of the development we stressed that the final result will be subject to the acceptance and involvement of the staff of the company.

3 IMPLEMENTATION

3.1 Where shall we begin?

The development of a marketing information system requires several years of work. Although the assignment of external consultants included the formulation of the concept of the system and the implementation of some "pilot study" type sub-systems, for which we allocated 18 months, we always said that we should prepare for very intensive work estimated for around 10 years in the technical literature. Our ideas concerning the project are illustrated very well through the fact that the development schedule was suggested to the client on the basis of the scheme often referred to in relation to the development of decision support systems. The steps of the scheme are the following:

- Definition of main problems and opportunities
- Definition of decision making problems in these key areas
- Analysis of the decision making processes and decision making environment
- Definition of the principles of modelling and formation of the model base
- Data base design, collection of data
- Software development and analysis
- Development of a user interface
- User testing and supplements
- Implementation

In fact, the assignment covered the support of the first five steps only. Essentially this involved the system design and functional specifications as well as the specification of requirements for the system. The further steps are rather technical and we did not deal with them directly, although made several recommendations for the IT solutions as it was kept in mind all the time that the system will work on computers.

Having studied the activities of the company, it became clear that the decision making processes and even the organisational structure focused on product and service categories. This is why the decision was made that the marketing information system had to follow this structure and development had to take place in a way that the product and service categories could be integrated into the system one after the other.

First we selected a product category which was competing at an expansive market, was still a market leader but was heavily threatened by the competitors. If we put this product into the portfolio matrix of the Boston Consulting Group, it would clearly fall within the "star" category. The distribution of the product requires an IT background and thus we had accurate data and, since it was a relatively new product all the chronological data were also available. However, it turned out in the case of this first example that the company stored mainly turnover data and there was no consequent data collection about the consumers of the product or the competitors.

The above information could only be used to assess the current situation but it should be noted that only one function could be fully supported, namely external reporting. The company had to provide regular reports for the supervising authority to which it belongs according to its profile and also to the Statistical Office. Within the company, information management was over-centralised and concentrated on the current information demand, computer systems of different philosophies were mixed up, information was managed passively and there was a total lack of collection of marketing information. At the same time it was clear that the right information could be used much more effectively as well. The performance of the company could improve if it were able to use the information to prepare marketing answers through which it could strengthen its position in the market.

For this purpose the marketing information system must provide at least three kinds of support.

- **Resource support,** which takes place in the form of data bases and model bases. In our specific case this means the definition of the data base which contains the main features of the analysed product categories, the variables describing the consumers of the product category and the typical features of the competitors who are active at the market. The model base collects the methods with which data are manipulated, e.g. through frequency histograms, calculation of indices, simulations, etc. The format of standard reports must be defined there too.

- **Process support** which means the definition of the tasks which may be performed better using the information available through the system. In the case of a product category it is a justified requirement for the marketing information system that it should support the segmentation of the consumers purchasing the product category and, on the basis of the turnover data, it should indicate where new points of sales should be set up and ways in which the company could improve its position at the market.

- **Intellectual support** which involves supporting of creative ideas and principles as well as structuring the problems. An example for that could be the integration into the system of the results of public surveys about the product which may suggest how potential consumers could be approached. Better planning of cross-selling actions could also promote acquisition of customers. Thinking about competitors could be stimulated by showing their strengths and weaknesses through which a better competitive strategy could be formed.

Usually marketing decisions have three dimensions. They affect the consumers as they try to influence them, they relate to the competitors, as is reflected in the competitive strategy, and they relate to the company products, as the market position of a company can be improved a lot through the modification and development of its products. These opportunities, directions and marketing tools had to be explicitly included in the information system as well. These requirements impacted mainly as the specification of the contents of the information system, but were also taken into account when the structure of the system was planned.

In our case, the data and analyses related to the various product categories appeared in three segments. These were called modules. The three modules in fact represented consumer-orientation, competitor-orientation and service management concept and this was also reflected in their titles: consumer analysis module, competitor analysis module and product analysis module. They may be summarised briefly as follows:

- **The consumer analysis module** is the basis of the consumer-oriented marketing strategy. The objective of the strategy is to get better information about the consumers which is only possible by completing the transaction data, which are mainly related to turnover, with other information of the behaviour, motivations and satisfaction of consumers. Naturally, in order to capture this information, one must use different methods, e.g. enquiry, observation. In addition to individual customers, company customer should be given special attention and existing and potential customers should also be distinguished.

- **In the competitor analysis module** the data of competitors are collected, managed and analysed. We had to make it clear that provided that the company intended to keep its market leading position and the wide range of products, it could not exist without most accurate information concerning the activities of its competitors. Two types of competition were distinguished. We dealt with global competition among companies of similar profiles e.g. for funds and with product competition which may be observed in a specific segment of the market.

- The information in **the product analysis module** is used to develop the products of the company and make their sale more successful. The most obvious marketing tool is improvement of the product and making it compatible with the market. Naturally the product analysis module consists of the sub-systems which represent the product categories of the company.

3.2 Problem owners and problems in decision making

After the concept of the system had been outlined, actual work began. Naturally the first task was to assess the currently used marketing information, the producers of that information and to define the users of the information. The first shock occurred when we learnt that more than one hundred information systems operated within the company in parallel with each other. It was no longer a surprise that they practically did not communicate with each other. We also came across not accounting type data, e.g. results of consumer enquiries, but awareness of those and their use were very limited. Consequently, the first achievement of the project was to identify the location and flow of information within the company.

The most difficult task was to identify the users. The mission of the internal and external specialists involved in the development could have been defined as trying to develop a system providing marketing information which can reduce the risks and stress involved in decision making and, as a result of the improved decisions, lead to better results. For this we had to find the future users as the information system must support their work in future.

As already stated, the structure of the company is product-oriented. Decisions are prepared in a decentralised manner, at the level of business categories, yet decision are made centrally. Decision making is based on the classic method of organisations with a hierarchy. The decision making levels are separated according to the volume of expenses resulting from the decision. It was then clear to the developers of the information system that the problem managers are the managers of the business categories and the top level decision makers sitting at the top of the hierarchy. However, since the products of the company are mainly services, which are sold to the customers directly, there was also a requirement that the system should also support the person who is negotiating with the customer and tries to sell the service and intends to convince the potential customer that his product was much better than that of the competitors.

Many people have addressed the problem many times that usually the decision makers are unable to specify the information they need for their decisions. Therefore developers of information systems must try to guess what their requirements are - and they fail most of the time. We also tried to achieve the impossible and asked the decision makers responsible for the "pilot study" about the types of marketing decisions they usually made and the information used for those decisions. Unfortunately, this interview took place at a very bad psychological moment as the managers had to report to the top management on the results of the product during the recent period on the same day. The managers responsible for the product were very frustrated as it became clear from the report that the company intended to change the strategy for the product and the former expansive strategy preferring the increase of volume had to be replaced with a strategy focusing more on costs. You might think that, for this reason, our questions caught them at the best possible time but in fact they had not been able to digest what they had heard at the meeting yet.

Our original intention was not an informal talk or an interview as in the given situation these methods would not even have worked. Instead we used the group work method and reduced the question to a list of decisions which were related to marketing and we even assisted them. We specified some typical decision making subjects in connection with marketing:

- decisions related to the access of the service
- decisions related to the service charges
- decisions on the promotion and advertisement of the service
- decisions on limiting or extending the choice for the service
- decisions related to the consumers buying the service
- decisions related to competitors

These unfortunate conditions were reflected in the quality of the answers. We had to get over it as it was more important to attract the attention of the problem owners and to get their support because our idea was that following the pilot study they would have to organise system management. This was only partly achieved. However, we also had more favourable experiences. In the product category, which was analysed next, we experienced much greater interest and intention for co-operation. Here managers actively assisted the work and the specialists worked continuously. It was also true that in this case the sales of the product had fallen drastically for the previous six months, mainly because of the significant reduction of purchasing power. As it was a product with lower costs but high sales revenues, the company wished to make it successful again, therefore the problem managers were committed to the objective.

As we were unable to specify all the user requirements for the system during the pilot study, we could only indirectly define the contents of the information system. Instead of the concept of a decision catalogue we introduced the concept of problem list which essentially meant a list of those subjects which covered the analytical areas and decision making dimensions, relevant for marketing. These were the following.

- The analysis of the users of the service involved the segmentation of consumers, analysis of the behaviour of customers and their satisfaction as well as identification of potential customers.
- In relation to the analysis of the access to service, we dealt with the functional and technical aspects of the service (in time, according to the form of service) and the current opportunities were compared to the customer requirements and expectations.
- In addition to simple turnover analysis, the analysis of the turnover of service extended to the definition of the priorities in sales, the impact analysis of the various sales promotion campaigns and the impacts of the changes in the service.
- The analysis of the market position of the service included the review of market tendencies, trends and participants, assumptions for the size of the market and market opportunities, a description of the economic environment, definition of the target groups, service positioning and market penetration.
- In relation to partners and competitors we collected the basic data which were available about them, all their known ideas, plans for possible co-operation and tried to identify the newcomers at the market.
- The analyses related to the quality of service were aimed at the foundation of a product policy within the marketing mix. Consequently, they extended to the review of the image of the product, product awareness, strategic importance of the product and its place in the portfolio, identification of the product objective and the processing of the history of the product within the company.
- The second element of marketing mix is the pricing policy, for the formulation of which the price flexibility of customers may need to be tested and some economic calculations may be needed. These analyses may clarify possible ways to increase profits.

- The third element of marketing mix is the sales policy which cannot exist without a thorough analysis of the sales channels, processing of consumer requirements for the channels and an analysis of the complaints against sales.
- The fourth tool of marketing mix is the communications policy which includes the sales promotion campaigns, and marketing communications for which an impact analysis of indispensable. The information gained from those may be integrated into the planning processes of the future campaigns.
- A lot of stress was put on the integration into the marketing information system of the results of relevant research related to the given services and products. In this case we did not refer only to research ordered or carried out by the client, but to all relevant research results which were available.
- A separate subject was the technical background of services as the analysed products and services could only be sold successfully with high-level IT support. Naturally, the stress was placed on development opportunities.
- Finally, the list of the subjects was closed with interesting items which included information that was a special treat for the users either because it is absolutely up-to-date in nature or substance, or simply because it was simply striking.

3.3 Logic of Information System Construction

Our recommendations concerning the building and documentation of the system were derived from the final result. On the basis of the list of problems and modules we had a better understanding of what the marketing information system had to support. As much as we could, we identified the decision making personnel and analysed whether the various decisions were regular or individual decisions. The identification of the decision making points and situations aimed at the medium and top management through the identification of the problem situations which were relevant to them, but it also included some sales decisions, that is open issues for the lower decision making levels.

Then we had to concentrate on the outputs which had to be generated at the analysed decision making points of the information system. The definition of this information base was the result of lengthy discussions. The discussion focused on the extent to which users can be authorised to search in the data base individually and to which set of outputs should be included in the system. There was a demand for the "ready-made" outputs, but we were aware of the danger that the information generated this way would mainly reflect the ideas and interpretation of the developers and not those of the decision makers.

Therefore outputs were interpreted as the services of the information system. Their format also confirmed this as they were designed on screen. Each output had a single format. It included a graphic summary figure which was completed with a short explanatory text. The data forming the basis of the graph were mostly shown in tables which could be reached through the same, or a different screen. Thus all the information used was made available right through to the primary data. Stress was put on indicating the exact source of the data and we also showed the frequency of updates and the person responsible for them. The main objective was that the outputs should directly support decision making without further calculations or editing.

Following the design of outputs, the necessary analyses were described. By analysis we meant operations that transform the primary or aggregate data available in the information system into outputs. Naturally, one decision making point was connected with several outputs and the generation of one output also could require several analyses or the same analysis could support several outputs.

Following the compilation of the collection of analyses, the necessary data were identified. These data were either imported from different computer data bases or were out into the system as external data, that is they were not generated within the system. We had to make sure that the analyses should only use data the regular generation of which will be assured in future too. For example, in the case of information gained from public surveys this meant that in future these surveys will have to be repeated periodically. In case of uncertain subjects, such as a consumer survey aimed at the analysis of purchasing power, there may be a need to acquire data from several sources and confirm them. Within the company the collection of data should be put on a new basis and we recommended that the existing centralised method will soon have to be replaced with a different practice in which the relevant information is collected by the various business units who provide the information by entering it into the marketing information system.

At a general level Kotler and Armstrong define a marketing information system as consisting of: "people, equipment and procedures to gather, sort, analyze, evaluate and distribute needed, timely and accurate information to marketing decision makers." It is well known that managers ask for information not raw data, consequently we need analytic tools to provide the necessary information to them. Sometimes retrieval questions come up of course, but most often the answers to these questions require nontrivial manipulation of stored data. Knowing this told us much about the kind of support required and made it clear that a simple data base management is not enough.

We met a company who is the Hungarian distributor of EXPRESS the world wide used commercial system with a strong business orientation and were convinced that EXPRESS is appropriate for our purposes. This software offers an easy-to-use, Microsoft Windows interface and can perform competitive analysis, track product introductions and promotional effectiveness, conduct market-by-market comparisons, isolate trouble spots, adjust marketing and sales strategies. It integrates sales and marketing data from multiple internal and external sources which was very important for us, because our modules use mainly external data and provides a full range of ad hoc analysis and reporting tools. Ranking and exception-based reporting capabilities allow marketing professionals to quickly target, track, and analyse results using their own specified criteria. Links to popular spreadsheets and word processing packages facilitate the sharing of information and eliminate the need to reformat reports and allow the use of a gallery of graph types for investigating trends. Measure-creation tools allow the addition of new marketing calculations for more detailed analysis. Support for multiple hierarchies lets users organise data to suit their specific business needs and thus transform marketing data into business intelligence.

To illustrate all this, let us look at a specific example, though the company will still not be named. The example shows the work performed in the different modules. The example is taken from the pilot study and analyses the opportunities of sales promotion in relation to the analysed products. As we saw before, this product may not be sold without a computer background and turnover could be increased in different ways, either by increasing the number of transactions or increasing the turnover in each transaction. Both methods result in a bigger market share and reduce costs. The decision concerning sales promotion is made by the management of the business unit and decisions may be made once every six months or they may be occasional decisions, depending on the actions of competitors.

Many outputs support the decision. Let us now concentrate on the one which shows the monthly sales of the product to consumers according to various income categories. Naturally, primarily the spending habits of the company's own customers are interesting for active marketing but the review of similar data of competitors may also give useful additional information. In this case the output could be a pie diagram showing the consumer proportions according to the income categories. It could be supplemented with a background table in which the lines show the income categories according per capita monthly income and the columns show the sales of the company and competitors. Thus the table illustrates the spending habits, comparing them with the similar figures for the competitors.

To analyse this output we need to know the spending and saving habits of customers, as well as the tendencies for changing them. The data required for the analysis should include the income categories, the number of customers falling into those categories and the turnover figures. Such data may be collected mainly through personal enquiries as people are reluctant to give information about their income in any other forms, e.g. in writing. Naturally, the sales figures are available at the company. It is practical to assign a market research firm to collect the data, at least to complete the enquiries, or to ask those members of the staff who are in contact with customers even if not in relation to this product, but through other products. The information generated this way will only be reliable if it is updated at least once every six months, as in a turbulent economic environment the purchasing power of the population cannot be considered stable.

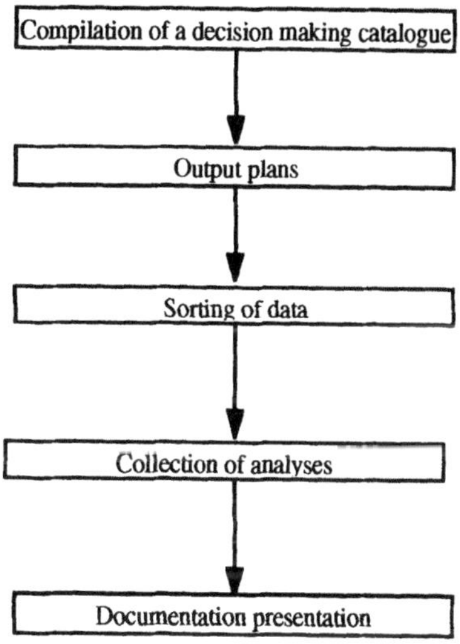

Figure 1 Scenario of the activities of the modules

How much does the shown output serve marketing? First of all it may indicate which of the customers of the company need more attention, and what should be concentrated on more: whether to increase the number of customers or to promote sales to existing customers. Targeted marketing campaigns may be prepared with it and thus the efficiency of marketing activities increases.

Figure 1 shows the algorithm for this work and the fact that development took place in practice at three levels. The first one could be called the planning or reconsideration level, characterised by assessments made by specialists. They covered different areas and summarised the dilemmas of experts. For example, this included the definition of parameters and features required for the decision making levels, the necessary but not quantified data for the decision concerning what should be stressed in the outputs for the various decision making levels. The issue of future operation of the information system, for which the developers intended to rely on the future users, also falls in this category. Experience shows thatpromoting the marketing information system itself requires serious marketing work before the users will agree to that task.

The second level involved the operation level where data are collected, verified and the data used in the analyses are generated. In fact data preparation and processing belong there. In the pilot study the main test of the operation level was loading data into the system from which we learnt a lesson, namely that many data could only be obtained with more difficulties than expected. This is mainly true for data related to the competitors and the internal expense figures of the company. It is natural that in the increasing competition the competitors protect the figures of their own operation and the expense figures were not available due to lack of controlling. However, it is promising that the controlling system is also being developed at the company and its level of completion makes it possible to pass on information to the marketing information system in the near future.

The third level of development is the user level. Convincing the users has always been a very important task. The system tried to provide them information classified according to dates, source and reliability and we continuously demanded feedback about the information put into the system and in relation to new requirements. The information system managed the user requirements in two dimensions. Information was generated for decision making levels and for special areas. We found that there was more interest in the latter group of information.

4 ROLE OF THE MARKETING INFORMATION SYSTEM IN DECISION SUPPORT

One of the most important successes of the assignment for the marketing information system was that those involved in the project understood the role of marketing, became aware of the importance of the market and that it was essential to share information about the market within the company. The information system was introduced to the organisation as a kind of collective memory and, although its development was suggested by the department responsible for marketing, we managed to involve representatives of other functions and business lines into the development.

The project organised for the development of the information system helped the participants to develop a new type of market-oriented thinking and provided a base of some classified information, though in specific areas only, which contains actual data about the given areas from marketing aspects. It is worth mentioning that, since marketing is an integrating function in the operation of the company, during the development we came across many strategic problems which do not strictly fall into the competence of developers. In such cases we did not go into the problems in depth but did not avoid them, either. Instead we tried to put into the information system further information assisting the marketing-oriented analysis of the analysed problems.

Data base marketing is becoming more popular in Hungary. In this case we chose a more tiresome way of marketing information system development, going beyond data base marketing, because we looked at system development as a learning process for the client company. The members participating in the project did not only represent their own organisational units but also acted as catalysers. They were creative, disclosed problems and requirements, collected and classified information and in the meantime they were thinking about the future of their company.

5 REFERENCES

Barabba, V.P. and Zaltman, G. (1991) *Hearing the voice of the market: competitive advantage through creative use of market information*. Harvard Business School Press, Boston.

Cats-Baril, W. and Huber, G.P. (1987) Decision Support Systems for Ill-Structured Problems: An Empirical Study. *Decision Sciences*, **18**, 351-371.

Checkland, P. (1981) *Systems Thinking, Systems Practice*. John Wiley and Sons.

Dockerry, E. (1991) *The strategic use of information systems technology in banking firms and building societies*. Working Paper No. 117, City University, London.

Doll, W.J. (1985) Top Management Involvement in Successful MIS Development, *MIS Quarterly*, March, 17-35.

Douglass, D.D. (1990) Building Marketing Information Systems. *I/S Analyzer*, **28**, 1-12.

Er, M.C. (1988) Decision Support Systems: a summary, problems and future trends. *Decision Support Systems*, **4**, 355-363.
Finlay, P.N. and Morteza, F. (1995) *A Consultant Advisory System for Decision Support Systems,* Research Series Paper 19, Loughborough University Business School.
Humphreys, P.C. and Berkeley, D. (1983) Problem Structuring Calculi and Levels of Knowledge Representation in Decision Making. in *Decision Making under Uncertainty* (ed. R.W. Scholz), North Holland, Amsterdam.
Humphreys, P.C. and Nappelbaum, E.L. (1995) Structure and communications in the process of organisational change: Eastern European experience and its general relevance. in *Decision Support in Organisational Transformation* (ed. B. Mayon-White, S. Ayestarán and P.C. Humphreys), Universidad del Pais Vasco, San Sebastian.
Kotler, P. and Armstrong, G. (1991) *Principles of Marketing*. Prentice-Hall, Englewood Cliffs, N. J.
Loebbecke, C.and Kronen, J.H. (1995) Fips sets the fashions: a DSS for purchase planning in a European department store. in *Decision Support in Organisational Transformation* (ed. B. Mayon-White, S. Ayestarán and P.C. Humphreys), Universidad del Pais Vasco, San Sebastian.
Meador, L.C., Guyote, M.J. and Keen, P.G.W. (1984) Setting Priorities for DSS Development. *MIS Quarterly*, June, 117-129.
Paprika, Z. and Zoltay, Á. (1994) *The Current Hungarian Business Climate*. BEAMS Doc. UR-RR-006. Department of Business Economics, Budapest University of Economic Sciences.
Phillips, L.D. (1992) Gaining corporate commitment to change. in *Executive information systems and decision support* (ed. C. Holtham), Chapman and Hall, London.
Porter, M. (1980) *Competitive Strategy*. The Free Press, New York.
Sol, H.G. and Vecsenyi, J. (1990) *Environments for Supporting Decision Processes*. North Holland, Amsterdam.

6 BIOGRAPHY

Dr. Zita Zoltay Paprika is an assistant professor at the Business Economics Department of Budapest University of Economic Sciences. She teaches decision making theory and decision making methodology at undergraduate, graduate and post-graduate levels. She is in charge of the minor organised for graduate students which is called "Managerial Decision Making". She also permanently works as a consultant during which activity she has been a project manager on several occasions. From 1991 to 1994 she was the Hungarian co-ordinator of the TEMPUS BEAMS (Business Economics and Management Support) JEP-2360 Project financed by the European Union. At the moment she is the manager of the follow-up project of the same project. She is also the manager of the Decision Making Methodology Project of the Competitiveness Programme, which is organised by the Business Economics Department, and studies the competitiveness of the Hungarian micro-sector.

23

Processes for managing project uncertainty with contingency planning

Cathy Roberts, Chris Wild, Kurt Maly
Old Dominion University Department of Computer Science
Norfolk, VA, USA, Phone: (804) 683-3915, FAX: (804) 683-4900,
[ccr|wild|maly]@cs.odu.edu

Abstract

One of the most pervasive problems faced by project managers is controlling a large project in an uncertain and distributed work environment. We believe that many of the inherent difficulties in managing large engineering and software projects result from difficulties in managing the uncertainty inherent in any lengthy, complex undertaking. Currently available project management tools allow the project manager to perform "what-if" and risk analyses, but do not support the management of an uncertain project environment. Existing decision support systems allow analysis of known facts about the project, but they focus upon what should be done with information after it is available. They do not support decision-making in the face of evolving and often insufficient project information, and they do not support the decision-maker when a plan must be enacted even before a decision can be made. Also, they assume that decisions are made once, instantaneously, and in isolation from the external project environment.

In our approach, we respond to the presence of project uncertainty by supporting the manager in developing and enacting competitive contingency plans. Competitive contingency plans are those plans which solve a particular project objective, and which are performed concurrently because sufficient information is not available to allow the manager to choose the single most appropriate plan. The competing plans are simultaneously enacted because project uncertainty precludes selection of a single correct course of action, and the manager must proceed with project tasks based only on the information at hand. In this paper, we address the management of contingency plans in the inherently uncertain environment of large-scale projects. Our major objectives for this research are to define and implement a process for decision-based contingency planning, and a knowledge structure to support this process. By utilizing this decision process model, we will be able to see the effects of new information upon the project and communicate the new information to affected project team members.

Keywords
Project management, decision-based system development, contingency planning, group communication, uncertainty

1 INTRODUCTION

Organizations are becoming increasingly linked to their information systems, and this "cyberorganization" provides a diverse set of services which are distributed in space and time. These services include engineering services (such as those provided by consultants), consumer services (such as those provided by stock brokers), consumer products (services provided by manufacturers), health care services, and so on. Management of system development projects in these various domains is impeded by many pervasive problems, and many of them involve uncertainty about the project and its environment. Projects have evolving goals, and have constraints introduced by agents external to the project. Because the cyberorganization's services are becoming more distributed and complex, the systems supporting the cyberorganization are also becoming larger and more diverse. They are developed by team members who may be distributed across wide geographic areas, and who often utilize a distributed information architecture. Also, this team is often composed of consultants or contract workers whose services are outsourced. The system development process must support complex collaborative efforts for a complex user, the cyberorganization. It also must support the uncertainty which results from this distributed, complex nature of the cyberorganization. Each step of this process involves decision management by team members and managers, regardless of their roles in the project or their geographic location. The impact of decisions upon each other needs to be represented, and changes which impact a decision need to be effectively communicated. Management of such a development process in the face of uncertainty requires the ability to understand and review the evolving web of decisions which results in the product which is being generated.

Support for project management has previously borrowed from techniques for managing traditional engineering projects. The structure of the organization which guides the project decision management process is often pictured as hierarchical or matrix-based. However, structuring the organization around the project decision-making process is a more appropriate approach when the projects involve a significant amount of problem-solving. The decision process guides the development of products for the cyberorganization, and this process should be reflected in the support for the organizational structure. The stakeholders in any single decision are a diverse group which often cut across organization boundaries (and may indeed involve members outside of the organization).

Traditional project management techniques also fall short in an attempt to manage projects for the cyberorganization. Techniques which allow the management of project budgets are available (traditional bookkeeping and accounting techniques, for example), as are good scheduling techniques and resource management methods. Decision support systems are effective in analyzing decisions when relevant project information has been gathered and is readily available. However, none of these methods provides integrated support for the on-going decision processes which drive the management of the uncertain project environment.

To deal with uncertainty, a manager often must be creative with his or her approach to solving problems and to project tasking, and will likely fall back on techniques such as contingency planning if he or she does not have sufficient information to select a single course of action from among many alternatives. None of the methods mentioned in the preceding paragraph was designed to continuously handle project uncertainties. The research presented in this paper identifies a process for managing competitive contingency plans when evolving project requirements exist. We do not propose a decision-theoretic approach, since we could not adequately deal with uncertainty in this manner.

Our approach for incorporating decision process support into project management has its roots in the Decision-based System Development (DBSD) paradigm. DBSD was developed at Old Dominion University to manage and record system development decisions and the artifacts which result from the development process (Wild and Maly, 1992). Its focus is upon the process of decision-making, as opposed to simply building the decision tree. Its initial application was to software projects which are small in scope (contract value of less than \$100,000); however, it has also been shown to be useful in managing more complex problems (Wild et. al., 1994). DBSD views system development as a series of problem-solving episodes which determines the characteristics of the system which is ultimately created. There are a large number of these episodes in any cyberorganization which much be managed, and they are partly driven by their distributed nature, the uncertainty of available information, the complexity of the project, and a need to take action before the scope of the project can be fully determined. Since decisions are not made once, forever, and instantaneously, it is necessary to provide support for managing decisions over time. DBSD emphasizes the need to support the key process elements (decisions) which lead to the design of the final product structure.

DBSD has been applied to five different system development projects. These applications span all phases of the software life-cycle. Most recently, the paradigm has been applied to NASA's Low-Visibility Landing and Surface Operations (LVLASO), and to the day-to-day management of the development of software tools supporting the Advanced Research Project Agency's (ARPA's) large distributed simulation software product called ModSAF. The LVLASO application focused on capturing the development process in its earliest phases by recording the decisions which defined the direction of the project. The application to ModSAF tracked the daily management decisions which guide the development of new ModSAF-related software tools. The focus of this application is upon project management.

2 A CONCEPTUAL MODEL FOR MANAGING UNCERTAINTY WITH CONTINGENCY PLANS

Decision-making plays roles in many facets of the management of system development projects. These decisions also have several characteristics common among these facets. They are not made instantaneously, since it often takes considerable time to identify alternatives, assign criteria for evaluating them, and then make the evaluation. For example, it may be necessary to build a simulation in order to better understand the nature of the problem being solved. The decisions are also not made in isolation. External factors often affect the choice which must be made from among alternatives. These factors include previous decisions made on the project which define the context in which subsequent decisions take place as well as environmental factors (such as changing government regulations, or new products from competitors or suppliers). Also, decisions are not always made exactly once. They are regularly revisited during a project, and are also relevant to other projects and can be reused. Because of these three characteristics of project decisions, uncertainty is prevalent in the project's scope. At any given point, information is being gathered for decision-making, decisions are being reviewed and revised, and the external project environment is changing. This uncertainty is not typically the result of bad project management practices, but does result from changing customer requirements, market conditions, and other factors outside the control of the project manager (Kraut and Streeter, 1995). This uncertainty causes the manager to utilize techniques such as conditional decision-making, risk analysis, and contingency planning. Our focus is upon managing competitive contingency plans, and is described in the following section.

2.1 Competing Contingency Plans

Contingency plans are often enacted when not enough information is available to make an informed decision, but tasks must begin anyway. In other words, they involve the paradoxical enactment of a decision before the decision is actually made. A plan is chosen contingent upon the receipt of some outstanding information, or perhaps upon the occurrence of some event. Although contingency planning can be supported by traditional project management methods such as PERT (Winstanley, 1991), there is a need to provide support for contingency planning which is more dynamic and decision-based than the traditional methods. A PERT view of a contingency plan would, for example, show the tasks being performed in parallel in the PERT network. PERT and CPM, however, provide a view of a project's status at a discrete point in time and do not show the decisions which resulted in the current status. They also do not allow the analyst to examine tradeoffs among contingency plans, the trigger points (i.e., events or decisions which allow the selection of one course of action from among the contingencies) which enact plans, and the risk involved in pursuing the contingencies. While contingency plans can be represented by these methods, they are not distinguishable from real concurrent plans, and therefore are not fully supported by traditional project management approaches. Also, the ability to re-use work done in support of the contingency plans is not addressed with these project management methods. Additionally, since decision-making is not an instantaneous event, it is not easily represented by these traditional project management tools (Roberts, 1994). This implies that the complete PERT chart may not be available when the project begins. Decision-making is, however, a process which is driven by a need to gather information to make the decision (March, 1991) . Often, this process requires a significant amount of effort and time. Previous decision support system designs (Stohr and Konsynski, 1992) attempt to assist in this effort by allowing the decision-maker to model the problem, establish weights for alternatives, and eventually extract a decision from the system. The process of building the initial model is not addressed. Further, no attempt is made to manage this modeling process.

Current approaches to contingency planning simply support a "what-if" analysis which is performed before a project plan is executed (Kartam, Tzeng, and Teng, 1993). The purpose of this what-if analysis is to optimize a set of discrete events rather than to manage a dynamic, group-collaborative, decision-based process. What-if analyses simply involve making a discrete decision before the tasks are undertaken, and they assume a stable environment (i.e., no residual uncertainty after task commencement) Because there is a need to provide a more dynamic approach to project planning, this proposed research will involve the support of competitive contingency planning in a group-collaborative environment. Competitive contingency plans differ from other contingency plans in that multiple solutions are enacted in competition with each other. Usually contingency plans can be stated in a sentence like "if A then B else C". Competitive contingency planning allows both B and C to be executed until the truth of A can be established. A simple example of these differing views of contingency planning would be the preparation of a conference presentation. Suppose we wish to make a conference presentation about a new Web-based software product, but we do not know whether the conference organizers are offering Internet connections, equipment to display computer screens, or simply overhead projectors. We prefer to demonstrate our product on-line using the World Wide Web and project the interface on a screen for the conference participants to see, but the conference organizers do not know if they can provide this type of equipment. We have three options for presenting our new system. First, we can do "screen dumps" of our interfaces and simply display them with the overhead projector. Second, we can give a typical presentation with overheads, and follow that later with a demonstration on a computer at a small "break-out" session. Third, we can perform the demo to the assembled participants using a Web-connected computer and computer screen projection equipment. As the time for the conference approaches, we must proceed with preparations for our presentation, although the conference organizers still are unsure about the resources we will have available. Because we do not want to risk preparing only an elaborate on-line presentation that we may not be able to give, we decide to pursue all three competing contingencies. We prepare a Web-based presentation, and from this prepare overhead transparencies that we can use if a live demonstration is not feasible. It is possible that the time spent preparing transparencies will be wasted if we can do our Web-based demo, but we determine that risk to be acceptable. Regardless of our ultimate course of action, the time spent preparing the on-line demo is not likely to be wasted, because it is used in all three scenarios (it is used to generate screen dumps, it is used for the small demo in the break-out session, and it is used if the full-blown demo can be given). We call this type of task a "robust" task.

Contingency planning does provide a means for managing risk by allowing the enactment of a plan based upon the best available information at any particular time. However, as shown in the example, some wasted effort could result. So, some competing plans require more resources before they can be enacted, or alternately it may be necessary to use fewer resources per plan (e.g., use fewer people to prepare the full demo). Good management includes knowing how to control this risk and knowing which contingencies are appropriately undertaken. Selection of contingencies is a complex problem which relates to schedules and deadlines, utilization of resources (e.g., an employee is hired before enough is known about the project for correct tasking, so the employee starts work on a contingency), changing requirements, reliability of available information, impact upon or by external organizations, lack of domain knowledge, maximization of learning experiences, and minimization of cost by reuse of the work performed. Therefore, contingency planning can be seen to be both a valid response to project uncertainty, and affected by these aspects of project uncertainty as well.

To support decision management scenarios in which competing contingency plans are enacted, we propose a paradigm which must allow multiple decisions to be enacted simultaneously, and must allow the evaluation of multiple alternatives against a set of criteria.

Further, the paradigm must support analysis of the tasks involved in each alternative which is enacted. Contingency plans are the result of a lack of information; therefore, new information from the tasks and the environment must be propagated to the team and to the manager in order to allow de-activation of contingency plans which are no longer relevant. This analysis of tasks should also support risk assessment based upon the "robustness" of contingent tasks. A "robust" task within a contingency plan, as illustrated previously, is one which is present in all contingencies; that is, it is performed regardless of which contingencies are enacted. Enactment of non-robust tasks carries a certain degree of risk which can be characterized by the probability that the contingency plan of which this task is a part is discarded. The potential of wasted effort which is put into a non-robust plan is itself one of the criteria that must be considered in choosing a contingency. Effort spent on a feasible contingency, which is later determined to be non-optimal, will often dictate the outcome. If a task appears in many contingencies, the risk is less than if it appears in only one contingency plan. If a task occurring in a single plan is performed, and then the plan is later abandoned, the work performed for this task is lost. If a task appears in several plans, it is more likely that the work performed will not be wasted.

Since each task in a contingency plan carries some risk of wasted effort, we can assign a probability value to the task representing this risk. We refer to this as the probability of wasted effort, or $\pi_w{}^i$. This probability value is computed from the number of contingency plans in which the task appears as follows:

$$\pi_w{}^i = 1 - (\text{number of contingencies in which task } i \text{ appears / total number of contingencies}). \quad (1)$$

For example, if four competing contingencies have been enacted, and a task appears in three of them, the value of $\pi_w{}^i$ would equal 1-(3/4), or 25%.

The analysis must also include evaluation of tasks shared among contingencies in terms of schedular and resource constraints. Adjustment of project schedules may be necessary to allow resources to work on these simultaneous tasks, and to exploit the availability of the necessary resources.

2.2 The Justification Matrix

The justification matrix provides structure to organize the various activities of the decision management process, and is particularly useful when managing decisions needed for competitive contingency planning. It also contains the primitives which are used in the decision-making process. These primitives include the alternatives (the columns of the matrix), and the decision criteria (the rows of the matrix). This justification data structure also contains fields which denote contingency plans (which can be stored in a project management software system or in another relation in the database). As the process of decision-making proceeds, rows and columns of the matrix are filled, and contingencies are tagged. Instantiating the matrix forces a comprehensive examination of the problem, promotes in-depth understanding of the relevant decision issues, has historical value, and captures a growing body of knowledge as a problem is evaluated. The contents of the matrix depend on the type of the decision being made. For example, budgetary decisions will often have "hard" (quantifiable) criteria such as cost savings or anticipated expenditures for each alternative. Personnel-related decisions will have softer criteria, such as improved morale or development of better work habits. Although we have not done so, it is likely that a basic set of criteria can be defined for each classification. These sets could be reused as justification matrices are developed for each new decision.

2.3 Group Communication For Contingency Planning

Project decision-makers require the most current information possible as they attempt to guide the project. Making each project-related decision requires the elimination of uncertainty by gathering information relevant to the decision. It also requires that the decision-makers in the group have the most current information possible about the status of each competitive contingency plan which has been enacted, and about trigger points which have been reached. The use of competitive contingency plans demands that team members are constantly aware of the internal and external project environment, so that decisions made by the group are informed and effective.

To support this group communication, clear channels of communication between the project manager and team members must be maintained, along with communication among the team members themselves. Commercial project management and group collaboration software developers have recognized the necessity of communication among team members, and support this with various e-mail enhancements. We also believe that group communication is a pervasive process, and define a process for effective group communication in the presence of contingency plans. This process focuses information flow around project decisions, so that uncertainty is reduced as efficiently as possible.

The communication model is based upon seven types of messages, which are directed to team members whose identifiers are resident in the decision database. The first message, a decision request (DR), is sent to the relevant decision-maker when a decision must be made that is outside the recognized domain of the requester. The decision-maker then responds to the requester with a Response to DR (RDR), which either contains a decision, advises that no decision is forthcoming, advises of a date when the decision can be expected, or gives a probability that a particular course of action will be taken. A user can also pose a Question (Q) to any team members, and a response is give by team members in an Information message (I). "I" messages can also be used to pass any information or data to others in the cyberorganization. Users can also make Status Queries (SQ) to find out the status of a Decision Request if the request has been pending too long. Another feature of the communication model is the ability of a user to assess consensus within the cyberorganization about a decision issue by issuing a Gauge Interest (GI). Others in the cyberorganization respond to this message with Response to GI (RGI) messages, and the original requester can evaluate the relevance of the issue to the cyberorganization as a whole.

The seven message types, DR, RDR, I, Q, SQ, GI, and RGI, are denoted in the mail header, and the messages are counted if necessary to determine demand for a particular decision. This communication model's implementation is currently being studied, and will most likely be implemented in the context of groupware or networked mail tools.

3 THE UNCERTAINTY REDUCTION PROTOCOL AND ITS IMPLEMENTATION

The use of Competitive Contingency Planning and the group communication paradigm discussed previously have as their stated goals the reduction of uncertainty in the cyberorganization. We propose a process for using these tools, and refer to this application as the Uncertainty Reduction Protocol (URP). The Uncertainty Reduction Protocol attempts to minimize uncertainty in the execution of project tasks by focusing team members' attention on project decisions and the resulting tasks. It also supports enactment of tasks even when decisions cannot be made due to lack of information or lack of consensus. The process presented here has two components. The first addresses a process for considering new decisions, and the second addresses the revisiting of decisions which have been previously entered into the system.

3.1 Process for Using the Protocol

The process for contingency planning is based upon the process used for the Decision-based System Development (DBSD), but carries it further. The process steps for newly introduced problems can be listed as follows:

- **Identify and articulate the problem to be solved**. In the URP implementation, this is done through a decision form interface.
- **Identify alternative solutions**. These are entered in the justification matrix.
- **Choose decision criteria**. These are entered in the justification matrix.
- **Justify alternatives**, using the data in the justification matrix.
- **Plan contingencies**, using project management software.
- **Enact contingency plans**, utilizing techniques defined in communication model. To obtain information about the status of pending decisions, the requester sends a status query to the person from whom the decision is needed. To request a decision from elsewhere in the cyberorganization, a decision request is submitted to the person(s) who must make the decision. An information message is sent when project information must be disseminated to others in the cyberorganization. Gauge interest messages are sent if consensus-building is required. A question message is sent as information is gathered, especially early in the enactment. A response to decision request message is sent as decision requests are addressed. This message can contain a decision, the date a decision can be expected, advice that no decision will be made, or the probability that a particular course of action will be followed. A response to a gauge interest message can be sent to inform original requesters of interest in the plan being enacted.

  During this step, data regarding risk are collected, and trigger points are tracked with the project management system. The contingencies are tracked in the project management system for as long as they exist.
- **Evaluate contingency plans**, using the project management system (cost, resource, schedular analyses) and using the decision database to track pending decisions' progress. Information about progress of the plans may come from elsewhere in the

cyberorganization, and these data are entered into the decision database and the project management package as necessary.

- **Evaluate conditional decisions**, and enter the effectiveness of the decision or contingency into the decision database.

One simple example of the use of this process would be the conference presentation example given in section 2.1 Competing Contingency Plans. Suppose we wish to enter our conference presentation contingency plan into our system. First, we prepare a concise statement describing the need to prepare this presentation, and our uncertainty about available resources for it. We type this into our decision database using the available form. Next, we identify the three alternative solutions for this problem (using transparencies, an off-line demo, and a full demo) and type these into the justification matrix spreadsheet. The criteria we will be using to select our presentation medium are listed in the justification matrix (namely, the availability of an appropriate platform and the availability of a network connection). Then, we plan our contingencies by listing tasks for all three alternatives in our favorite project management software, and we link the tasks to the decision database (we use Time Line Solutions' TimeLine® product for project management, and we take advantage of the project management software's Object Linking and Embedding (OLE) capability to accomplish this). Then, we proceed to prepare the three presentations, after confirming that we have adequate resources to do this. Finally, after reaching the conference site, we can evaluate the contingencies by determining which hardware resources are available, and select one presentation from our contingencies. We then enter this selection into the decision database for future reference in case we submit a paper for this conference again at a later time.

Revisiting decisions is usually prompted by the receipt of information from elsewhere in the cyberorganization. It can result from the receipt of a structured message as required by the group communication model when contingencies are enacted. The communication model defines how this message is handled.

If incoming information is unstructured, or comes from a source other than the email system, the following process is used to handle the information:

- The decision database is queried for a list of all decisions, or an SQL query can be used to search for a known keyword. The user extracts pertinent decisions and reviews them. The information obtained is entered into the justification matrix and decision database as appropriate.
- A "closure generator" is then used to trace through other related decisions. This tool traces through the decision database to find all decisions which are logically linked (i.e., parent decisions which spawned sub-decisions, etc.). The new information is entered in any relevant decisions.
- The new information is then placed into the project management tool if it involves schedule, budget, or resources. The appropriate tasks can be found from links from the decision database.
- A "mail propagation tool" is next used if others in the cyberorganization must be notified of changes resulting from the new information. The contact list from the decision database is used to determine to whom the information message should be propagated.

- If the new information requires that a decision should be made elsewhere in the cyberorganization, the decision request is generated and sent.
- If the new information enables response to a decision request, the response to decision request is sent.
- If the new information raises questions, the question message is prepared and sent using the mail propagation tool.
- If the new information spawns contingencies, they are entered as described in the previous section. The probability of wasted effort is calculated for the plans by the system, and this information can be used to analyze the contingencies' risks. The process then follows the steps outlined for new problems.

As an example, referring again to the conference presentation example, suppose we are preparing the three presentation formats as outlined. Before we have completed the preparation of the demonstrations, we receive a letter from the conference organizers informing us that we will only have an overhead projector available to us for our presentation at the conference site. Therefore, we can use this information to select the single contingency which is appropriate: the preparation of a transparencies. We search the decision database for the relevant problem using the query mechanism we have available, then we enter the decision which was made (i.e., to use transparencies for our presentation). We update the tasks in the project management tool, then use the mail propagation software to inform the team members to concentrate on the development of the presentation using the overhead projector only.

3.2 Implementation of the Protocol

The implementation of the Uncertainty Reduction Protocol is being done in the context of enhancements to commercially available software products. The main reason for this approach is so users will feel comfortable using the protocol in the familiar context of project management software, spreadsheet software, and groupware. The architecture being implemented consists of a decision database, which can be maintained in any ODBC-compliant database or spreadsheet system, a communication form implemented in groupware, a decision interface, the justification matrix (currently implemented in a Microsoft Excel® spreadsheet), and data from the user's project management software package (we are using Time Line Solutions Corporation's TimeLine® project management software). The user is expected to use any problem-solving methodology he or she wishes. The architecture is illustrated in Figure 1.

By using the protocol as described in the process outlined previously, and an implementation of the proposed architecture, we would expect the system to answer user questions such as the following:

1. I receive an email relating to a decision. It has a predictable structure containing keywords. How do I find decisions relevant to this email in the decision database?
2. I receive an email or phone call relating to a decision, or I got information about the decision in a meeting. The information is not structured and may not be in the system at all. How do I find decisions which are relevant to this unstructured message?

3. I make or change a decision. Which other decisions and tasks are affected by this modification?
4. I am tracking competing contingencies with a project management tool. New information arrives about these contingency plans. What happens?
5. I am tracking competing contingencies with a project management tool. A trigger point is encountered. What happens?
6. I make or change a decision and need to alert others in the cyberorganization with need-to-know. How is this accomplished?
7. I need some consensus in the cyberorganization about a pending decision I must make. How do I get this?
8. I made an important decision which should be made known to some other people in the cyberorganization. How do I do this? How do I find out which people have need-to-know?
9. I have to make a decision, and I wonder who else in the cyberorganization cares about it. How do I find out?
10. I need my management to make a decision for me. How do I request this?
11. I need to know the status of a decision I requested. How do I find out?
12. I got a Gauge Interest (GI) message about a decision I'm interested in working on. How do I let the sender know that I'm out here and interested?
13. I need some information from elsewhere in my cyberorganization before I can make a decision. How to I get it?
14. I need to change my schedule and resource allocation for the project. Which decisions are affected?
15. I need to change some decisions I made. How is the schedule/resource allocation/budget changed to correctly reflect this? How do I pick up all decisions in this "closure"?
16. How do I know how robust a task is (i.e., what is the value of $\pi_w{}^i$)?
17. I need a list of all decisions that have to do with "x".
18. I need to know the financial and schedular risk of pursuing a couple of contingency plans. How do I get this?
19. How do I optimize contingency plans so that I waste the least work?
20. What is the global uncertainty of my project?
21. I can't make up my mind about "z". What is this indecision costing me? Do I have to make a decision, or can I afford to defer it?

Answering user questions such as these requires the presence of some new system features. These features include a mail handler, which builds a query upon receipt of a structured message, and then searches the database for decisions based on the keywords in the message. A decision list generator is needed for presenting the user with a comprehensive list of decisions if a structured query cannot be build from the received message. A closure generator should trace up and down links in the decision database and present the user with a list of decisions which are related logically in the database. A mail propagation tool uses the contact list in the database to send structured messages to relevant people in the cyberorganization. Finally, the computation of the wasted effort in a contingency plan should be performed for the user upon demand. We are currently implementing these features and will subsequently evaluate their usefulness.

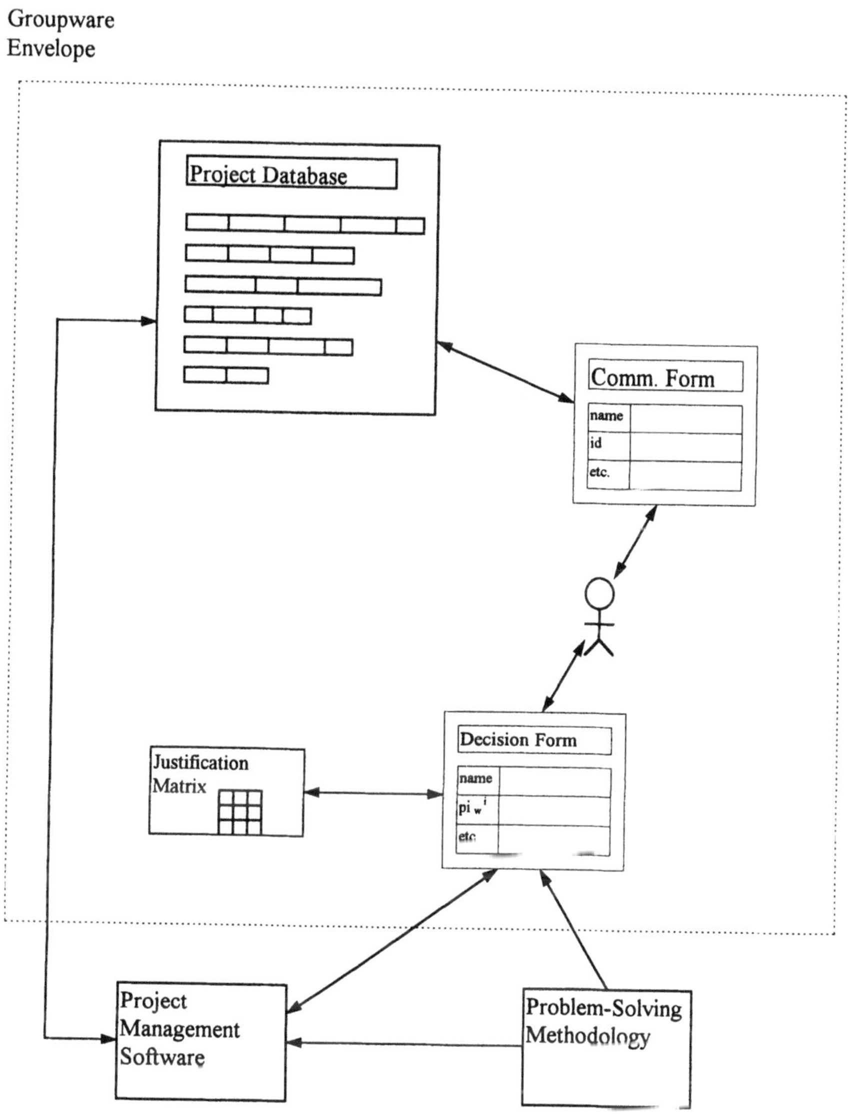

Figure 1 Uncertainty Reduction Protocol Architecture

4 SUMMARY

This paper has discussed processes for contingency planning and group communication which support the management of uncertainty in large system development and engineering projects.

We believe that the responding to project uncertainty with enactment of competitive contingency plans is a widely-used project management technique which is not currently well-supported. We propose a decision-centered process with a supporting information and communication structure for managing contingency planning. This ensures that team members in a decision-making capacity are aware of all current information about each of their impending decisions, and that they know when contingency plans have been resolved.

Future work will involve the evaluation of the success of this application. We anticipate revisions of the Uncertainty Reduction Protocol as necessary based upon these evaluation studies.

5 REFERENCES

Kartam, N., Tzeng, G.-H., and Teng, J.-Y. (1993) Robust Contingency Plans for Transportation Investment Planning. *IEEE Transactions on Systems, Man, and Cybernetics,* **23:1**, 5-13.

Kraut, R., and Streeter, L. (1995) Coordination in Software Development. *Communications of the ACM,* **38:3**, 69-81.

March, J. (1991) How Decision Happen in Organizations. *Human-Computer Interaction,* **6**, 95-117.

Roberts, C. (1994) A Decision-based System Development Paradigm for Support of Contingency Planning and Group Collaboration. Old Dominion University Ph.D. Thesis Proposal.

Stohr, E., and Konsynski, B. (1992) *Information Systems and Decision Processes.* IEEE Computer Society Press, Los Alamitos, CA.

Wild, C., and Maly, K. (1992) Software Life Cycle Support - Decision-based Software Development. *Information Processing 92,* **1**, 72-78.

Wild, C., Maly, K., Zhang, C., Roberts, C., Rosca, D., and Taylor, T. (1994) Project Management Using Hypermedia CASE Tools. *1994 Conference on Data and Knowledge Systems for Manufacturing and Engineering,* 722-727.

Winstanley, G. (1991) *Artificial Intelligence in Engineering.* John Wiley and Sons, New York.

6 BIOGRAPHY

Cathy Roberts is a Ph.D. candidate in Computer Science at Old Dominion University. She received her B.S. degree in Industrial Engineering and Operations Research from Virginia Tech in 1983, and her M.S. degree in Computer Science from Old Dominion University in 1992. She has held industrial engineering, systems engineering, and project management positions in industry. Her current research interests include decision-based systems development, project management issues, and software engineering.

Chris Wild received his Ph.D. degree in Computer Science from Rutgers University in 1977 in the area of computer vision. He worked for eight years at Bell Telephone Laboratories on computer graphics, robotics, CAD/CAM, data base and communications network systems. He is currently an associate professor at Old Dominion University. His research interests are software testing, decision-based systems development, distance learning and medical support systems.

Kurt J. Maly received the Dipl. Ing. degree from the Technical University of Vienna, Austria, and the M.S. and Ph.D. Degrees from the Courant Institute of Mathematical Sciences, New York University, New York, NY. He is Kaufman Professor and Chair of Computer Science at Old Dominion University, Norfolk, VA. Before that, he was at the University of Minnesota, both as faculty member and Chair. He also is Visiting Professor at Chengdu University of Science and Technology, People's Republic of China and is Honorary Professor at Hefei University of Technology, PRC. His research interests include modeling and simulation, very high-performance networks protocols, reliability, interactive multimedia remote instruction, Internet resource access, and software maintenance.

Implementation of information technology: Issues connected with revision of business processes in transition

Henryk Sroka and Stanislaw Stanek
Institute of Management of the K. Adamiecki Academy of Economics
ul 1 Maja 50 , 40-287 Katowice, POLAND
Phone +48(32) 598-421, FAX :48(32)586831
Email:sroka@legato.ae.katowice.pl, stanek@legato.ae.katowice.pl

Abstract

Implementation of Information Technology is nowadays seen as a means, available to organizations, of improving their competitive position. However, the question arises, "What is it that makes improvement in one organization quick and successful but unsuccessful in another?" Analyzing the implementation requirements is crucial since it sets the initial direction and thereafter guides the evolution of the improvements. In this work we would like to present the suggested preconditions of, and our experience in, the implementation of innovative processes that are connected with the revision of the business processes in an organization in transition, with a special focus on the implementation of Information Technology. Soft system methodology requires that we perceive an organization as a whole. In organizational settings this kind of perception is strongly connected with the leader who is in a position to perceive the process of improvement in its relation to his vision, or concept. In this context it must be emphasized that technology now calls for general management leadership.

Keywords

Implementation of Information Technology, Implementation requirements, Revision of Business Processes, Organizations in transition, Organizational support, Innovative process, Supporting management decisions

1 DETERMINING IMPLEMENTATION REQUIREMENTS

Merely launching hardware and software at an existing organization problem does not necessarily cause this problem to be solved. Even after the introduction of new methodologies (Application Implementation Methodology, Business Process Re-engineering/Redesign, Information Centre...), the implementation of improvement remains an art which turns ideas into money. In this work we will present the preconditions of, and our experiences in, the successful implementation of innovative processes which are connected with the revision of business processes in an organization in transition, with a special focus on the implementation of Information Technology. Questions like "Where are the main difficulties in the process of improvement implementation?", "Which are the factors that decide whether an improvement is successful or not?", "What is it that makes improvement in one organization quick and successful but unsuccessful in another?" are vital. Due to extensive investigation in which took part some major computer companies (IBM, Oracle, ICL, and others) we have a lot of empirical material to analyze. This material allows us to see a light in the dark cave.

Figure 1 Dialectics of Improvements in organizations

Let us start with the basic scheme given in Figure 1. Every organization performs a number of activities aimed at a better adaptation to the conditions imposed by external environment, according to the contemporary models of successful organizations. Unfortunately, many of them lack the necessary balance on two planes of interaction: the management - leadership one, and the other involving organization structure, Information Technology, and individuals and their aspirations. The organizational culture is the element which entails the inertia of the system. Moreover, accidental effects such as uncertainty, equivocality, and the differentiation of strategies of decision makers also come into play. In neutralizing these effects we may find helpful the principle of balance between the actions of leadership and management, adequate distributions of roles, and changes in the organization structure which are consistent with the Information Technology being implemented. The inertia of each organization is usually so great that without taking these preliminary measures the organization would quickly revert to the original state, or break up. Let us, therefore, move on to the implementation requirements.

1.1 Allowing for the culture of an organization as a precondition of a successful innovative process

Let us start with the old doctor's adage: "first of all, not to harm". De Lisi (1990) pointed out the interplay of forces of technology and culture which is at work in organizations. Major changes in technology, and then the difficulties in their adaptation into patterns of behaviour may cause a downfall (the lesson of the steel axe). Brook (1995) compared changes in the existing organizations with the volcano and a tree, and made a critical appraisal of the treatment of human resources. The observations made during the research had implications for recruitment, training, and career structures. By focusing on people rather than on technology, the main concern became, not the software's life cycle, but the employee's life cycle. A deeper understanding of the rapidly developing body of experience and knowledge about "cultural diversity" and management (Morden 1995), as well as opening our eyes to see, enable us to avoid serious mistakes. We have to learn the local norms, preferences, practices - perhaps even a new language or way of speaking - in order to fit in (Harris, 1985). Furthermore, the humanistic school which advises us to see information "as symbol rather than signal" is in agreement with this view (Symons, Waisham 1988).

1.2 Enhancement of the leader's impact as the first precondition of a successful innovative process

In an organization's reality the power of decision making rests with the decision maker (DM). On the one hand, DM is supported by experts (E) who only know certain aspects of the problem, but not its entirety, and on the other, the decision should be consistent with the general vision promoted by the leader (L). The leader's operations are well described by two words: vision and empowerment (D'Egidio, Moller 1992). These two are interrelated. The "vision" is the dream of the future we wish to create for our group (Matejka, Kurke, Gregory 1993). You need to have a vision in order to strengthen, inspire, and unite. The purpose of the organization - the goal it sets for itself - is contained in this vision. Information processes are the barometer of the effectiveness of leadership in an organization. Nowadays, as the competitive environment pushes an organization to its limits, there is an urgent need to establish the balance of power between the leader, the manager, and the experts. Huber (1988) concluded that the use of computers in the process of decision making and technologies supporting communication led to an increase of the influence of experts in organizational decision making. The results of Harvard's study (Kotler 1990) clearly indicated that in American enterprises there was much more traditional management than leadership. Empirical studies by Keely and Roure (1990) led to the conclusion that management is an important determinant of success, but its main contribution is through the implementation, and not through the formulation of the initial strategy. At this point we have to take into our account all the different kinds of problems an organization has to grapple with. If we distinguish: the rapidity of changes (the obsolescence of technology, the turbulence of the environment, strong competition), quantitative problems (multi-dimensionality, dispersion, the number of products and services), qualitative problems (complicated technology; legal, financial, accounting problems), and place, for simplicity, the roles of the leader, the decision maker, and the expert in three different dimensions, then the importance of each respective role is in proportion to the weight of the three groups of problems.

The topic of executive leadership in strategy research provides a tremendous opportunity for further development. We have very well developed and thoroughly tested models, and there is much room for further integration of leadership style in strategy formulation and implementation and in organizational performance (Nahavandi, Malekzadeh 1993, Taylor 1995).

1.3 Success in Organizational Structure, Processes, and Personnel Development

Implementation of Information Technology, along with the effective utilization of human resources, are now seen as the last remaining mechanism available to organizations to improve their competitive position (Leyland 1993, Morley & Heraty 1995). But applying Information Technology calls for inductive thinking (Hamer & Champy 1993): the ability to first recognize a powerful solution and then seek the problems it might solve; problems the company probably does not even known that it has. We have determined, too, that the condition being fulfilled that computer based communications systems are economically efficient at all levels of an organization, with tasks involving the processing of information (Huber 1984, Holt 1990), the interactions between the organization structure and its supporting technology could become so intense that maximum effectiveness would require their joint design. Recent studies have been sceptical of the importance of the internal structure in explaining a business company's performance. It is recommended however, that the U-form structure be used for small to medium sized firms, and the M-form structure for large firms (Weir 1995).

The case has been also argued for flattening the organization structure - so that it is no longer fragmented - the orientation of jobs or case teams around processes, and for making decisions (a task that managers formerly performed) by computer supported workers (Hamer Champy 1993, Young 1988). The novel approach to work design in a high technology environment includes the conception of high performance work systems. Designed to achieve the best "person - environment fit", high performance work teams are typically small groups of individuals (between 5 and 12) who work with the same facilitator, sponsor or coordinator. Normally, team members undergo training and development in brainstorming, effective interpersonal skills, problem solving, conflict handling, consensus building and decision making, as well as specific training designed to increase the organization's functional flexibility so that the team member has the ability to deploy acquired competence across a broader range of areas (Garavan, Moreley 1992; Moreley, Hearty 1995).

1.4 Orientation on leadership

We have pointed out above the schema of the three interactions in an organization: leader (L), decision maker (DM), expert (E). What should be their roles in the context of Information Technology? Technology now requires general management leadership. Bob L. Martin (1995), President and CEO of Wal-Mart Stores, said "I think that CEOs increasingly recognize the impact that technology decisions have on their business and their corporate culture. As a result, they are becoming less comfortable delegating technology decisions to others. ... Chief information officers are in a critical role. CIOs who share the language and vision of the CEO and have a strong link with the business will help the CEO understand the business and organizational risk of new communications technologies." In speaking about the problems facing those who want to implement new information technology, it is important to stress the different level of complexity of the systems involved (see Figure 2). The new solutions that have been developed (e.g. EIS, DataWarehouse) enable us to formulate a more coherent strategy of organization support, and aid the leaders of an organization in transition.

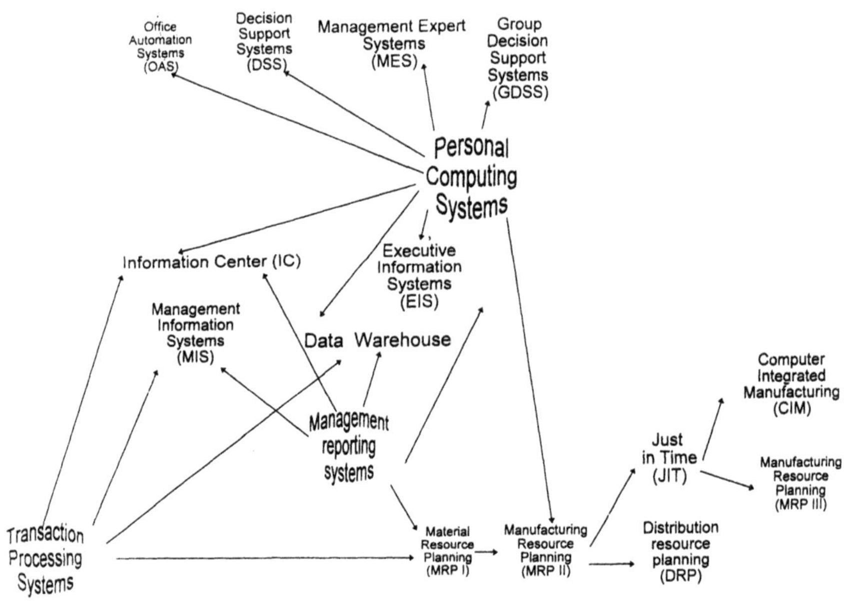

Figure 2 Dynamics in the development of management information systems

1.5 Rich communication, group systems, triggers, and knowledge providing as means to avoid uncertainty, equivocality, and the differentiation of strategies of decision makers

An organization which is in transition has to cope with many obstacles. Delegation of the power to make functional strategy decisions (Burgeois, Eisenhardt 1988), attempts to obtain many ideas from many sources (Kelly, Roure 1990), and the need to look for political alliances (Williams, Zmud 1990), can potentially escalate several well known shortcomings such as:

- uncertainty (in organizations where interdependence is high, uncoordinated actions of one department can force another department to change or adjust its actions or decisions accordingly)
- equivocality (managers from different departments may not share a common perspective and, thus, will have different interpretations of the same data, information, or events)
- differentiation of strategies (in transition there is a strong temptation to resolve known problems by informal, political means.

The remedy for these maladies is in using high technology that allows us (Daft, Lengel 1986, Latherwood, Dilla, Boland 1990) to:

- establish rich communication independent of place in which decision makers are staying at a given moment,
- focus our creativity on tasks such as generating ideas and actions, choosing alternatives, negotiating solutions by groupwork support systems,
- build execution triggers in managers' personal support systems,
- provide information along with the possibility to acquire knowledge (quick development of research on hypermedia in connection with decision support offers very interesting possibilities (RADA 1991).

1.6 Aspiration to form a new culture of the organization in which the staff can feel more involved and which stands for the best service for clients

Successful case study analysis (Stork, Compaq, ICI, Chrysler, Scandinavian Airlines etc.) pointed to the cultural change that had taken place. McGregor listed a number of characteristics observed in the operation of effective teams:

- The members listen to one another; every idea is given a hearing.
- The group is comfortable with disagreement, showing no signs of having to suppress conflict resulting in "open warfare", or the need for resolution through a vote.
- Decisions are reached by a kind of consensus in which it is clear that everybody is in general agreement and willing to go along.
- Successful organizations, wishing to develop their business, need to obtain many ideas from many different sources.

Inexpensive ways to obtain ideas should be developed, these ideas should be subsequently screened for strategic merit, and then a (relatively complete) management team should be assembled.

Knowledge has become the most crucial component in the struggle for competitiveness. Several years ago we reached a stage where the question had to be posed, "How can we build organizations in which continuous learning occurs?" (Senge 1990). Developing learning organizations requires new tools that enhance the leader's conceptual abilities, and foster communication and collaborative inquiry. The total quality movement has been the first wave in building learning organizations (Senge 1990b). To be able to make correct decisions and to stop redefining our objectives all too often, we need to be capable of distributing the limited improvement resources among these overlapping approaches: (1) total cost management, (2) total productivity management, (3) total quality management, (4) total resource management, (5) total technology management. There is a necessity of supporting the five methodologies (Ernest & Young's technical report 93.001 lists the major tools used by each methodology). Acquiring the knowledge of joint venture partners through a process of organizational learning is now under consideration (Richter, Vettel 1995). Japan's experience in this area is of most significance for developing countries. Means should be found to spread knowledge internationally regardless of historical divisions.

2 EVIDENCE ON THE IMPLEMENTATION OF INFORMATION TECHNOLOGY IN THE CONDITIONS OF TRANSFORMATION OF THE POLITICAL AND ECONOMIC SYSTEM

We have been working on new ideas on supporting management with Information Technology (MIS, DSS) since late 70's. Since that time the Polish political and economic system has undergone substantial and consequential changes. Four stages can be distinguished:

2.1 Centrally planned economy

In the declining centrally planned economy of the early 80's we started by determining an executive's information needs in the largest Polish steel plant "Katowice". It was a methodological error: the problem solving process proved that those information needs were not easily determined in advance. When an immense body of data on the potential information needs of executives had been collected, using very sophisticated methods, the usefulness of the data stored in our data bases turned out to be illusory. In a centrally planned economy the managers tended to maintain a high level of hidden resources while negotiating a low level of plan targets, which was usually followed by effectively attaining the objectives or slightly exceeding the targets. As a consequence, it was rather hard to generate any interest in computer aided decision making.

2.2 The illusion of a parametric economy

With the unsuccessful attempt made in the years 1982–1985 in mind, we developed corporate models of RYFAMA, a small enterprise specializing in mining equipment. At that time in Poland's economy became prevalent the trend to switch from a centralized system to a parametric one, which inspired some managers with some interest in analyzing company's profit. Using the very friendly software for the ICL 4.50 (which was compatible with the ODRA 1305 computer produced in our country), e.g. statistical packages, PROSPER (profit simulation and risk), etc., we built an application which executives appeared to like, and which we then further developed in the desired direction indicated by the executives' reactions to the subsequent interim versions. At the time the global economic parameters were altered by the central government all too frequently and the persistent central interventions obscured the situation to such an extent that an informal (small) DSS seemed more appropriate. In general, an alliance of directors of enterprises with the organizations of workers would force the central government to give ground. The organization (i.e. RYFAMA) started to build up a vision of computerization which was not feasible, given the contemporary level of microcomputer technology and in view of the restrictions that were imposed on high technology by western countries and caused a delay in the introduction of Information Technology in Poland.

2.3 Market oriented economy

The transformation from the concept of a parametric economy to a market oriented one began in Poland in the 1990's. However, we lacked the necessary know-how and high Information Technology. We tried to test two approaches:

1 Much hope was placed in the development of knowledge-based systems. For example, the problem of labour valuation was solved by choosing several simple heuristics which controlled the user - system dialogue and the recording of the valuation procedures in a knowledge base. However, upon implementation, it turned out that, in these complicated and controversial areas, a simple knowledge-based system was too difficult for the users to accept. It was necessary to develop this prototype into a GDSS with a knowledge base module. After that, the system was introduced on a trial period of 18 months in many different business organizations (a large steel plant; civil engineering, electronics, clothing and foreign trade companies). During the test period of the labour valuation package, both the commercial system and the service approach were examined (cf. eg. Stanek, S. 1990a).

Later, encouraged by this success, we tried to build expert systems on the basis of a pre-prepared shell (cf. eg. Michalik, K. 1990, Sroka, H 1991). It was very easy to build prototypes of systems e.g. in students' MA projects, but developing these prototypes into products was very often a failure. Some of them, however, were at least partly successful, and have been further developed and updated, up to the present moment. An example of such an application could be the "Expert system for credit risk assessment". The first version of this system was created as a MSc project (Palonka, P. 1993). Later, it was handed over to the PKO S.A. bank for verification, but fell very short of the user's expectations. Most of all, the Credit Department of the bank complained about the incorrect allotment of point weights to particular factors, and the terminology used, but also requested the addition of a module to handle the creation of fund reserves. The bankers' comments received the careful consideration of the members of the special research group and set the direction for improvement and modifications (Stanek, S., Palonka, J., Palonka, P., 1994). The revised and enhanced version of the system was returned to the bank to undergo comprehensive tests on authentic data. A comparison of the results obtained by bank inspectors, who have analyzed the same cases, with those generated by the system revealed (cf. Palonka, P., 1995) that when evaluating credit risk involved with business entities that are not legally bound to produce detailed financial reports the system and the inspectors were agreed in 80% of cases. The bank's managers concluded that in the course of the tests the application had proved to function correctly, both in terms of the results generated and its technical reliability, and expressed much appreciation for its usefulness and functionality. At the request of the bank's management, the system was licensed to the bank as a handy tool in training bank personnel in credit risk assessment, and in rating the creditworthiness of applicants for loans.

2 Taking into account the difficulties in the maintenance of a DSS, we tried to utilize a DSS generator, developed as an extension of the Symphony package. Experience gained in the process of development indicated that the correct organization of the implementation process is just as important as the characteristics of the design itself.

Let us illustrate this with the example of a manufacturer of men's suits employing around 4,000 people, with a production capacity of 1 million suits per year and three major target markets: home market, western Europe, and the Soviet Union. In 1987 the activities of the existing electronic data processing unit in that large manufacturing business consisted mainly in maintaining data input systems (data on inventory of materials, fixed assets, work-in-progress, sales, direct work and use of materials) based on MERA 9150 data loggers (produced under licence from a British company REDIFON) with 22 data input stations. Those data were then processed using obsolete software in rented time on an Odra 1305 computer (ICL 1900 compatible third generation computer) owned by another company based in the vicinity. Toward the end of each year, as a large amount of data had been accumulated, computing would take a lot of time, causing delays in supplying the results to the Company's managers (it was not unusual for the Managing Director to pay penalties for failing to turn in the company's statistics to the Central Statistical Office on time). The Financial Director, to whom the EDP Section reported, was willing to start collaboration, yet he insisted on instant effects even before deciding on any purchases.

We decided to offer them a three months' lease of an Academy owned XT microcomputer so that they could test the capabilities of IBM PC microcomputers, along with the software generator we had been working on. It turned out that all the data that had formerly been batch processed by a mainframe computer could just as well be processed on a day-to-day basis by an XT microcomputer connected to the multi-station MERA 9150 data logger. When the lease period expired, the company had already become the owner of several IBM PC AT computers. Having started cooperation with the Financial Director as well as other section managers (EDP, Planning, Finance, Wages & Salaries, Sales), we were able to analyze varied partly structured decision making problems and immediately generate adequate computing models using our decision support systems generator (cf. e.g. Sroka, H. and Stanek, S. 1989; Stanek, S. 1990b).

As to the breakdown of decision support systems into those oriented on data, models, or of logical nature, the principle of disproportional gradation of the difficulty level in the implementation of systems was verified true (cf. e.g. Alter, S 1980, Camussone, P 1985, Stanek, S. 1994b). The data procurement system was the easy part. An initiative to found this sort of system may well come from an EDP department or an information centre staff, who know the company's information needs, are aware of its possibilities in terms of hardware and software, and are acquainted with decision support systems. As decision makers and experts become involved, there arises the need to analyze the data. At the next stage of development - a model-oriented decision support system - we thus faced a qualitative barrier. Very little of previous experience could be directly transferred and applied. At this point it was the decision makers who had to take the lead, any attempt to shift the initiative away from them or impose any solutions would result in opposition. In each case the scope, time and form of support had to be individually determined by the particular decision maker. The computer was only one of the many items his view of the organization encompassed. With every single problem, however, advice had to be provided concerning the choice and application of quantitative techniques, their allocation depending not solely on the type of problem but also on the data, time and resources available (contribution of the Information Centre).

The transition toward logical models constitutes another substantial qualitative change. The pivotal problem was usually the necessity to allow for a great number of additional conditions when moving from concept to practical implementation. Further development of the company's information system and its better adaptation into global competition required increased capital spending (computer networks, increasing computing power, fourth generation tools, intensive staff training). In spite of a slump on the Russian market (initially, large outstanding payments, and subsequently reduction of orders from a market that used to account for as much as 1/3 of the company's sales), the company adopted a strategy aimed at retaining its position.

2.4 Adaptation into global competition

The next step in the transformation of our economy is the necessity of a better adaptation of organizations into global competition. With little alternative to domestic sources of financing, it is hoped that the privatization of the former state-owned enterprises (SOEs) will be accompanied by a growth in foreign investment, particularly through joint ventures. Foreign capital cannot only underwrite the modernization of the industrial base, it can be the mechanism of introducing modern business practices and technologies (Ferris, Joshi, Makhija 1995). A more global view of using Information Technology is essential.

The most difficult problems are connected with coal mining. Coal mines are characterized by huge differences in the cost of production; in some of them this cost happens to be even several times higher or lower than the average. A political decision was taken to the effect that a gradual transfer of resources between mines would take place. Obviously, this will require a powerful support system. The largest Polish software house, the Centre of Information Systems for Mining Industry (COIG), is responsible for the construction of information systems. As indicated by the experience in the implementation of decision support systems discussed above, the work started with the formulation of the concept of a system oriented on input of data.There is a plan to build DataWarehouses to link all the different systems working for each specific coal mine. As a first step, a prototype of EIS was created by graduate students of our Academy working for the COIG, using SAS software and based on data and guidelines provided by the COIG analysts (cf. Koszowski, Z. 1995).

The prototype of the DataWarehouse is now in the process of construction - SAS and Oracle software is used - and will be distributed depending on the needs of the specific coal mines. Another example of our activities will be the implementation of Information Technology for health care service, developed in cooperation with OPTIMUS, the largest Polish computer company, and for banking.

3 CONCLUSIONS

In view of the above discussion, it seems that the following conclusions can be drawn:

1. Where decision making processes are centralized the introduction of computer based support systems may facilitate the consolidation of existing relations, resulting in inefficient operation, which can pose a serious threat to an organization operating in a competitive environment.
2. Providing computer support for single, isolated decision making processes may aggravate conflicts, increase disagreement about the strategic goals, and induce informal political actions, with only slight, and short term, beneficial effect on the company's global performance indicators.
3. Ensuring a proper balance between rich support, teaching/learning and imparting information in a cooperation oriented environment may bring about qualitative changes in the process of managing the organization, providing the framework for inspiring actions (empowerment) on which the leader's impact is based.
4. The high rate of development of information technology - including the technology of knowledge base systems, graphical work environment, multimedia solutions, groupwork support systems, etc. - is an important factor in eliminating such threats as mutual uncertainty of the managers, equivocality of information, and the differentiation of decision makers' strategies.
5. It is our recommendation that the basic elements of the concept of decision support systems insisting on orientation on an individual decision maker be further developed towards focus on the decision maker *within, and as part of,* the organization, which will make it necessary to incorporate the design of Information Technology in the design of the organization structure itself.

4 ACKNOWLEDGEMENTS

In the present work have been used the findings of the following Central research programs:

- MR.I.30 "Development of methods of system analysis and their application in national economy" (*Rozwój method analizy systemowej oraz ich zastosowanie w gospodarce narodowej*): 1980-1985;
- CPBP 02.15 "Development of system research and its top-priority applications" (*Rozwój badañ systemowych i ich priorytetowych zastosowañ*): 1986-1990;
- RPBR.0.2 "Selected Applications of Information Systems" (*Wybrane zastosowania informatyki*): 1987-1990;

Grant 828/91 "Management Information Systems in Support of Decision making in an Organization in a Market Economy" (*Informatyczne wspomaganie decyzji kierowniczych w organizacji w warunkach gospodarki rynkowej*): 1990-1995.

5 REFERENCES

Alter, S.L. (1980) *Decision Support Systems: Current Practice and Continuing Challenge*, Addison Wesley

Brook, E.C. (1995) Volcanoes and trees: identifying a suitable working environment', *Management. Decision*, **33**, 5-11

Camussone, P.F. (1985) *I Sistemi Informativi Direzionali*, Industrie Pirelli Spa, Milano 46-60

D'Egidio, F. and MOLLER, C. (1992) *Vision & Leadership*, Franco Angeli.

DeLisi, P. (1990) Lessons from the Steel Axe: Culture, Technology, and Organizational Change, *Sloan Management Review*, **83**, 83-93

Ferris, S., Joshi, P. and Makhija, K. (1995) Valuing an East European Company", *Long Range Planning*, **28**, No 6, 48-60

Garavan, T. and Morley, M. (1992)Organization change and development: introducing flexible working groups in a high technology environment", in Winstanley, D. and Woodhall, J. (Eds.) '*Case Studies in Personnel, Institute of Personnel Management*, 1992

Hammer, M. and Champy, J. (1993) *Re-engineering the corporation. A manifesto for business revolution*, Nicholas Brealey Pub.

Harris, P.R. (1985) *Management in transition*, Jossey-Bass, 305-322

Holt, C.C. (1990) Conceptual environment for Organization Support Systems: Design and Use of Information Technology in Organizations, in Vecsenyi, J., Sol H.G. (Ed.), *Environments for Supporting Decision Processes*, Proceeding of IFIP WG 8.3 Working Conference on Organizational Decision Support Systems, June 1990

Huber, G.P. (1984) The nature and design of postindustrial organizations, *Management Science*, **30**, No. 8, 928-951.

Huber, G.P. (1988) Effects of Decision and Communication Support Technologies on Organizational Decision Processes and Structures, in Lee, R.M., McCosh A., Migliarese,P (Ed.), *Organizational Decision Support Systems*, Proceeding of IFIP WG 8.3 Working Conference on Organizational Decision Support Systems, June 1988

Keely, R. and Roure, J. (1990) Management, strategy and industry structure as influences on the success of new firms: a structural model', *Management. Science*, **36**, No.10, 1256-1267

Koszowski, Z. (1995) Koncepcja wykorzystania systemu SAS we wspomaganiu planowania ob≥o¿enia kadrπ przodków w kopalniach wêgla kamiennego, (*A Concept Of Using The SAS System In Support Of Planning The Working Face Staffing In Coal Mines*), II Konferencja U¿ytkowników Systemu SAS w Polsce (*II Polish Users of SAS System Conference*), Warszawa, 1995

Kotler, J.P. (1990) *A Force for Change*, New York

Leyland, V. (1993) *Electronic data interchange. A management view*, Prentice Hall, 1993

Matejka, K., Kurke, B. and Gregory, B. (1993) Mission Impossible? Designing a Great Mission Statement to Ignite Your Plans , *Management Decision*, **31** No. 4, 34-37

Michalik, K. (1990) Prototypowy system ekspercki, w H. Sroka (red.) *Reprezentacja i modelowanie z≥o¿onych i nieustrukturalizowanych decyzji* (Expert System Prototype in H. Sroka's (ed.) *Representation And Modelling Of Complex And Unstructured Decisions*), AE Katowice, 76-86

Morden, T. (1995) International culture and management, *Management Decision*, **33** No.2, 16-21

Morley, M. and Hearty, N. (1995) The high performance organization: developing teamwork where it counts, *Management Decision.*, **33** No.2, 56-63
Morley, M. and Hearty, N. (1995) The high performance organization: developing teamwork where it counts', *Management. Decision* , **33**, No. 2, 56-63
Nahavandi, A. (1993) Leader style in strategy and organizational performance: an integrative framework, *Journal of Management St.*, **30**:3, 405-425.
Perspectives (1995) The end of delegation? Information Technology and the CEO, *Harvard Business Rev.*, September-October, 161-172
Palonka, P. (1994) *System ekspertowy do oceny ryzyka kredytowego* (*Expert System for credit risk assessment*), a thesis presented in part fulfilment of the requirements of the MSc degree at AE Katowice
Palonka, P. (1995) System ekspertowy do oceny ryzyka kredytowego, w Sroka, H. oraz Stanek, S. (red.): *Inteligentne systemy wspomagania decyzji w zarzπdzaniu* (Expert System For Credit Risk Assessment, in Sroka, H. and Stanek, S. (ed.): *Intelligent Decision Support Systems in Management)*, AE Katowice , 251-256
Rada, R. (1991): Hypertext and paper: a special synergy, *International Journal of Information Management,* March
Senge, P. (1990b) The leader's New Work: Building Learning Organizations, *Sloan Management Review*, Fall , 7-23
Senge, P. (1990) *The Fifth Discipline: The Art and Practice of the Learning Organization*, New York: Doubleday/Currency
Sroka, H. and Stanek, S. (1989) Anwendung spezieller DDS - Generatoren fur die Entscheidungsfindung, Konferenzbeitrag zur Tagung 'Rechneruterstutzer Arbeitsplatz des Okonomen', Sektion Wirtschaftsinformatic, Hochschule fur Okonomie 'Bruno Leuschner' Berlin, 30-35
Sroka, H. (1994) *Systemy ekspertowe* (*Expert Systems*), AE Katowice
Stanek, S. (1990a) SWD dla wartoúciowania pracy, w H. Sroka (red.) *Reprezentacja i modelowanie z≥o¿onych i nieustrukturalizowanych decyzji* (Decision Support System For Work Valuation, in H. Sroka (ed.) *Representation And Modelling Of Complex And Unstructured Decisions*), AE Katowice, 59-76
Stanek, S. (1990b) Generator SWD "Eureka", w H. Sroka (red.) *Reprezentacja i modelowanie z≥o¿onych i nieustrukturalizowanych decyzji* (The "Eureka": A Decision Support Systems Generator, in H. Sroka (ed.) *Representation And Modelling Of Complex And Unstructured Decisions*), AE Katowice, 87-97
Stanek, S., Palonka, J. and Palonka, P. (1994a*) System ekspertowy do oceny ryzyka kredytowego* (*Expert System For Credit Risk Assessment),* Grant 828 Technical Report, AE Katowice
Stanek, S. (1994b) Systemy bazujπce na wiedzy w formu≥owaniu strategii organizacji (*Knowledge-Based Systems In Determining An Organization's Strategy*), AE Katowice
Symons, V. and Walsham, G. (1988) The Evaluation of information systems: a critique, *Journal of Applied Systems Analysis*, **15**, 119-132
Taylor, B. (1995) The new strategic leadership - driving change, getting results', Long Range Planning, 28, No.5, 71-81.
Weir, C. (1995) Organizational structure and corporate performance: an analysis of medium and large UK firms, *Management Decision*, **33** No. 1, 24-32.

Young, L. (1988) Worker participation Support Systems: A missing link in Organizational Computer Support?, in Lee, R.M., McCosh A., Migliarese, P. (Ed.), *Organizational Decision Support Systems*, Proceeding of IFIP WG 8.3 Working Conference on Organizational Decision Support Systems, June.

6 BIOGRAPHY

Henryk Sroka is Professor of Management and Business Informatics at the Academy of Economics in Katowice, Poland. He is the author of more than 250 articles, monographs, projects, case studies and 15 books (including Organizational DSS" - 1986, Representation and Modelling of Complex and Unstructured Decisions" - 1990, Expert Systems in Finance and Banking" - 1994, "Intelligent DSS in Management" -1995). Professor H. Sroka studied at the University of Wroclaw, Osaka University, and Tohoku University. He earned his research and honours degrees and titles including PhD, assistant, associate and full professor at the Academy of Economics in Katowice. He has held many positions in the field of information systems (Corporate Computer Centres, Polish Academy of Sciences, the Technical University of Silesia, Management and Business Informatics Colleges in Bielsko and Katowice) such as developer, manager, educator and researcher. He has been president of the organization committee of an annual scientific conference on DSS in Poland since 1980, member of editorial review boards in several conferences and scientific institutions and societies, visiting professor of Japanese and European universities.

Stanislaw Stanek is Associate Professor of Management and Business Informatics at the Academy of Economics in Katowice, Poland. He embarked on his academic career after 10 years of research work - of those 4 as director of a research project team -,in the Institute of Management of Polish Academy of Sciences, and in industry (BZPO Bytom Co.). He received his MSc degree in Applied Mathematics from the Technical University of Wroclaw and his PhD in Economics from the Central Business School (Szkola Glówna Handlowa) in Warsaw. He has held many positions in the field of information systems such as developer, manager, educator and researcher. He is a computer consultant specializing in MIS, GDSS, EIS and DataWarehouse. He took part in many research projects (Polish Government Central Research Programs, TEMPUS Projects, grants). He has been member of the organization committee of an annual scientific conference on DSS in Poland, and member of an editorial review board. He is the auhor of more than 100 articles, monographs, projects, case studies and 5 books (including "Representation and Modeling of Complex and Unstructured Decisions" - 1990, "Knowledge Based Systems in Formulating Organizational Strategies" - 1994, "Inteligent DSS in Management" -1995).

INDEX OF CONTRIBUTORS

KEYWORD INDEX

GPSR Compliance
The European Union's (EU) General Product Safety Regulation (GPSR) is a set of rules that requires consumer products to be safe and our obligations to ensure this.

If you have any concerns about our products, you can contact us on

ProductSafety@springernature.com

In case Publisher is established outside the EU, the EU authorized representative is:

Springer Nature Customer Service Center GmbH
Europaplatz 3
69115 Heidelberg, Germany

www.ingramcontent.com/pod-product-compliance
Ingram Content Group UK Ltd.
Pitfield, Milton Keynes, MK11 3LW, UK
UKHW020132290926
15471UKWH00003B/435
* 9 7 8 1 4 7 5 7 5 4 5 2 0 *